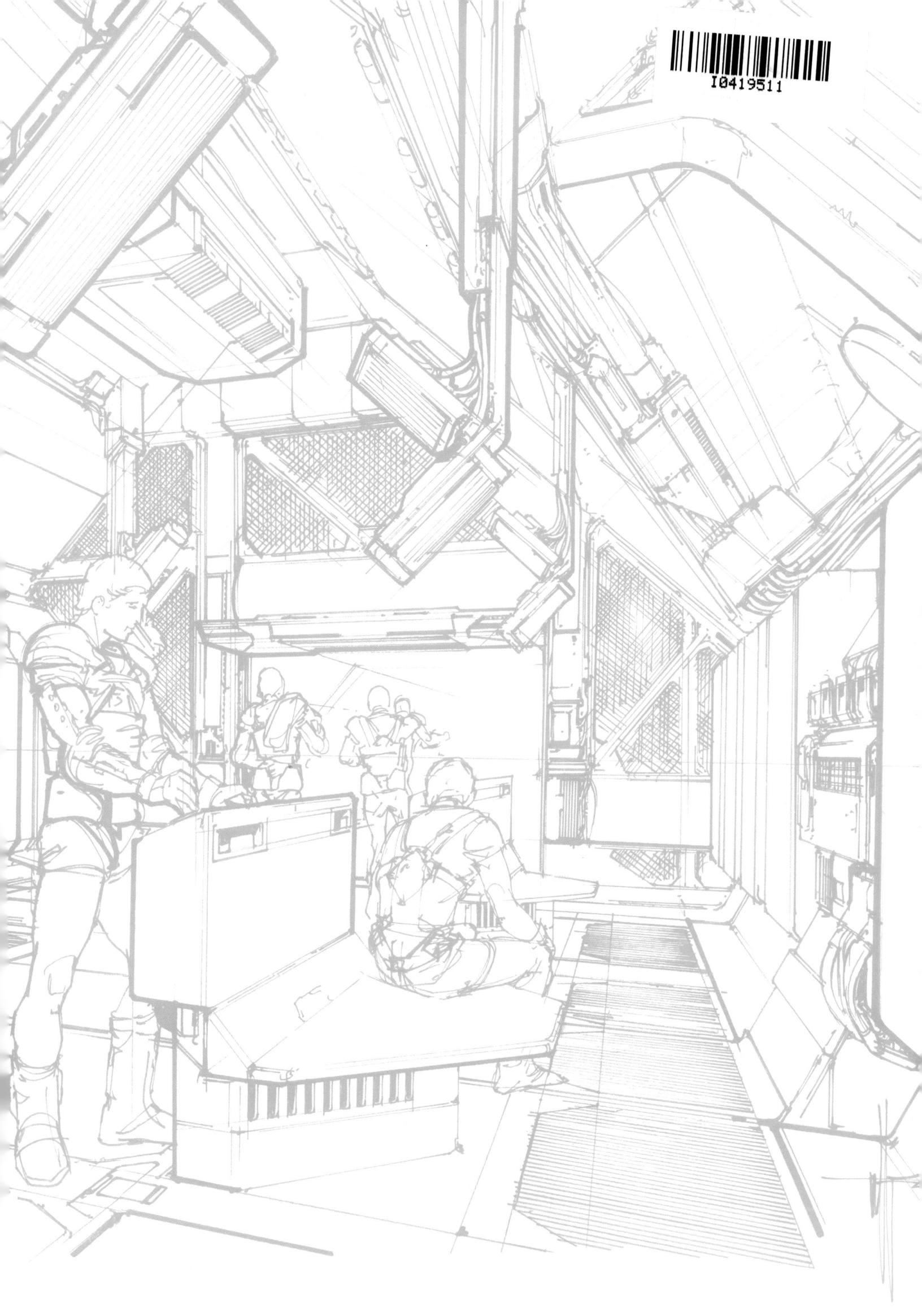

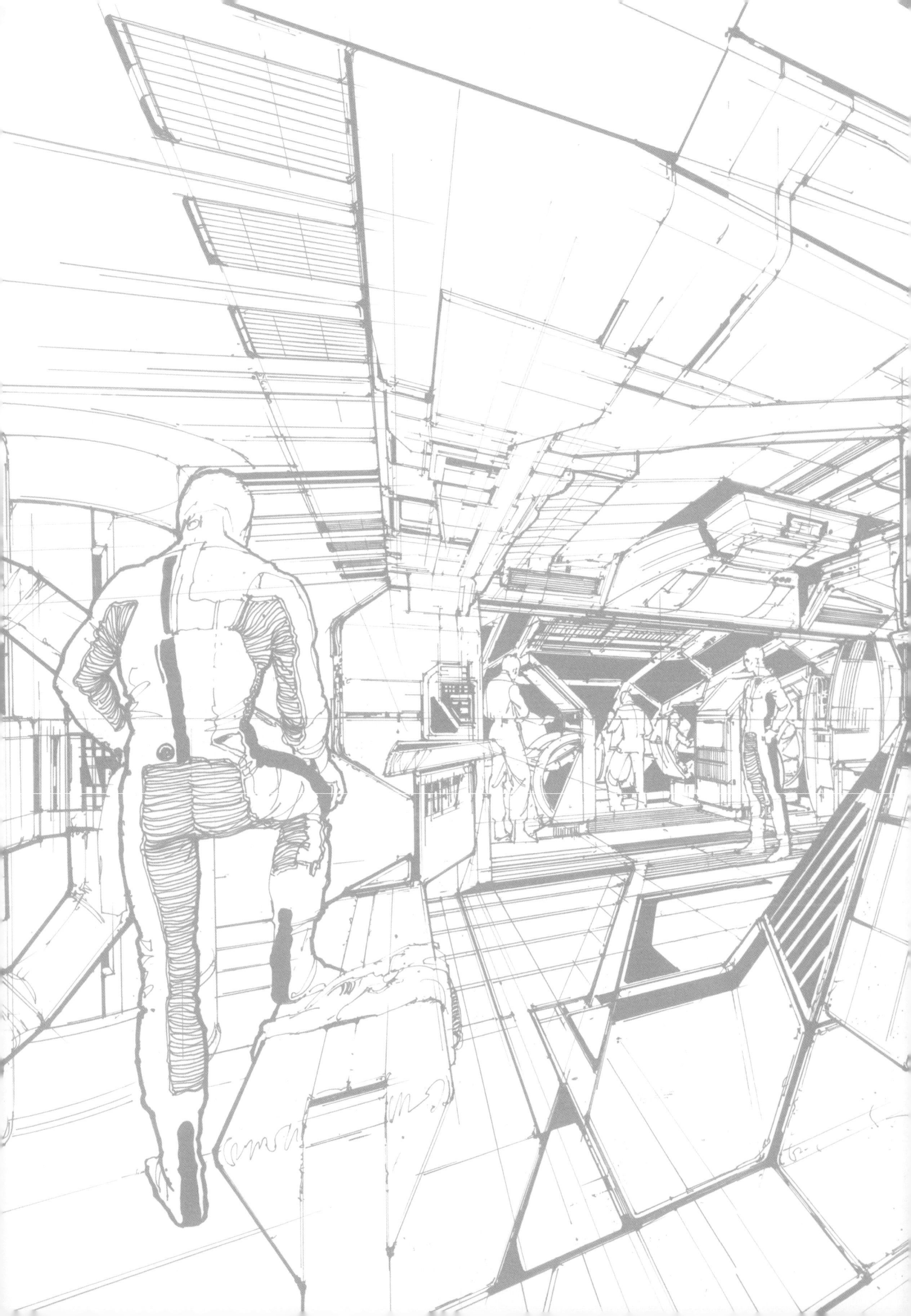

THE MOVIE ART OF
SYD MEAD
VISUAL FUTURIST

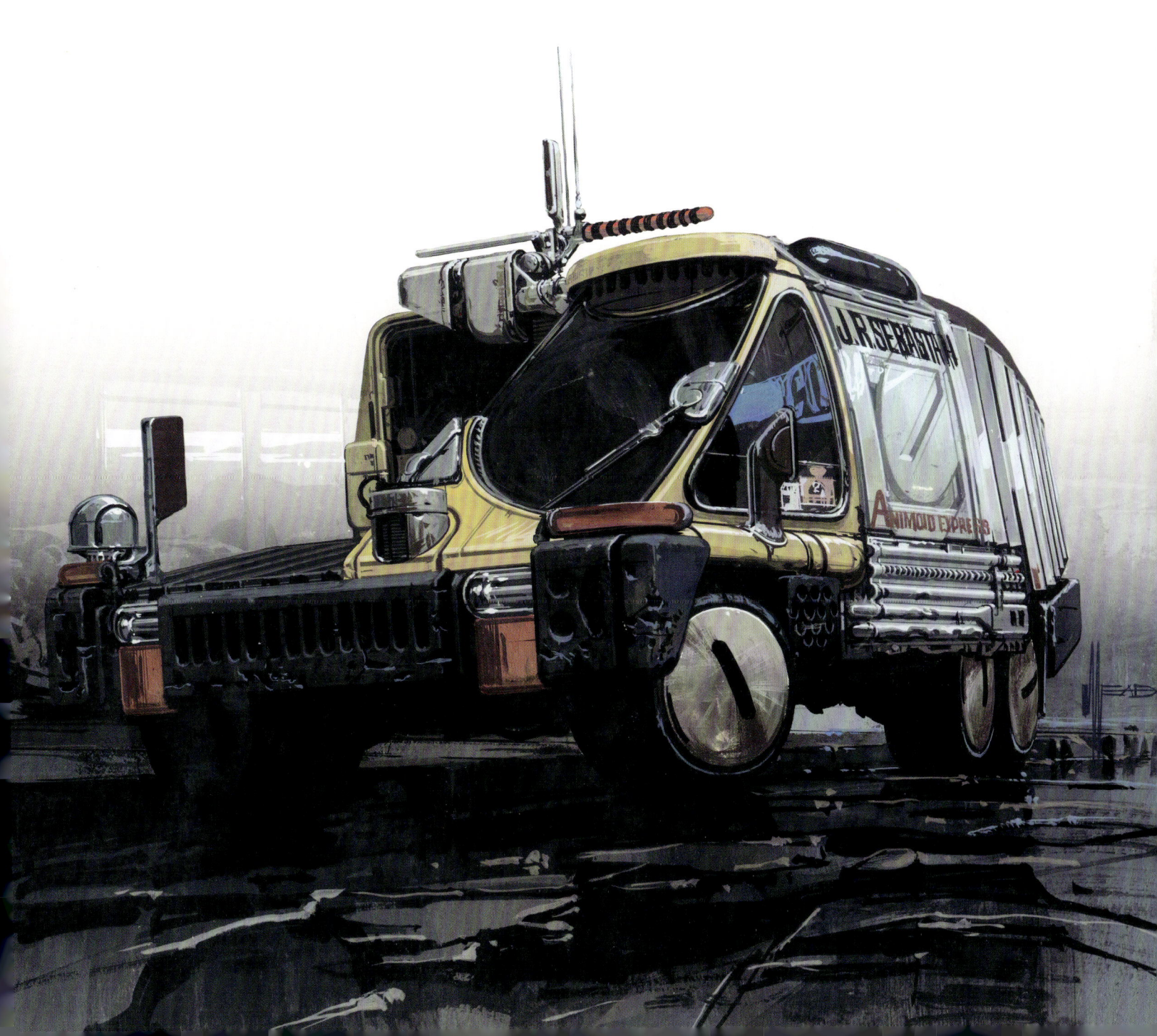

THE MOVIE ART OF SYD MEAD: VISUAL FUTURIST
ISBN 9781785651182

Published by
Titan Books
A division of Titan Publishing Group Ltd
144 Southwark Street
London
SE1 0UP

First edition: September 2017
10

EU RP (for authorities only)
eucomply OÜ Pärnu mnt 139b-14 11317
Talinn, Estonia
hello@eucompliancepartner.com
+3375690241

Did you enjoy this book? We love to hear from our readers.
Please e-mail us at: readerfeedback@titanemail.com
or write to Reader Feedback at the above address.

To receive advance information, news, competitions, and exclusive offers online,
please sign up for the Titan newsletter on our website: www.titanbooks.com

A CIP catalogue record for this title is available from the British Library.

Printed and bound in China.

THE MOVIE ART OF
SYD MEAD
VISUAL FUTURIST

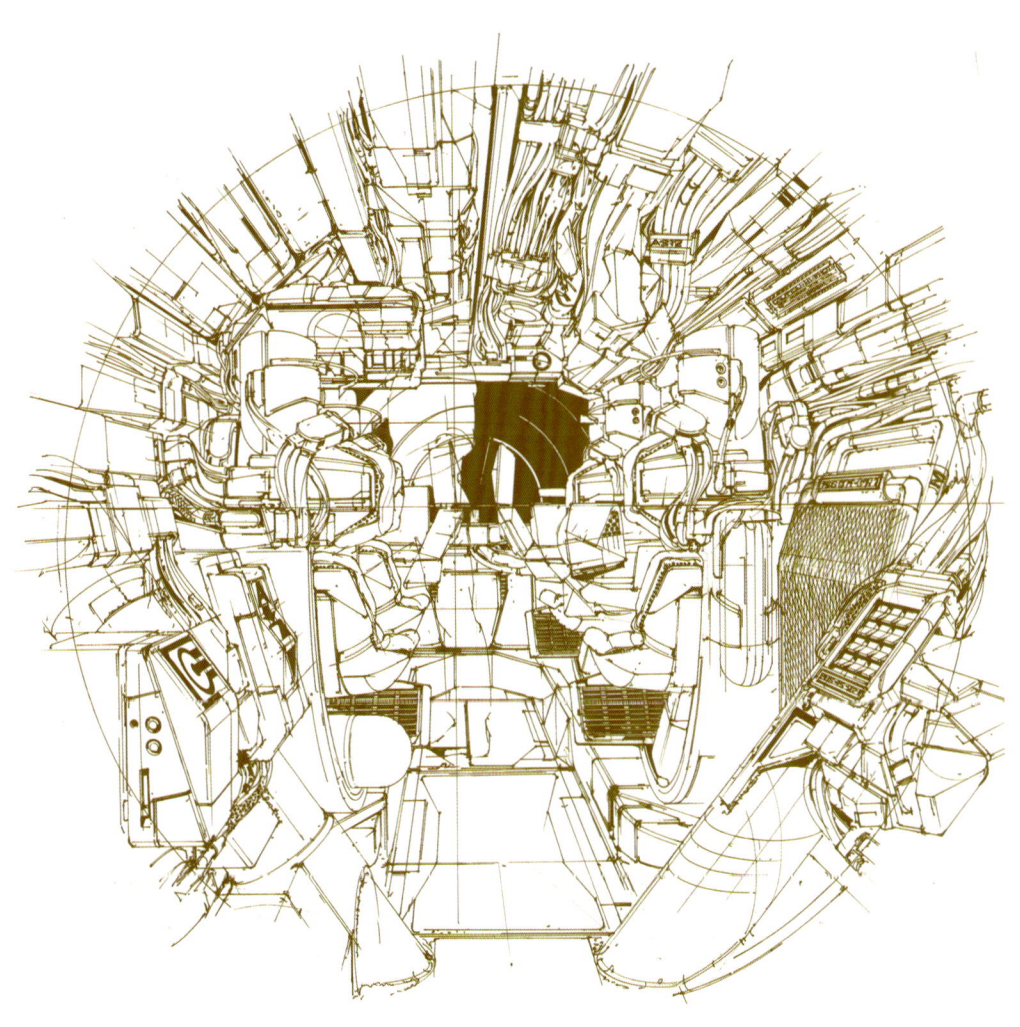

WRITTEN BY
SYD MEAD &
CRAIG HODGETTS

FOREWORD BY
DENIS VILLENEUVE

TITAN BOOKS

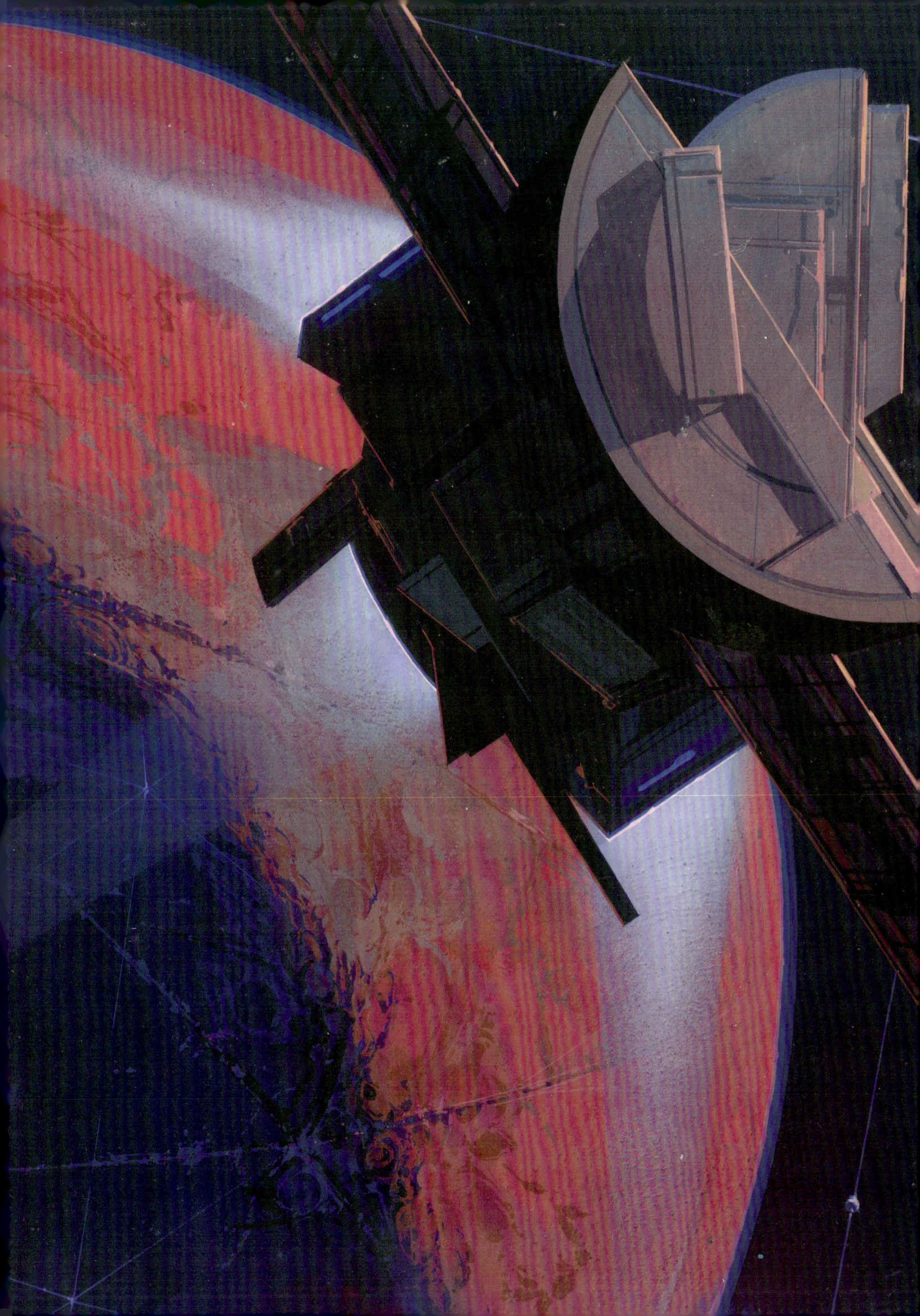

CONTENTS

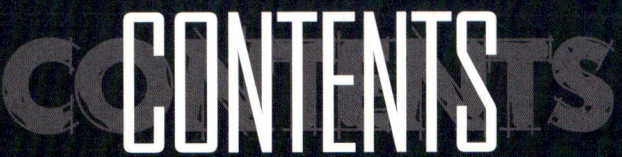

WHY AM I SO DEEPLY MOVED BY SYD MEAD'S ART?

BY DENIS VILLENEUVE

Is it normal to feel nostalgia when looking at visions of a futurist? That is exactly how I feel when I dive into Syd Mead's unique world.

The only way to explain it is to say that deep inside, I've always dreamed of living and evolving in Syd's worlds. Their sensuality and stunning beauty offer such a magnificent contrast with the brutality of our reality. I am convinced they exist somewhere, in a parallel dimension and I have this strange sensation that I have been there, even strolled through them. I always come away with this sense of longing, like remembering moments from my own childhood.

I am also deeply moved by Syd Mead's art because he's one of the last great utopians of our time, and I am in desperate need of optimism. Now that we are in the future of the 20th century, we realized that we aren't able to stop the repetitive patterns of history. Who dreams about the future these days, without having nightmares? While most of humanity is afraid of its own future, we need, more than ever, advised dreamers that can make tangible the visions of a better tomorrow.

I suspect that Syd's universes are fueled by the strength of the optimism of the 50's, when the World was rising from its ashes, when everything seemed possible, again. He used this force to create a future where pure elegance of design and social peace would reign, where humanism and science would win over chaos, where progress and nature would evolve in harmony. Still today, he is ahead of our time, wandering in distant perfect tomorrows, as a tourist who visits his own creation.

I may be wrong but I think Syd's traveled in dystopia only once, and it was because of Ridley Scott. Syd's first drawings of Los Angeles for *Blade Runner* were pure, bright and peaceful but Ridley wanted his new world to be more claustrophobic and oppressive. And Syd dived into the darkness.

As I was creating the universe of *Blade Runner 2049*, I realized only one person could reimagine the city of Las Vegas and give it the magnetism it needed to be worthy of *Blade Runner*'s dystopian landscape. So, I asked the master to go back to the future for me. He came back with stunning images. I never thought Las Vegas could be as pure, beautiful, devoid of cynicism. I didn't ask Syd to go darker. I needed this powerful beauty, maybe for my own sake. Now, I look forward to losing myself in those streets, while missing them already.

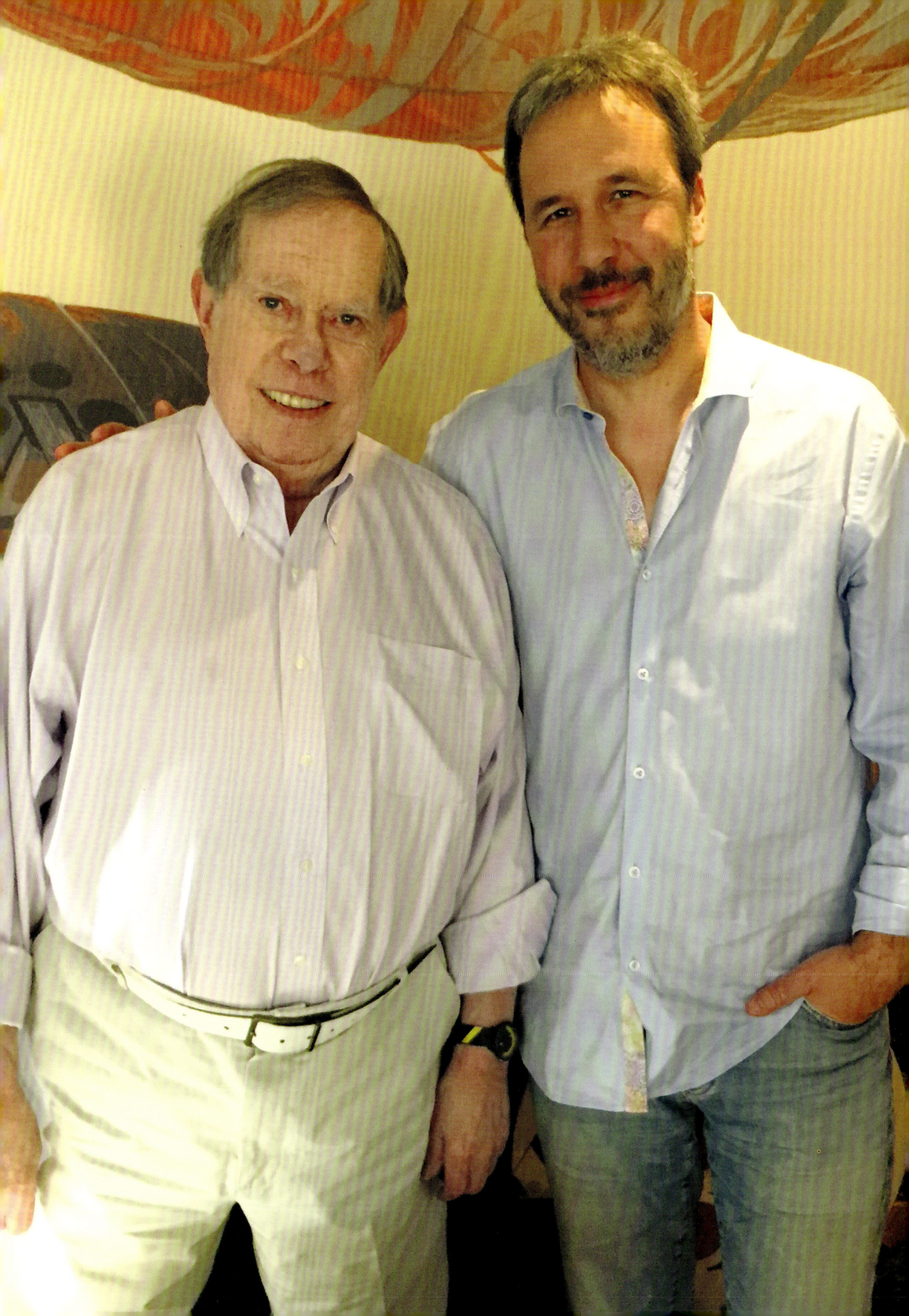

THE FUTURE ACCORDING TO MEAD

In the beginning, there was pulp sci-fi. Lurid cartoons of future cities riddled with aerial tramways and flying cars, and throbbing with atomic power. *Whoosh!* You could almost hear them. *Whirrrrh! Whoosh!* Smoke trailing from pulsing exhausts, transmission lines disappearing into the distance, the acrid smell of spent rocket fuel —a gaudy mix of techno-optimism, repressed desire, and artistic freedom was setting the bar for the foreseeable future.

For the most part they populated the covers of newsstand offerings like *Popular Science* and *Amazing Tales*. But all that was before Syd Mead. He changed all that. He was a futurist. He invented the term. He created a new genre.

By now there are millions, maybe even tens of millions of Earth's residents, who have formed an idea of the future as visualized by Syd Mead. They program computers and fix cars, teach school and write stories, go to movies and eat hamburgers. What they have in common is a view of the world, and man's place in it, in which stylized objects loaded with advanced technology are sought-after harbingers of things to come. They have come to understand, through Syd's imagination, and the films based on it, that among the endless possibilities of a technically mature culture, that man and machine can, and perhaps should, share a seamless, symbiotic environment.

Mead is perhaps best known as the visionary designer whose work on 1982's *Blade Runner* set the stage for the edgy, post-apocalyptic style that shoved postmodernism into oblivion. Originally hired as an ArtCenter "car–thug" to visualize Rick Deckard's (Harrison Ford) hovering cop car, he couldn't resist plunging the auto, in true Mead fashion, into imaginary street scenes

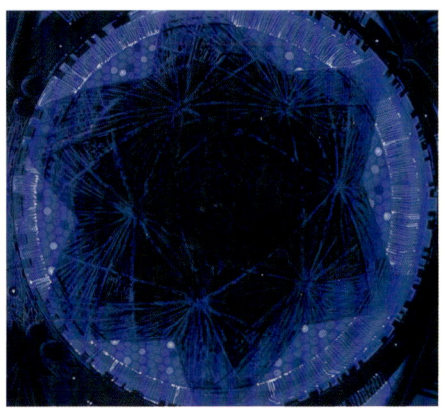 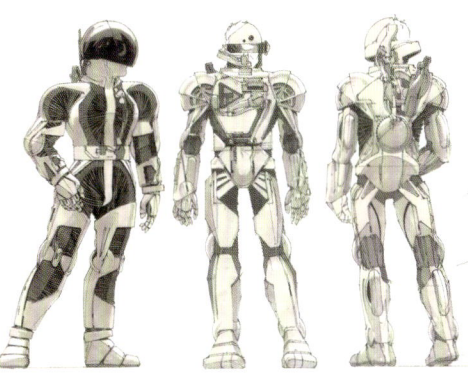 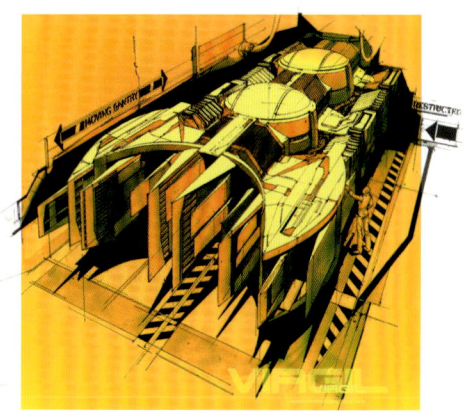

cluttered with a goulash of cryptic signs and symbols and draped with a spaghetti of cables and pipes, as though the whole of Los Angeles was on life support. Those images, now part of our collective subconscious, propelled Mead into a stratosphere of designers whose vision embraced everything the consumer could see, down to the typography on a food cart.

For many, the idea of such a future reached escape velocity about the time Cape Canaveral launched the final Apollo moonshot. But America's—indeed the world's—determination to embrace a glamorous, high-tech future seemed to evaporate overnight. Those Vogue magazine covers with Twiggy in astronaut gear, and Caddy's with ready-for-take-off fins were replaced with tattooed smiley faces and Whole Earth compost pits, and we woke up from the dream.

But Syd Mead was, and is, a true believer.

He developed his famous signature while at ArtCenter College of Design in the late fifties. The school was still in its infancy with classrooms tucked away in cubbyholes in the Larchmont area of Los Angeles, but it boasted a faculty conscripted from Disney, LA's car culture, and then-nascent arts culture, and had quickly made a name for itself as the premier place in the states to study industrial design. Saul Bass, Raymond Loewy, and Henry Dreyfuss were within easy reach, and an adventurous Maurice Tuchman was busy assembling the now famous "Art and Technology" shows at the nearby Los Angeles County Museum of Art.

Drawing at ArtCenter had little to do with traditional charcoal and pen washes. Instead, it was seen as a way to convey the sleek, polished surfaces of industrial products, with color and flashes of chromium to accent the form. New technologies like the airbrush and vividly colored wax pencils made their debut, capable, in the right hands, of transforming illustration from the nostalgia of Norman Rockwell to the sleek, hard-edged sensuality of pin-ups and automobiles. These "renderings" as they were soon dubbed, were to become the designer's preferred way to "wow" a client, and soon Mead's prowess led to assignments, first with Ford where, in Mead's words:

"The excitement and elan of the automobile mystique was elaborately expressed by combining product reality and fantasy. The lacquered surfaces mirror the surrounding world in the flowing cascade of reflection; the chrome ignites with a hundred blue-white suns."

The process itself takes a journeyman's hand, but what Mead brought to it was passion and imagination, setting his vehicles in dramatic environments, positioning glistening bodies languishing in the sun, stabbing streaks of chrome through a dark sky; already, in a context of mundane corporate assignments, bringing a theatrical, IMAX-worthy image to the page. In 1965!

Four years on, Mead was recruited by Phillips, the European leader in domestic appliances, located in the Netherlands.

It was while at the Phillips office in the Netherlands that Mead got a call from Robert Wise, who had seen his renderings in a Phillips brochure, tracked him down, and asked him to put his imagination to work on a movie version of television's *Star Trek*.

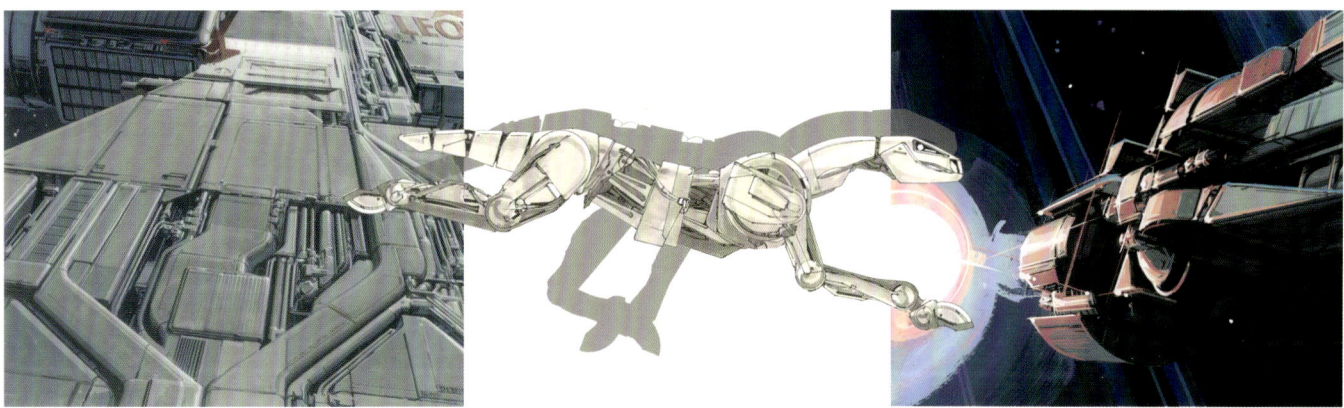

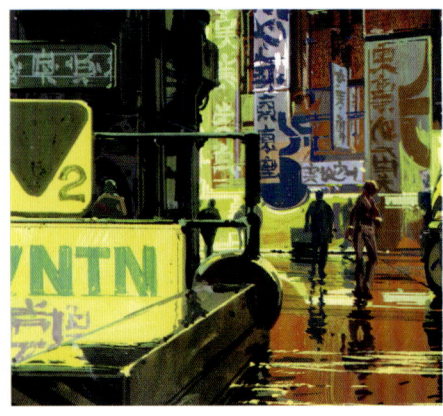 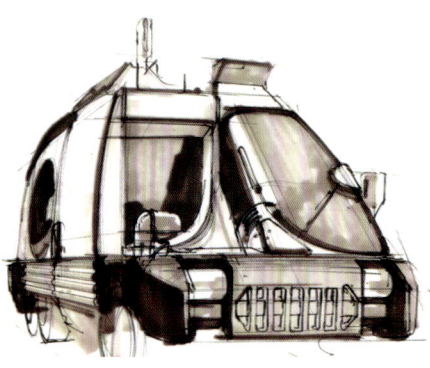 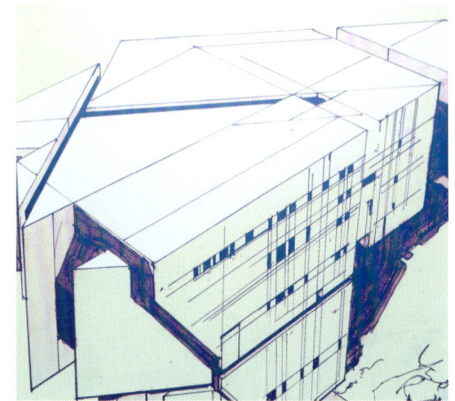

In spirit, as well as substance, Mead's ingenuity, coupled with design *elan,* can be compared to Norman Bel Geddes, the American stage designer, engineer, and architect who had the responsibility for many of the well-known icons from the 1939 New York World's Fair. Bel Geddes, like Mead, had a flair for the future, as well as clean but sensuous design, based on solid technical references, and a persuasive feel for iconic design that still endures today.

It follows that, for sheer technical bravado, Mead has few peers. Famed science fiction film designers, like Ron Cobb and Geiger, are rightly celebrated, and even venerated, for their singular creations, but it is Mead who has established the milestones in the industry.

And of course, it is Mead, whose images, many published here for the first time, visualize a production far in advance of the elusive "green light". A number of these outings, often based on a simple story outline or even less, prompted some of Mead's most original visions, some of which, sadly, were never realized. Others, like *Johnny Mnemonic,* helped producers and directors secure funding.

COMPOSITIONS

The products of Mead's imaginings are often situated in star fields and endless interplanetary space, or in the purple haze of an otherworldly sunset reflected from the spit-polished canopy of an idling coupe. But what's important is the existence of, indeed the *fact* of those reflections, the *fact* of the sunset, the *fact* of the coupe in the foreground, framing a distant view of a many-spired city, and the *fact* of the deeply textured fabric of the driver's jacket,

that conjures references to Velázquez and Tintoretto. The paintings do exalt a now-banished monarchy, and the bejeweled courtiers do embody the self-indulgent posture of the aristocracy, but those issues do not displace the astonishing artistry compressed into a few millimeters of paint.

Like the great classical artists, Mead's primary palette is light. Limpid, hard-edged, violent even. It splashes, spurts, and eddies in mercurial pools, restlessly articulating his subjects. One cannot detect Mead's hand in this. His brushstrokes melt into the subject matter, revealing first the glint of a visor, then the almost imperceptible texture of a darkly shadowed overhang. The overhang, the shadow, and the barely visible activity within might be framed by a highly reflective pool, leading the eye to an off-camera transaction scorched into a jagged rockscape. There is intrigue, a mesmerizing stillness, and a fully realized yet improbable culture framed as carefully as a tourist poster. The geometry, rendered in great, sweeping gestures that bind the composition, would have provided a feeding frenzy for art scholars like Rudolph Arnheim, but for poor mortals, it is the proto-erotic, fetishized imagery itself that lingers in the memory.

Many of Mead's concept illustrations, when subjected to the analytical tools first proposed by Arnheim, employ an abstract composition of arcs and lines which serve to organize not only the objects portrayed but the overall thrust and parry of dark and light, reflective and mute. These primary pictorial devices, in Mead's hands, are able to produce effects of extreme depth or overwhelming scale.

The high view of Deckard's spinner (page 108) employs the

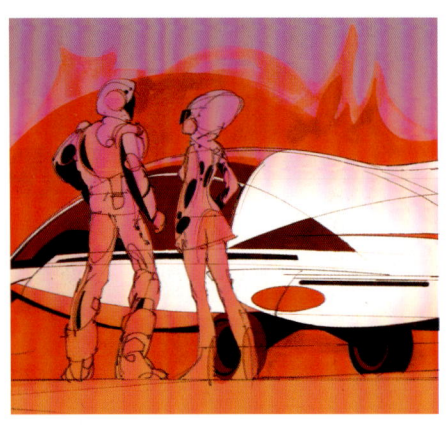 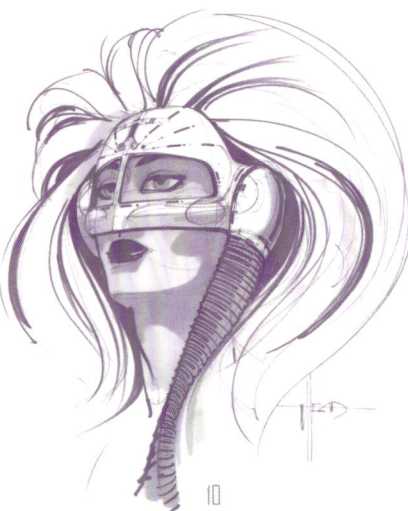 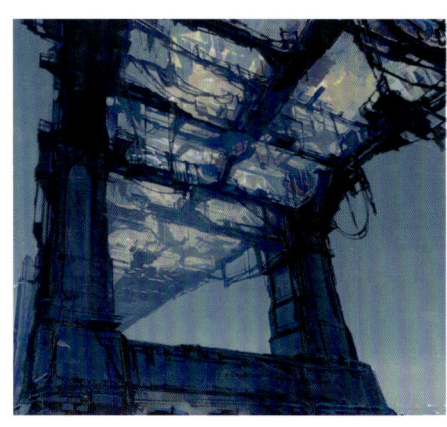

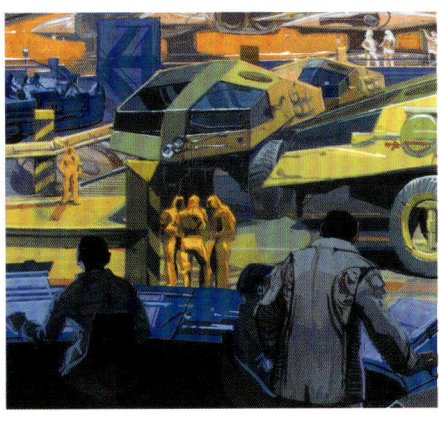 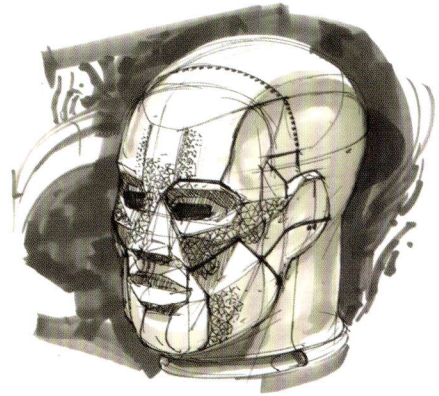 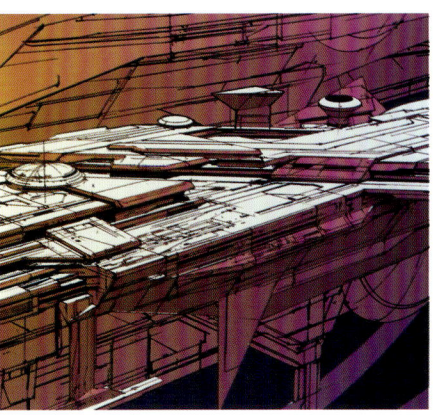

geometry of the extended wheels to produce a powerful diagonal thrust from edge to edge of the picture frame, while the arc of the cockpit established an internal focus which helps to lead the eye to a somewhat diffuse street scene far below. The intensity of the cockpit detail, its precision and density, juxtaposed to the scene below transforms both time and space.

More often than not, light—the edges of louver-like surfaces, or the glint on a polished strut—will dance through a scene in an almost choreographic sequence, again establishing an axis, a sub-axis, or even a sub-sub axis which can enhance our sense of scale.

Mead's remarkable ability to produce effects of monumental scale, even as our senses tell us otherwise (after all, the images in this book fit easily into one's hand) creates a feeling of hyper-reality. Those same spaces and objects, were they to be faithful to 'reality' would no doubt seem impressive, even very large, yet lack the sensation of awesome space conveyed by Mead's sketches.

The landscape photography of Ansel Adams owes much of its vast scale to a similar technique whereby Adams subtly manipulated the printing process to enhance the experience of depth.

In contrast, for the most part, most Twentieth Century art has sought to minimize the duality of the flat "picture plane" and the perspectival portrayal of objects and spaces. Warhol, Wesselman, and artists of the "pop" movement took care not to violate the "picture plane", while Mead uses every device in his arsenal to destroy it. And it works!

But far from being a faithful depiction of reality, even of an imaginary reality, Mead uses precisely those arguments, precisely that tension between the plane of the picture and what is going on within it to create a "for your eyes only" image which seems to act directly on one's visual receptors.

Is this what makes him perhaps the greatest future visionary ever? Actually, not even close.

The future he envisions is multi-layered to be sure, and rich with the non-sequiturs of reality—but a reality extruded from, and familiar with, the everyday reality of our time. Mead seems especially attuned to the trajectory of technology, of progress as defined by man's ability to synthesize materials, processes, even information, to achieve rewards, and to use imagination to wrest control of the environment from natural forces. Such a repertoire, given the deep cynicism of today's political and social climate, seems a welcome antidote to the futility preached by many.

What makes Syd's vision so compelling is not only the means he employs to convey it, but the acute physical and environmental awareness; the endless curiosity about how the world works; the precise level of detail and the practical engineering knowledge that he brings to even the most fantastic devices.

Mead's images—confident, manifestly manmade, and culturally unapologetic—represent a technology-positive and aware worldview but at the same time, have a powerful ability to summon heroic, even idealistic emotions. In this artistic, futuristic space, Syd Mead has become an icon and here presented are both his best known and unknown works chronicling a career unparalleled by any living artist.

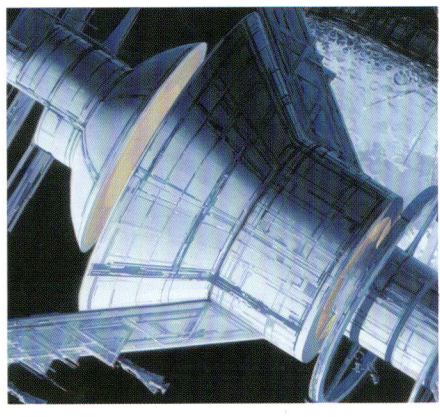 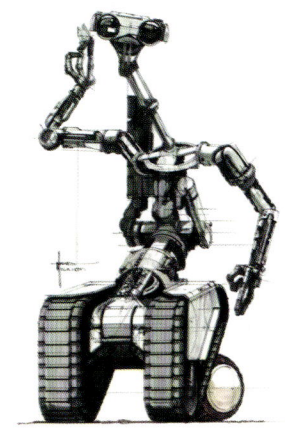 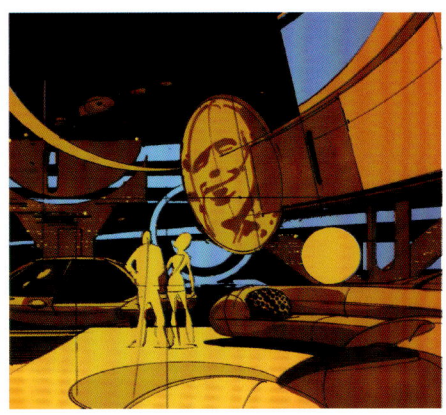

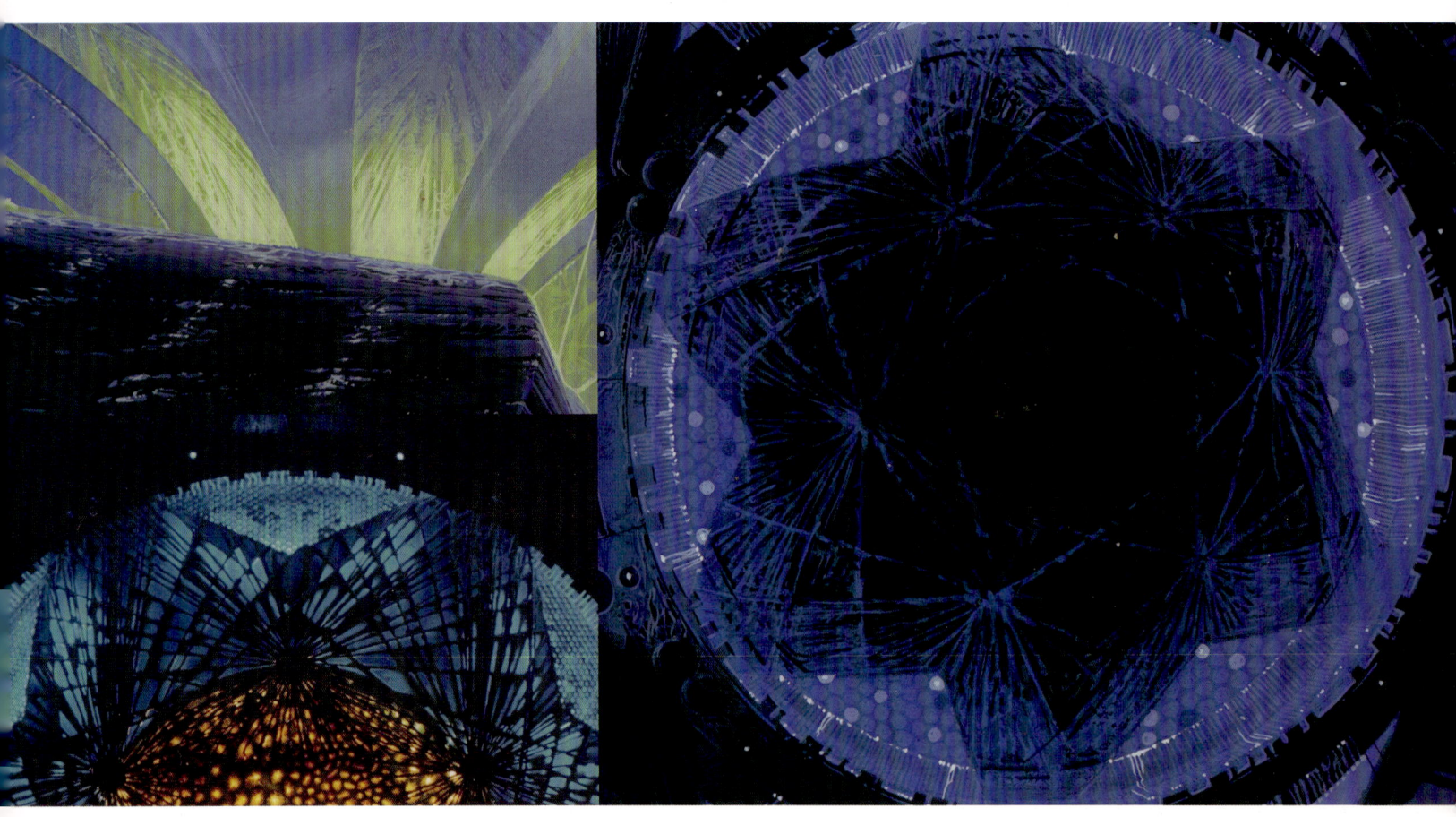

STAR TREK
THE MOTION PICTURE

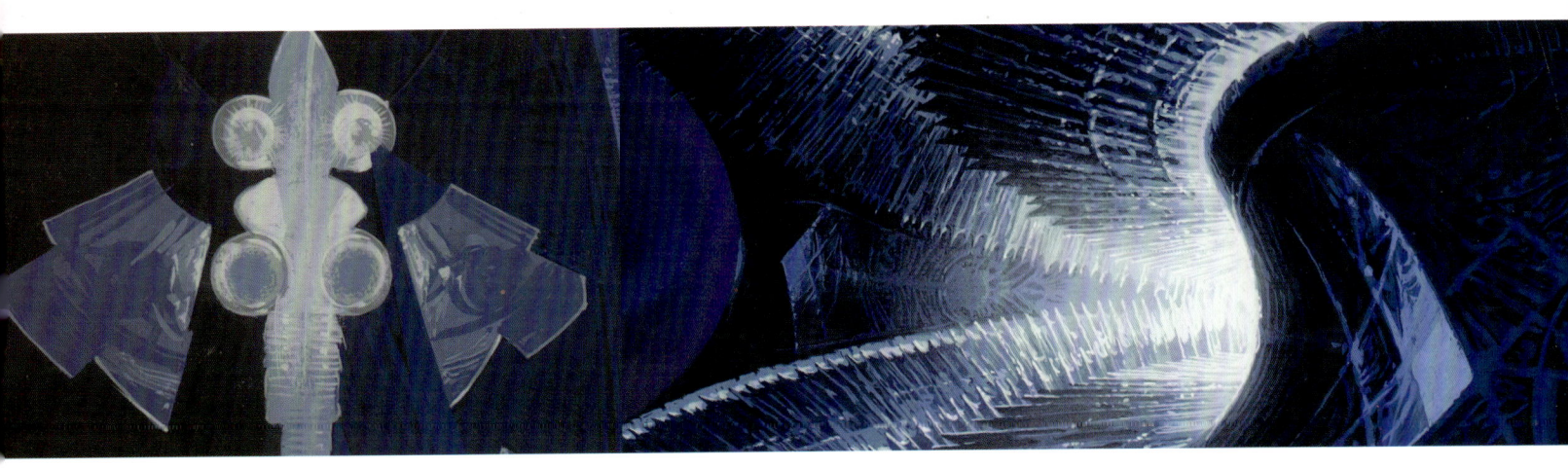

tar Trek: The Motion Picture (1979) brought widescreen imagery to the fabled TV series. As Mead's first venture into motion pictures, it also brought an around-the-clock schedule, as he juggled a day job as an illustrator for Phillips with the demands of John Dykstra and Jeffrey Katzenberg, who were overseeing the visual effects for seasoned director Robert Wise. For Wise, helming what was to become a major motion-picture franchise, the character of the visual design was a make-or-break opportunity to step away from the admittedly "cheesy" design of the original, and he figured Mead was the untried man to do it. By overnighting the artwork from his office in Amsterdam, they kept the schedule on track, and the rest is history.

The creation of an object which director Robert Wise demanded, "no man had ever seen" was Mead's first motion picture assignment.

These images of the *V'ger* described in the script are able, by Mead's handling of light, texture, and elements of pure geometry, to convey an almost inconceivable magnitude even in the incalculable void of outer space. Cloaked in mystery, and ordered by precise 60-degree geometry, the concept is primordial, ecstatic, and deeply spiritual all at once. But most of all it embodies both religious iconography and references to infinity.

Mead envisioned the plasma-rich, unfolding *V'ger* itself to be a mechanical apparatus as large as a planetoid, which had been created to guard *the V(oya)ger* on an eons-long return to its makers on earth. With specific references to gothic architecture and the evocation of an eternal triangle, the phenomena of "black holes" confer existential meaning, while an enormous maw opens with a grave and deliberate choreography.

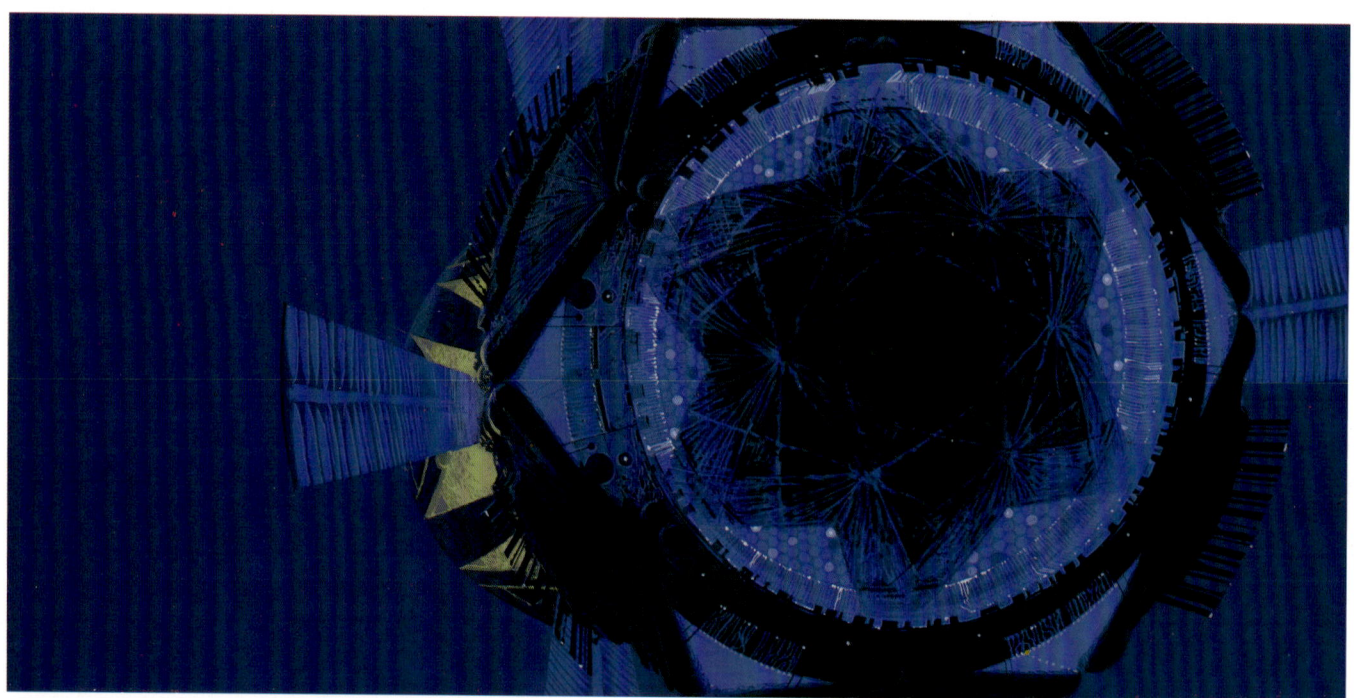

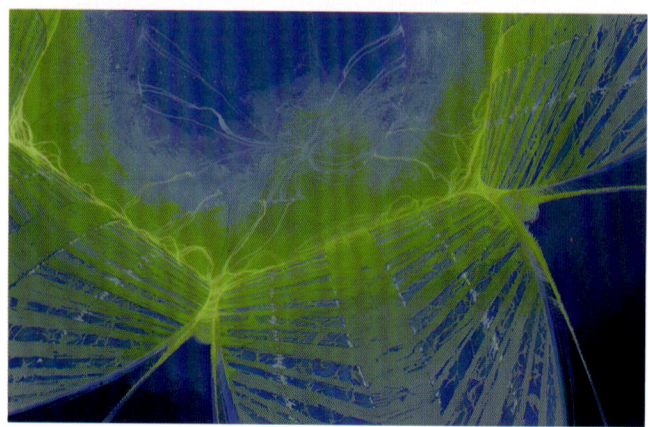

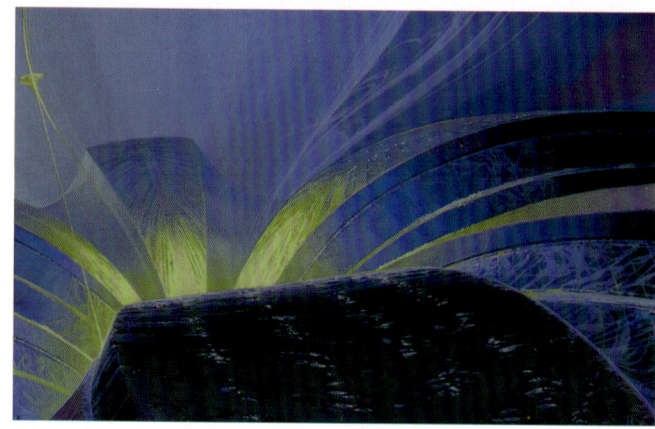

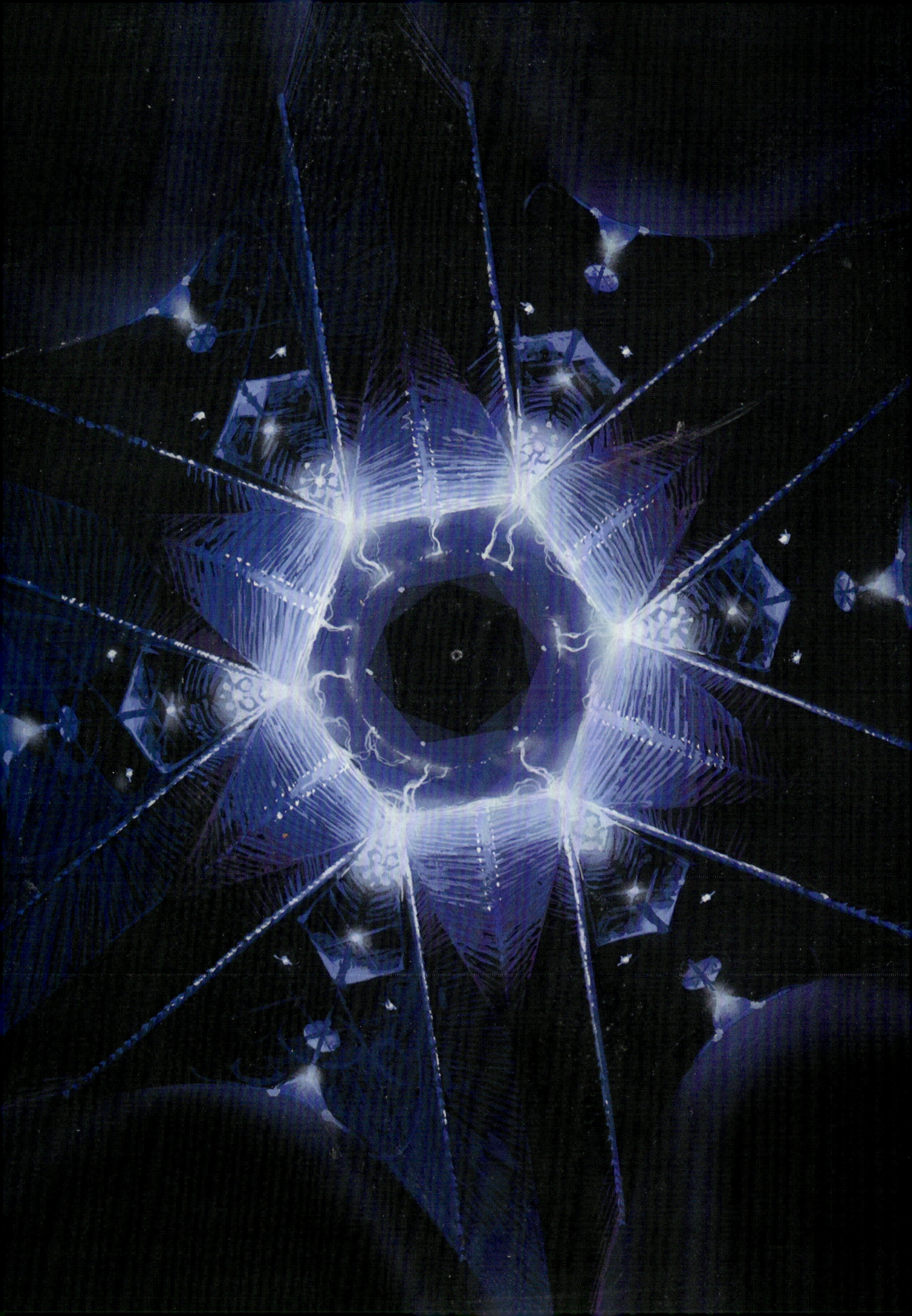

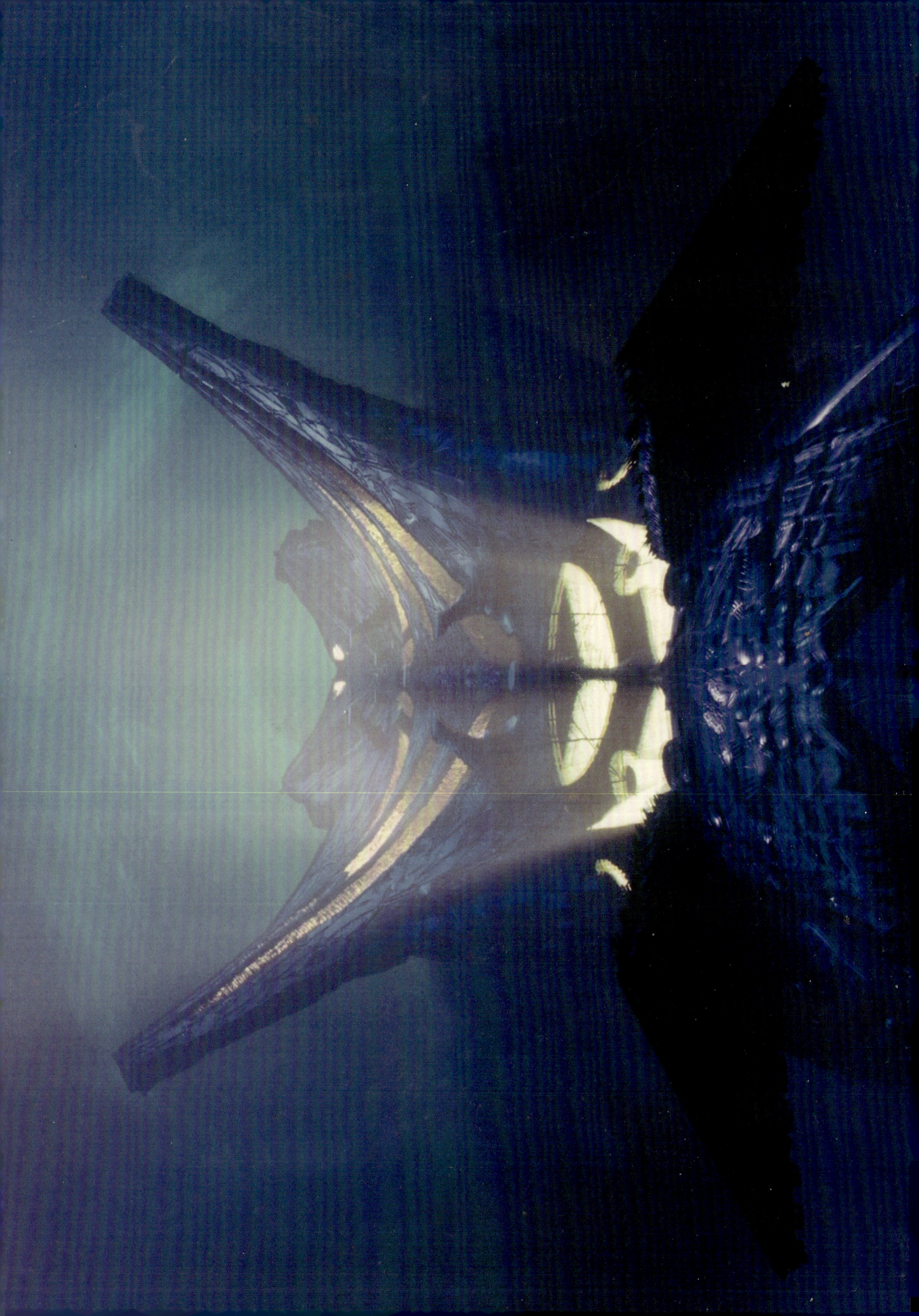

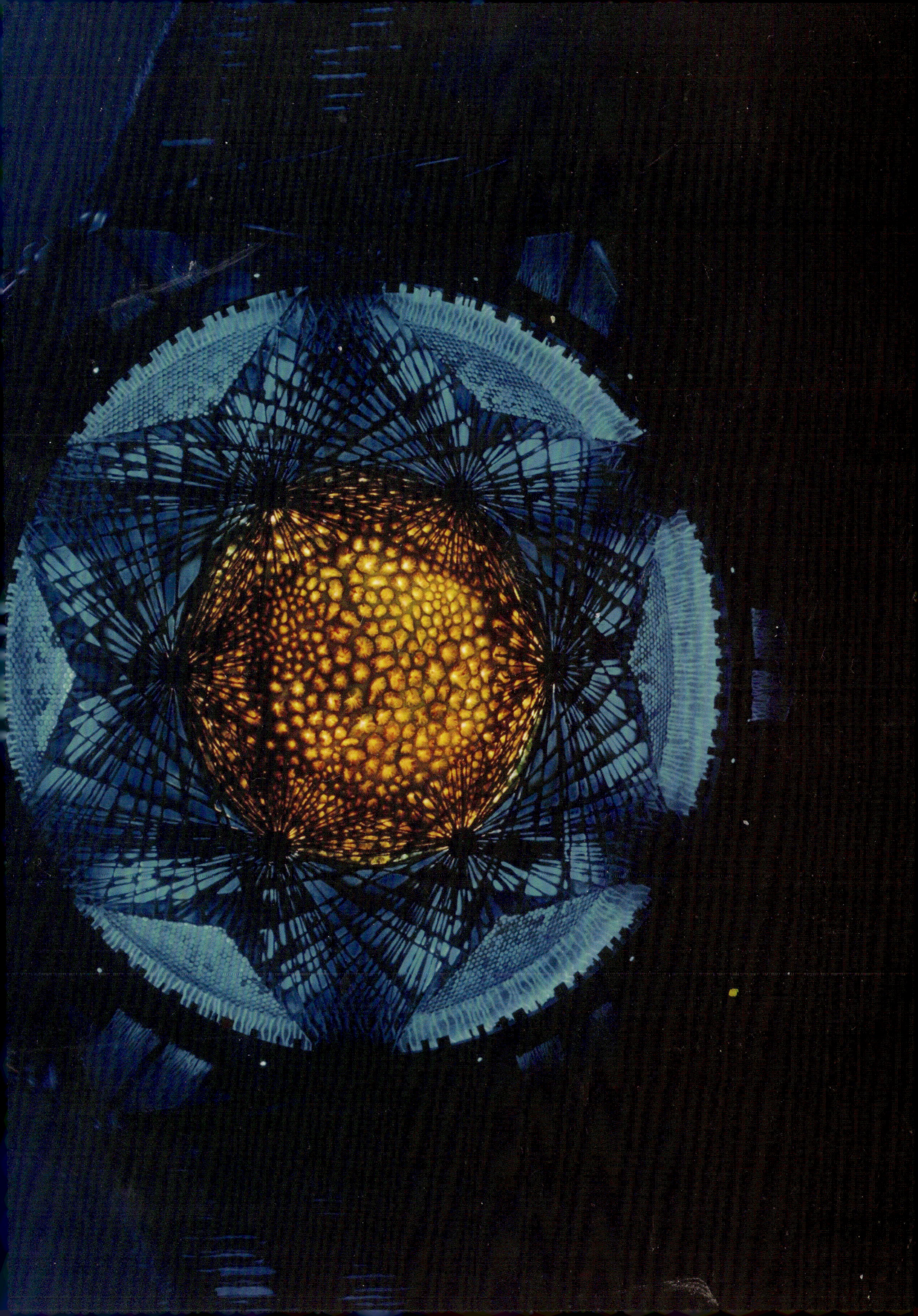

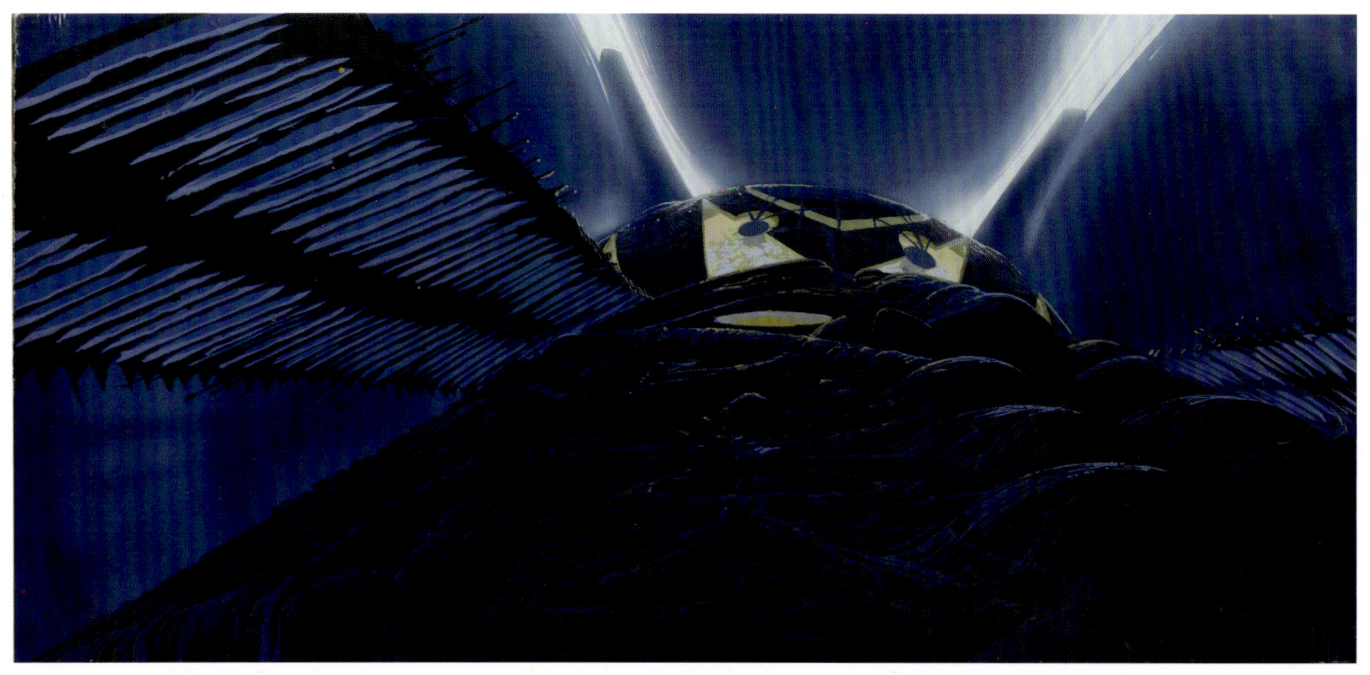

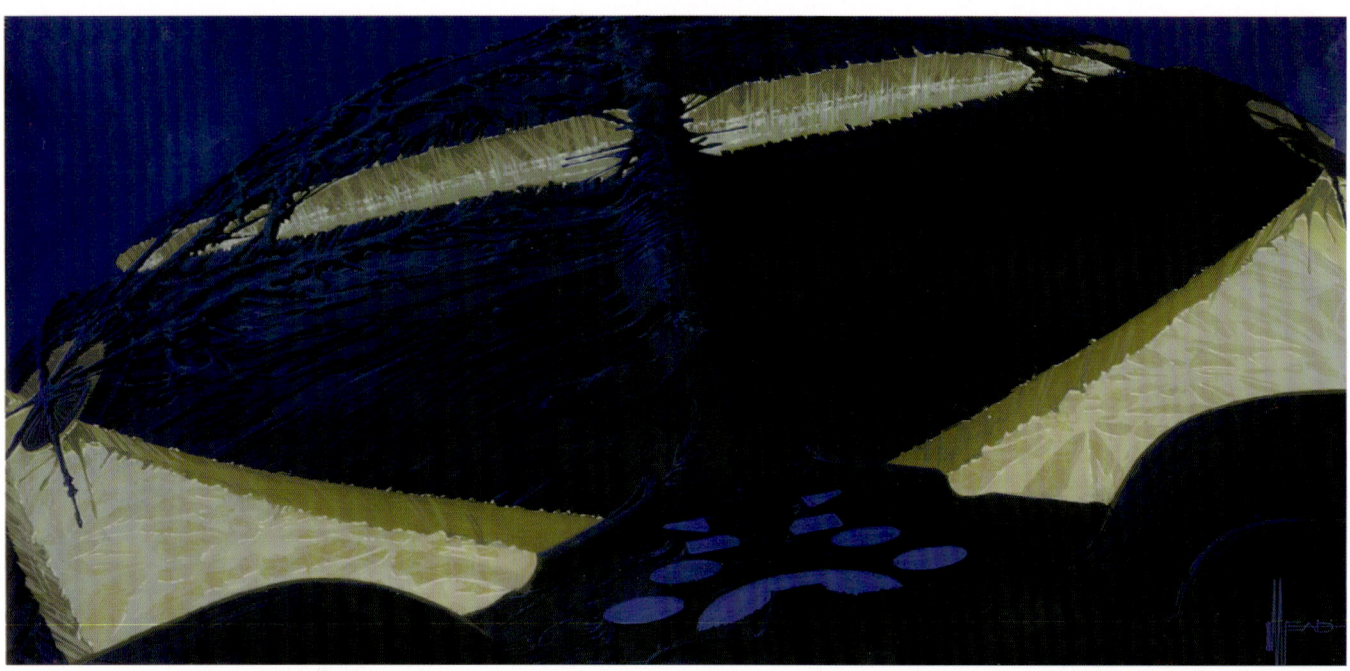

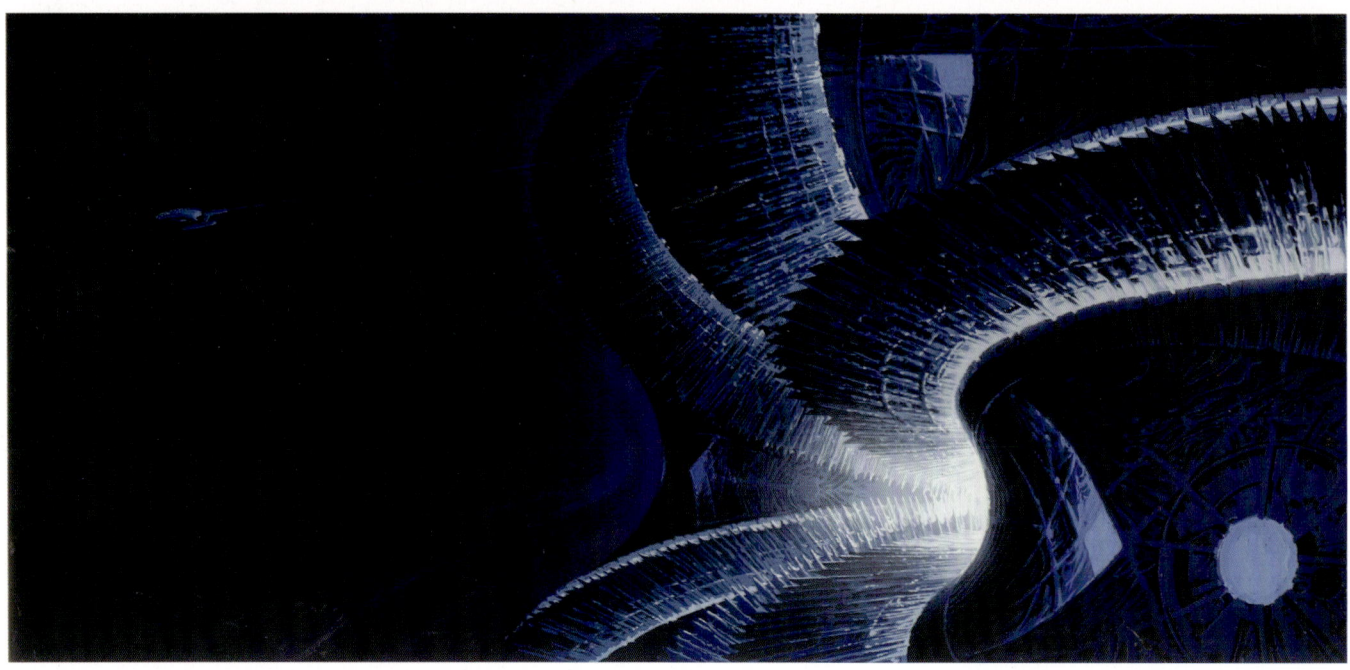

V'ger's maw opens via a mechanical cam arrangement, which confers a hexagonal geometry to both the surface design and the detailed patterns within. The frontal view features dark and light kaliedoscopic imagery which, in lateral disposition, can be seen to resemble alien facial features.

A quasi-organic surface treatment avoids simplistic interpretation bringing a mysterious, hybridized identity to the curving tentacles as they reach into the depths of infinite space.

WITHIN, A MAGNIFICENT CHAMBER ANIMATED BY
OVERLAPPING TRIANGULAR PLATES SUGGESTS
AN OVERWHELMING KALEIDOSCOPIC SPACE

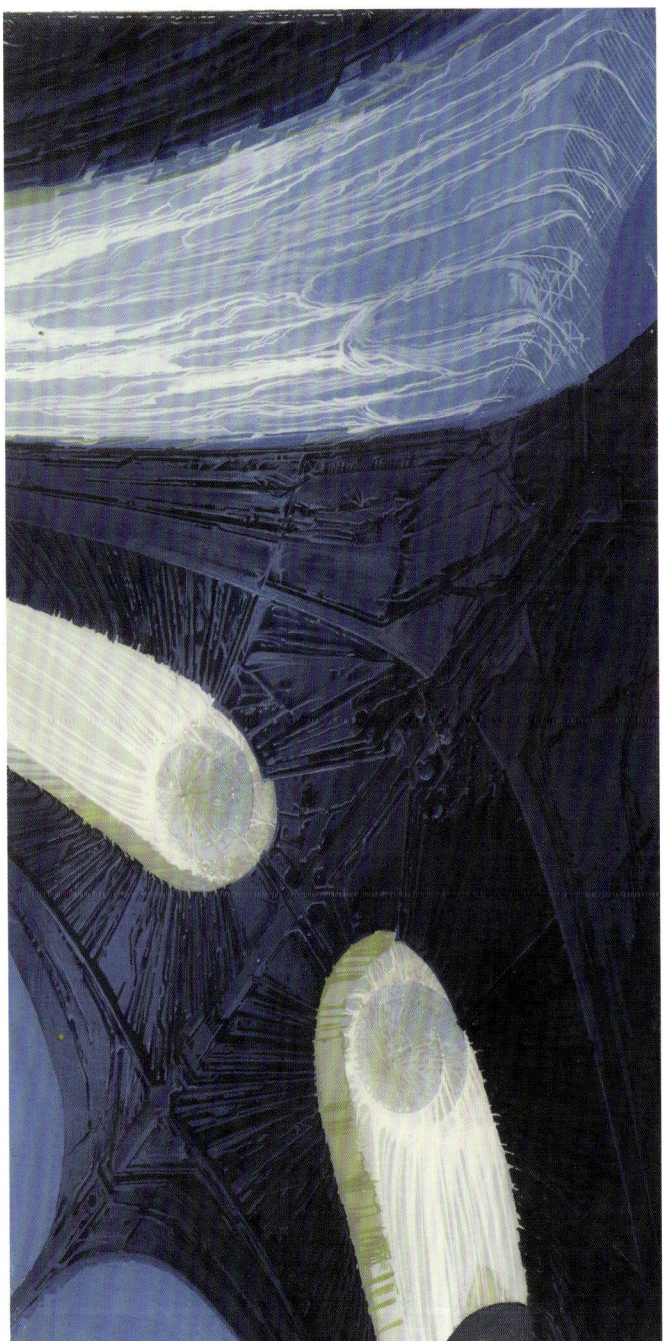 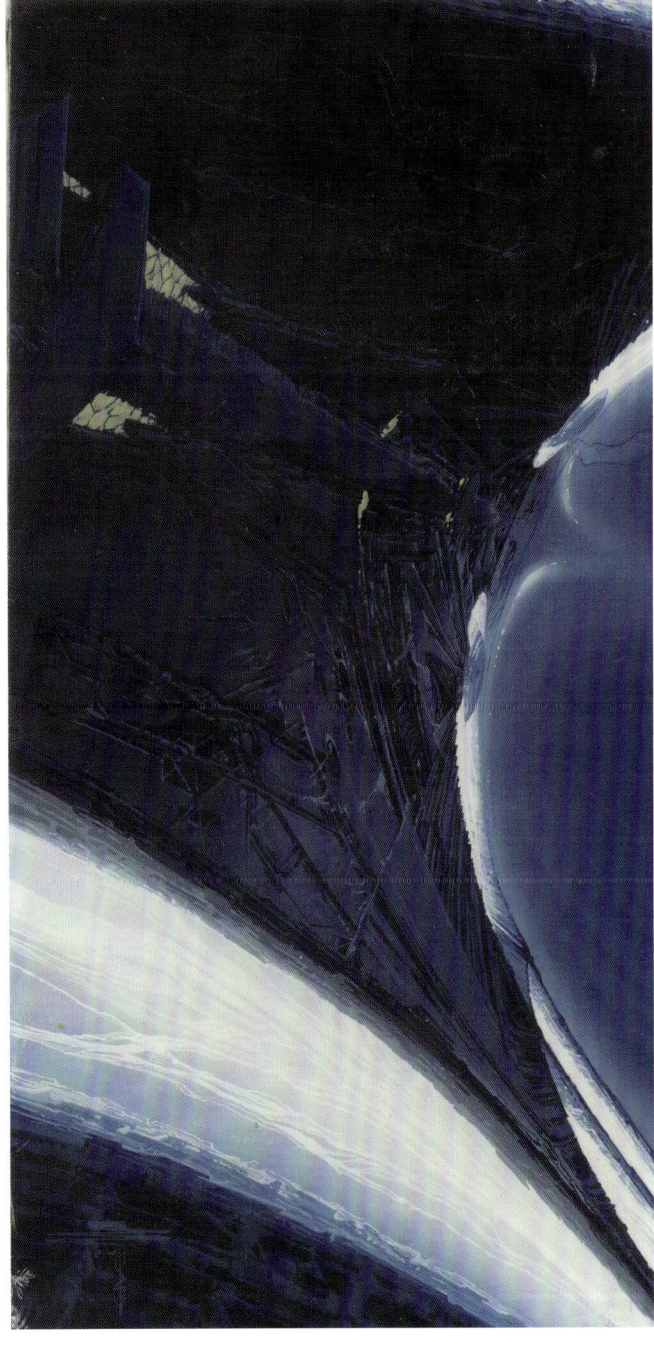

"The director of Star Trek: The Motion Picture, Robert Wise, handed me a portion of the screenplay which said, 'They were looking at something no man had ever seen before'," explains Mead. "The V'ger entity was conceived as a mechanical chaperone of planetoid size given intelligent, self-generative powers in order to protect the fragile Voyager 6 on the journey back to its 'Creator' on Earth. The surface relief and organic pattern arrangement were designed to suggest an organic complexity of organization and a layered, evolutionary growth."

This treatment, in retrospect, represents a dramatic departure from the conventions of futurist imagery, initiating a trend in depictions of other worlds that continues to the present day.

RIGHT AND BELOW: THE DETAILED SURFACE OF THE V'GER FORWARD OF THE VANES

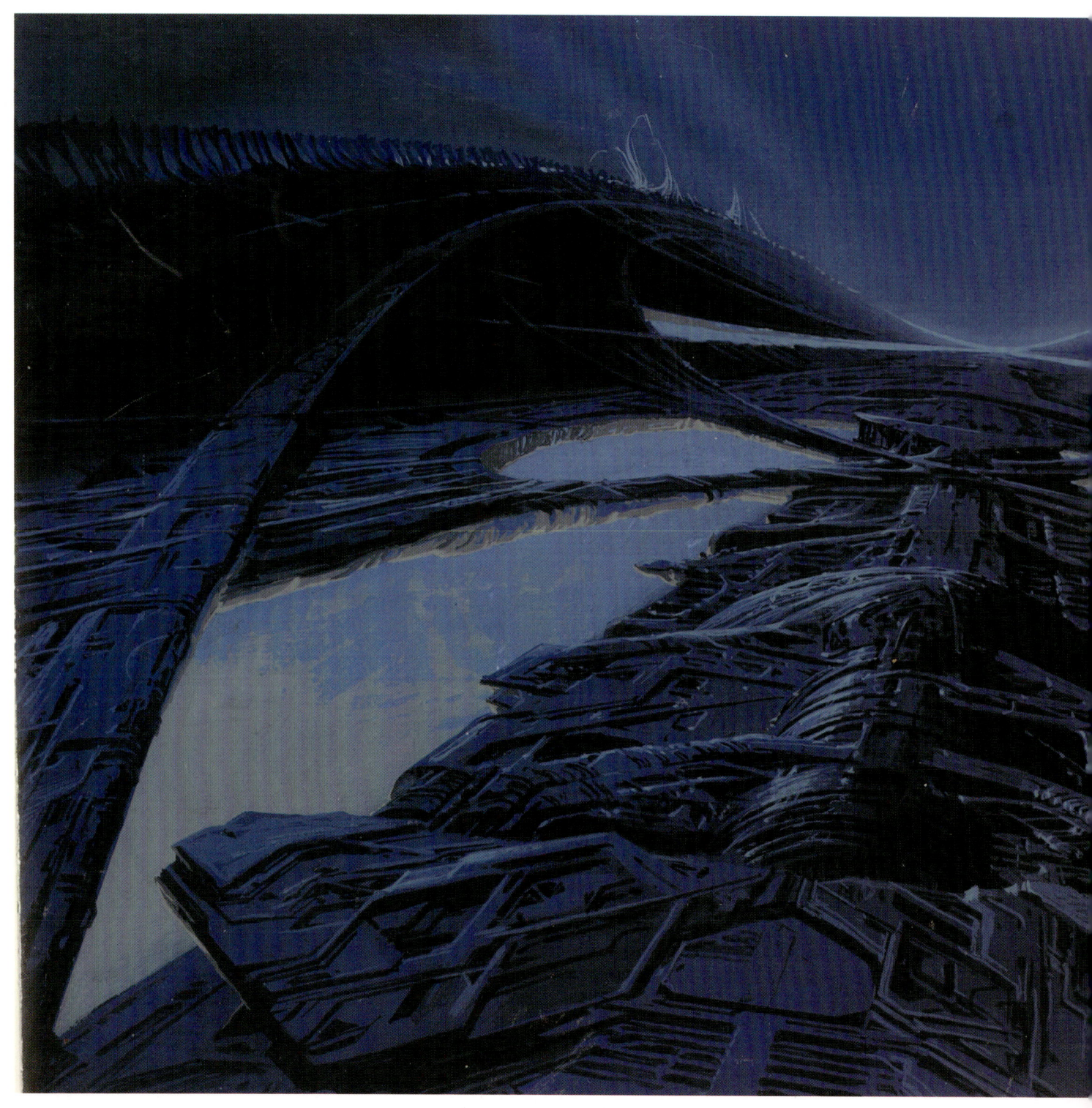

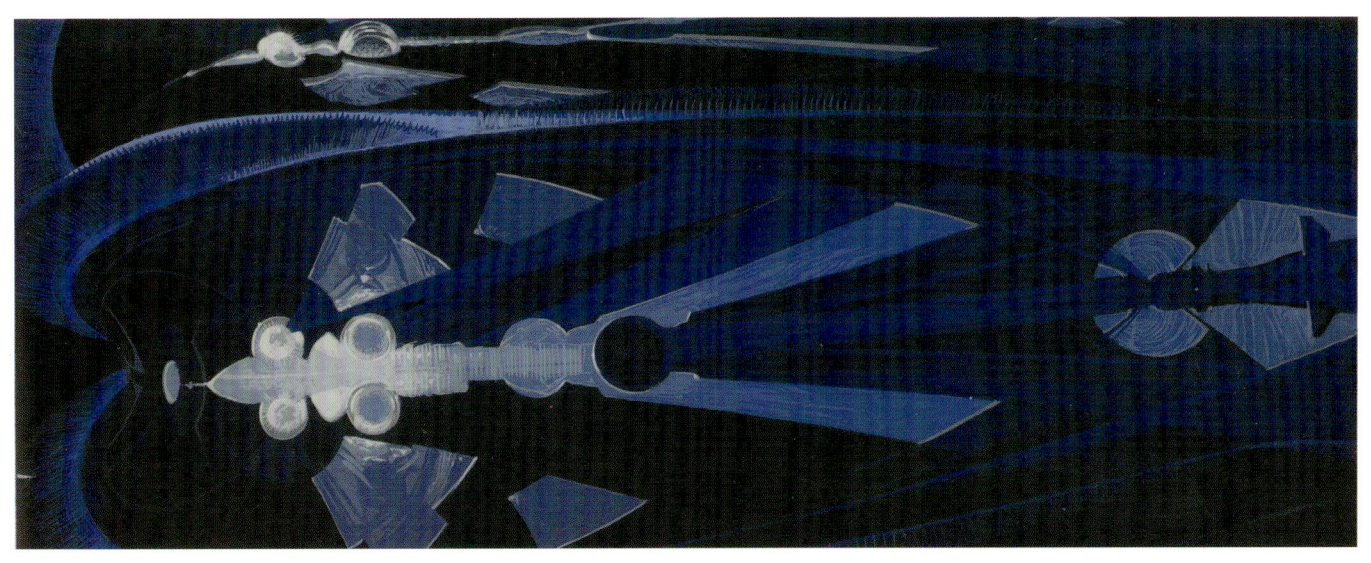

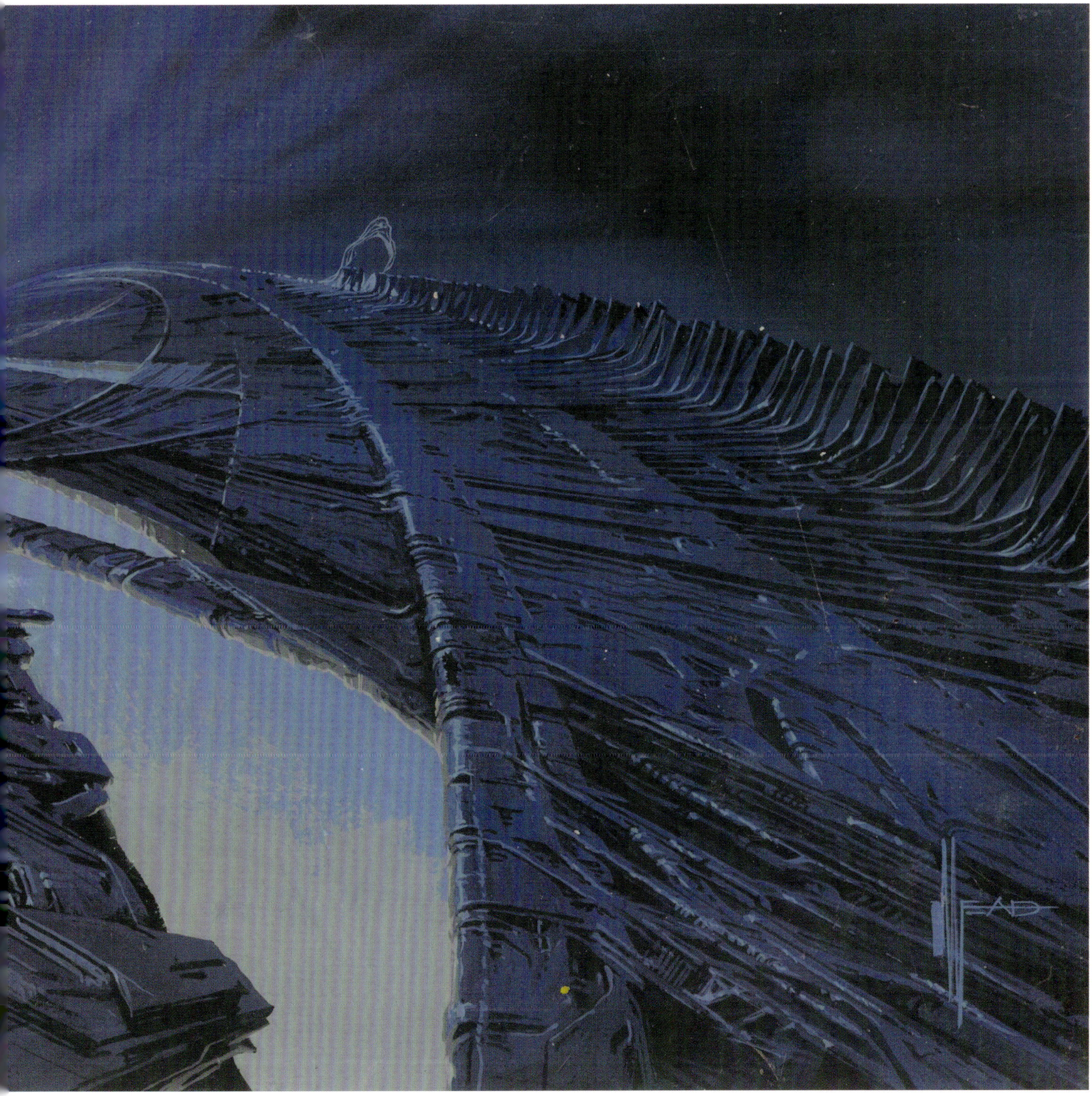

STRANGE DAYS

MIND GRABBER

Strange Days was released in 1995 but originally conceived of by James Cameron in 1986. It marks the directorial debut of Katherine Bigelow, featured a story that mixed snuff films, drugs, and desert action in a scenario that depended on a biomechanical device that transferred instructions and sensations directly into the brain. Mead was recruited to design the device with only a concept draft of the script, and little in the way of visual references. Mead's design pioneered the "look" of today's virtual reality headsets with a tight-fitting, four-fingered, vaguely medical headpiece which came to be called a S.Q.U.I.D.

As the first version of the script envisioned a piece of "head jewelry" to be worn on a shaved head, and none of the movie's characters had "shaved heads" the final S.Q.U.I.D. would be worn by actors with long hair. That device, complemented by an electronic device connected by a translucent umbilical, wound up visually similar to a giant centipede clutching the actor's head.

THESE IMAGES SHOW AN EARLY CONCEPT OF THE HEADSET PIONEERING A MORE ORGANIC APPROACH TO TECHNOLOGY DESIGN. THE CONNECTORS ARE REMINISCENT OF AMPHIBIAN 'HANDS' AND 'FEET'.

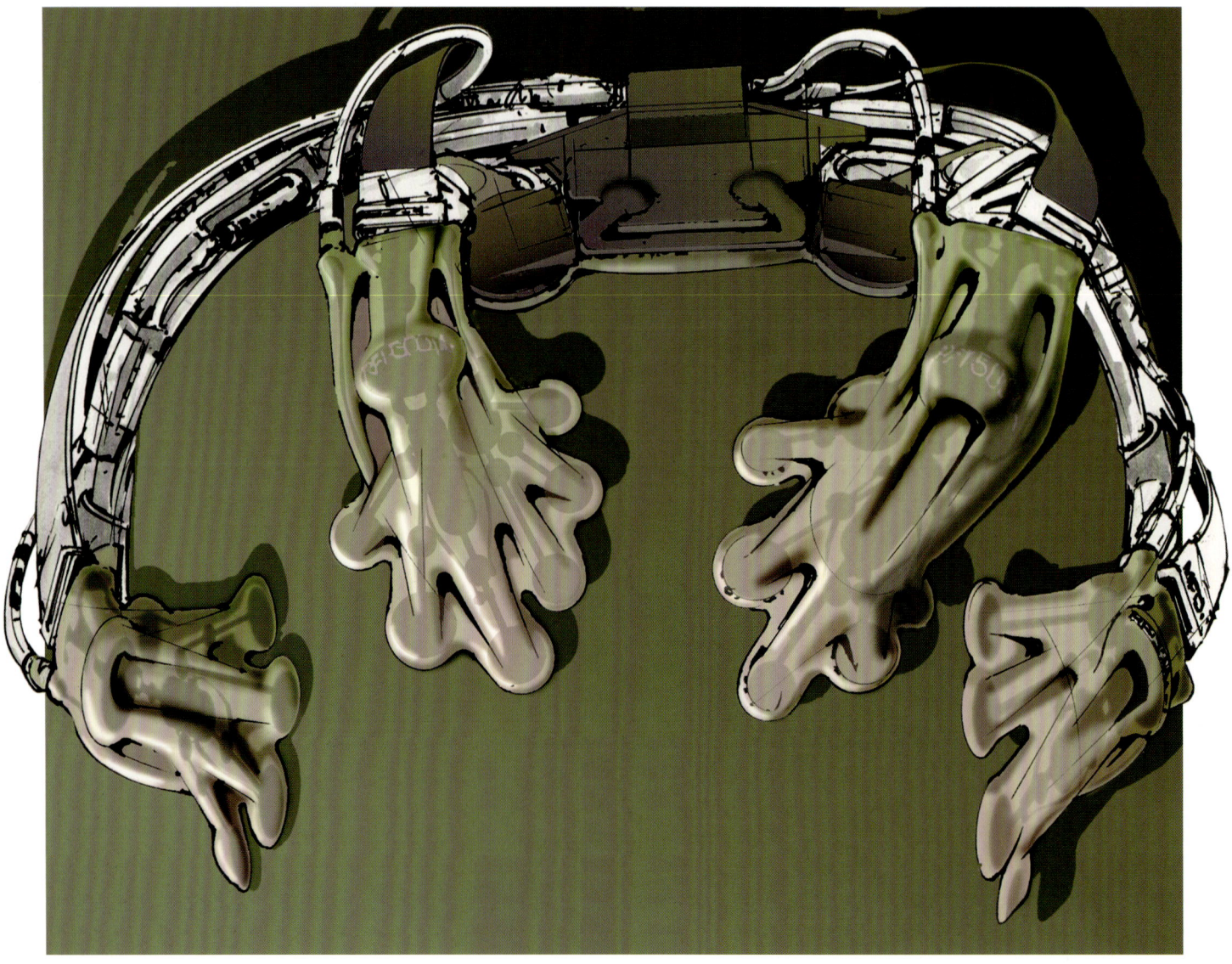

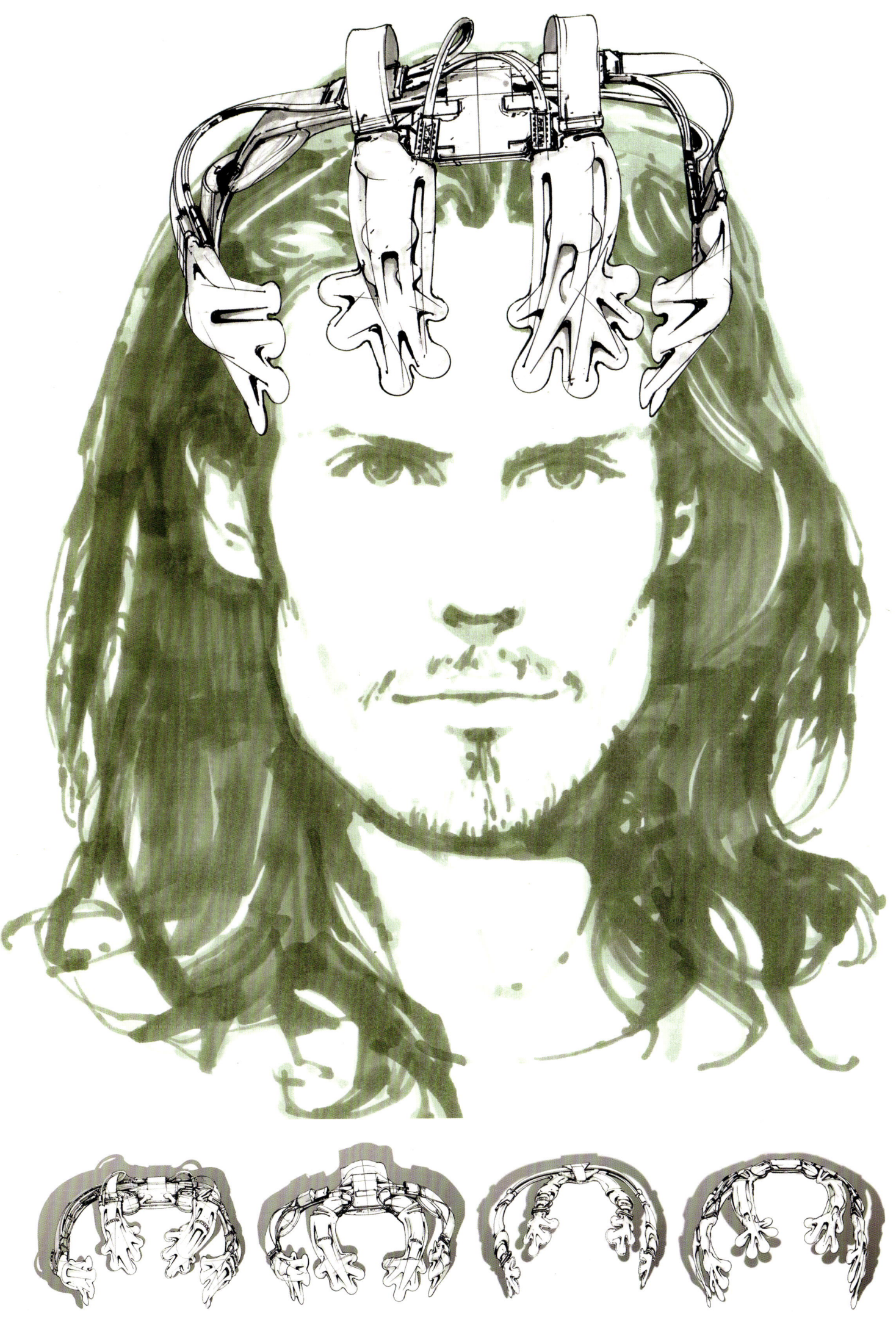

THE CORE

"WE'LL REWRITE, SYD"

As a reboot of the Disney classic *Journey to the Center of the Earth*, the storyline of *The Core* requires its crew to burrow deep beneath the earth's crust in order to avoid a planetary meltdown. As the drilling mechanism was to be a central feature, almost a character unto itself, the producers put their faith in Syd Mead to come up with a plausible "look" for the machine, and Syd, upon reading the script, informed them of a flaw in the engineering logic of the script: that the writers had failed to understand that the debris from the excavation would need to be disposed of behind the advancing machine. Mead then went further to hypothesize that a high-powered laser might liquefy the solid rock, thus allowing it to be expelled more efficiently.

Director Peter Hyams agreed to the changes, tweaking the script and completing the movie, which was released in 2003.

THIS PAGE: MEAD'S ORIGINAL SKETCHES FOR *VIRGIL*, THE CENTIPEDE-LIKE VEHICLE WHICH TAKES THE HEROES DEEP INTO THE EARTH.

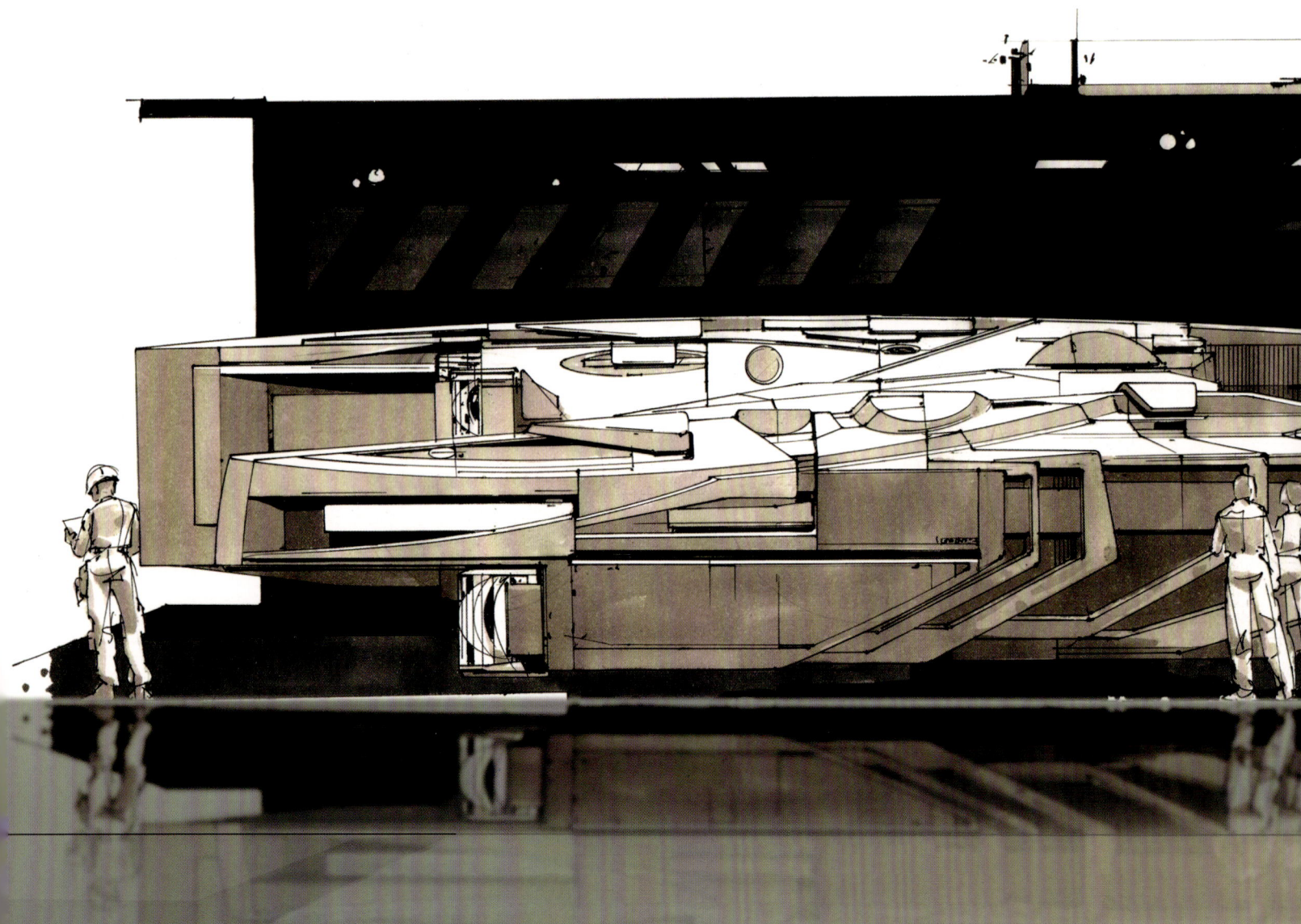

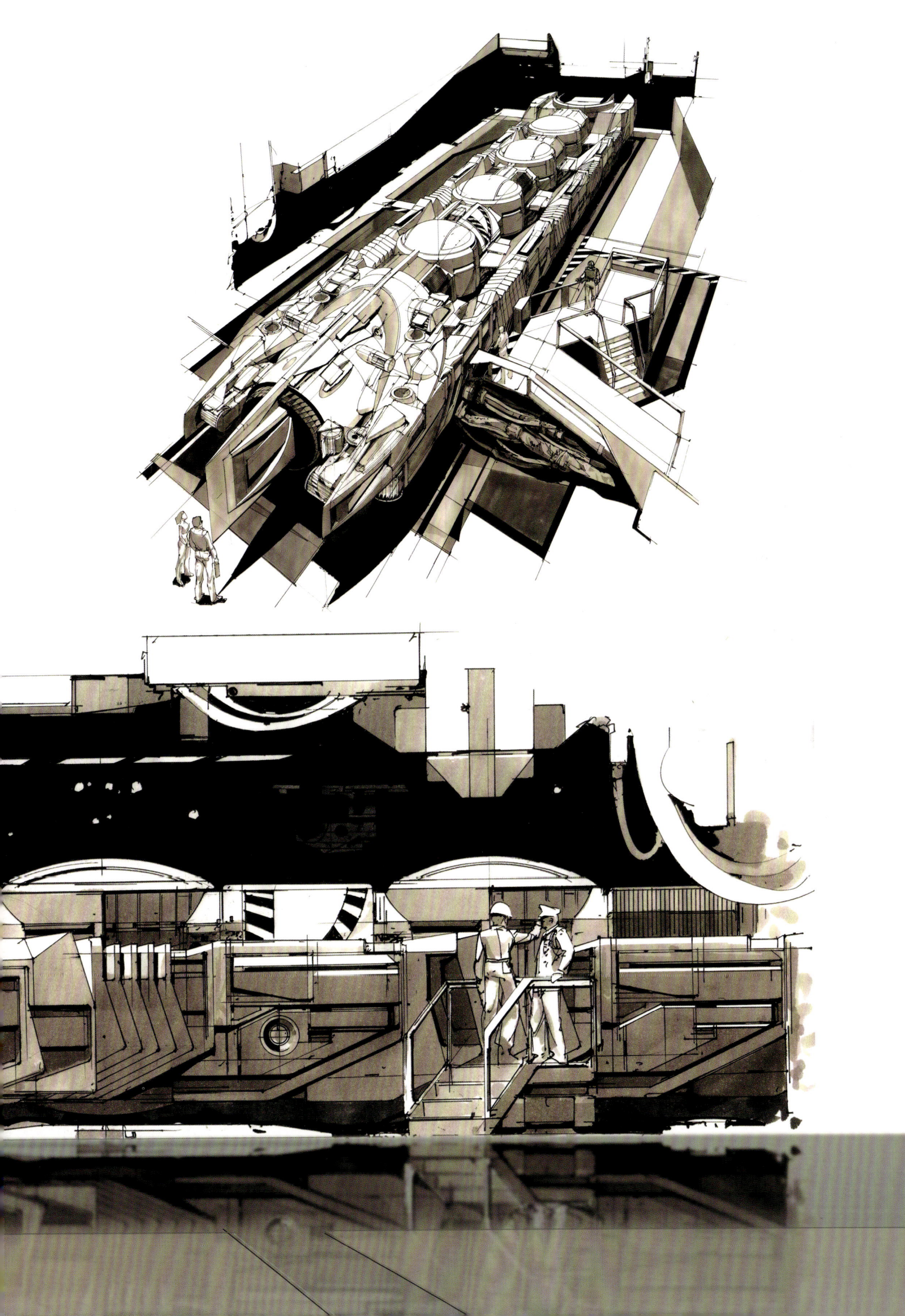

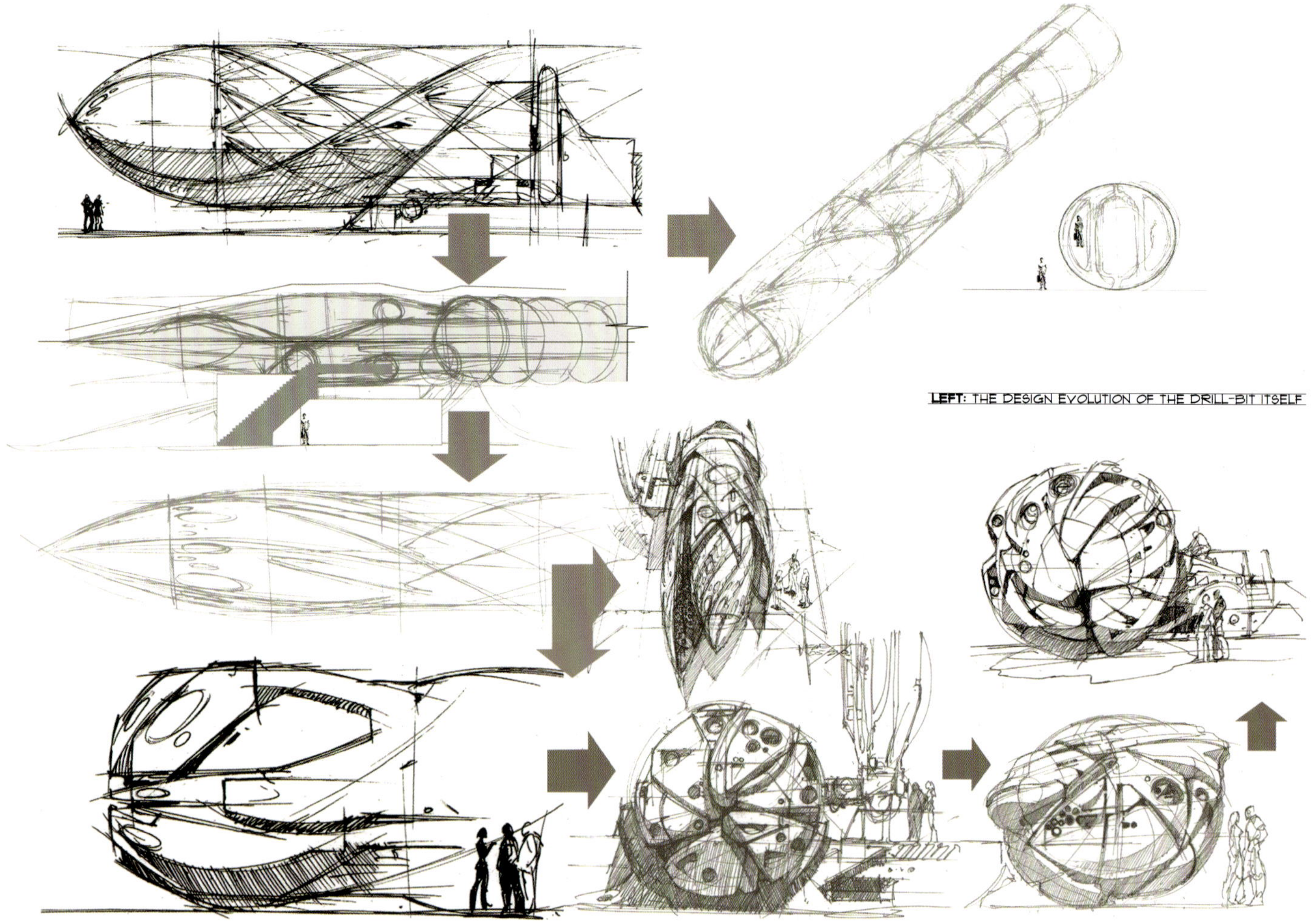

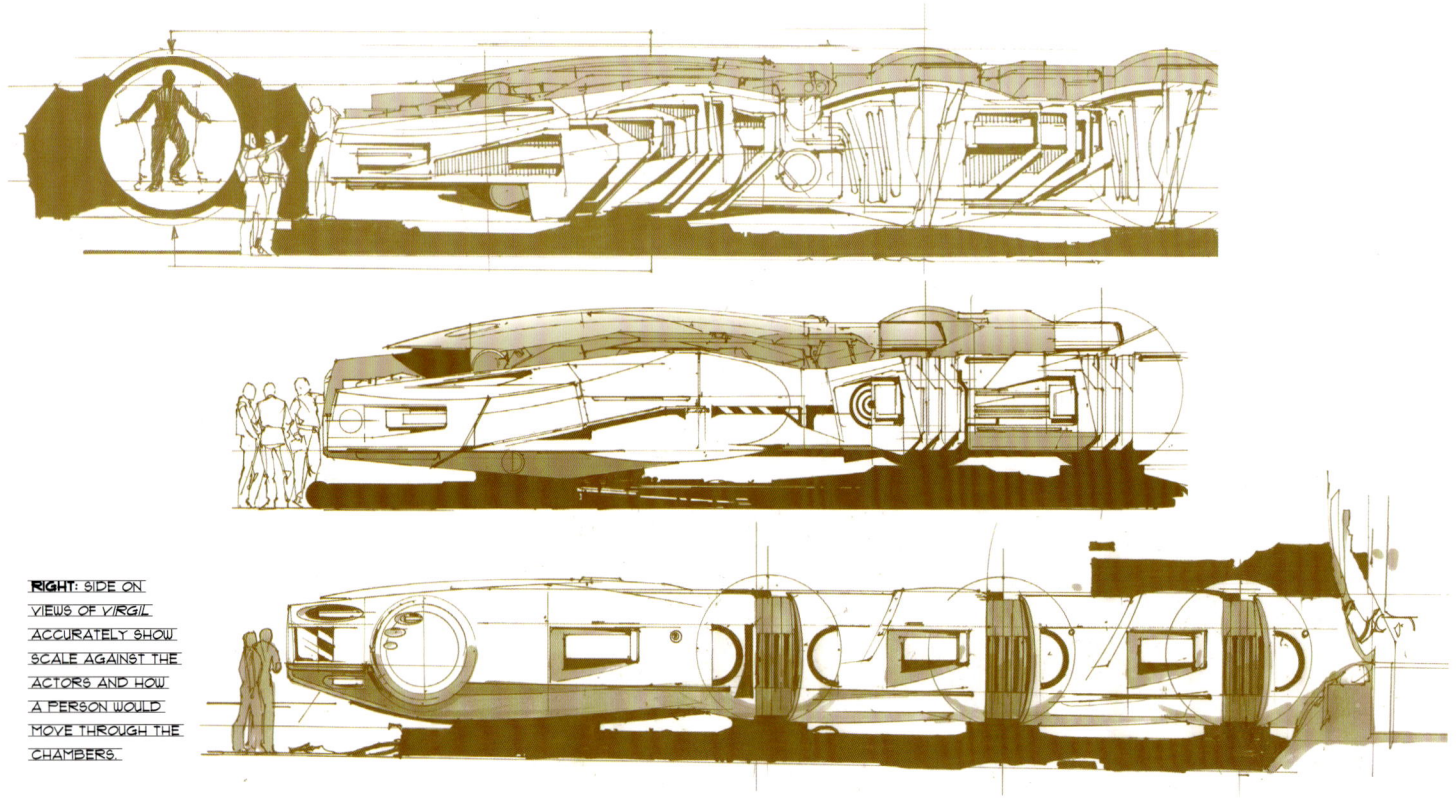

LEFT: THE DESIGN EVOLUTION OF THE DRILL-BIT ITSELF

As these sketches demonstrate, in the evolution of the machine dubbed *Virgil*, Mead sought to combine the engineering logic of an Archimedes Screw to remove the dross with the anthropomorphic image of a larger-than-life hand.

Blending the imagery and devising a plausible means to uncouple sections of *Virgil* as the story evolved led to a final design with specialized capsules, each devoted to a specific task.

RIGHT: SIDE ON VIEWS OF *VIRGIL* ACCURATELY SHOW SCALE AGAINST THE ACTORS AND HOW A PERSON WOULD MOVE THROUGH THE CHAMBERS

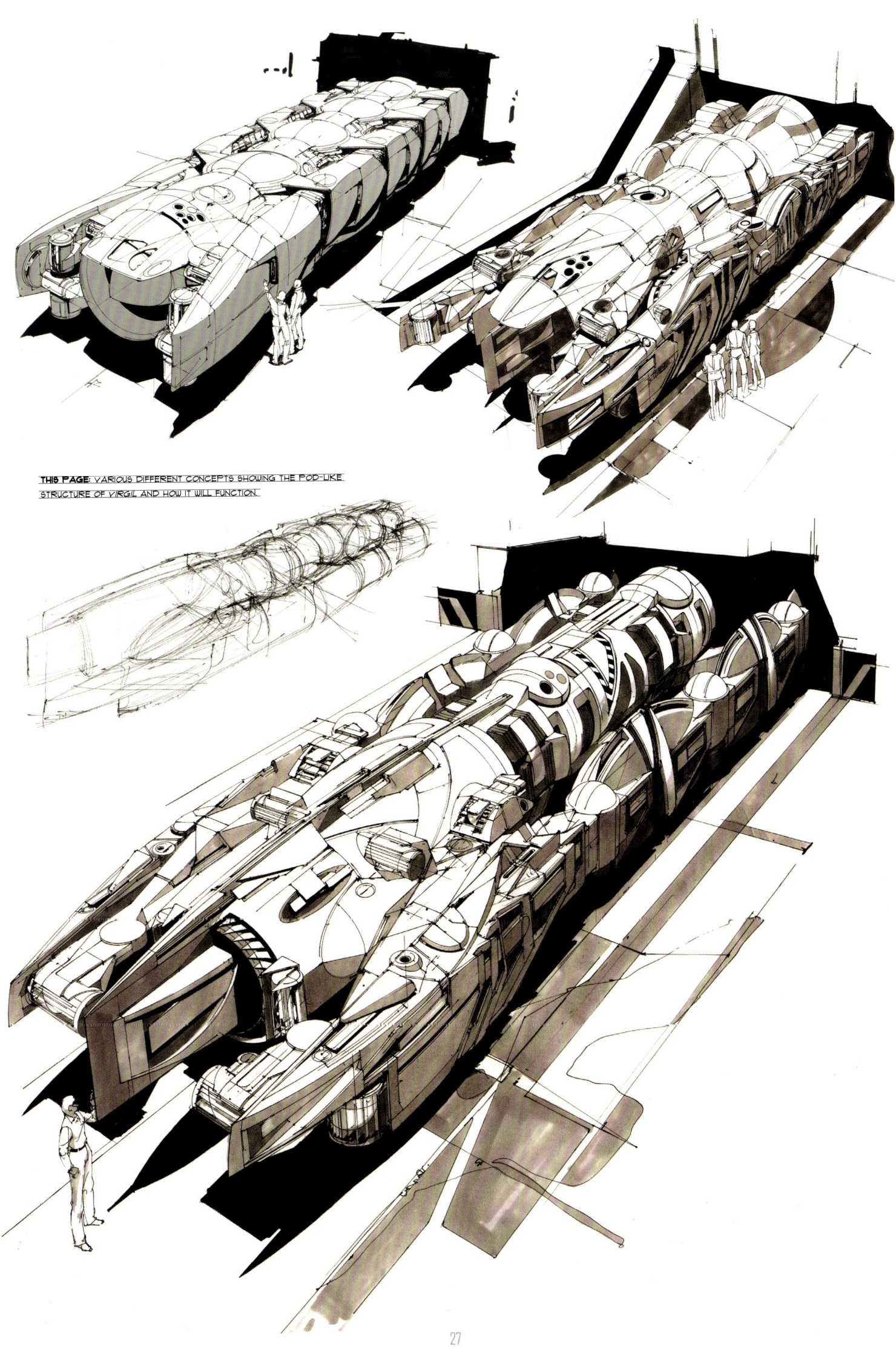

THIS PAGE: VARIOUS DIFFERENT CONCEPTS SHOWING THE POD-LIKE STRUCTURE OF *VIRGIL* AND HOW IT WILL FUNCTION.

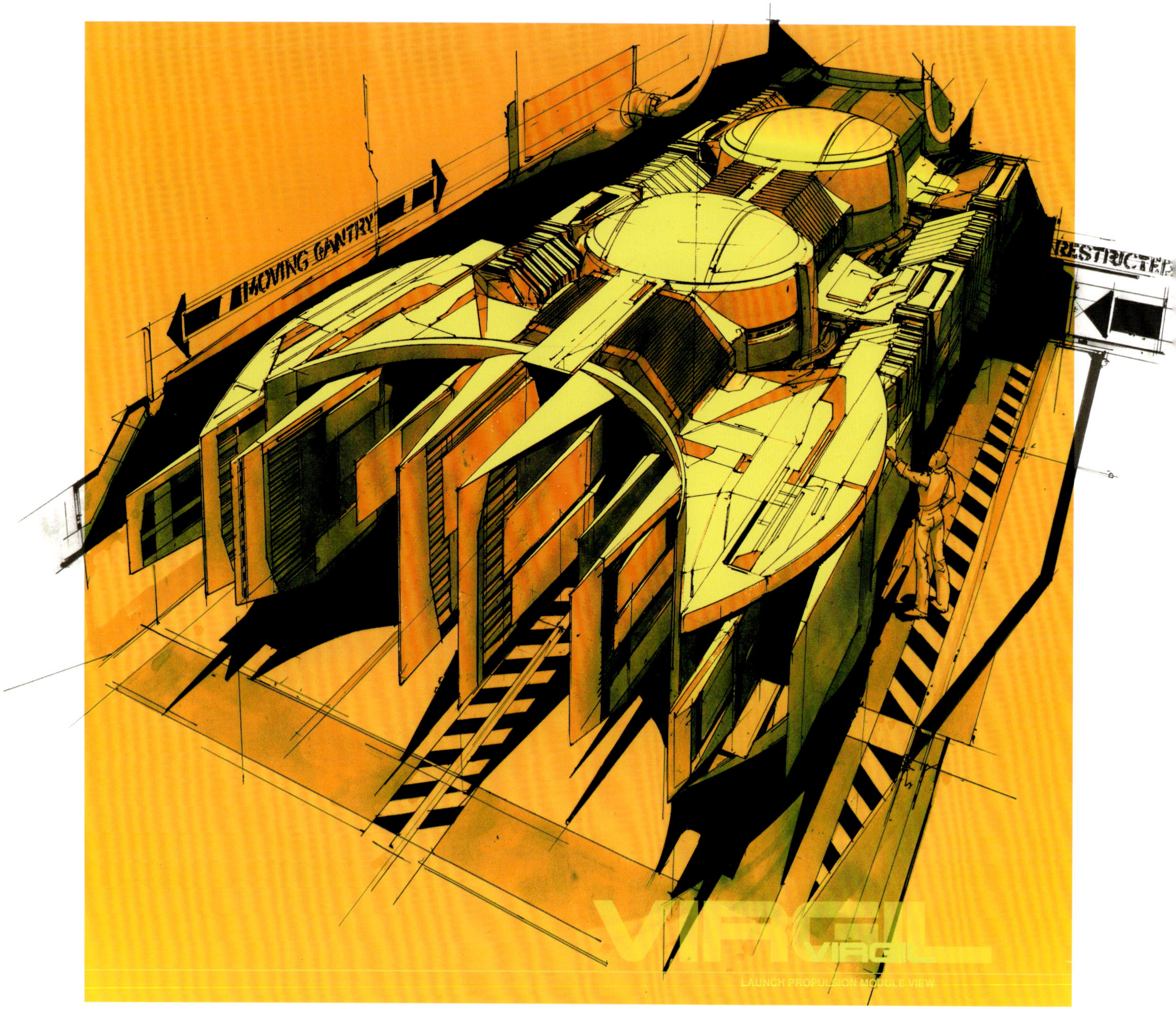

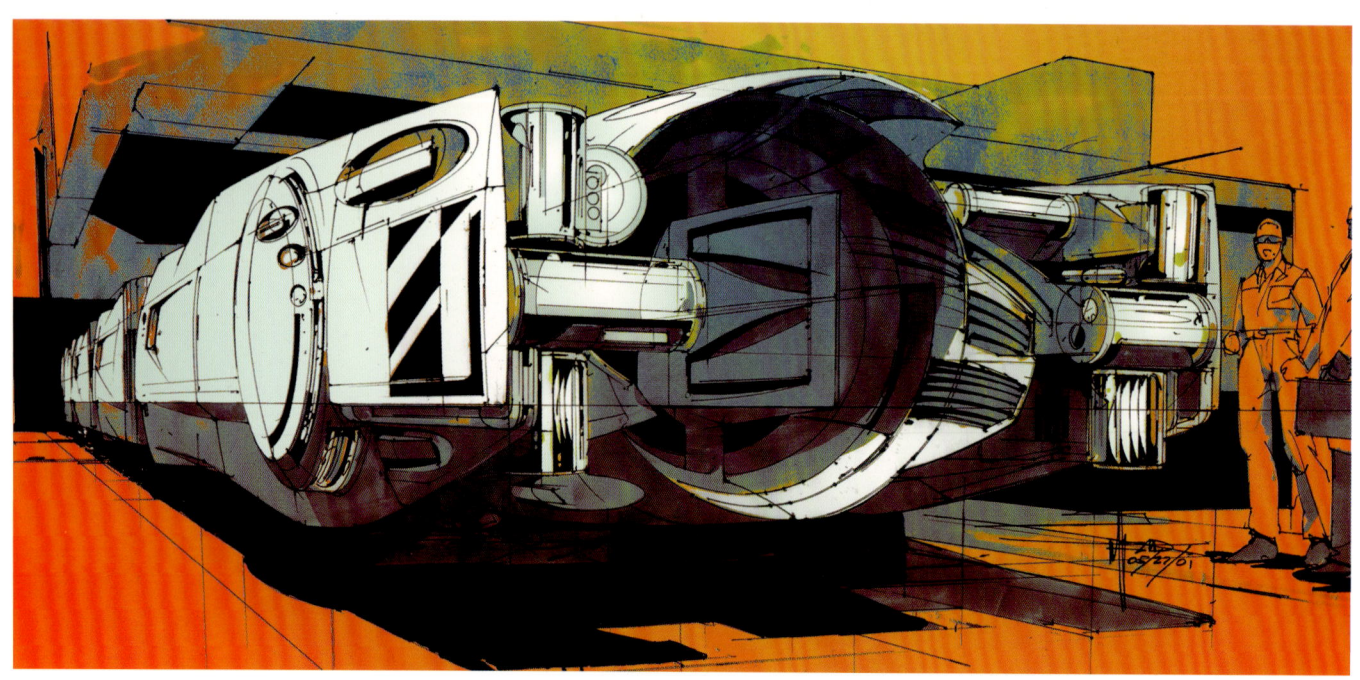

MOVING GANTRY

RESTRICTED

VIRGIL
LAUNCH PROPULSION MODULE VIEW

AS MEAD'S RESEARCH REVEALED A HIGH-POWERED LASER MIGHT BE ABLE TO LIQUEFY THE ROCK, HE REVISED HIS INITIAL DESIGN WITH THE ARCHIMEDES SCREW TO A MASSIVE BURROWING MACHINE FEATURING BLADE-LIKE APERTURES HOUSING HIGH-POWERED LASERS WHICH COULD SAW THROUGH THE ROCK AND CHANNEL THE MOLTEN LAVA FLOW THROUGH THE ADVANCING RIG.

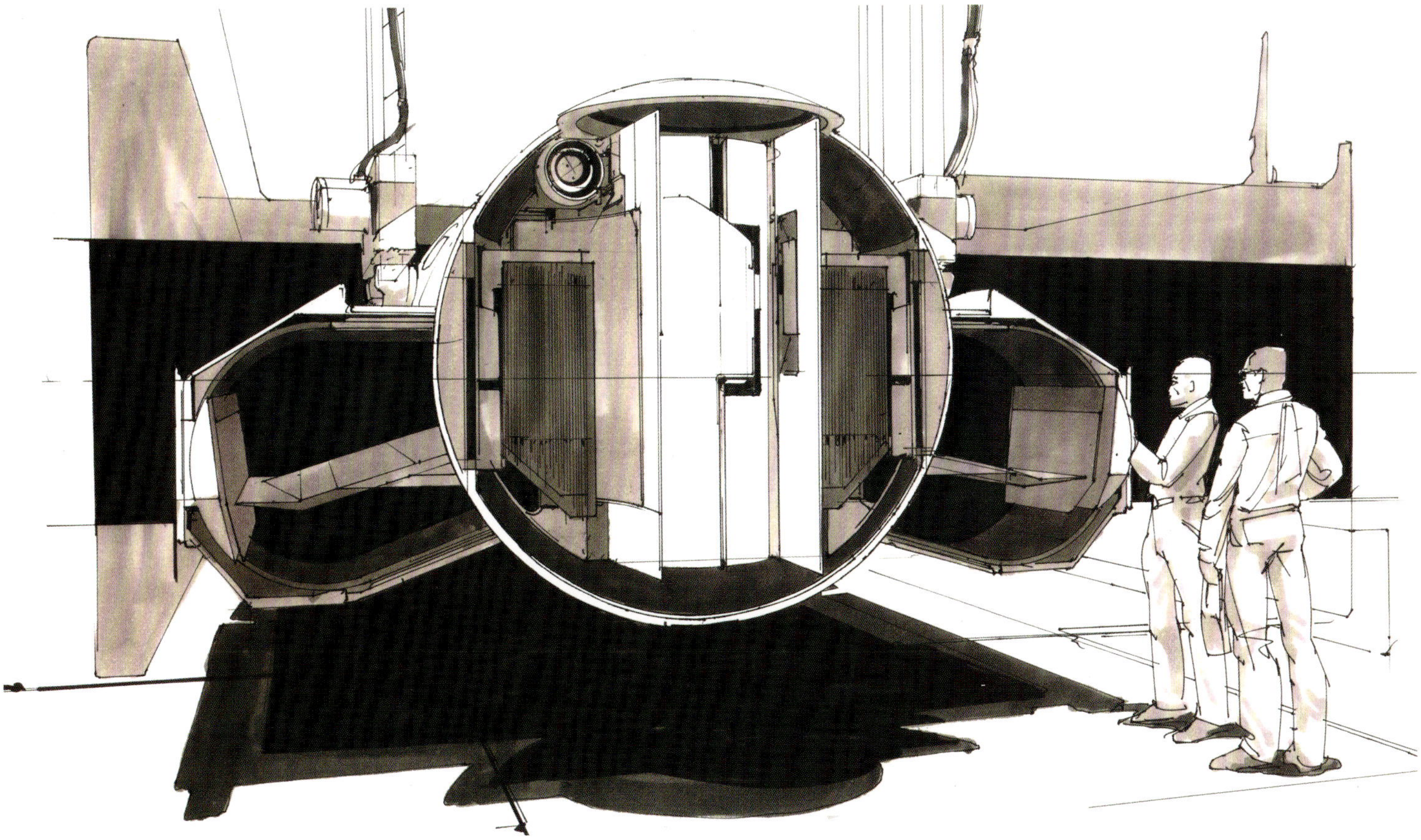

THE BUSINESS END OF THE RIG FEATURES A SERIES OF
ADJUSTABLE LASER-ARMED BLADES WHICH CAN BE EXTENDED
AND MANIPULATED LIKE RUDDERS TO CHANNEL MOLTEN ROCK
AS IT BORES EVER DEEPER INTO THE EARTH'S CRUST.

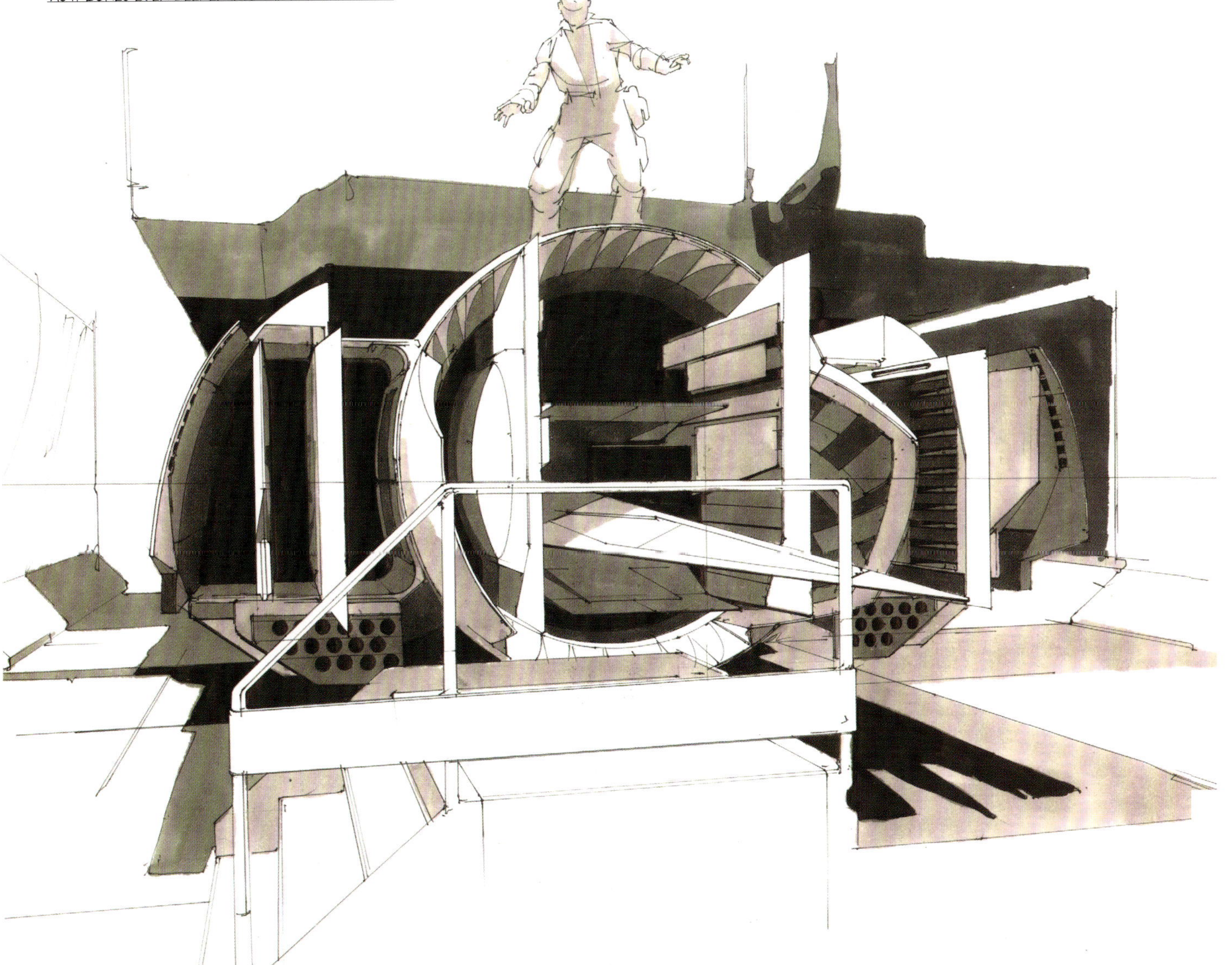

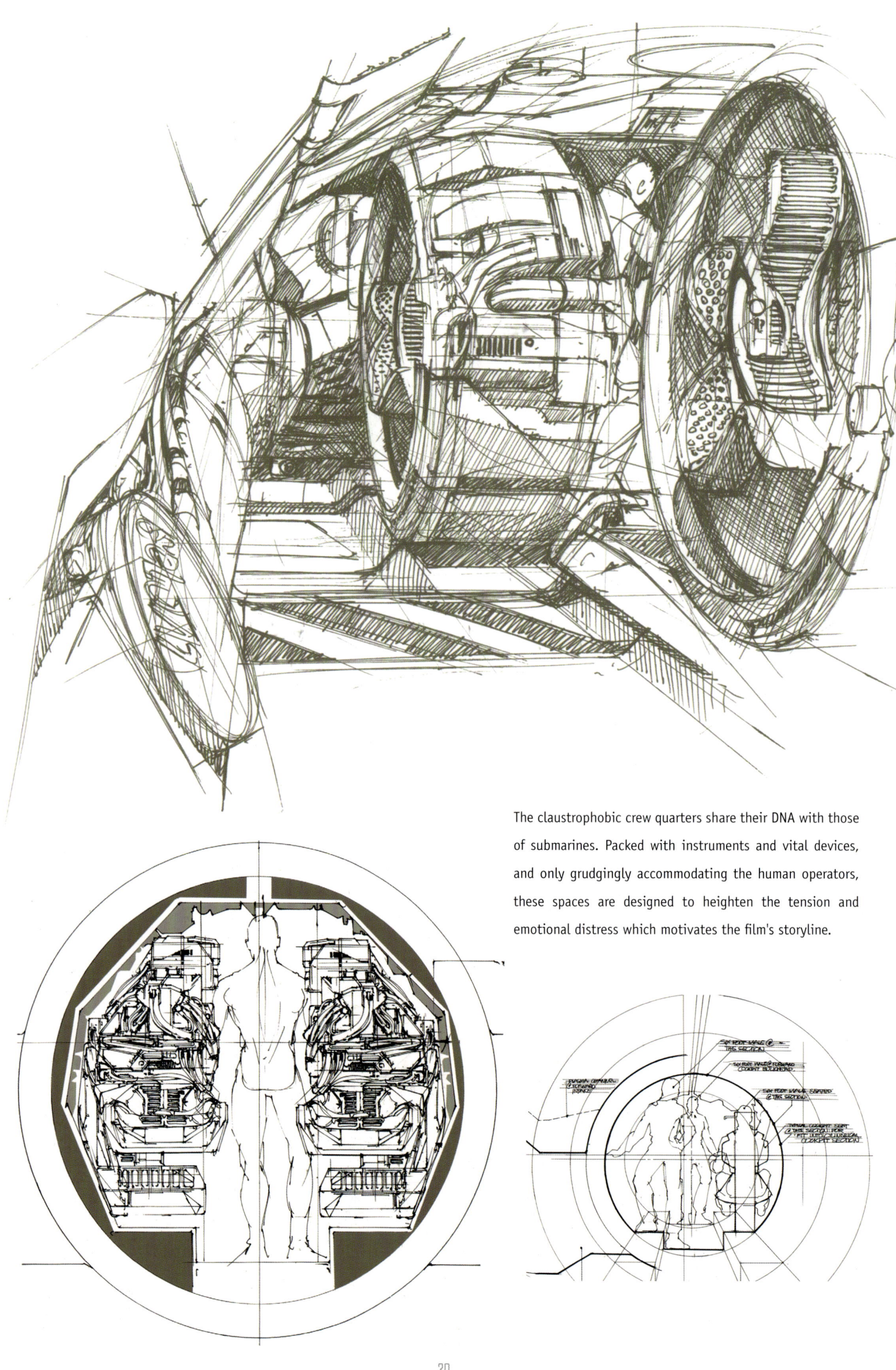

The claustrophobic crew quarters share their DNA with those of submarines. Packed with instruments and vital devices, and only grudgingly accommodating the human operators, these spaces are designed to heighten the tension and emotional distress which motivates the film's storyline.

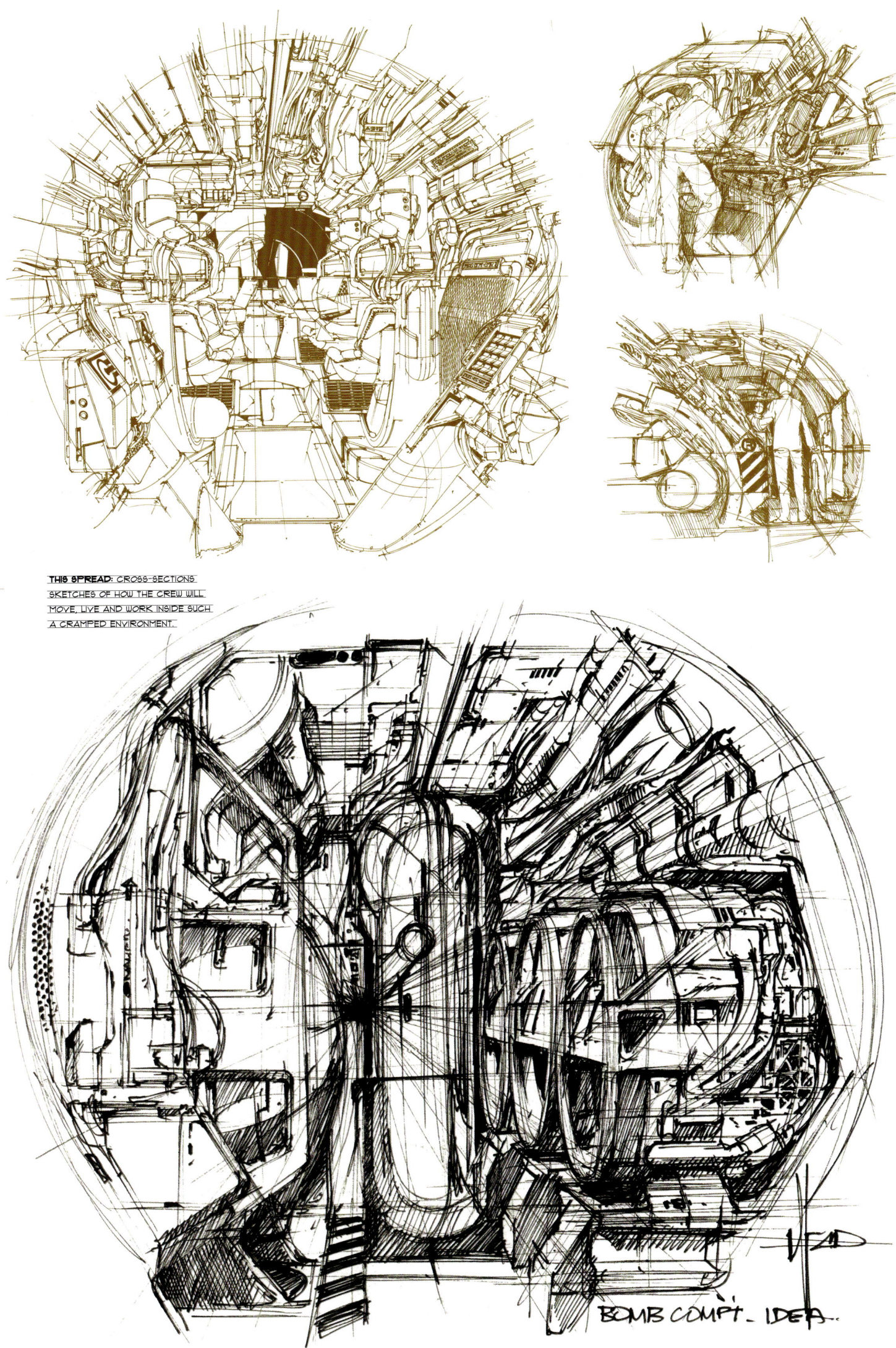

THIS SPREAD: CROSS-SECTIONS SKETCHES OF HOW THE CREW WILL MOVE, LIVE AND WORK INSIDE SUCH A CRAMPED ENVIRONMENT.

BOMB COMP't _ IDEA...

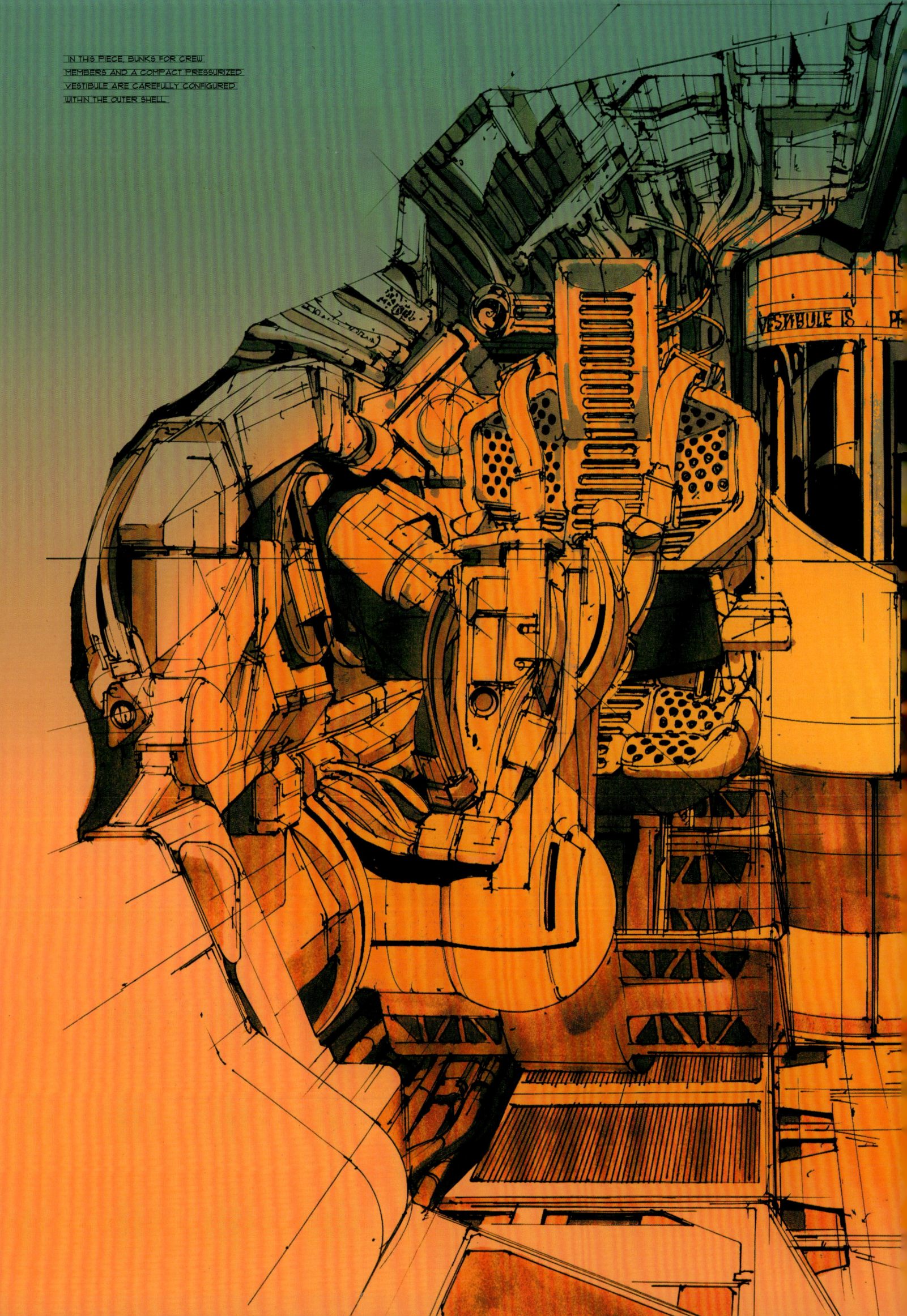

IN THIS PIECE, BUNKS FOR CREW
MEMBERS AND A COMPACT PRESSURIZED
VESTIBULE ARE CAREFULLY CONFIGURED
WITHIN THE OUTER SHELL

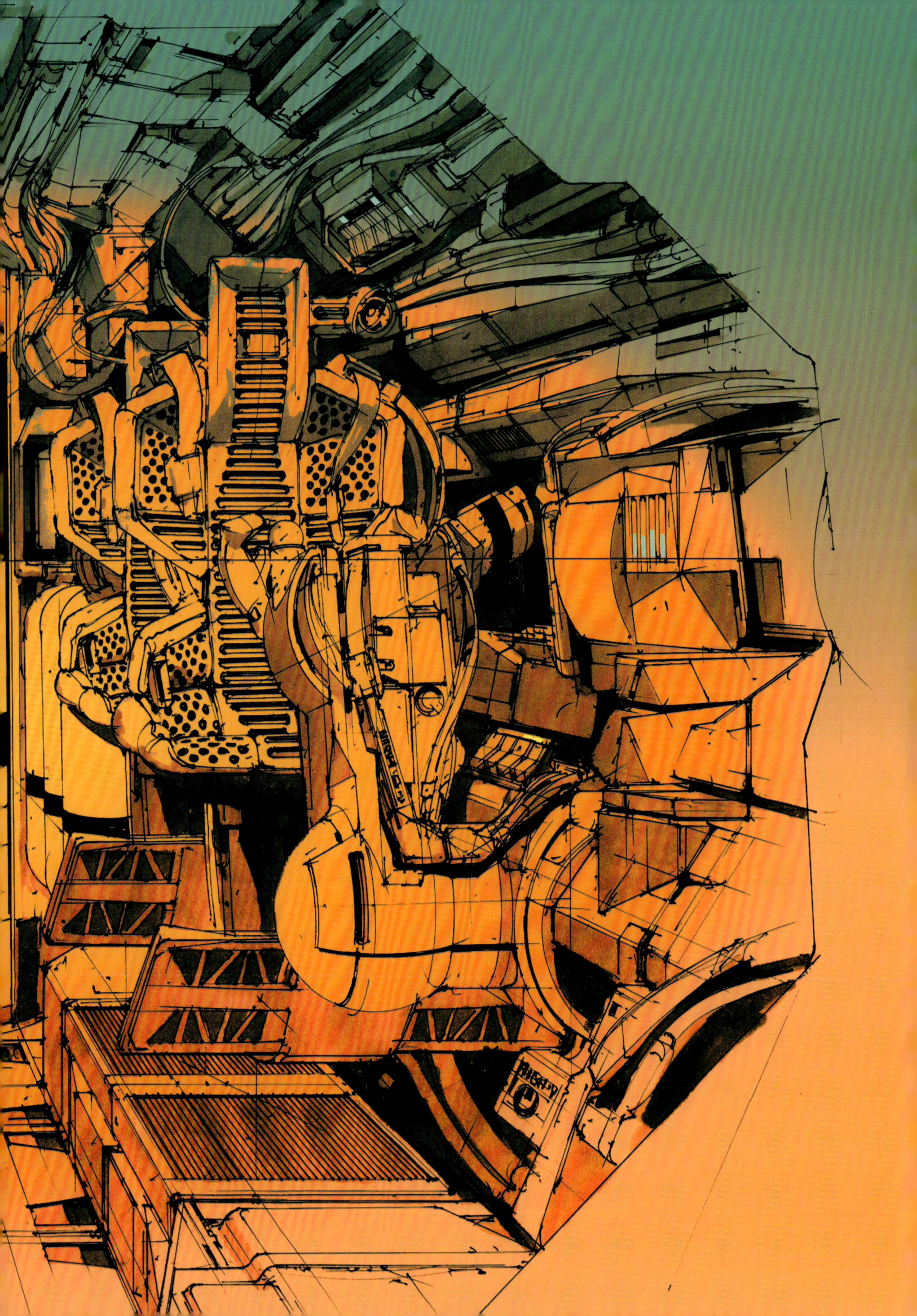

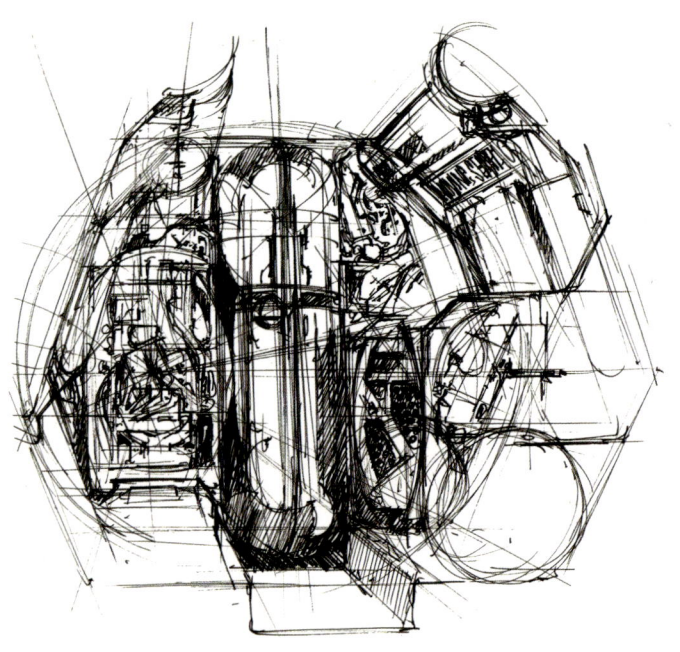

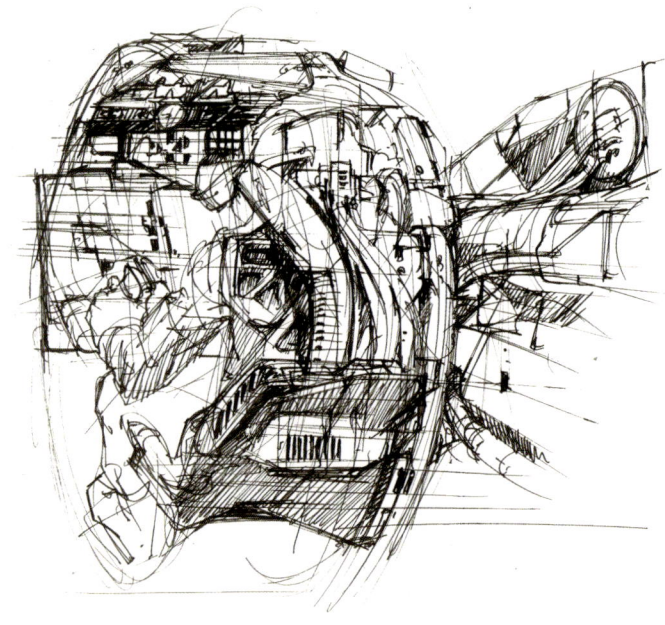

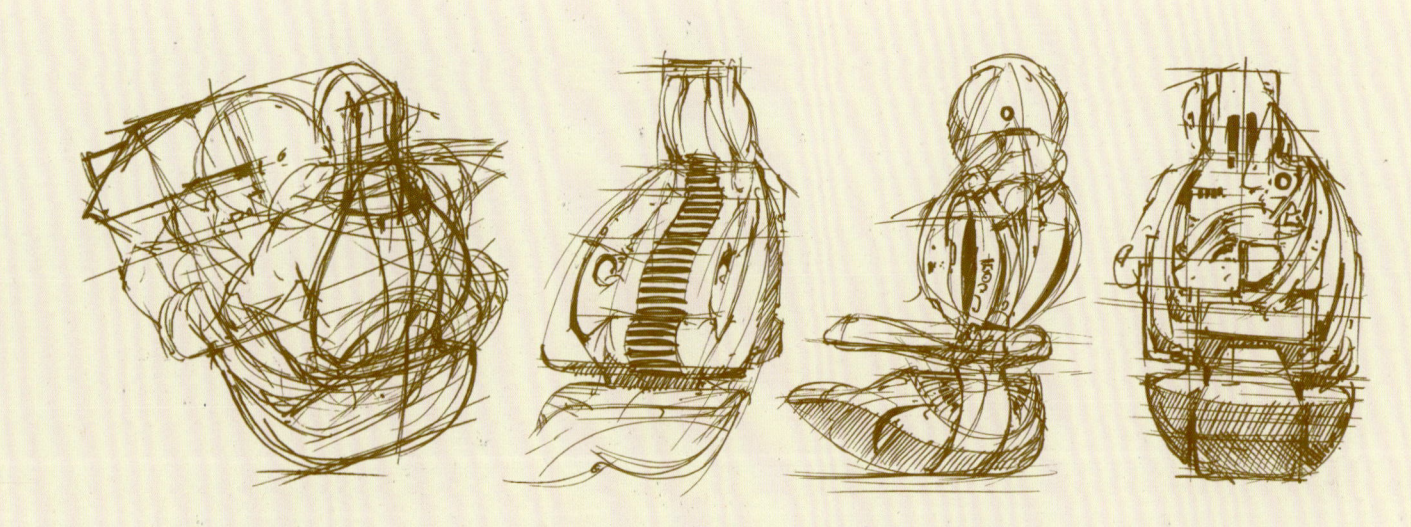

DETAILED STUDIES FOR THE COCKPIT OPERATIONS CENTER REVEAL MEAD'S NEAR OBSESSION WITH THE PARTICULARS OF THE TASK OF OPERATING *VIRGIL* AS IT MAKES ITS WAY TOWARDS THE CENTER OF THE EARTH.

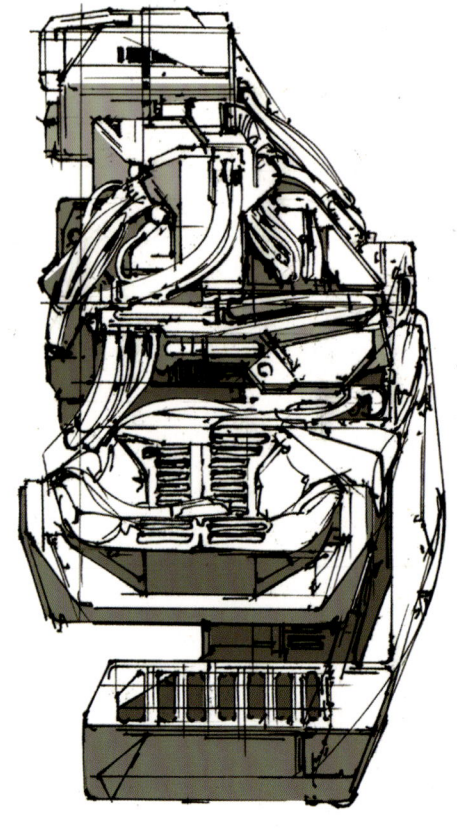

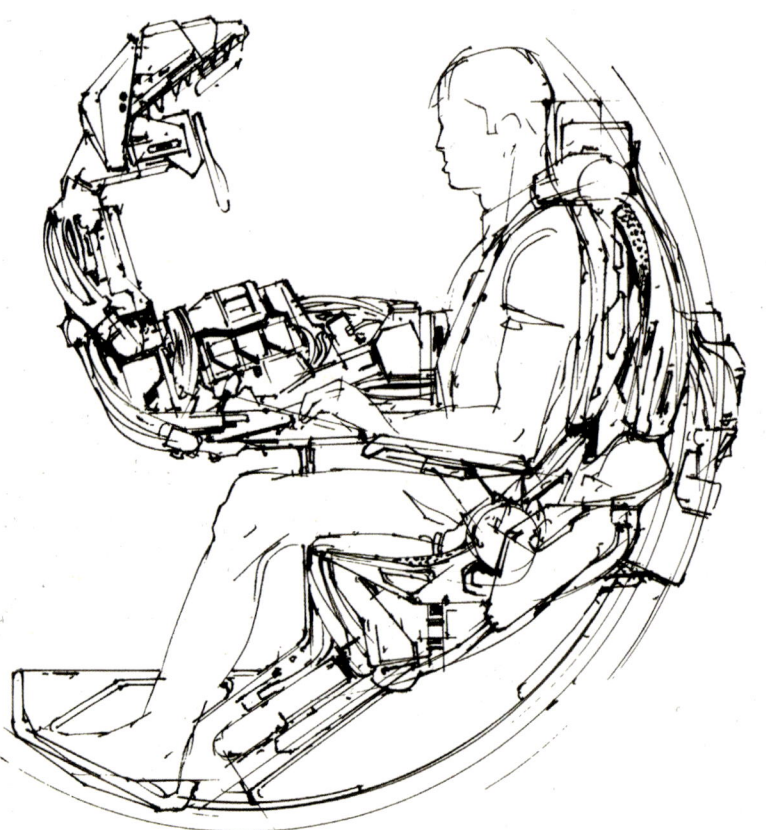

THE GYROSCOPICALLY STABILIZED, ERGONOMICALLY CORRECT SEATING, WITH A SWING-AWAY CONTROL CONSOLE, IS DESIGNED TO PIVOT THE OPERATOR INTO AN ERECT POSTURE REGARDLESS OF THE ORIENTATION OF *VIRGIL*.

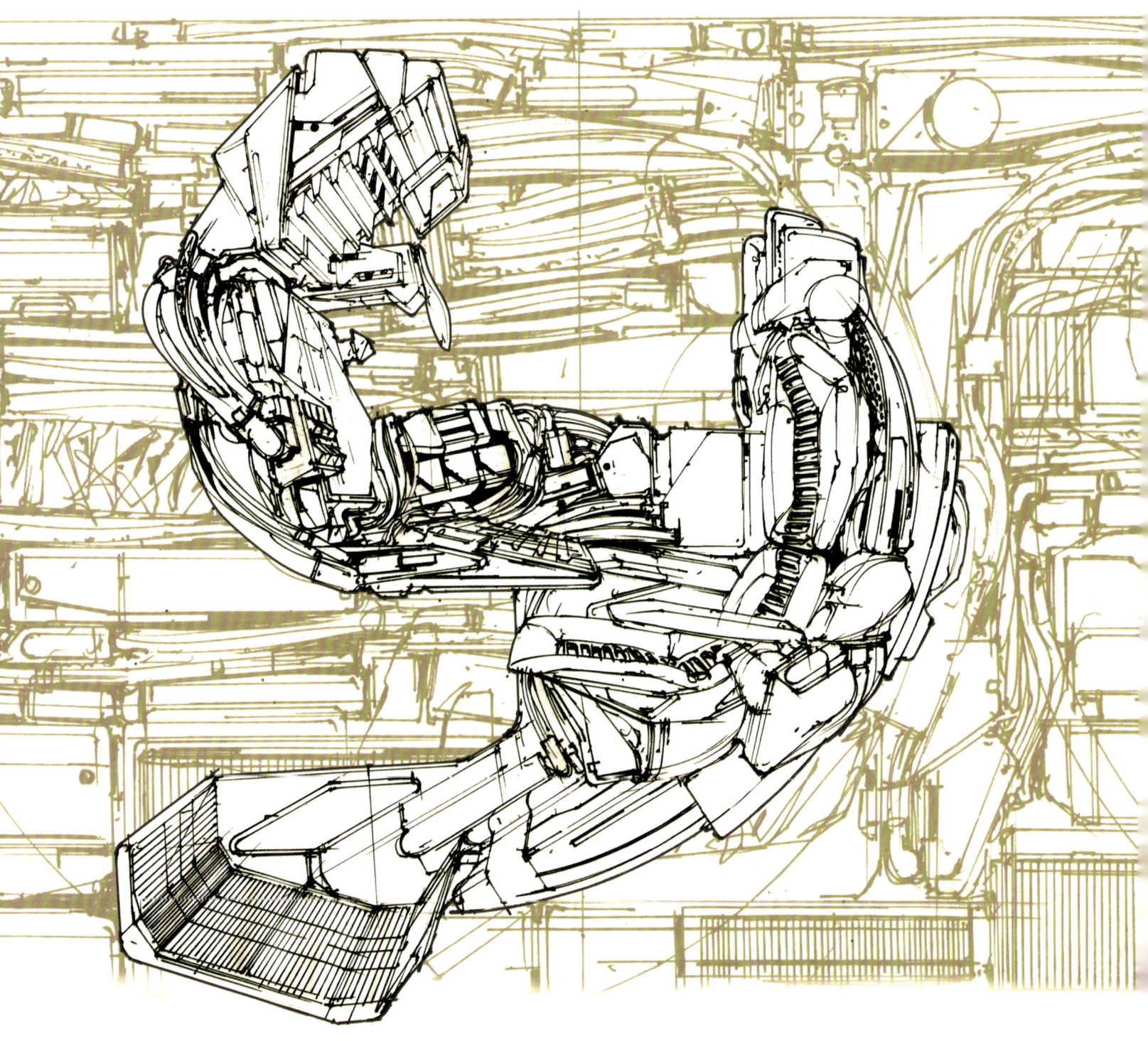

TOPEKA
PUNKED UP

The storyline—a high tech conflict between rebellious Native Americans and an aggressive government agency—juxtaposed after-market ingenuity with corporate resolution, resulting in an exciting challenge to Mead's design methodology. Here was an opportunity to portray the aesthetic and economic barriers between cultures with design features that underscored and highlighted the differences.

By pushing existing trends to the limit, the world of *Topeka* was to become a vivid clash between officials in electro-luminescent uniforms and the shaggy hodgepodge of *Topeka's* do-it-yourself culture.

Based on an ambitious story featuring a none-too-well disguised metaphoric conflict, *Topeka* found Mead immersed in the realm of prosthetics and D.I.Y. creative ingenuity. This was relatively new territory for Mead, whose background in industrial design had the usual elements of ergonomics, and man-machine interface, but this assignment was the first in which an intimate working knowledge of human and animal anatomy would spell the difference between success and failure.

FROM EXOSKELETAL COSTUME TO A FULLY REALIZED ROBOTIC MENAGERIE, MEAD'S COMMAND OF MECHANICAL DEVICES, LOADED WITH SERVOS, VALVES, AND HYDRAULICS, SERVED HIM WELL, LENDING NASA-LIKE ENGINEERING AUTHORITY TO THE CAST OF SLEEK YET TERRIFYING HUNTERS.

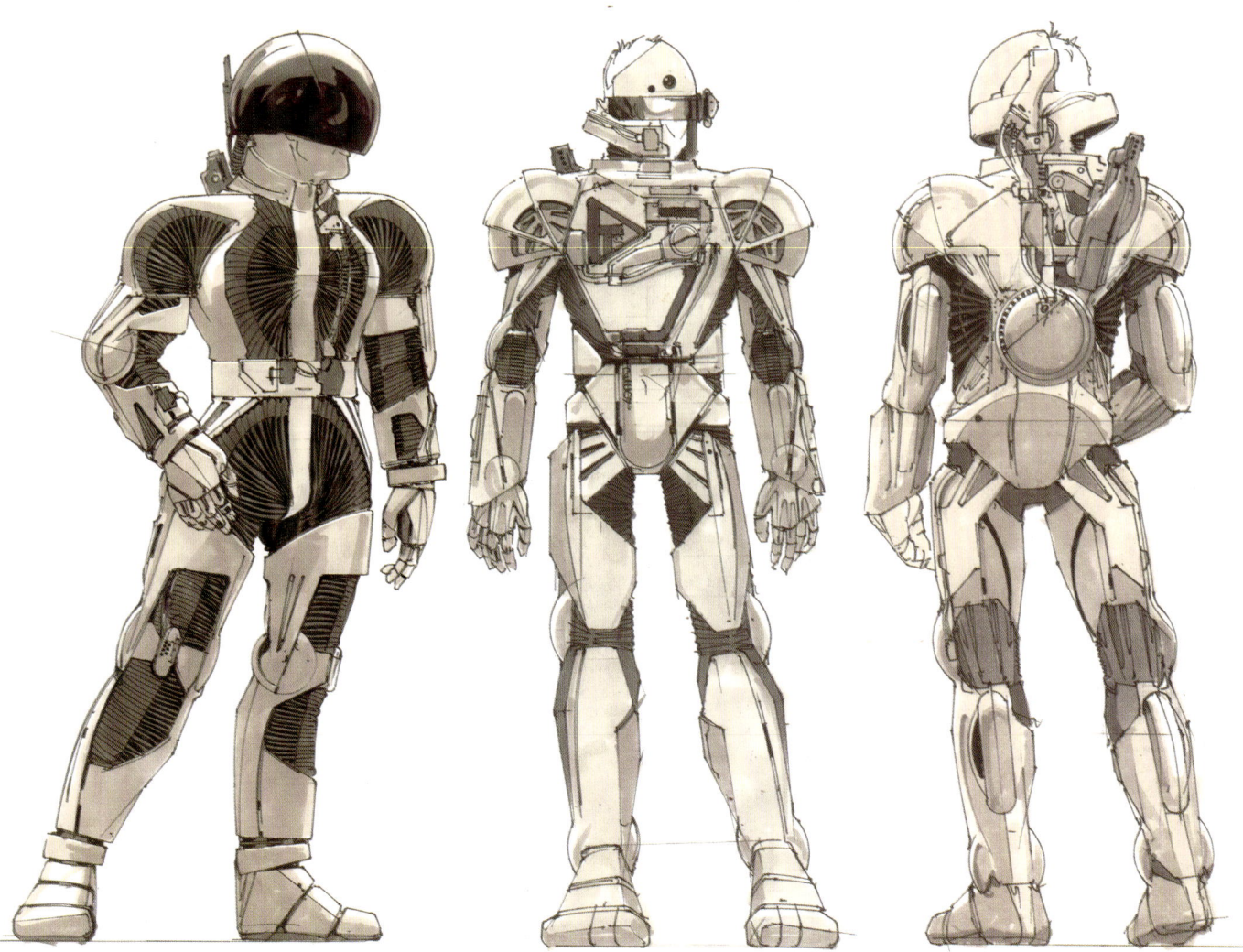

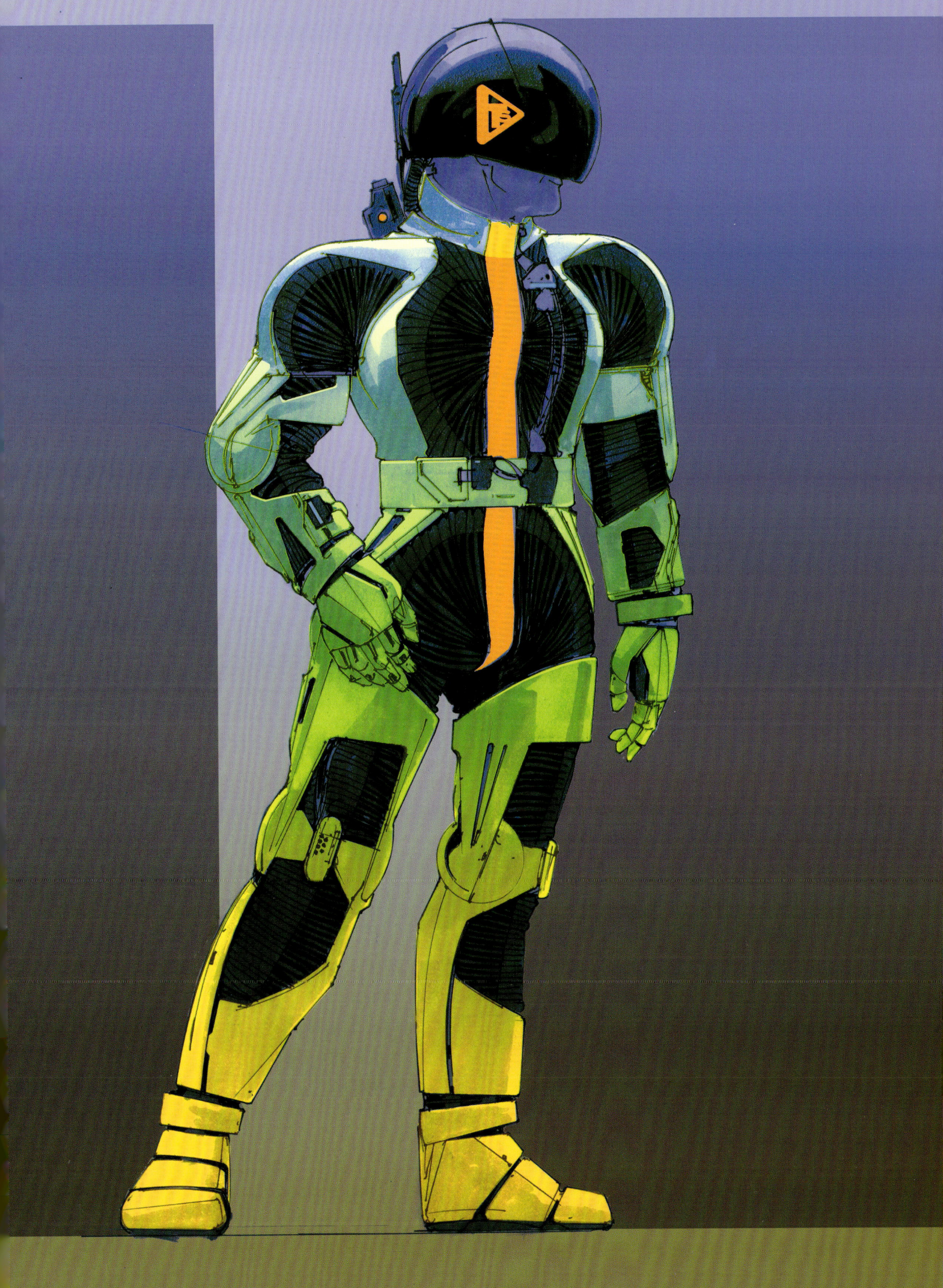

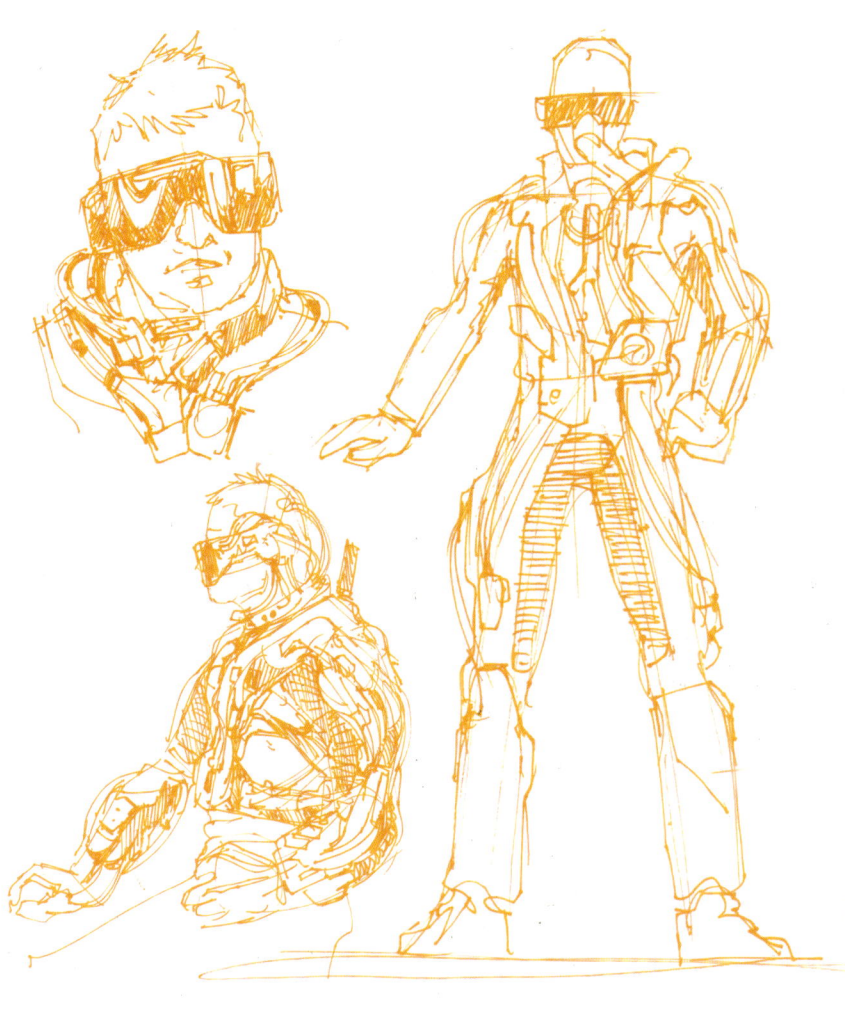

The iridescent ziggurats on blocky silhouettes, somewhat reminiscent of tribal patterns, while the retrofitted jalopy (overleaf) might have been rescued from the run-down front yard of a desert-rat trailer park. The stew of references, seemingly plucked from thin air, create a cauldron of imagery, all held together by Mead's over-arching machine aesthetic, sometimes veering into the cult of steampunk, but always returning to the confident center, where geometry reigns supreme. Here too, the tropes of southern California's hot-rod culture—the bolt-on residue of three generations of Detroit iron—come to a delicious climax in this robber-baron's desert cruiser.

HERE TOO, ARE MEAD'S FIRST VENTURES INTO THE REALM OF CHARACTER DESIGN WITH HARNESSES, FUTURISTIC CHAPS, AND VISORS, MEAD'S QUICK SKETCHES DEFINE A PROTEAN *MAD MAX* WITH A GLOSS OF PSYCHEDELIC STYLE

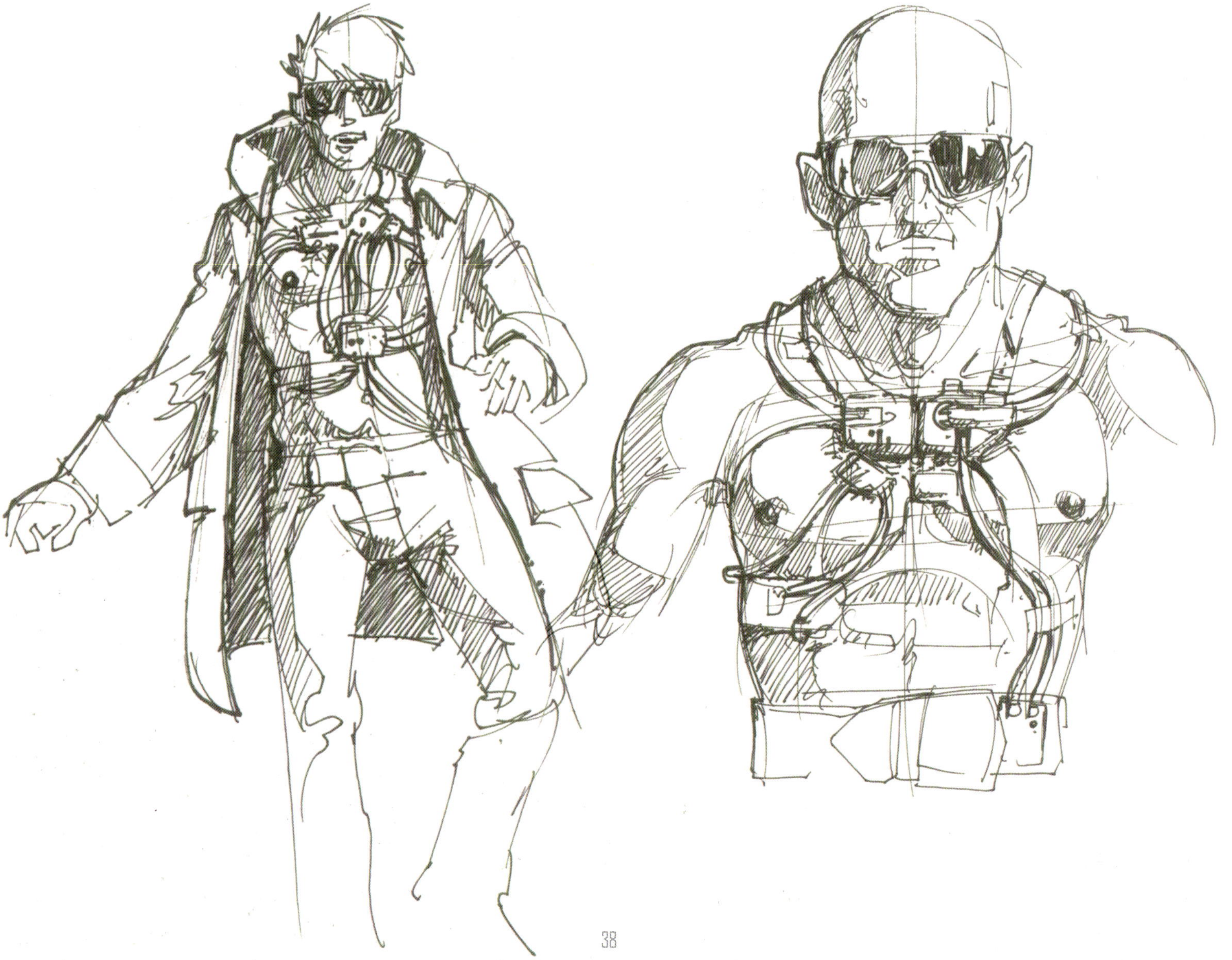

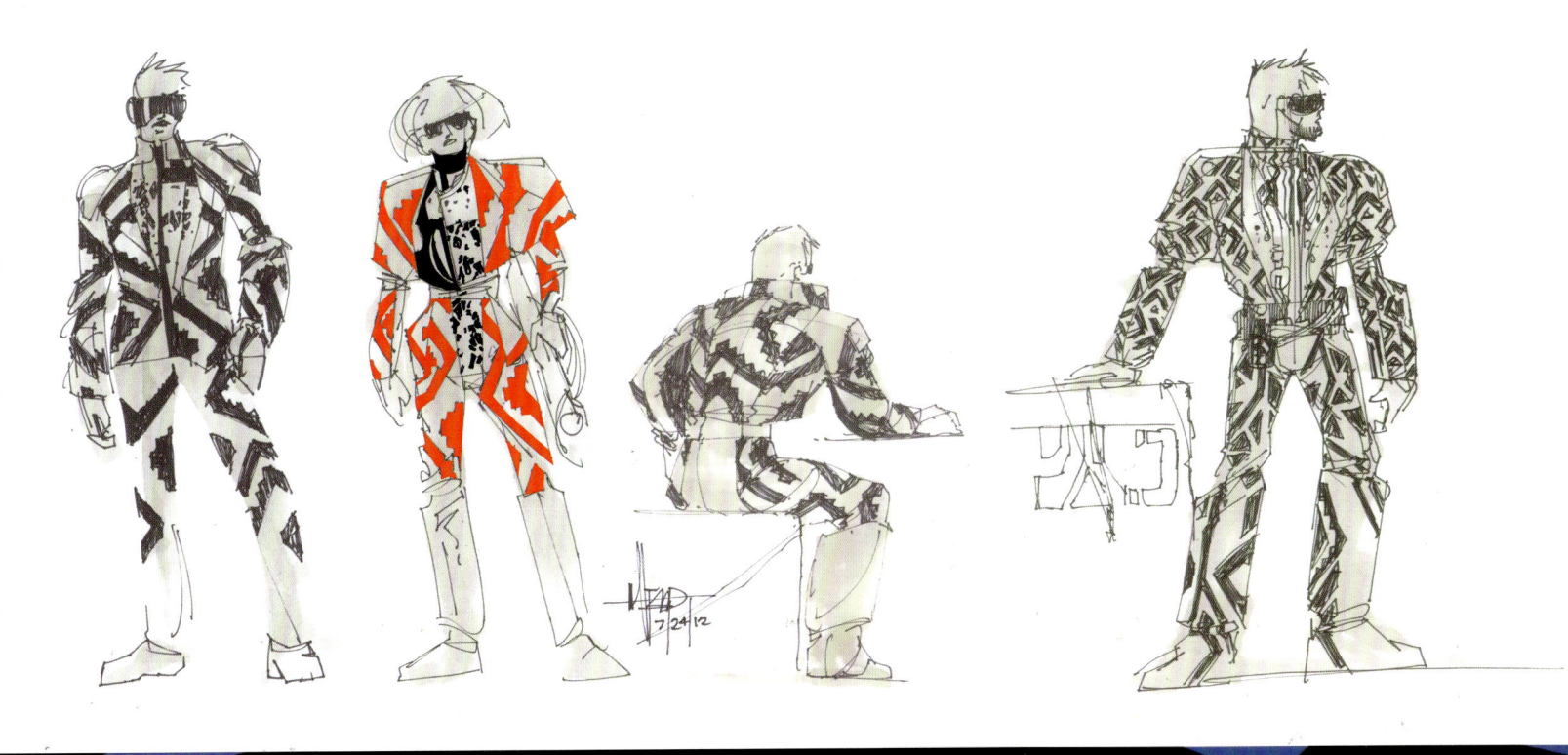

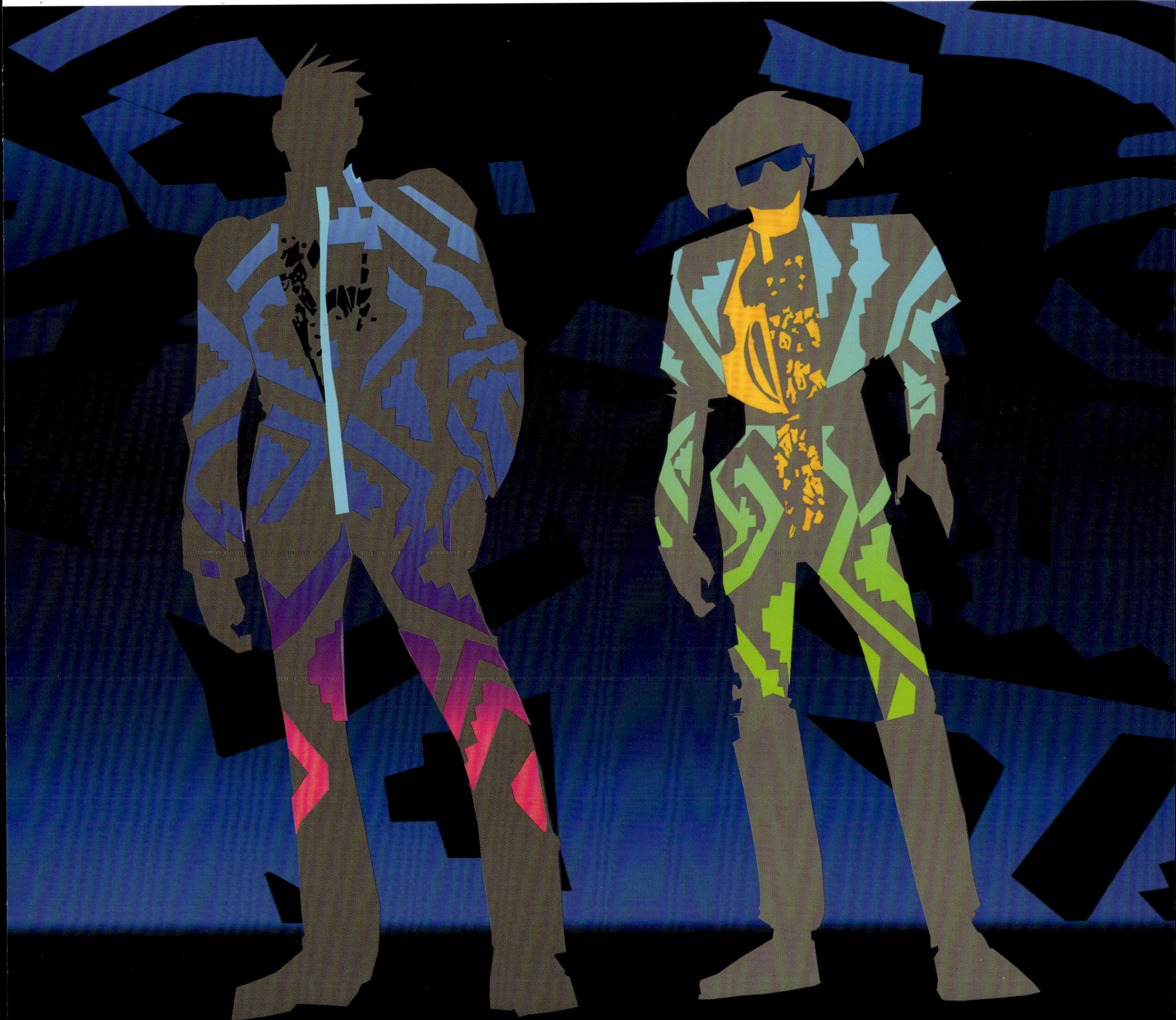

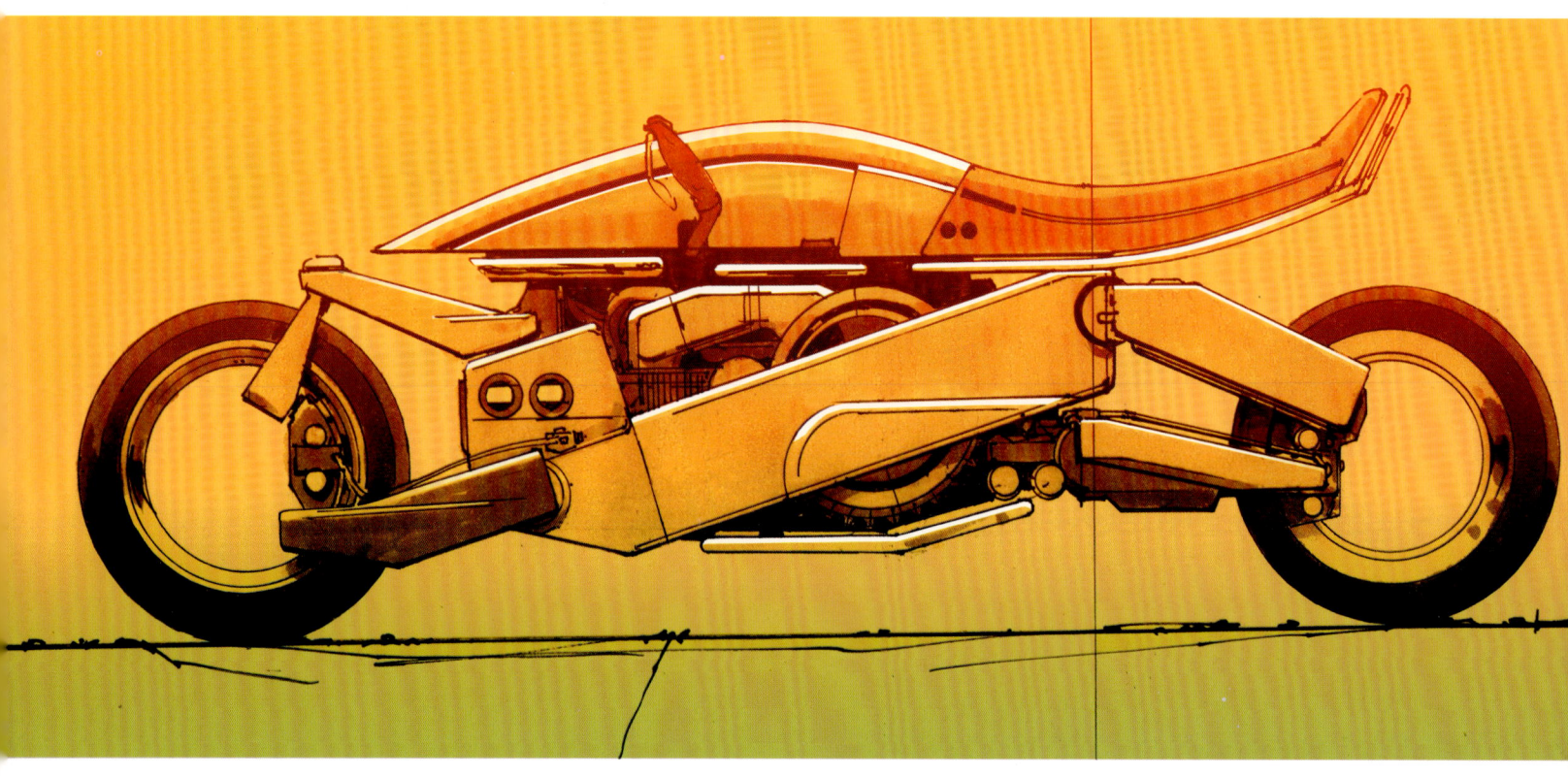

The phantasmagoric motorcycle pictured here—wheels without hubs, a limber animalistic frame, what appears to be a scorpion-like 'stinger' and a hypersonic profile—can change its wheelbase according to need, emulating the stride of a very quick, almost feline creature.

A close look at the desert rat jalopy opposite reveals the hood ornament from a Jaguar saloon affixed to the nose of the vehicle, low-rider style chrome fender skirts, and a plush, prohibition-era interior all in a grand mash-up worthy of DJ LL Kool. The flat-bottomed wheels represent a futuristic evolution of today's after-market rimes, in this case equipped with blowers that are designed to float the car on a cushion of sir, thus relegating rotating wheels to a thing of the past.

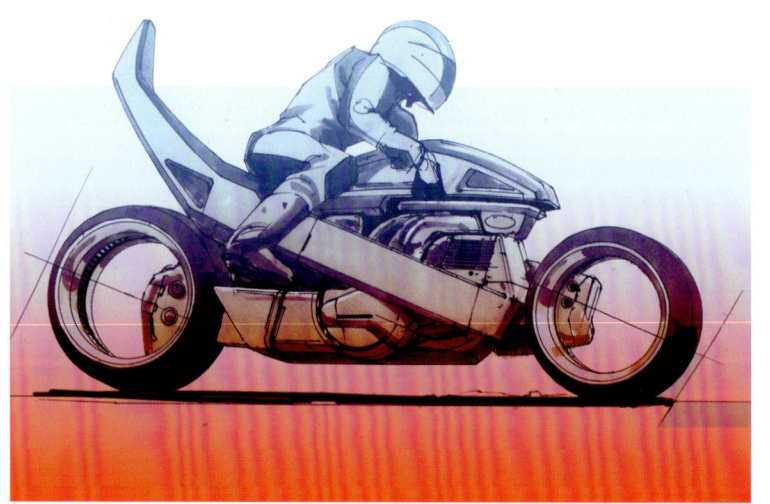

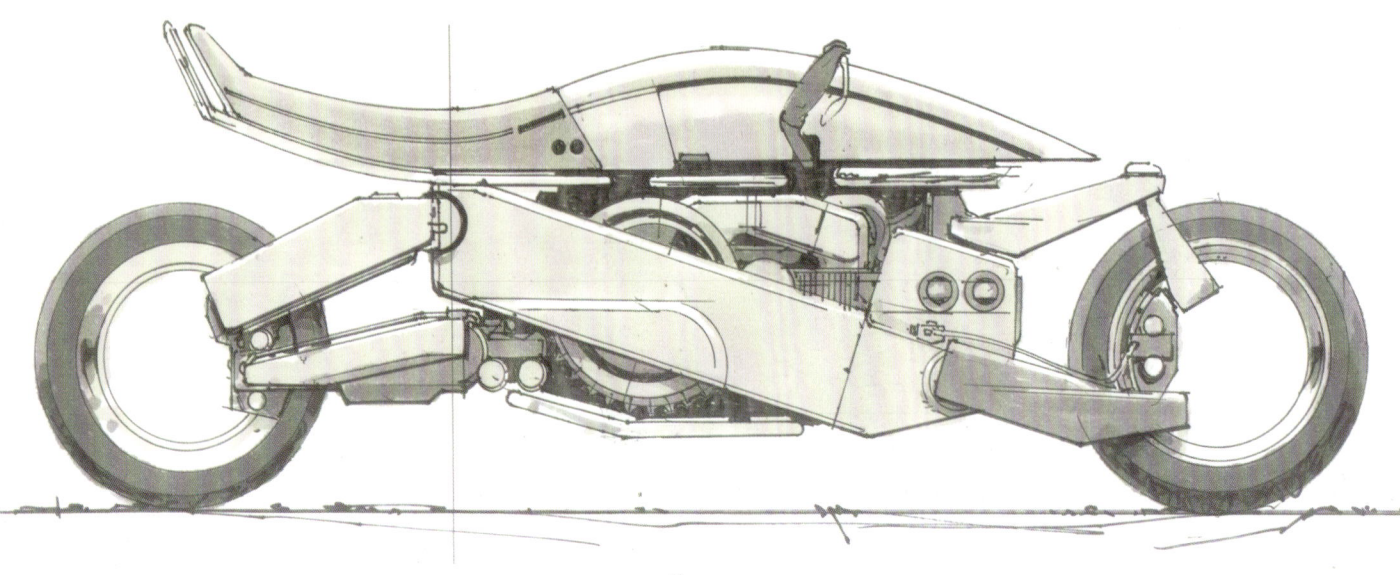

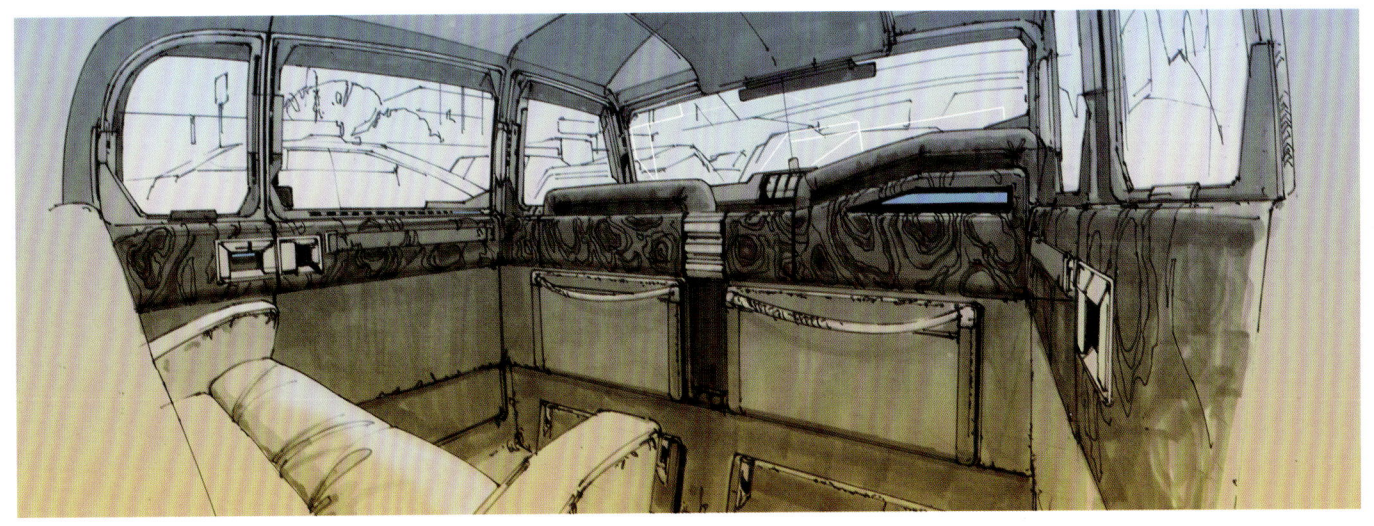

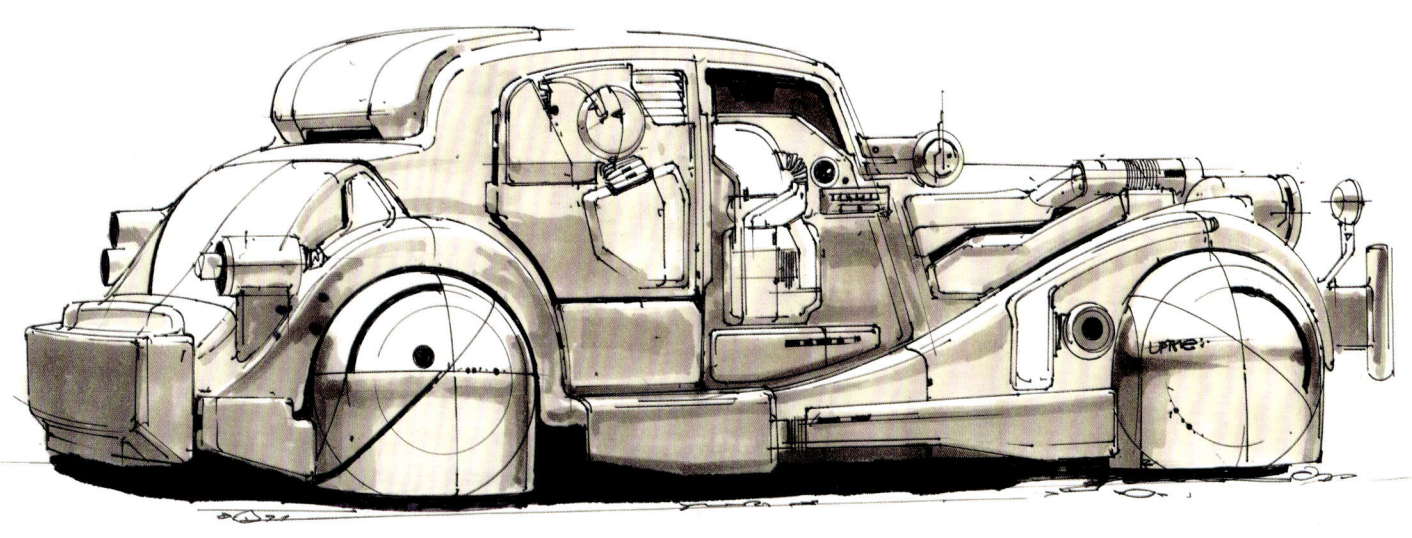

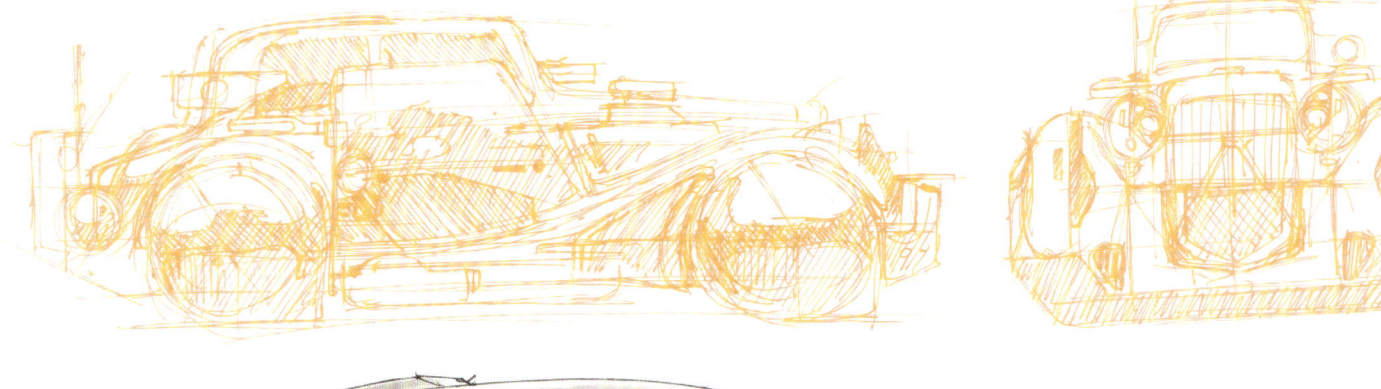

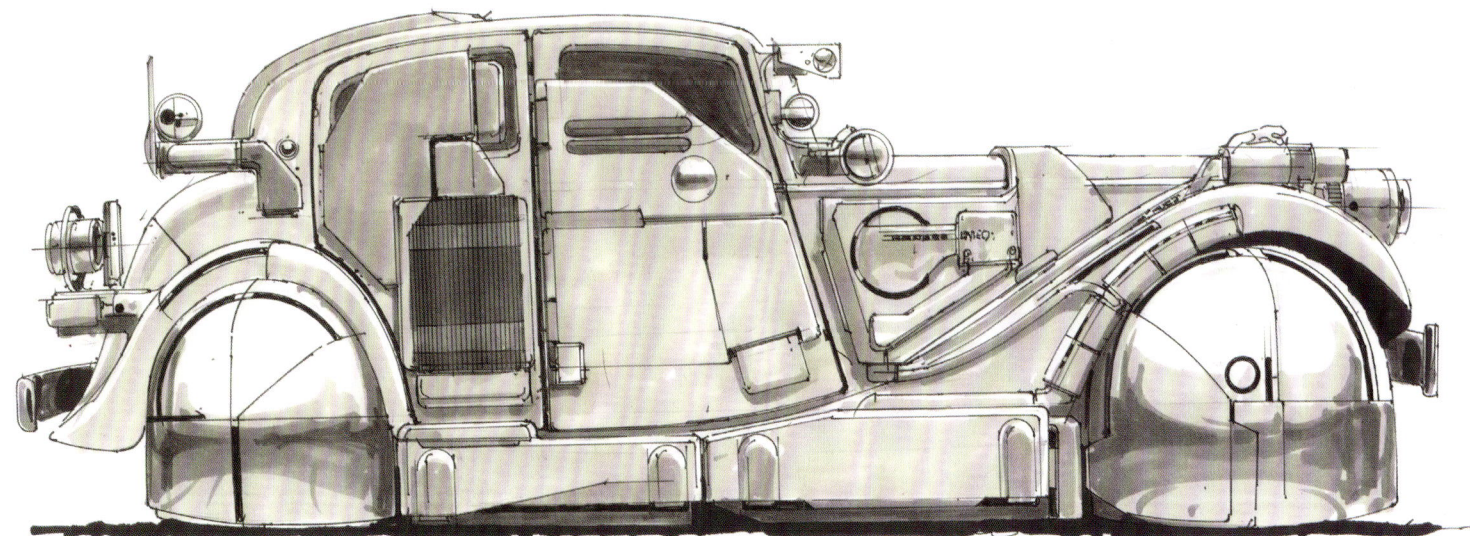

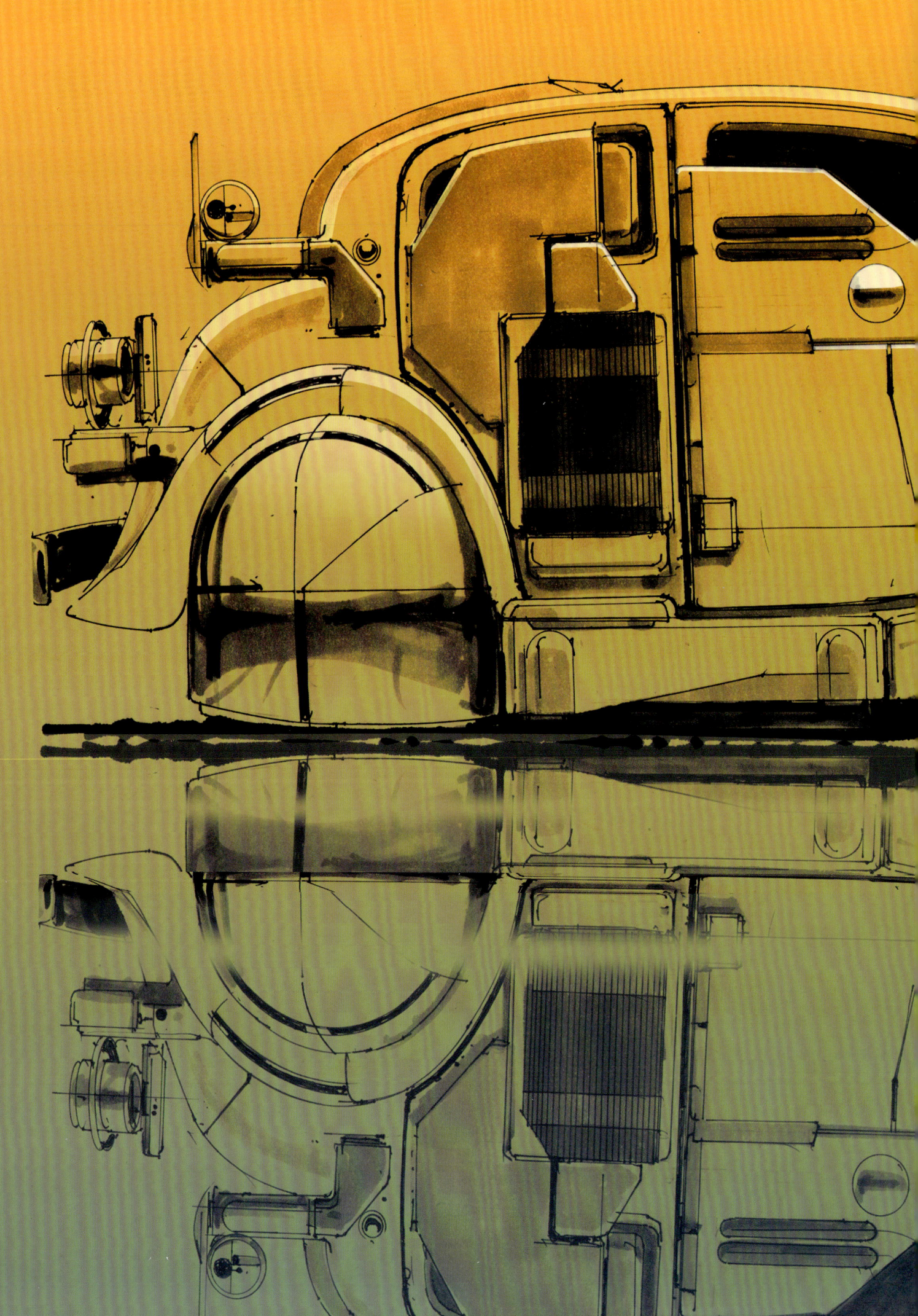

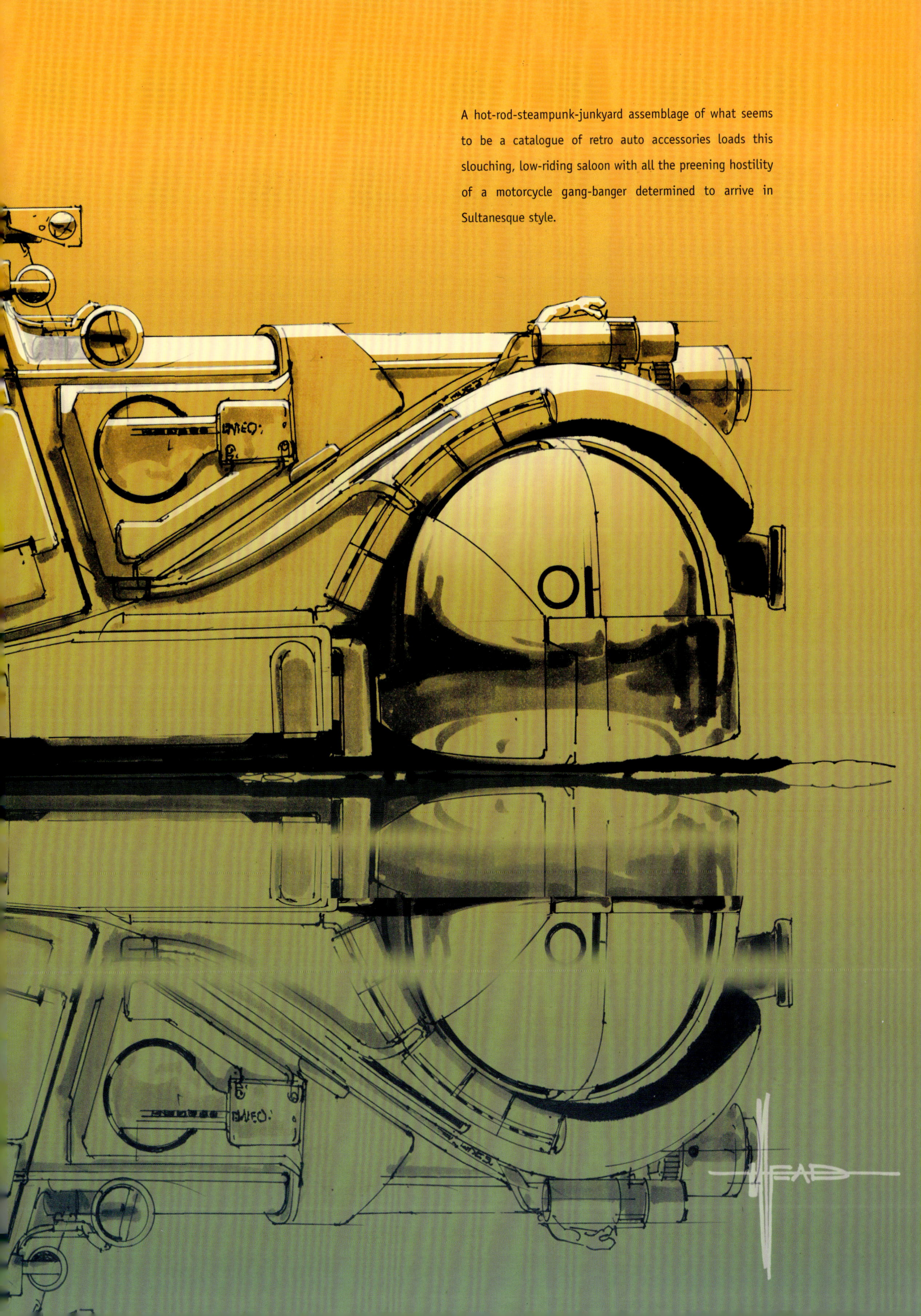

A hot-rod-steampunk-junkyard assemblage of what seems to be a catalogue of retro auto accessories loads this slouching, low-riding saloon with all the preening hostility of a motorcycle gang-banger determined to arrive in Sultanesque style.

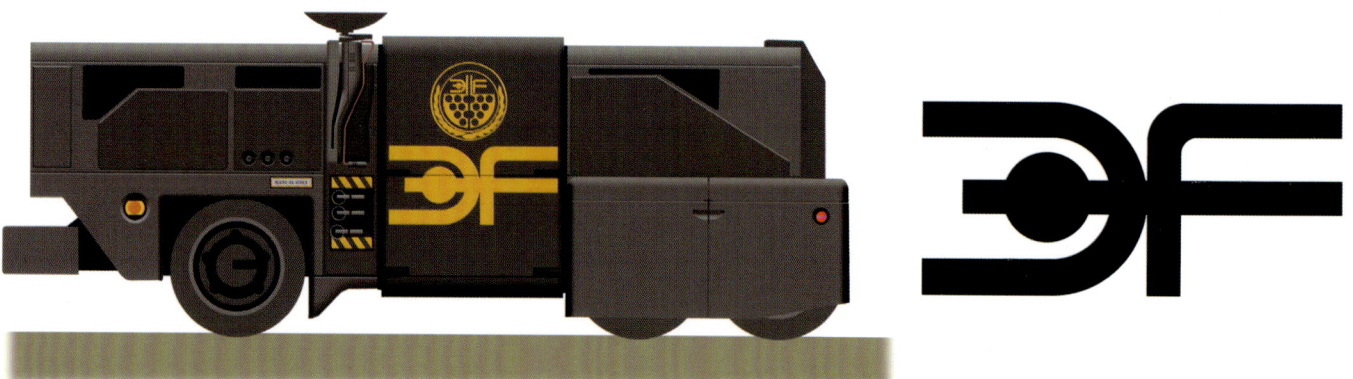

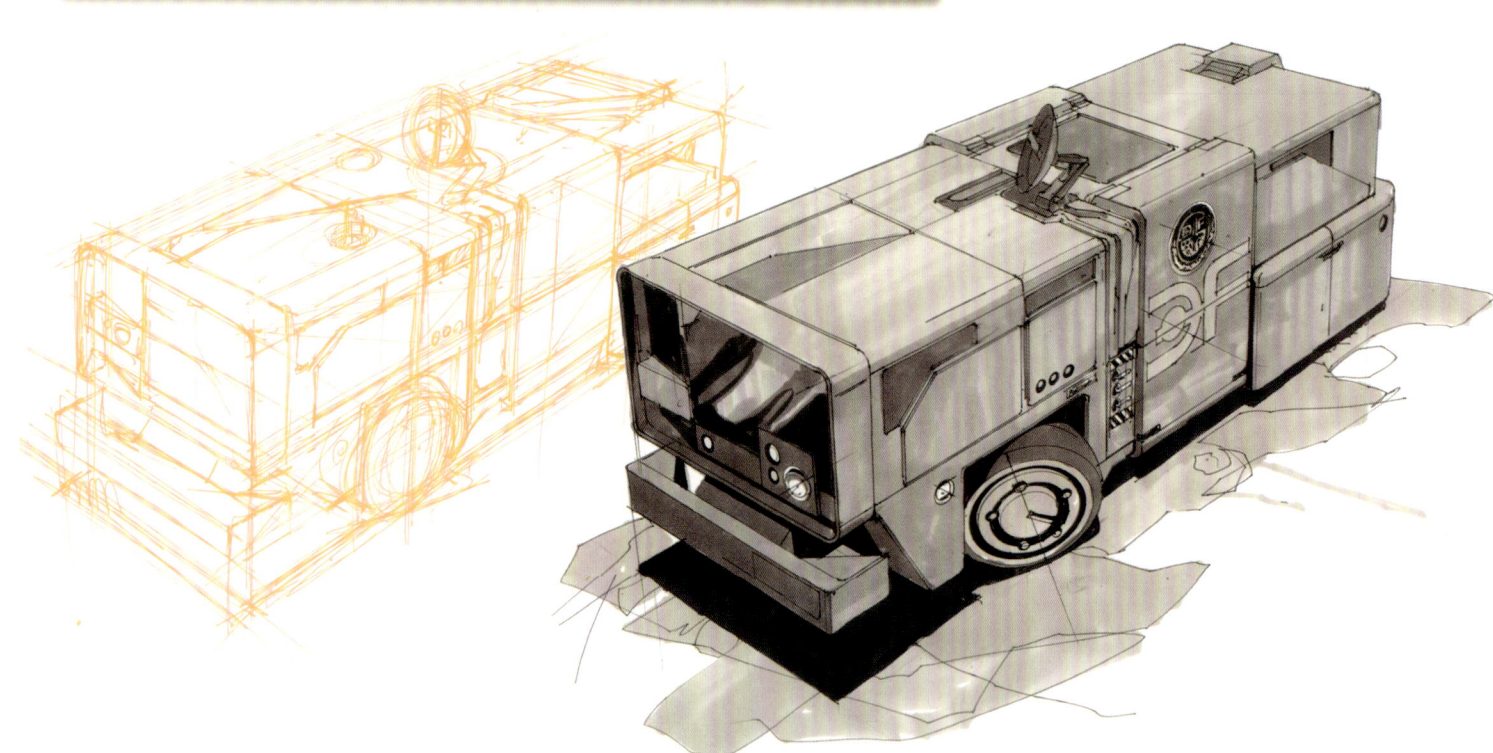

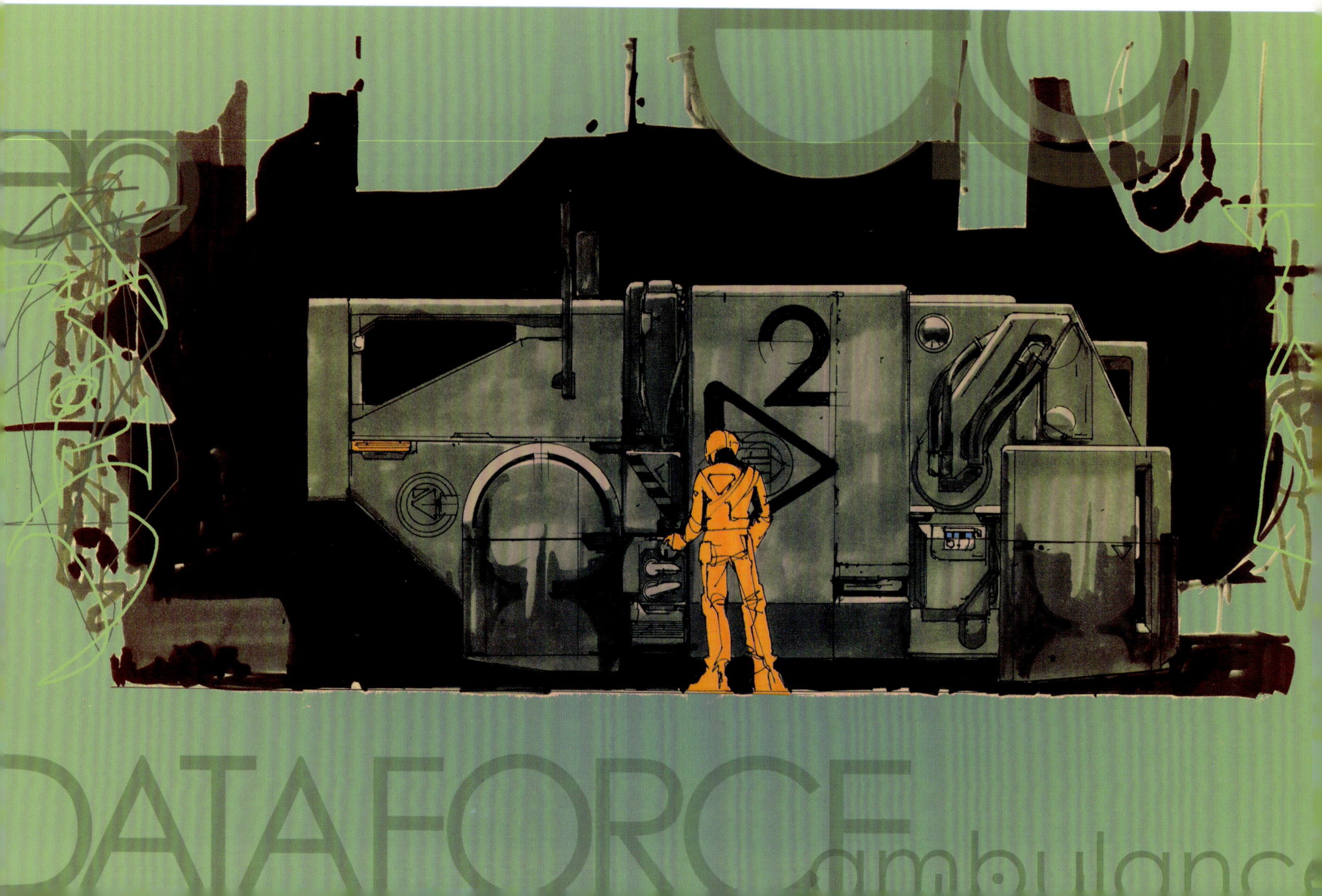

DATAFORCE ambulance

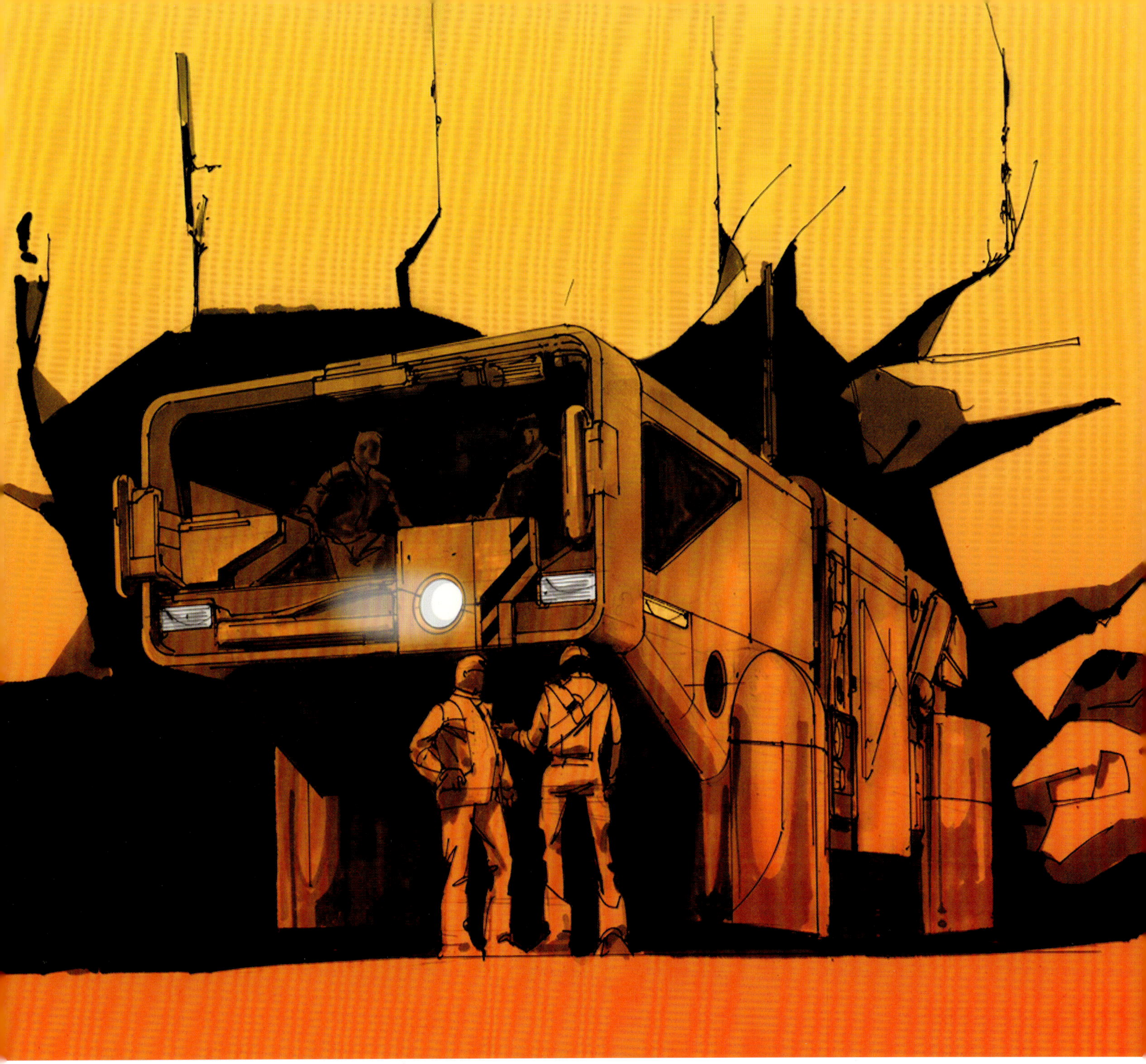

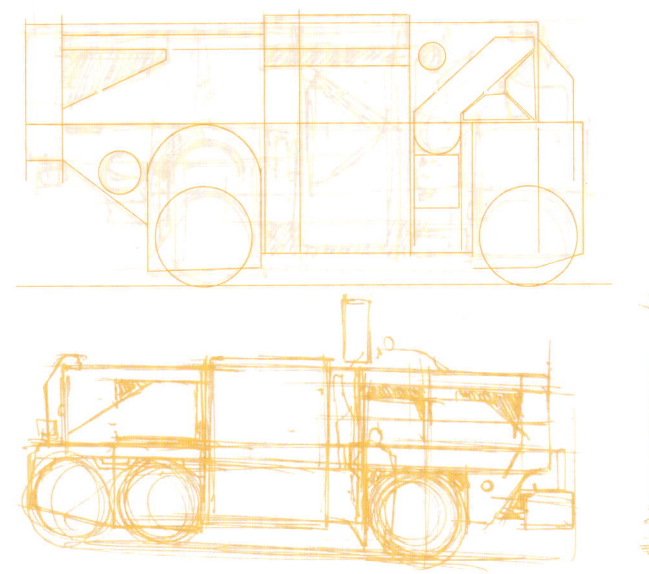

THE HEAVILY ARMORED DATA FORCE AMBULANCE, THE DATA FORCE LOGO, AND THE PATINATED SURFACE ARE VIVID REMINDERS OF MEAD'S ATTENTION TO DETAIL. THIS OVER-ARCHING AESTHETIC REGIME WELDS ALL OF THE FILM'S ENVIRONMENTS INTO A SINGLE, UNIFIED WHOLE.

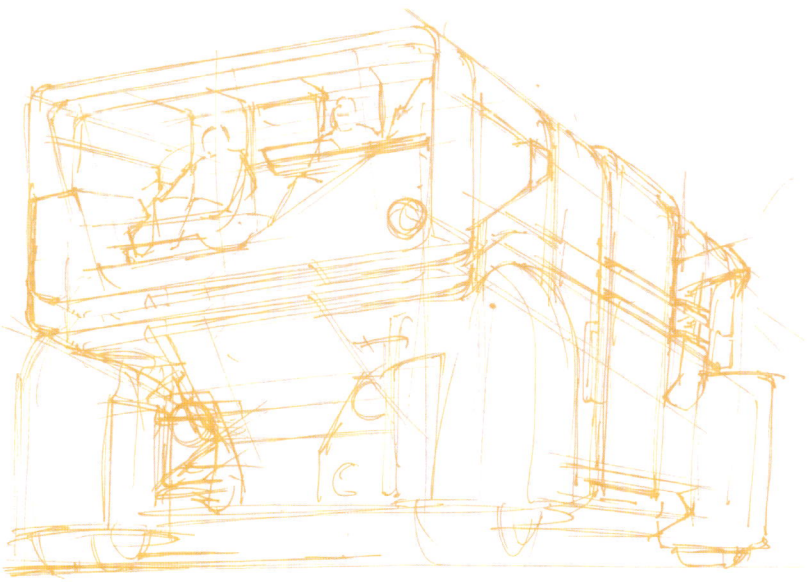

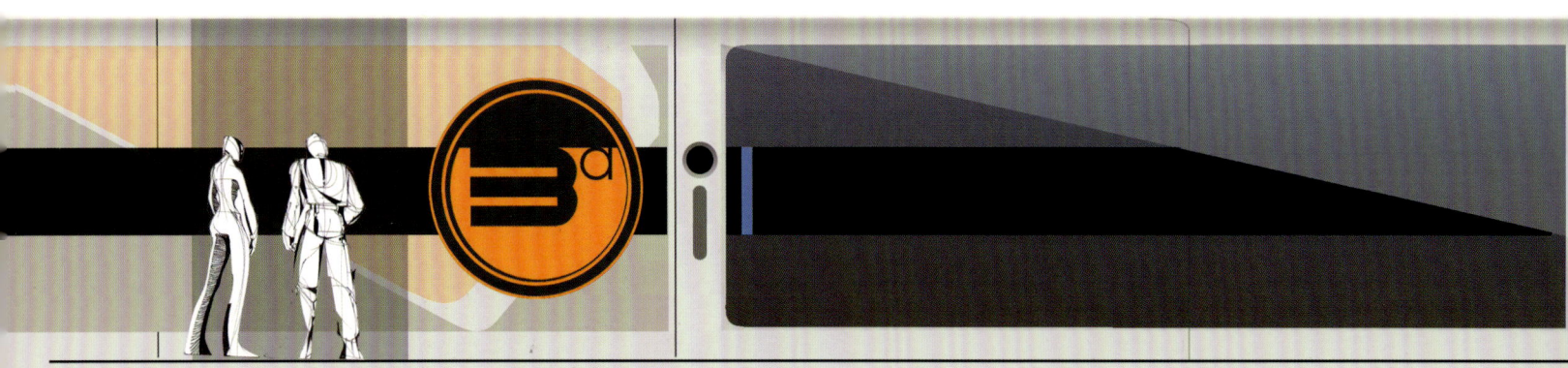

TRAIN:BOARDING SIDE

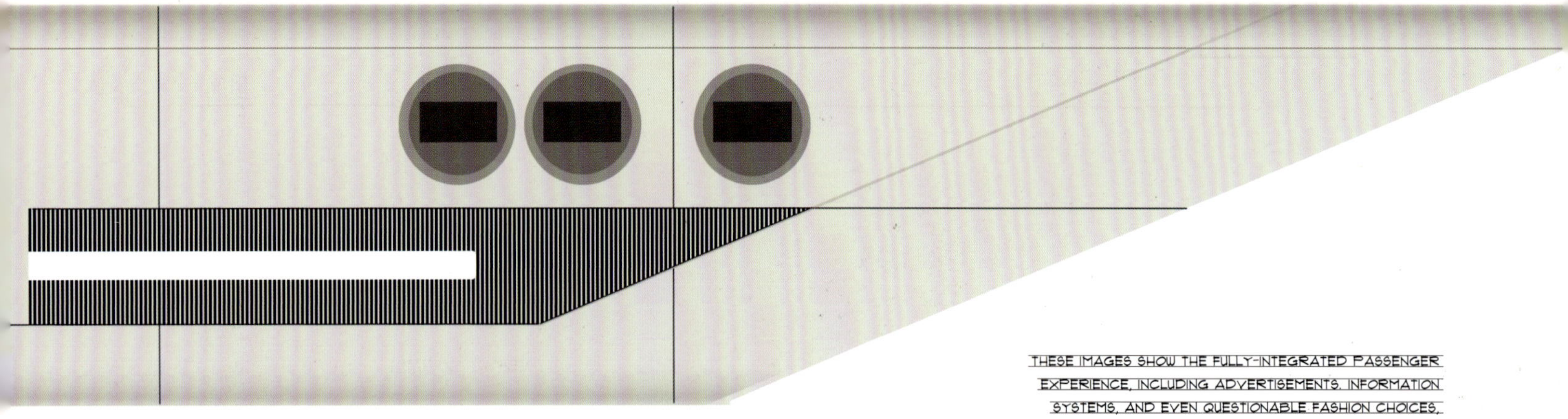

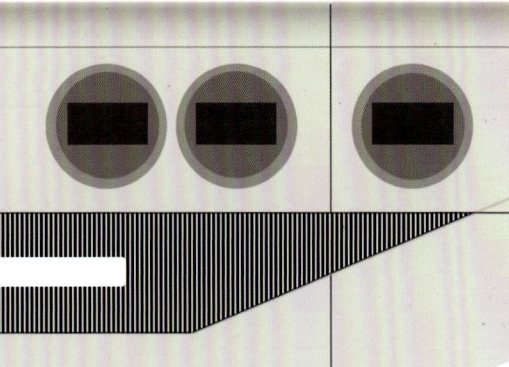

THESE IMAGES SHOW THE FULLY-INTEGRATED PASSENGER
EXPERIENCE, INCLUDING ADVERTISEMENTS, INFORMATION
SYSTEMS, AND EVEN QUESTIONABLE FASHION CHOICES,
ALL OPERATING IN UNISON WITH THE TRAIN TO FORM A
SINGLE, COHESIVE VISION.

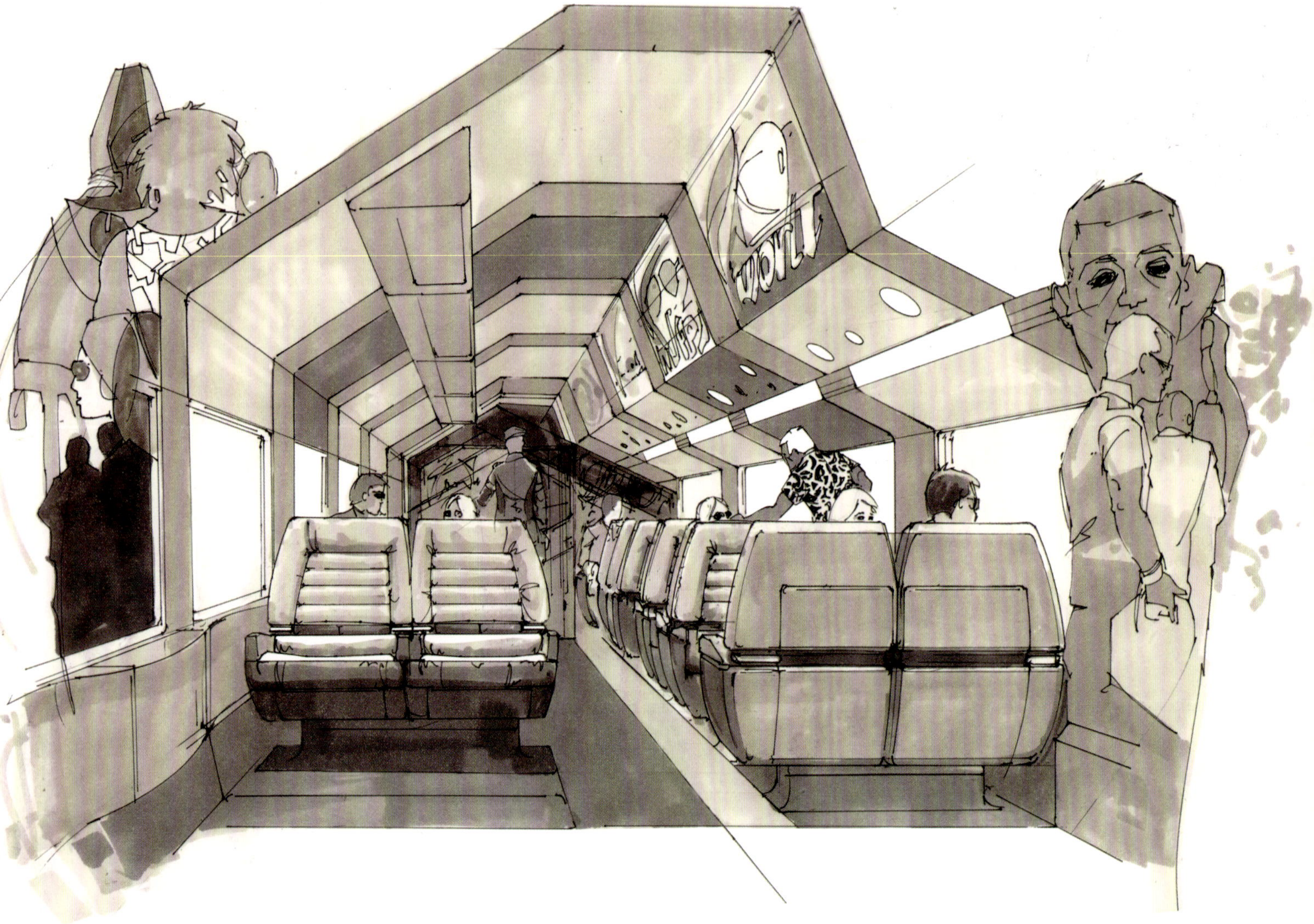

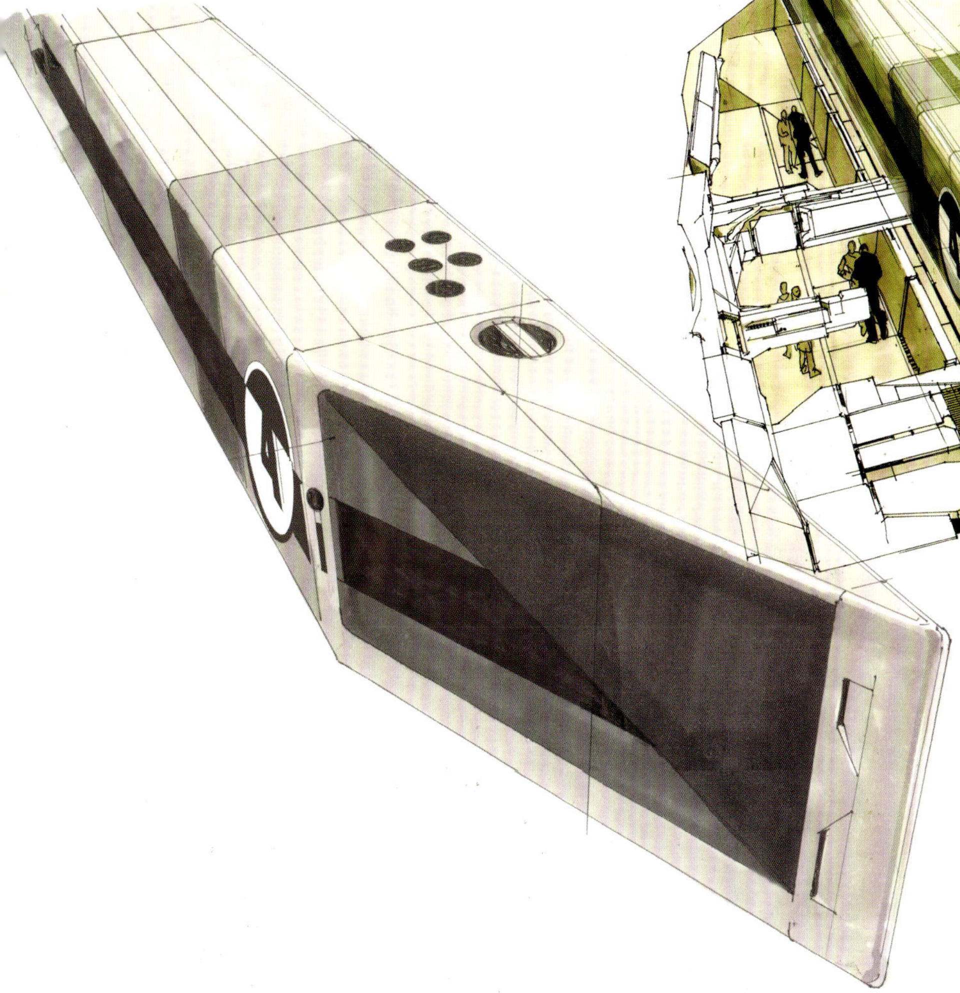

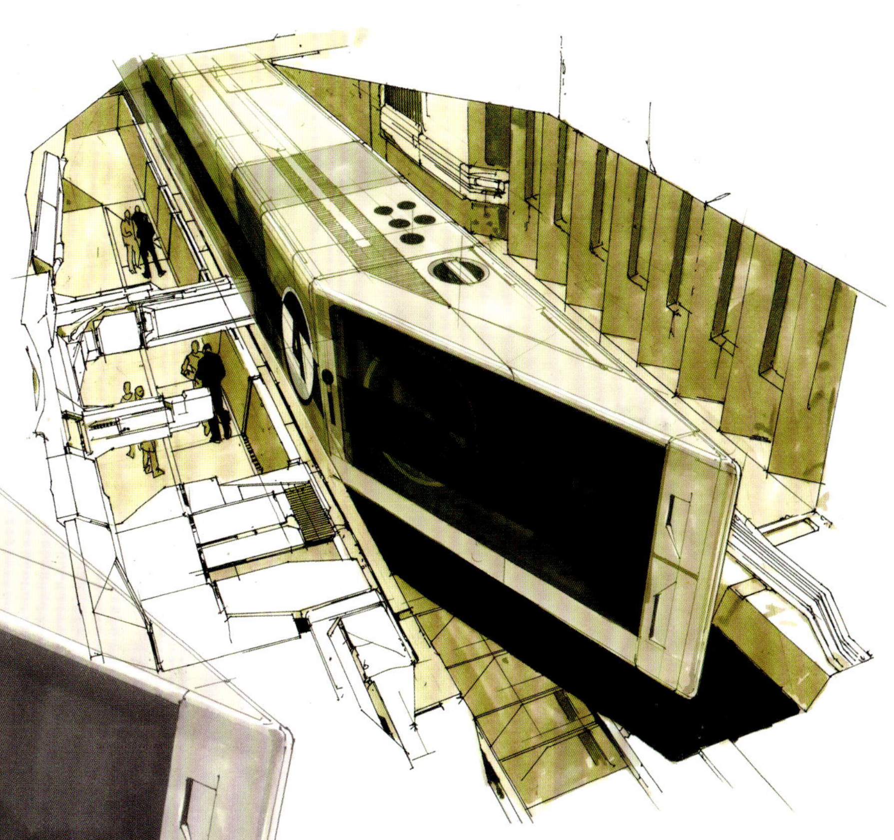

There is a radical logic in the design of the Topeka train's interior which posits a unique allocation of space and amenities as a response to the 'picture-window' concept of the motorman's cockpit, shown here in plan as well as section.

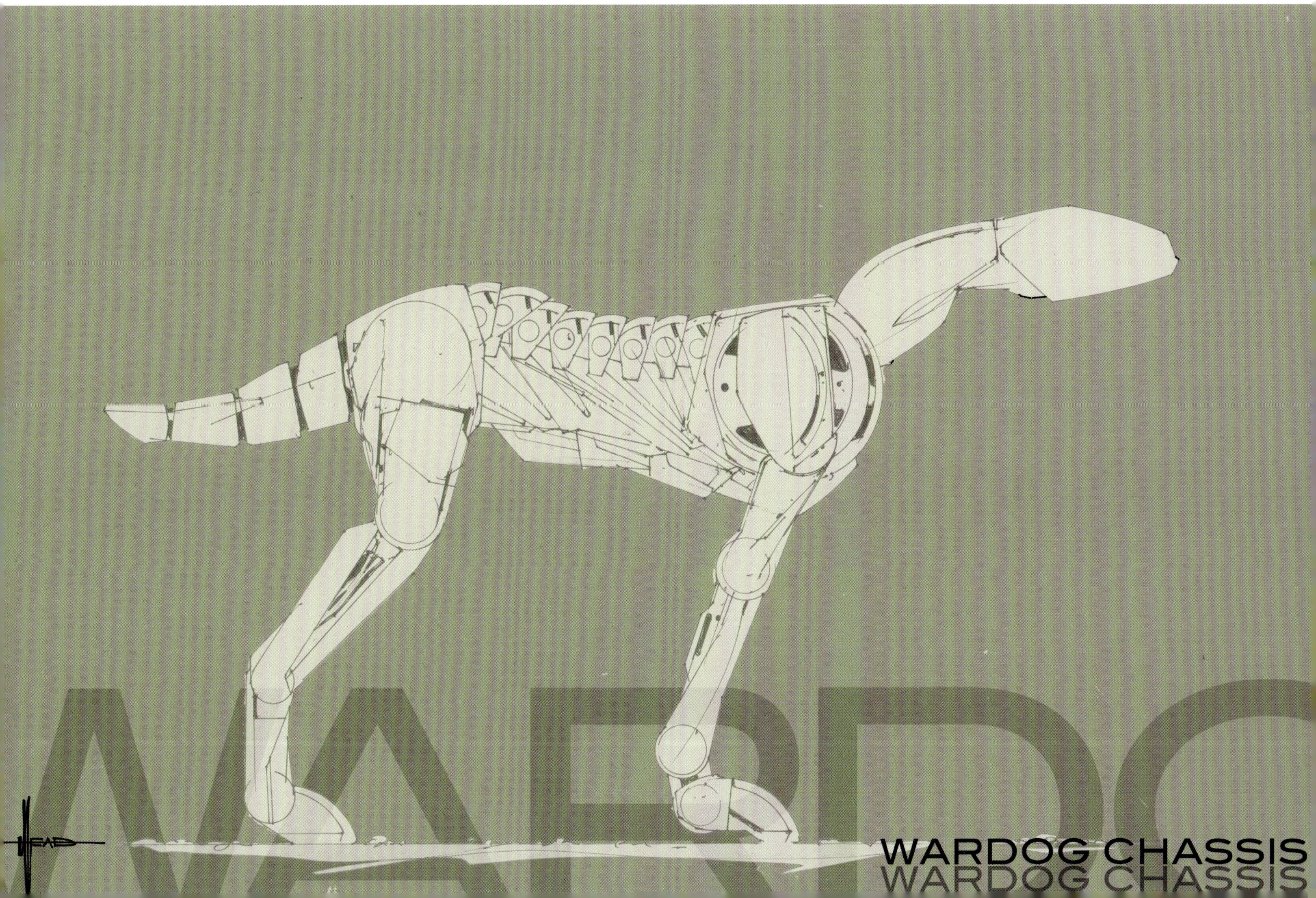

WARDOG CHASSIS
WARDOG CHASSIS

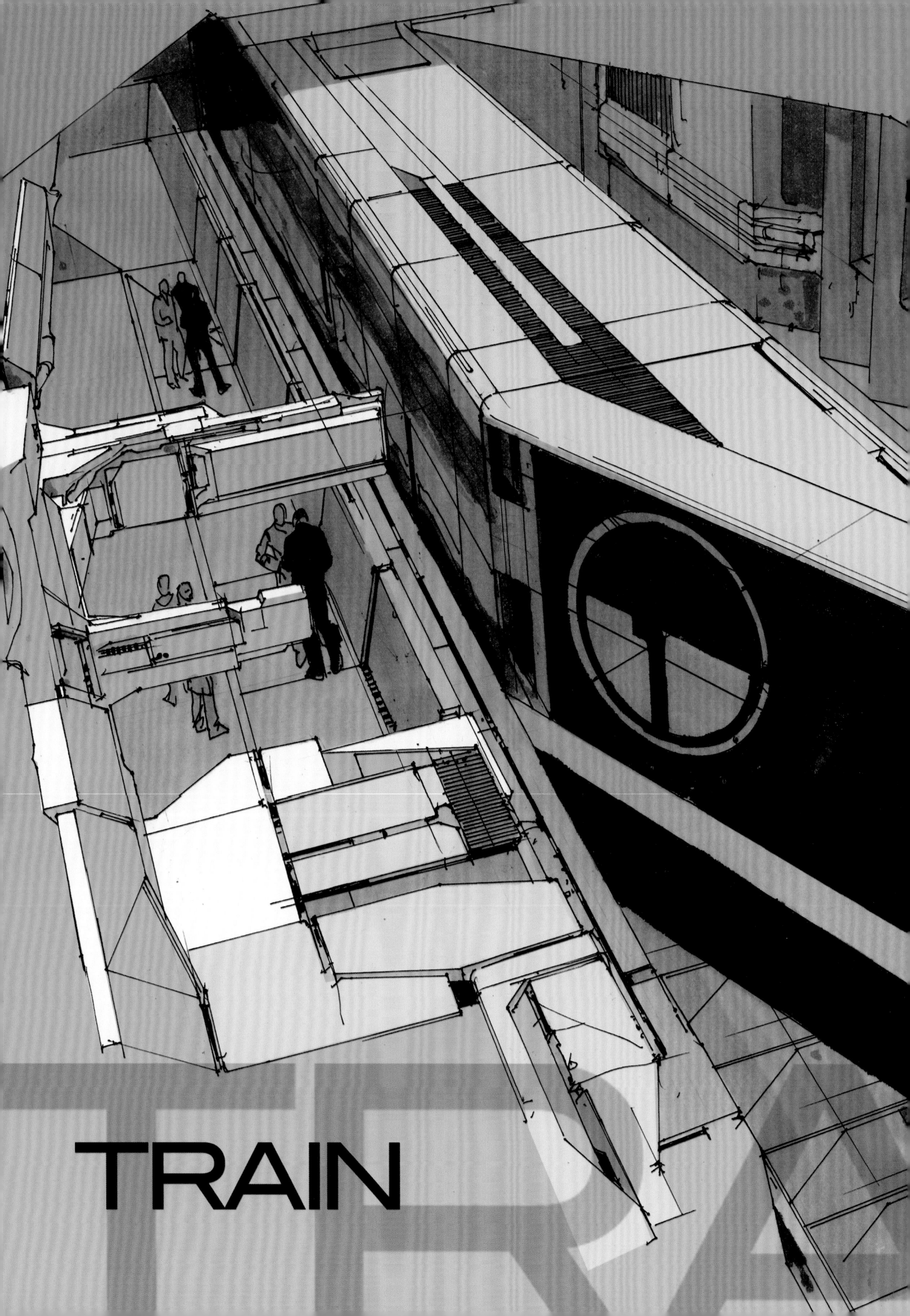

TRAIN

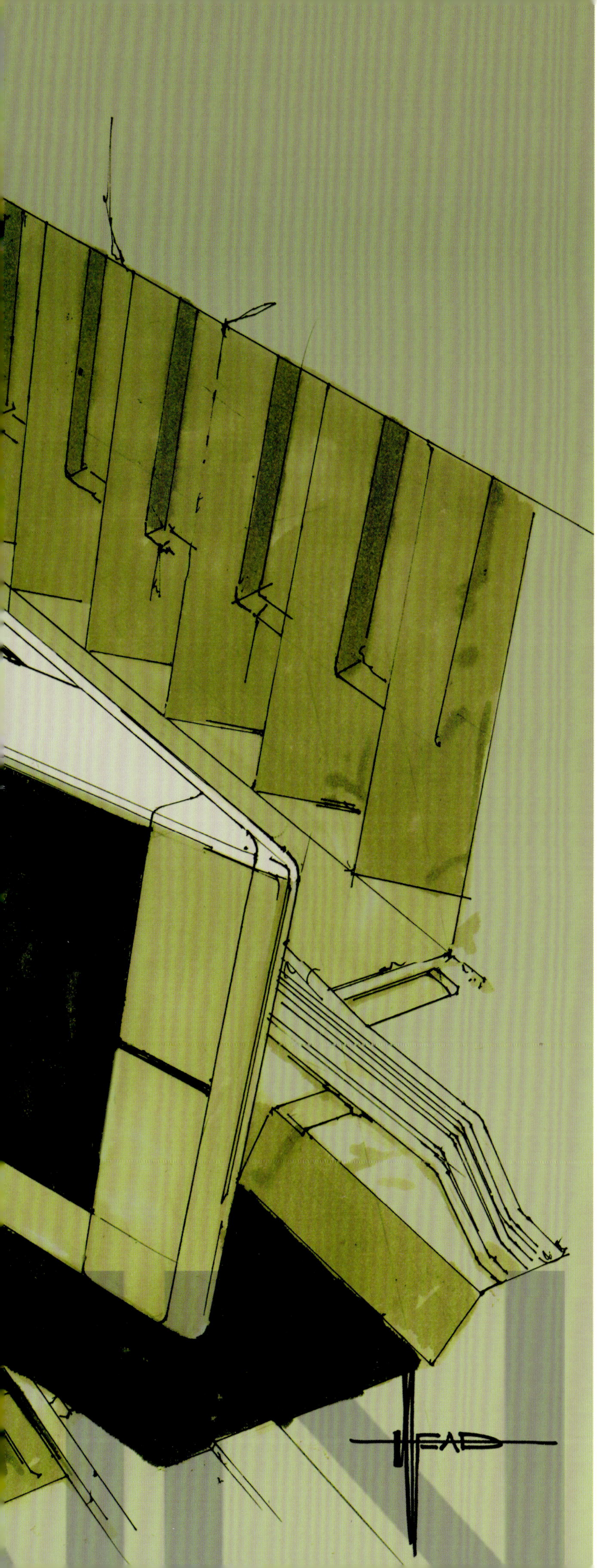

Regardless of aerodynamics, the asymmetrical train proposed for the film epitomizes Mead's irresistible urge to challenge stereotypes and propose often startling alternatives to the norm. Both the interior and the beveled picture-window of the locomotive/motorman's cockpit reflect a re-thinking of the conventions of train design which would have profound reverberations if implemented in the real world. Also apparent in this view are the interactive information systems in the foreground, a favorite Mead device to add depth and complexity to an otherwise ordinary image.

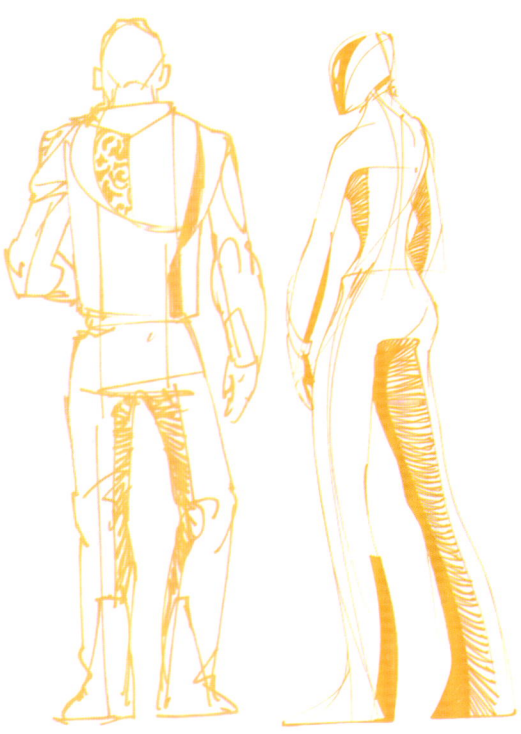

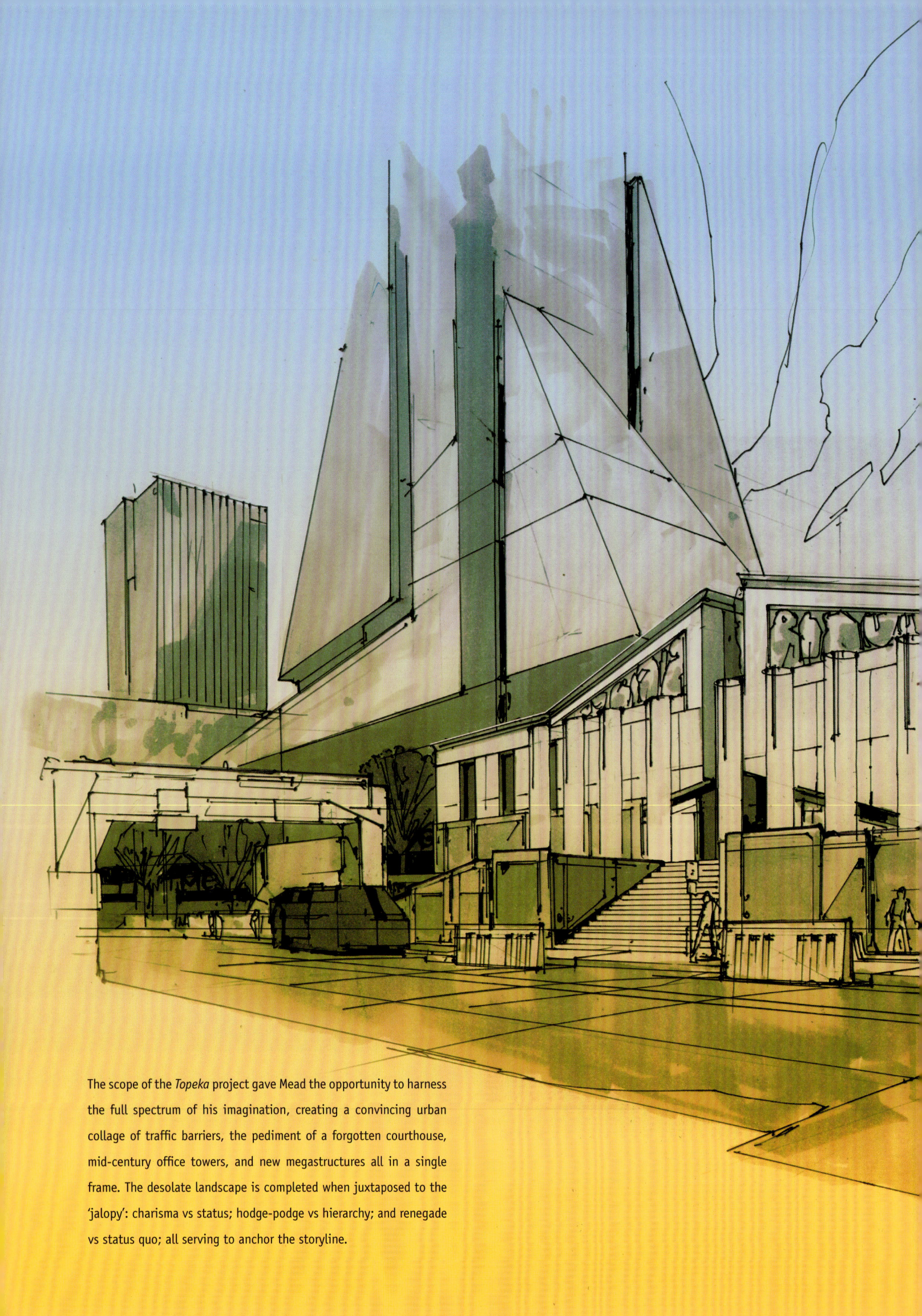

The scope of the *Topeka* project gave Mead the opportunity to harness the full spectrum of his imagination, creating a convincing urban collage of traffic barriers, the pediment of a forgotten courthouse, mid-century office towers, and new megastructures all in a single frame. The desolate landscape is completed when juxtaposed to the 'jalopy': charisma vs status; hodge-podge vs hierarchy; and renegade vs status quo; all serving to anchor the storyline.

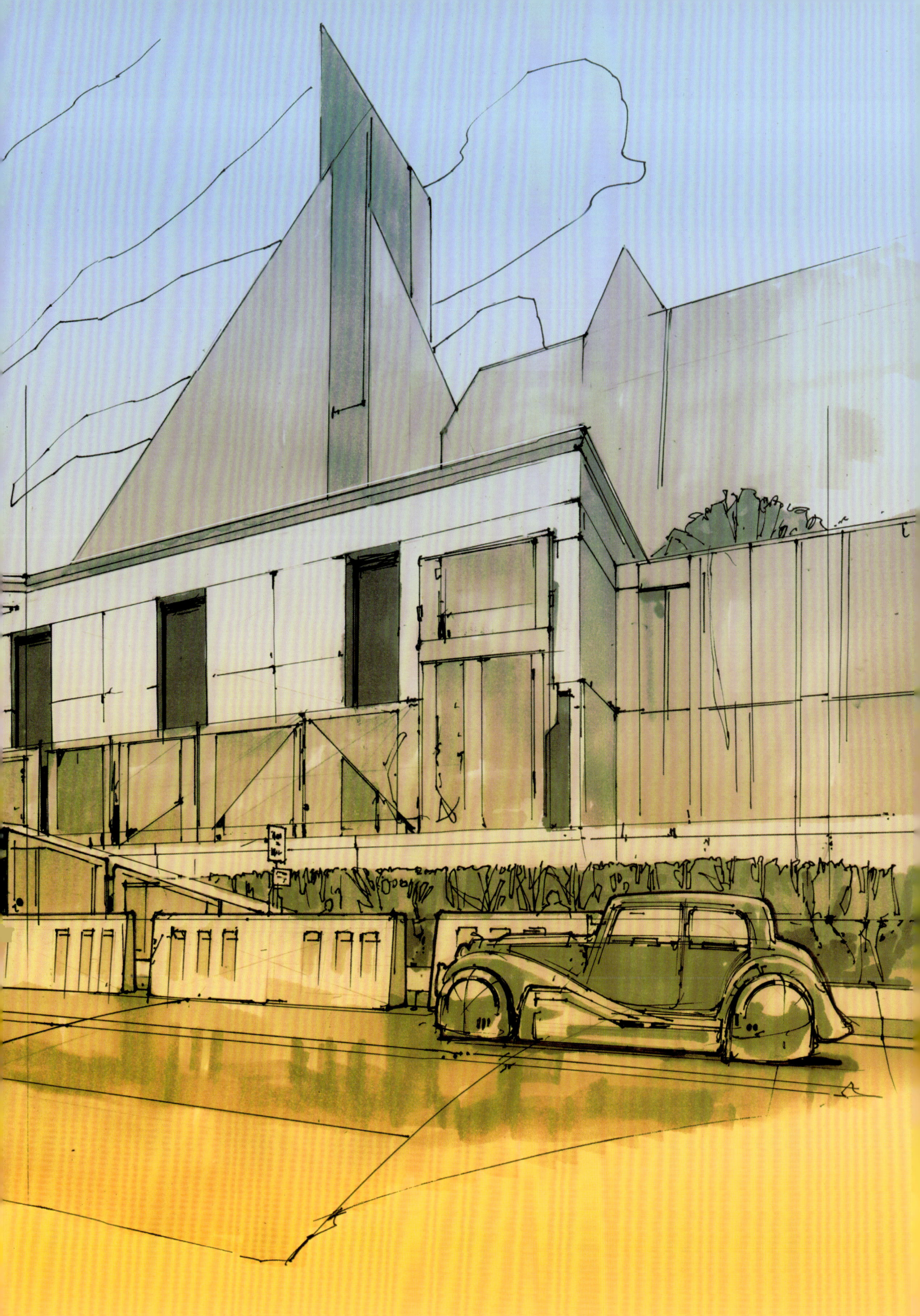

Since the turn of the millenium, architects have increasingly created forms much like this for high-profile projects, so that, in retrospect, Mead's vision is not only 'futuristic', but prophetic as well. Examples abound, in Malaysia, Turkey, China, and Korea, where entrepreneurs have pushed the envelope to new heights. This gigantic megastructure, with splayed 'legs' and flaring, pantaloon-like shapes would not be out of place in the skyline of Dubai.

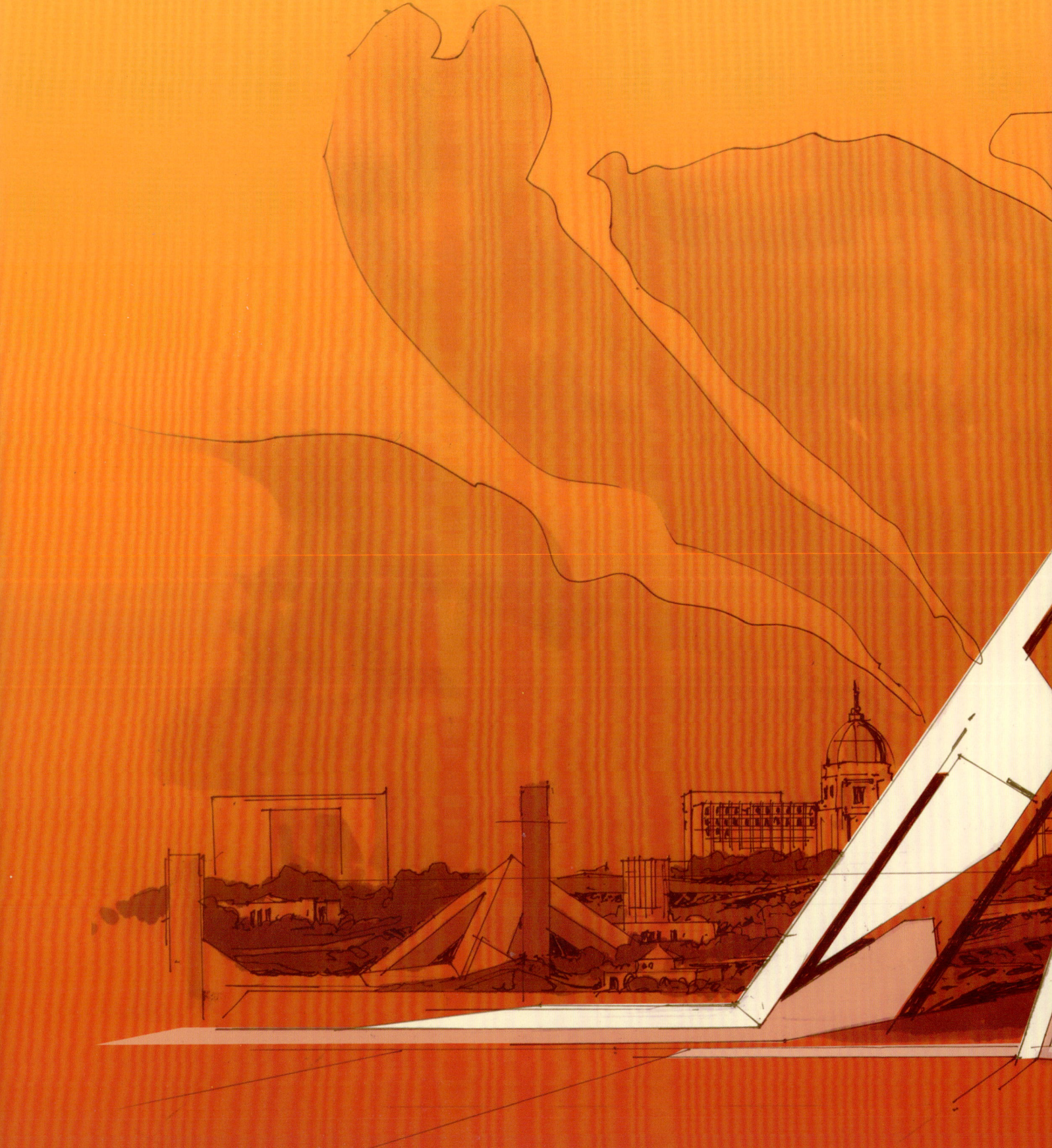

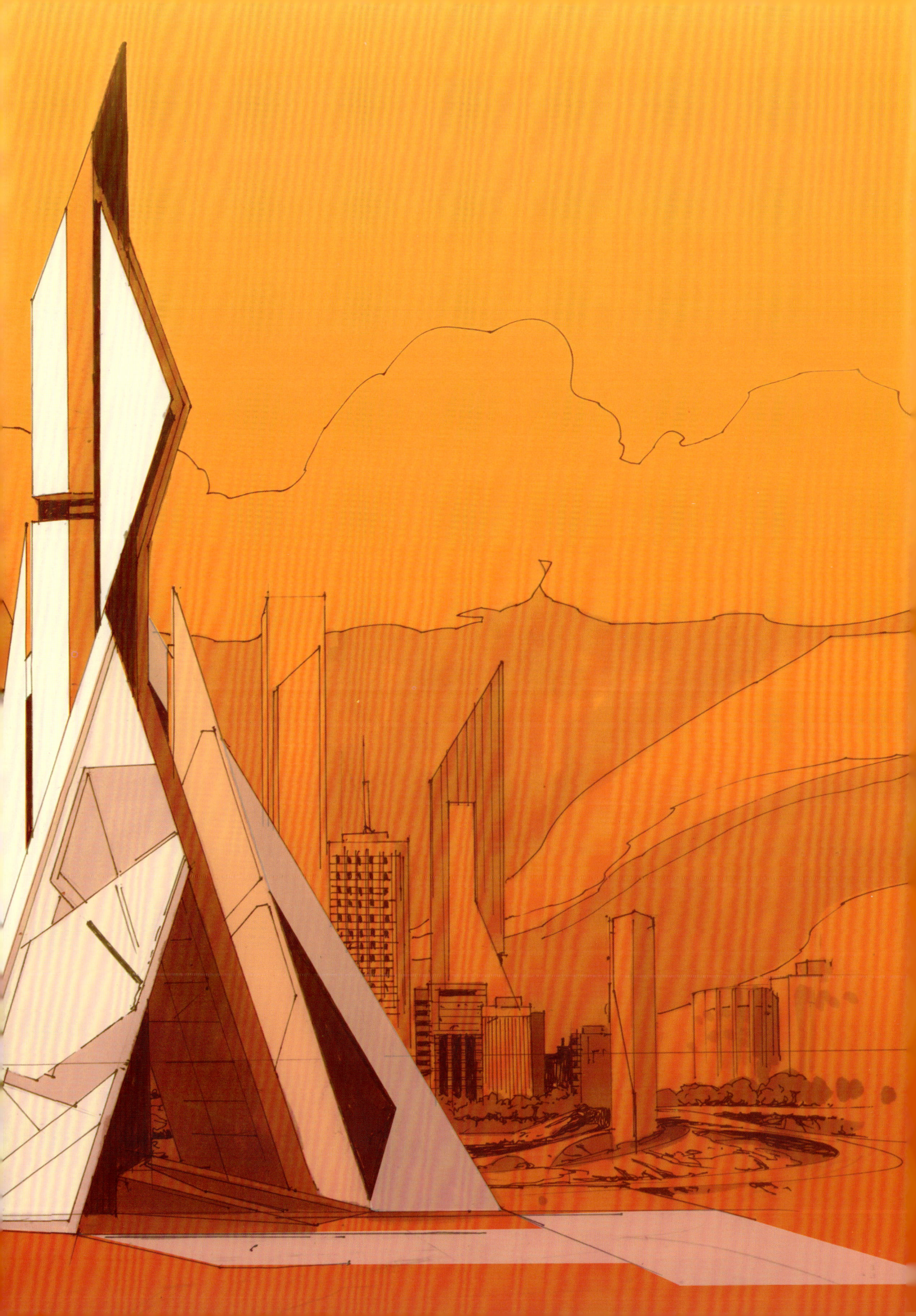

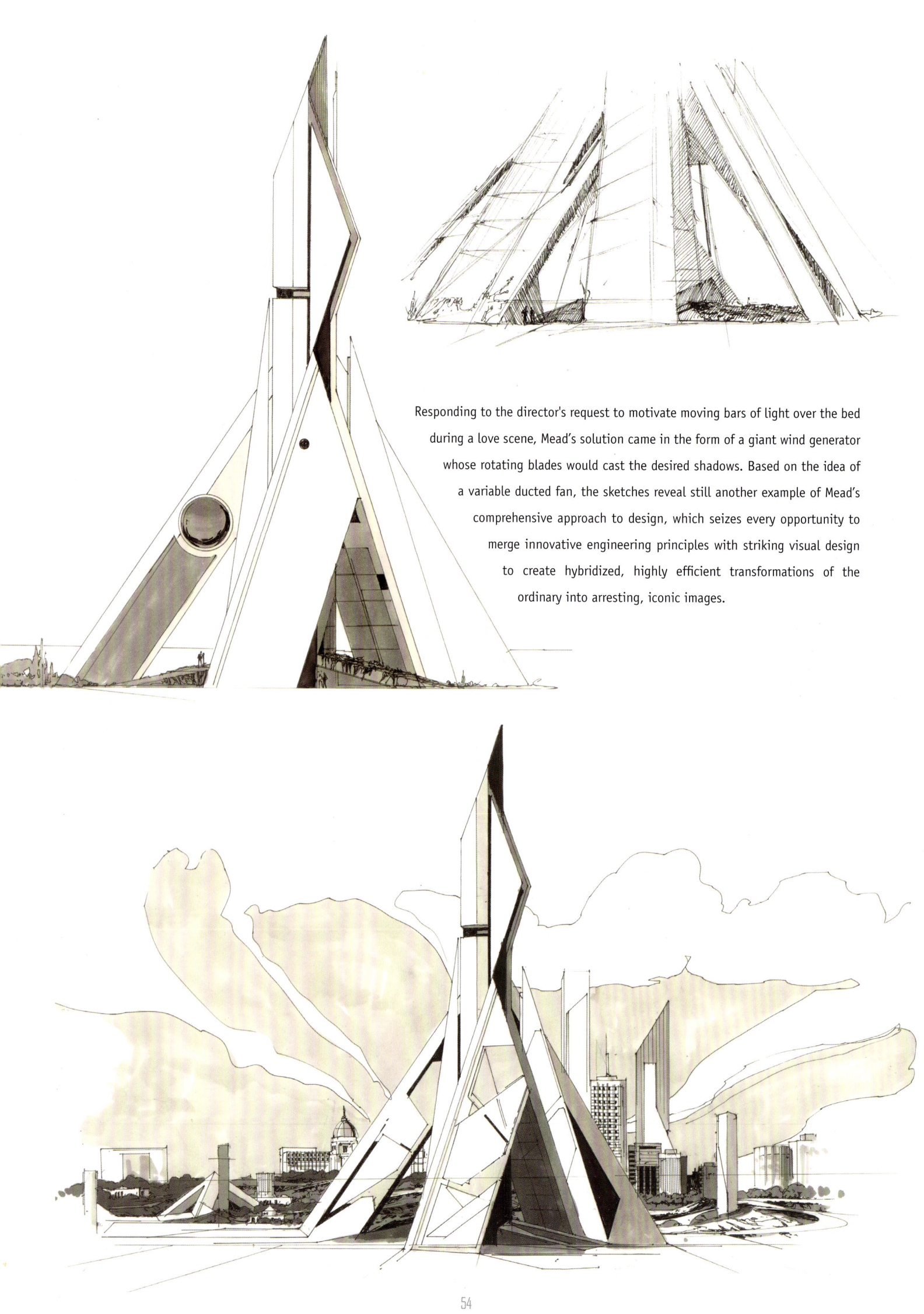

Responding to the director's request to motivate moving bars of light over the bed during a love scene, Mead's solution came in the form of a giant wind generator whose rotating blades would cast the desired shadows. Based on the idea of a variable ducted fan, the sketches reveal still another example of Mead's comprehensive approach to design, which seizes every opportunity to merge innovative engineering principles with striking visual design to create hybridized, highly efficient transformations of the ordinary into arresting, iconic images.

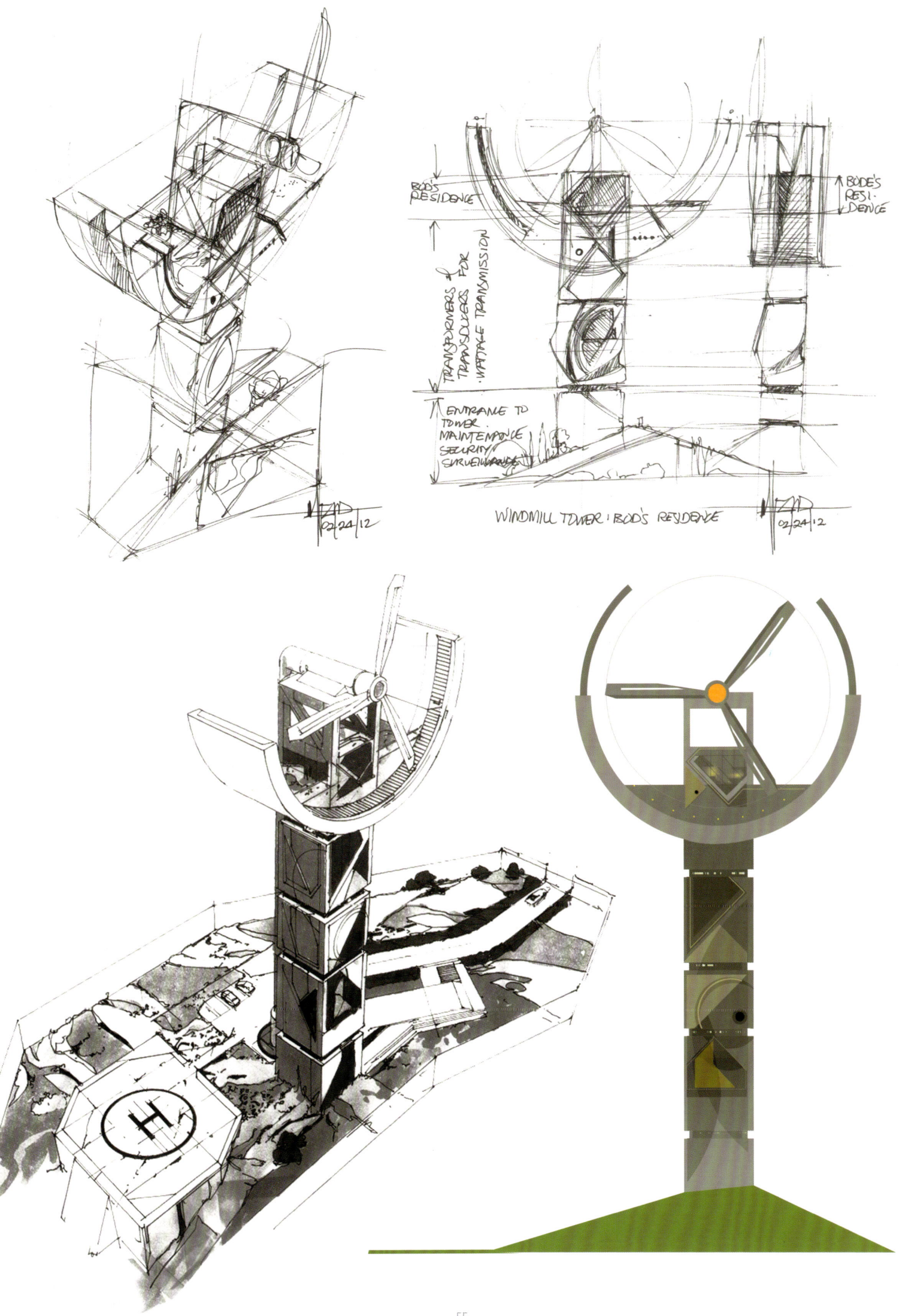

BOD'S
RESIDENCE

BOD'S
RESI-
DENCE

TRANSFORMERS & TRANSDUCERS FOR WATTAGE TRANSMISSION

ENTRANCE TO TOWER MAINTENANCE SECURITY SURVEILLANCE

WINDMILL TOWER : BOD'S RESIDENCE

02/24/12

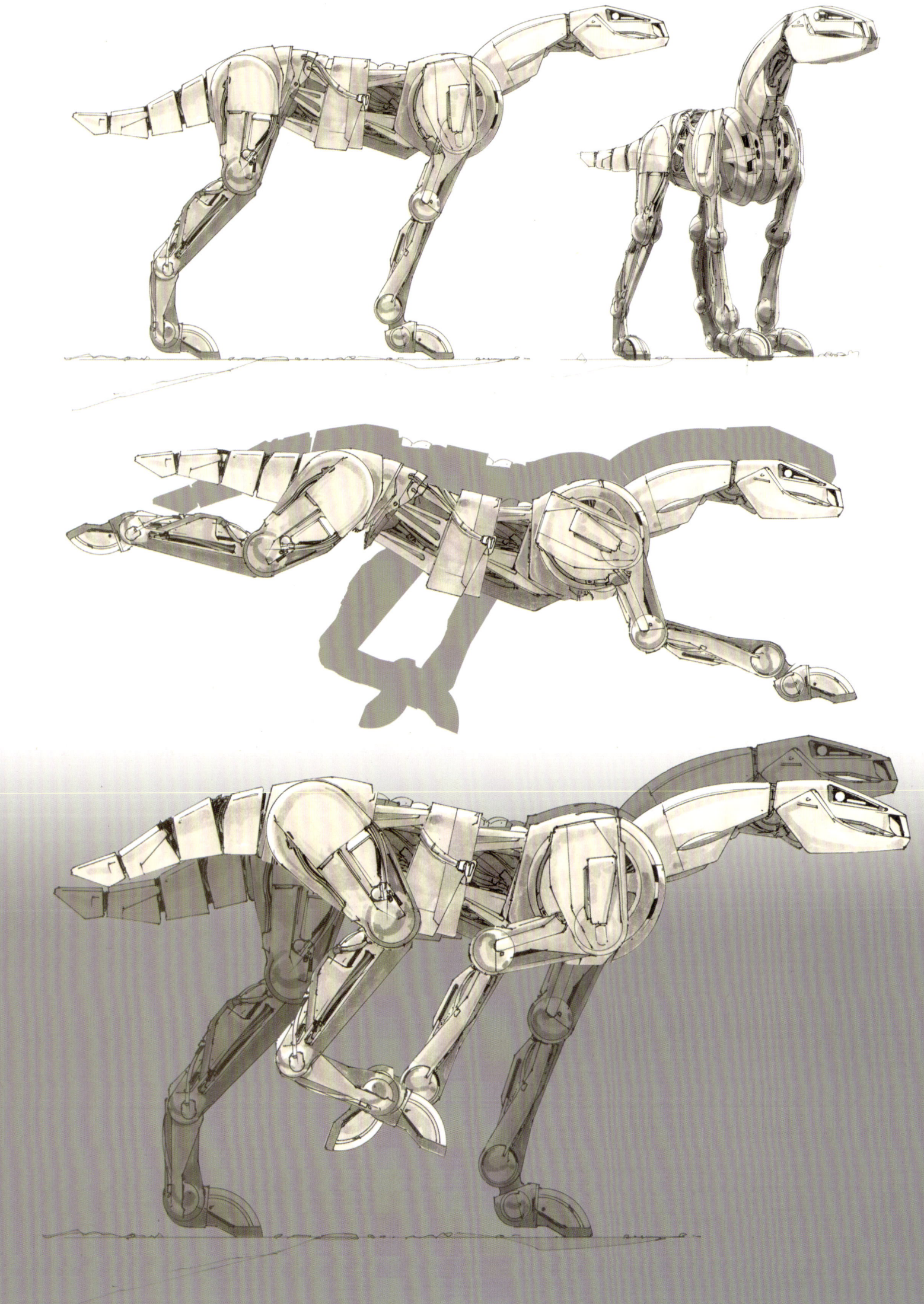

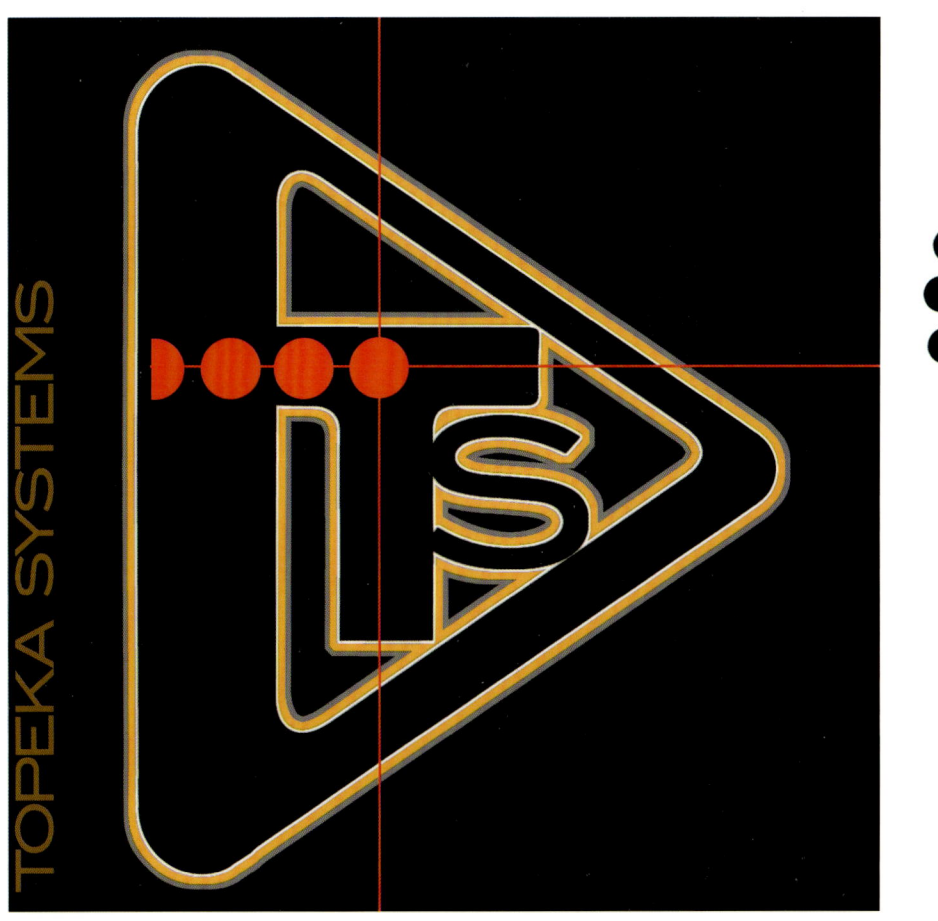

TOPEKA SYSTEMS

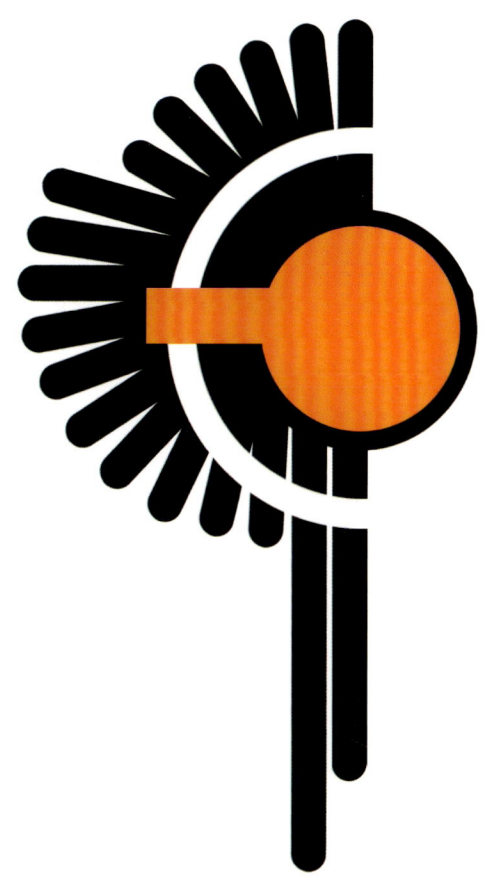

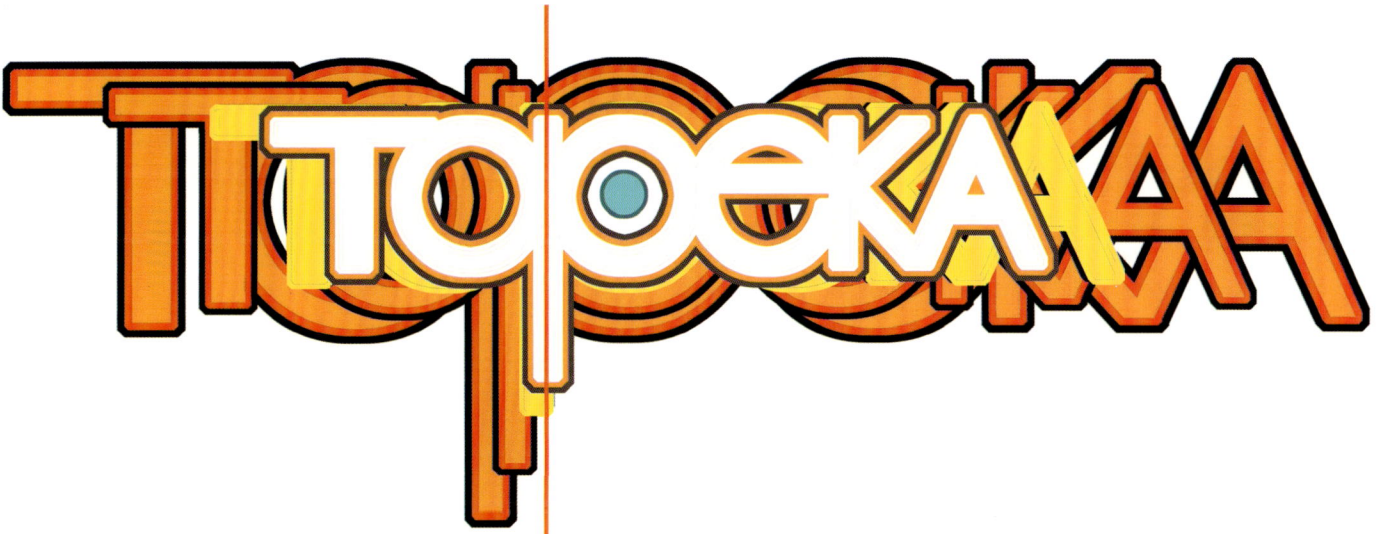

Metallic musculature over a robotic skeleton moves in a post-Muybridge fashion with a convincing gait in these sketches, which accurately depict mechanical motion, complete with hubs, actuators, and high-pressure lines. Mead's enthusiasm for depicting these assemblies will be seen again in his designs for *Blade Runner* and *Aliens*. Further development of the *Topeka* war dog and final design elements were introduced as the production struggled for a green light which never came. Asked whether the process was frustrating, Mead answered, "everything you do off and on is getting ready for the next challenge".

THE *TOPEKA* LOGO WENT THROUGH NUMEROUS EVOLUTIONS AS MEAD REFLECTED ON THE NUANCES AND OVERTONES OF VARIOUS GRAPHIC STYLES

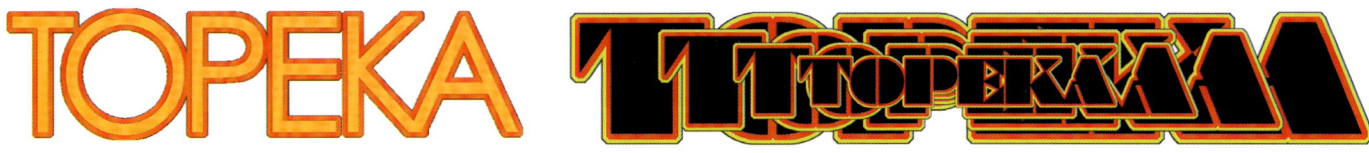

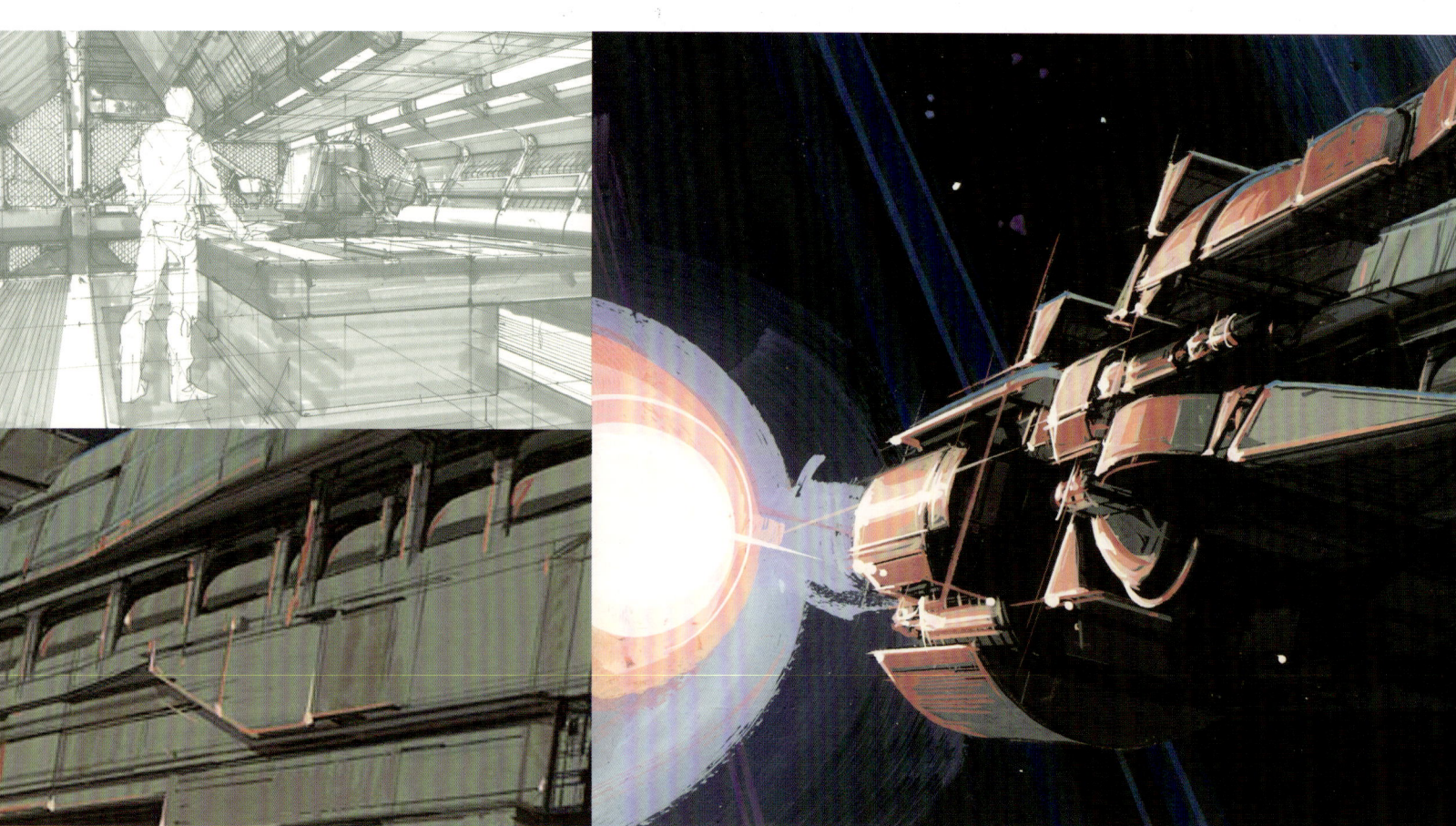

ALIENS

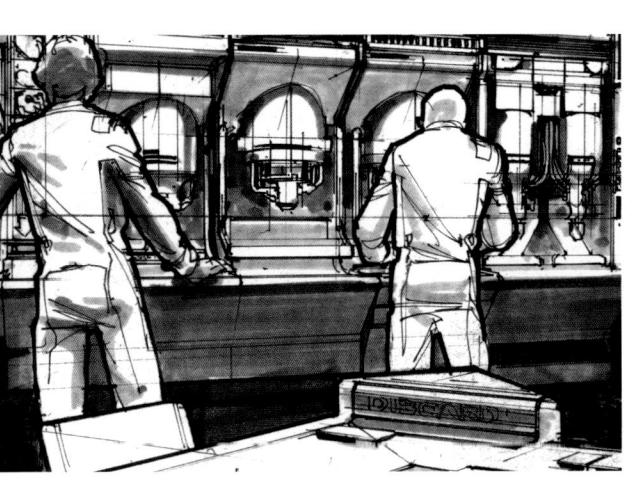

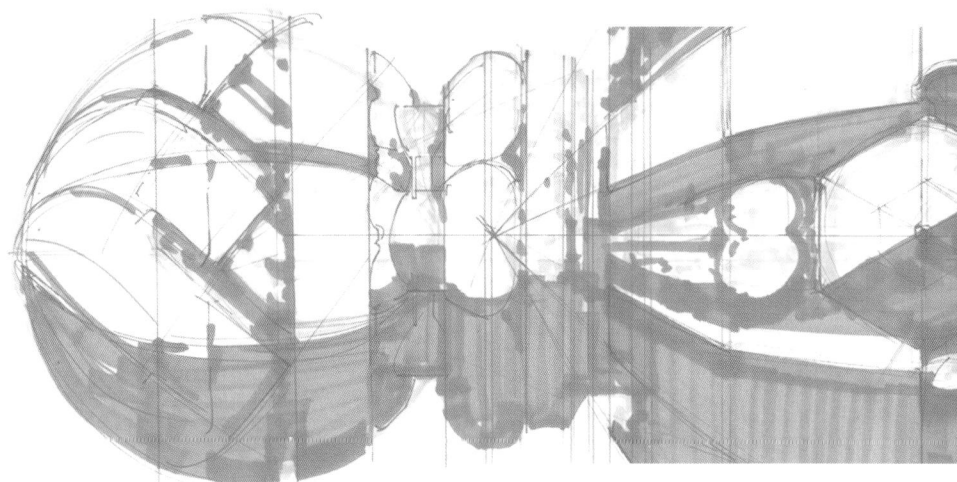

BEAUTY AND THE BEAST

One must admit that there was a certain irony to the assignment, as Mead received the invitation to design the *Aliens* sequel while in Florida to judge the Ms. Universe competition. The follow-up to Ridley Scott's ground-breaking sci-fi horror film was to be directed by James Cameron and again was to star Sigourney Weaver as Ellen Ripley. However it was in many ways far different from its predecessor, as the initial setting was to be aboard the USS *Sulaco* which Cameron envisioned as bristling with antennae, and configured in such a way that it would not be necessary to "pull focus"—a technical term for the manual operation required to keep a very large physical model in sharp focus as the camera moves across the frame. Upon landing, subsequent action takes place within a claustrophobic labyrinthine habitat called *Hadley's Hope*, which is infested with the alien from the original film.

For Mead, the devices and environments have to work. They must be based on some principles which, while speculative, hew close to what sets Mead apart. What lends his images authority and plausibility, whether of a flying vehicle or an otherworldly planet, is established norms that take their cue from developing technologies (Mead is an autodidact when it comes to technologic innovation, an arena he closely monitors).

In order to create narrative tension within the ship, Mead drew upon the anomalous nature of a medieval town, where, he says, "[you] can't predict where you are going to end up", and then just "added stuff". Cinematically, the claustrophobic atmosphere thus created is a pitch-perfect complement to the almost unbearable tension of the narrative.

Many of the following sketches are a textbook on kinetics – vehicles open up, lower ramps, and transform; the canopies of

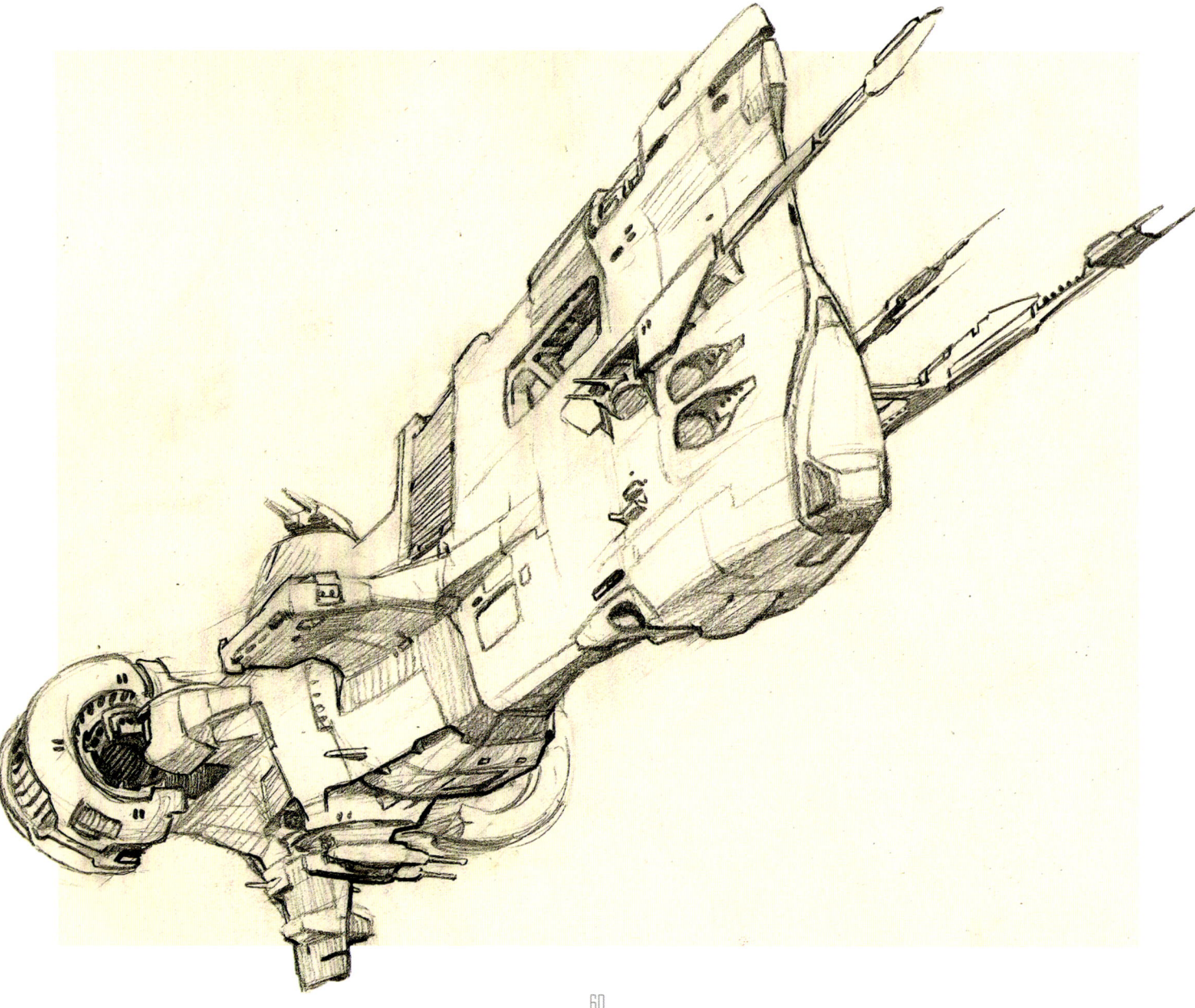

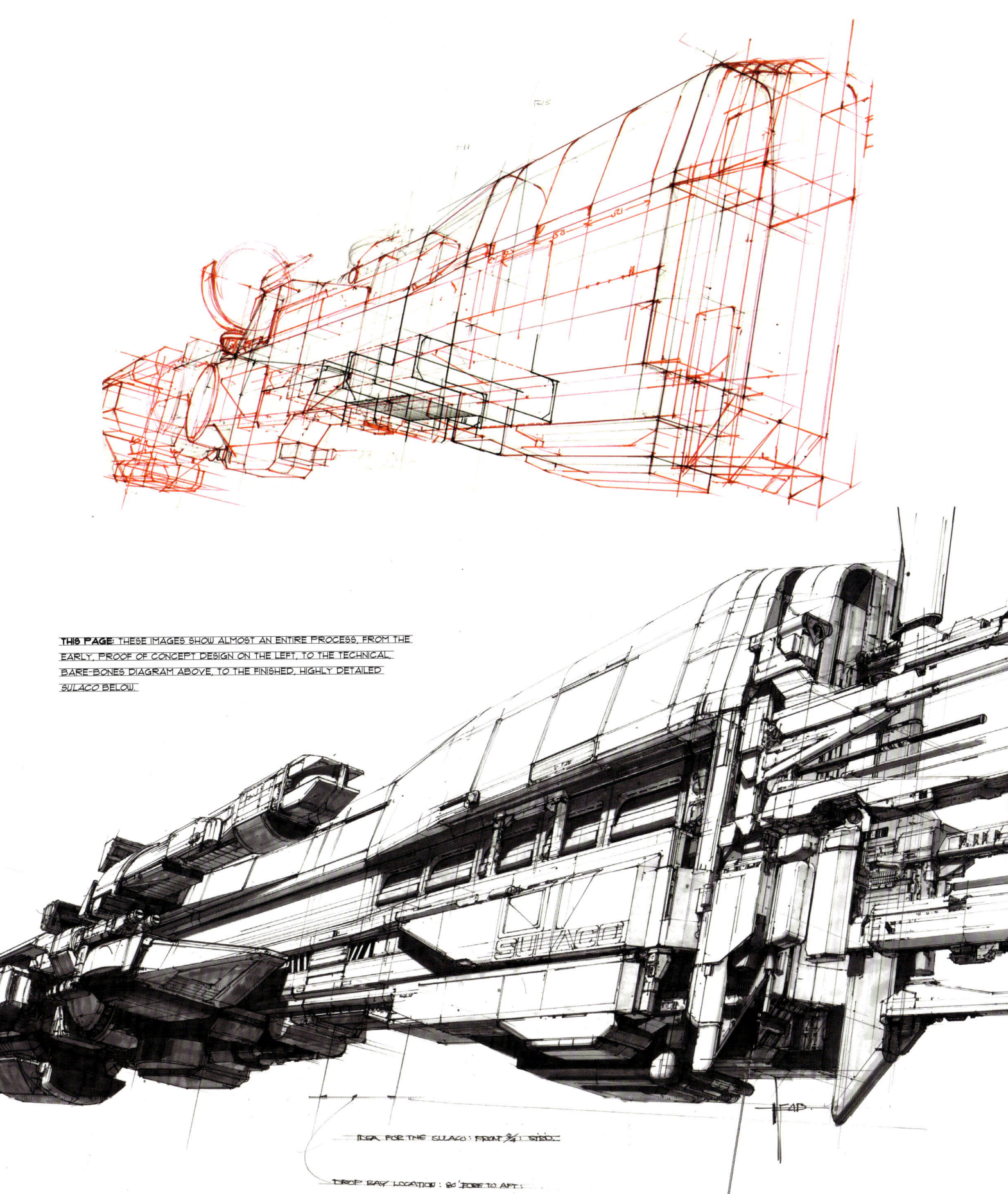

IDEA FOR THE SULACO: FROM 3/4 STBD.

DROP BAY LOCATION: 80' FORE TO AFT.

hibernation capsules slide open, and hatches to some unspecified place dot the floor, underscoring Mead's fascination with mechanical motion. The imagery is seminal, with a rare emphasis, for Mead, on repetition, perhaps to telegraph the soon to appear hordes of alien creatures, but certainly to convey spatial depth and a sense of impending crisis. The detail is uniquely Mead's. The tangles of umbilical tubes that serve the capsules are precisely located, with an engineer's logic, to serve pairs, rather than single units.

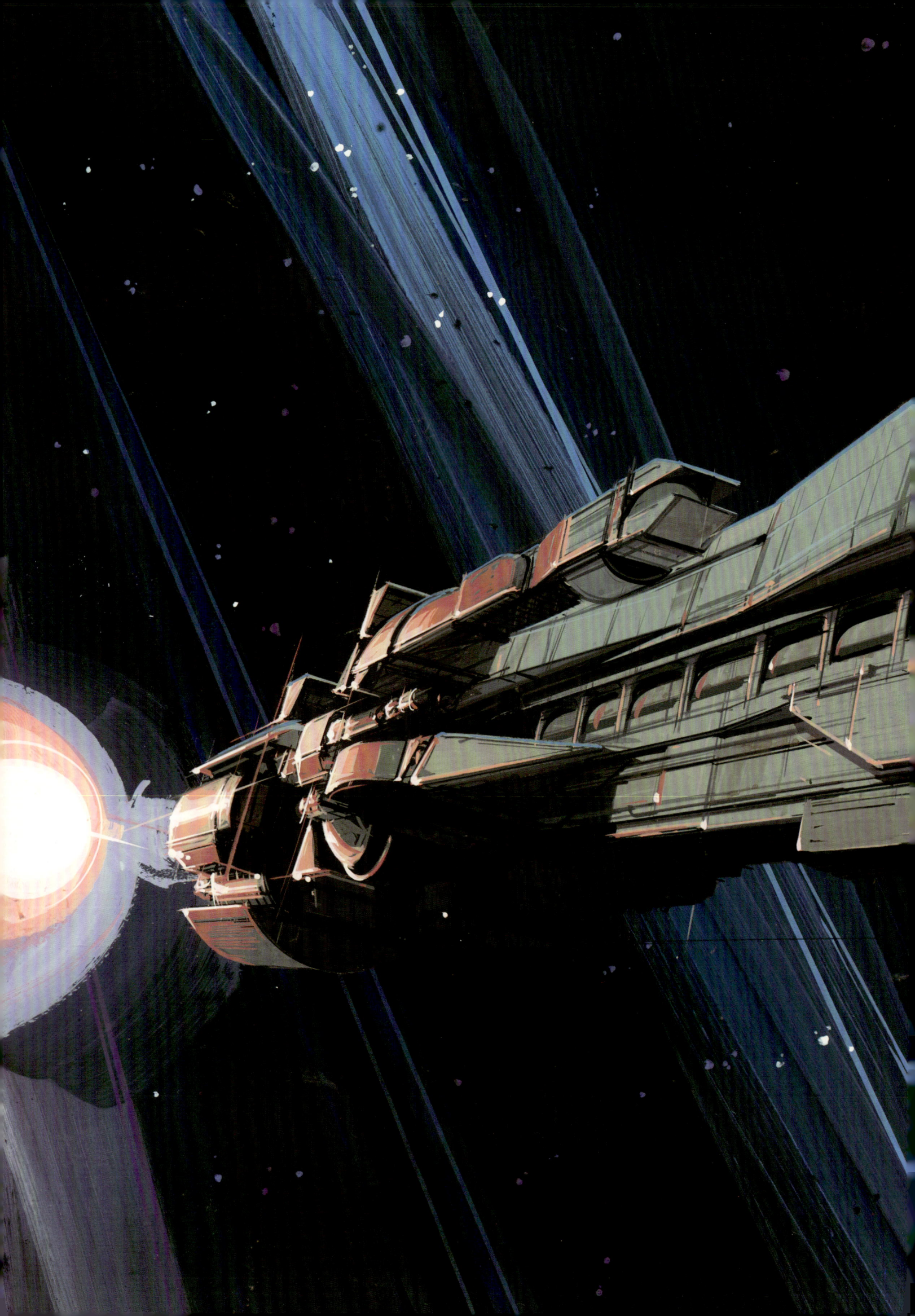

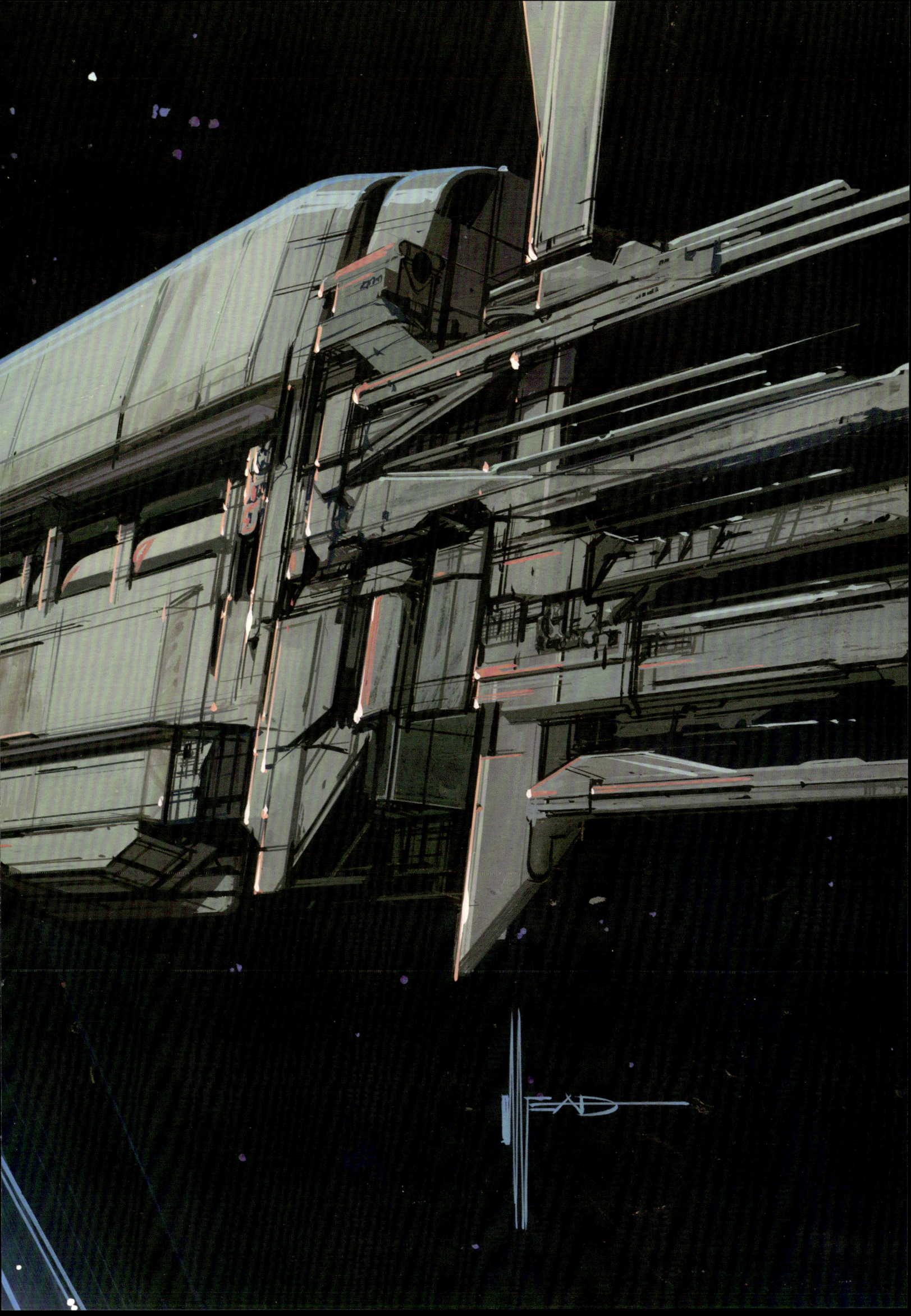

The preliminary sketches for the spaceship USS *Sulaco* which Mead submitted to Cameron were drawn while on the plane returning to Los Angeles. Showing an elongated craft made up of various specialized modules, each with its own form, coupled together to create a brooding, elegiac configuration which instantly conveys the solemn urgency of the mission.

This vessel had little to do with the slick shapes of *Star Trek*, and avoided the *greebles* of *Star Wars*. For *Aliens*, he designed a functional, section-by-section ship which gave the impression of a highly-engineered, purposeful vessel. That same logic led to a more open, visually accessible area, in which the capsules themselves dominate the frame, rather than the surrounding enclosure.

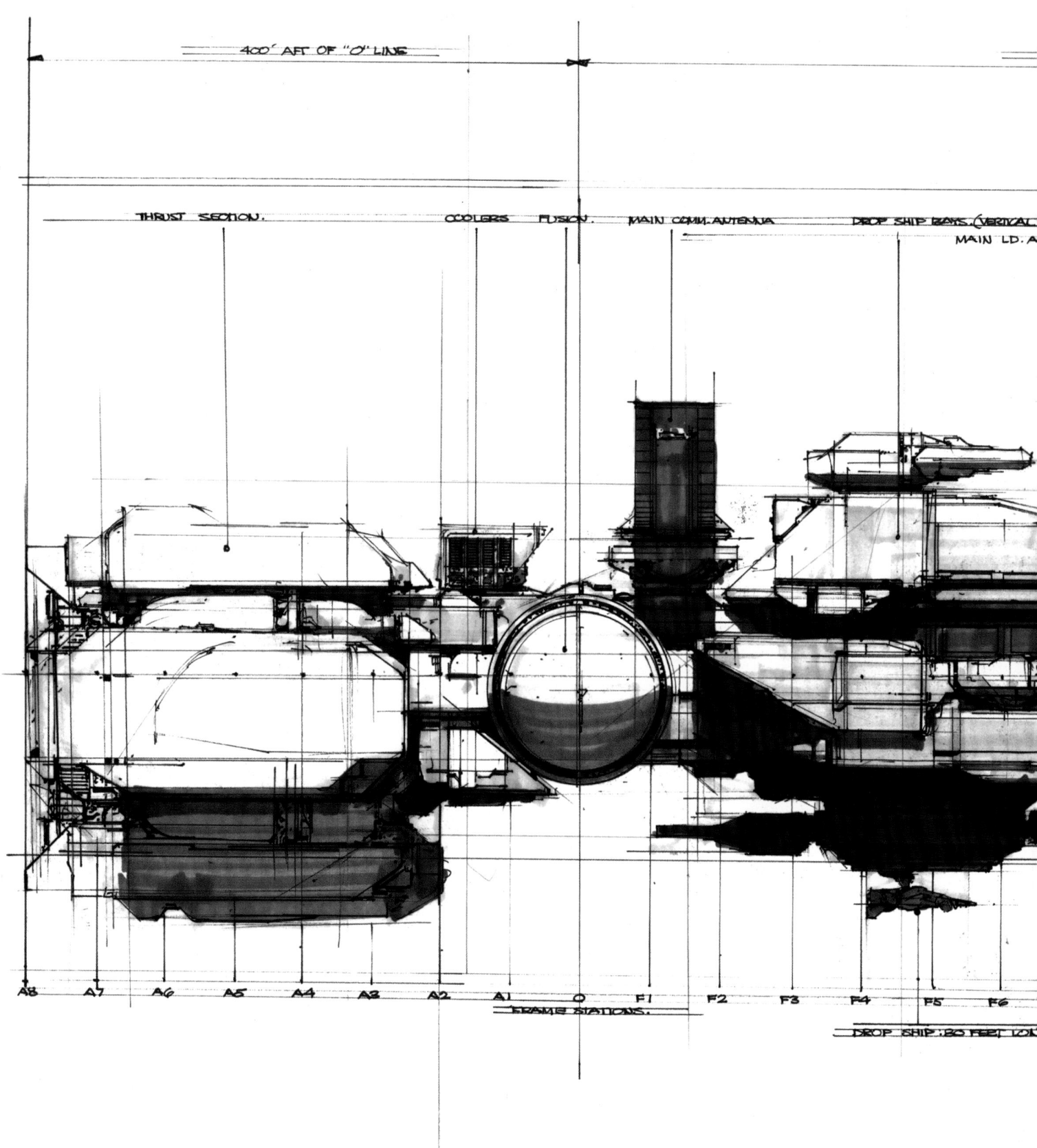

Mead's vision is all encompassing, lavishing ingenuity and visual order on every detail. Here a weapon, there a voracious opening he describes as a drop bay, and proceeds to explain how, in theory, the thing works. It all works in a kind of blissed-out harmony of lines, surfaces, and 'purposeful anomaly' that Mead creates with the calm assurance of a seasoned travel guide. In his imagination, no doubt, these astounding visions are simply part of a world he inhabits every time he puts his hand to paper, but to those whose future is circumscribed by adverts for 'futuristic' machinery, he resets the stage.

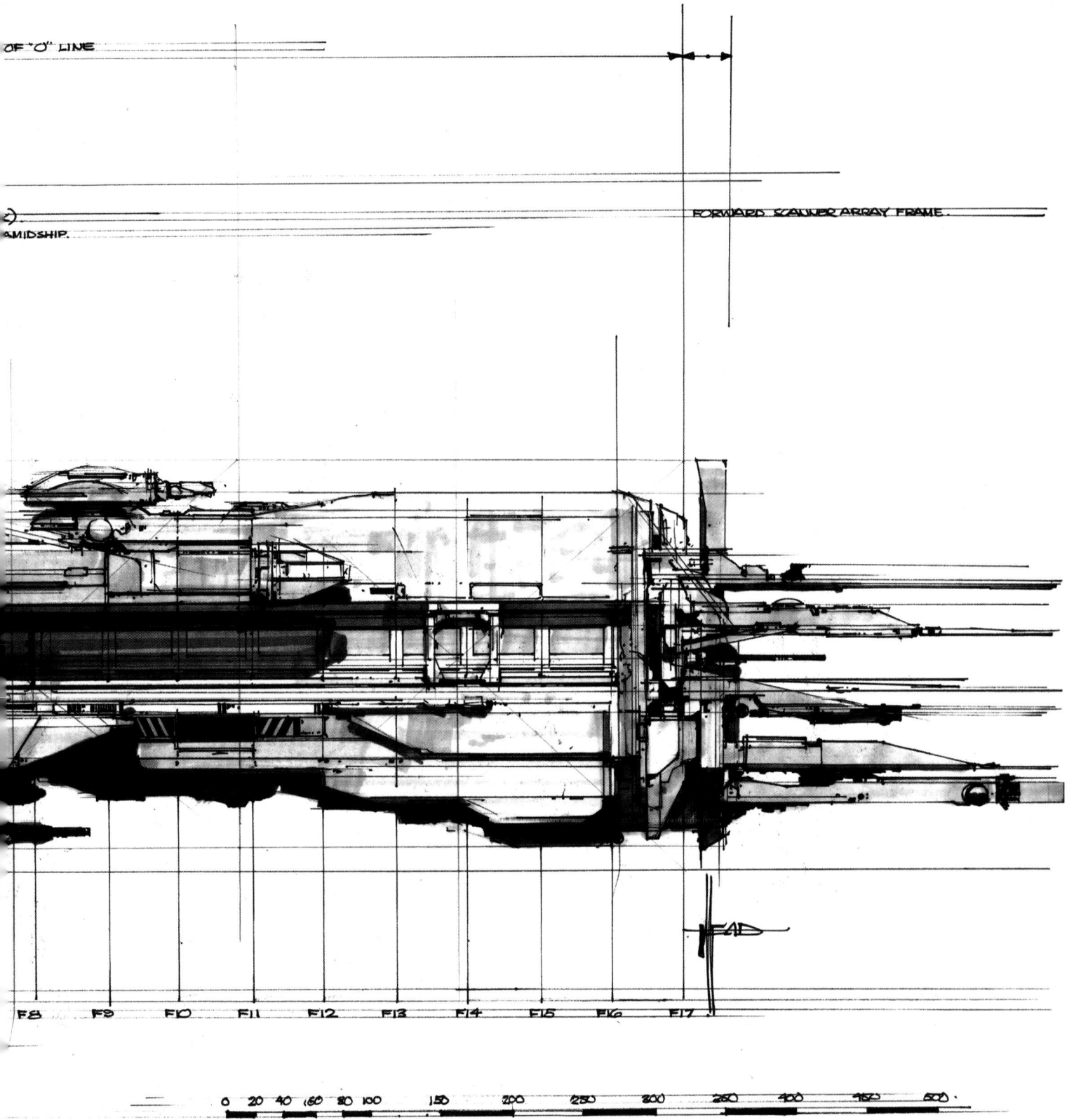

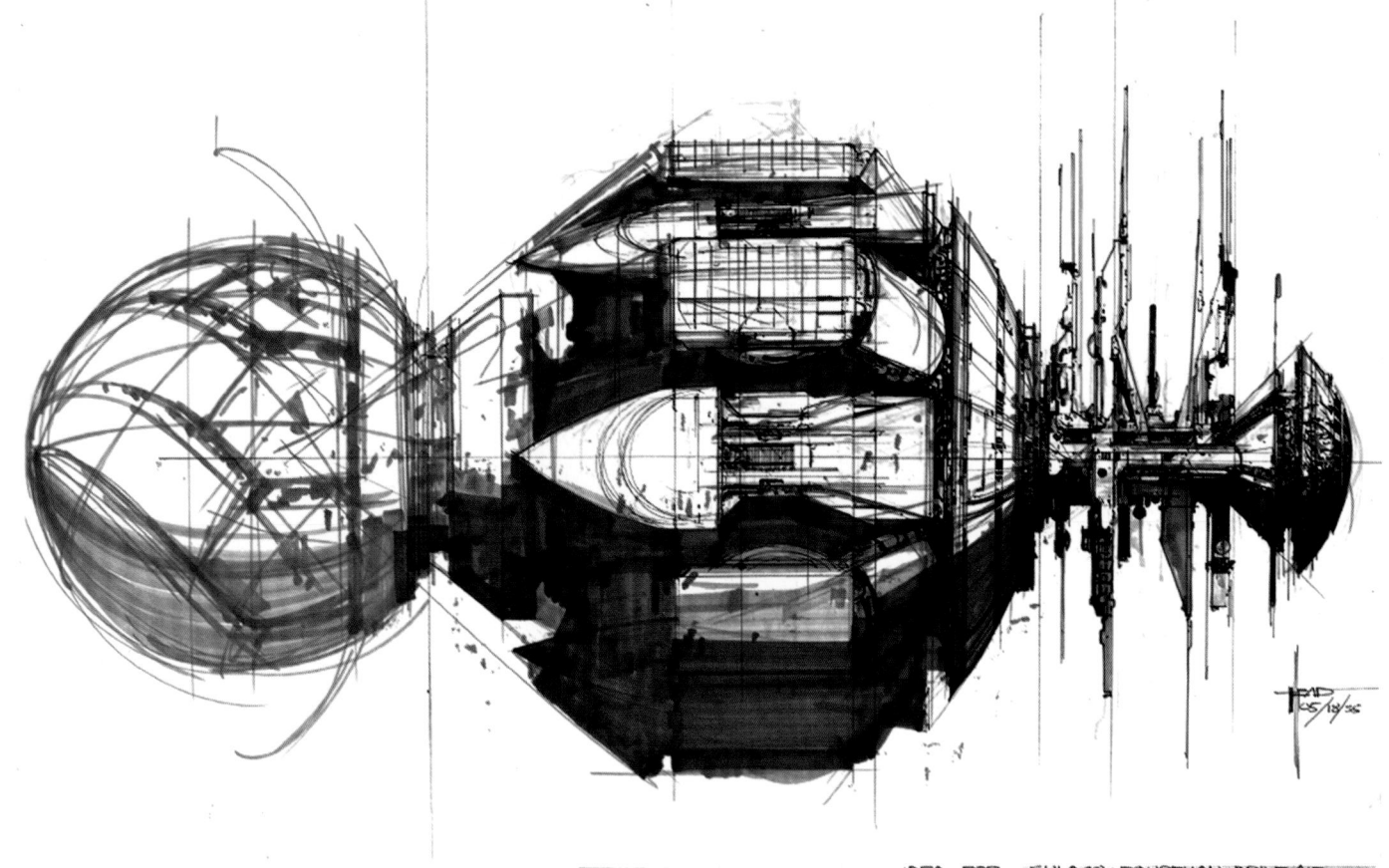

IDEA FOR SULACO: ROHREMAN DRIVE: ALT.

SCALE

THIS SPREAD: FIRST CONCEPT DRAWINGS FOR THE *SULACO* BEFORE MEETING WITH JAMES CAMERON

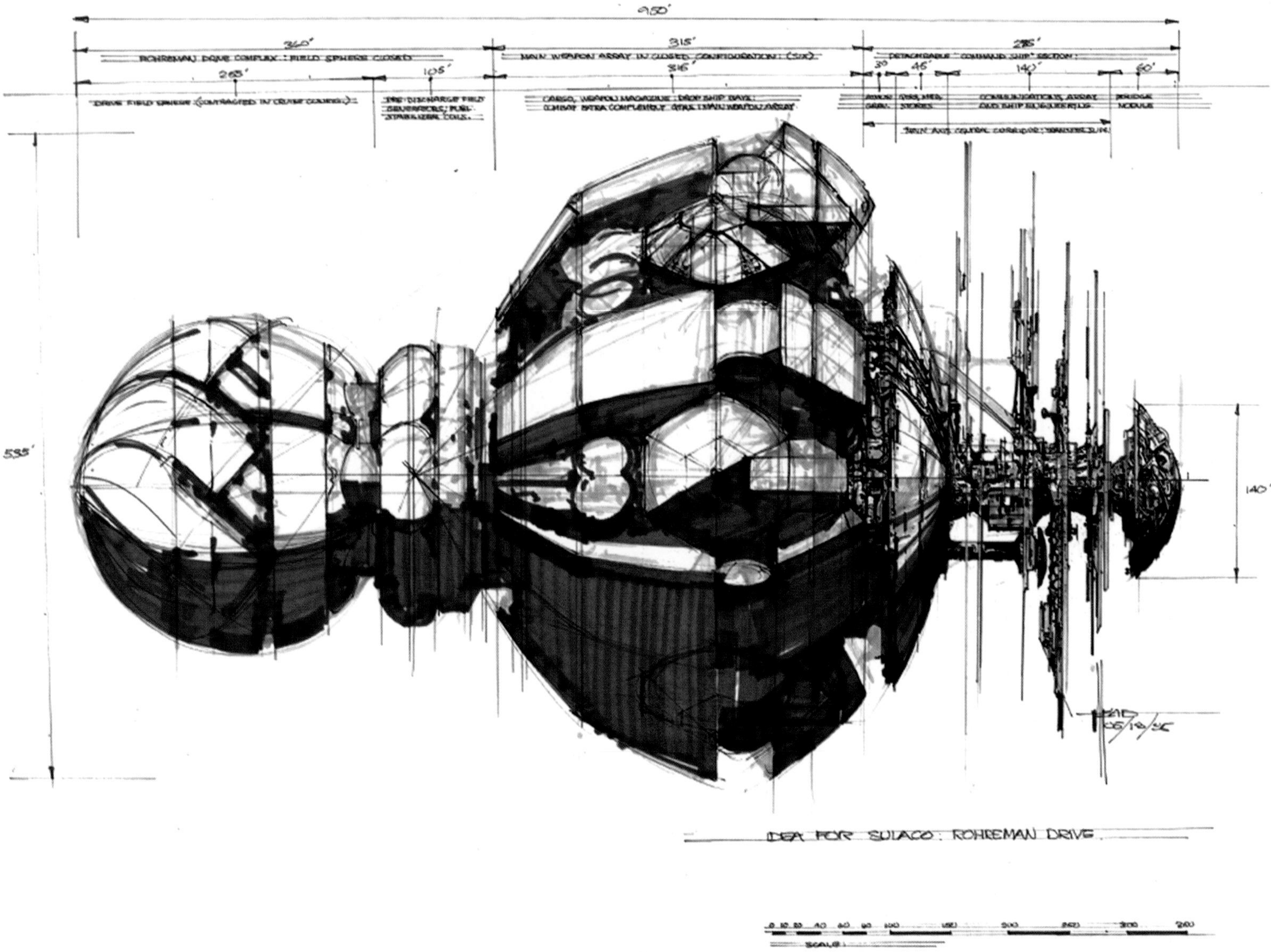

950'

360'   315'   285'

ROHREMAN DRIVE COMPLEX: FIELD SPHERE CLOSED   MAIN WEAPON ARRAY IN CLOSED CONFIGURATION: (SIX)   DETACHABLE "COMMAND SHIP" SECTION

265'   105'   345'   30'   45'   140'   60'

DRIVE FIELD SPHERE (CONTRACTED IN CRUISE CONFIG.)   PRE-DISCHARGE FIELD   CARGO, WEAPON MAGAZINE, DROP SHIP BAYS   ARMOR ENG. MED. COMMUNICATIONS ARRAY   BRIDGE
                                                     SILVERBORE/FUEL   COMBAT EXTRA COMPLEXES, STRUCTURAL MONTOU ARRAY   GRAV. STORES AND SHIP SUBSYSTEMS   MODULE
                                                     STABILIZER COILS   SHIP AXIS CENTRAL CORRIDOR: TRANSFER TUBE

535'   140'

IDEA FOR SULACO: ROHREMAN DRIVE

.8 10 20   40 60 80 100   150   200   250   300   200

SCALE

66

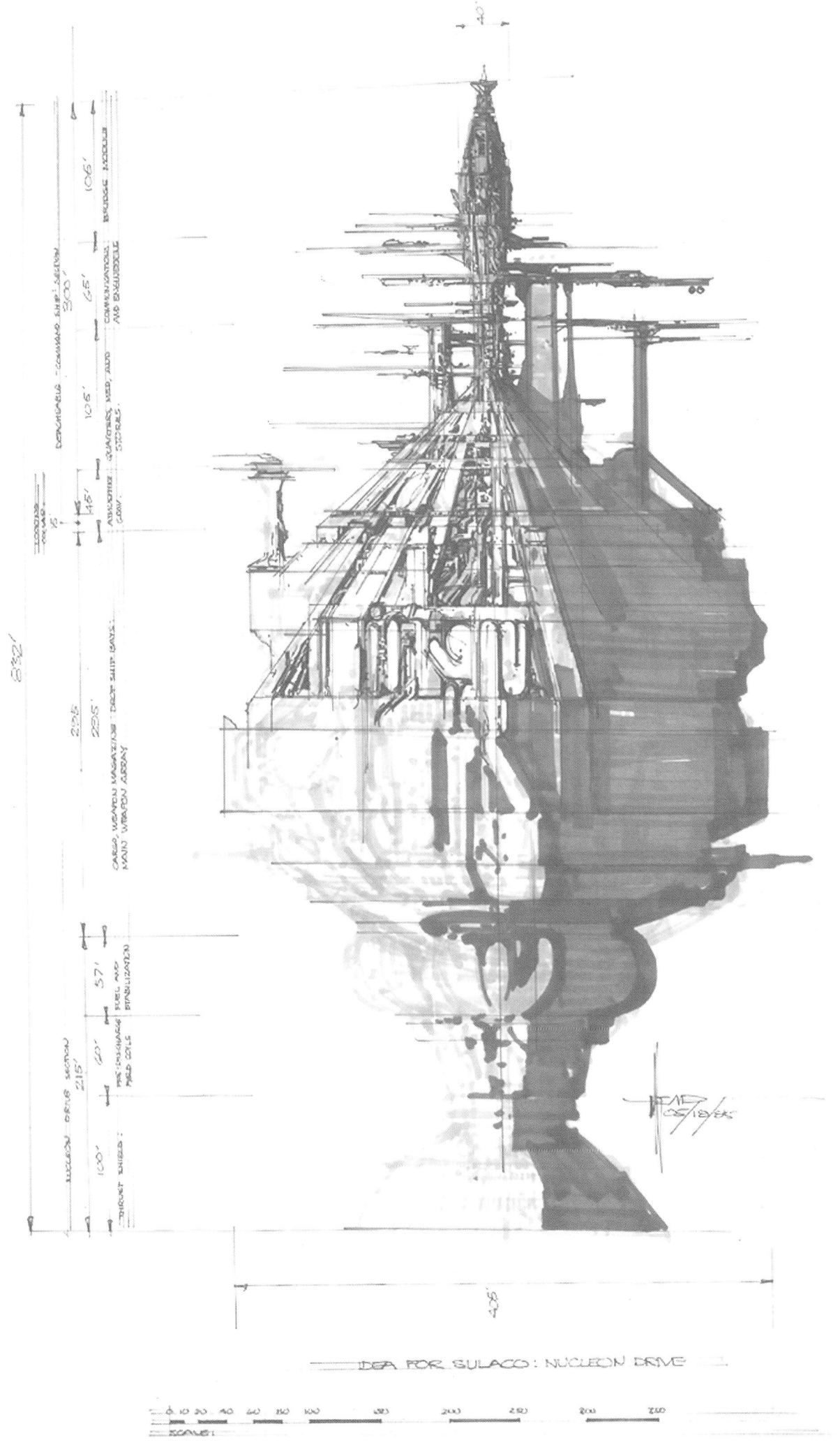

IDEA FOR SULACO: NUCLEON DRIVE

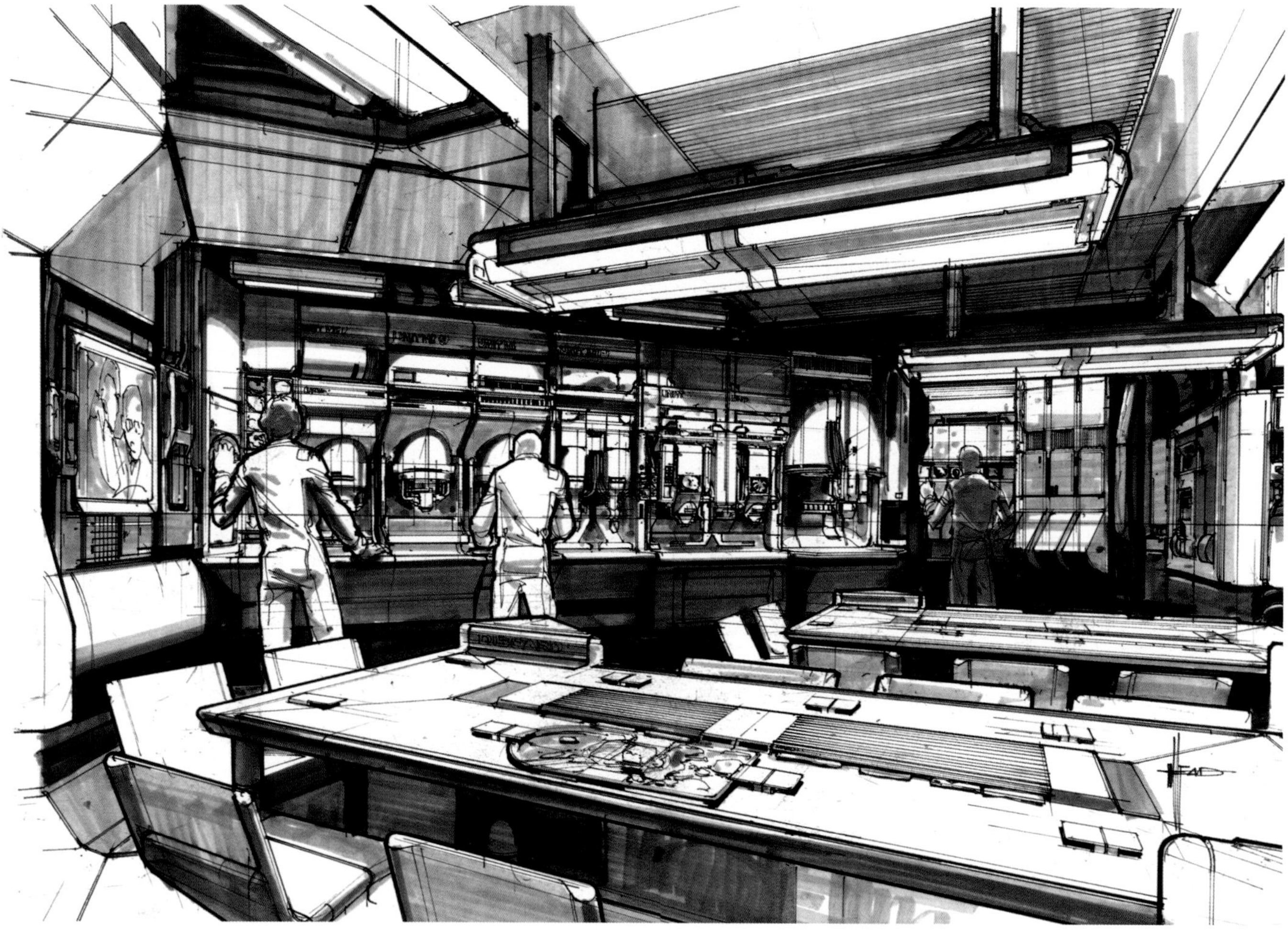

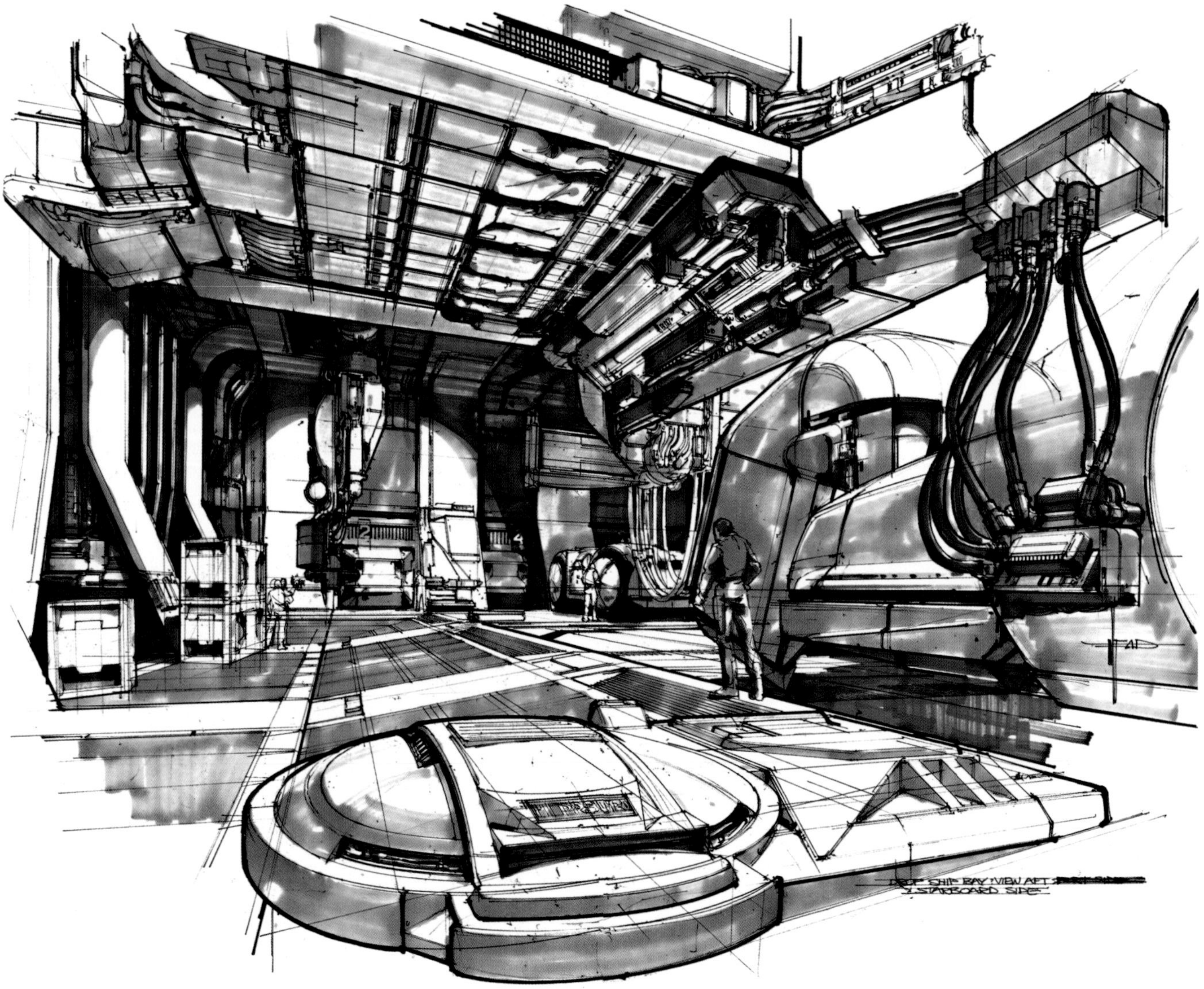

DROP SHIP BAY VIEW AFT
STARBOARD SIDE

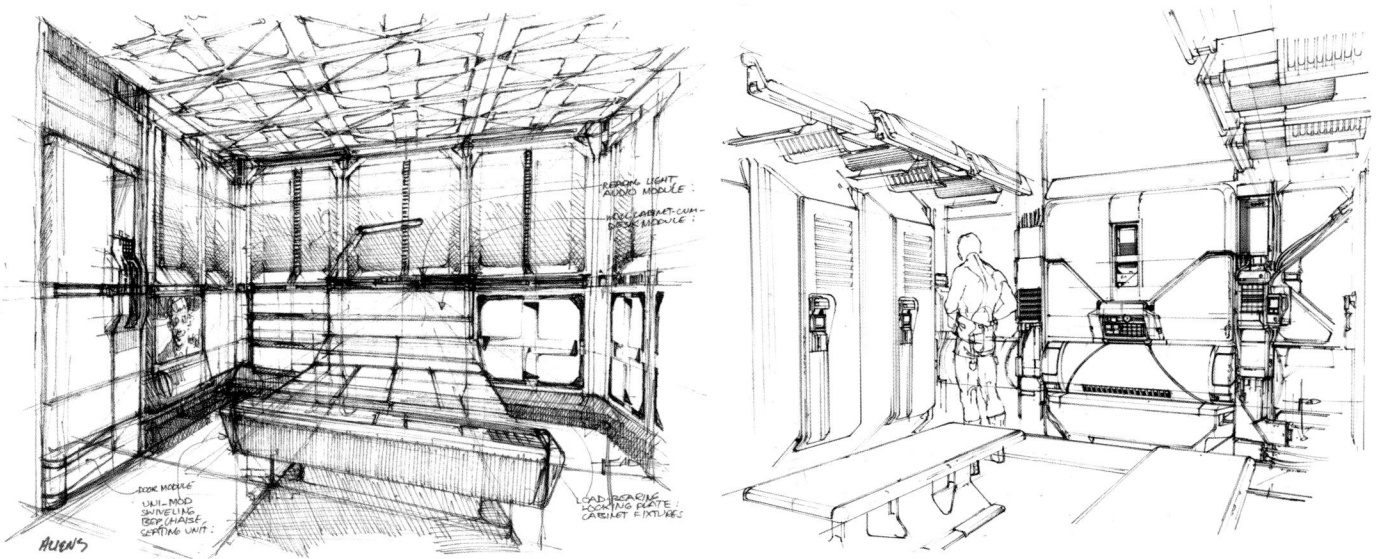

For the most part, Mead's images can be seen as snapshots of an unfolding scenario. As such they can be seen as one of a burst of images capturing a particular scene – people and objects suspended in a (future) time tableau.

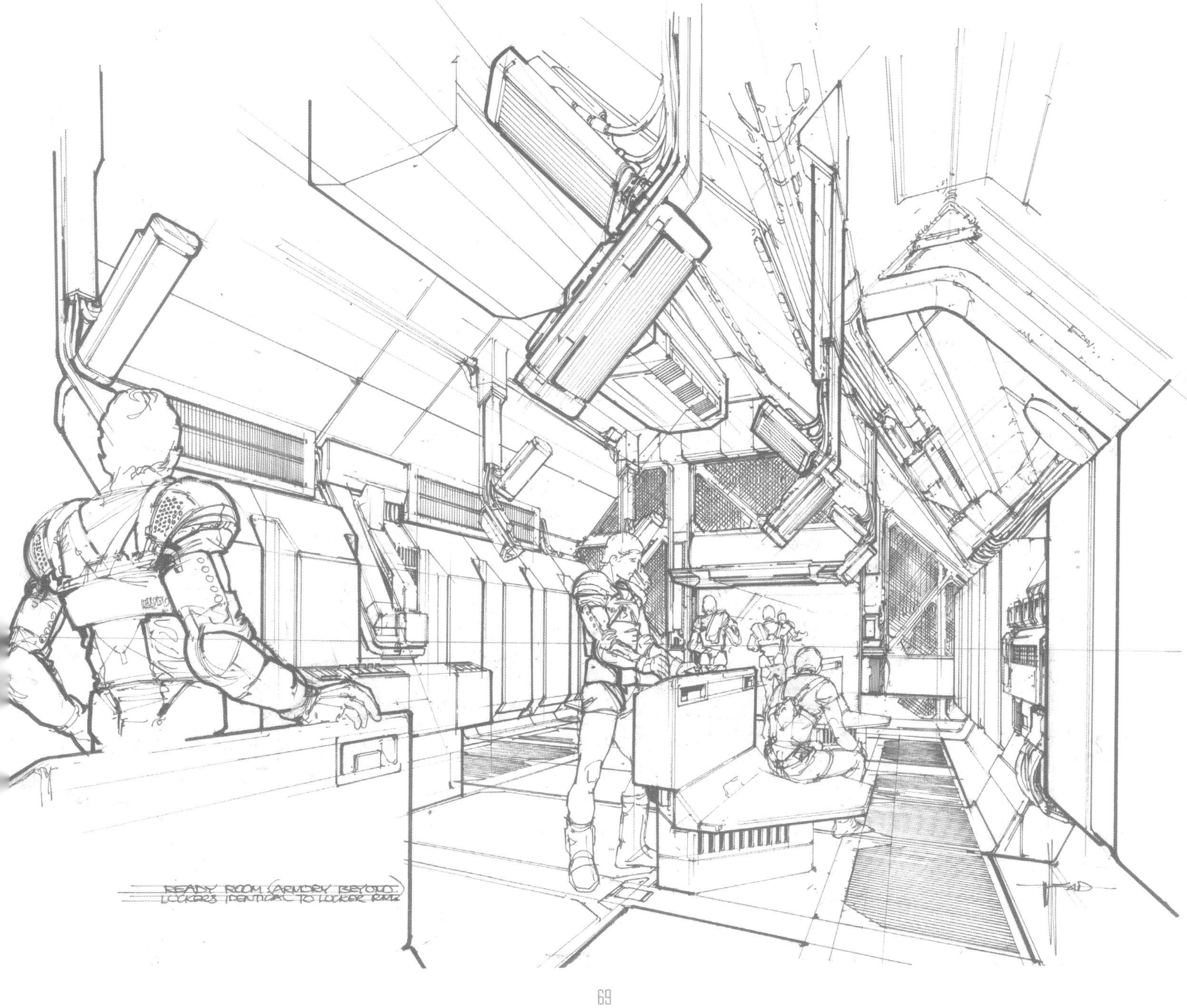

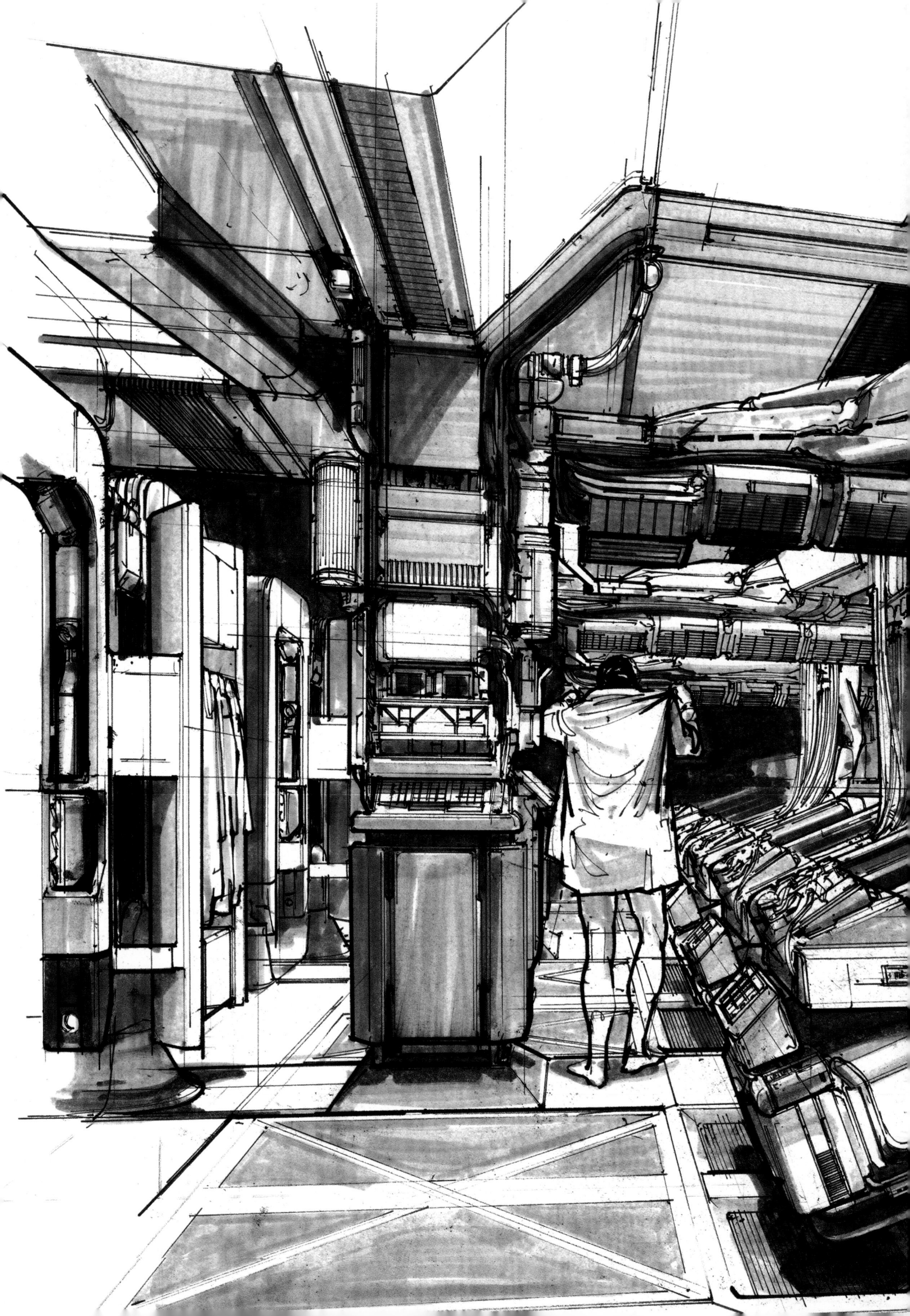

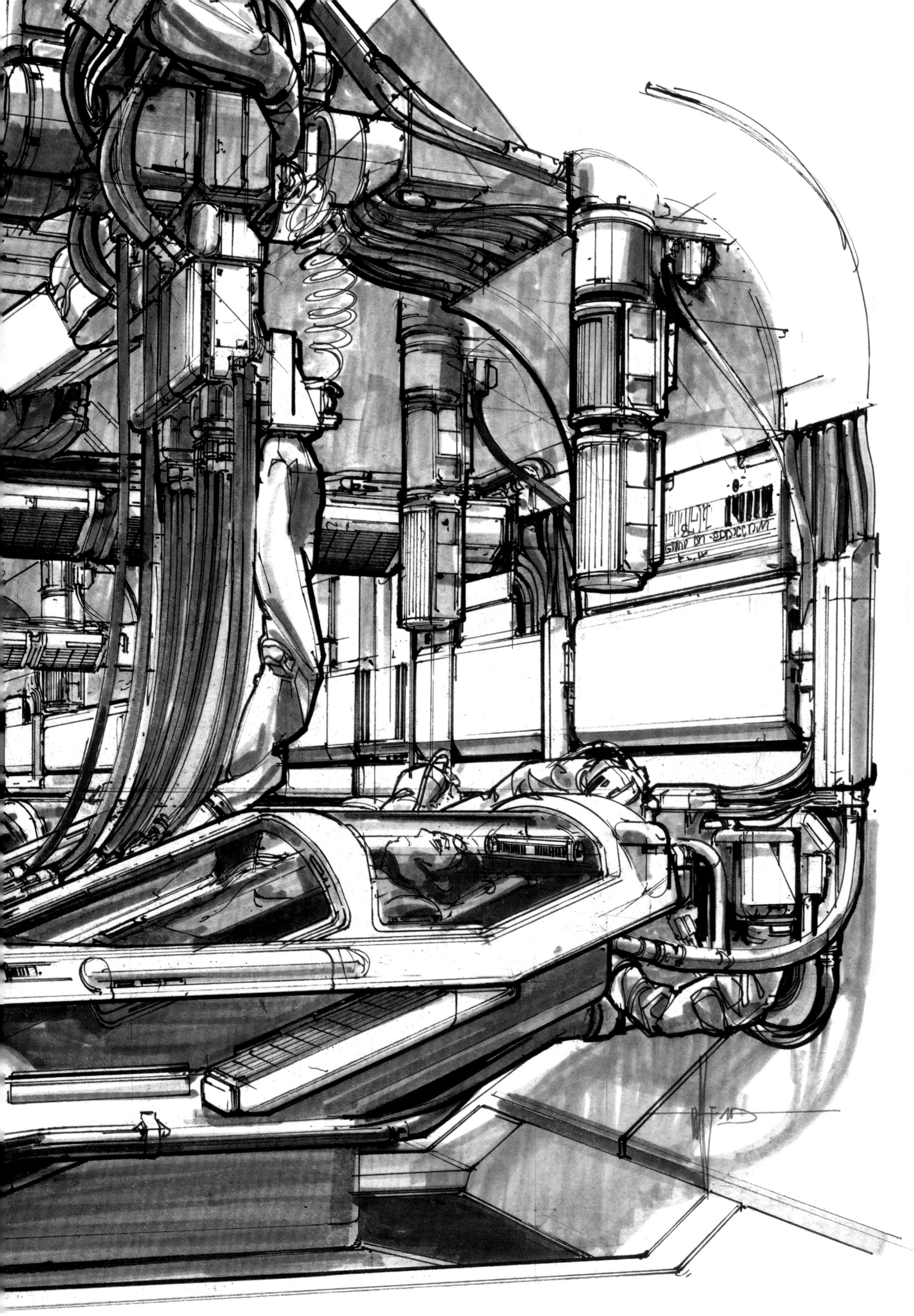

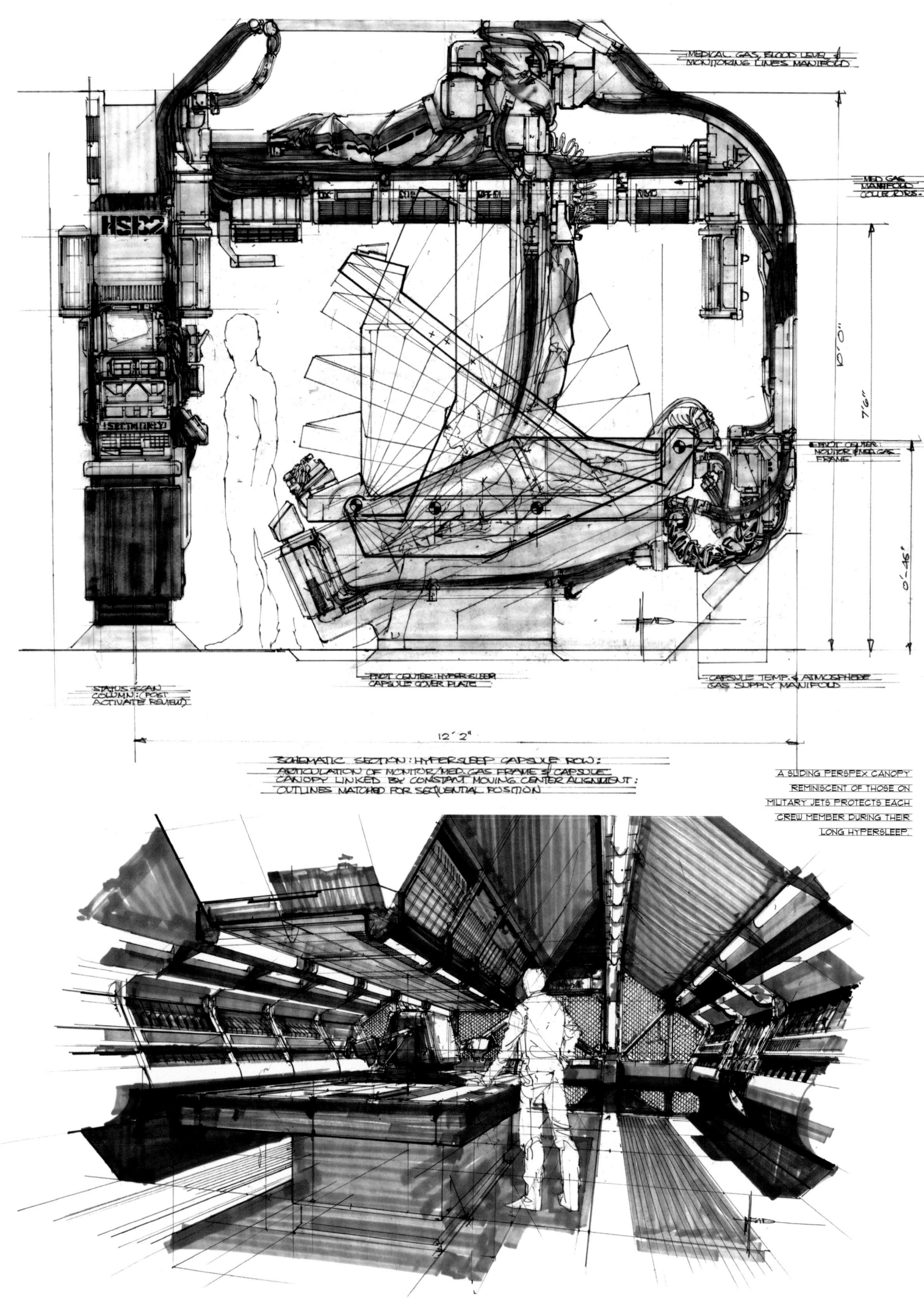

MEDICAL GAS, BLOOD LEVEL &
MONITORING LINES MANIFOLD

MED GAS
MANIFOLD
COLLECTORS.

10'0"

7'6"

PIVOT CENTER
MONITOR & MED.GAS
FRAME

0'46'

HSE2

SECONDARY

STATUS SCAN
COLUMN: (POST
ACTIVATE/ REVIEW)

PIVOT CENTER: HYPERSLEEP
CAPSULE COVER PLATE

CAPSULE TEMP. & ATMOSPHERE
GAS SUPPLY MANIFOLD

12'2"

SCHEMATIC SECTION: HYPERSLEEP CAPSULE ROW:
ARTICULATION OF MONITOR/ MED.GAS FRAME & CAPSULE
CANOPY LINKED BY CONSTANT MOVING CENTER ALIGNMENT:
OUTLINES MATCHED FOR SEQUENTIAL POSITION

A SLIDING PERSPEX CANOPY
REMINISCENT OF THOSE ON
MILITARY JETS PROTECTS EACH
CREW MEMBER DURING THEIR
LONG HYPERSLEEP.

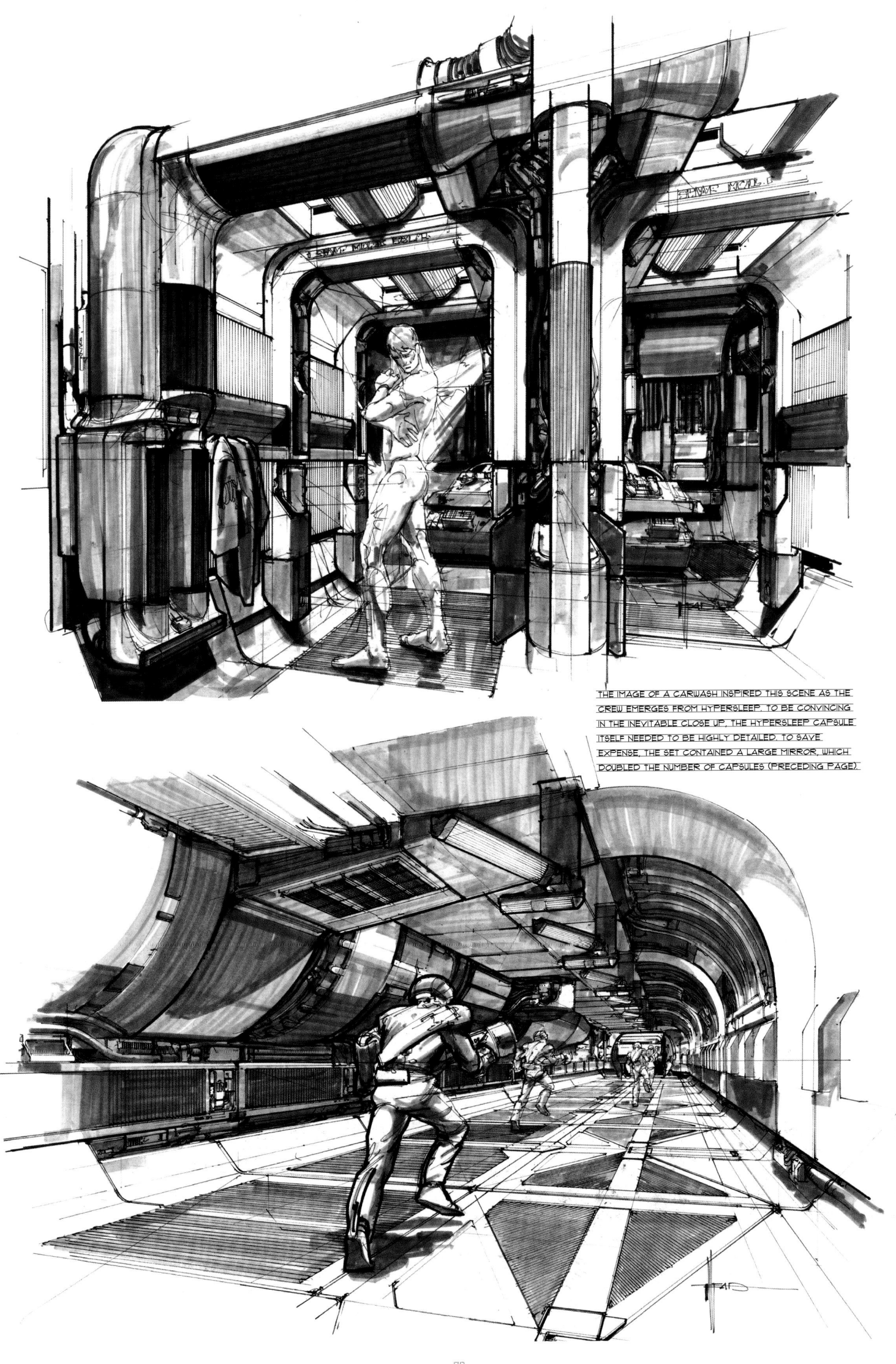

THE IMAGE OF A CARWASH INSPIRED THIS SCENE AS THE
CREW EMERGES FROM HYPERSLEEP. TO BE CONVINCING
IN THE INEVITABLE CLOSE UP, THE HYPERSLEEP CAPSULE
ITSELF NEEDED TO BE HIGHLY DETAILED. TO SAVE
EXPENSE, THE SET CONTAINED A LARGE MIRROR, WHICH
DOUBLED THE NUMBER OF CAPSULES (PRECEDING PAGE)

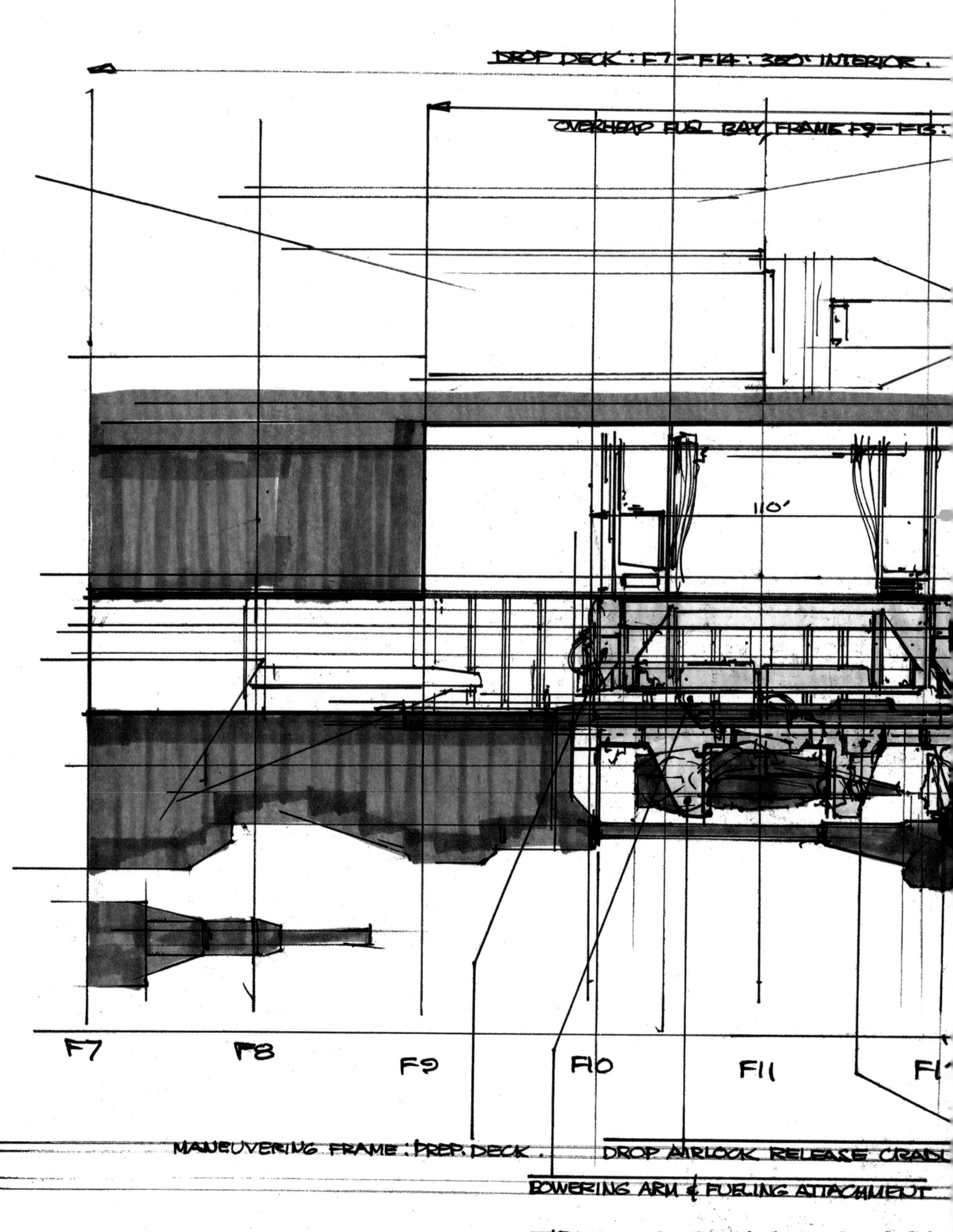

DROP DECK : F7 - F14 . 360° INTERIOR .

OVERHEAD FUEL BAY FRAME F9 - F13 :

110'

F7   F8   F9   F10   F11   F1

MANEUVERING FRAME : PREP. DECK .   DROP AIRLOCK RELEASE CRAD

BOWERING ARM & FUELING ATTACHMENT

IDEA SCHEMATIC : SULACO

74

The lateral and horizontal sections of the USS *Sulaco* were created to guide the set-building crew as they prepared a full-size version of the ship for principle photography. Without a diligent translation from concept to disciplined, dimensional drawings, much of the conceptual rigor is often lost. Fortunately, for the *Aliens* production, Mead was able to follow through with detailed, dimensioned drawings of this nature, calling out the gantries gripping the drop capsule, the hanger bay above, and a cross section of the capsule bay below, all of which, of course, was constructed in such a way that they can be pulled apart and separated for principal photography.

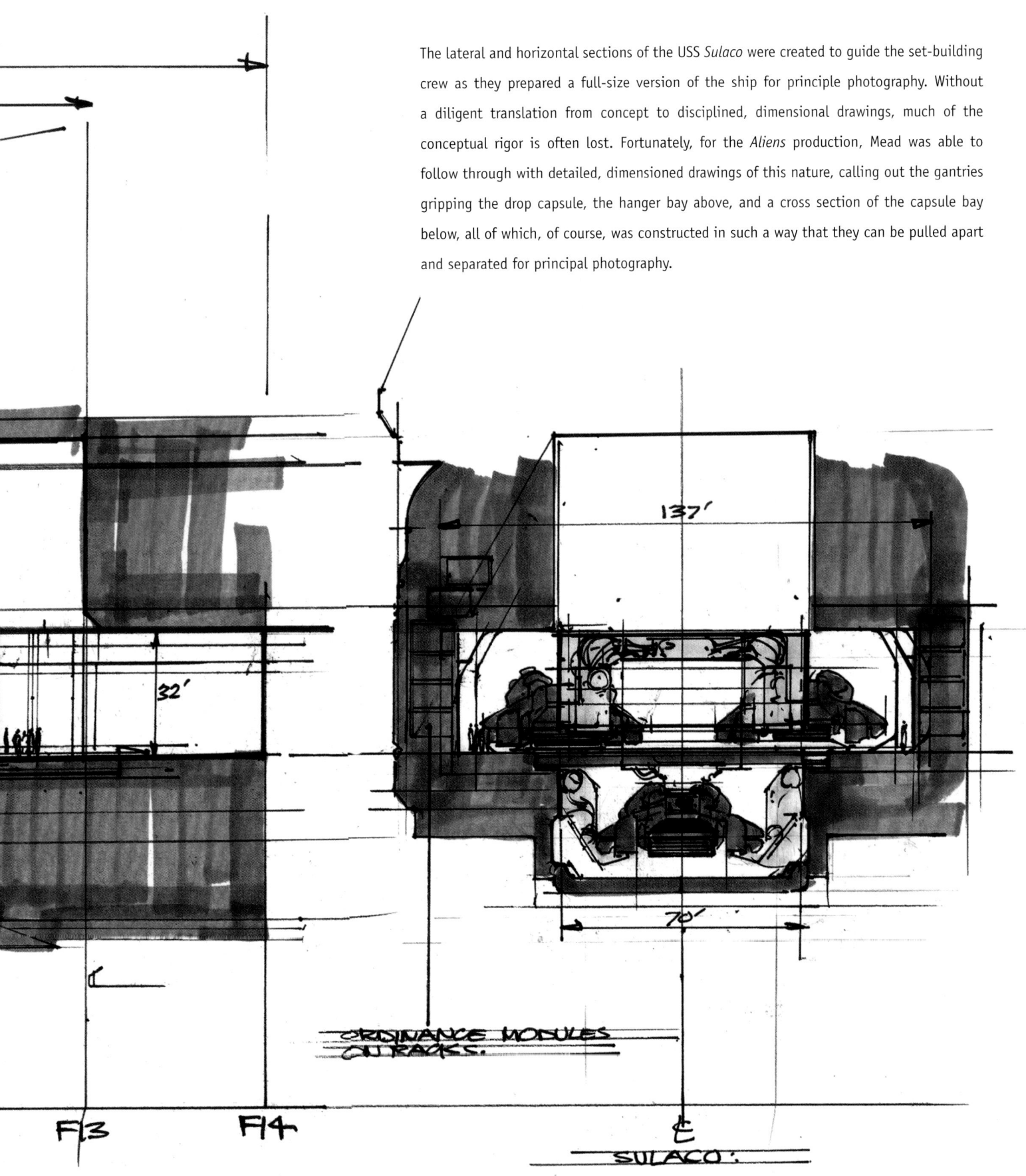

137'

32'

70'

ORDINANCE MODULES ON RACKS.

F13   F14   ℄

SULACO.

ABORT PERSONNEL EVAC. AIRLOCK.

SHIP PREP BAY s) DROP AIRLOCK : RELATIVE SIZES.

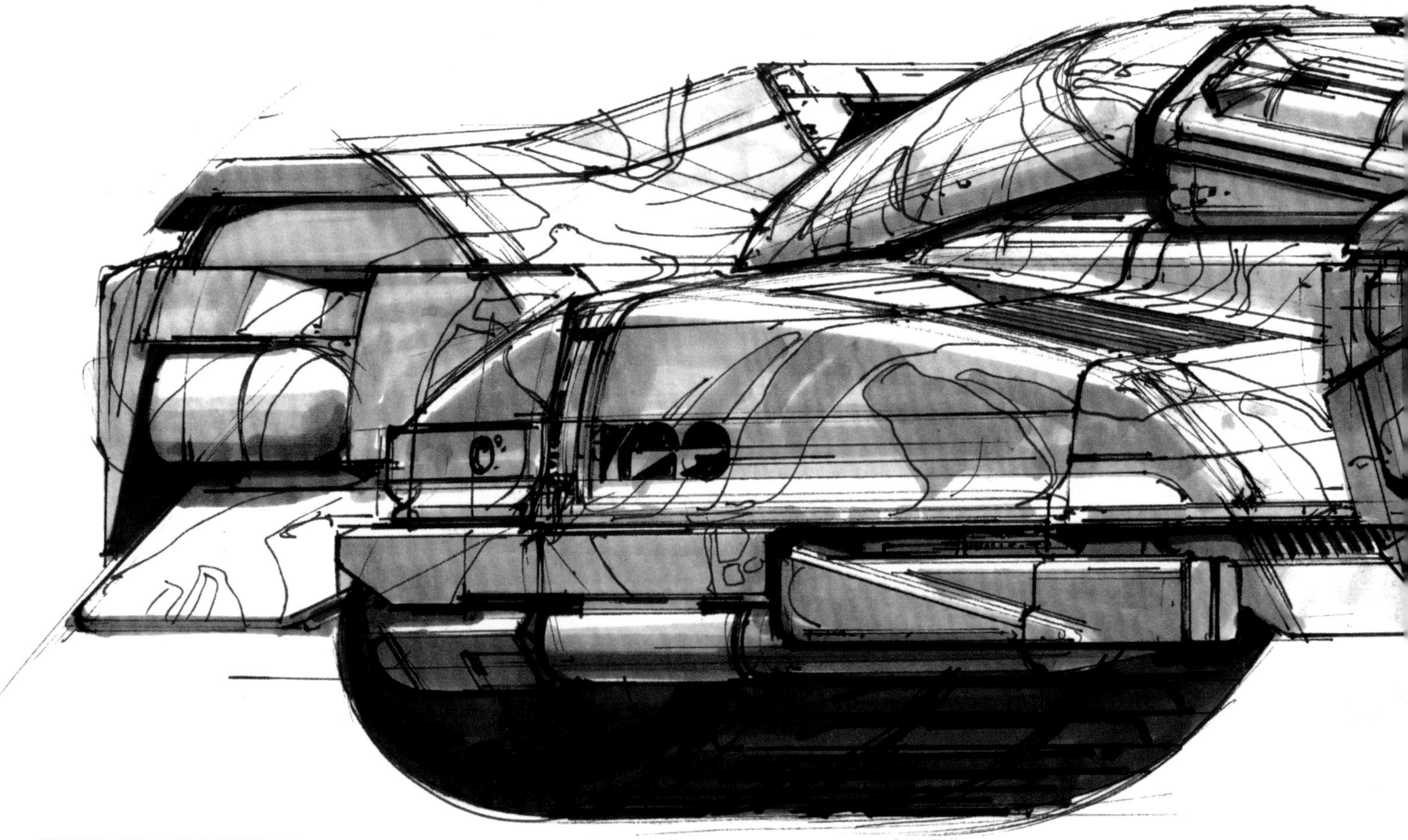

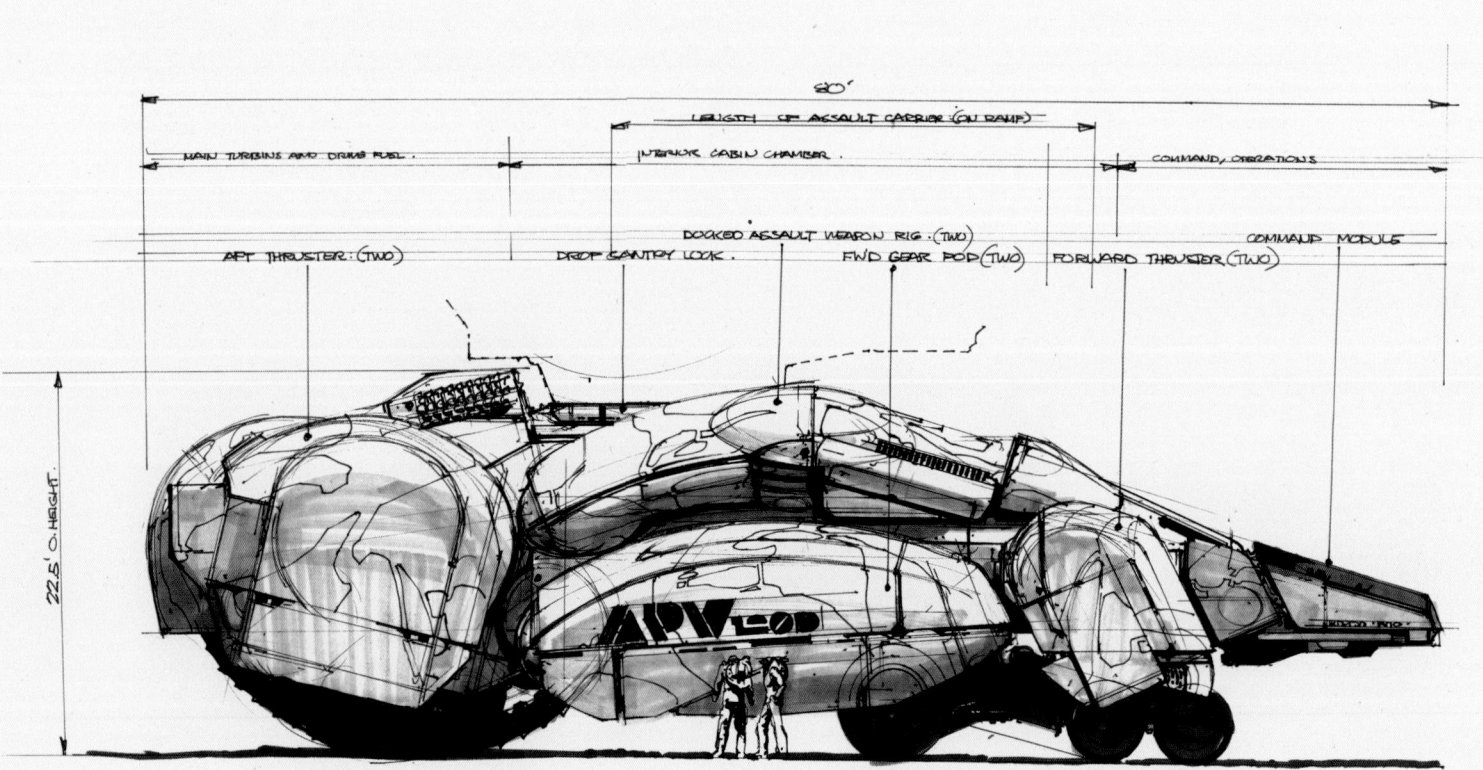

DIMENSIONED DRAWINGS SUCH AS THIS
GUIDED DYKSTRA'S SFX SHOP AS THEY
CREATED PHYSICAL SETTINGS FOR LIVE
PHOTOGRAPHY.

IDEA FOR DROP SHIP: 3

80'

LENGTH OF ASSAULT CARRIER (ON RAMP)

MAIN TURBINS AND DRUMS FUEL.   INTERIOR CABIN CHAMBER.   COMMAND, OPERATIONS

DOCKED ASSAULT WEAPON RIG (TWO)   COMMAND MODULE

APT THRUSTER (TWO)   DROP GANTRY LOCK.   FWD GEAR POD (TWO)   FORWARD THRUSTER (TWO)

22.5' O. HEIGHT.

APV 600

"IDEA FOR DROPSHIP: IMPACT CARRIAGES IN PARK CONFIGURATION.

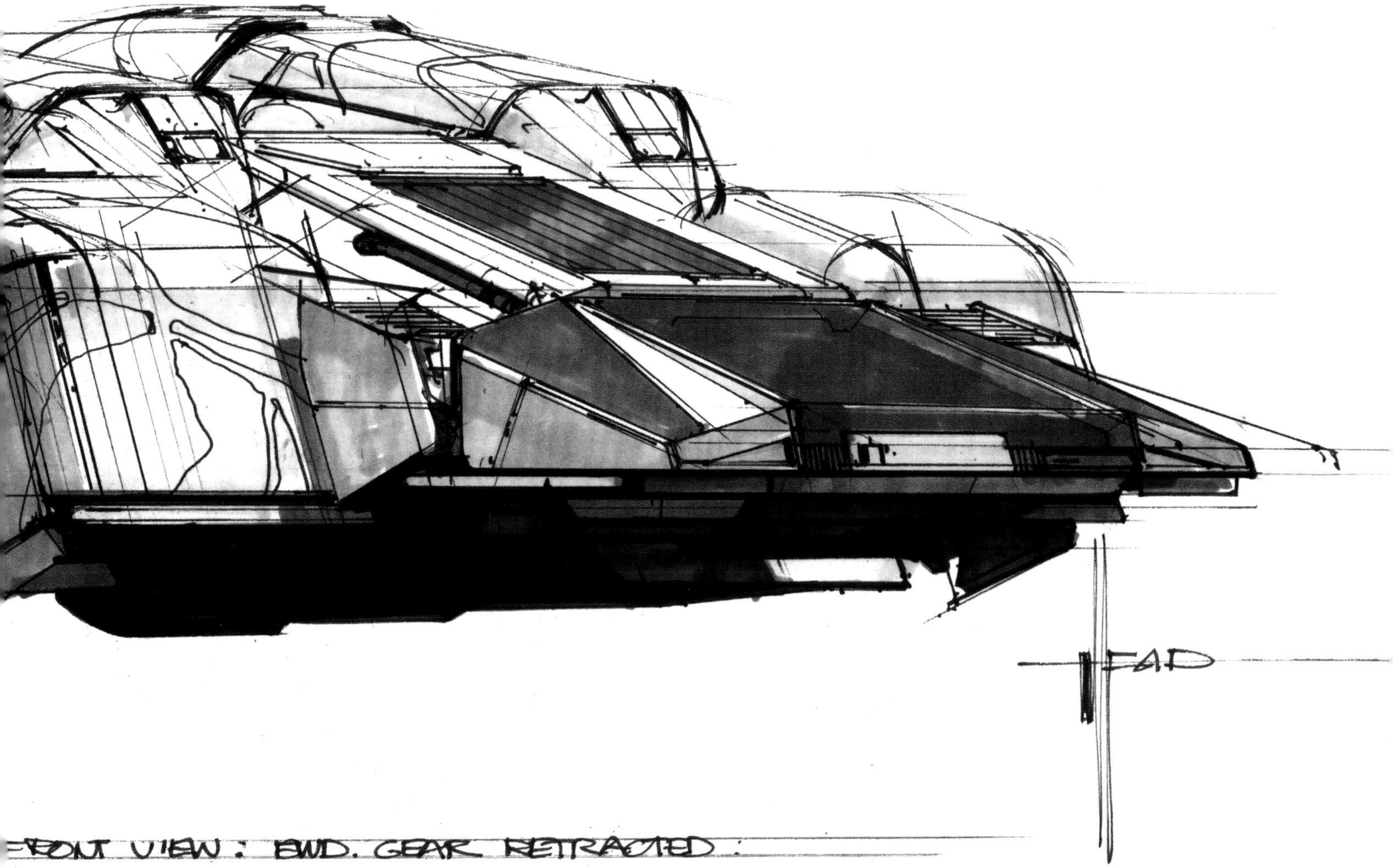

FRONT VIEW : FWD. GEAR RETRACTED :

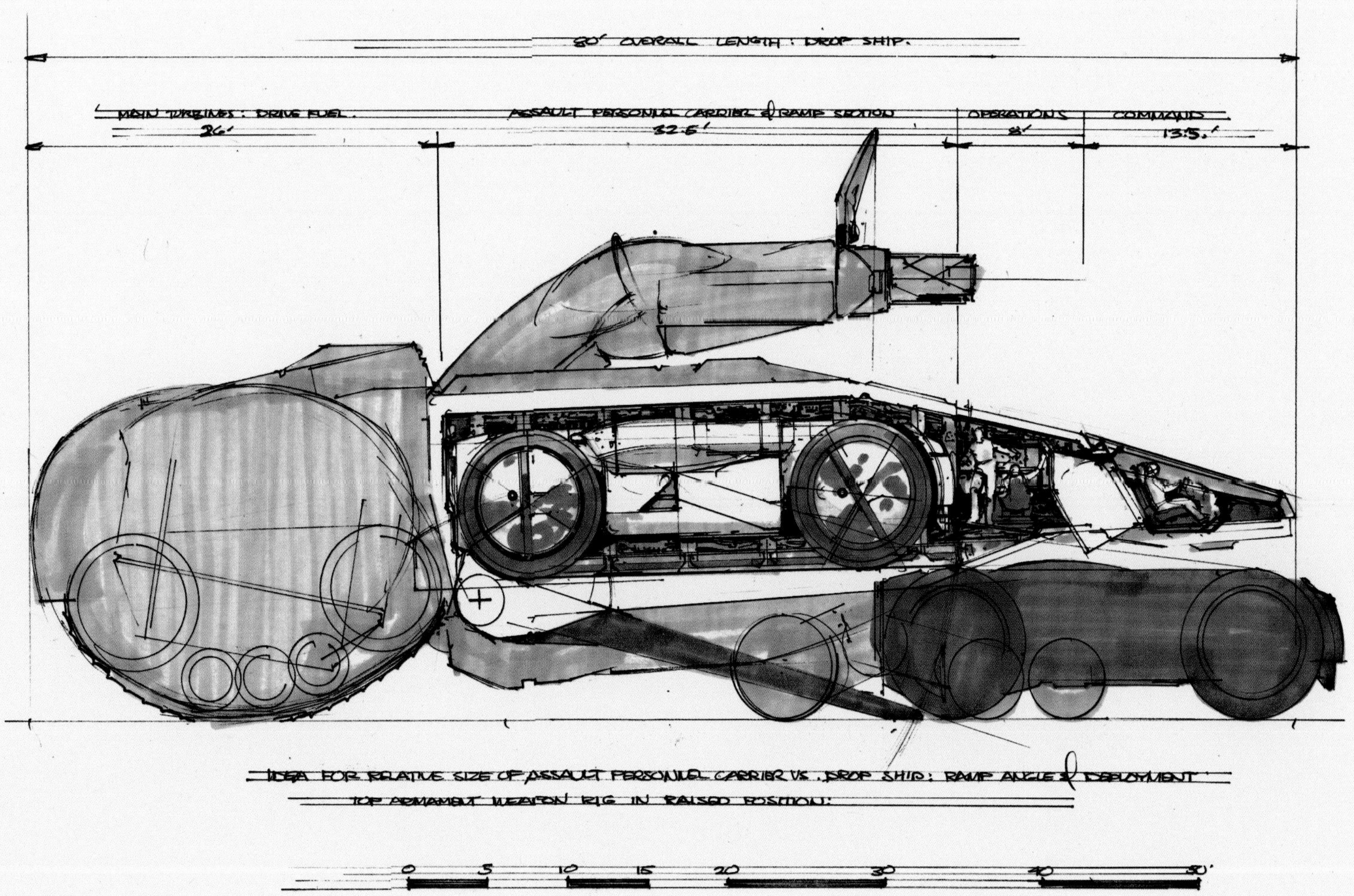

80' OVERALL LENGTH : DROP SHIP.

MAIN TURBINES : DRIVE FUEL.	ASSAULT PERSONNEL CARRIER & RAMP SECTION	OPERATIONS	COMMAND
26'	32·5'	8'	13·5'

IDEA FOR RELATIVE SIZE OF ASSAULT PERSONNEL CARRIER VS. DROP SHIP: RAMP ANGLE & DEPLOYMENT

TOP ARMAMENT WEAPON RIG IN RAISED POSITION:

0   5   10   15   20   30   40   50'

2010

THE YEAR WE MADE CONTACT

ONE HELL-OF-A-PIECE OF STUFF

Released in 1984, Peter Hyam's sequel to Stanley Kubrick's *2001: A Space Odyssey* (1968), takes place nearly ten years after the failed excursion to Jupiter of the spaceship *Discovery*. A joint U.S.-Russian expedition mounted to investigate its fate leads, inevitably, to a tense standoff between the commanding officers, as back on earth the two superpowers are on the brink of war. Notable for its special effects achievements, especially a bone-chilling flight through Jupiter's upper atmosphere, the film was anchored by Syd's design of a Russian-U.S. style spaceship which seemed to personify many of the cultural differences evident in the newscasts of the time.

The challenge for Hyams and Mead was to create a design that stood on its own, while achieving or even surpassing, the meticulously detailed images created by Kubrick's team. It was assumed that during those nine intervening years, space travel would have evolved to the point where the *Leonov*, would be powered by "big, blowing" ion engines, and capable of creating micro-gravity which, from a practical point of view, reduced production expenses for special zero-gravity effects.

BELOW: AN INTERIOR DESIGN OF THE *LEONOV* CONTROL CONSOLE, UTILIZING A NOVEL APPROACH TO OPERATING THE SHIP.

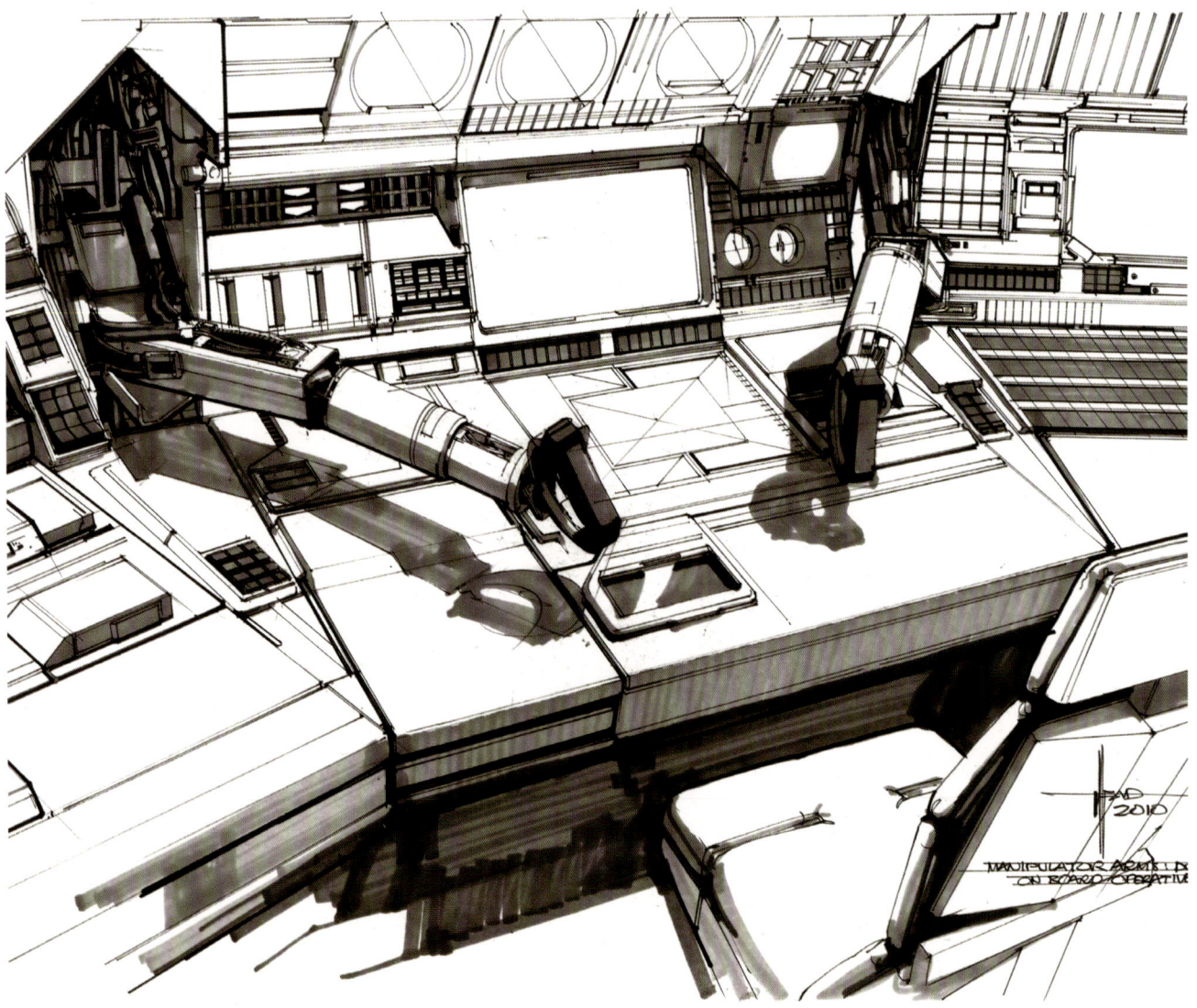

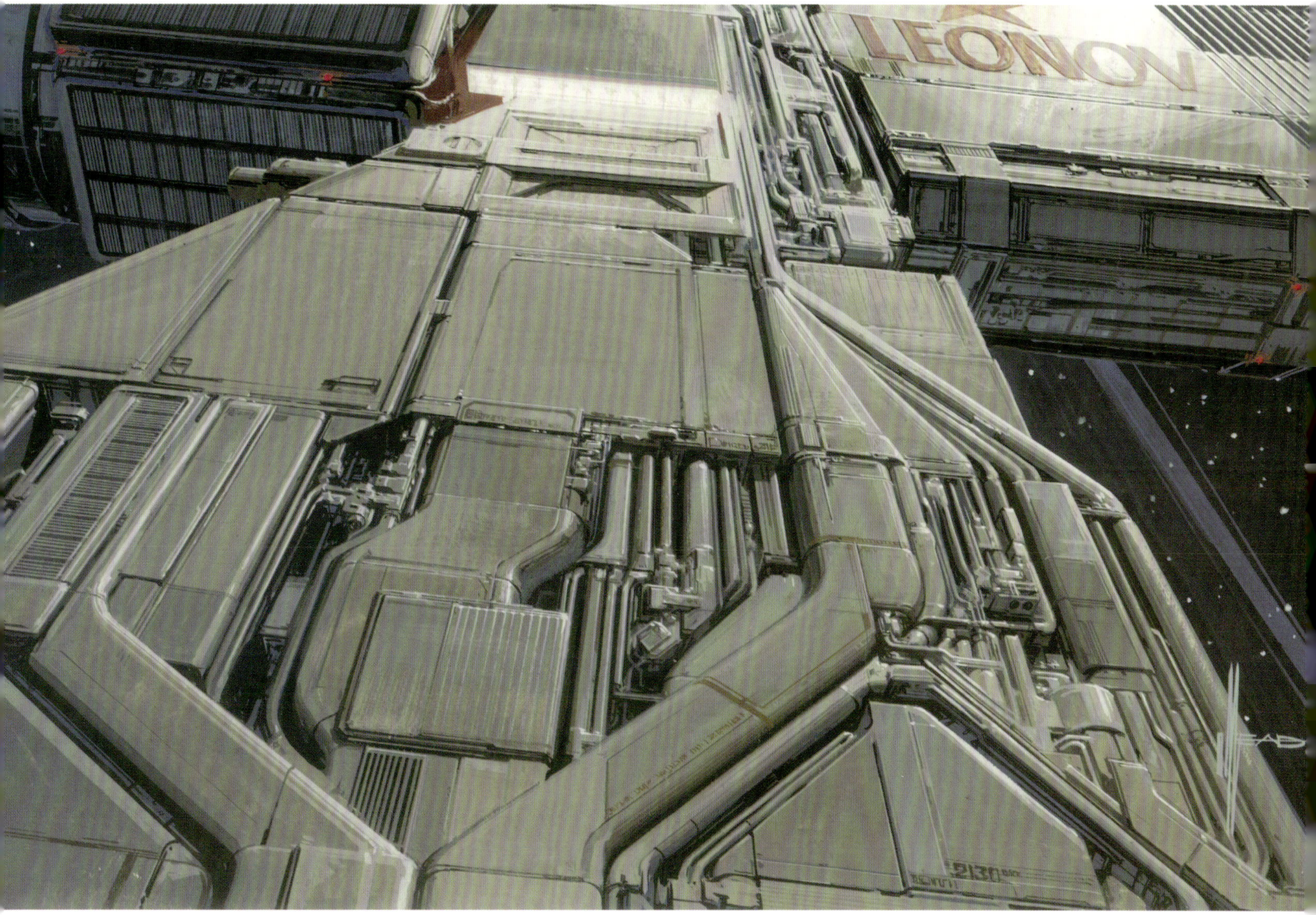

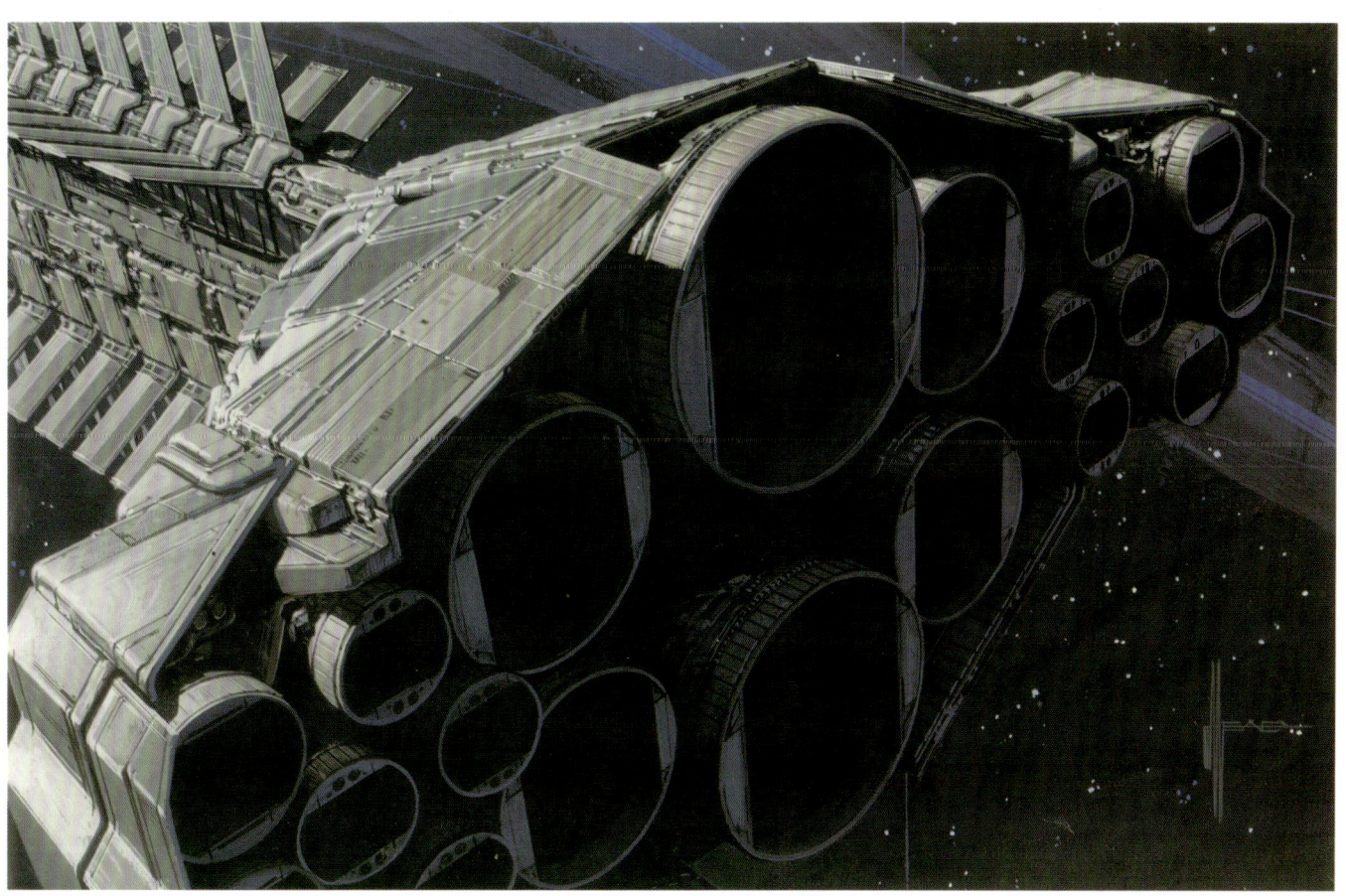

ABOVE: THE DETAILED, FINAL RENDER OF THE OUTER SHELL OF THE *LEONOV*. BELOW: THE "BIG, BLOWING" ION ENGINES.

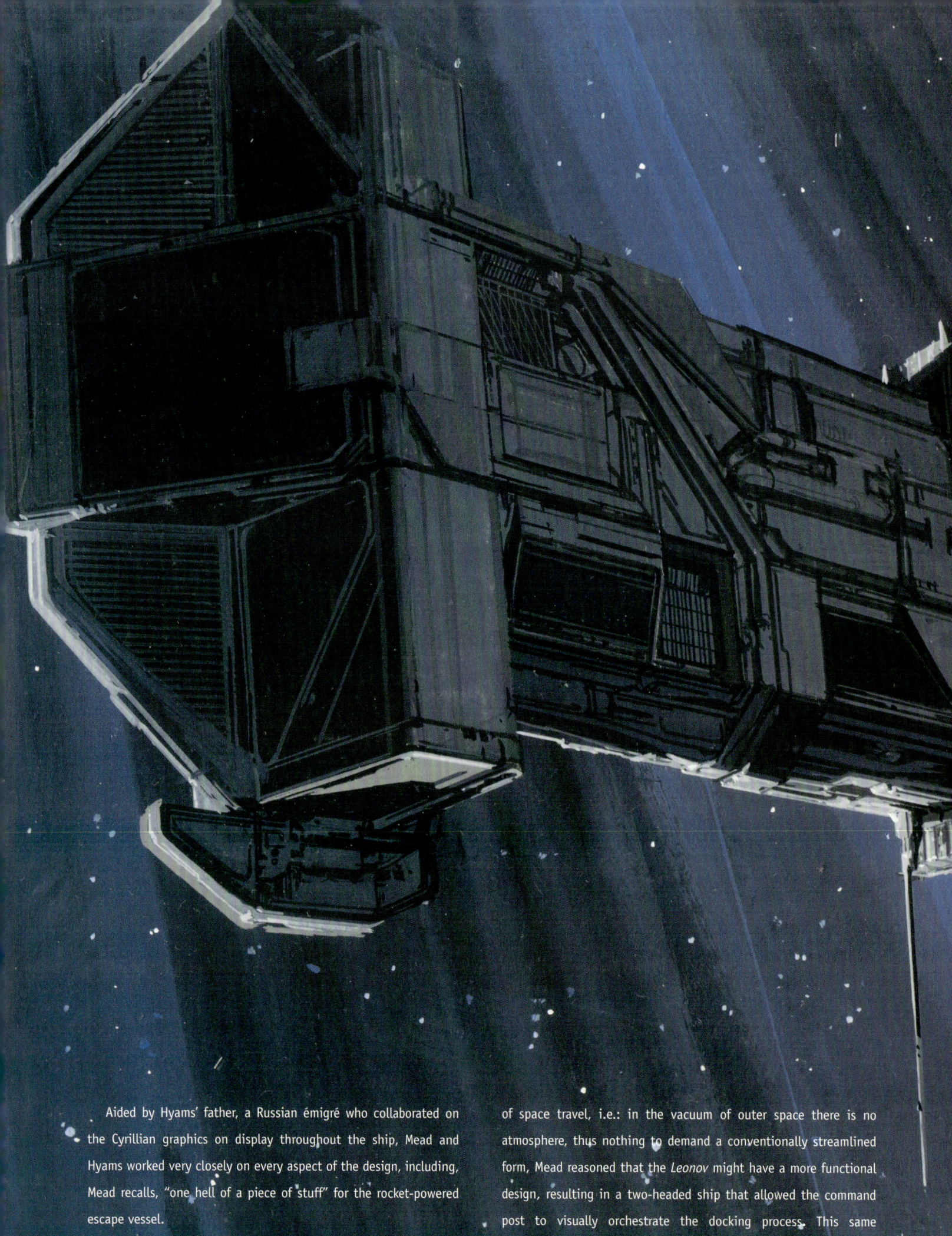

Aided by Hyams' father, a Russian émigré who collaborated on the Cyrillian graphics on display throughout the ship, Mead and Hyams worked very closely on every aspect of the design, including, Mead recalls, "one hell of a piece of stuff" for the rocket-powered escape vessel.

By abandoning the "aeronautical" idiom that had until then governed the depiction of spaceships and 'fessing up' to the realities of space travel, i.e.: in the vacuum of outer space there is no atmosphere, thus nothing to demand a conventionally streamlined form, Mead reasoned that the *Leonov* might have a more functional design, resulting in a two-headed ship that allowed the command post to visually orchestrate the docking process. This same logic could lead to establishing plausible points of view in the principle photography.

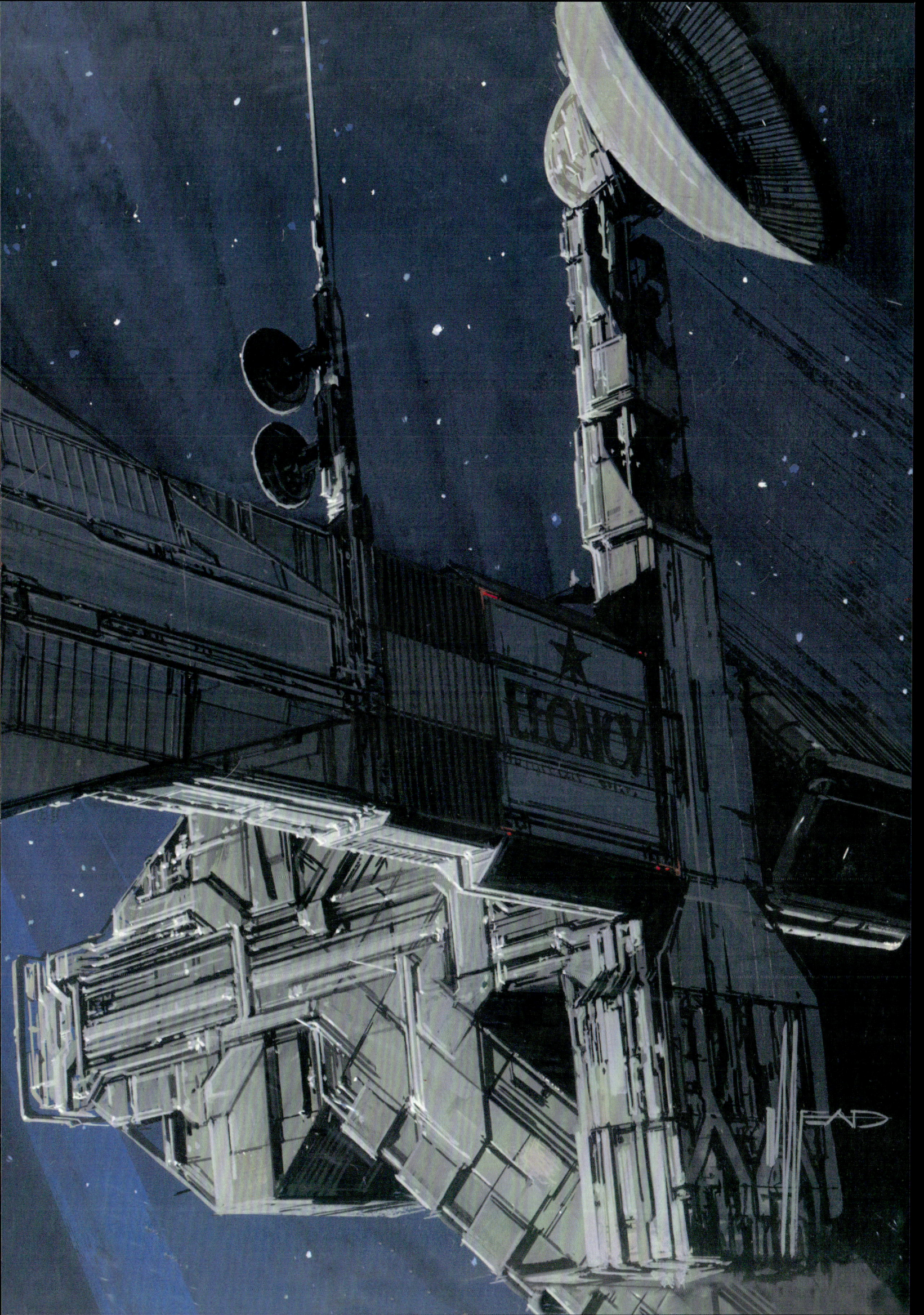

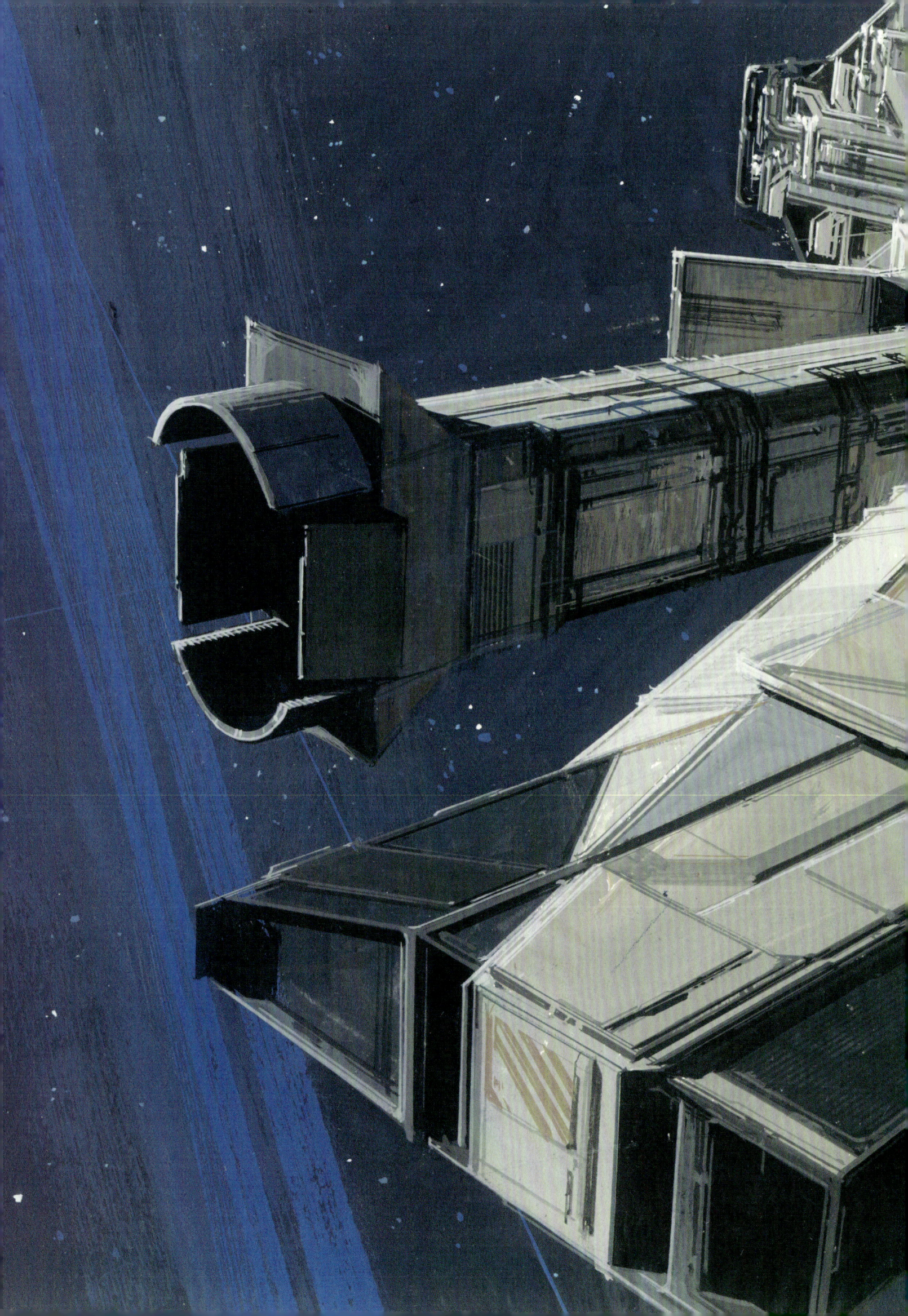

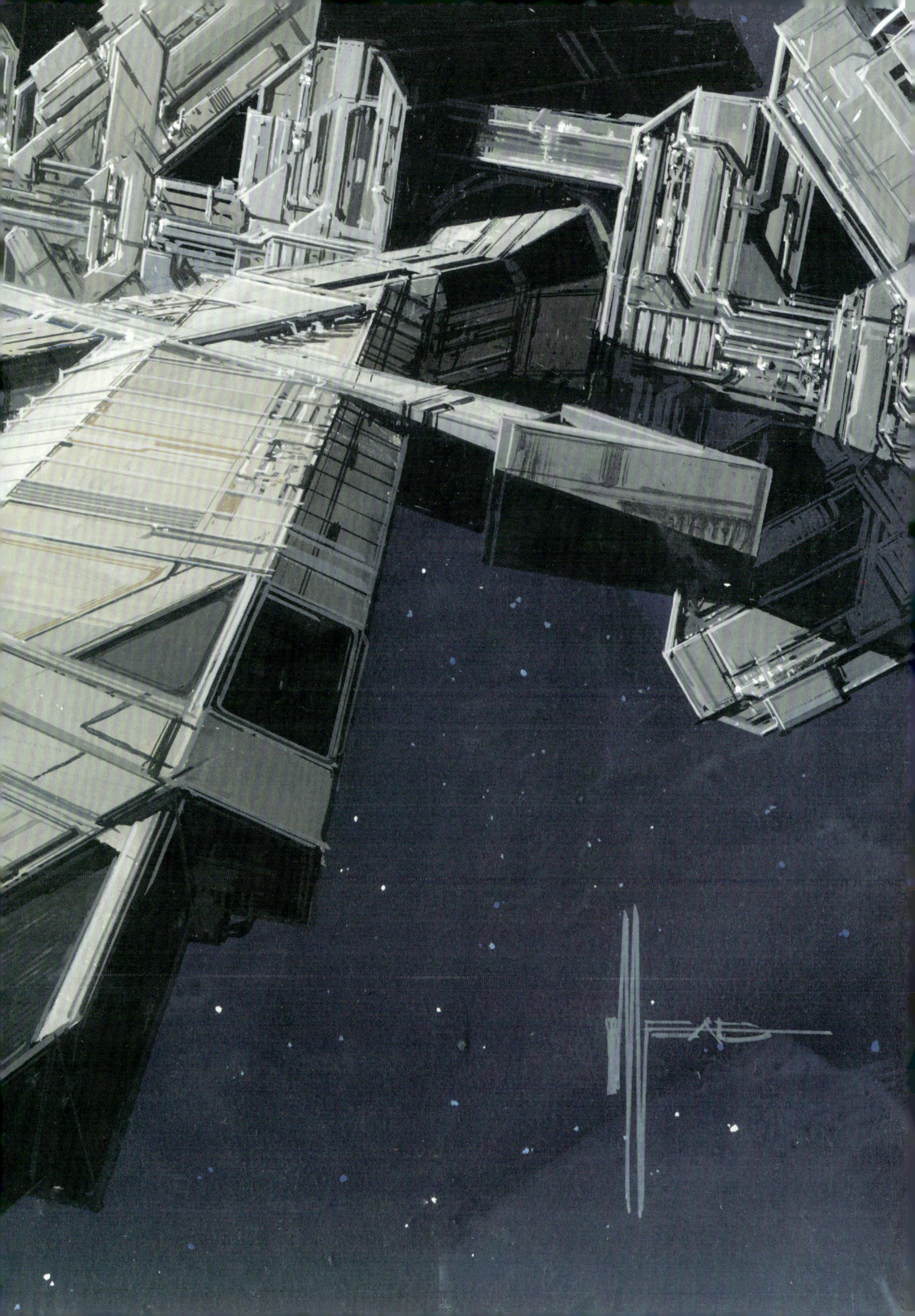

BELITTLED

MITES WITH WEAPONS

The pitch for *Belittled*, with Peter Hyams slated to direct, was based on an idea to market toys at 'real' scale with a storyline midway between a militarized rat pack caper and *Fantastic Voyage*. The protagonists, shrunk down to Lilliputian scale to enable them to sneak into high security spaces, were to be equipped with a full line of miniature high tech equipment, including a helicopter (below). As the miniature armada would encounter such a variety of surfaces, such as pile carpeting, and would be required to scale walls and other vertical surfaces, Mead proposed a high contact air cushion which one supposes would crawl over surfaces like a reptile. Unfortunately, in spite of Mead's enthusiasm, the picture never found financial backing and resides, even today, in development purgatory, so that these sketches, provocative as they are, are unlikely to find their way onto the screen.

A close look will reveal a pair of aviator glasses (a Syd Mead favourite), a set of keys, several books, and a pair of leather gloves surrounding a miniature helicopter as shrunken personnel ready its armament for an attack.

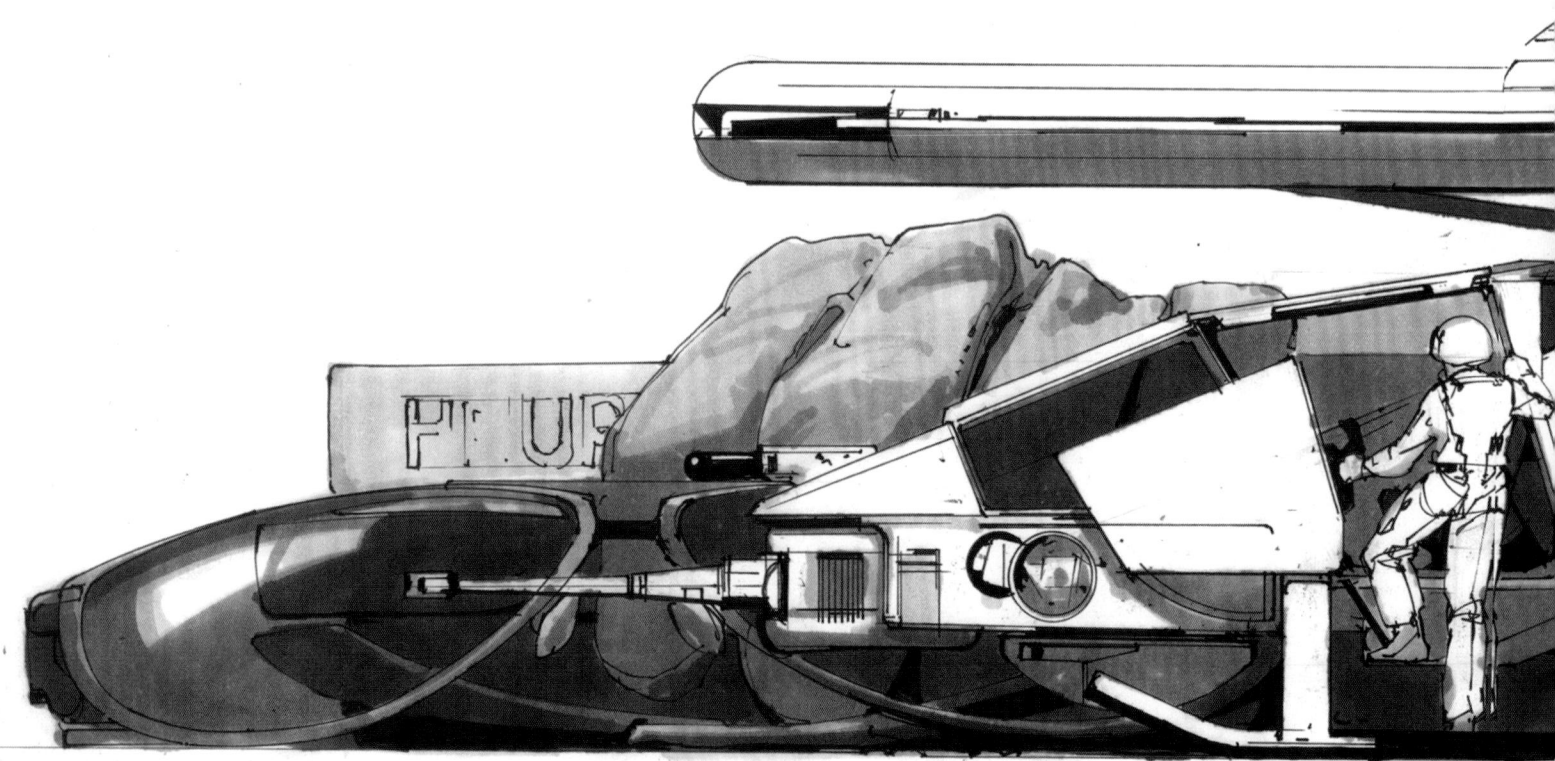

"AIR SSCALPEL" ATTACK HELICOPTER : SHROUDED ROTOR : TOW MISSILE PAK : ATG. MISSILE RACK.

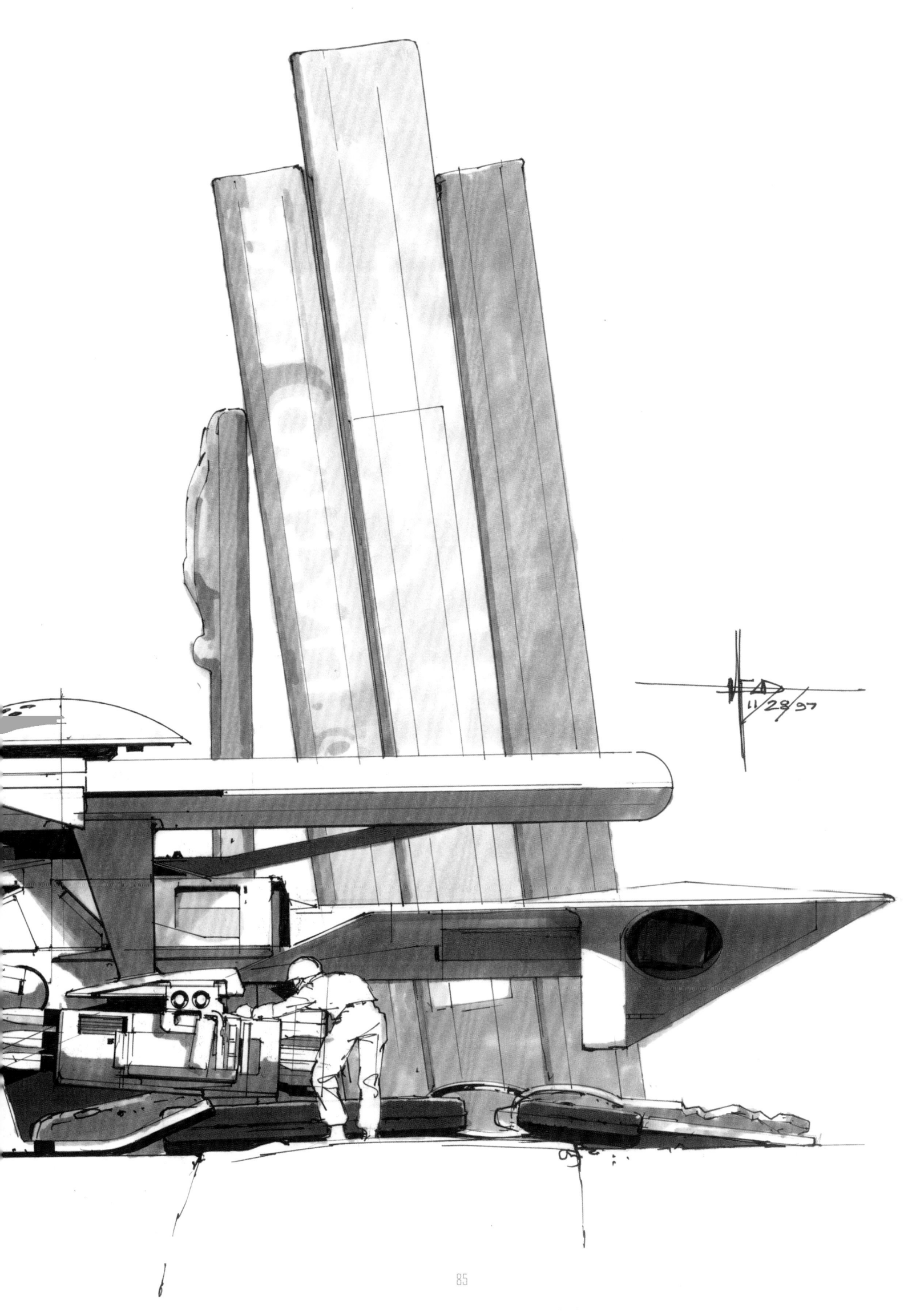

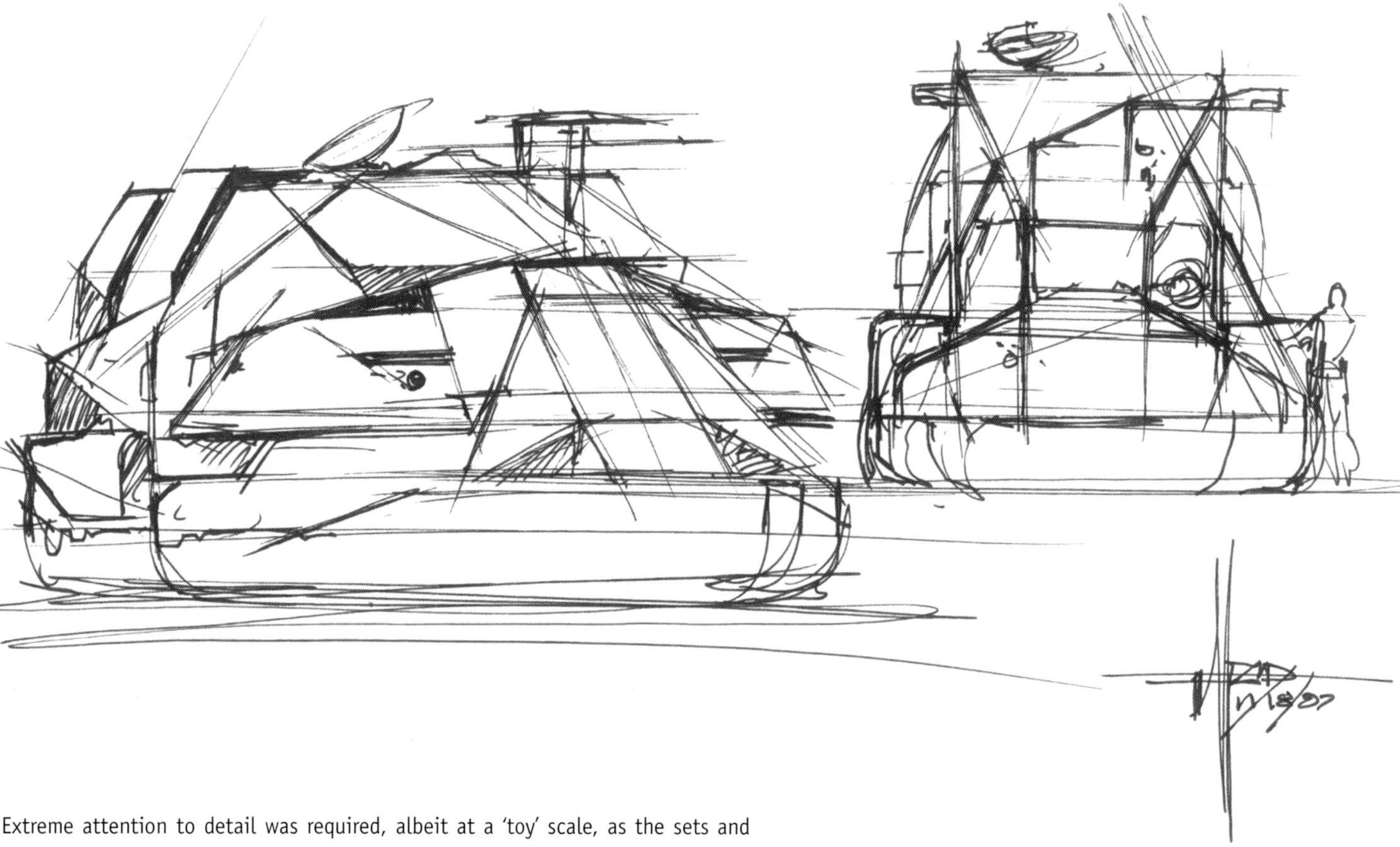

Extreme attention to detail was required, albeit at a 'toy' scale, as the sets and props would be shot at full scale prior to being reduced by the magic of the green screen process.

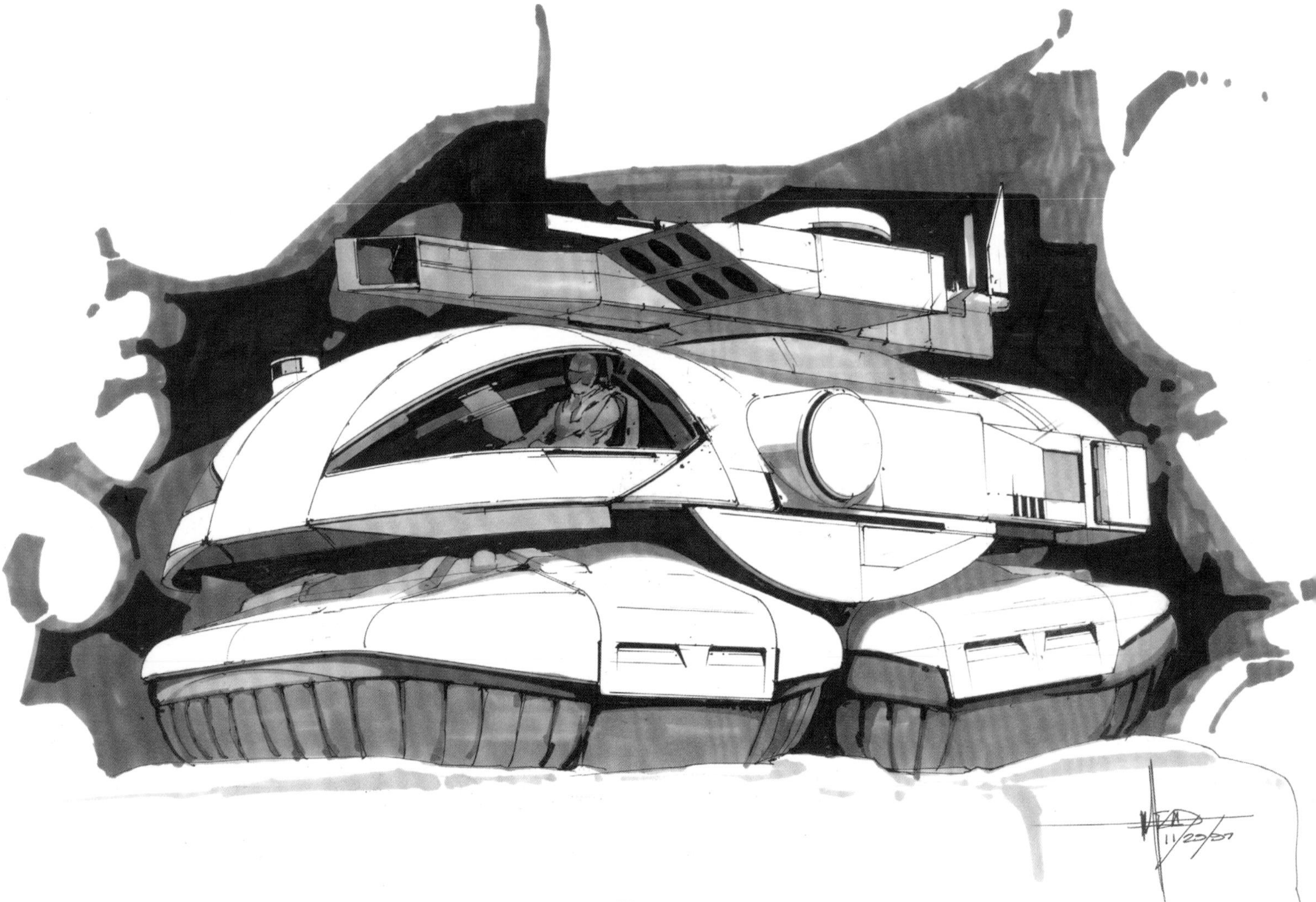

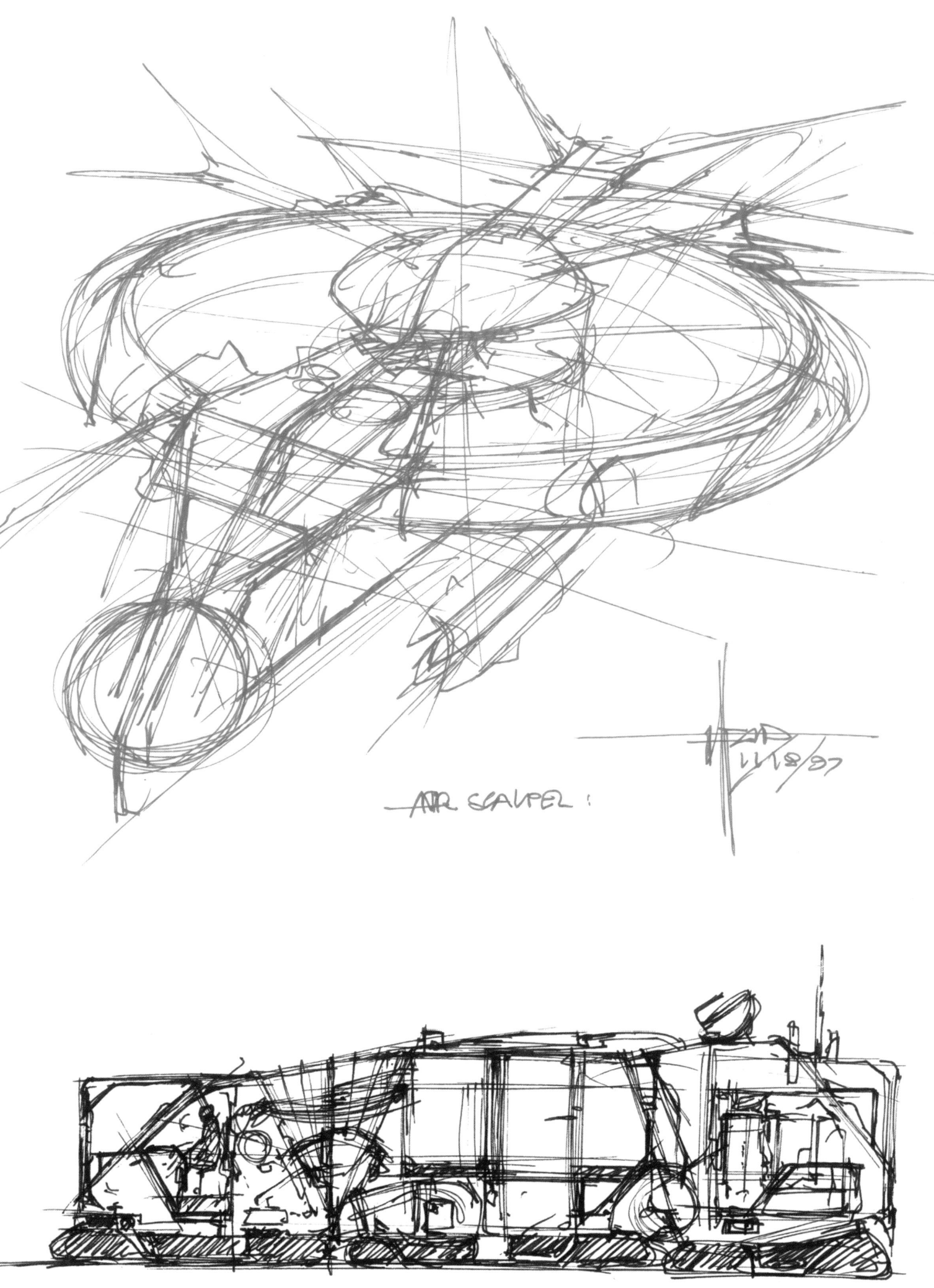

AIR SCALPEL!

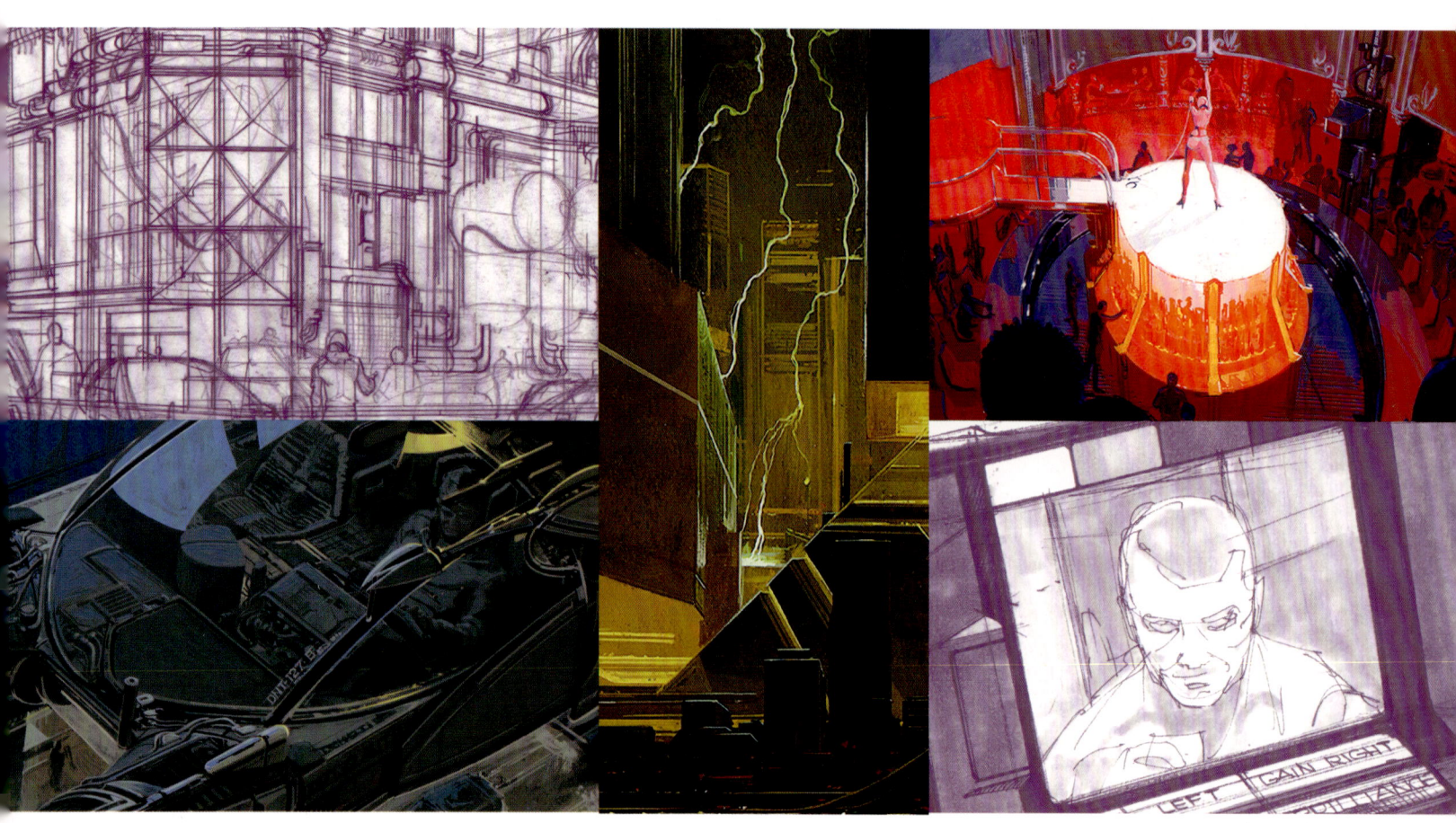

BLADE RUNNER

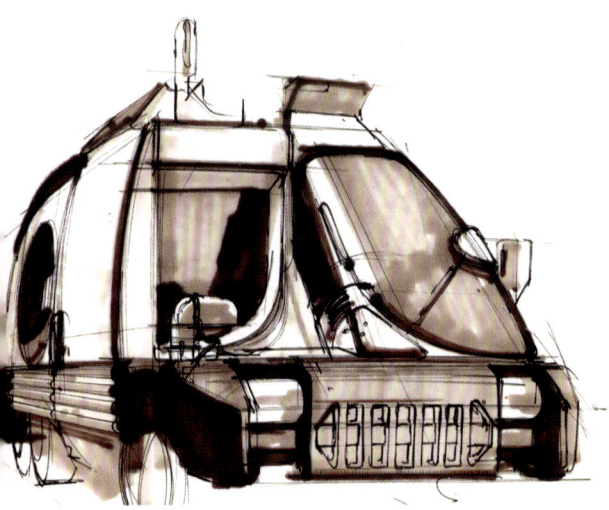

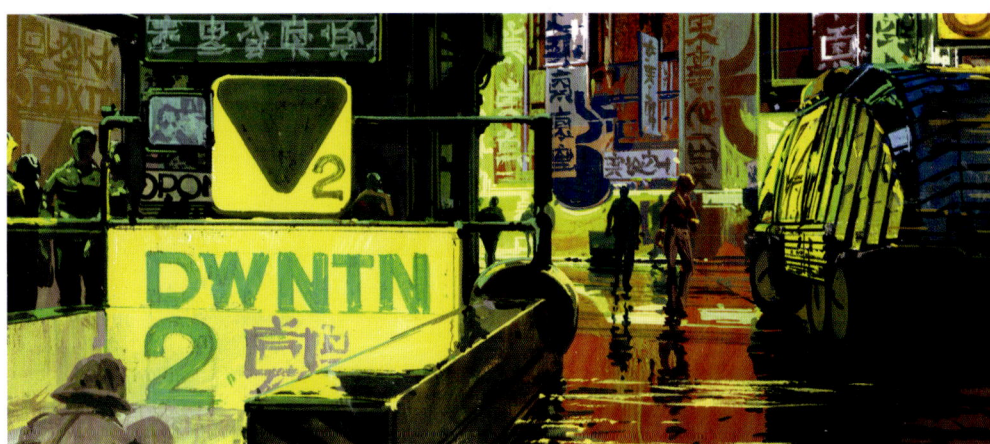

INDUSTRIAL DESIGN IN REVERSE

hillip K. Dick's dystopian novel, *Do Androids Dream of Electric Sheep?* with its off-axis query as a title, sets the tone for this cerebral but intense discourse on man's fraught relationship to the things he creates. Ridley Scott's 1982 adaptation, *Blade Runner,* is high-toned but has a pulp detective story at heart. Its dark, noir sensibility combines decrepit high tech with Mead's love of incidental detail to create a devil's brew of death and redemption.

Director Ridley Scott and Syd Mead speak the same language. Both are tinkerers at heart, channeling probable and improbable situations into a singular artistic vision. The project began with

Mead's sketch for a taxi bearing the scars of years in the urban muck, and brushstroke hints of the surrounding metro mash-up. Mead imagines a vehicle assembled from spare parts, like the city around it. He explains, "[It's] disheveled and dystopian (with) unexplained light sources. You think of it as nice and then you slowly and deliberately muck it up. [It's] fun to do".

The city he imagines, with its wan light perpetually on, the shop windows a riff on Edward Hopper's desolate cityscapes, and an armored force constantly patrolling polyglot streets, provides the background for the fascist society that Scott envisions.

THIS SPREAD SKETCHES THROUGH TO FINISHED, IN-SITU RENDERS OF THAT MOST UBIQUITOUS CITY VEHICLE – THE TAXI.

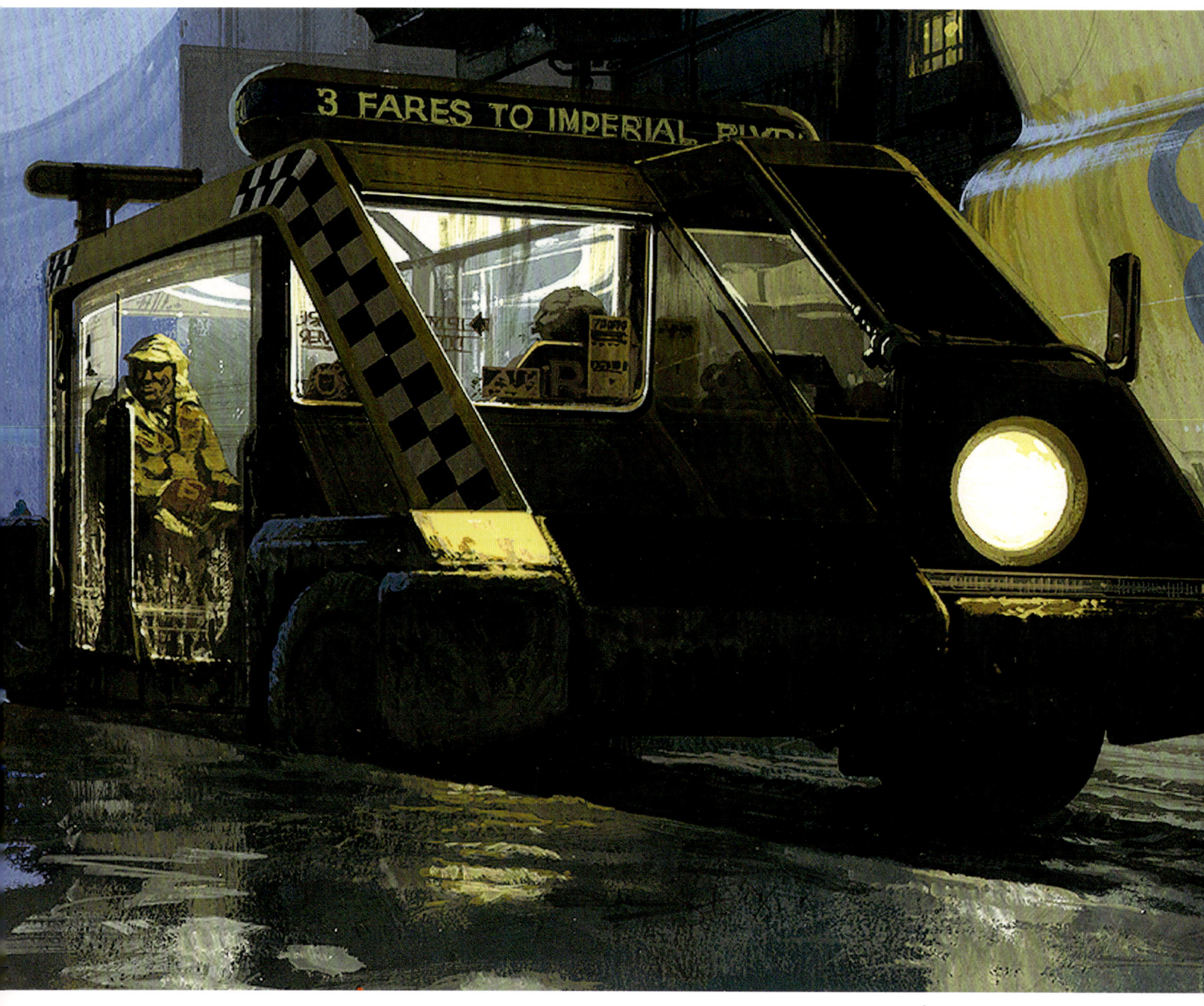

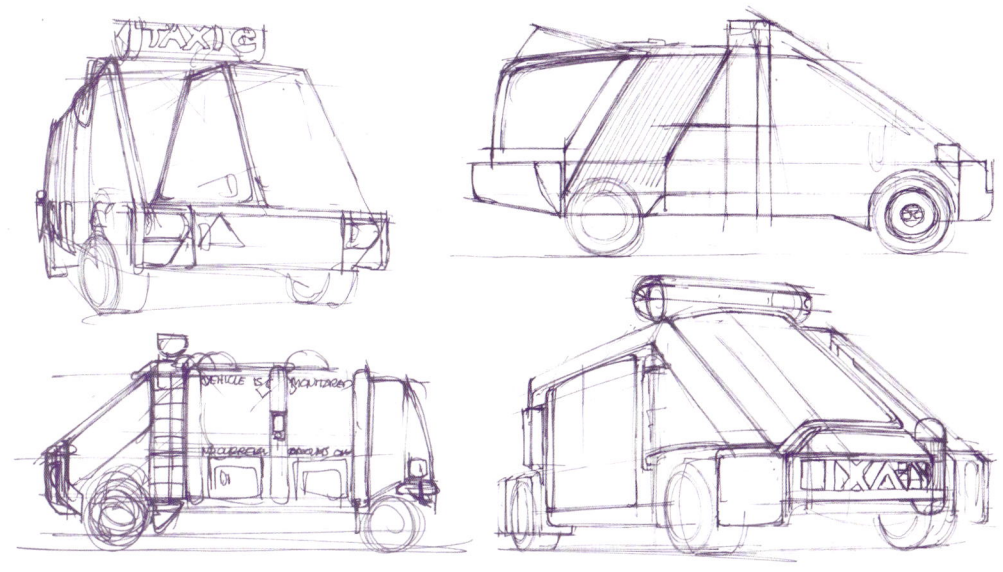

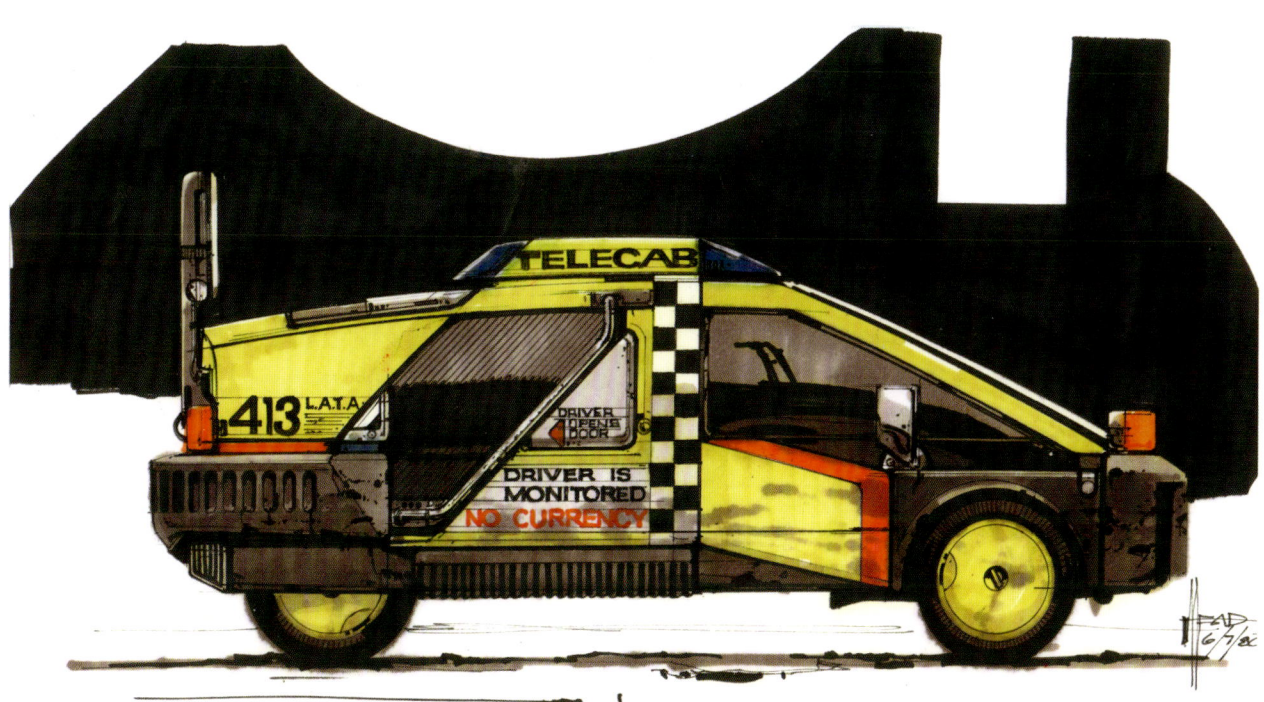

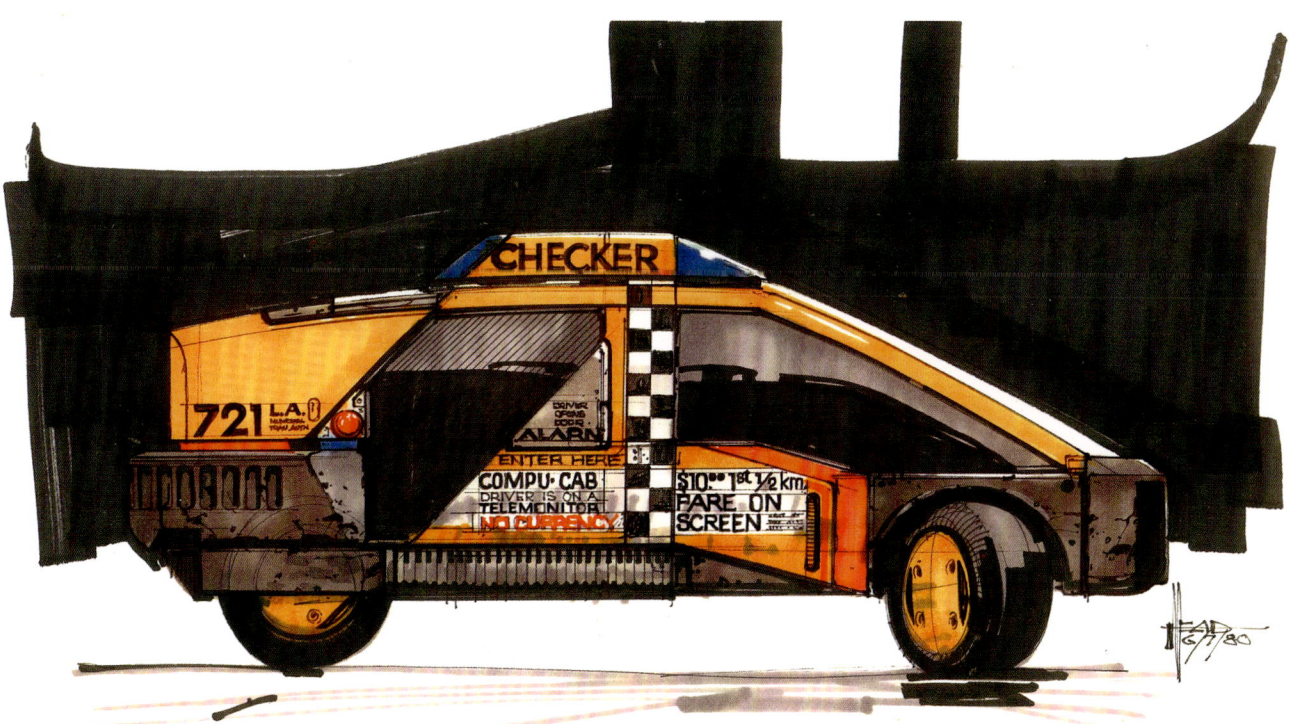

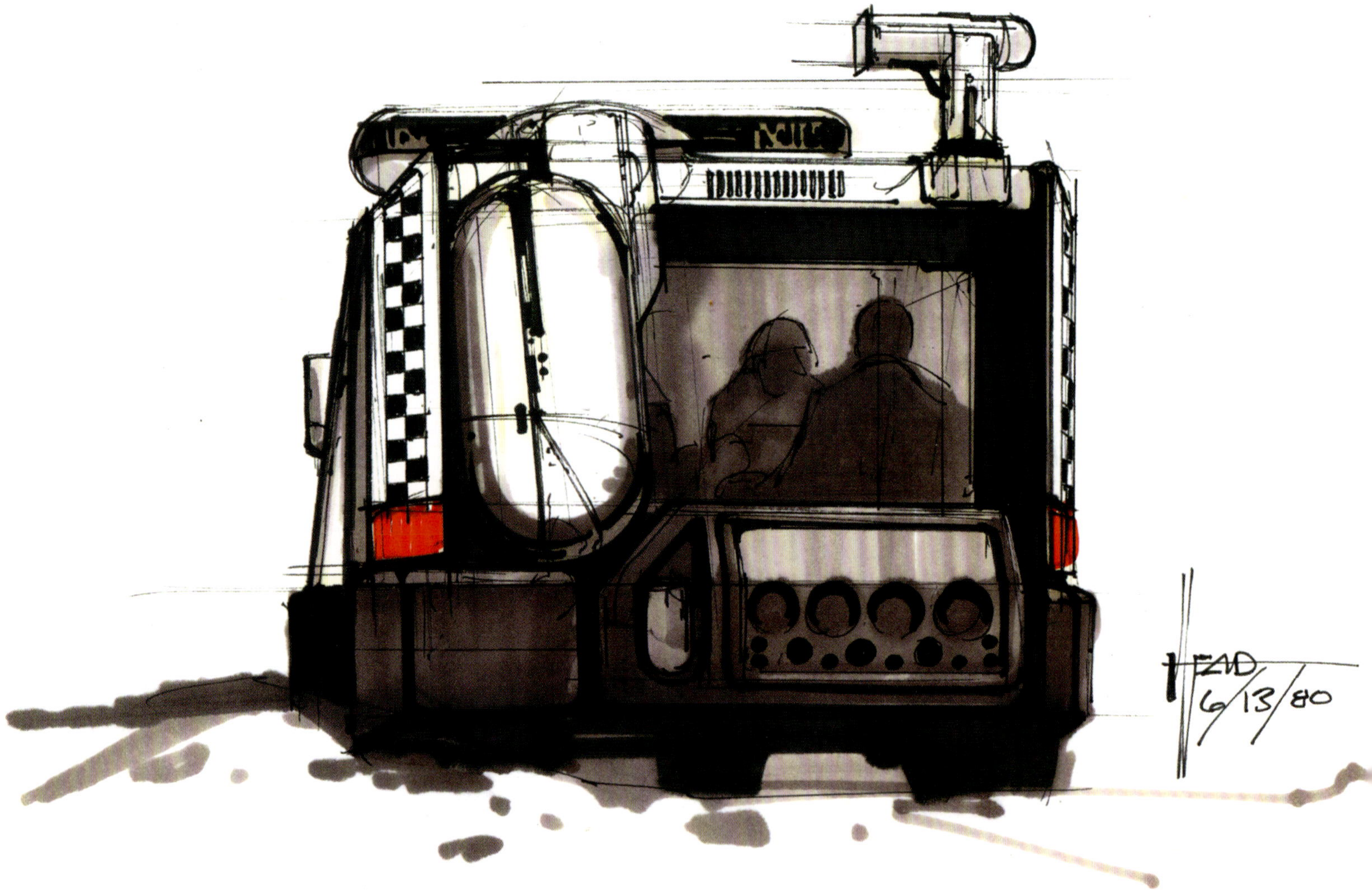
MEAD
6/13/80

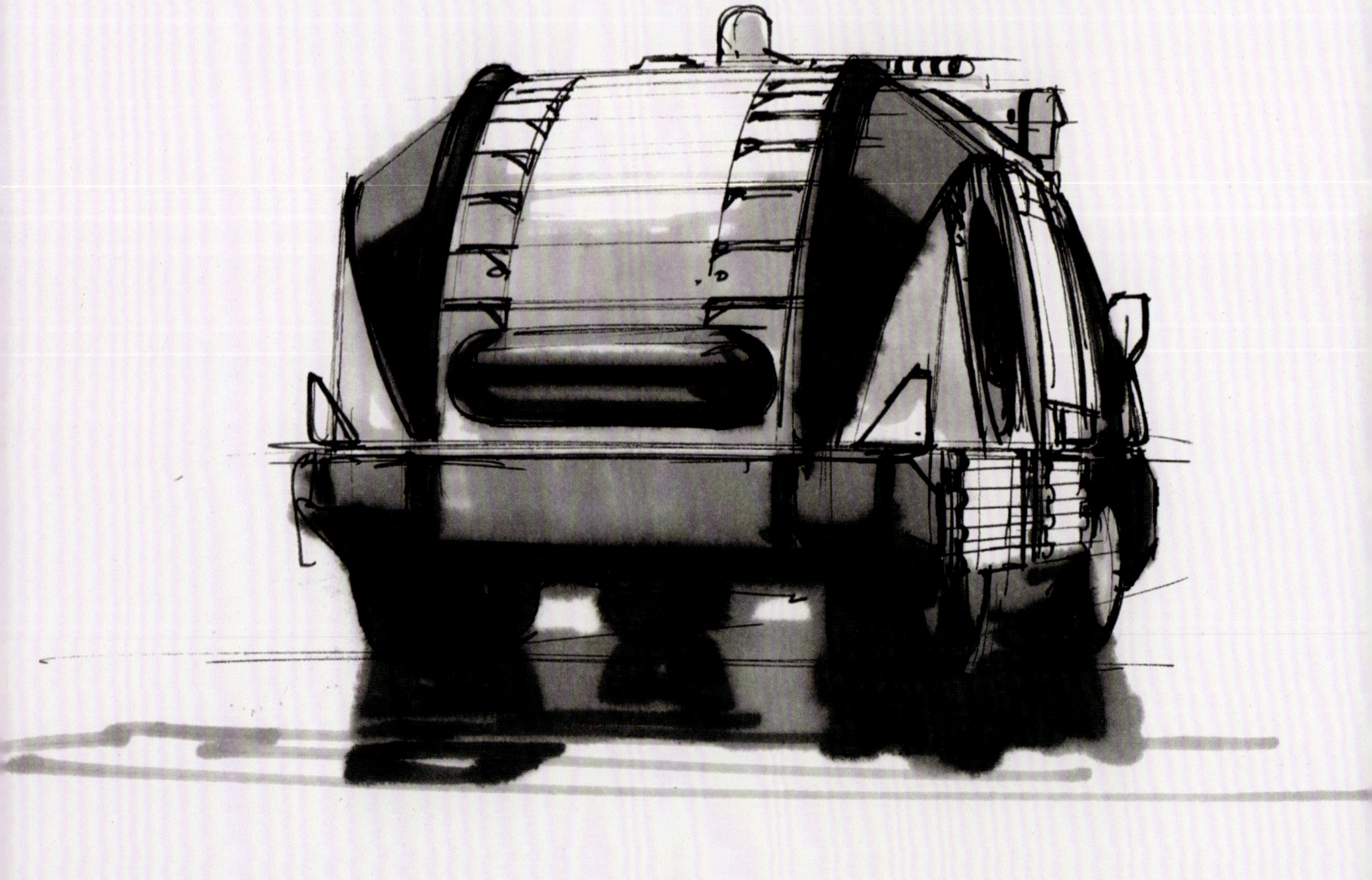

Mead's designs were instrumental in giving form to the concept of 'retro-fitting', the process of creating a unique object by means of a strategic assemblage of allied components. That is, by harvesting parts from abandoned or obsolescent donors and re-assembling them, a new entity is created.

Long a staple among visual artists like Robert Rauschenberg and Richard Stankewicz who created collages and crafted sculptures from scraps and junkyards, in the literary world the concept was immortalized in the writings of William Gibson, who established a sub-genre of science-fiction imagery with novels like *Mona Lisa Overdrive* and *Neuromancer*.

With *Blade Runner* that genre was given its first visual expression in the form of concepts developed by Mead.

Set in the near future, *Blade Runner* takes place in an environment uncomfortably close to a marriage of present third-world destitution and our own contemporary ruling class. A provocative story by legendary science-fiction writer Phillip K. Dick, and directed by *Alien* director Ridley Scott, the assignment offered the perfect opportunity for Mead to express the breadth of his imagination.

What is apparent in the sketches on these pages is the sheer visual force—the dramatic energy—which Mead brought to the assignment.

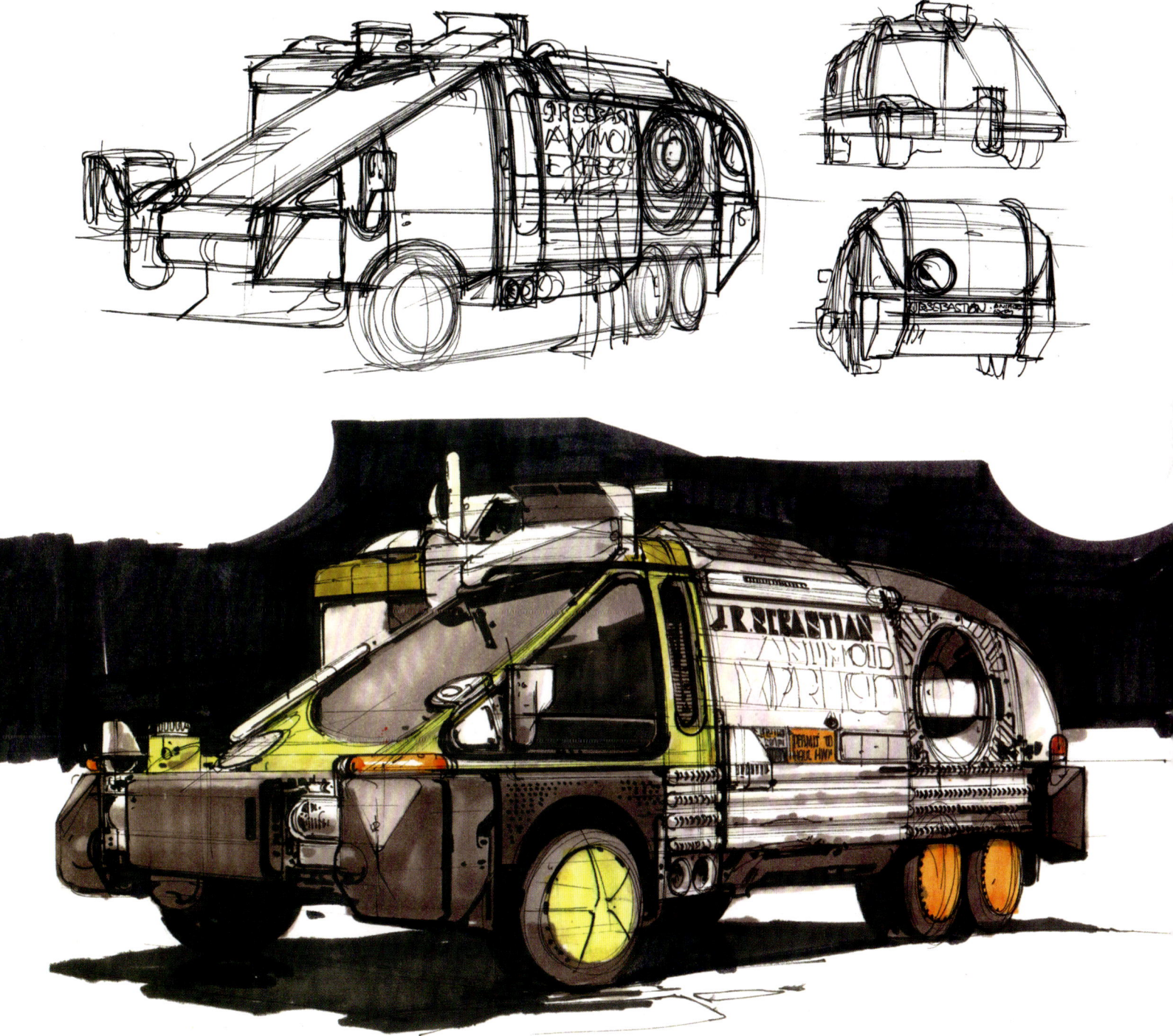

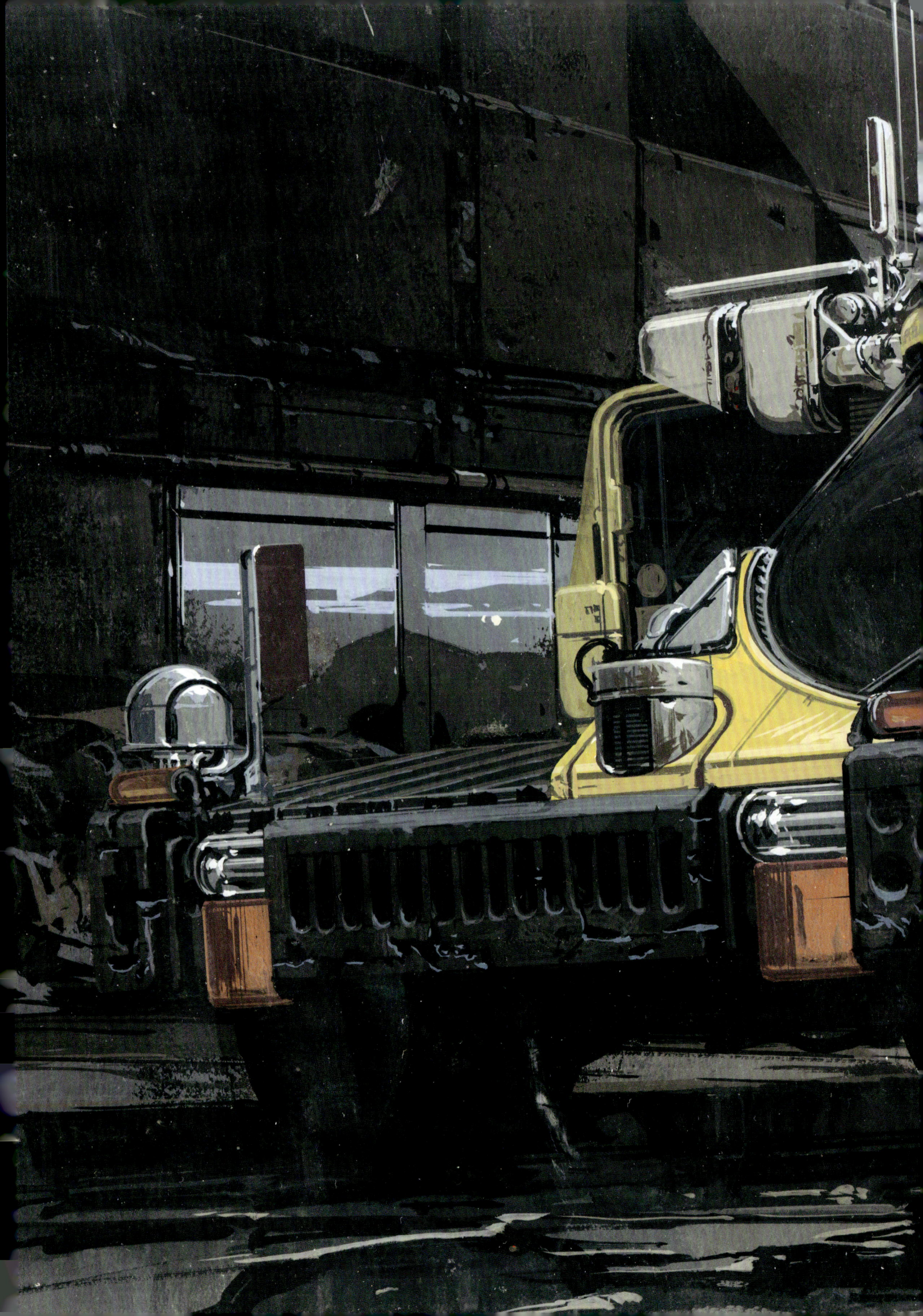

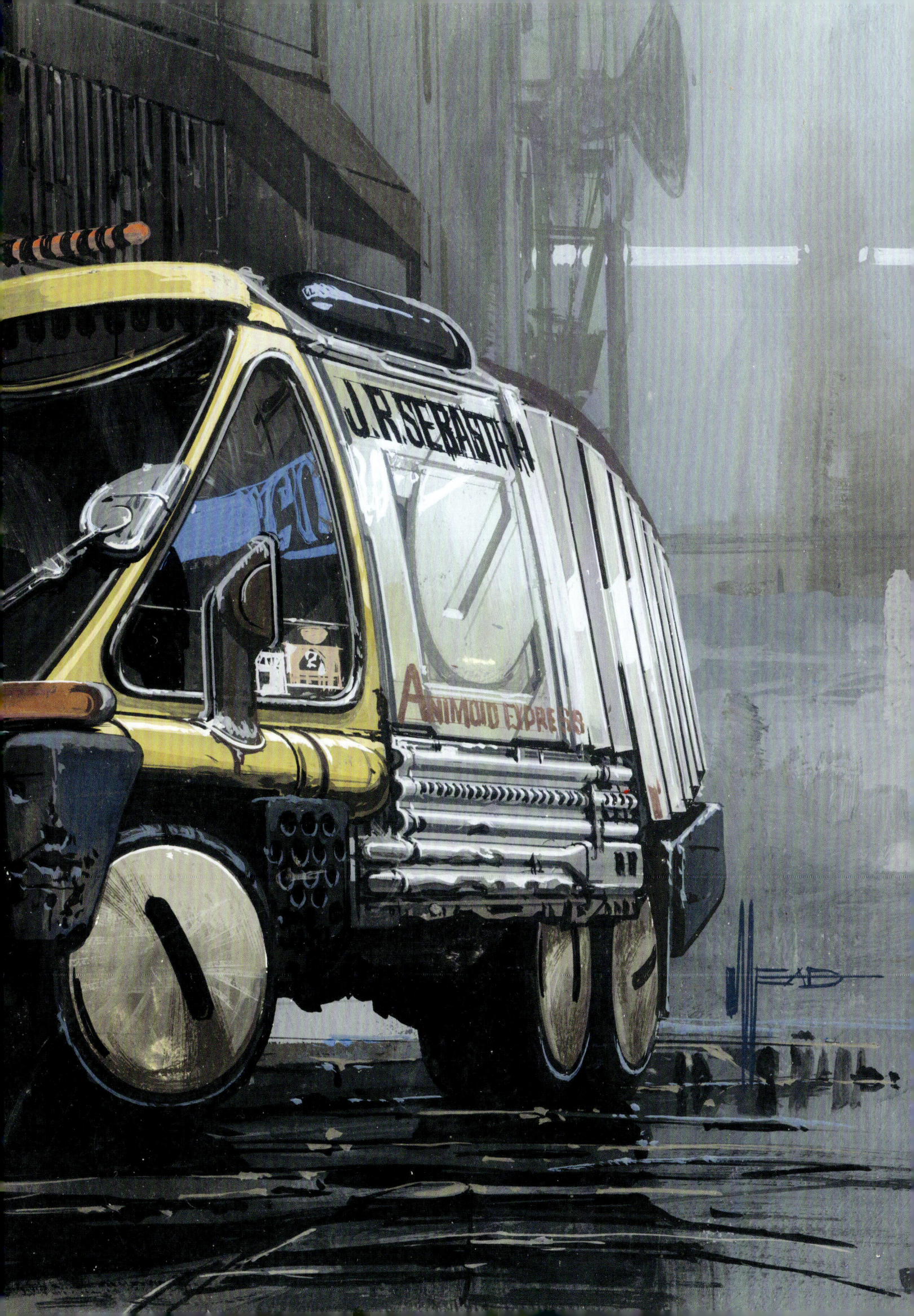

Never one to shrink from a full-bore engagement with challenging subject matter, Mead is in in his element here, almost jubilant in the forced marriage of a bus and the front section of a construction crane—with an architectural dome thrown in for good measure.

Such constructions, borne from years in industrial design, were not only plausible—they invigorated a medium which had long been represented by a cartoonish, disconnected future vision, and lent intensity to a story in which emotional depth was never far from the surface.

Even such quick sketches exhibit the wealth of incidental detail which contributed so much to the sense of reality in *Blade Runner*, and helped to dispel the critical dismissal of the science fiction film as an art form.

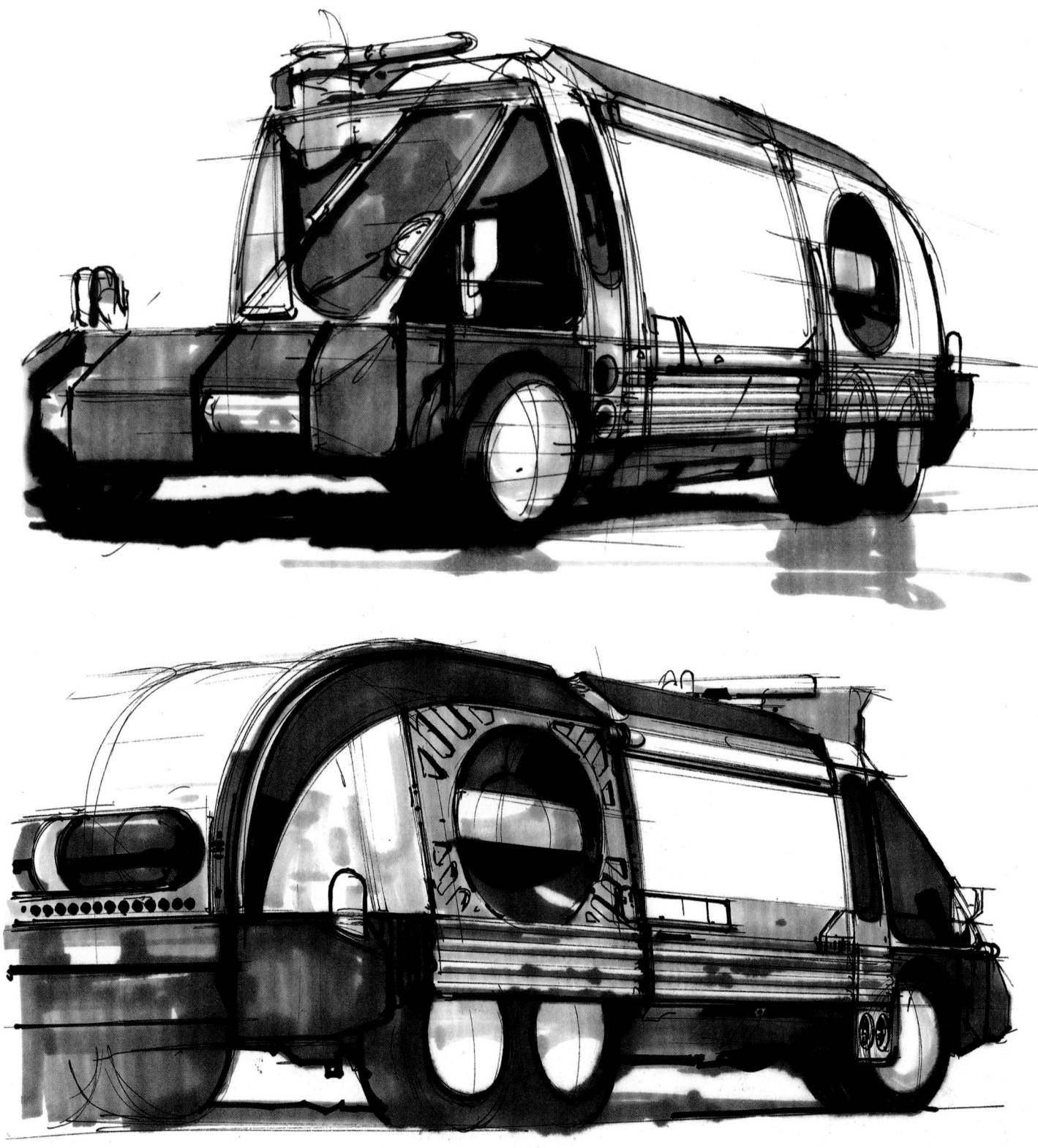

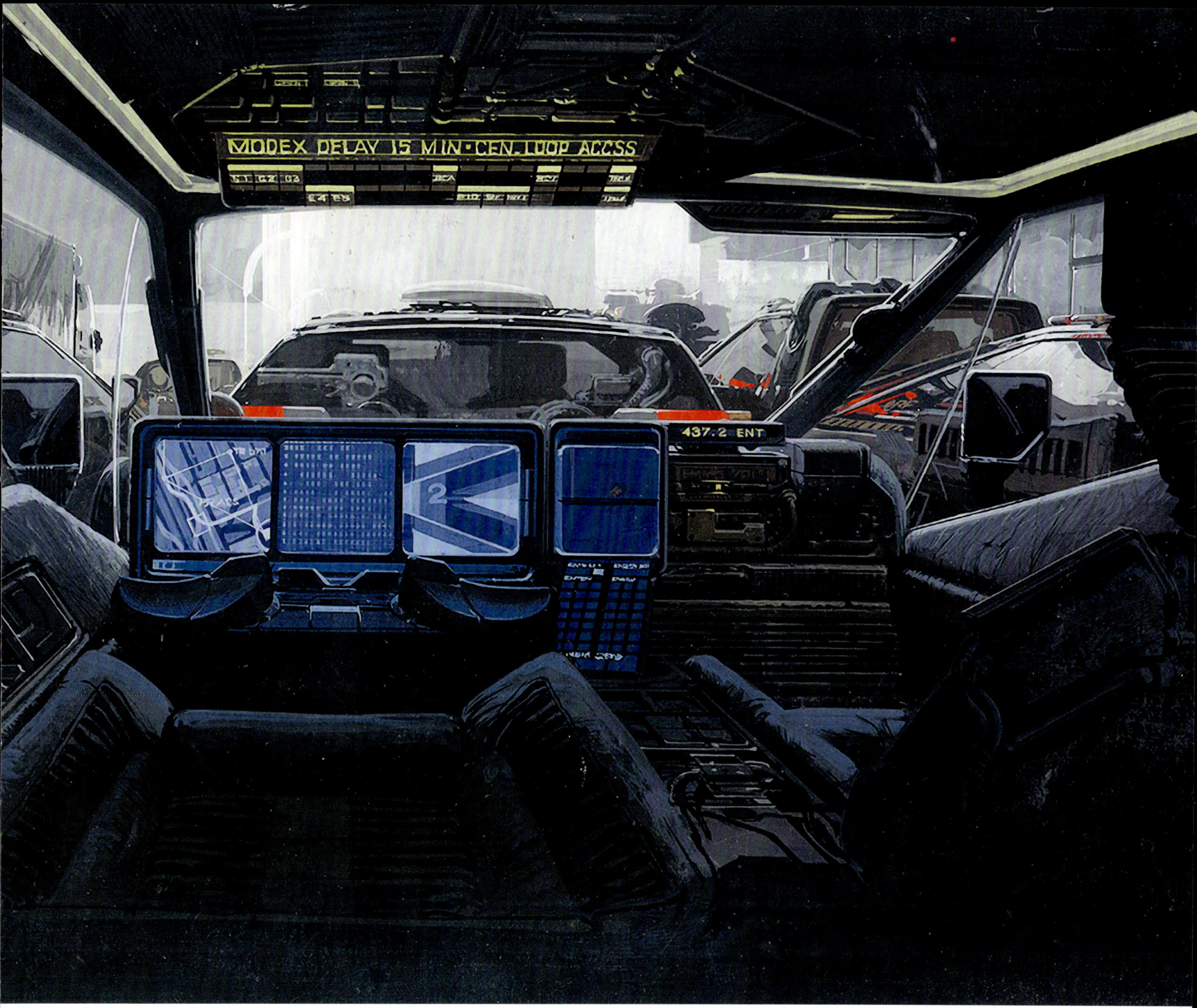

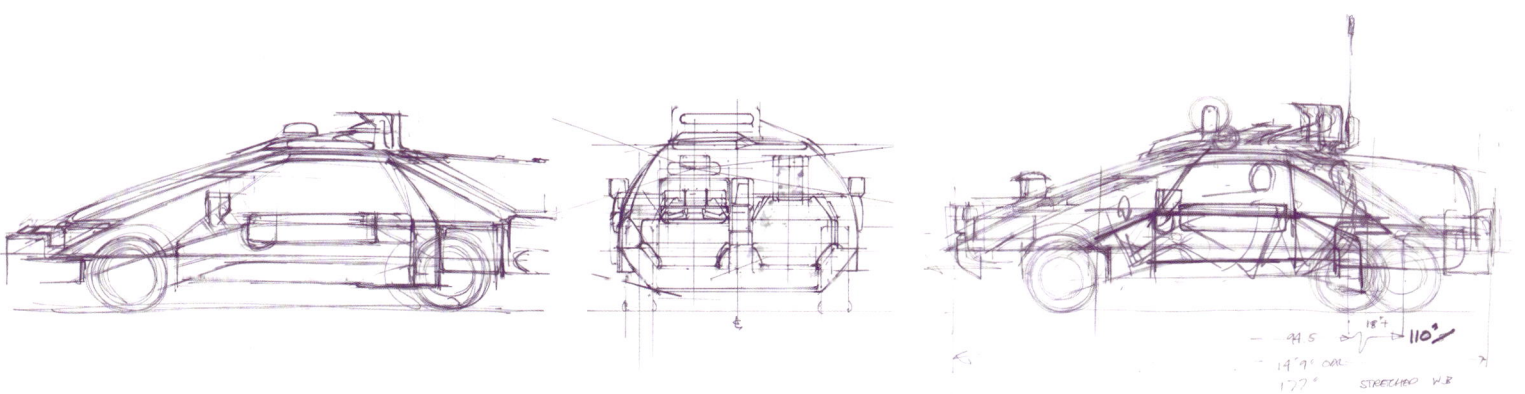

The vehicles Mead developed for *Blade Runner* are explicit. They are able to be realized down to the passenger accommodations, with critical details that reinforce the characterization of Deckard (Harrison Ford), and emphasize important story points.

As many of the vehicles in *Blade Runner* were projected to be maneuvered under their own power, Mead's designs were often based on an existing frame and power train. Thus the notation indicating the wheelbase for this taxi, for which Mead designed a barrage of stickers and notations to connote the legal and bureaucratic stranglehold of the overseers.

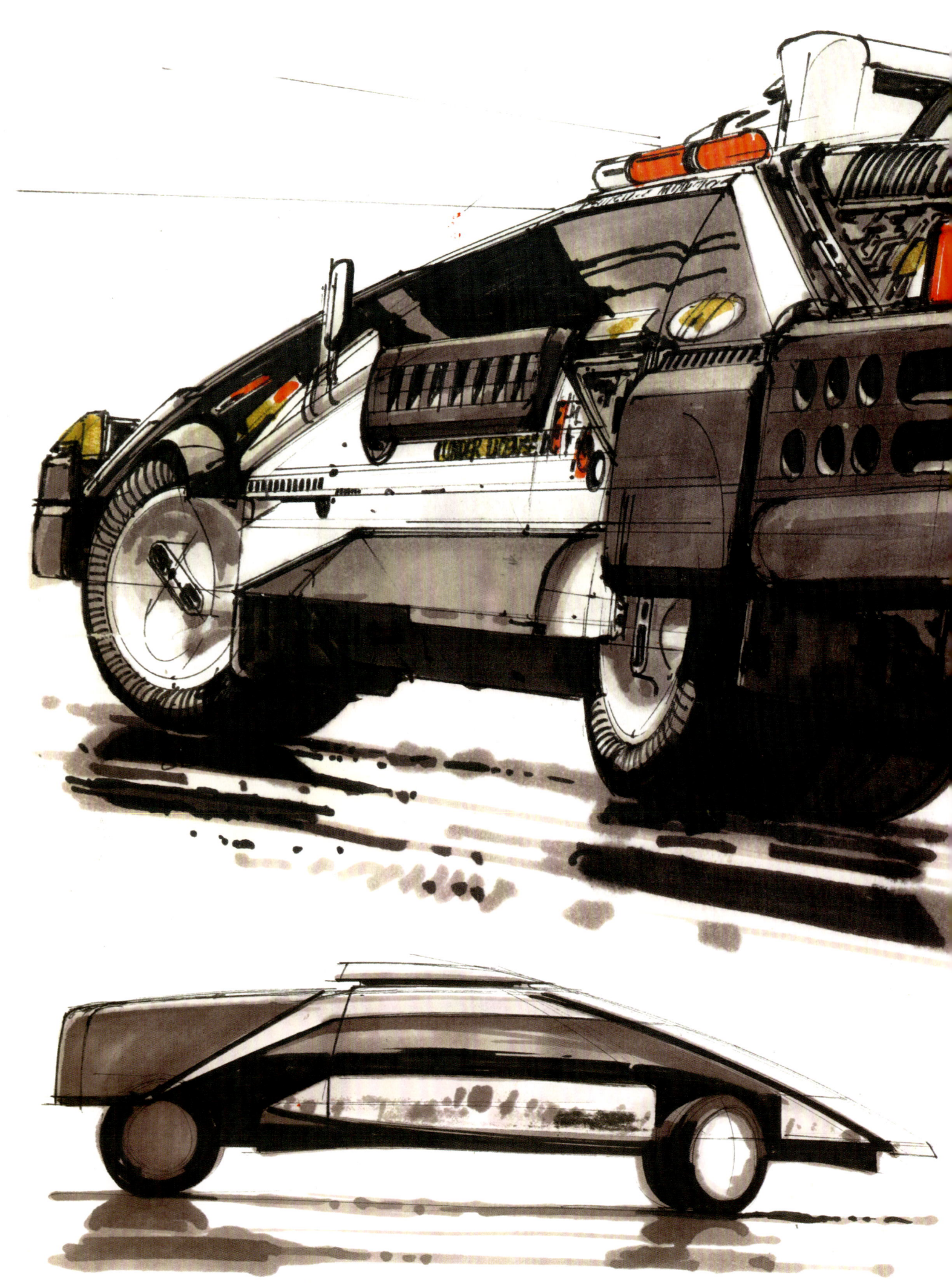

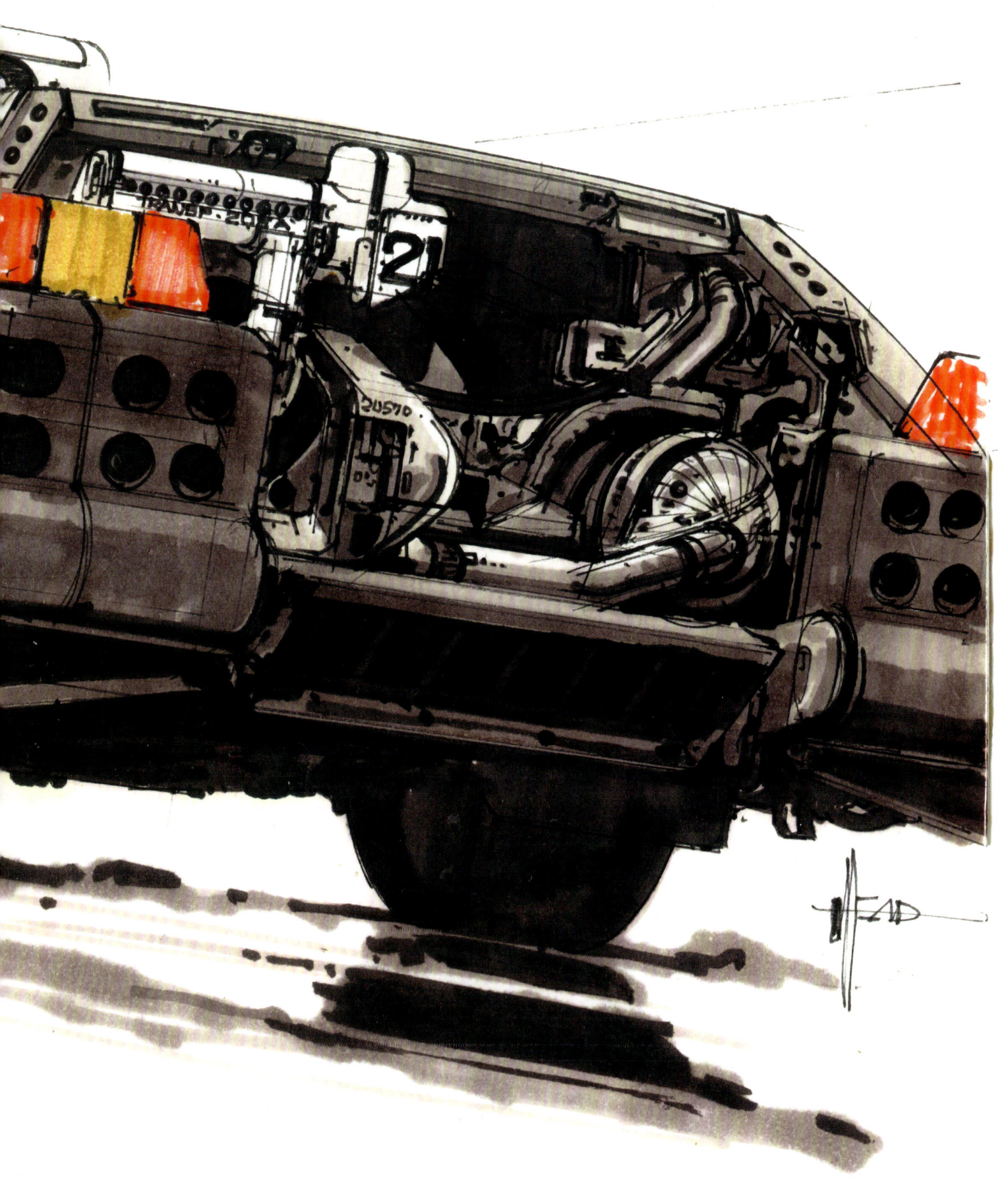

THIS SPREAD: EARLY CONCEPT DEISNGS OF DECKARD'S VEHICLE AND THE BASIS OF THE POLICE CARS.

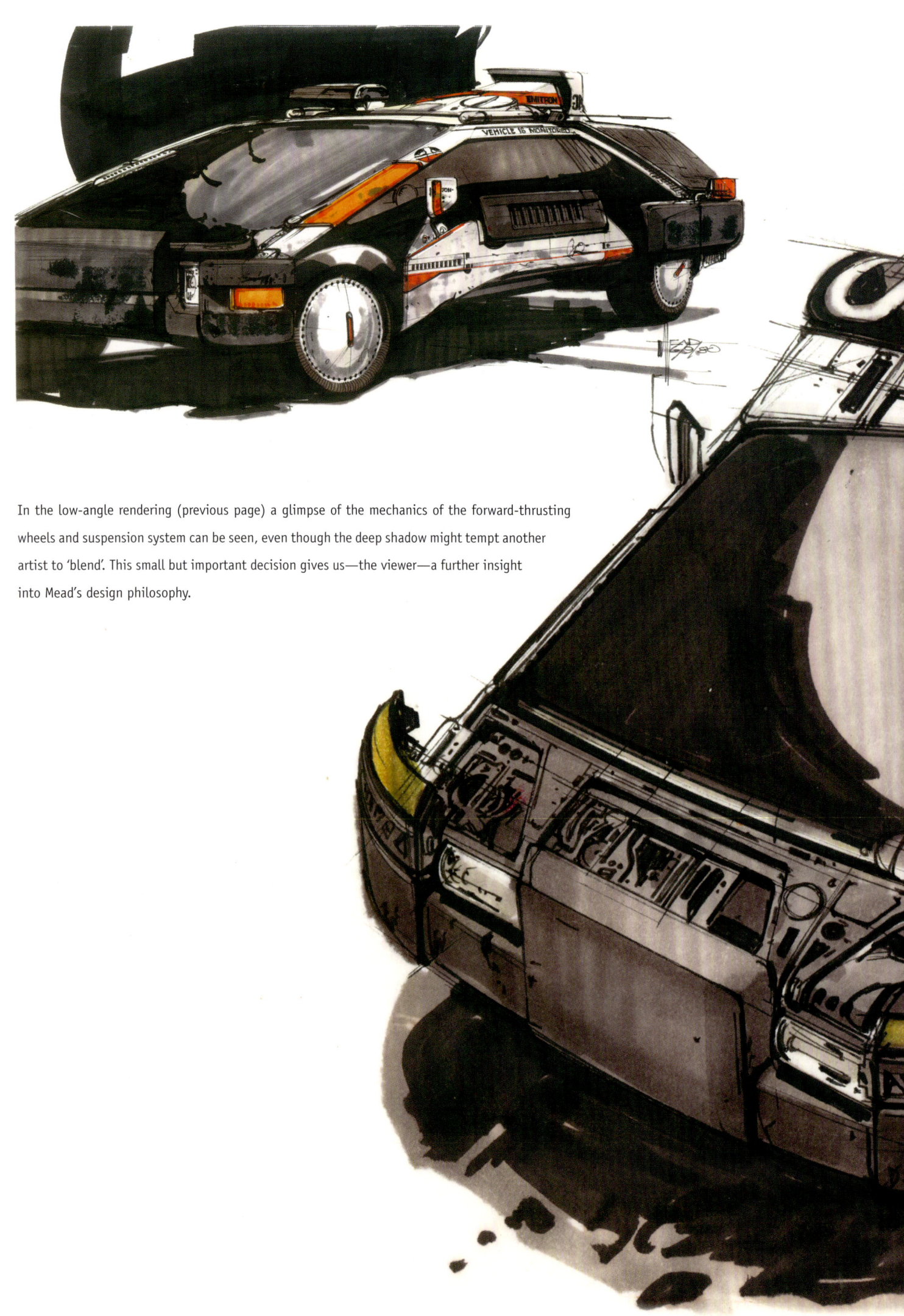

In the low-angle rendering (previous page) a glimpse of the mechanics of the forward-thrusting wheels and suspension system can be seen, even though the deep shadow might tempt another artist to 'blend'. This small but important decision gives us—the viewer—a further insight into Mead's design philosophy.

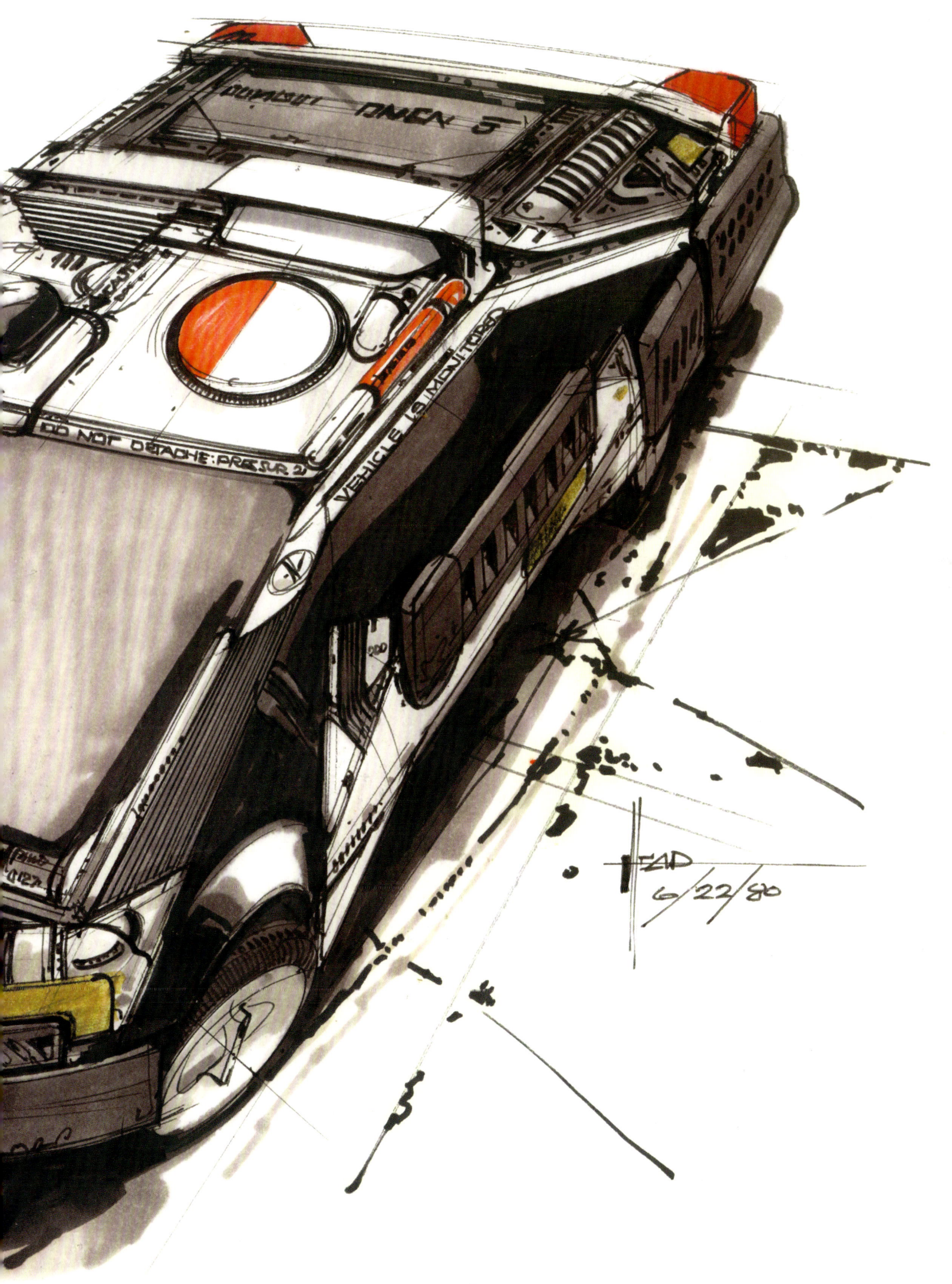

VEHICLE IS MONITORED

DO NOT DETACHE: PRESSUR 2

OMEN 5

EAD
6/22/80

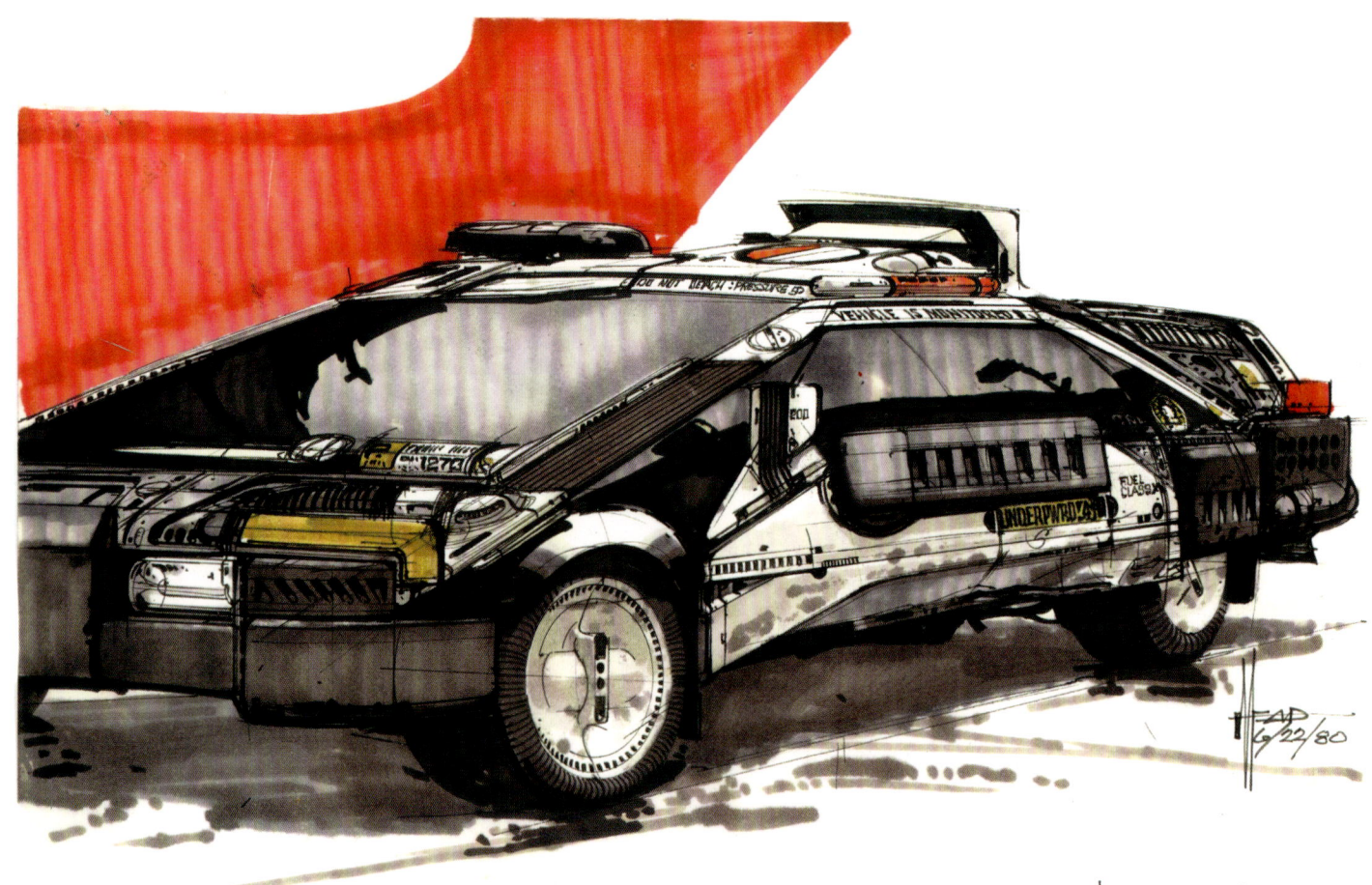

DECKARD'S VEHICLE: DECOMM'D AERODYNE:
REAR SPOILER REMOVED: BYPASS VENTS SEALED
SURFACE TRAFFIC IMPACT PACKAGE ADDED: PERI-
METER VISIBILITY GROUP: HI-CAP A/C PACKAGE:
CONTACT SWEEP WIPERS: PERMIT APPLIQUÉ:
THEFT/ASSAULT WARNINGS. AIRBORNE LIGHT
PANELS BLACKED OUT:

Other vehicles for *Blade Runner*, such as the police cars on these pages and overleaf,
were to be built 'from the ground up', with fully detailed bodywork and interior fittings.
The extended glass from the passenger compartment will be theme of many subsequent
Mead commissions, notably the *Jetsons*.

THIS SPREAD: EARLY STUDIES OF
CARS FOR BLADE RUNNER

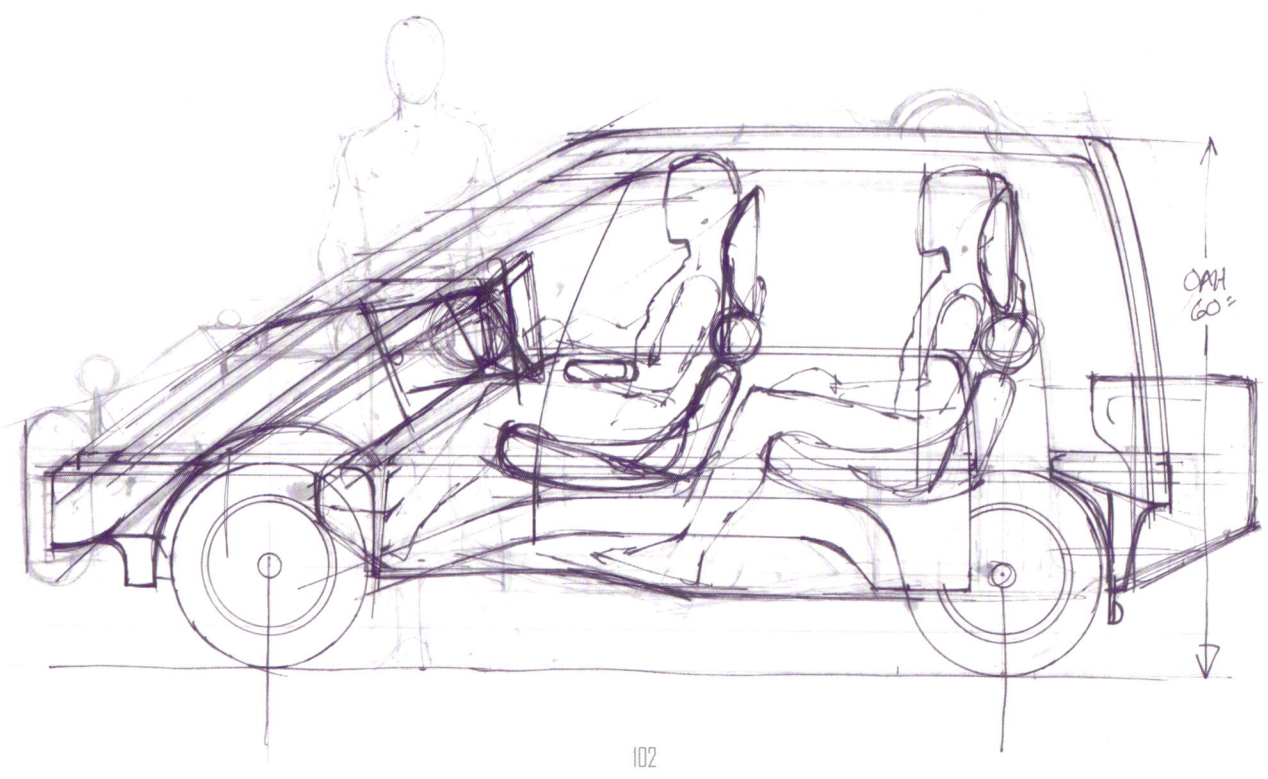

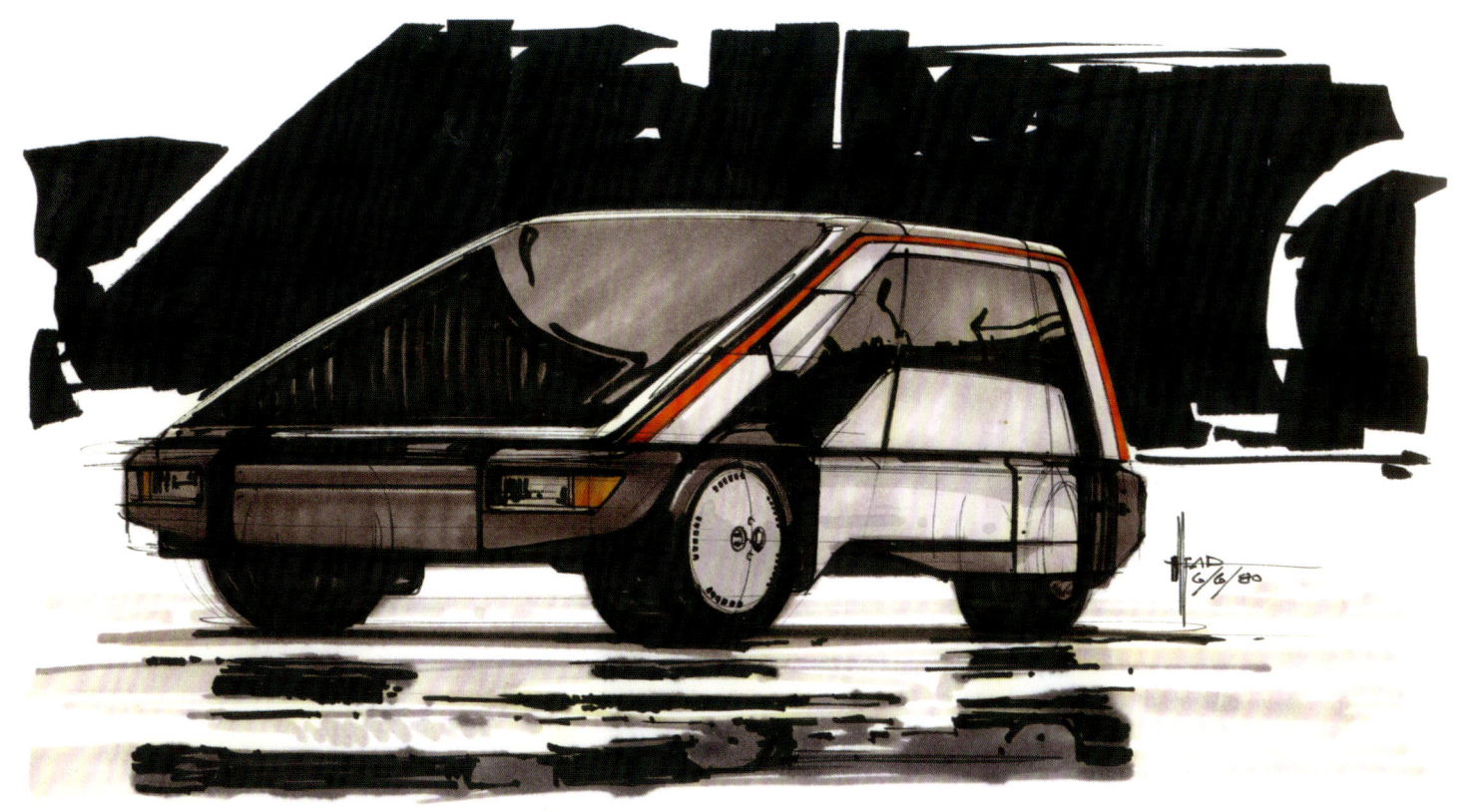

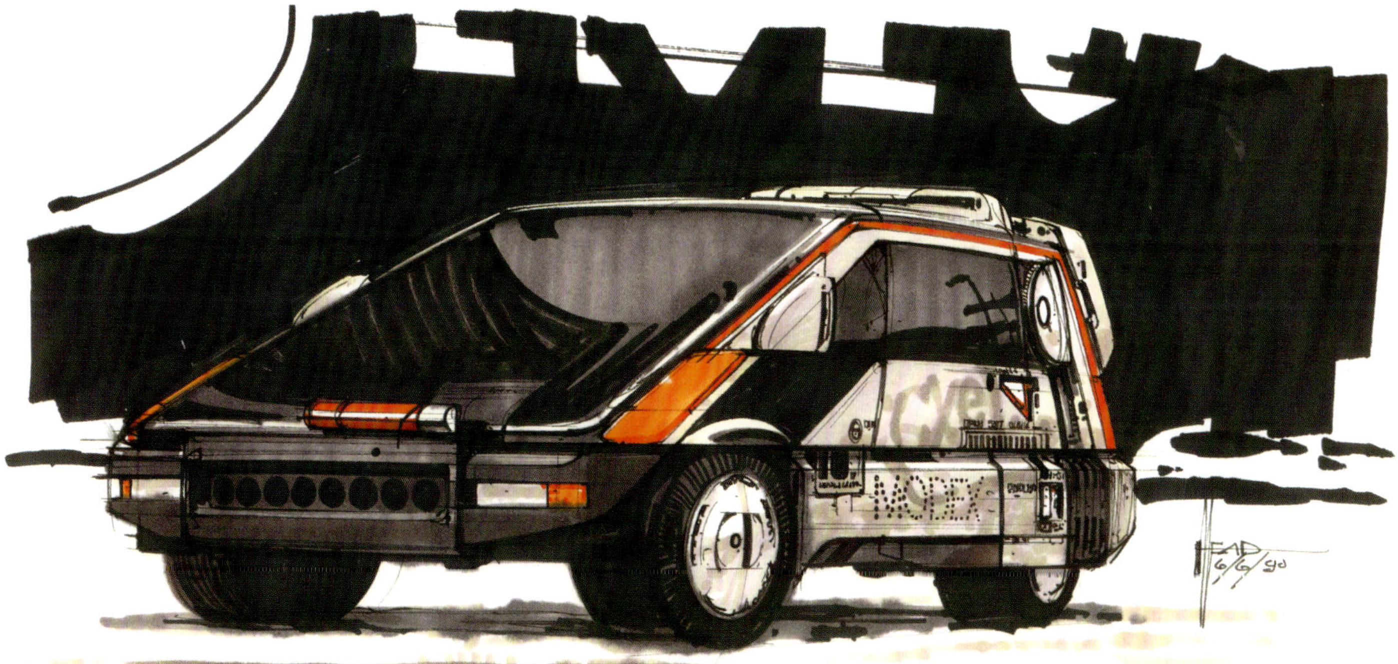

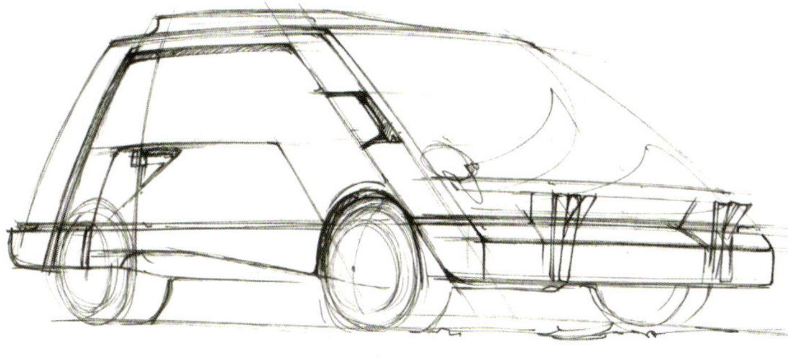

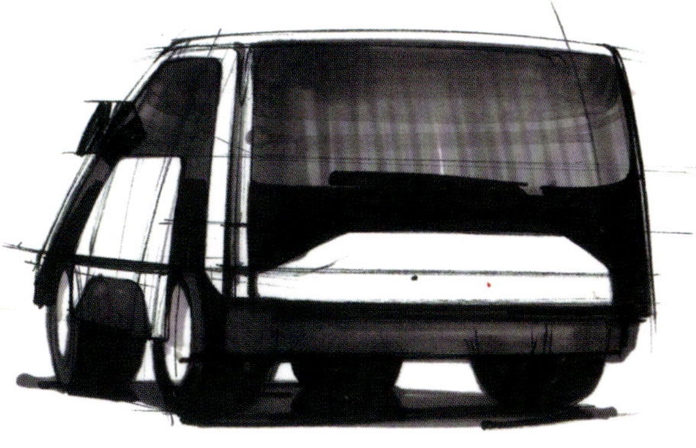

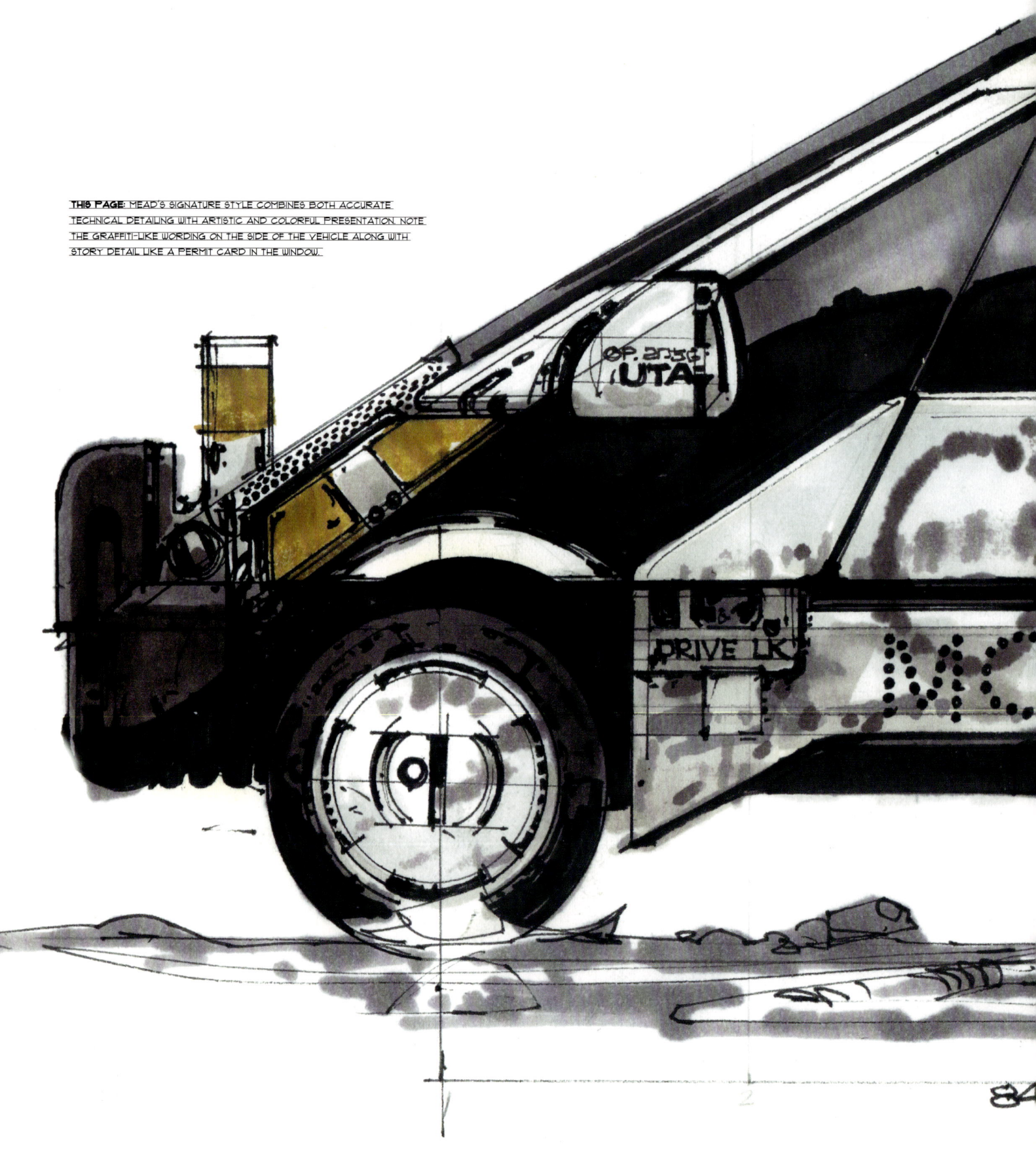

THIS PAGE: MEAD'S SIGNATURE STYLE COMBINES BOTH ACCURATE TECHNICAL DETAILING WITH ARTISTIC AND COLORFUL PRESENTATION. NOTE THE GRAFFITI-LIKE WORDING ON THE SIDE OF THE VEHICLE ALONG WITH STORY DETAIL LIKE A PERMIT CARD IN THE WINDOW.

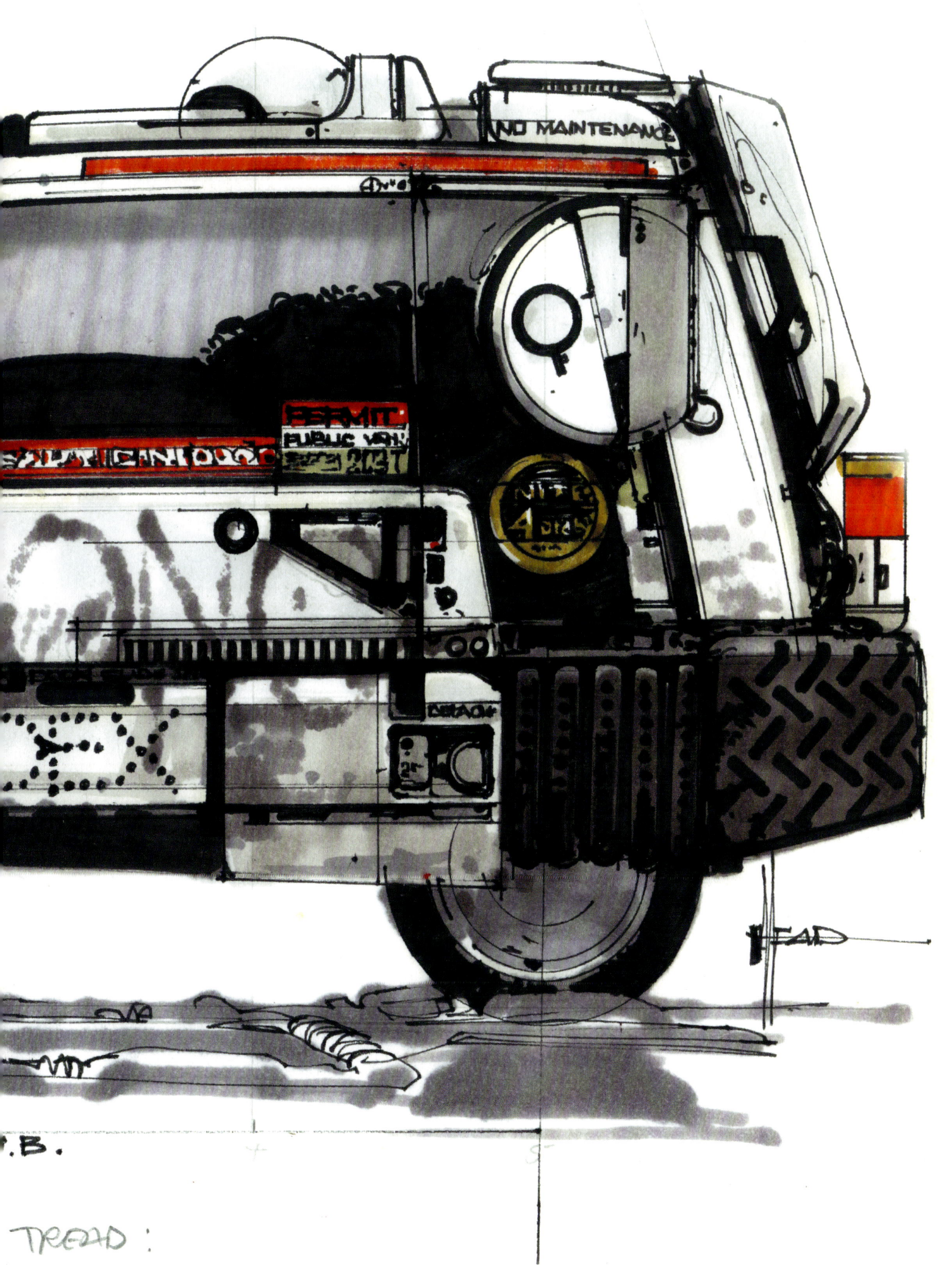

NO MAINTENANCE

PERMIT
PUBLIC VEH

NITE
4 DAY

.B.

TREAD:

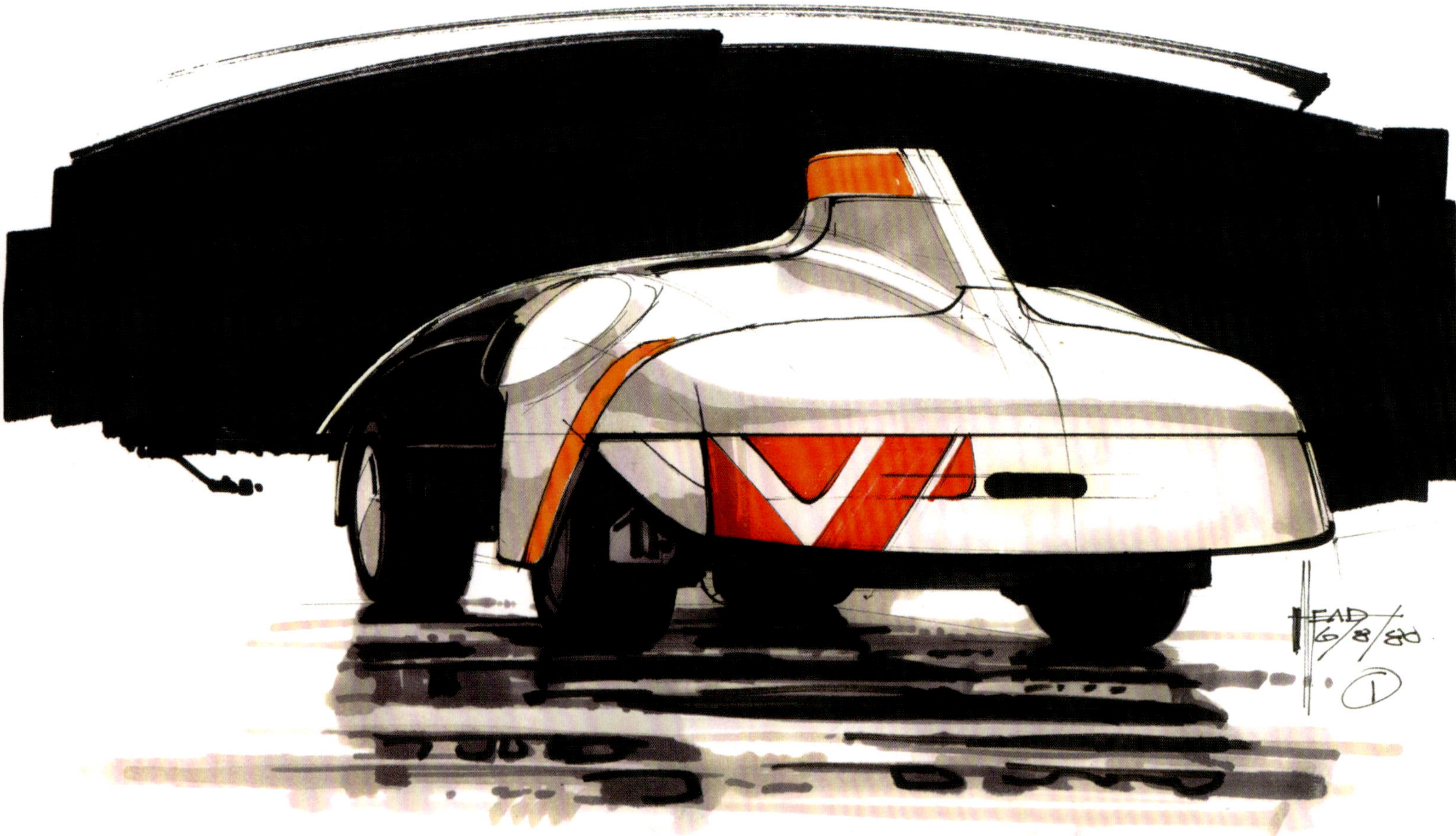
HEAD 6/8/80
1

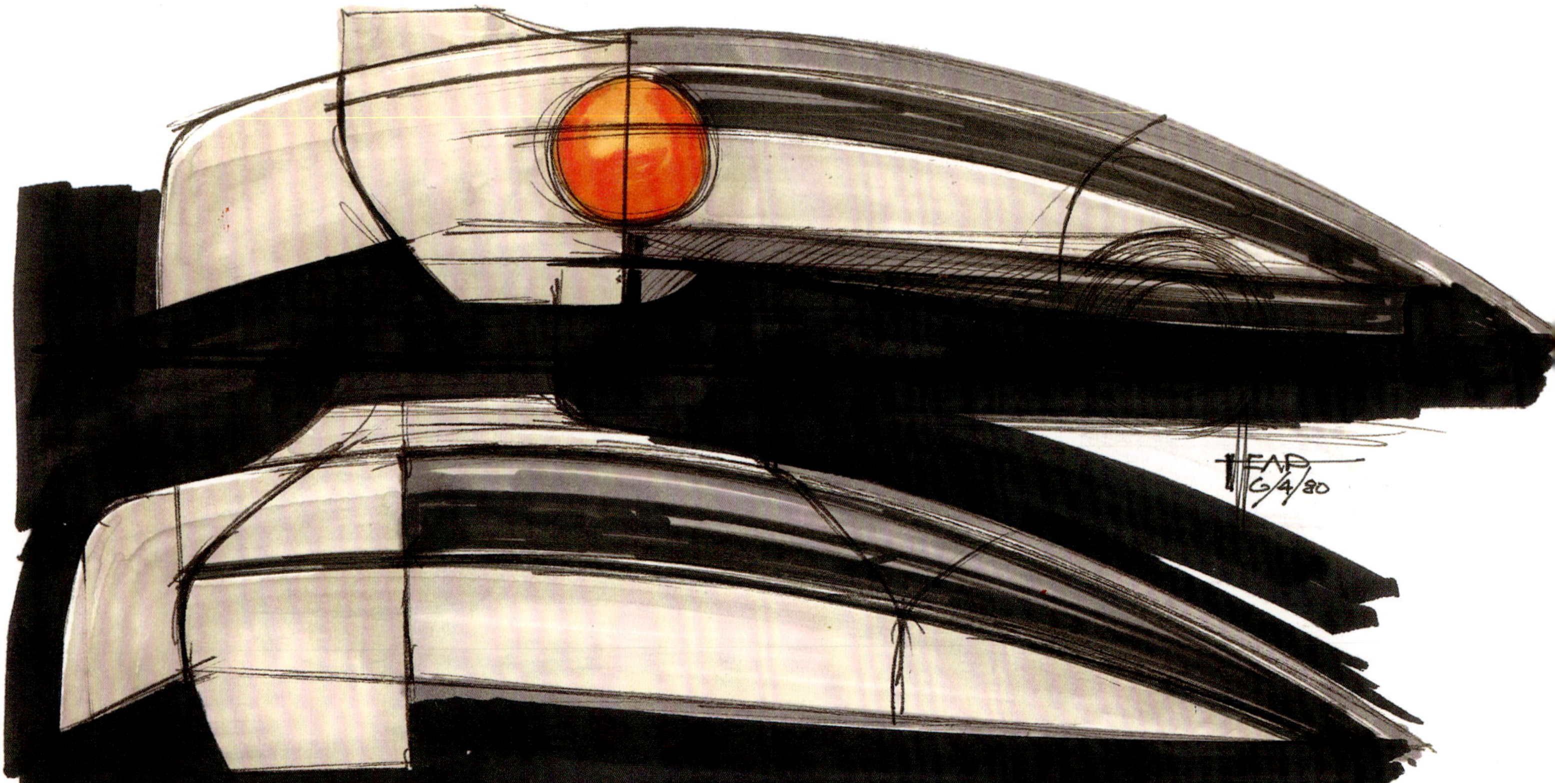
HEAD 6/4/80

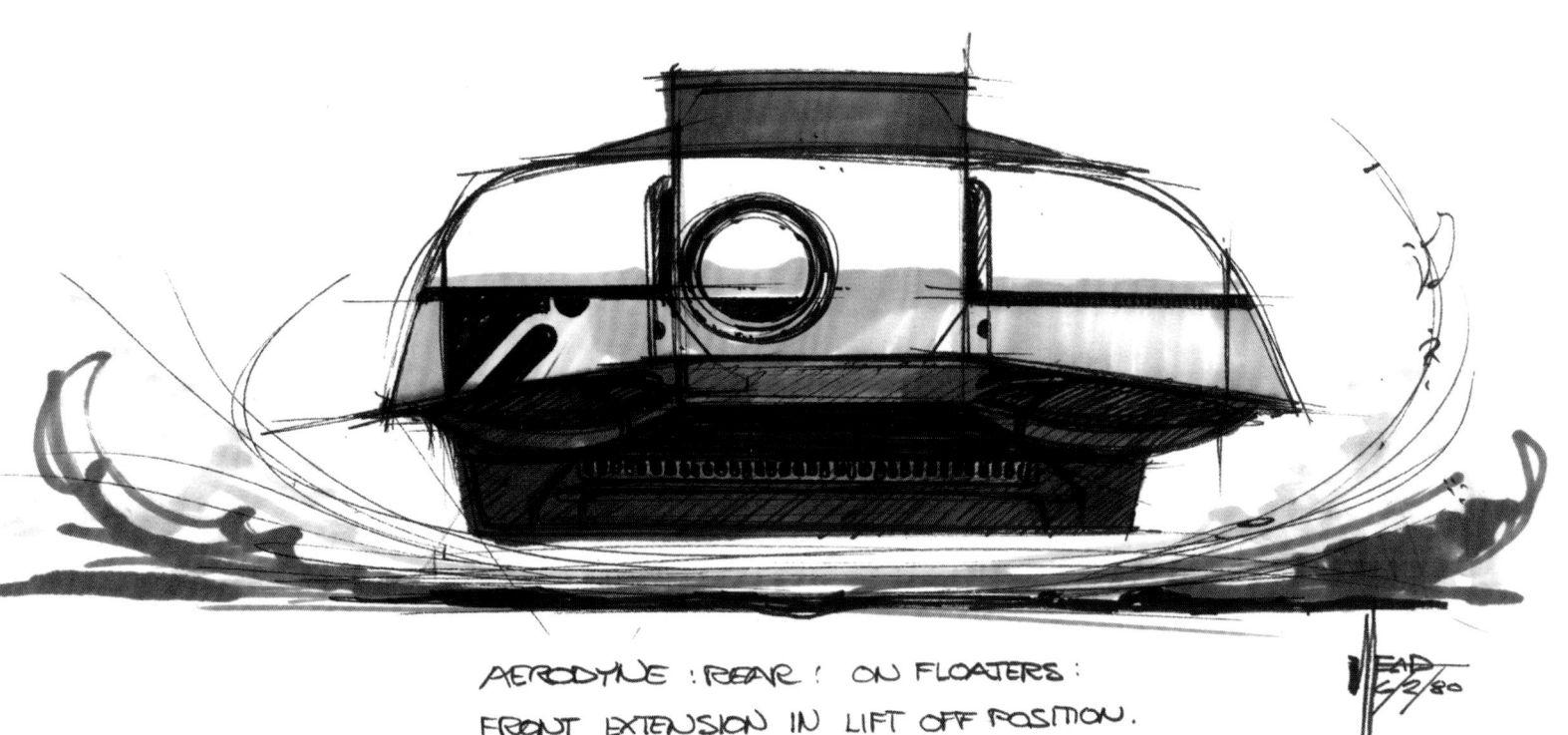

AERODYNE : REAR : ON FLOATERS :
FRONT EXTENSION IN LIFT OFF POSITION.
REAR AIR INTAKE PANEL RAISED :

Further detailed studies explored the geometry—always a central fact of Mead's design *oeuvre*—and deployment of a roof-mounted laser weapon which, while not explicitly called for in the script, was thought to add to the fidelity of the visual design.

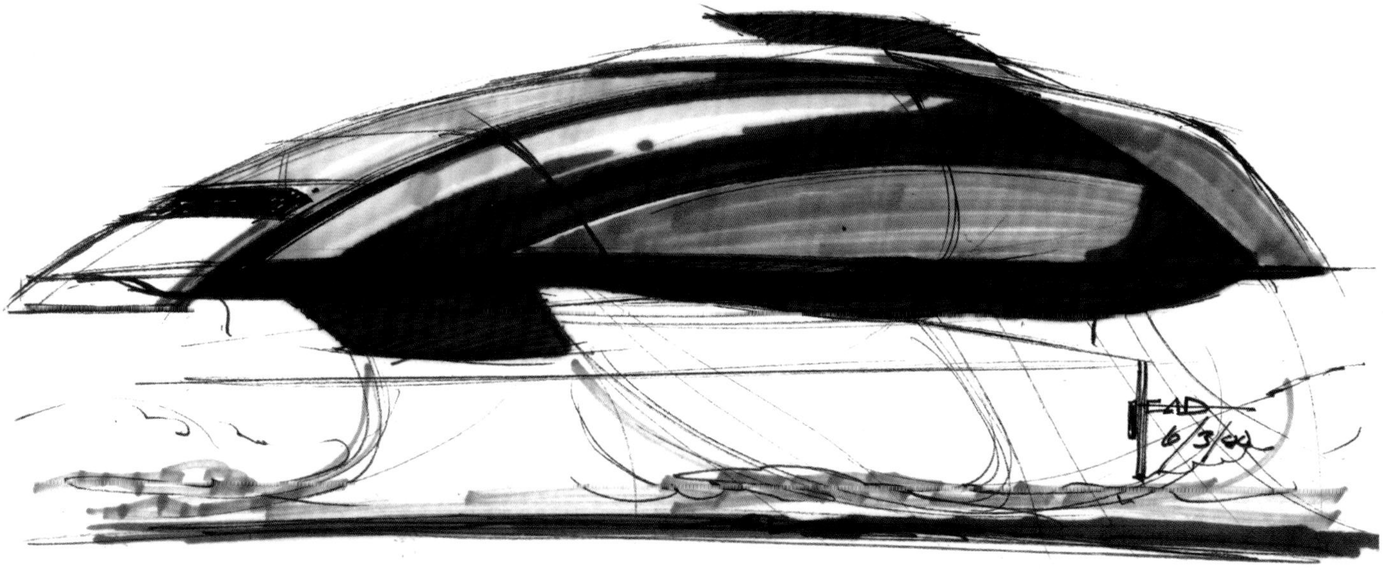

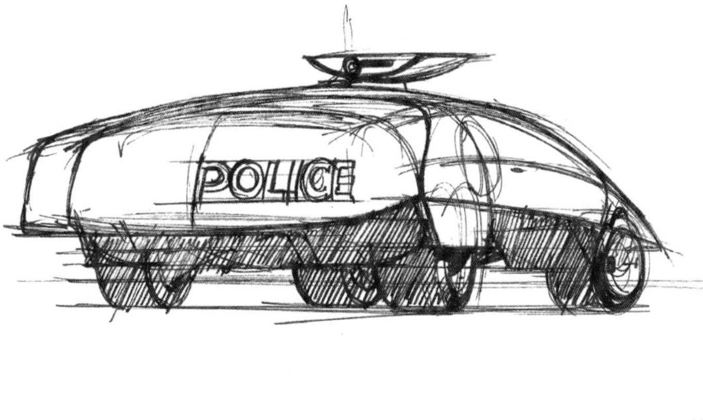

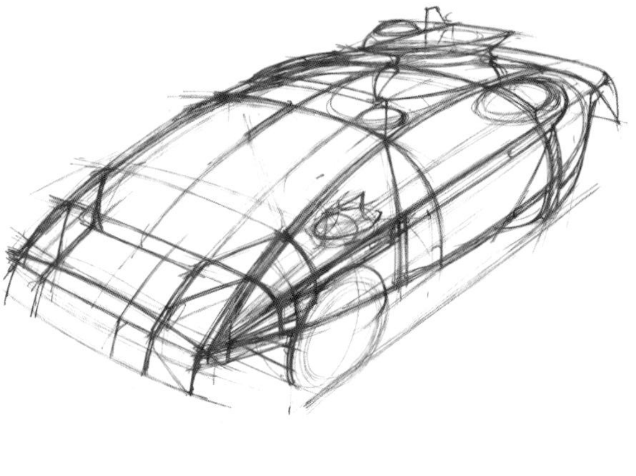

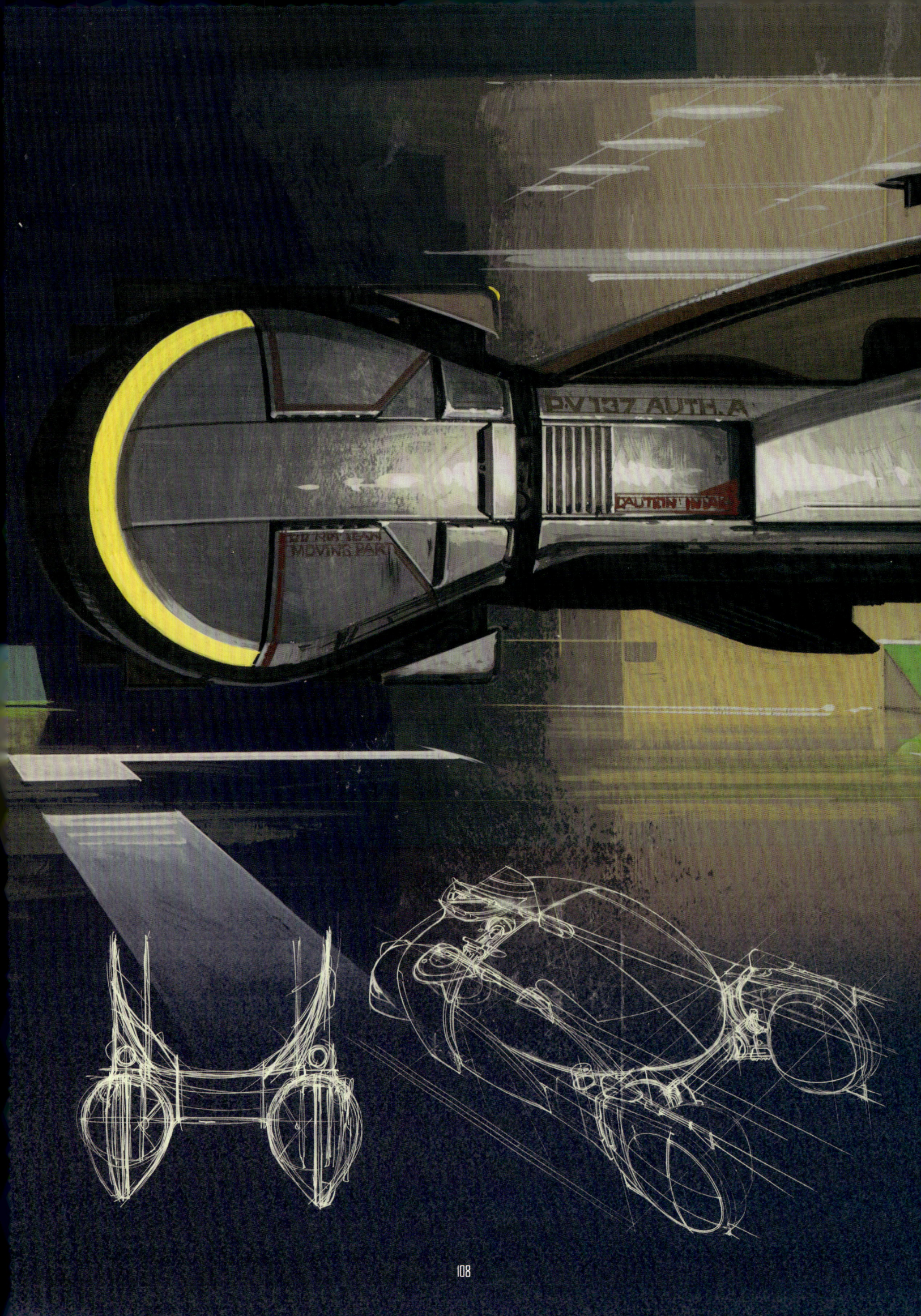

PV 137 AUTH. A

DO NOT LEAN
MOVING PART

CAUTION: INTAKE

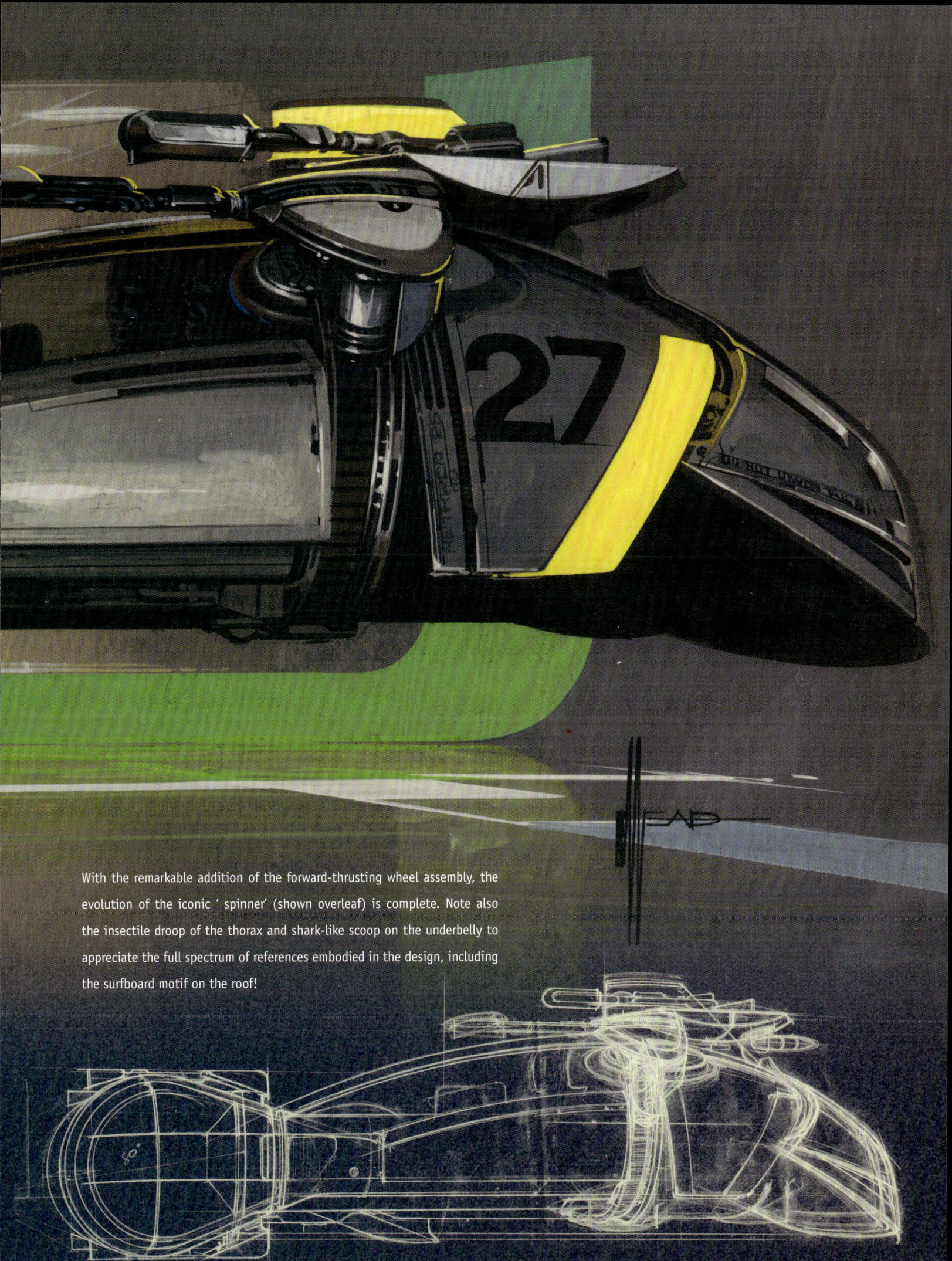

With the remarkable addition of the forward-thrusting wheel assembly, the evolution of the iconic ' spinner' (shown overleaf) is complete. Note also the insectile droop of the thorax and shark-like scoop on the underbelly to appreciate the full spectrum of references embodied in the design, including the surfboard motif on the roof!

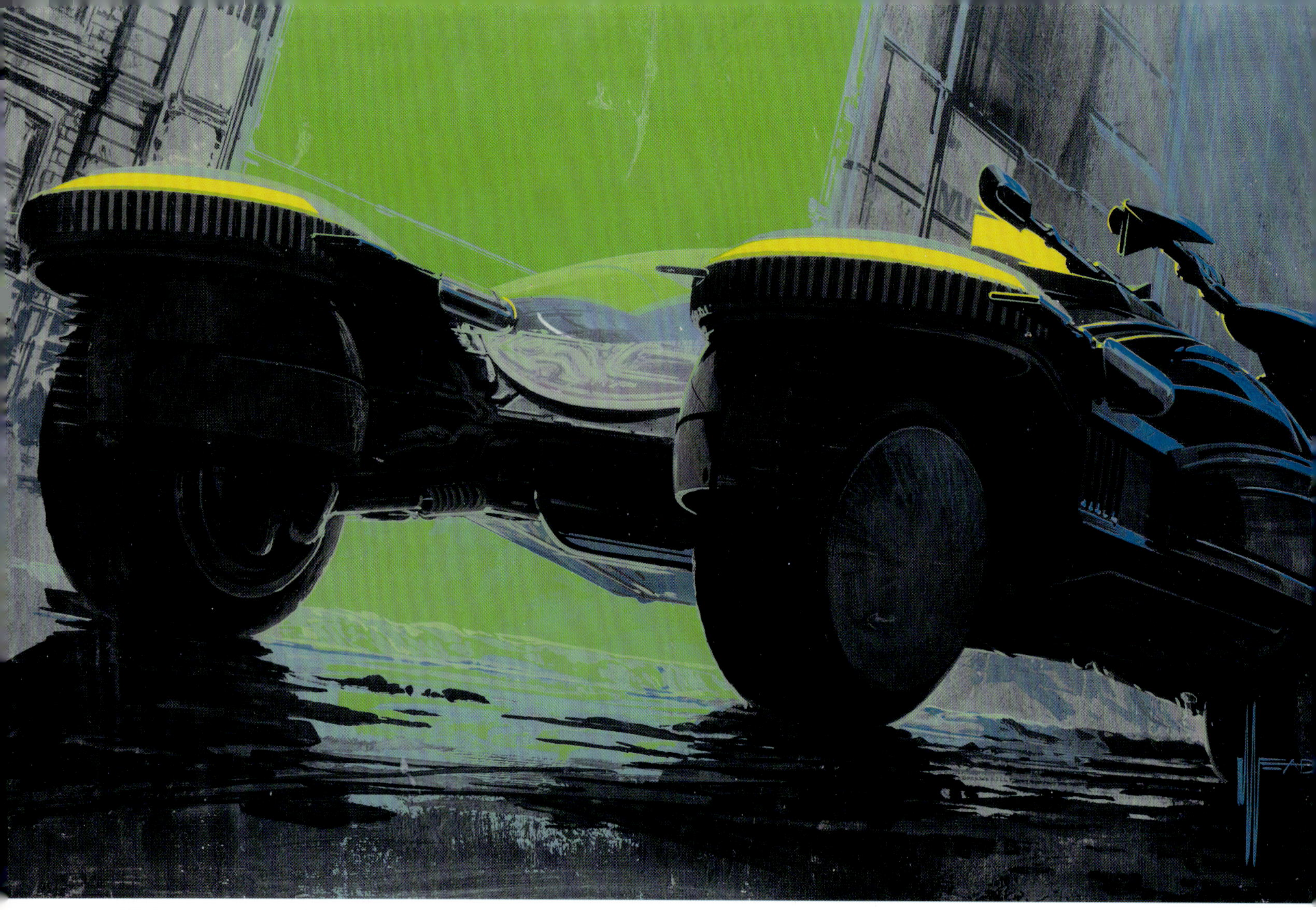

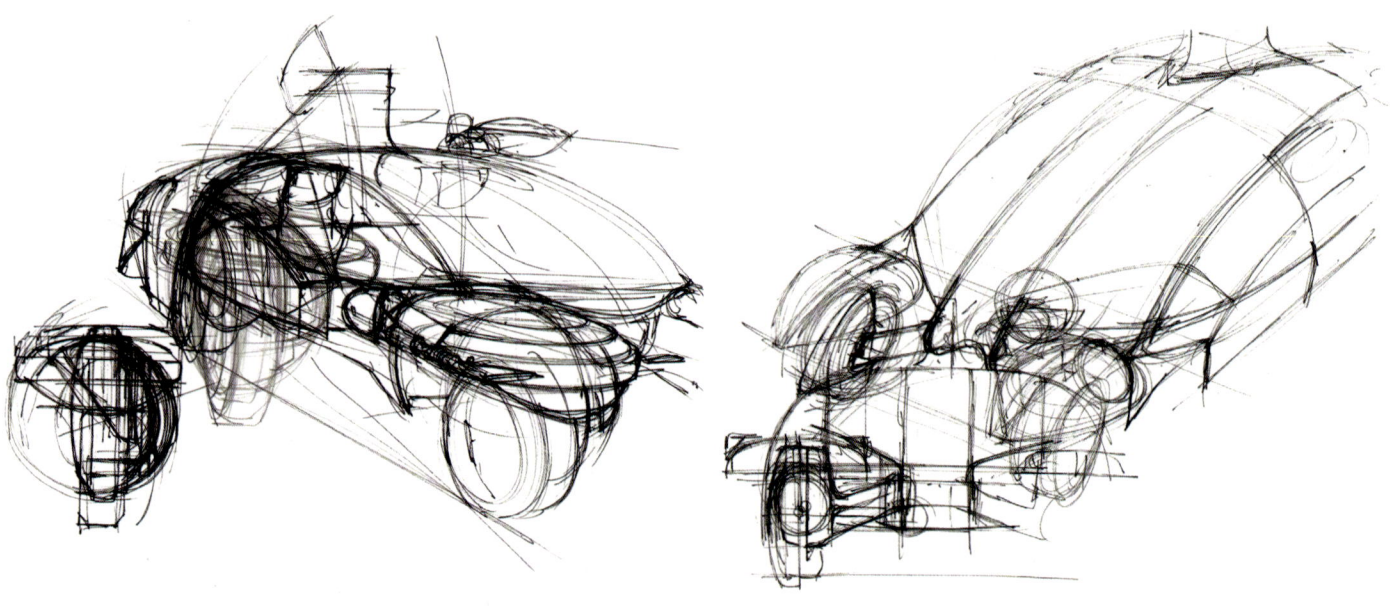

The final rendering (overleaf) depicts Deckard's spinner above the Chinatown district as everyday ground-based traffic continues to flow by. Here, Mead allows atmospheric perspective to reinforce the extreme perspective of the view, which becomes increasingly granular as the eye wanders from the crystal-clear depiction of the spinner to the chalky glow from headlights below. The intricate detail of the wheel housings, the fully rendered interior, and the glowing accents combine to create a high-impact hyper-realistic image fitting to the role of the spinner in the completed motion picture.

The interior of the spinner is no less detailed, as Mead brings his early training as an auto designer at ArtCenter College to consider the placement of read-outs, navigation systems, and advanced system controls as might be required in such a vehicle. Such dazzling detail would be unusual in a digital rendering. In a pencil and gauche medium with no prior references it is simply astounding.

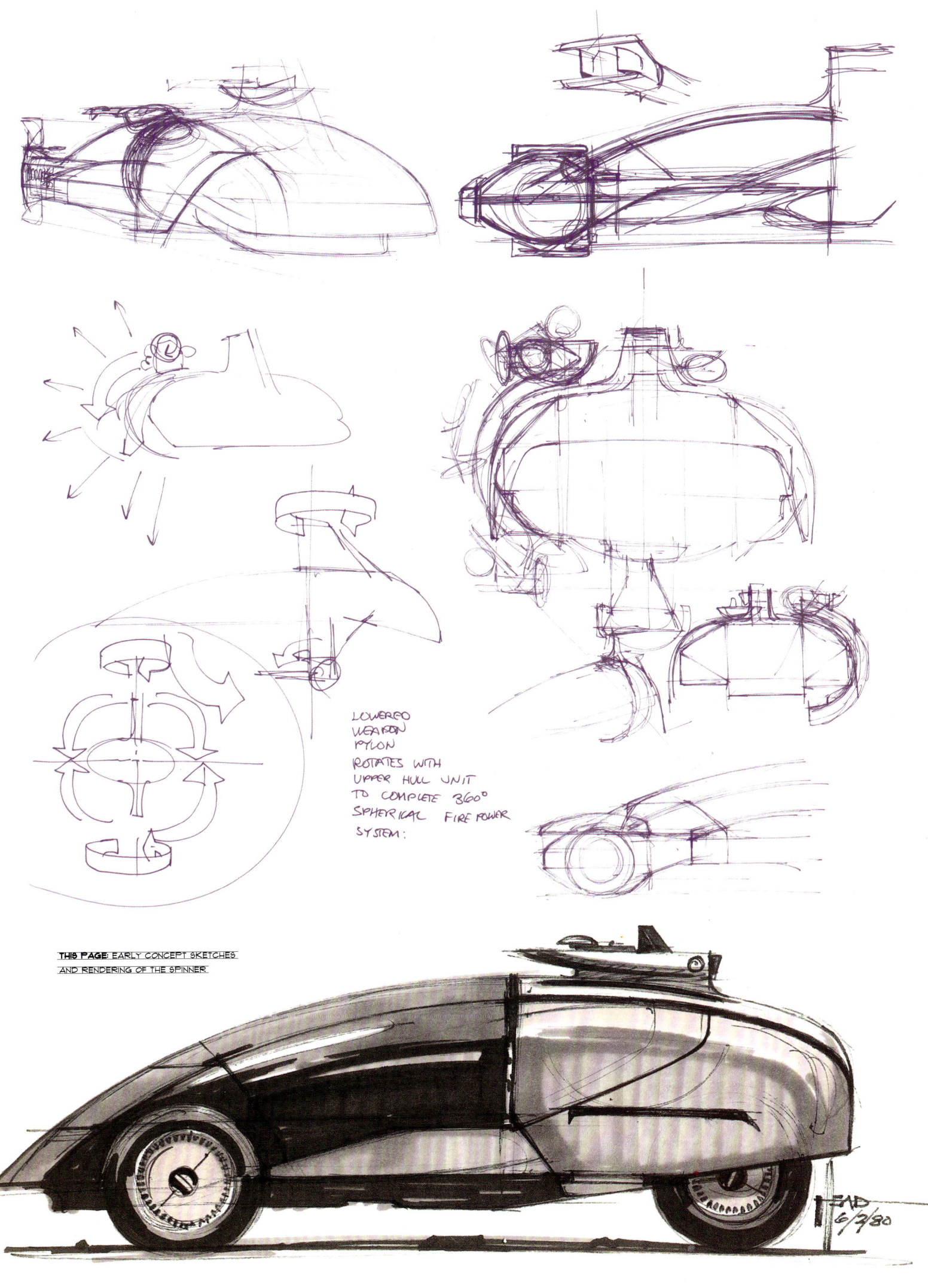

LOWERED
WEAPON
PYLON
ROTATES WITH
UPPER HULL UNIT
TO COMPLETE 360°
SPHERICAL FIRE POWER
SYSTEM:

THIS PAGE: EARLY CONCEPT SKETCHES
AND RENDERING OF THE SPINNER

EAD 6/3/80

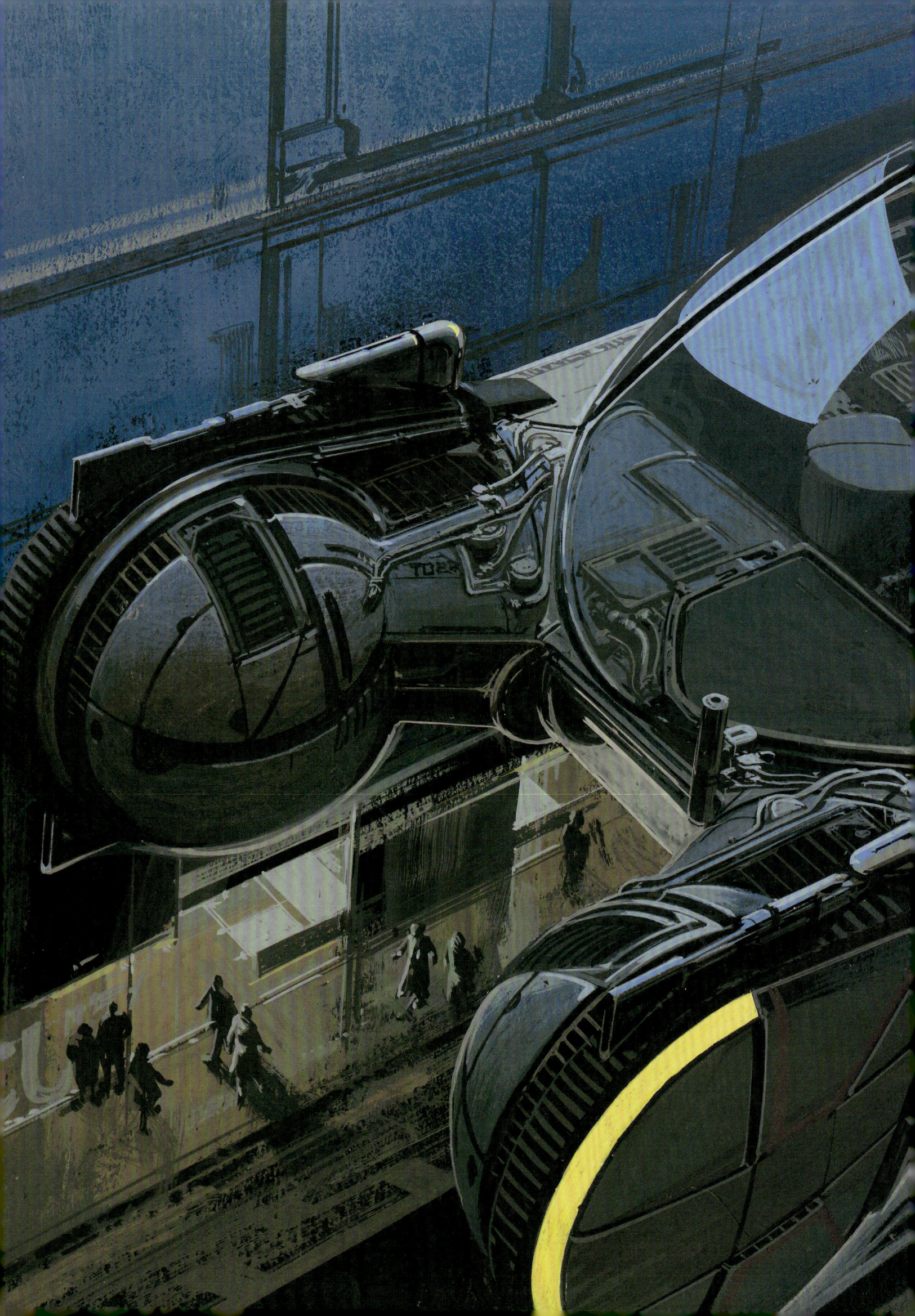

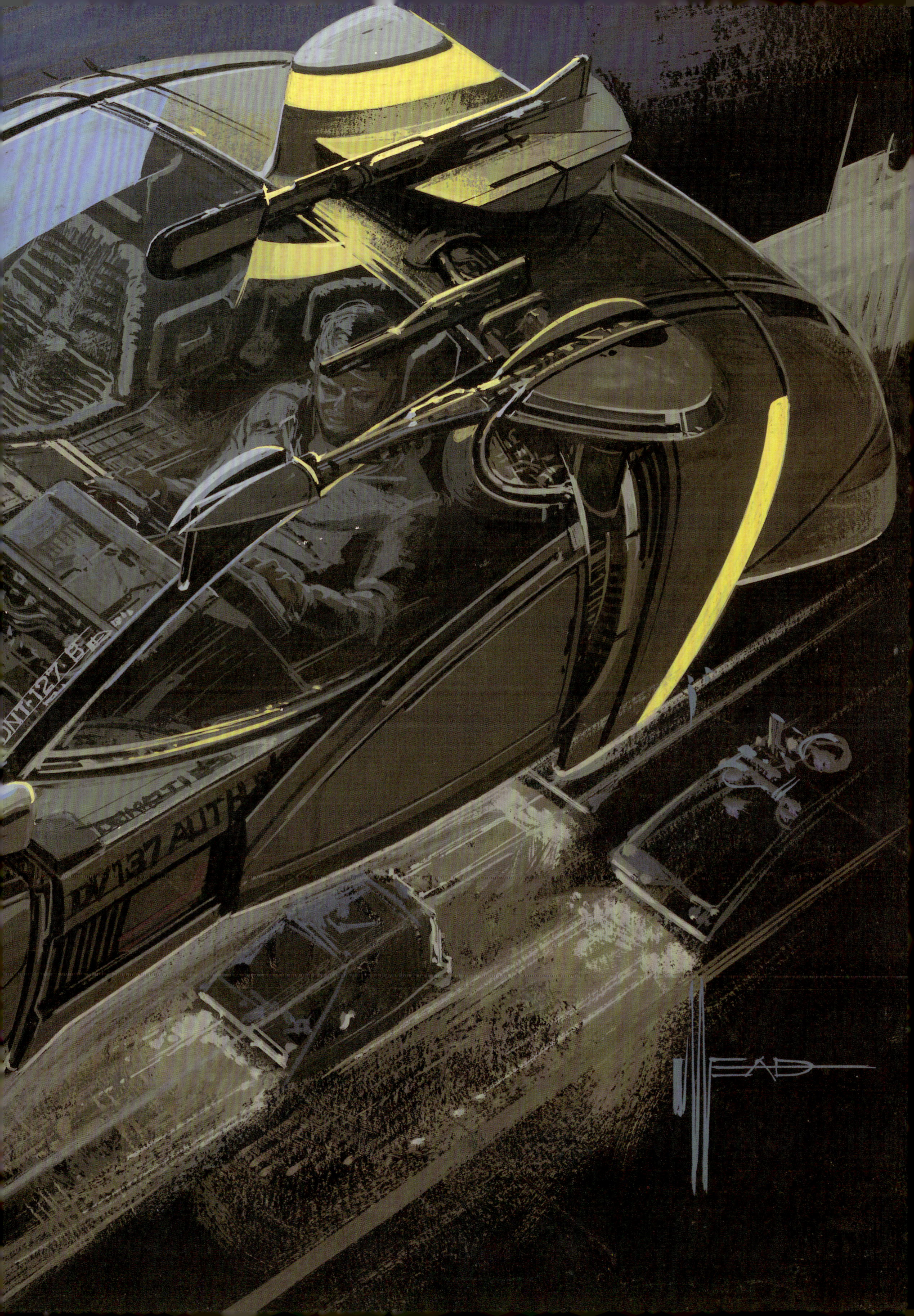

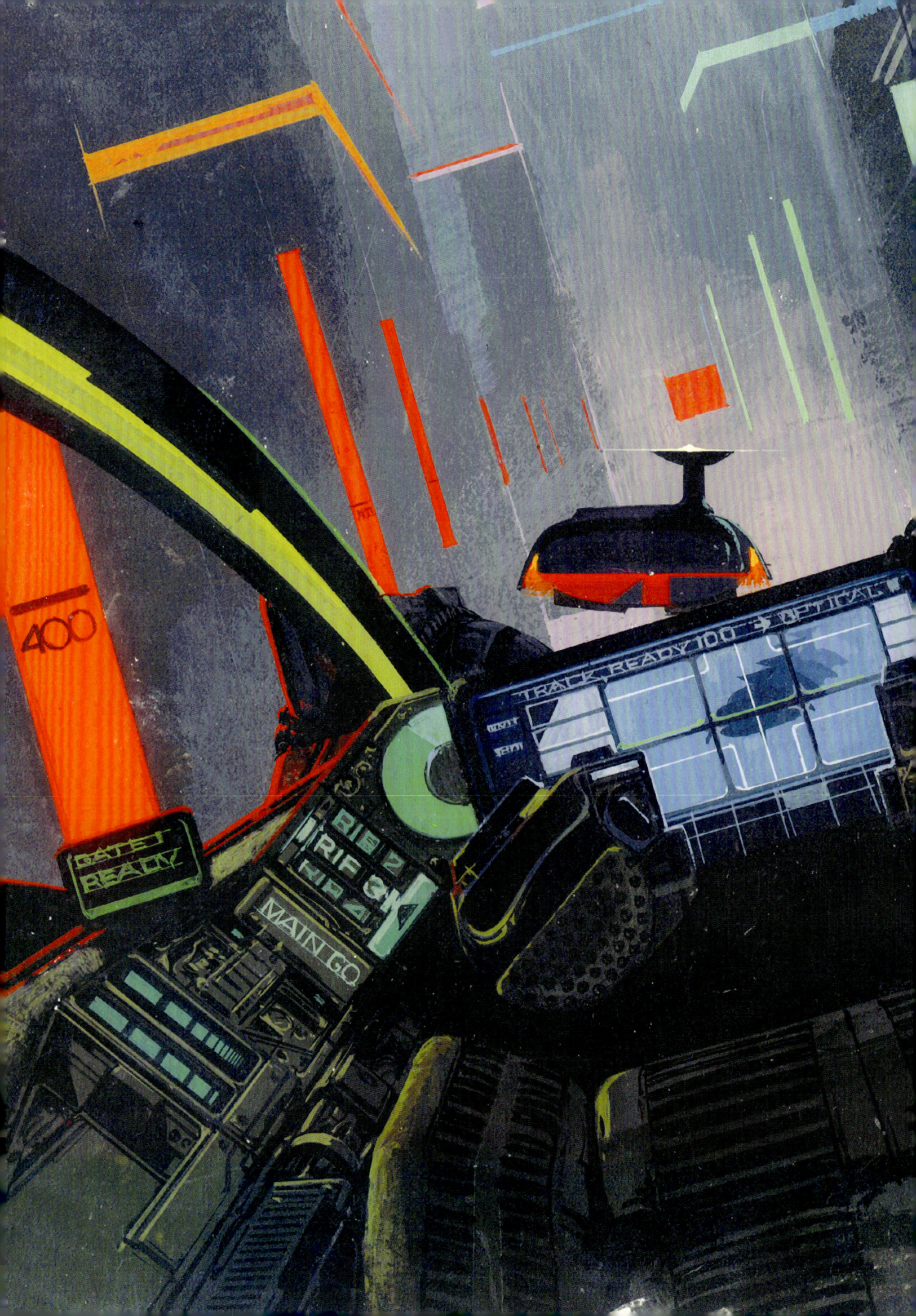

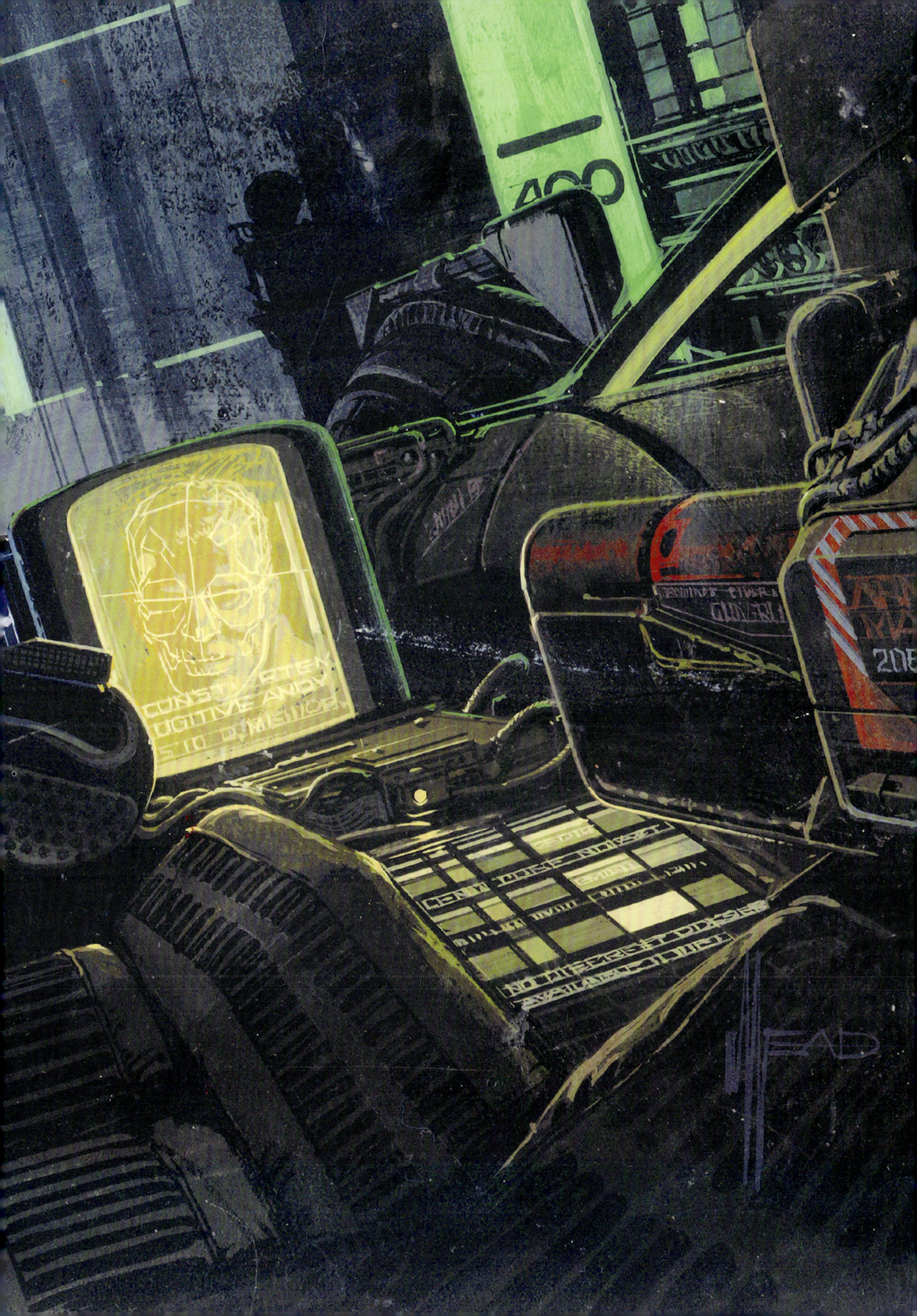

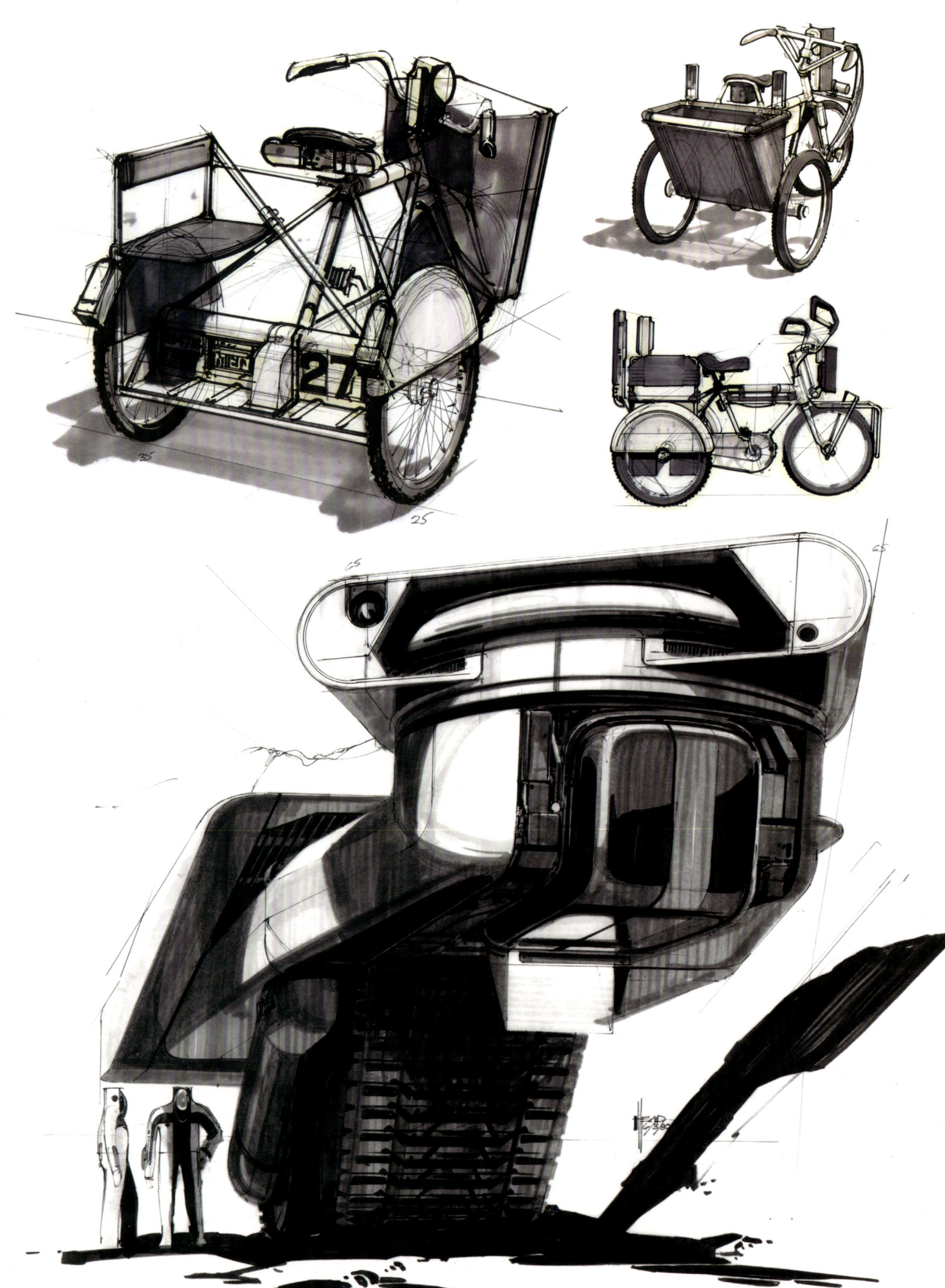

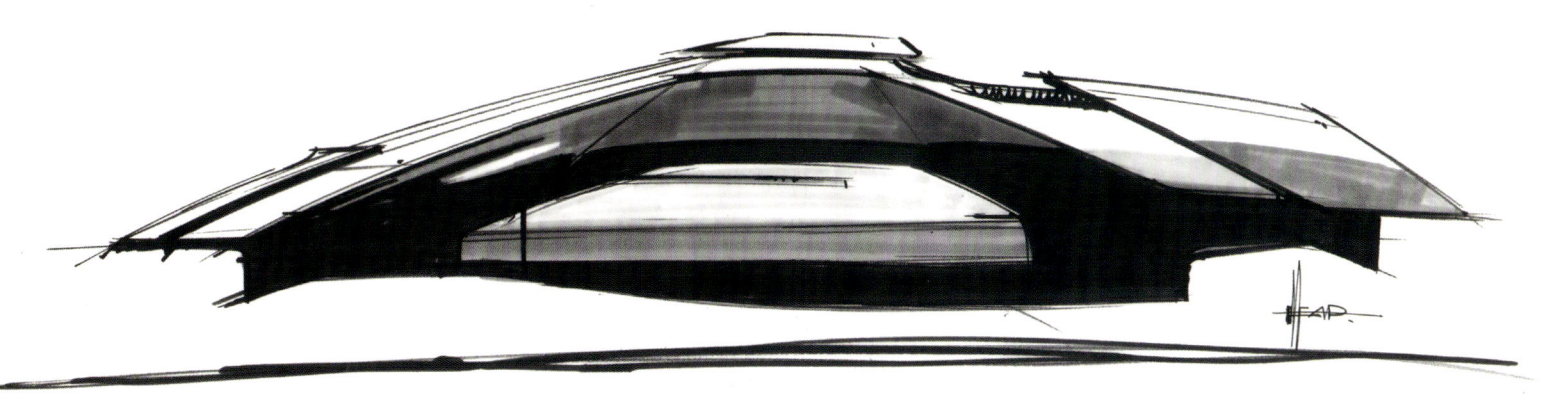

The incidental vehicles, from rickshaw-like delivery trikes to service vehicles are the 'extras' crowding the polluted streets with convincingly tattered frames, scarred paint and bleary lights, all in the service of a compelling portrait of a dystopian future society.

Mead, with a characteristic eye for distinguishing detail, provides each with a unique history as well as a provocative point of view, such as this from beneath the chassis of a massive truck (bottom of the left page).

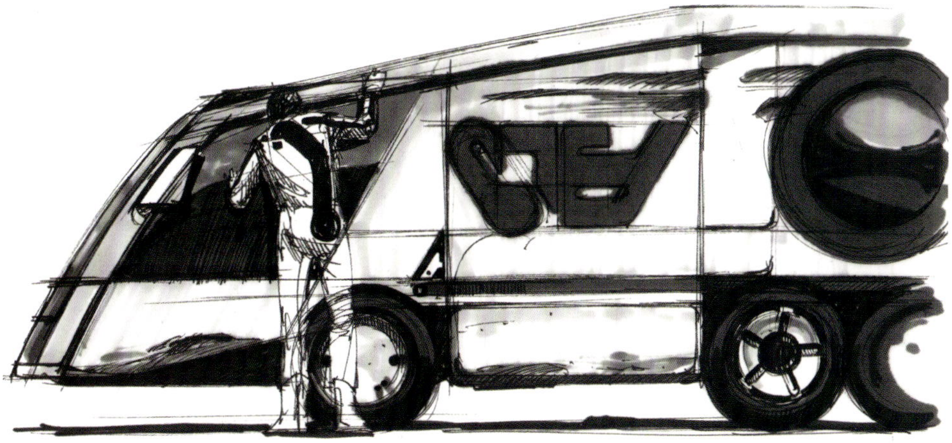

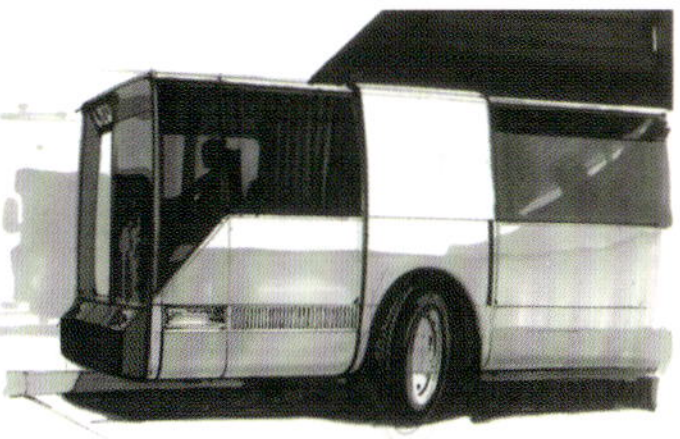

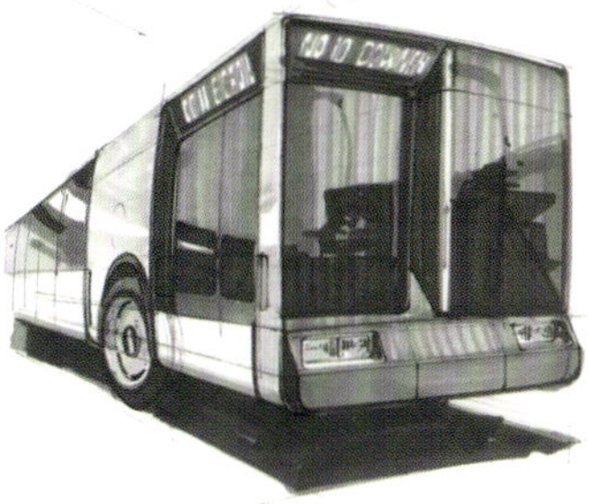

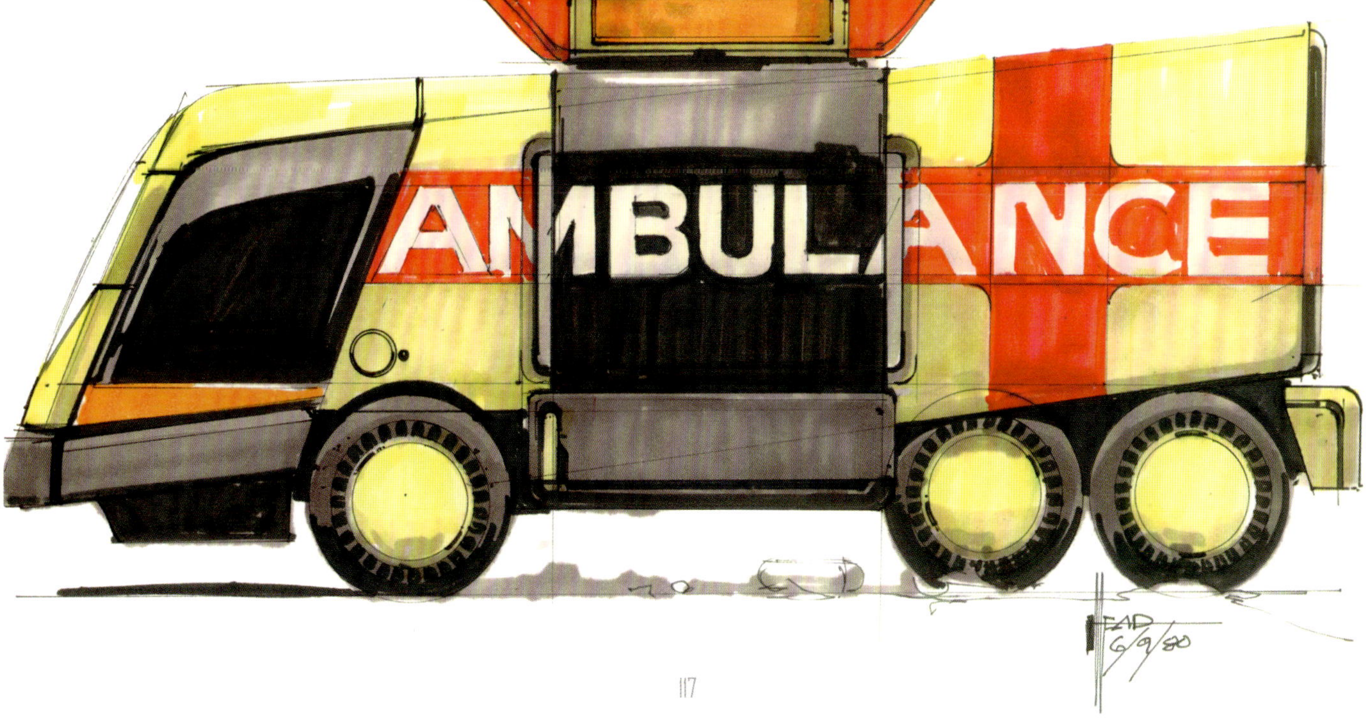

events as they unfold. That those images were initially created to support Mead's vision of the vehicles he had been asked to design is one of the great attributions of contemporary artistic process, and one that rewards immersion in the drawings.

Mead's ability to create a template for those settings with little more than a colored marker set the bar for the film's designer, Lawrence Paul, who, in Syd's words "just went for it!"

RIGHT: ROUGH SKETCHES OF THE SKYLINE SHOWING THE COMPLEXITY AND SPRAWL OF THE CITY. THE WILD VARIATIONS IN BUILDING HEIGHT SERVE TO REMIND US THIS IS A NEW WORLD AND A NEW FUTURE, SEEN STARKLY IN THE RECOGNISABLE OUTLINES OF MODERN DAY SKYSCRAPERS DWARFED BY THE COLOSSAL SCALE OF THE REST OF THE CITY.

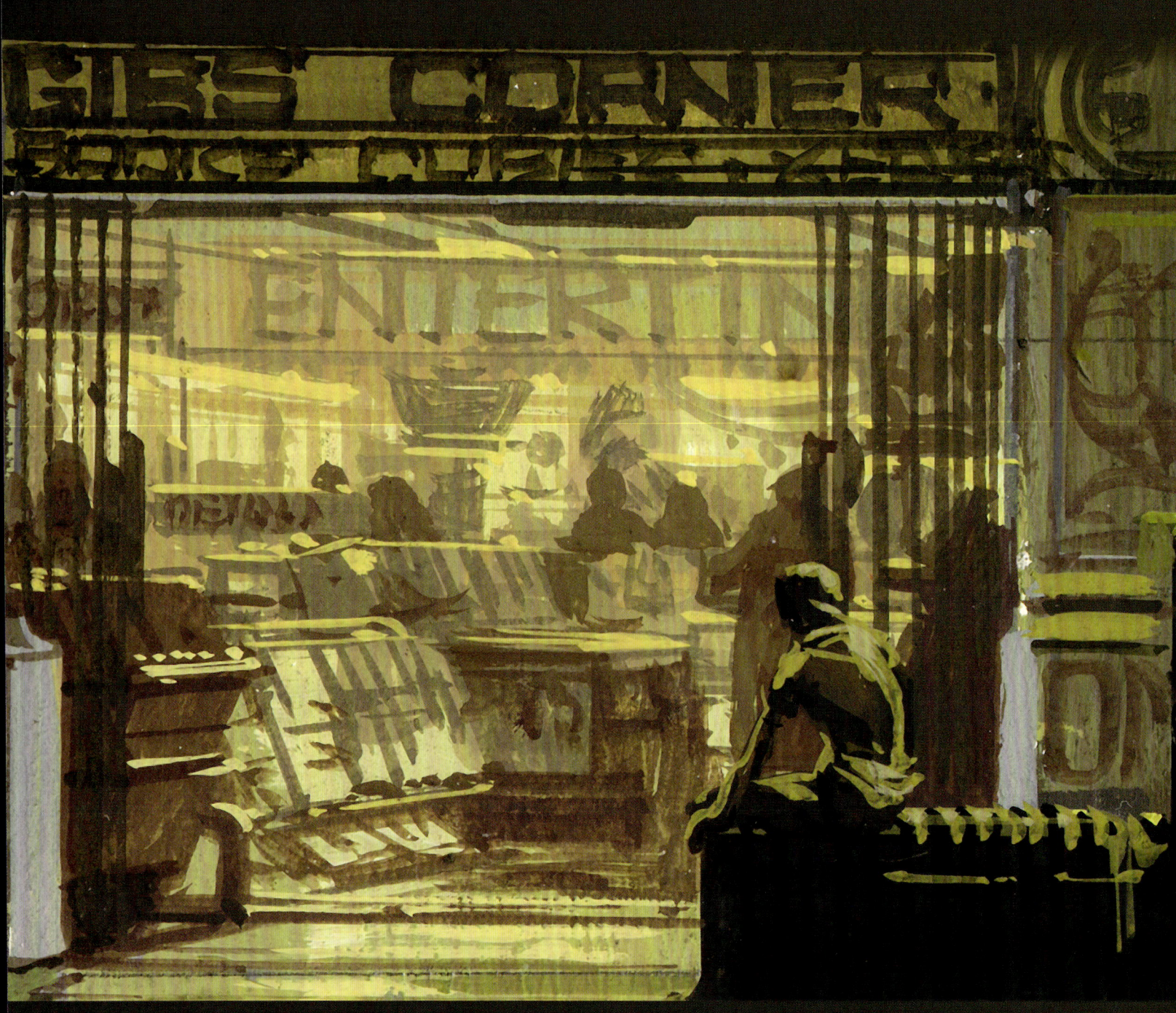

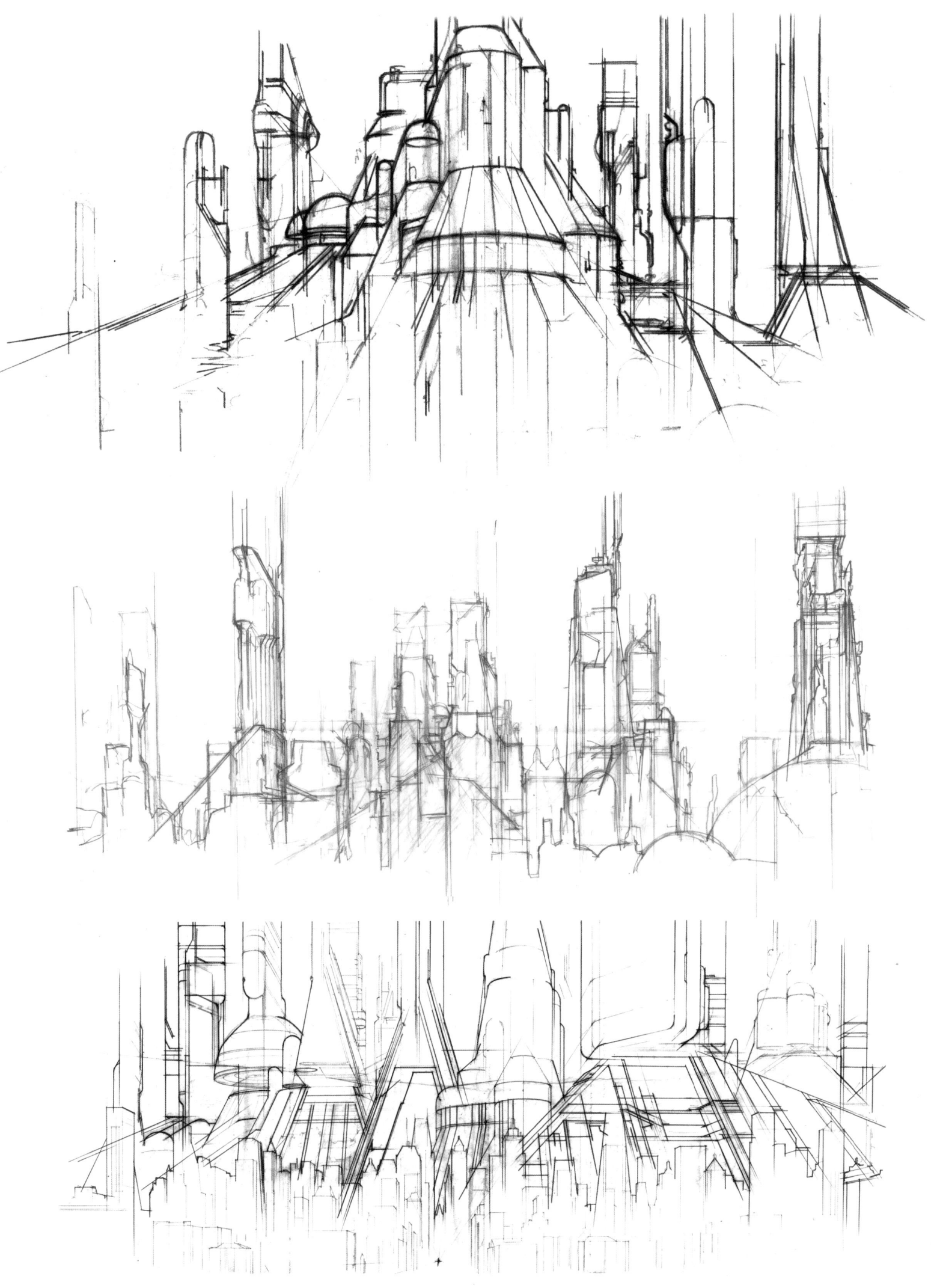

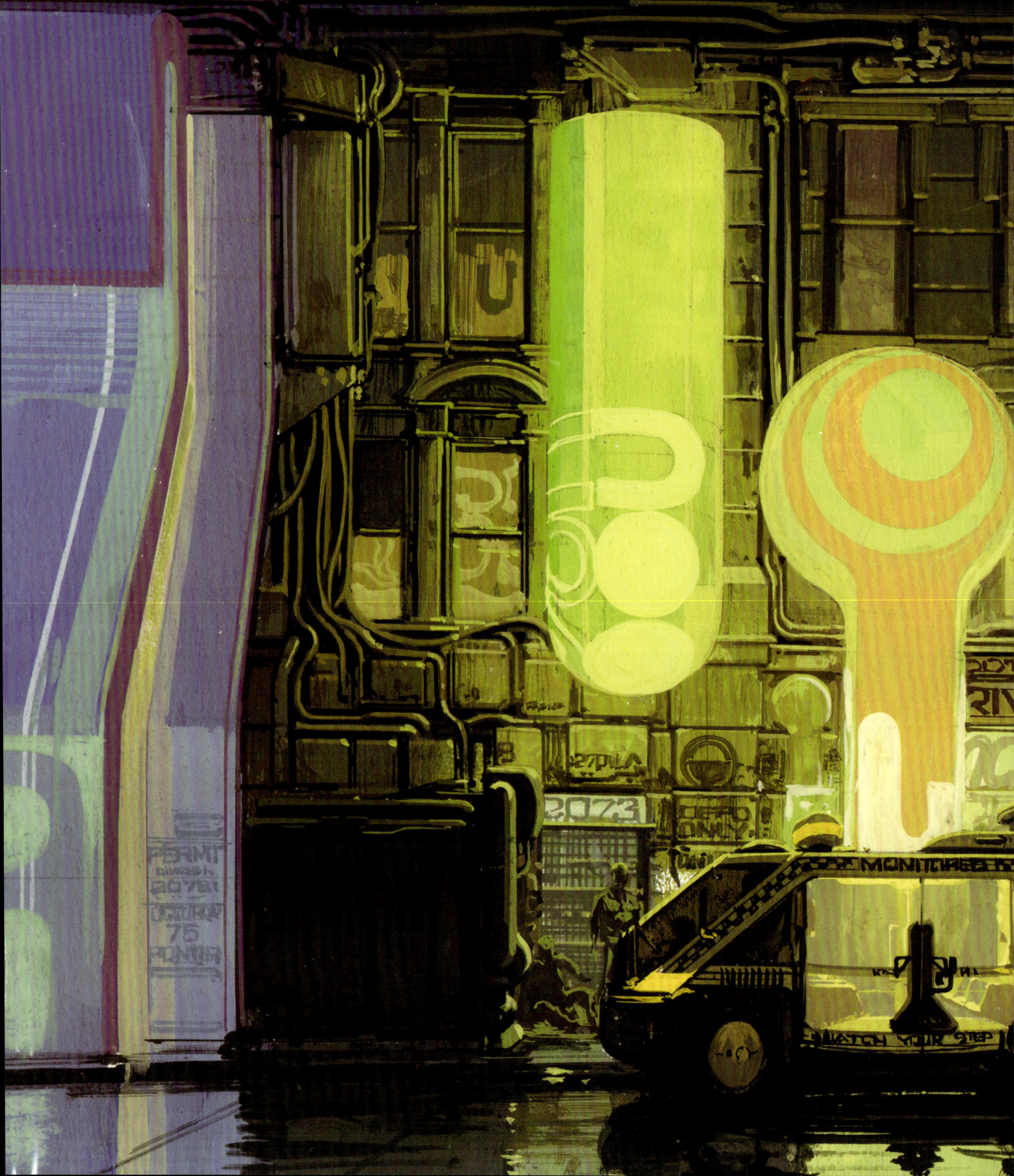

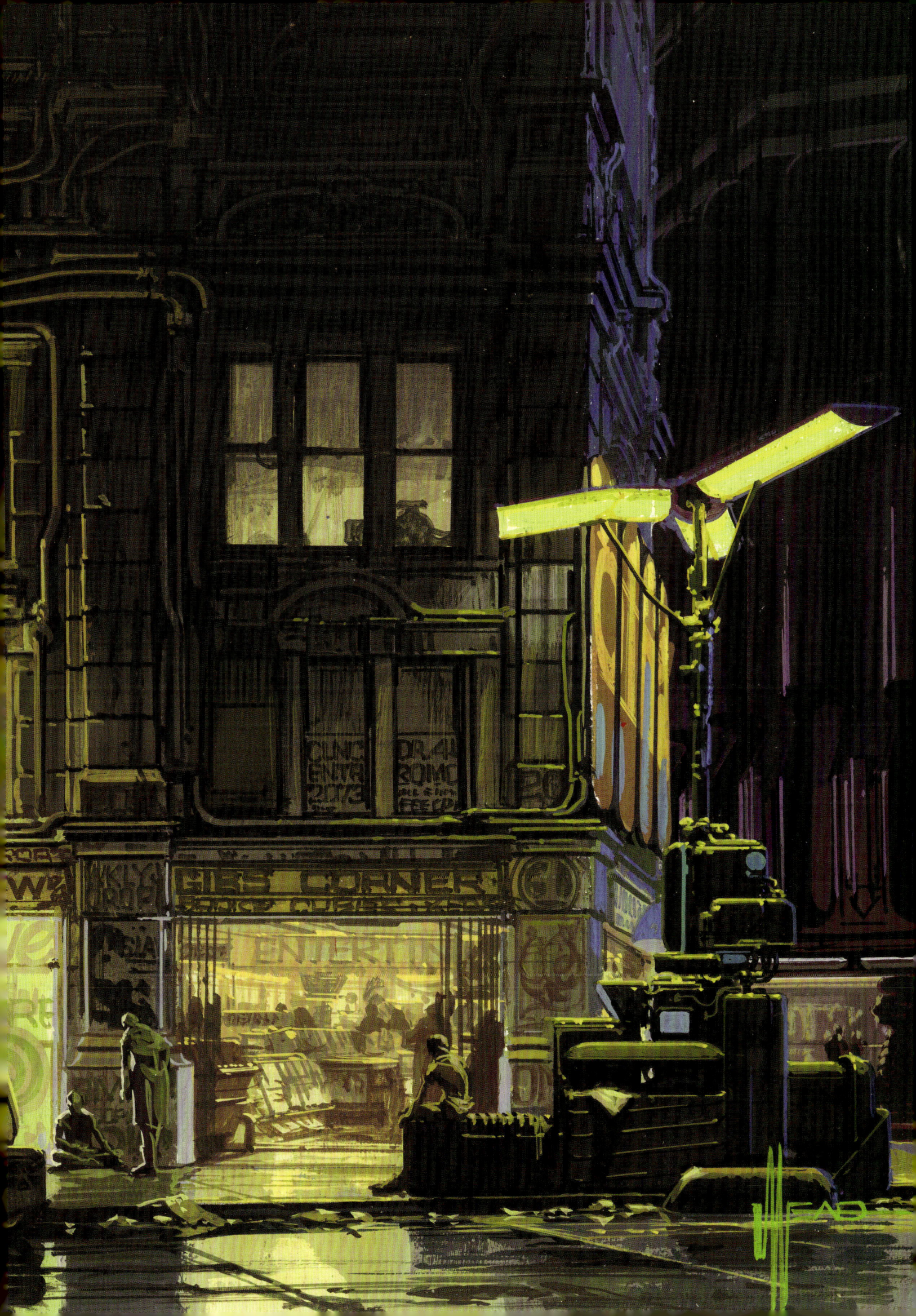

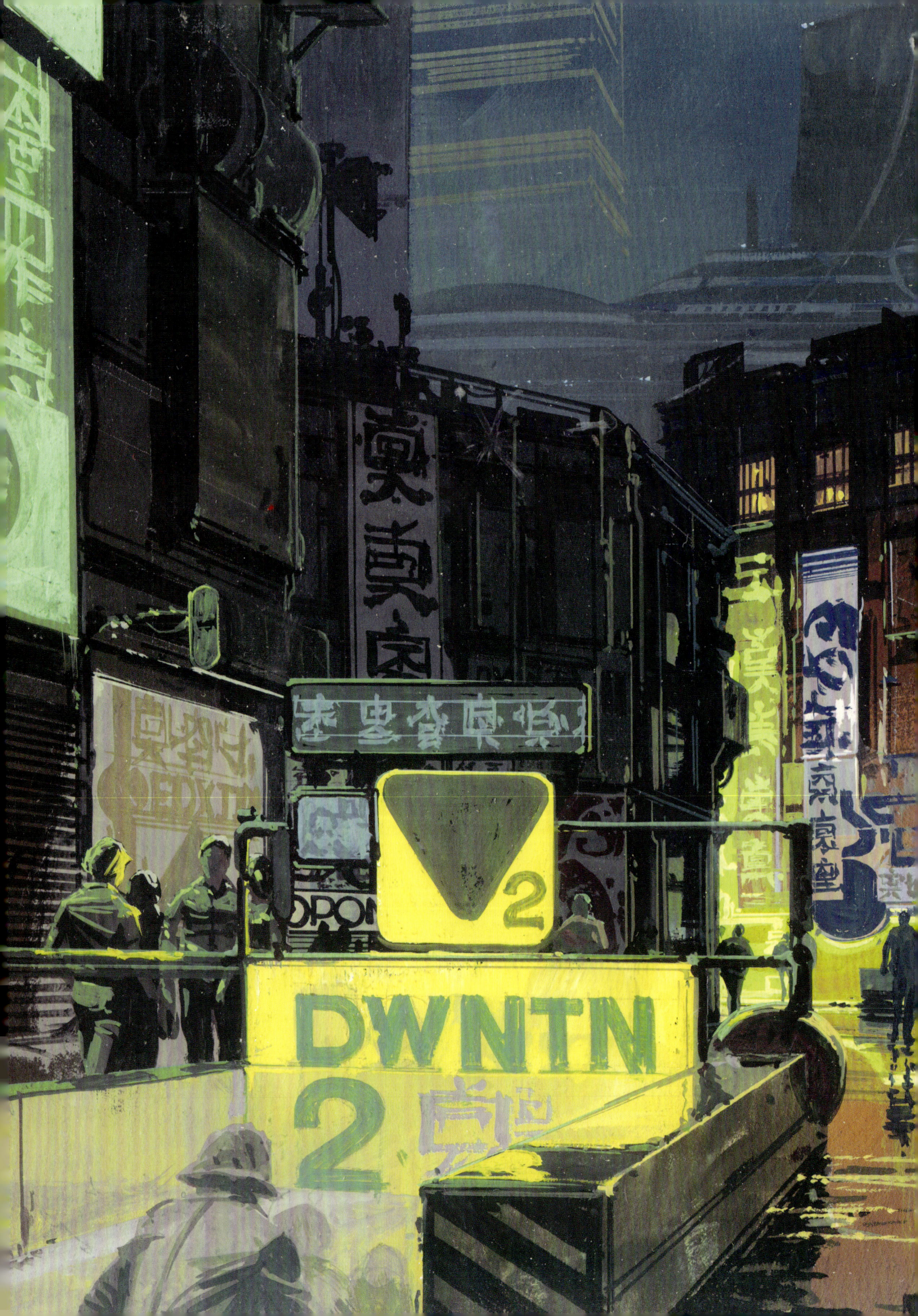

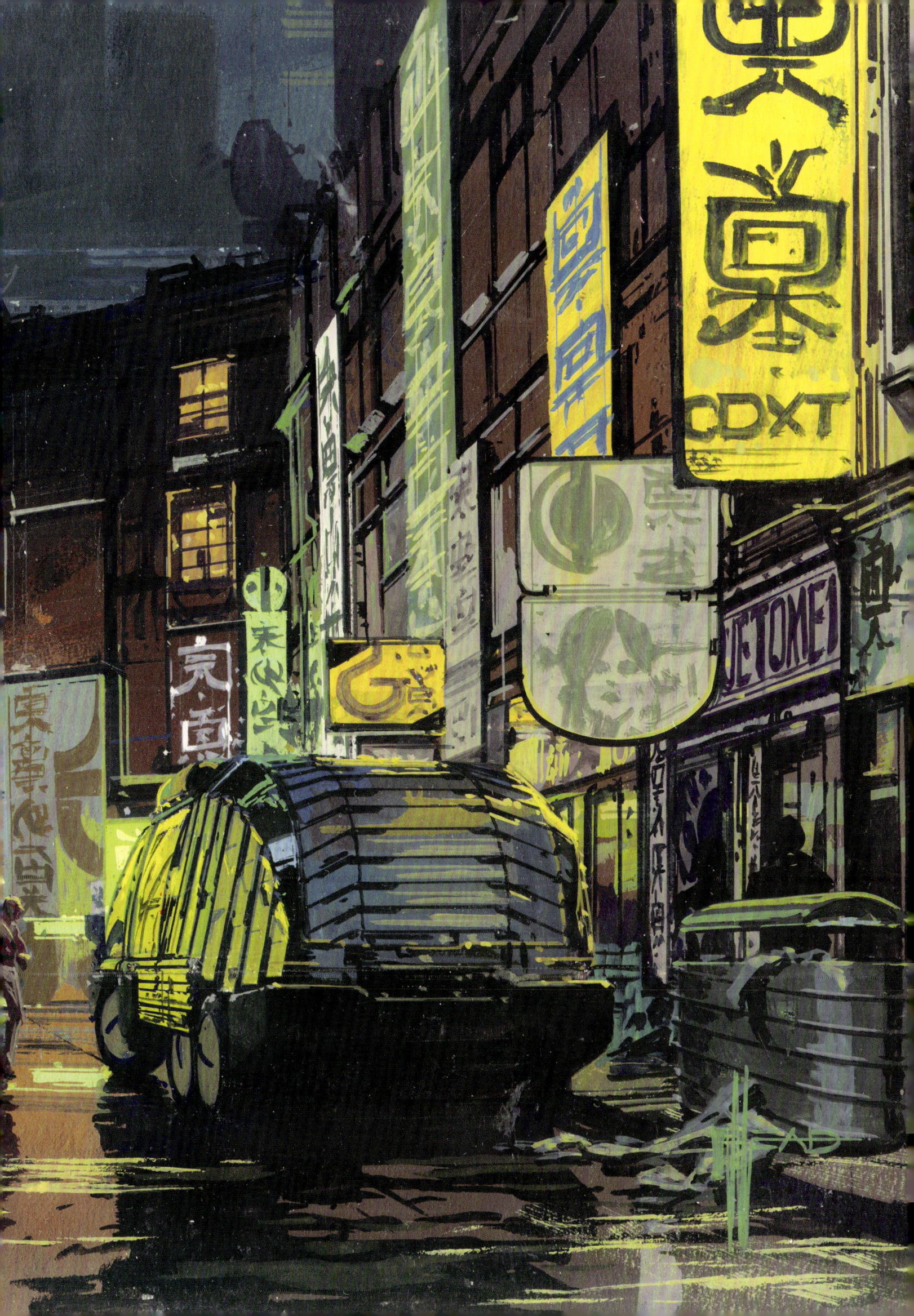

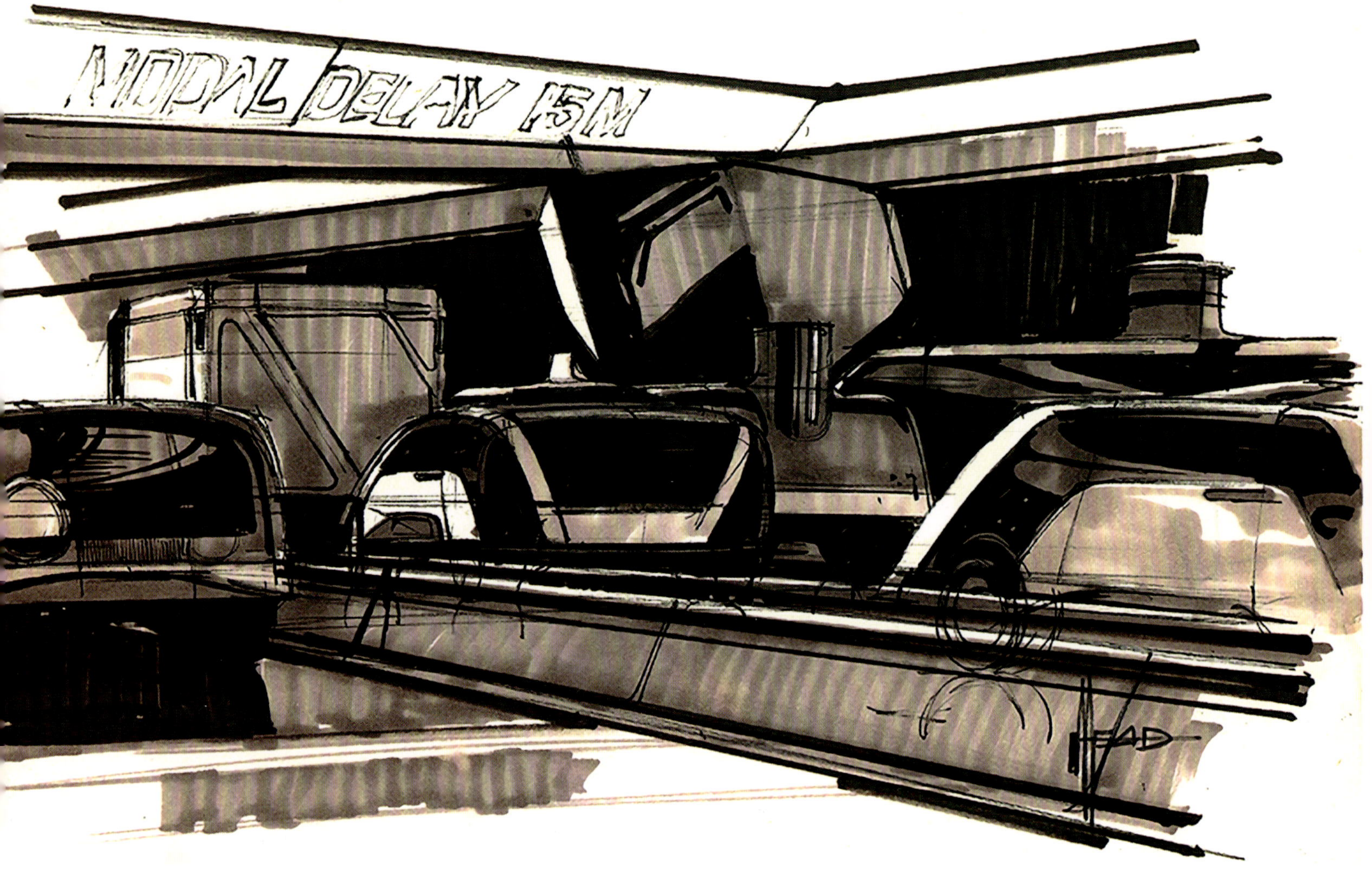

DENSE WITH DETAIL (PREVIOUS PAGES), PUNCTUATED BY BLINDING ILLUMINATED
ADVERTISING HUNG FROM DILAPIDATED BUILDINGS WITH A SCUM OF CABLES AND GRIMY
BOXES, EVEN THE SHOP FRONTS OOZE A POISONED LIGHT, AS THOUGH THE CITY HAD
GIVEN UP ON ITSELF, AND SUCCUMBED TO AN UNSPEAKABLE DEBILITATING DISEASE.

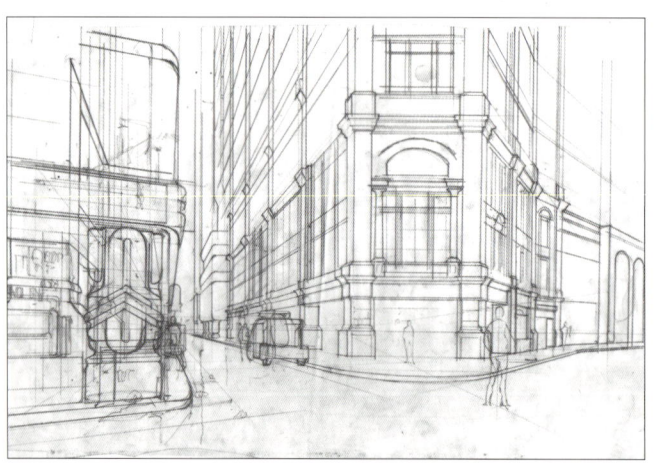

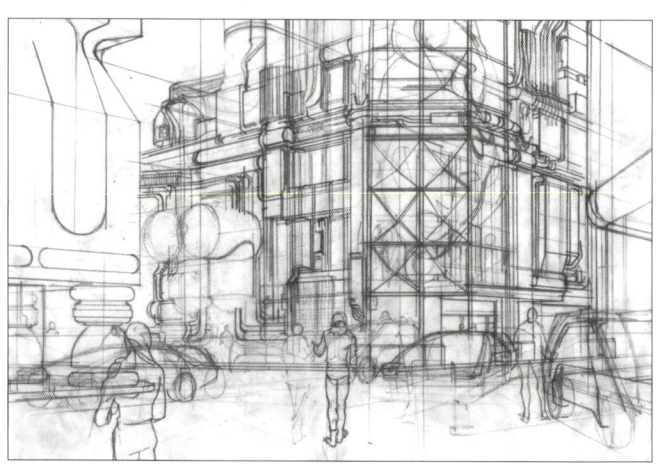

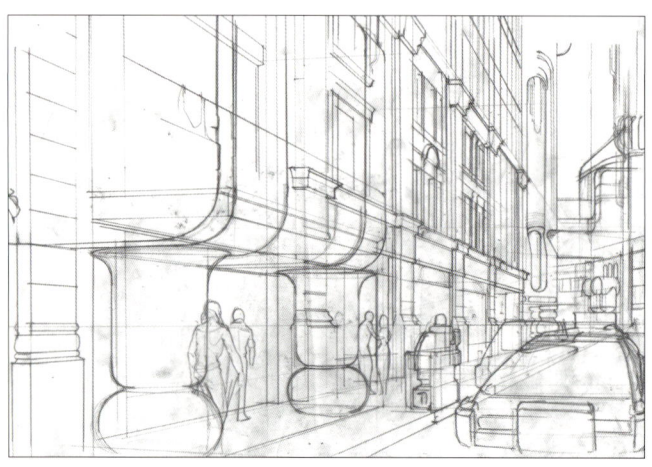

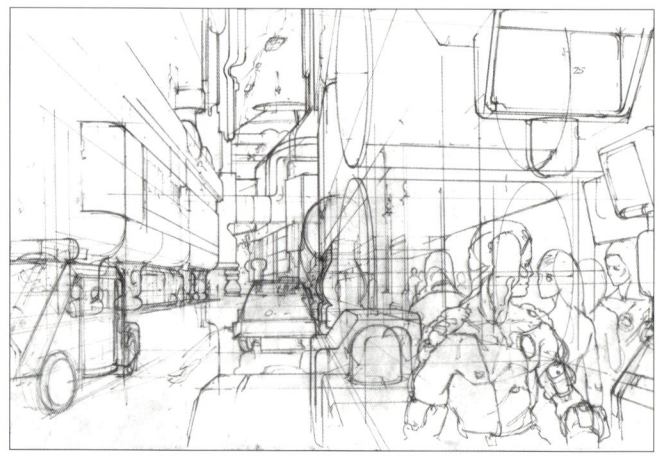

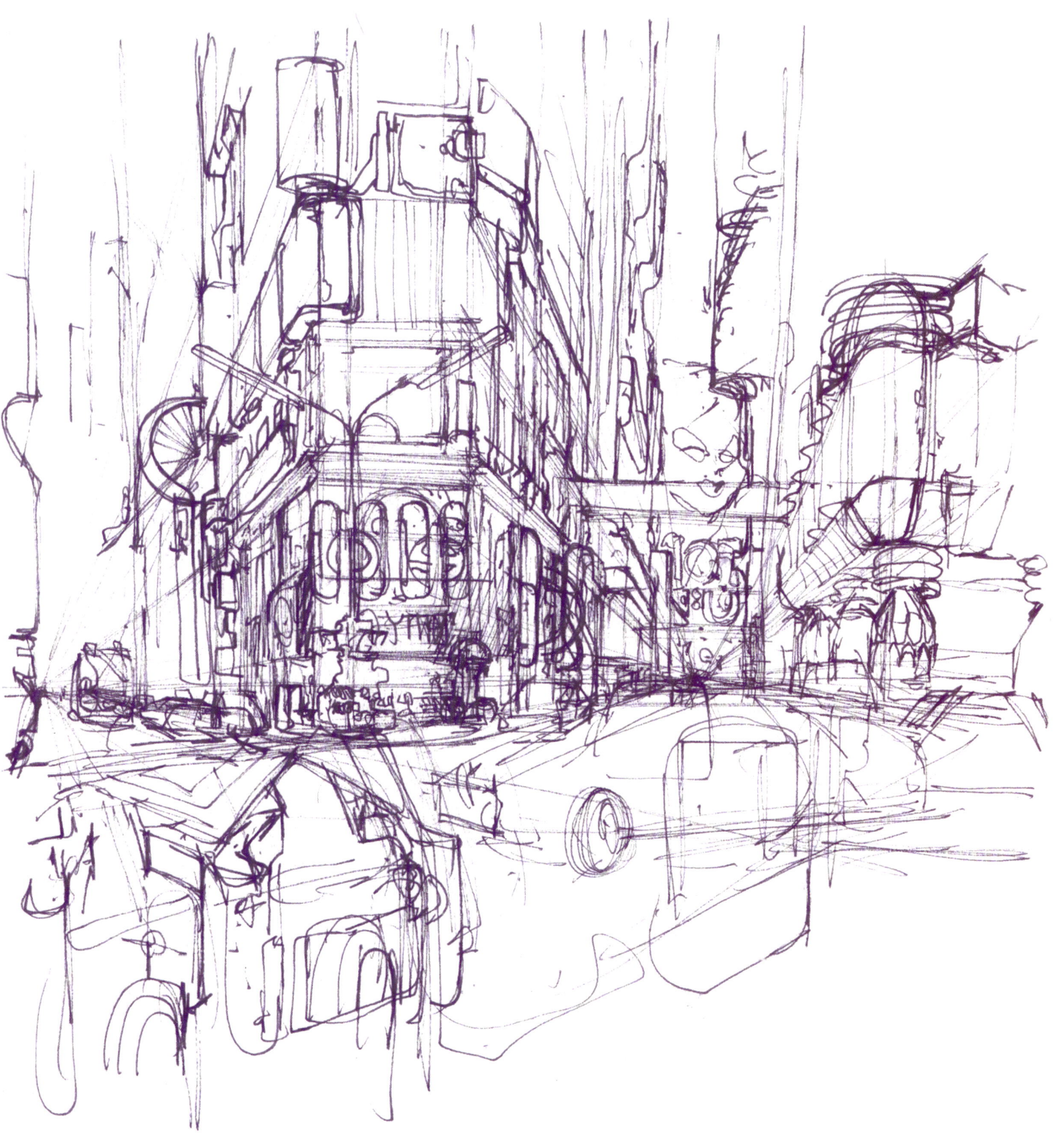

Mead's portrayal of the city touched a nerve. Architects, galvanized by the images, proffered their own visions of a heroic yet corroding architecture. Shades, shadows, and volumes on a par with the legendary architectural visions of Hugh Ferris articulate a skyline full of foreboding.

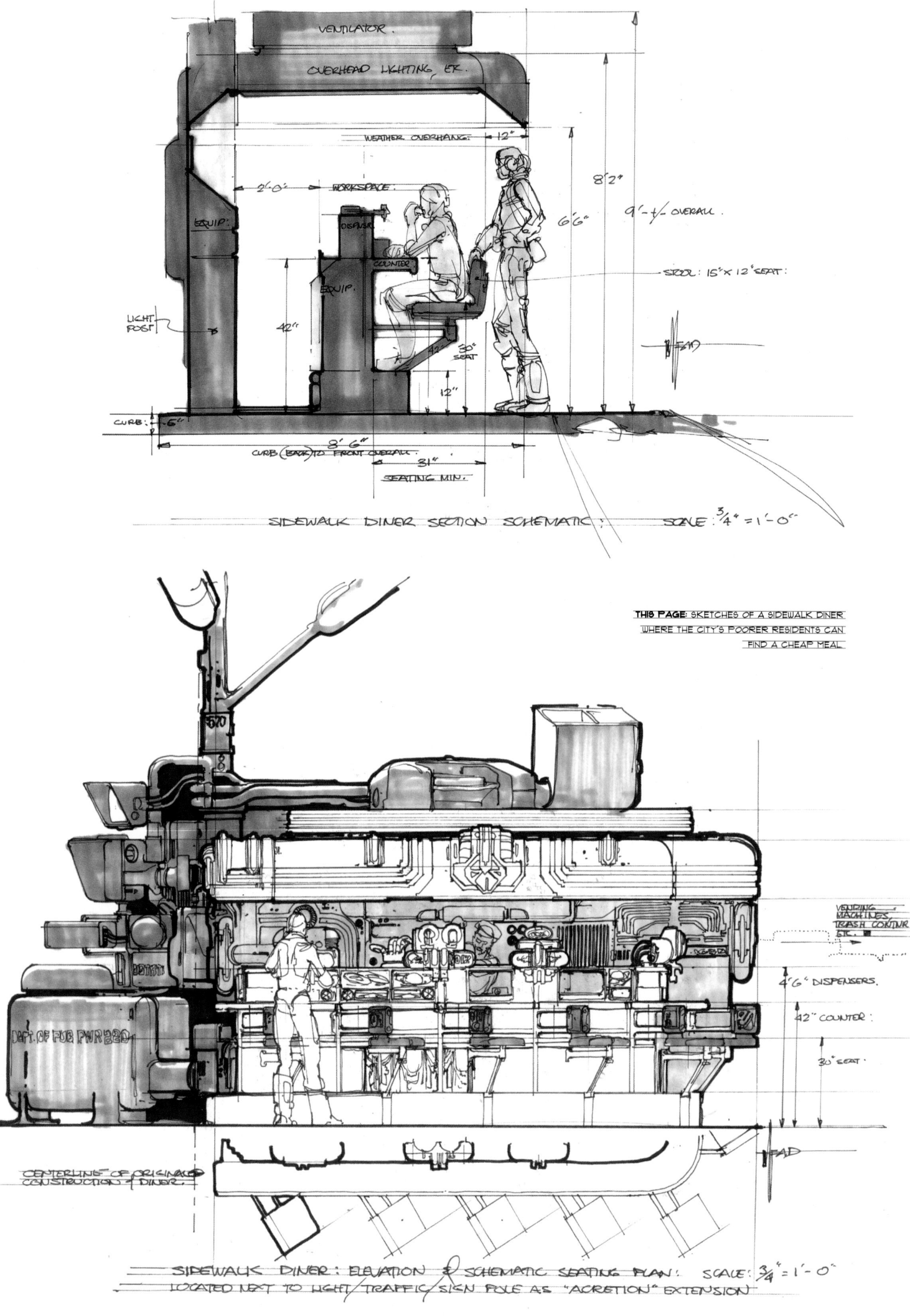

VENTILATOR

OVERHEAD LIGHTING, ETC.

WEATHER OVERHANG: 12"

WORKSPACE: 2'-0"

EQUIP:

DISPENSER

COUNTER

EQUIP.

LIGHT POST

42"

12" SEAT

30" SEAT

12"

CURB: 6"

8'-2"

6'-6"

9'-± OVERALL.

STOOL: 15" x 12" SEAT:

8'-6"

CURB (BACK) TO FRONT OVERALL.

31" SEATING MIN.

SIDEWALK DINER SECTION SCHEMATIC: SCALE: 3/4" = 1'-0"

DEPT. OF PUB. PWR. 220

VENDING MACHINES TRASH CONTAINERS, ETC.

4'-6" DISPENSERS.

42" COUNTER.

30" SEAT.

CENTERLINE OF ORIGINAL CONSTRUCTION OF DINER.

SIDEWALK DINER: ELEVATION & SCHEMATIC SEATING PLAN.   SCALE: 3/4" = 1'-0"
LOCATED NEXT TO LIGHT/TRAFFIC/SIGN POLE AS "ACRETION" EXTENSION

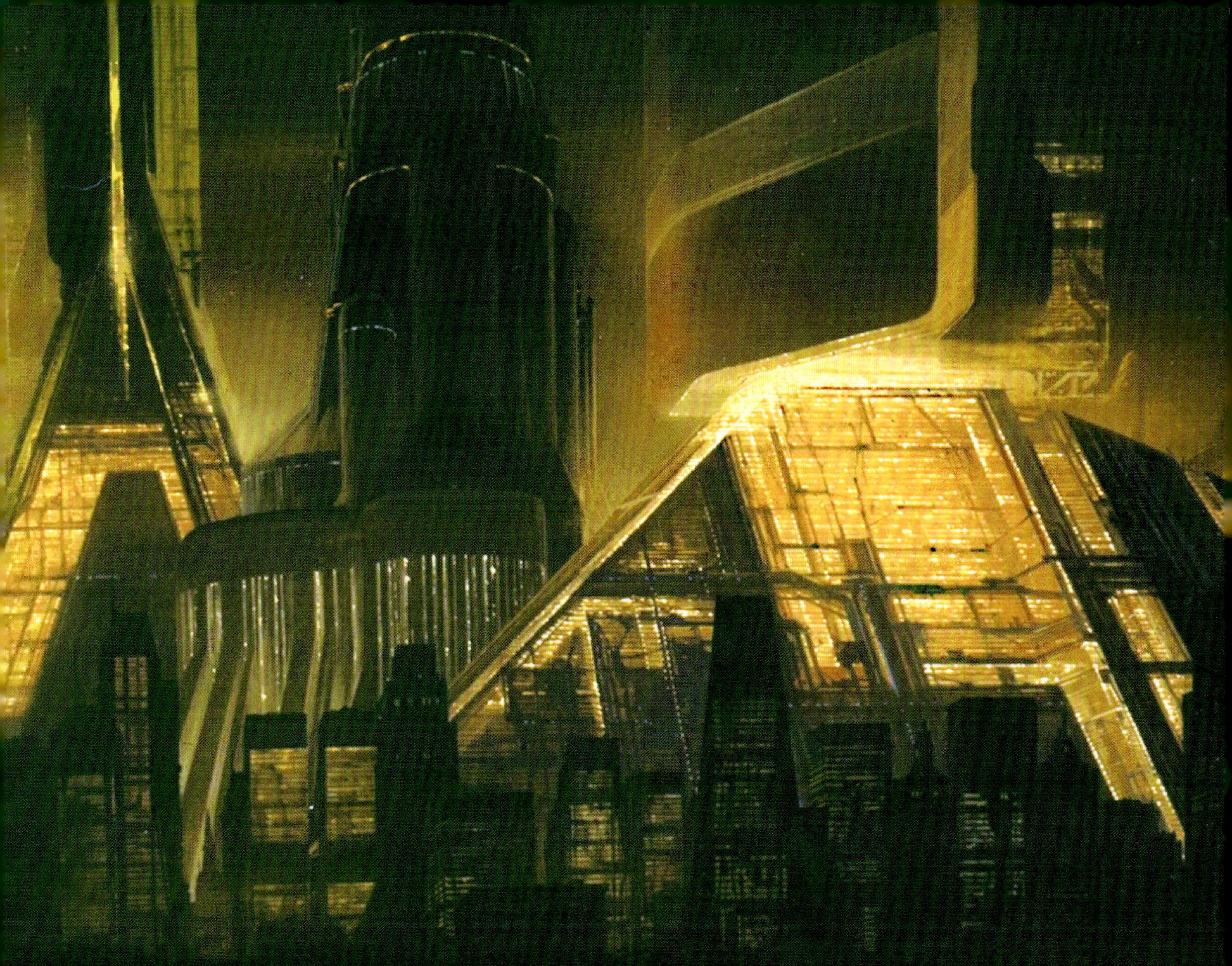

Here, Mead's command of light inspired director and cinematographer alike, resulting in one of cinema's most indelible sequences as Deckard searches for Sebastian.

Luxury megastructures tower over the corroded streets to emphasize the wealth and privilege of Tyrell, the replicant's 'father', who inhabits them with an artificial owl and his replicant mistress. Asked by her if he ever 'retired' a human by mistake, Deckard demurs.

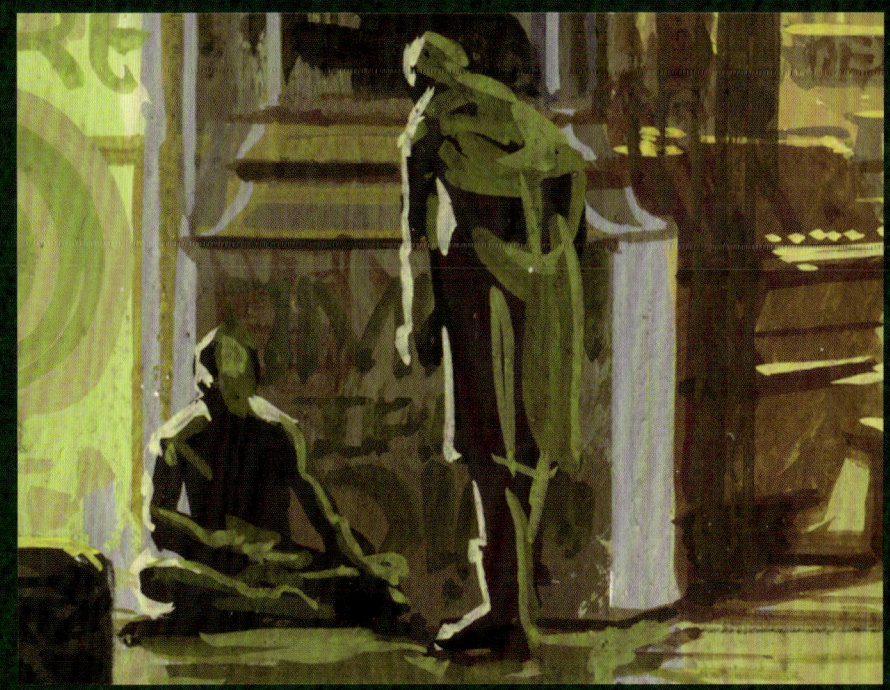

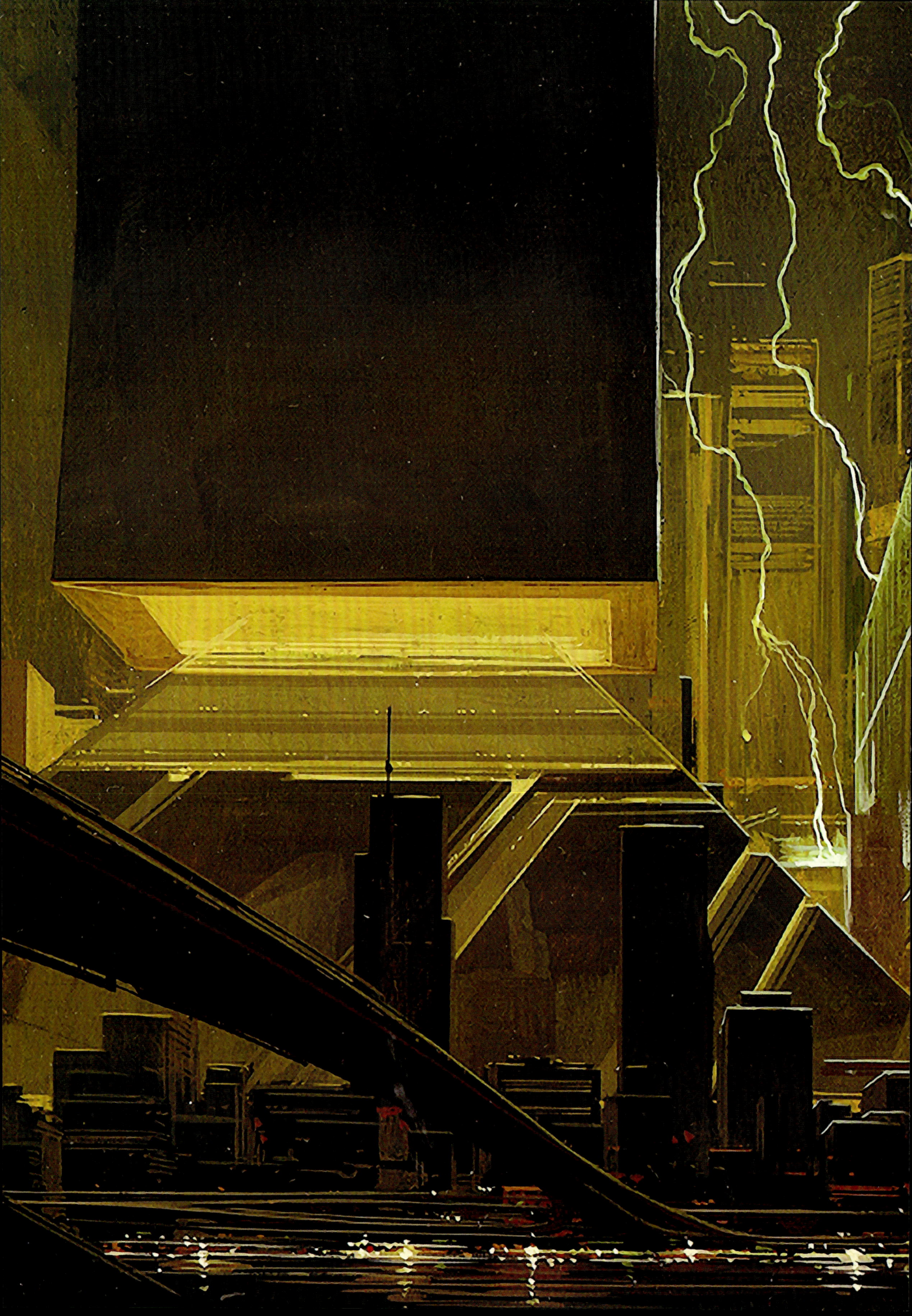

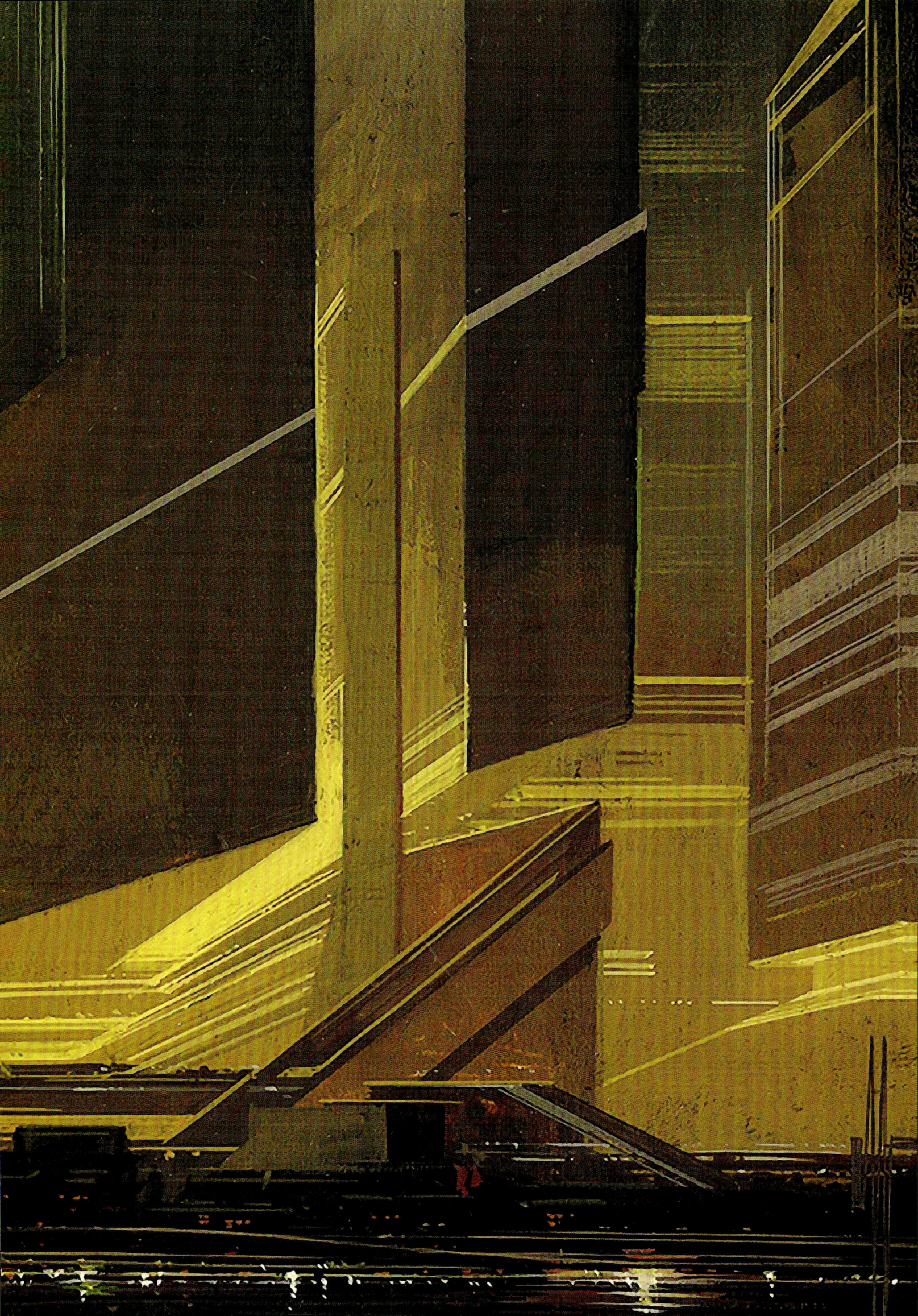

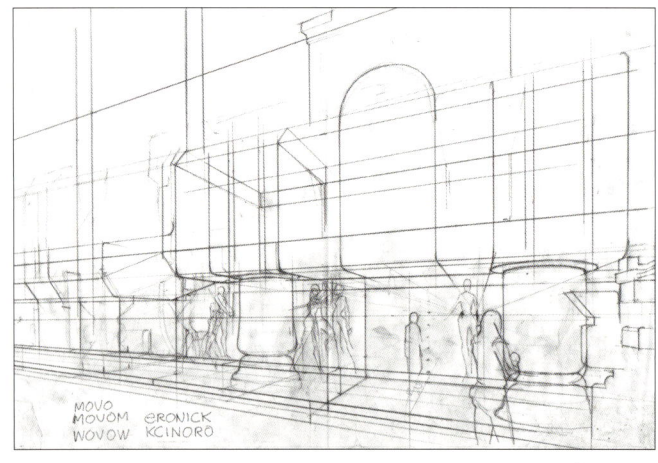

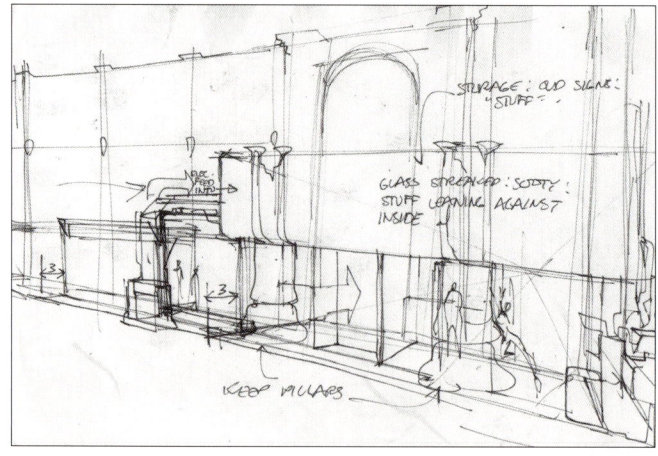

The seedy storefront lab where the sequin from an artificial snake is deciphered departed from Mead's concept to become a den of visqueen drapes and harsh fluorescent lights under which vats of liquid nitrogen released white clouds of steam.

With a nod to the streets of Hong Kong and 1960s Times Square, the storefronts in *Blade Runner* exude a sordid atmosphere, perfectly expressed here with pallid lighting – a 'hole-in-the-wall' setting which contrasts with the worn masonry of decaying structures.

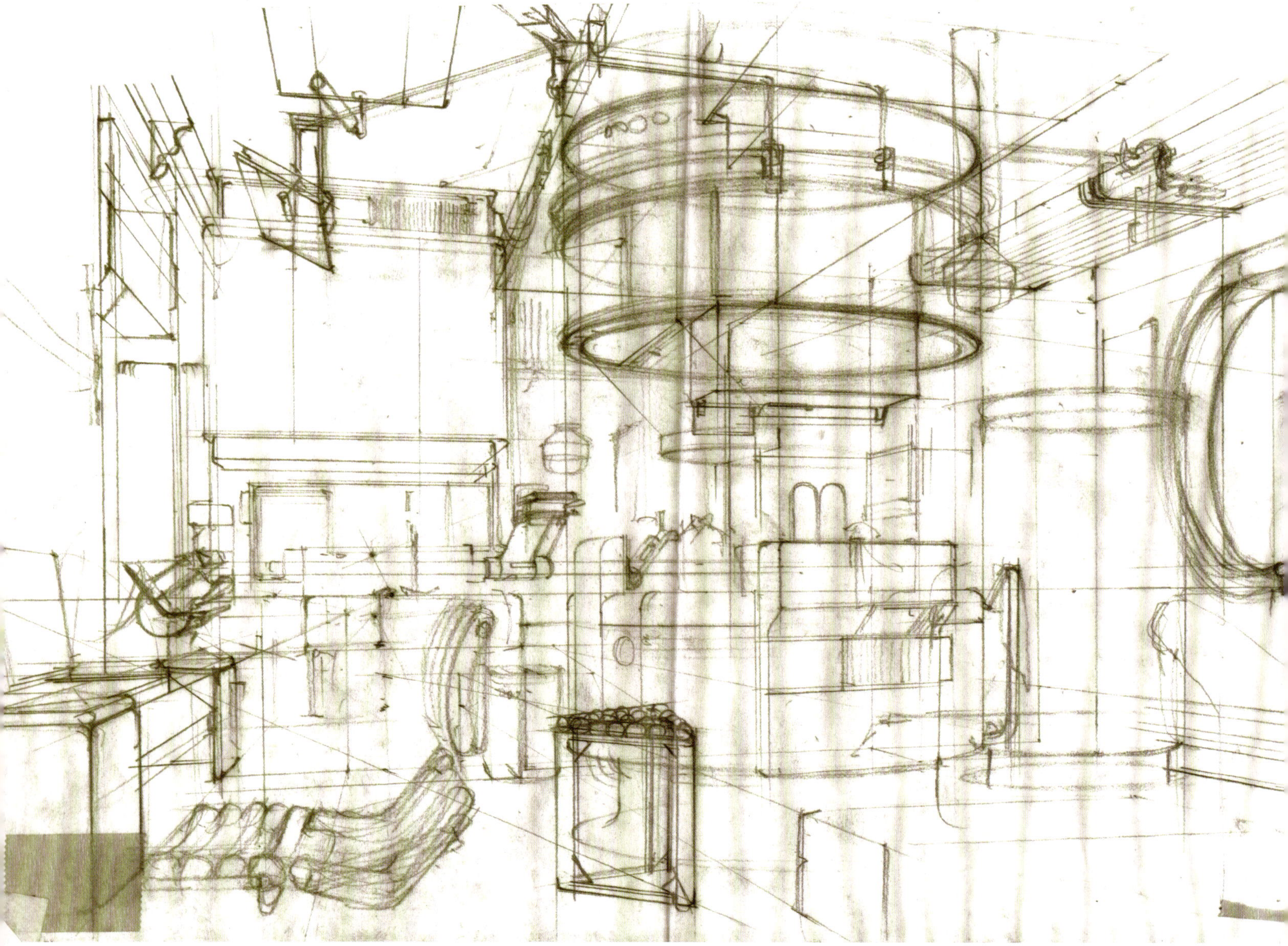

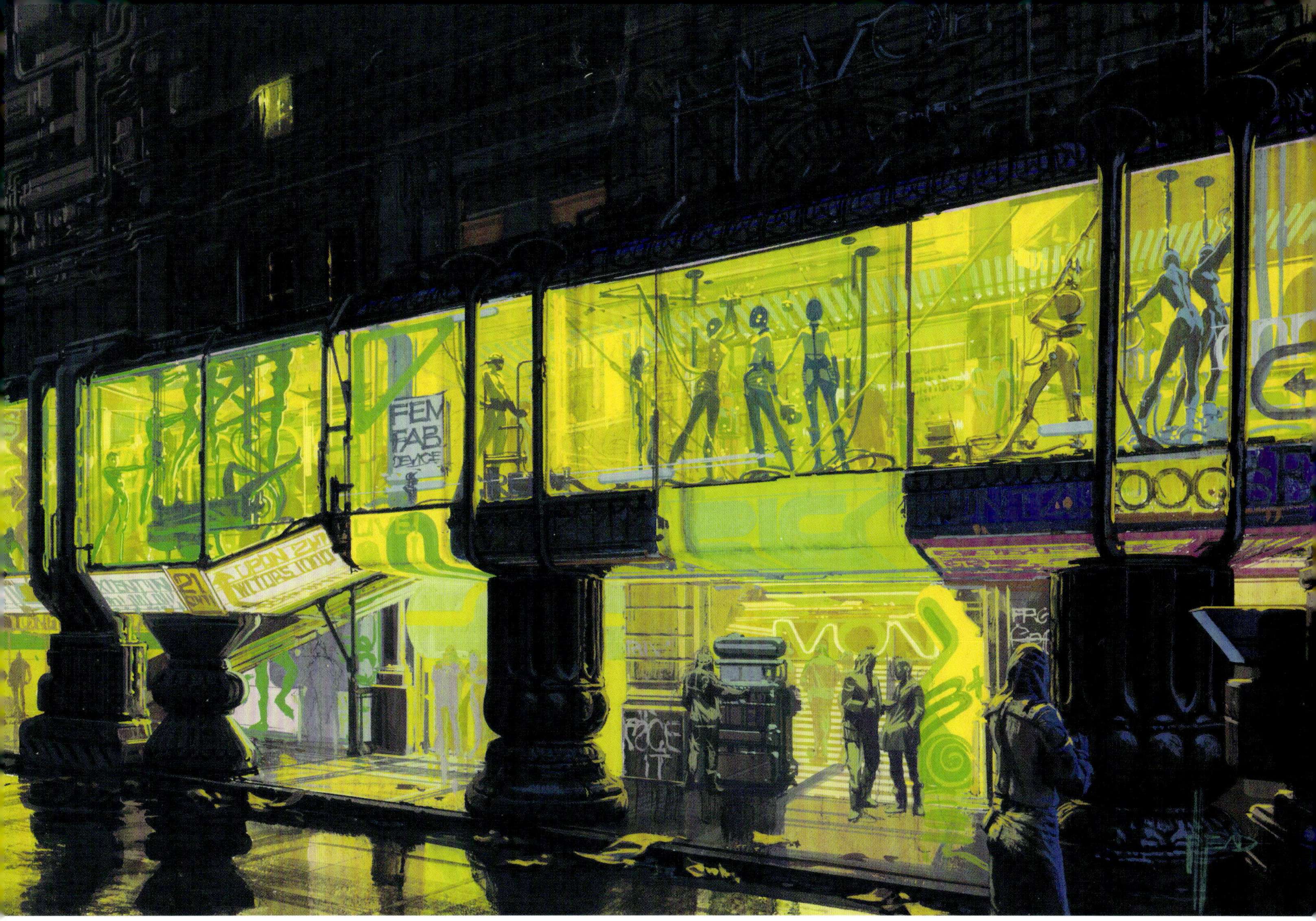
FEM
FAB
DEVICE

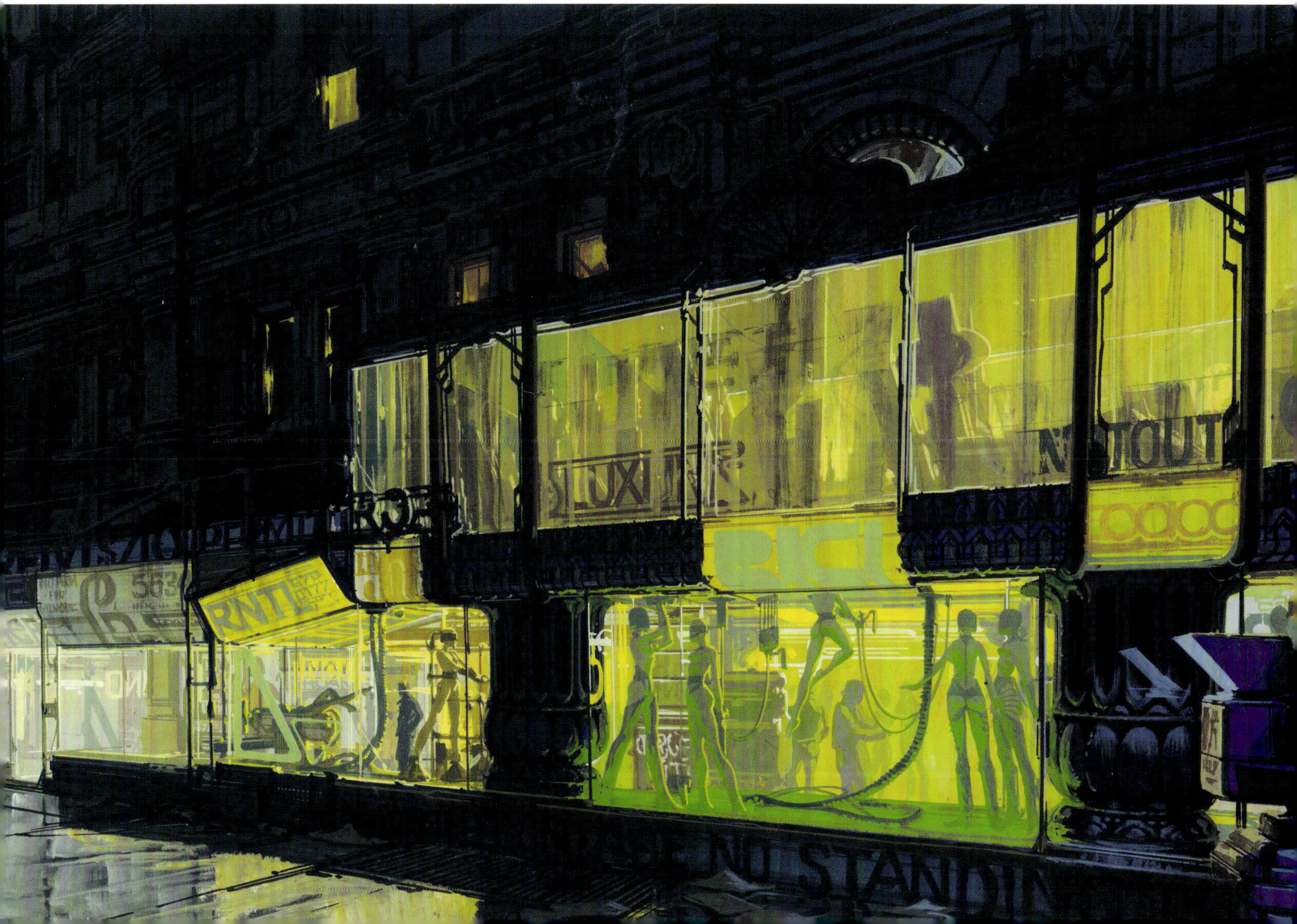

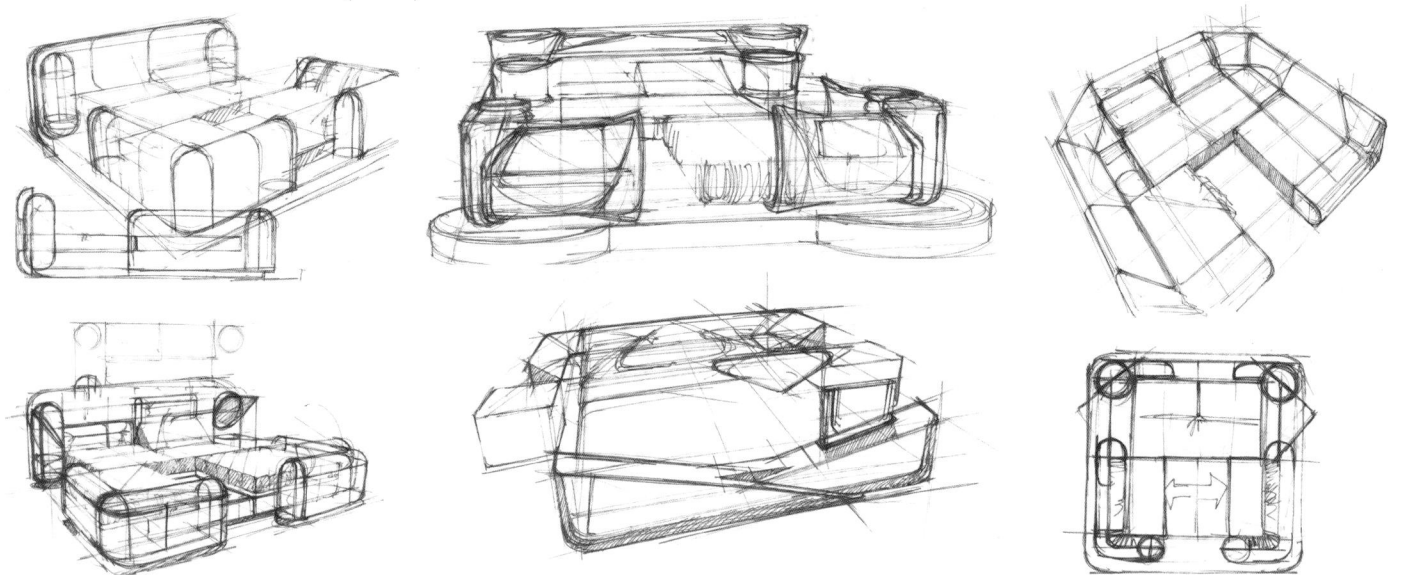

Deckard's cramped apartment, jammed with tech and analytic devices, was to be full of contradictions. There was to be a piano keyboard alongside an automated kitchen, the futuristic tech surrounded by the detritus of a classic noir detective. There was only one problem—how to access the bed—which Mead solved by having the sections slide apart.

In today's increasingly congested cities, architects and city planners are proposing changes to city codes in order to promote the creation of 'micro-living units' much like the one designed by Mead for the film. Such units are already a reality and in use in various parts of the world, most notably Tokyo, where the demands of over-population are painfully apparent.

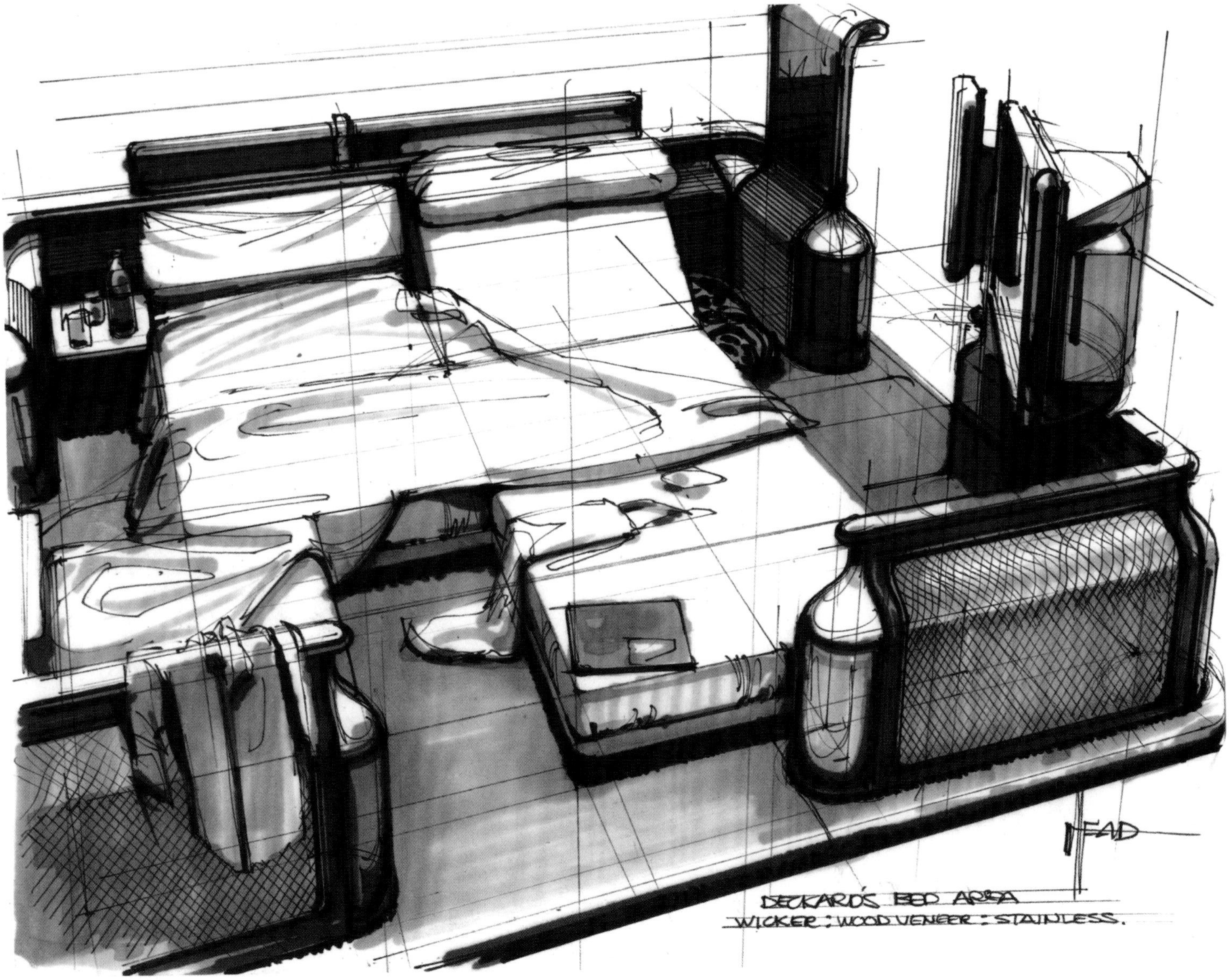

DECKARD'S BED AREA
WICKER : WOOD VENEER : STAINLESS.

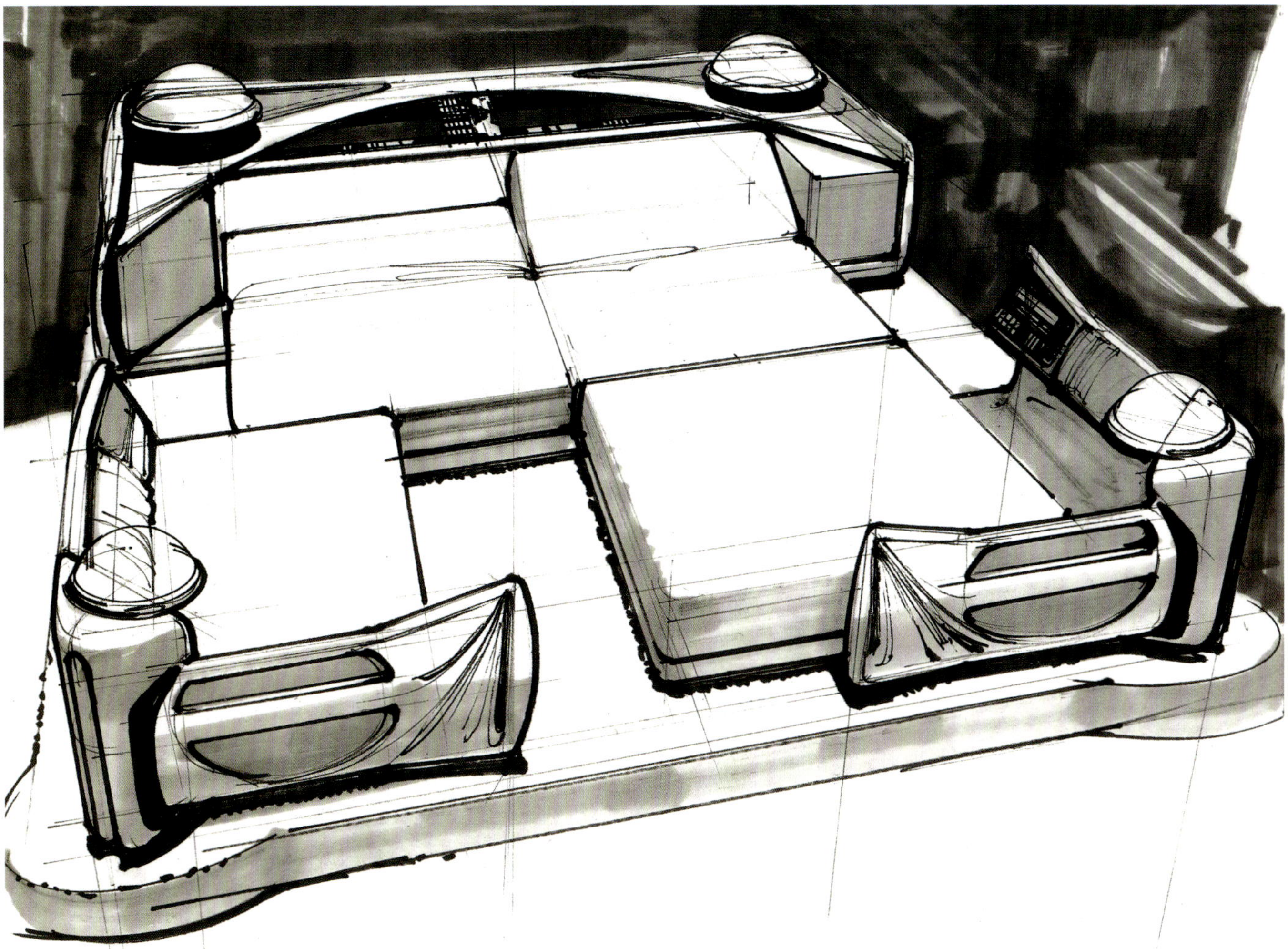

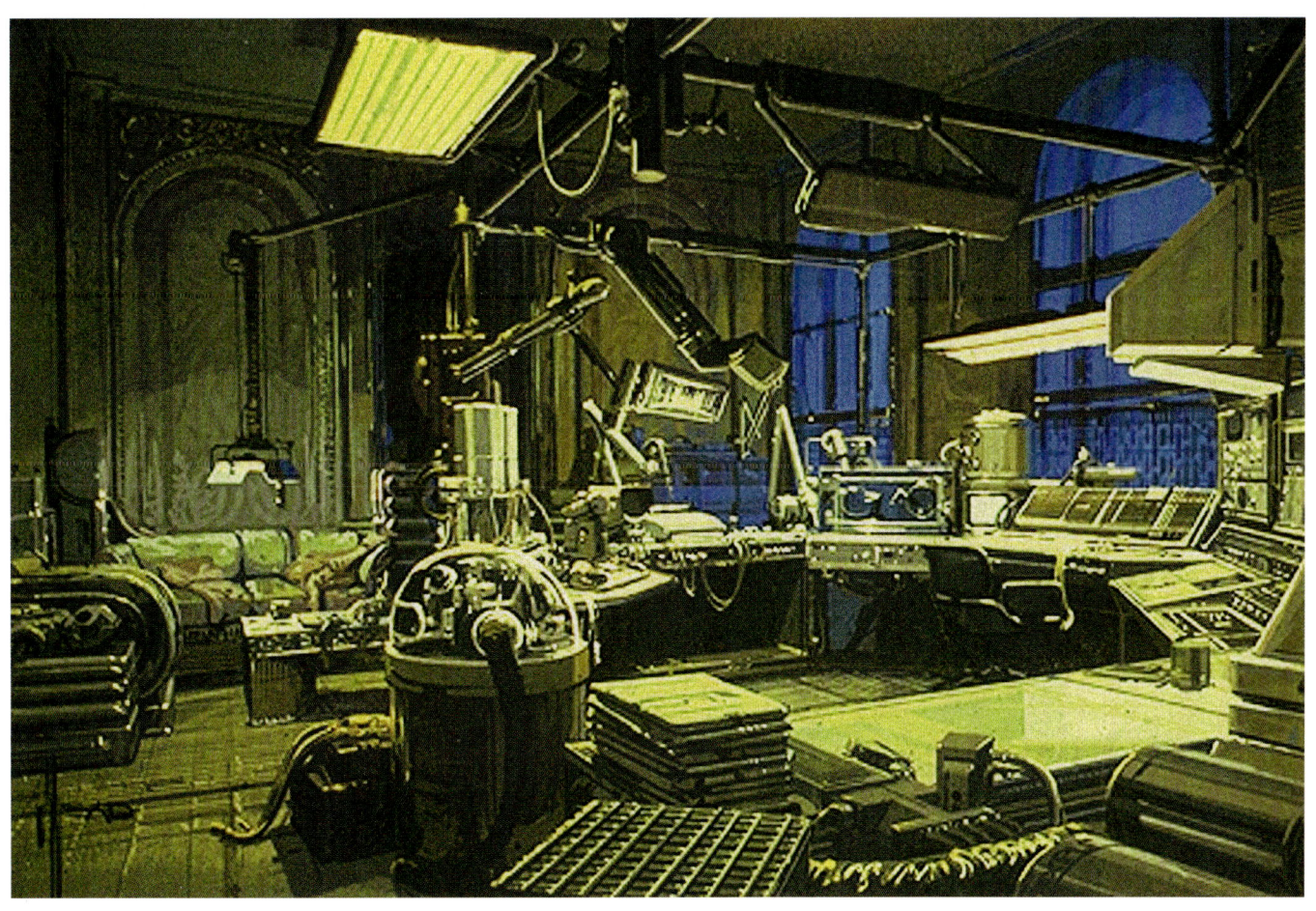

THIS SPREAD: FROM THE EARLIEST SKETCH TO THE FINAL RENDERING , THE EVOLUTION OF DECKARD'S APARTMENT
ARE SHOWN HERE, IN PARTICULAR THE INNOVATIVE APPROACH TO HIS BED.

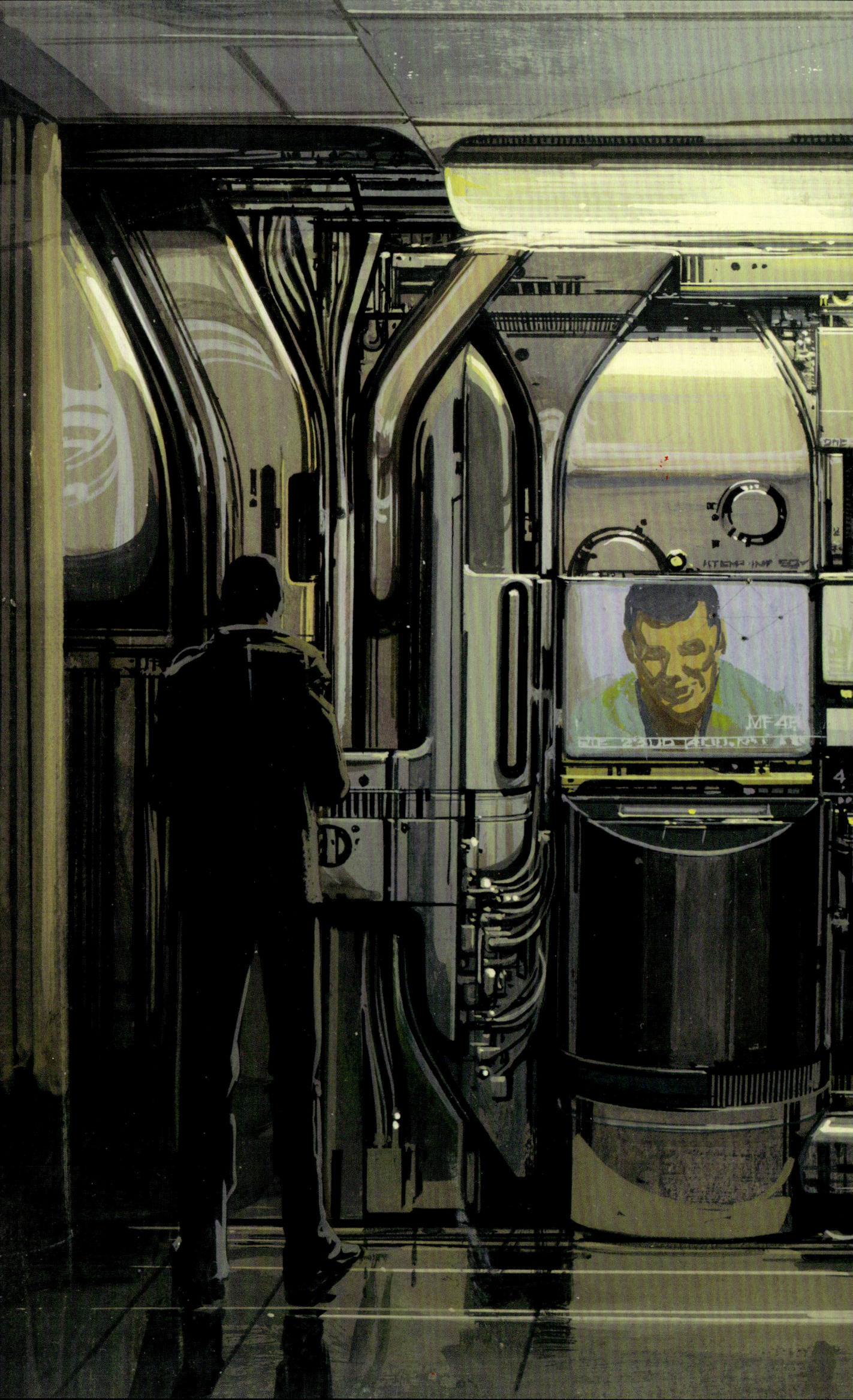

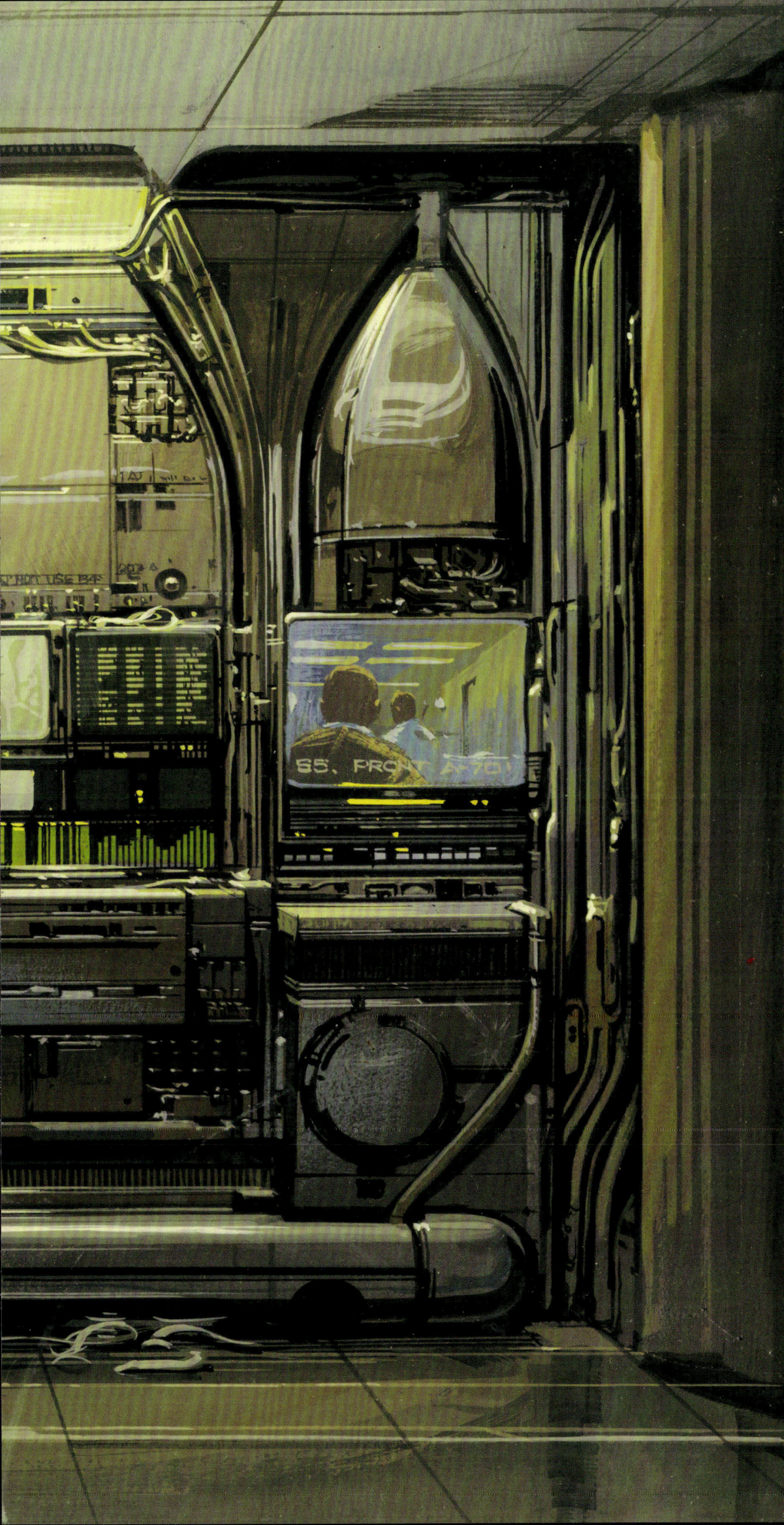

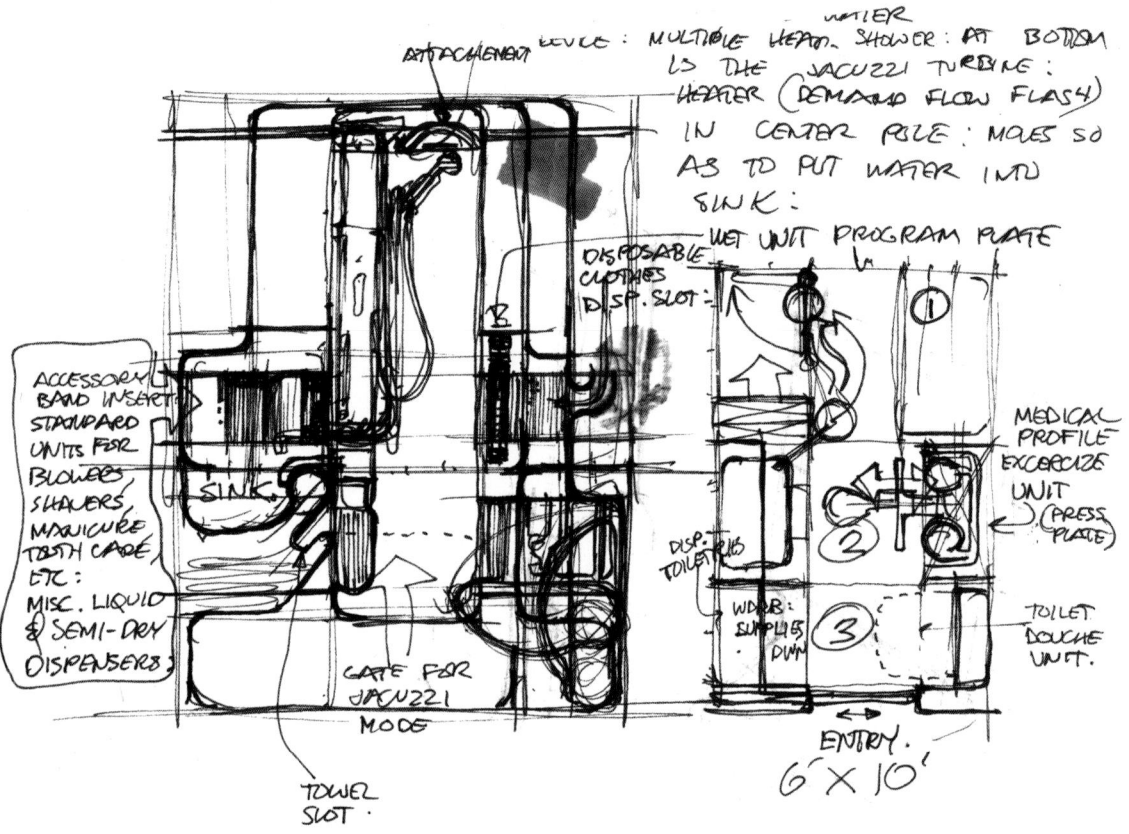

WATER
LOUVRE: MULTIPLE HEADS. SHOWER: AT BOTTOM
IS THE JACUZZI TURBINE:
HEATER (DEMAND FLOW FLASH)
IN CENTER POLE: MOVES SO
AS TO PUT WATER INTO
SINK:

ATTACHMENT

WET UNIT PROGRAM PLATE

DISPOSABLE
CLOTHES
DISP. SLOT:

ACCESSORY
BAND INSERT:
STANDARD
UNITS FOR
BLOWERS,
SHAVERS,
MANICURE,
TOOTH CARE,
ETC:
MISC. LIQUID
& SEMI-DRY
DISPENSERS:

SINK.

MEDICAL
PROFILE
EXCERCIZE
UNIT
(PRESS
PLATE)

DISP.
TOILETRIES

WDWR:
SUPPLIES
DWN

TOILET
DOUCHE
UNIT.

GATE FOR
JACUZZI
MODE

TOWEL
SLOT.

ENTRY.
6' X 10'

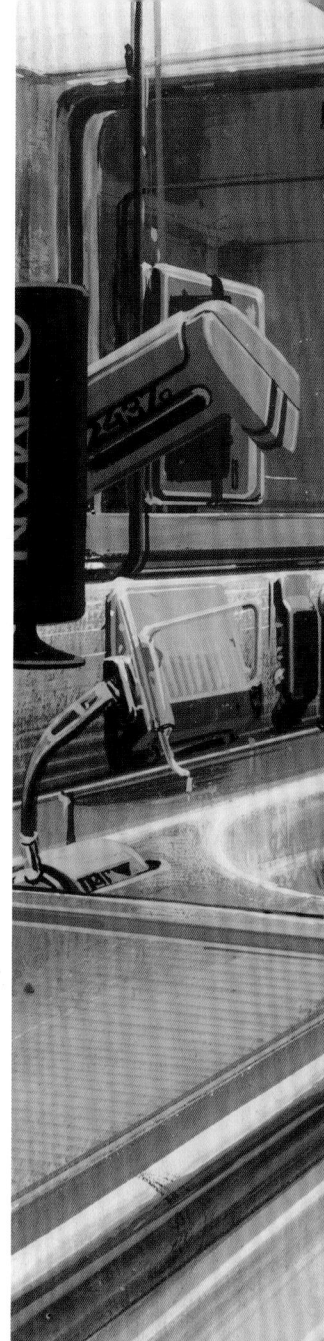

WHILE ON A TRAIN TO LOCATE SITES FOR THE FILM, SYD MEAD AND RIDLEY SCOTT TOOK
NOTE OF THE STAINLESS STEEL BATHROOM FITTED TO THEIR PULLMAN CAR WHERE,
TRANSPOSED TO THE TWENTY-FIRST CENTURY, IT SERVED AS THE PROTOTYPE FOR
DECKARD'S APARTMENT.

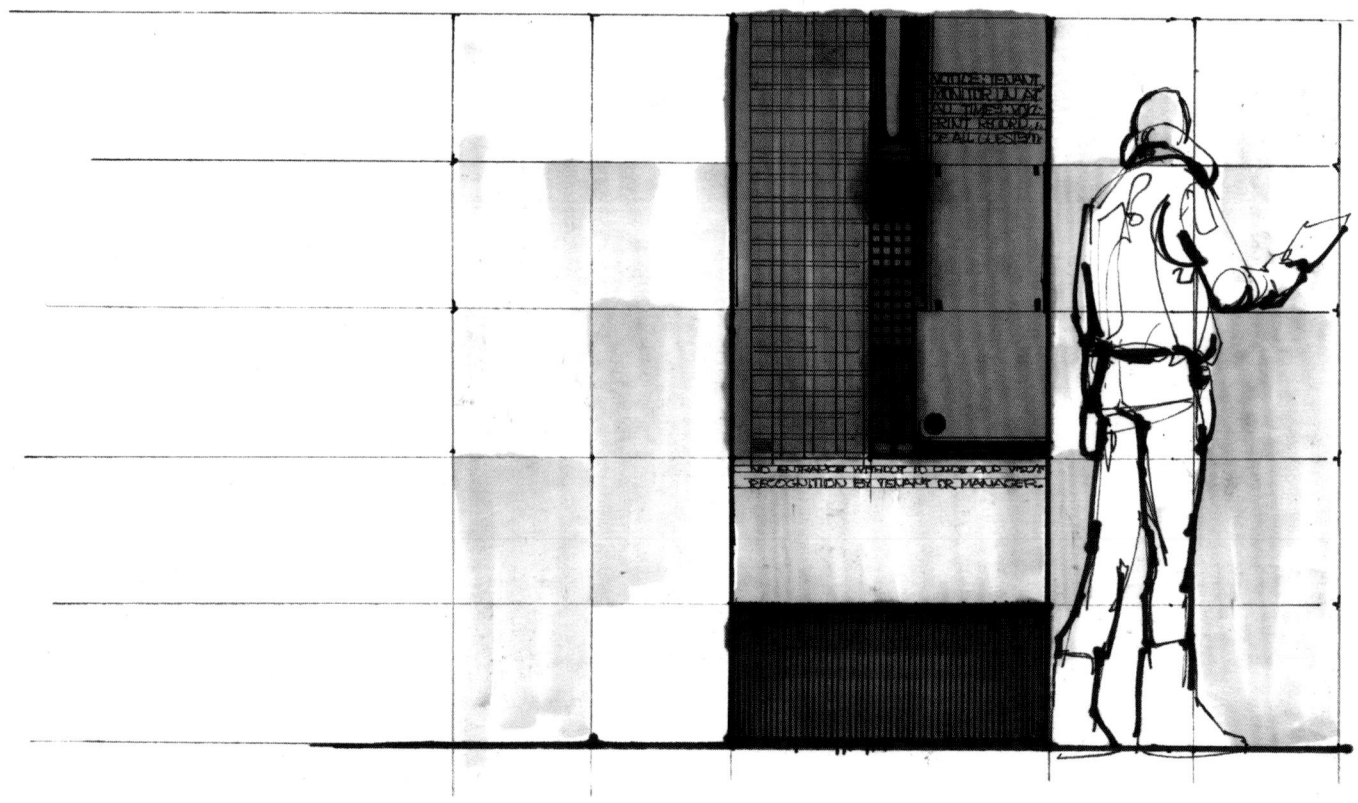

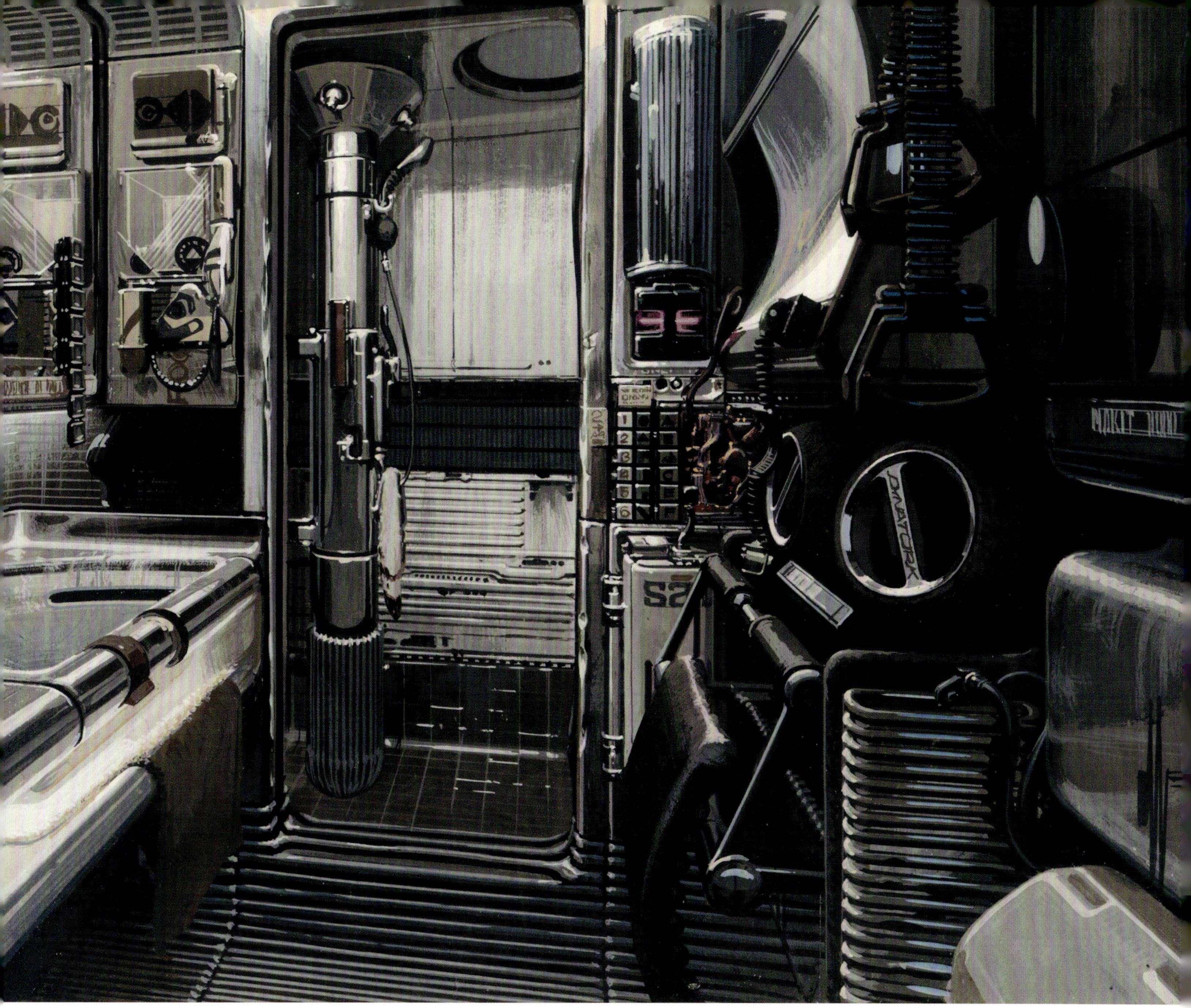

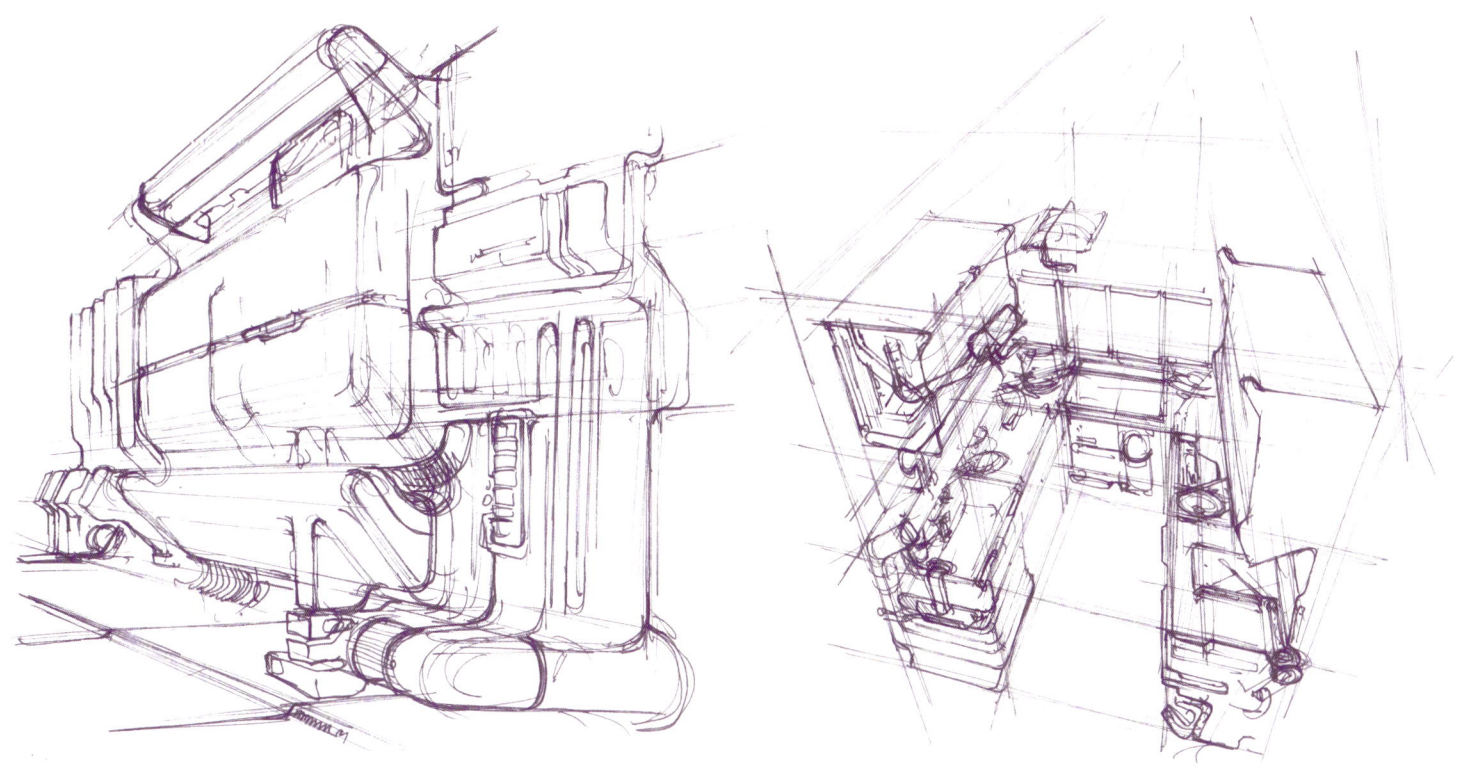

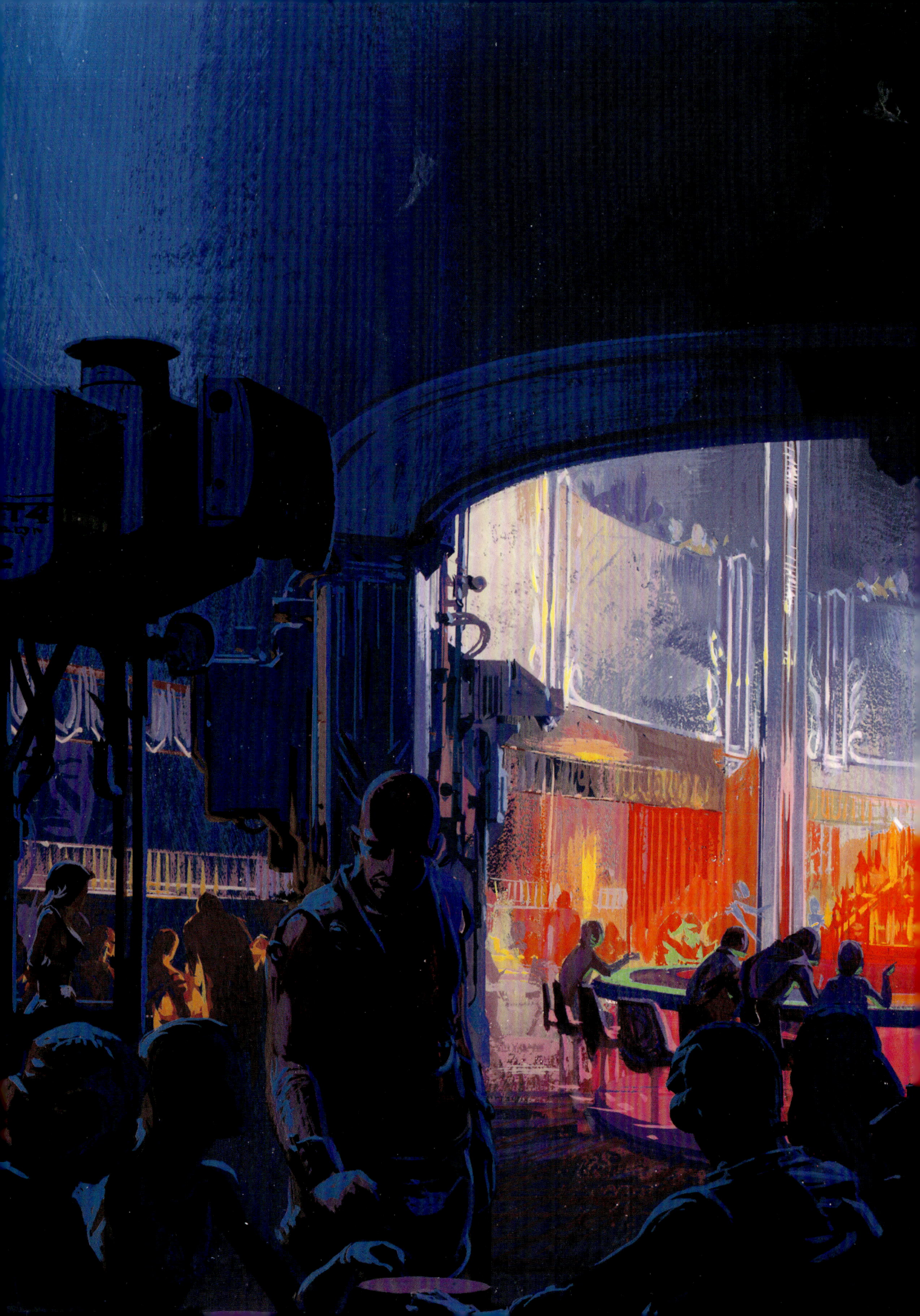

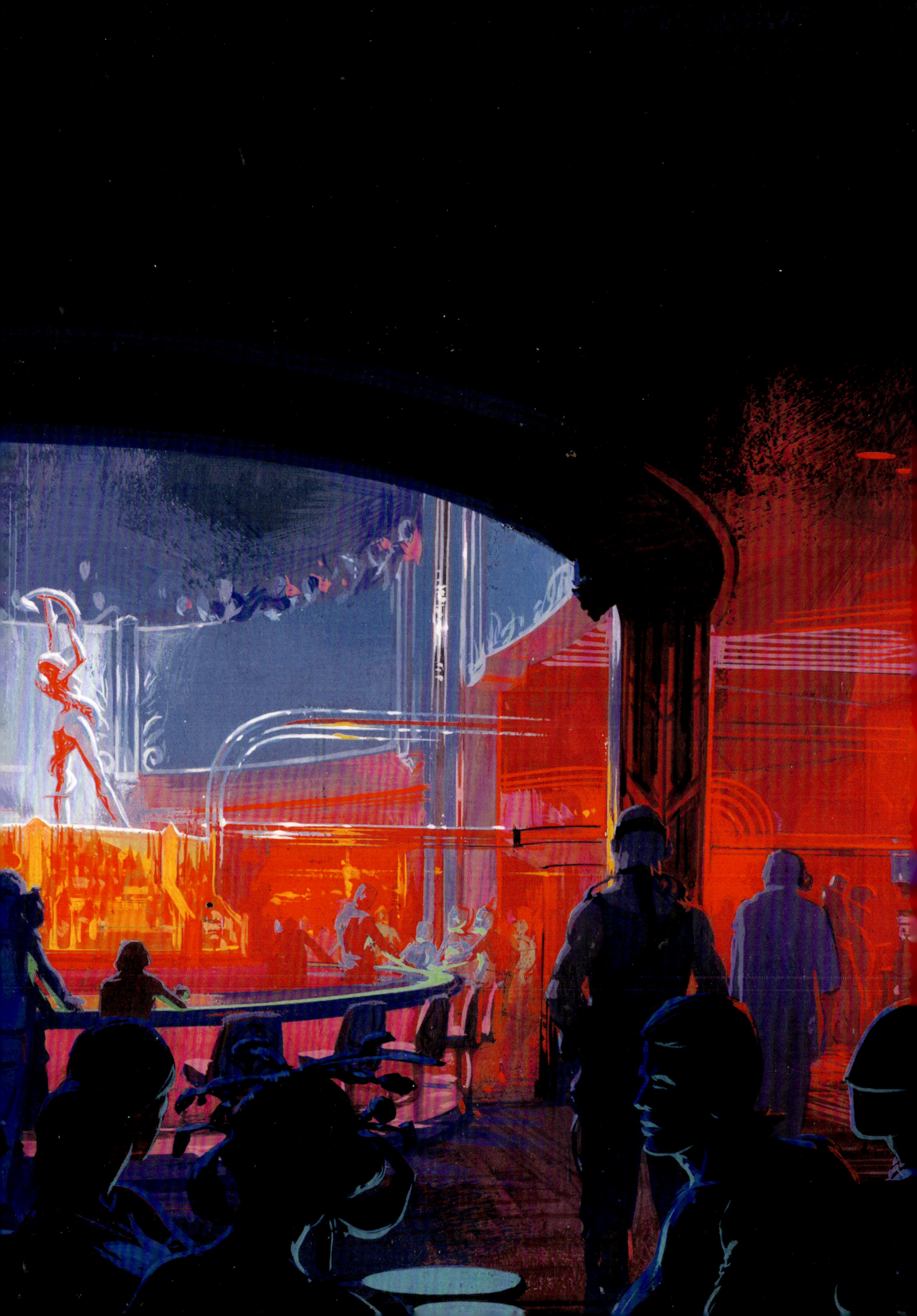

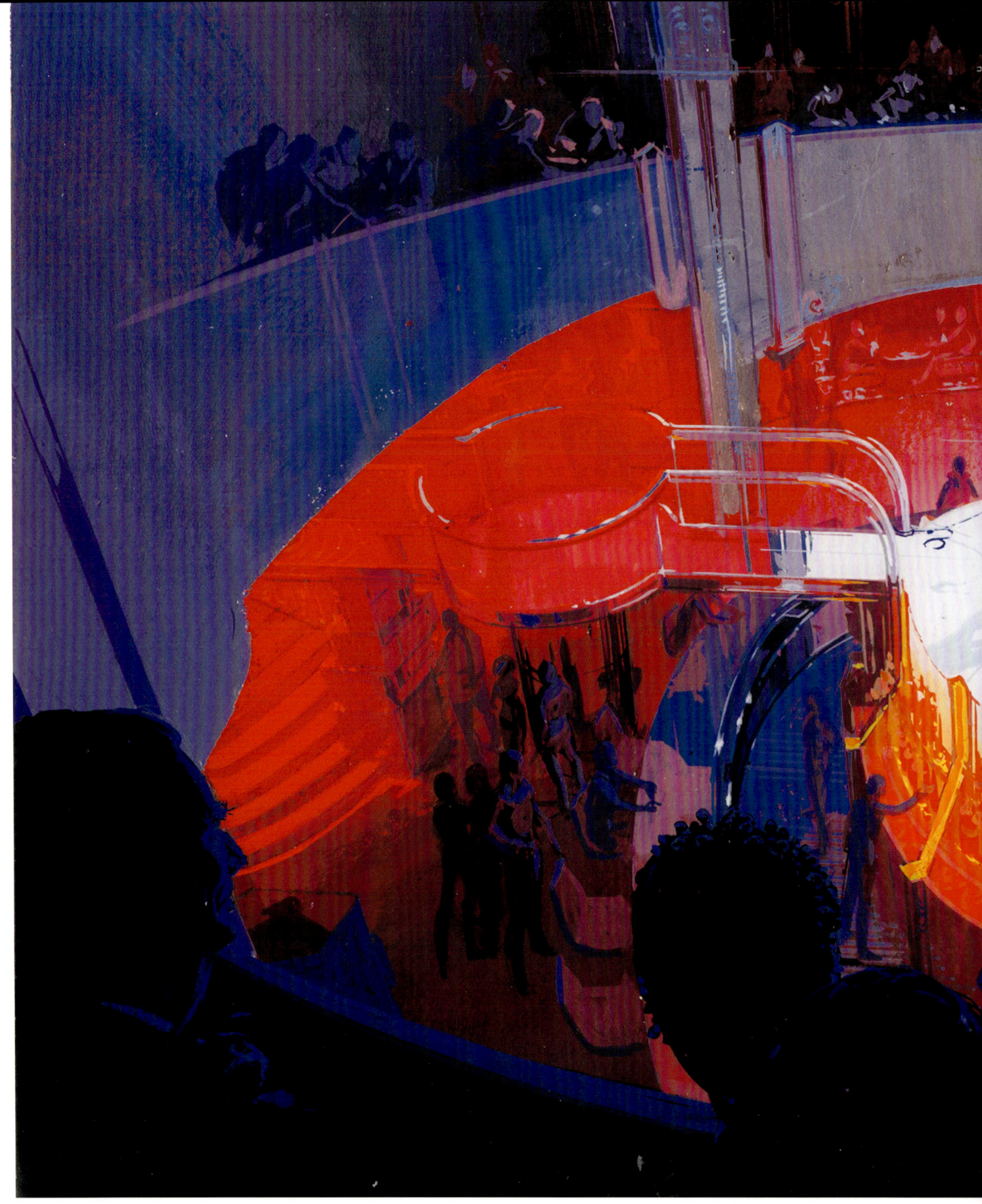

Originally planned to be shot in the lobby of the Wiltern Theater in downtown Los Angeles, the club scene reflected the after-hours culture then sweeping the country. Although the Wiltern's circular mezzanine overlooking the dance floor survived in Mead's sketches, the shoot was ultimately transferred to a sound stage because the expected funding due to the historic nature of the building did not materialize.

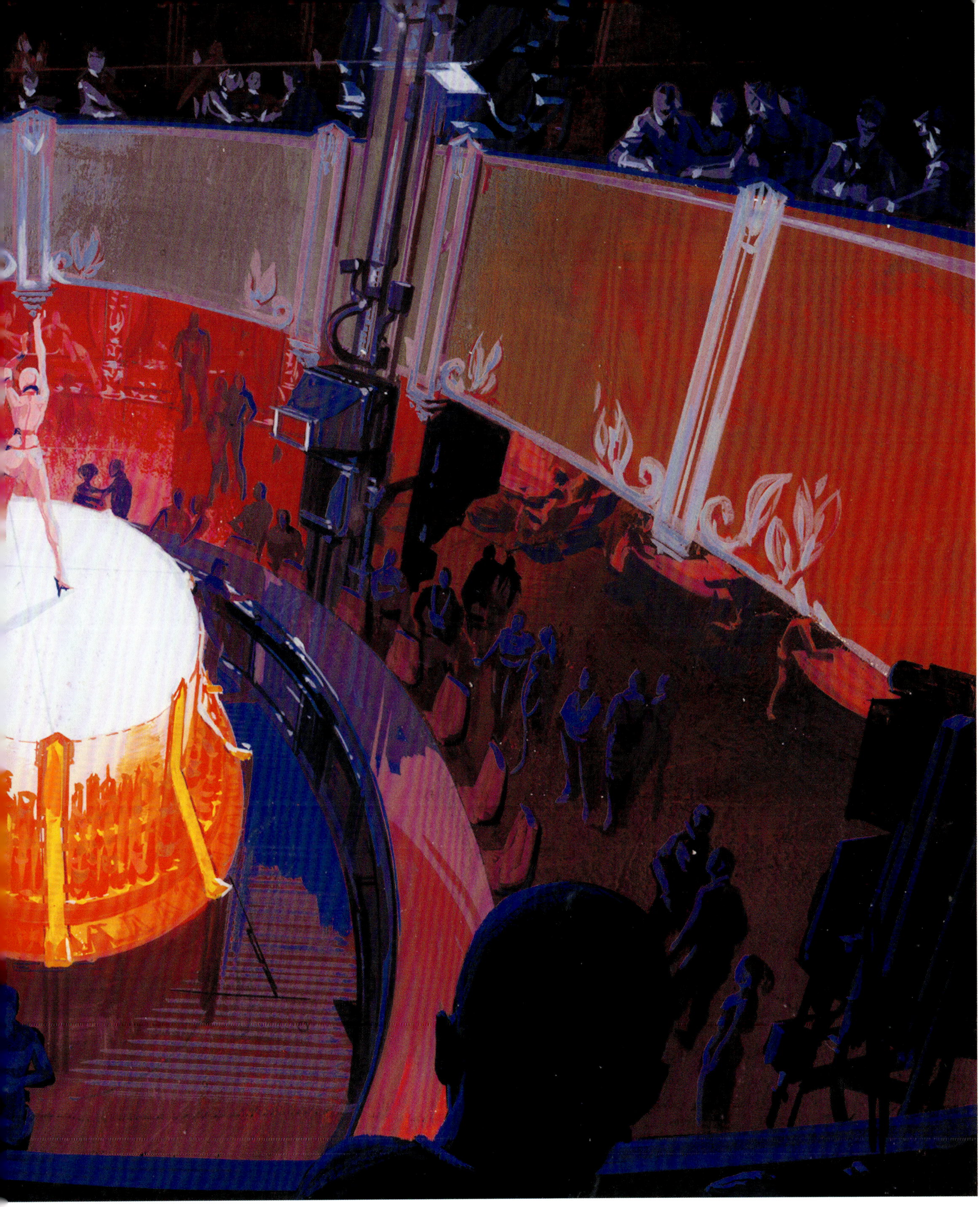

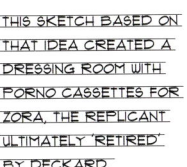

THIS SKETCH BASED ON
THAT IDEA CREATED A
DRESSING ROOM WITH
PORNO CASSETTES FOR
ZORA, THE REPLICANT
ULTIMATELY "RETIRED"
BY DECKARD.

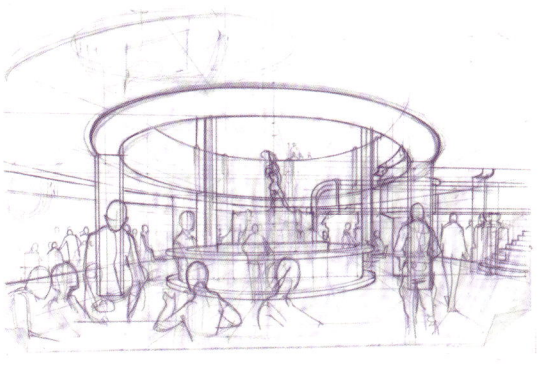

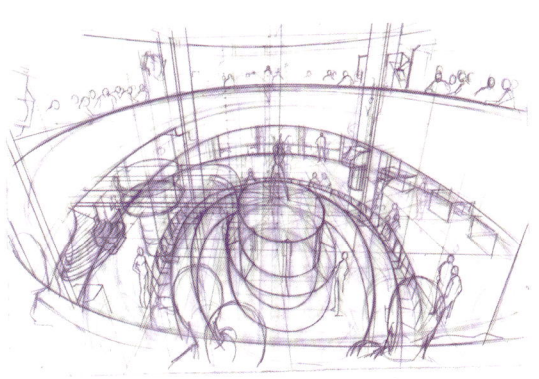

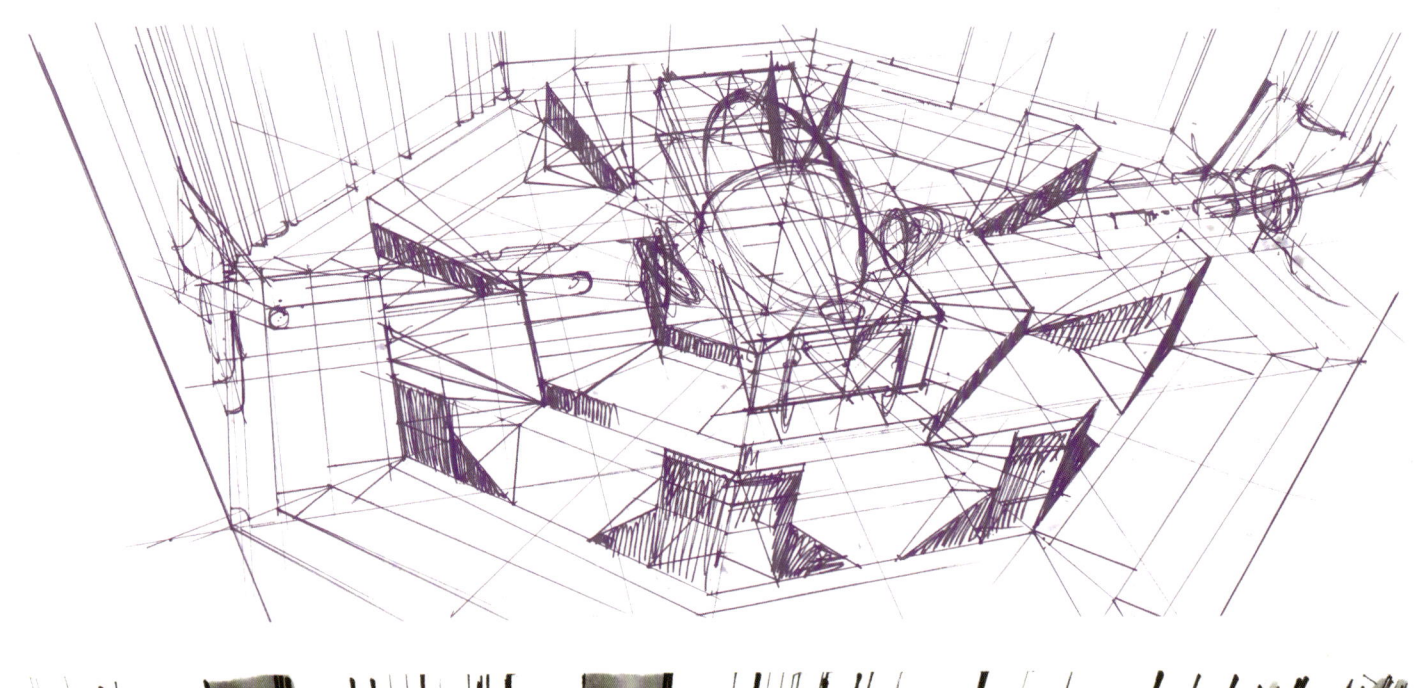

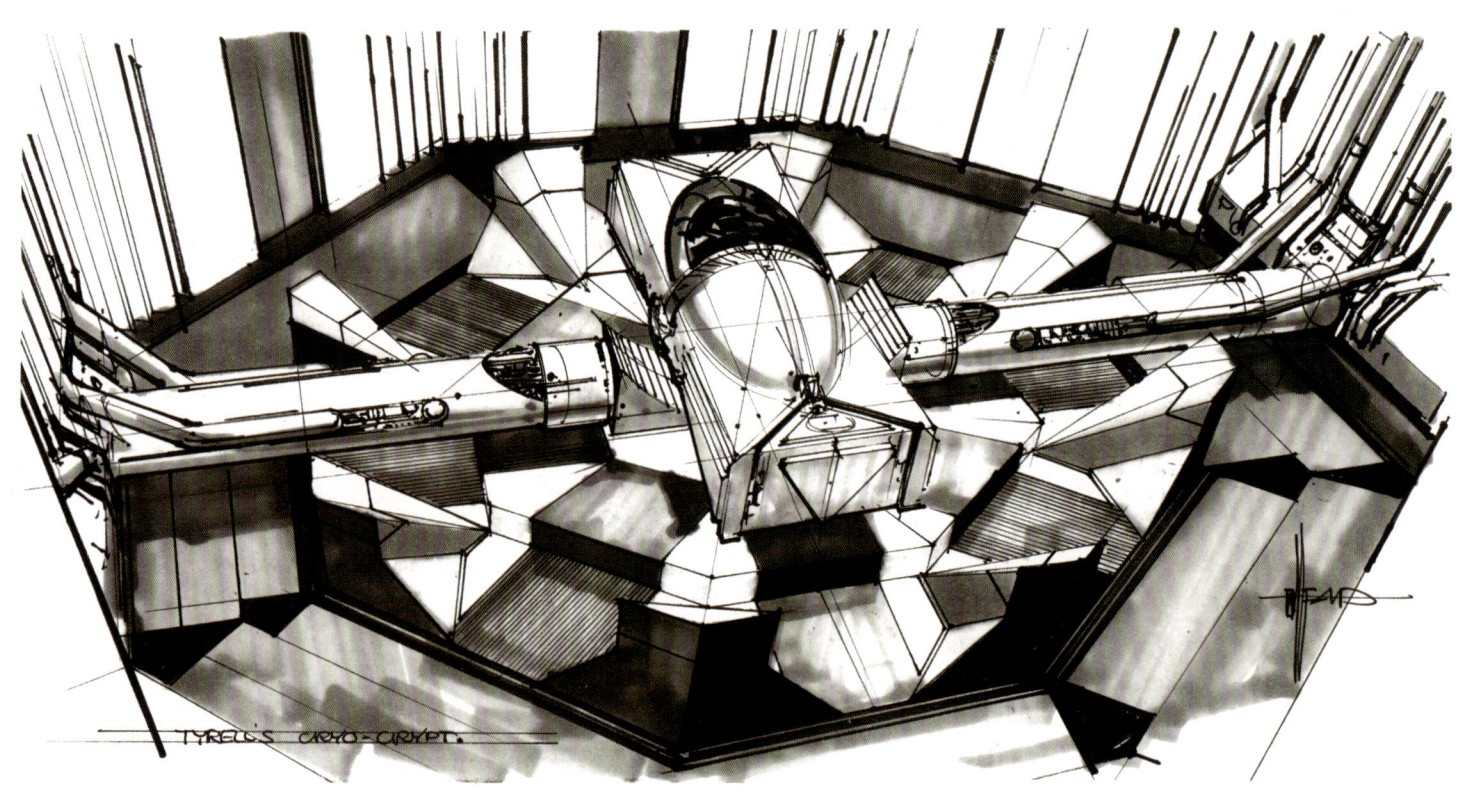

TYRELL'S CRYO-CRYPT.

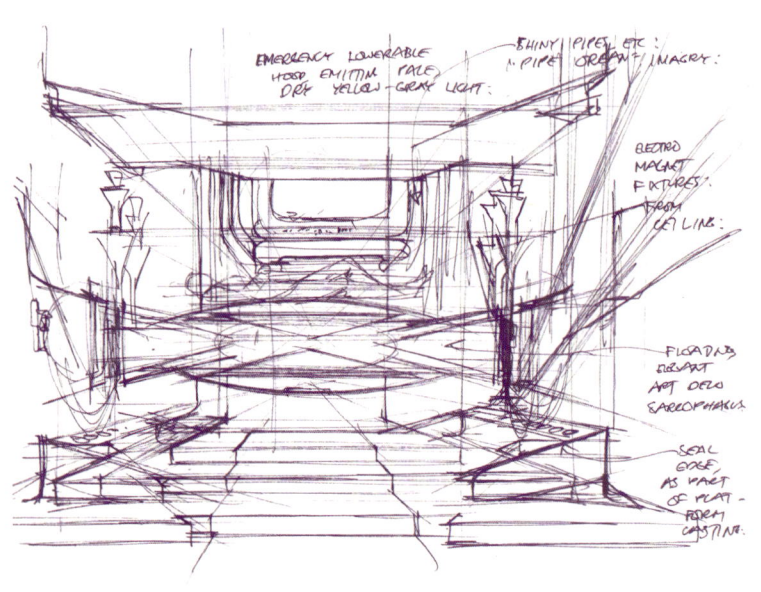

EMERGENCY LOWERABLE
HOSE EMITTING PALE,
DRY YELLOW-GREY LIGHT.

SHINY PIPES, ETC:
PIPE GREEN/MAGENTA.

ELECTRO
MAGNET
FIXTURES.
FROM
CEILING.

FLOATING
ELEGANT
ART DECO
SARCOPHAGUS.

SEAL
EDGE,
AS PART
OF PLAT-
FORM
CASTING.

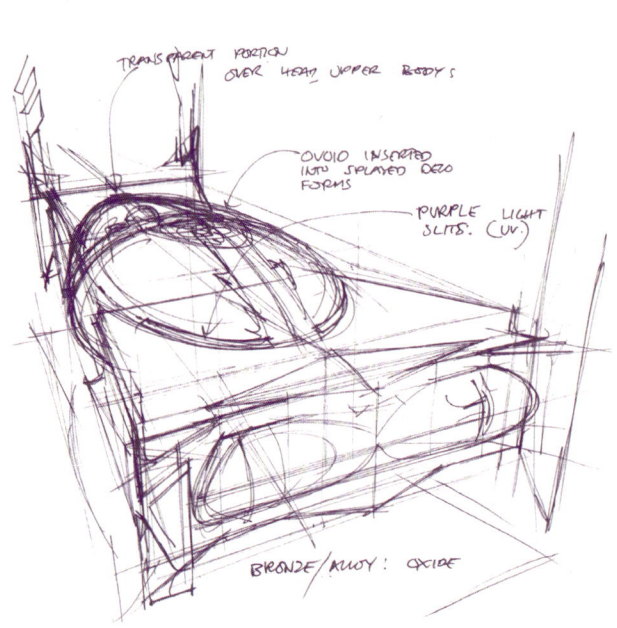

TRANSPARENT PORTION
OVER HEAD, UPPER BODY.

OVOID INSERTED
INTO SPLAYED DECO
FORMS.

PURPLE LIGHT
SLITS. (UV.)

BRONZE/ALLOY: OXIDE.

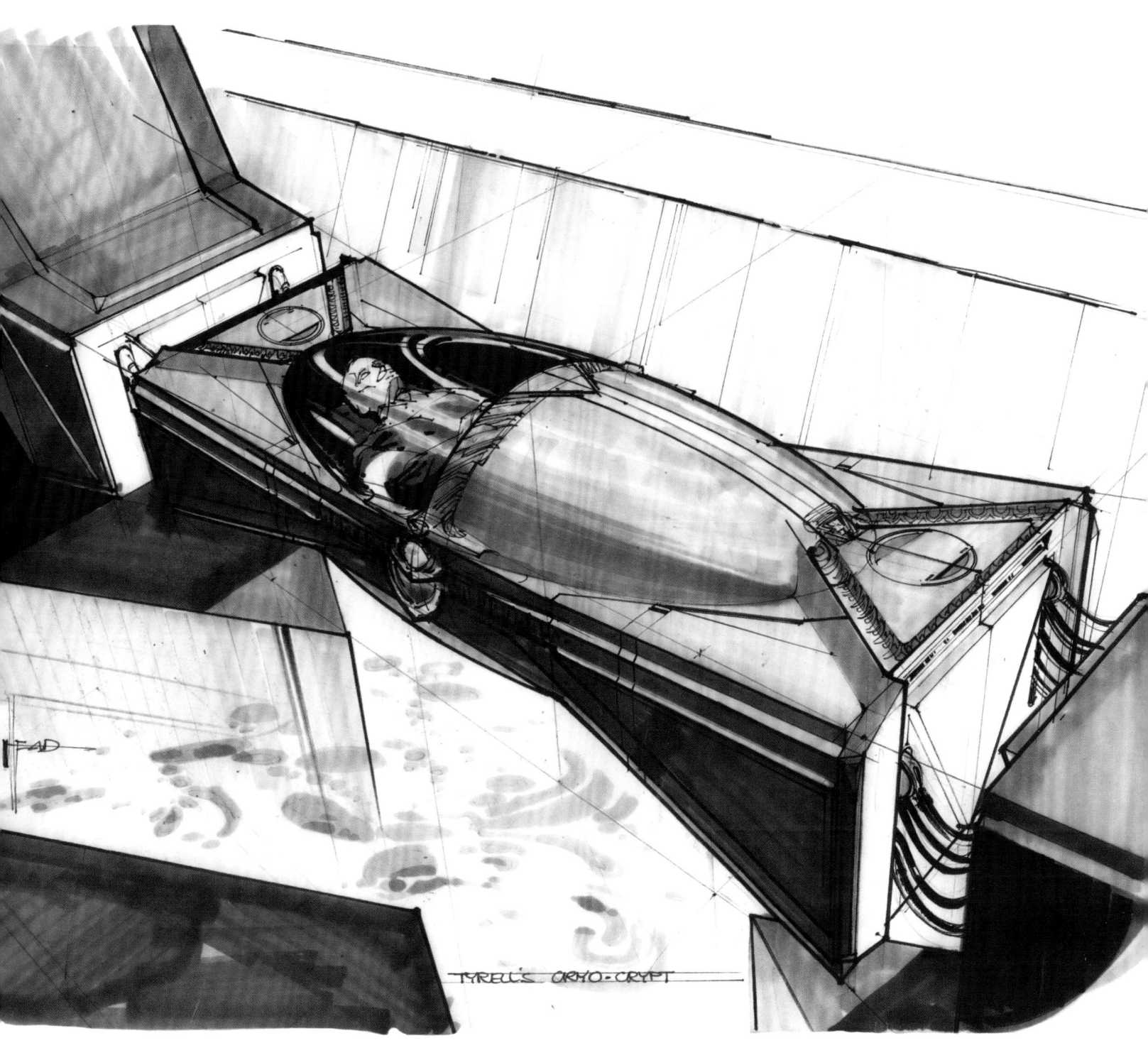

TYRELL'S ORMO-CRYPT

The original script called for an opening sequence featuring the transport of replicants from a far-off planet via a 'slave ship'. Mead's image of hundreds of replicants encased in tomb-like containers was never used, as the sequence was abandoned during pre-production.

Although Scott ultimately decided against a plot line revealing the outer planet origins of the replicants, Mead's sketches, based on the original script, reveal a complex, mechanized production system which appears fully capable of bottling-plant-like efficiency. Such fidelity to an actual process even at an early stage in the production brings into focus Mead's early career as an automobile designer, where his familiarity with the assembly line was honed by experience. Of particular note is the turntable which, from a cinematic perspective, would allow the camera to capture the entire process from a single point of view.

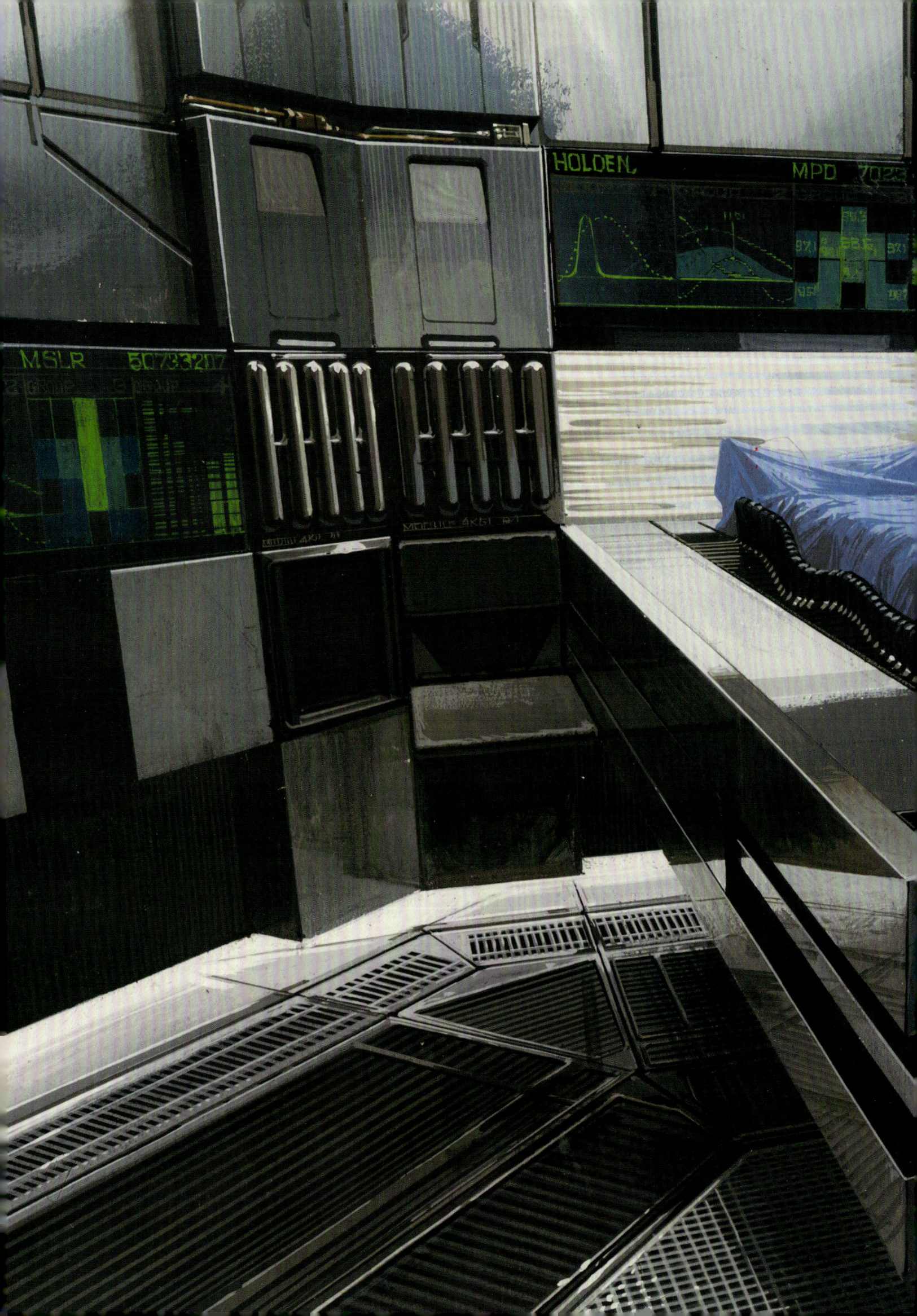

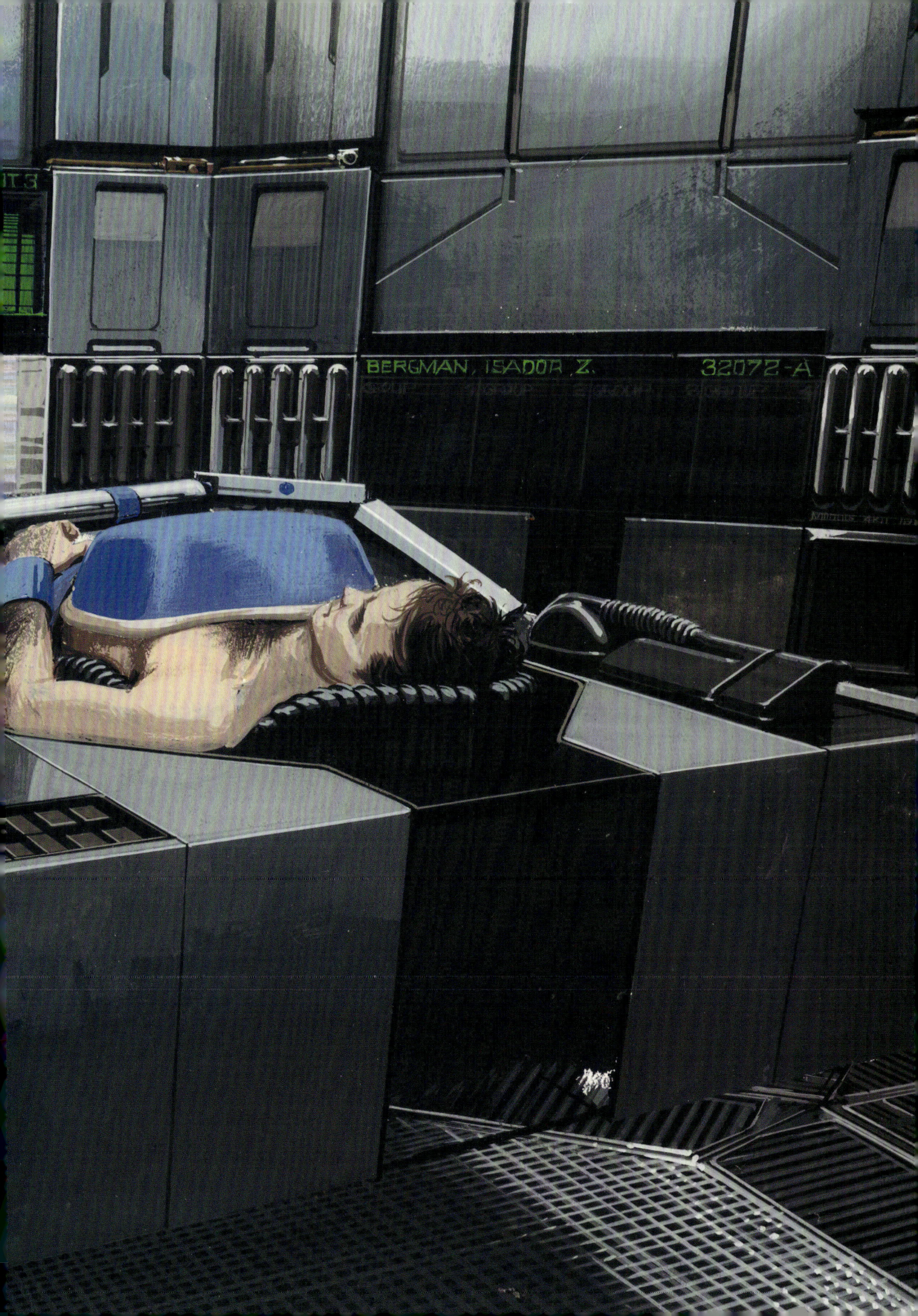

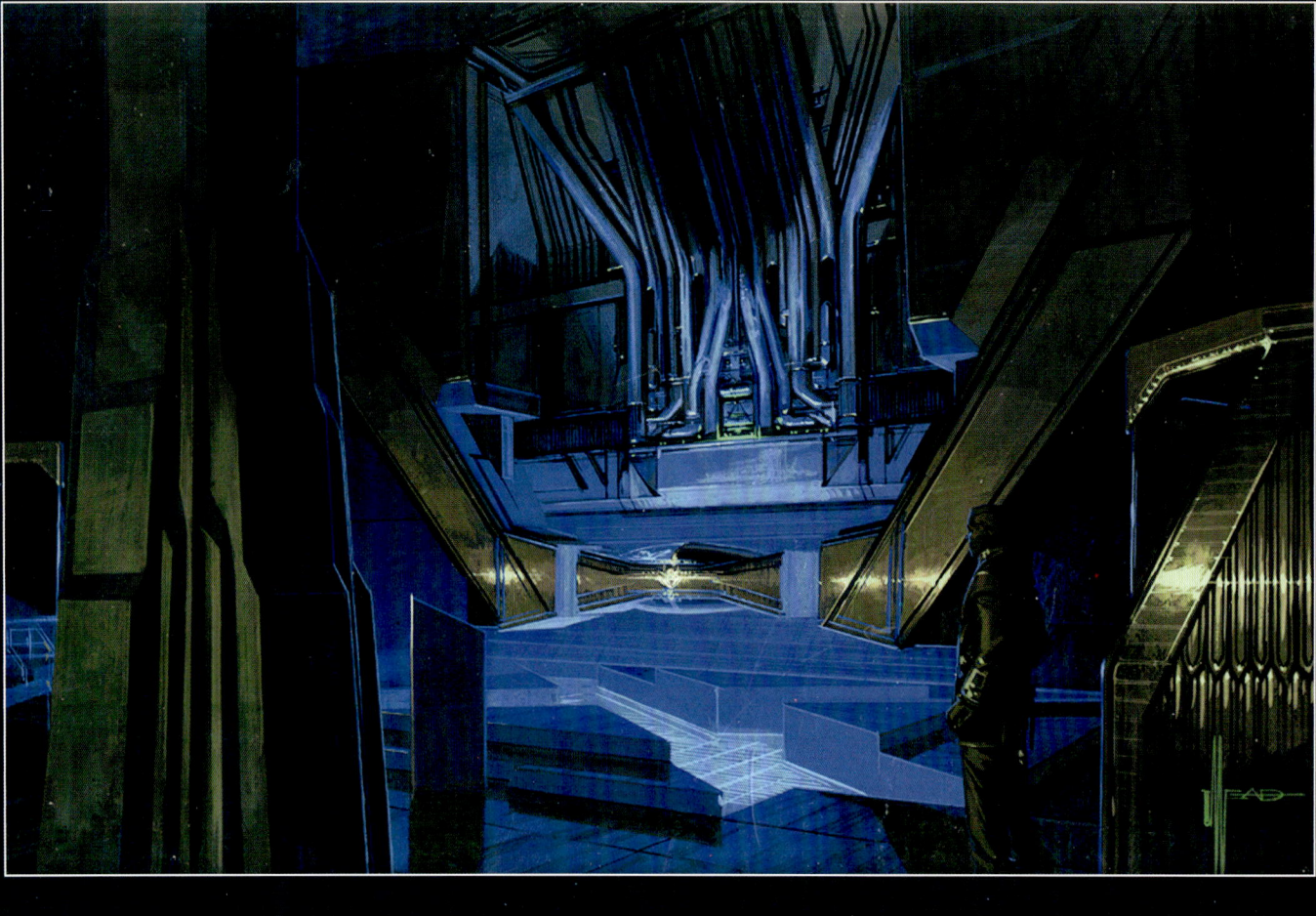

Never used sketches such as these are fascinating for what they reveal about Mead's total immersion in the *Blade Runner* project. In mood, in the color palette, and even the geometry, he establishes a unique dystopian visual vocabulary which permeates even the paper on which the images are created. This is especially apparent in the rows of abandoned seats on the train-car opposite which seems to have arrived at its last, despondent terminal.

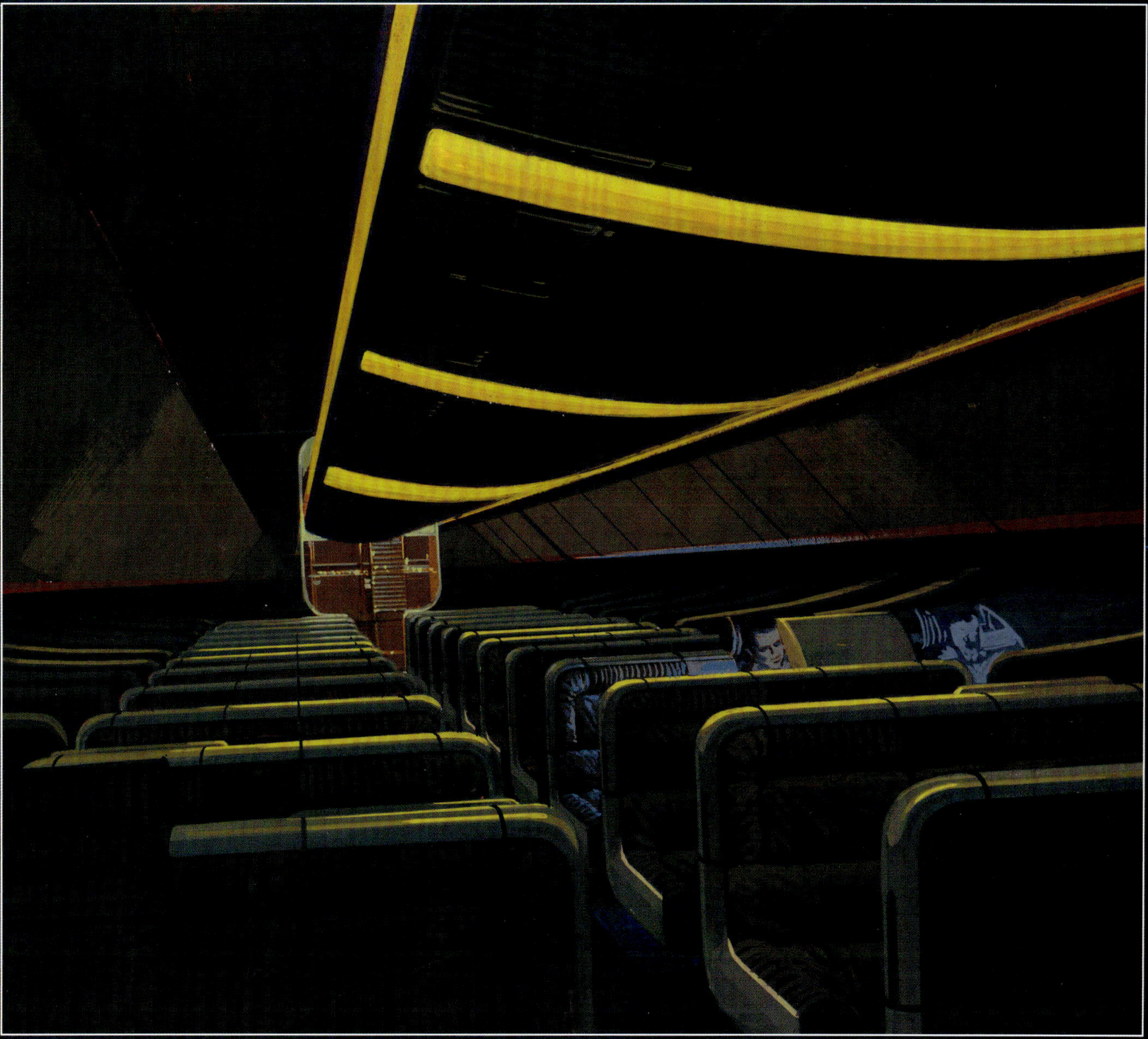

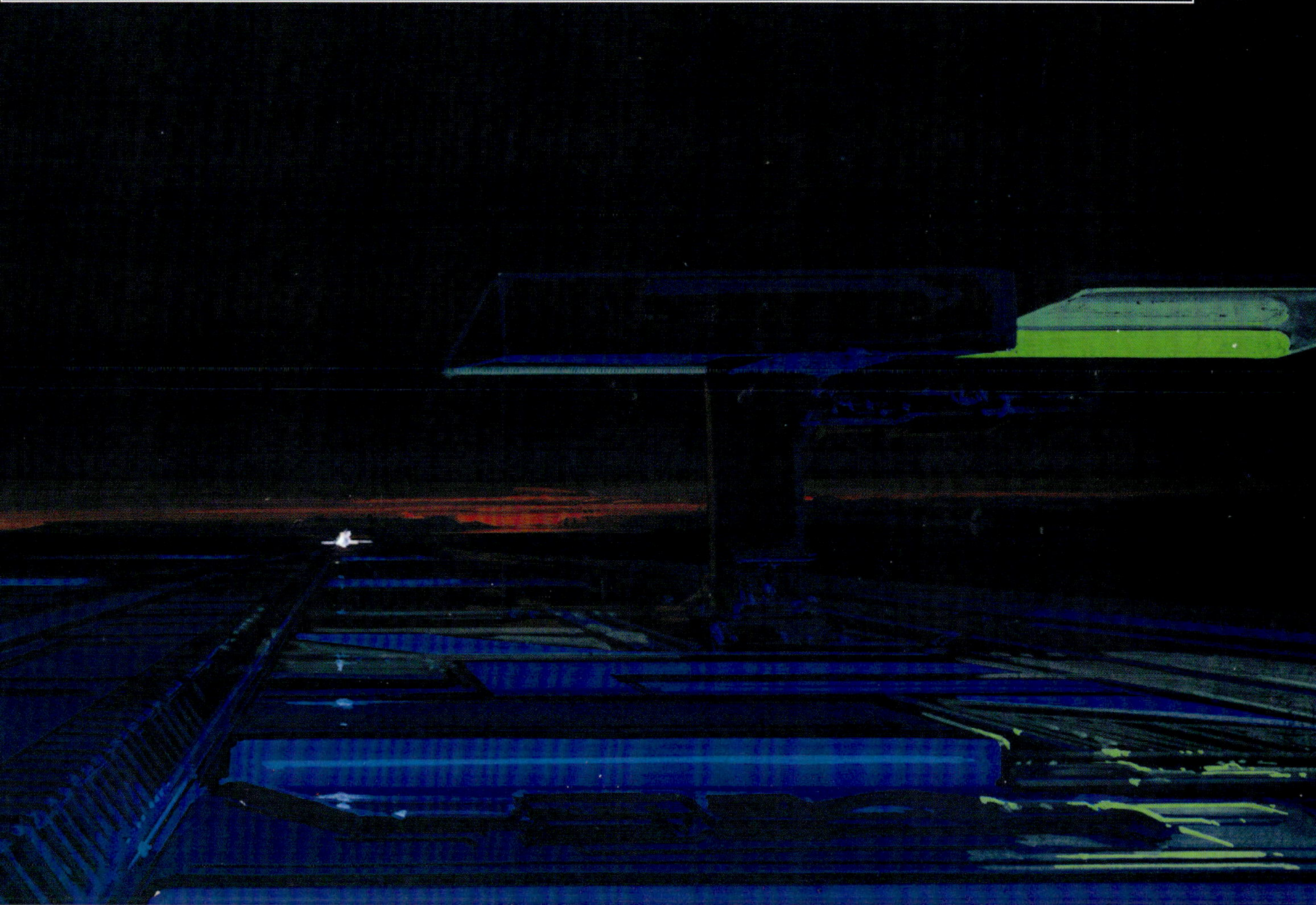

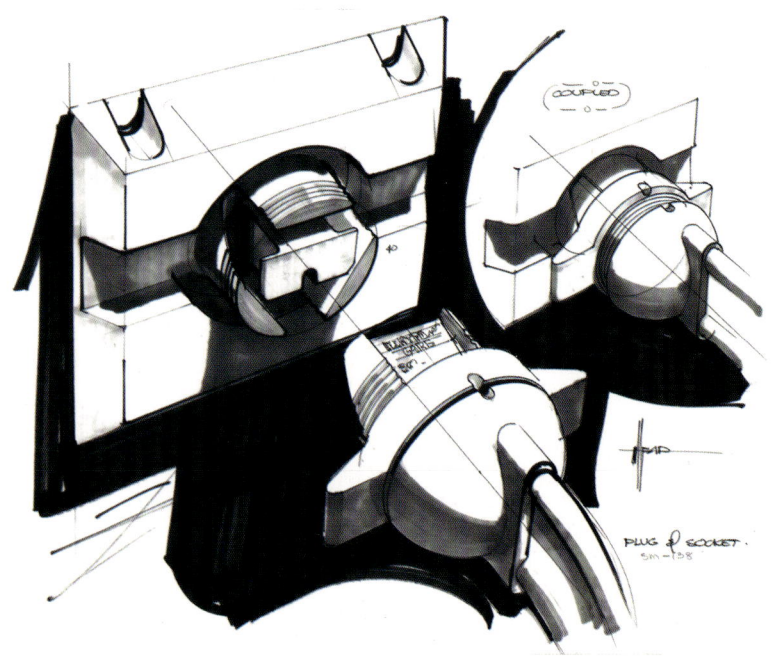

The malevolent presence of the Voight-Kampff machine in the first few minutes of *Blade Runner* sets the stage for the desperate tale to follow with its crouching shape, but also by the merciless rise and fall of its bellows as it samples the air for tell-tale pheromones. For Mead, the breathing of the machine was critical to the scene, and evolved as he speculated about how one might differentiate a replicant from a human being while sowing fear in the mind of the subject.

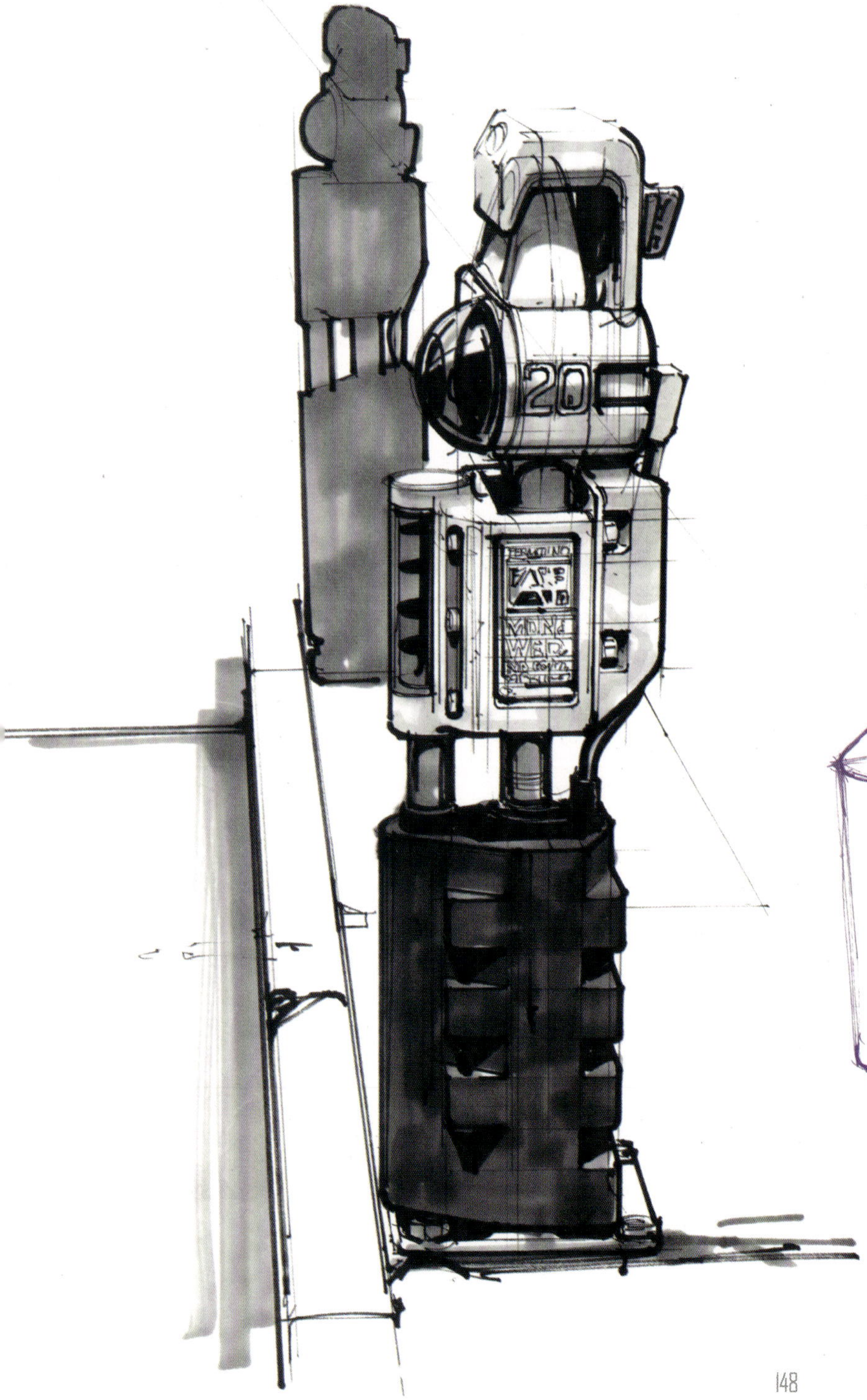

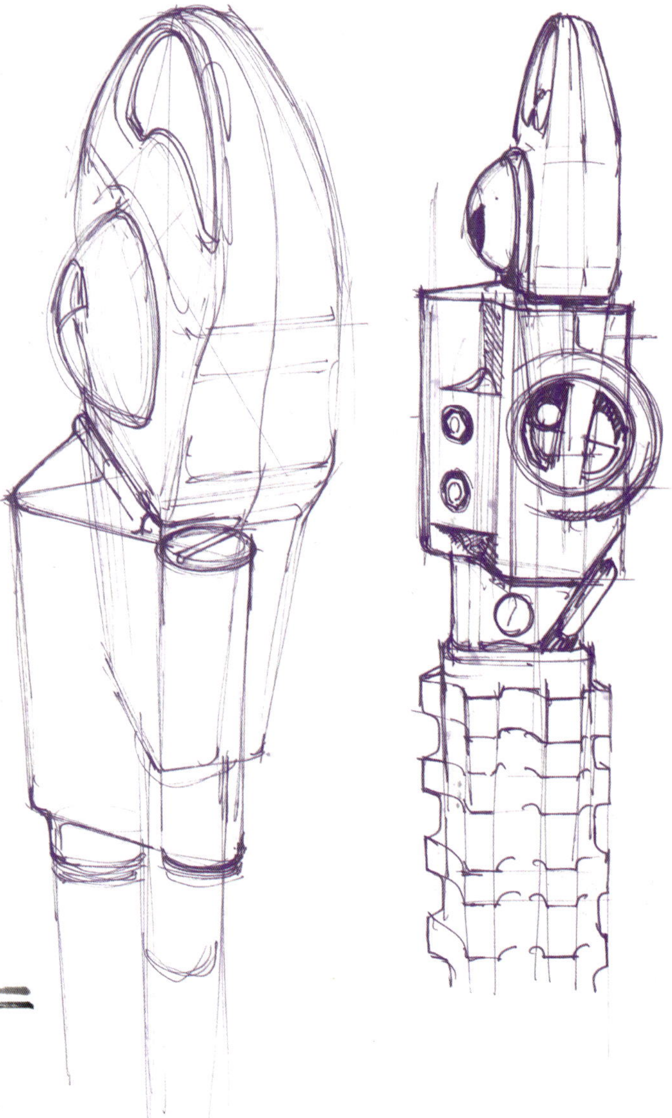

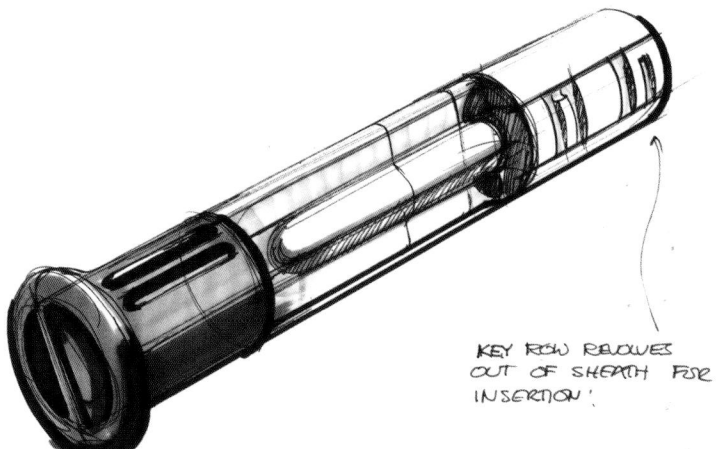

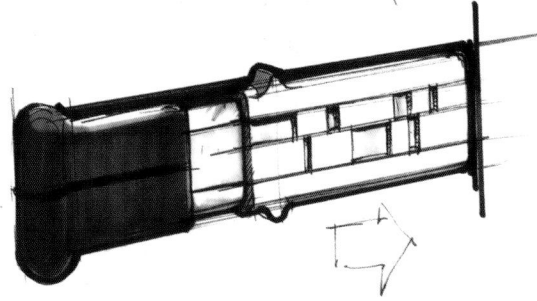

KEY ROW IS SERIES OF SMALL INSERTS: WHEN SHEATH IS PUSHED FORWARD SPRING PLATE PROPS THEM OUT TO FORM CODED NOTCH PATTERN ON ONE OR BOTH SIDES OF KEY.

KEY ROW REVOLVES OUT OF SHEATH FOR INSERTION.

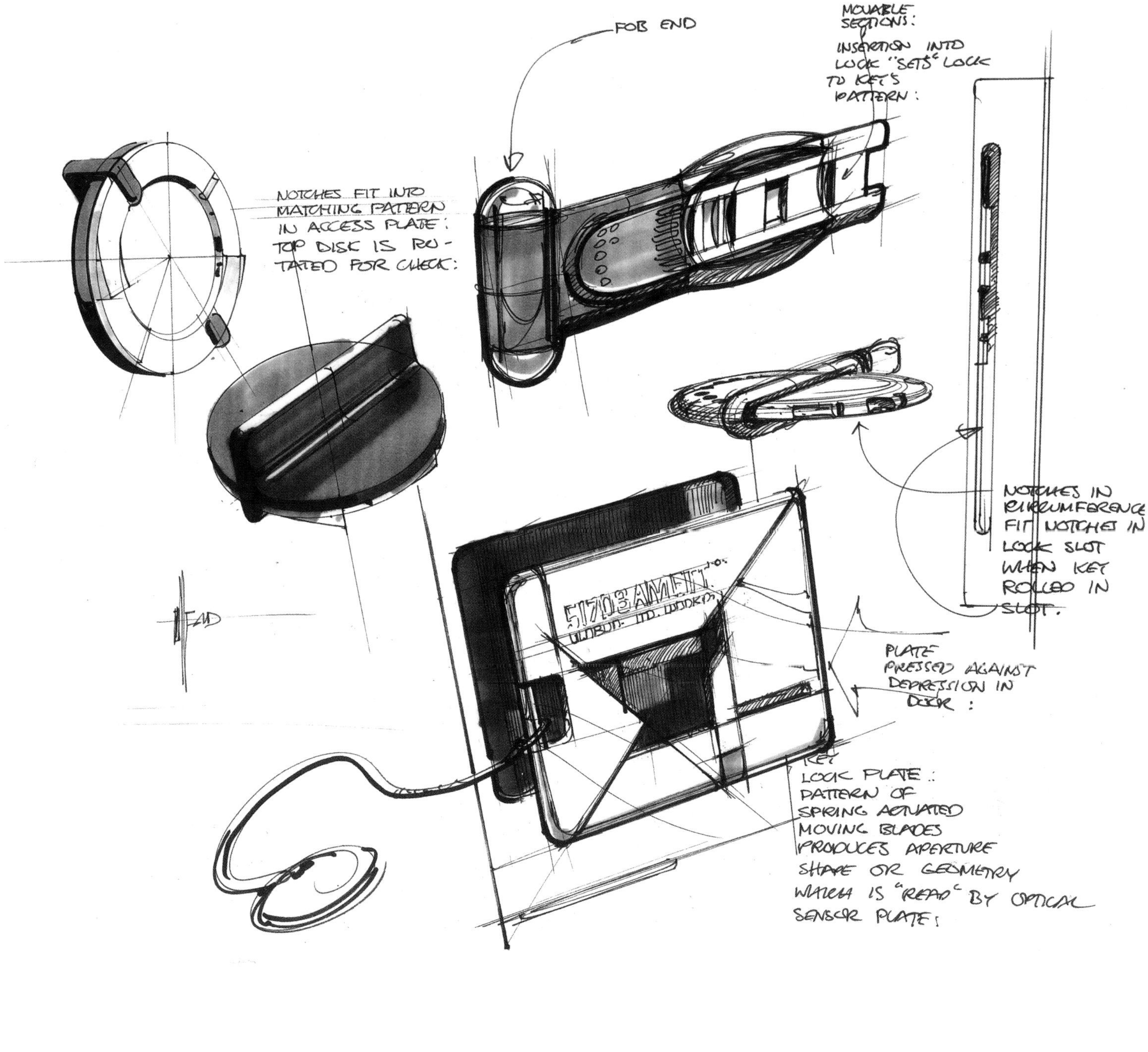

FOB END

MOVABLE SECTIONS: INSERTION INTO LOCK "SETS" LOCK TO KEY'S PATTERN.

NOTCHES FIT INTO MATCHING PATTERN IN ACCESS PLATE. TOP DISK IS RO-TATED FOR CHECK.

END

51703AMFIT
GLOBUS LTD. BROOKLYN

NOTCHES IN CIRCUMFERENCE FIT NOTCHES IN LOCK SLOT WHEN KEY ROLLED IN SLOT.

PLATE PRESSED AGAINST DEPRESSION IN DOOR.

KEY LOCK PLATE: PATTERN OF SPRING ACTUATED MOVING BLADES PRODUCES APERTURE SHAPE OR GEOMETRY WHICH IS "READ" BY OPTICAL SENSOR PLATE.

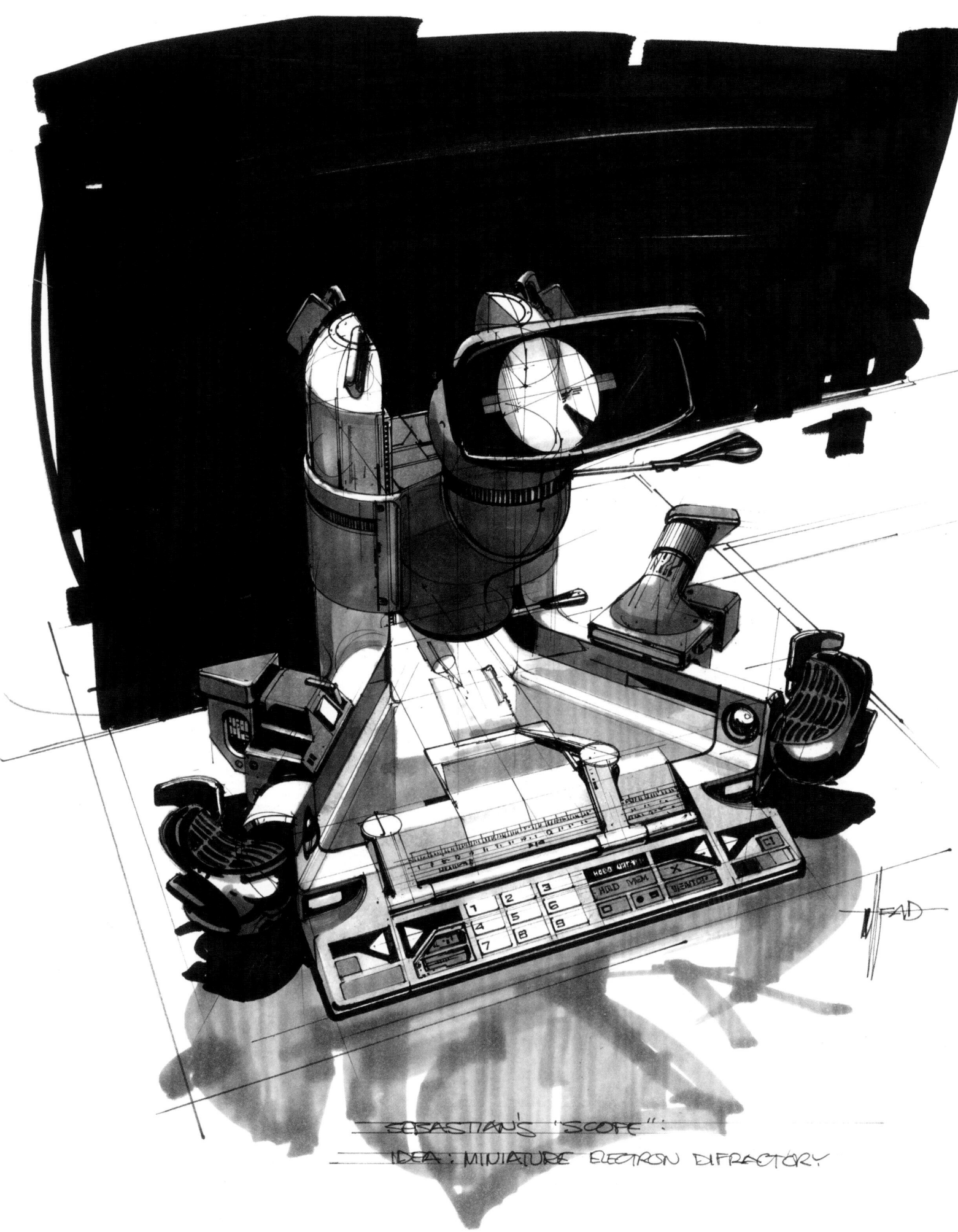

SEBASTIAN'S "SCOPE":
IDEA: MINIATURE ELECTRON DIFRACTORY

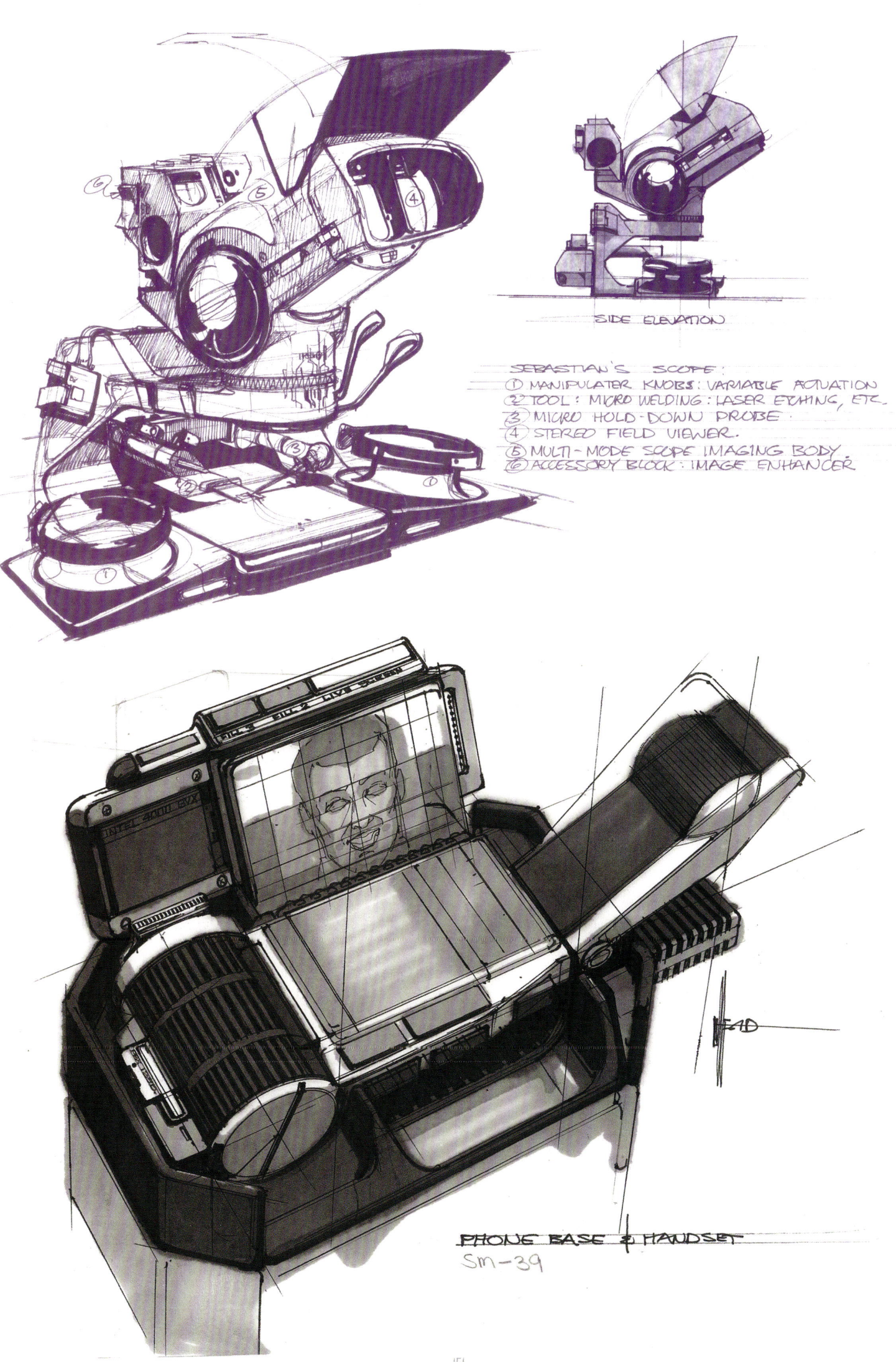

SIDE ELEVATION

SEBASTIAN'S SCOPE:
1. MANIPULATER KNOBS: VARIABLE ACTUATION
2. TOOL: MICRO WELDING: LASER ETCHING, ETC.
3. MICRO HOLD-DOWN PROBE.
4. STEREO FIELD VIEWER.
5. MULTI-MODE SCOPE IMAGING BODY.
6. ACCESSORY BLOCK: IMAGE ENHANCER

PHONE BASE & HANDSET
SM-39

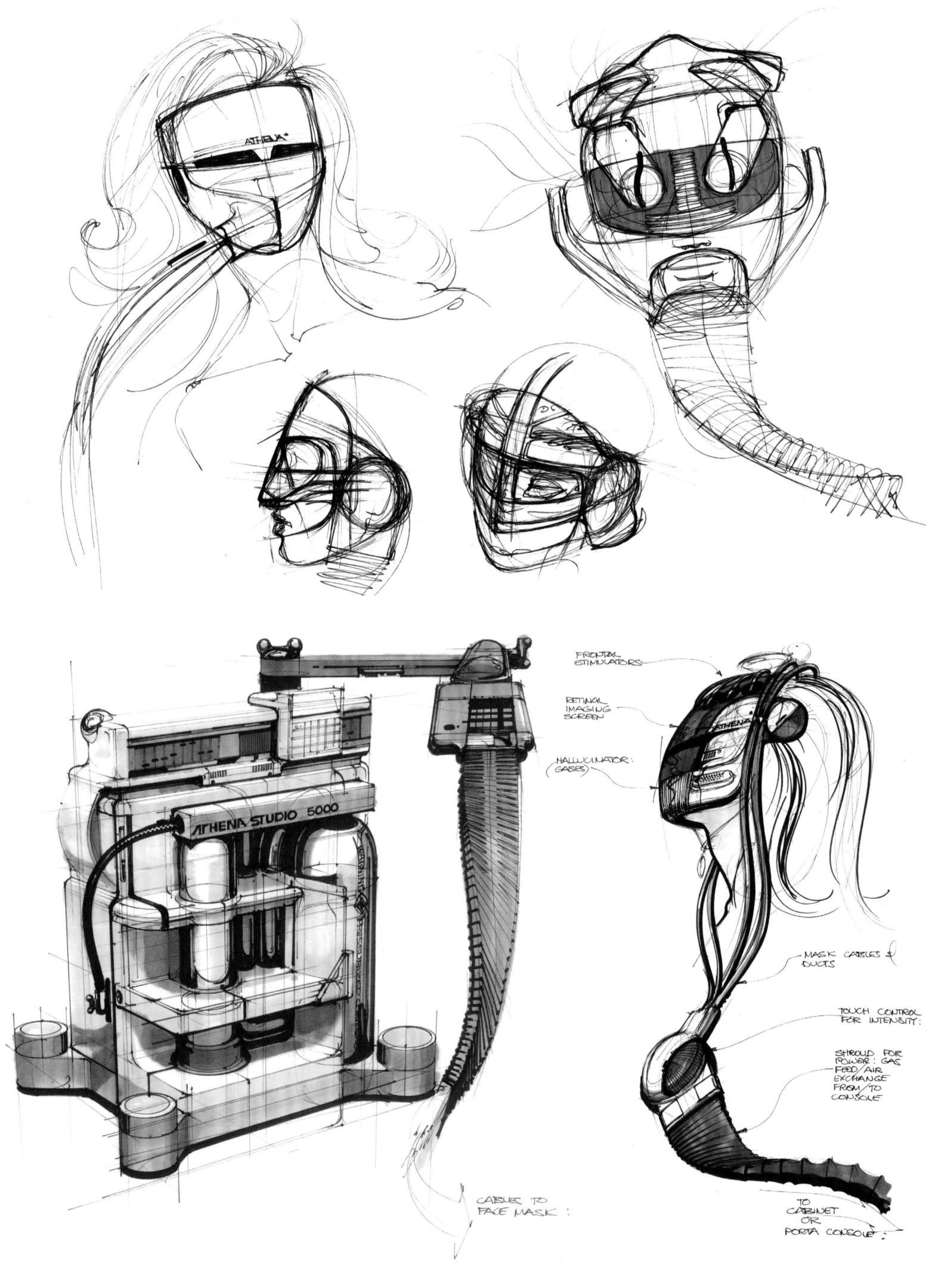

ATHENA

ATHENA STUDIO 5000

FRONTAL
STIMULATORS

RETINAL
IMAGING
SCREEN

HALLUCINATOR
(GASES)

ATHENA

MASK CABLES &
DUCTS

TOUCH CONTROL
FOR INTENSITY

SHROUD FOR
POWER, GAS
FEED/AIR
EXCHANGE
FROM/TO
CONSOLE

CABLES TO
FACE MASK

TO
CABINET
OR
PORTA CONSOLE

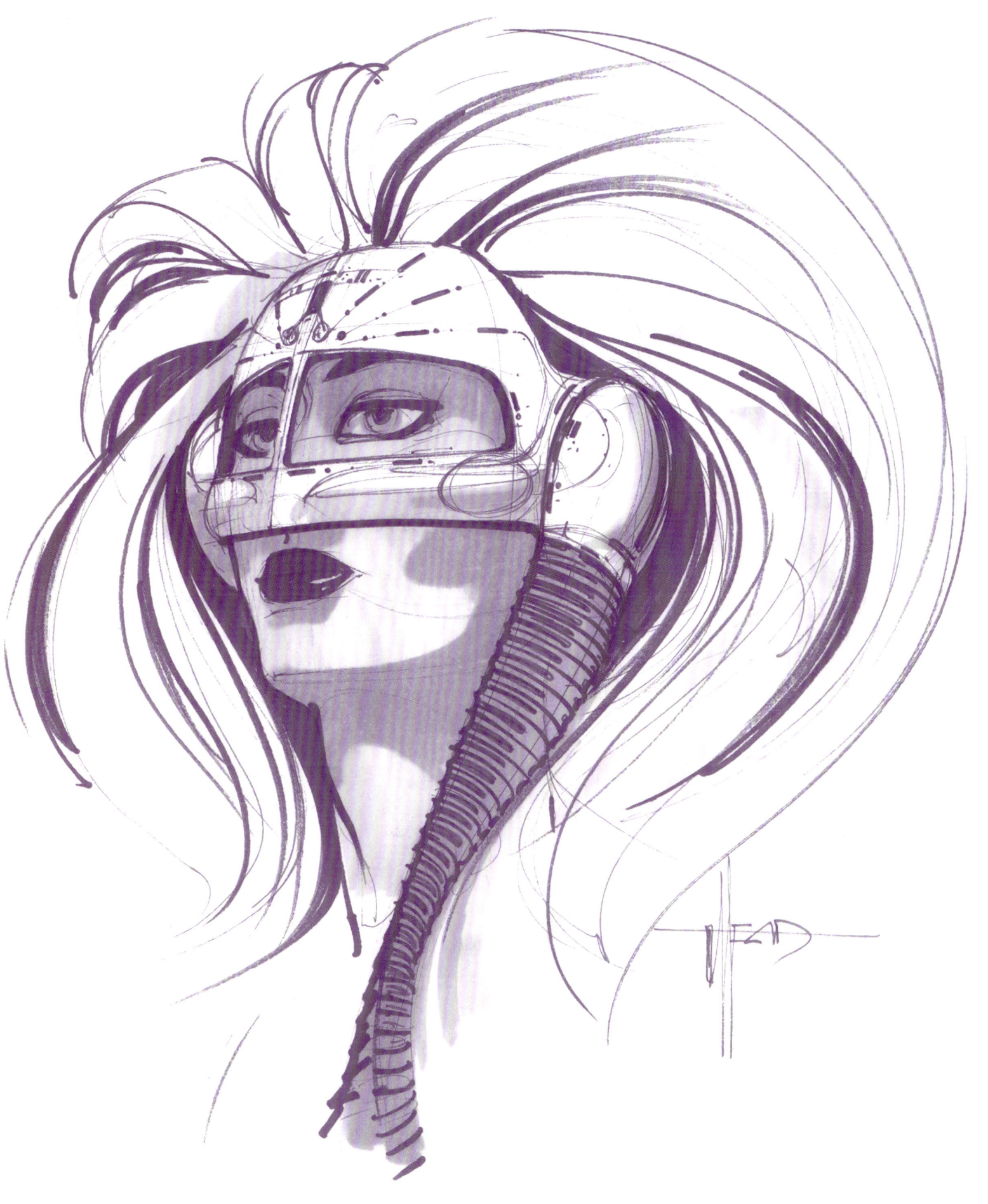

For the exotic club dancer ultimately retired by Deckard as she crashes through layer after layer of glass and visqueen, the plot revolved around the artificial cobra with which she performs a sensuous dance. It is a scale from this cobra, containing the manufacturer's identity that leads Deckard to the club and provides a final clue to unlock the puzzle. Here alternatives to the dancer's hair and mask, are studied, and resolved.

EKTOPIA

CIRCULAR THINKING

Mead imagined an "ideal village, with all the services buried underneath" as the prime setting for this family-friendly TV series set in the near future. As with many TV shows, this one, unfortunately, was never given a green light.

As a vision of a future city based on ecological principals, and with a form vaguely similar to that of the Oscar Neimeyer-designed capital of Brazil, the sketches reveal a multi-layered urban habitat in which freeways disappear under richly planted plateaus, and dwellings cluster around semi-circular public spaces embedded in an artificial life-sustaining structure.

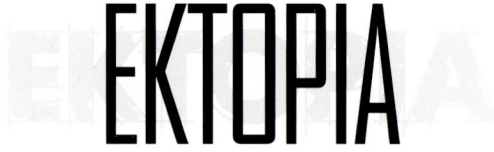

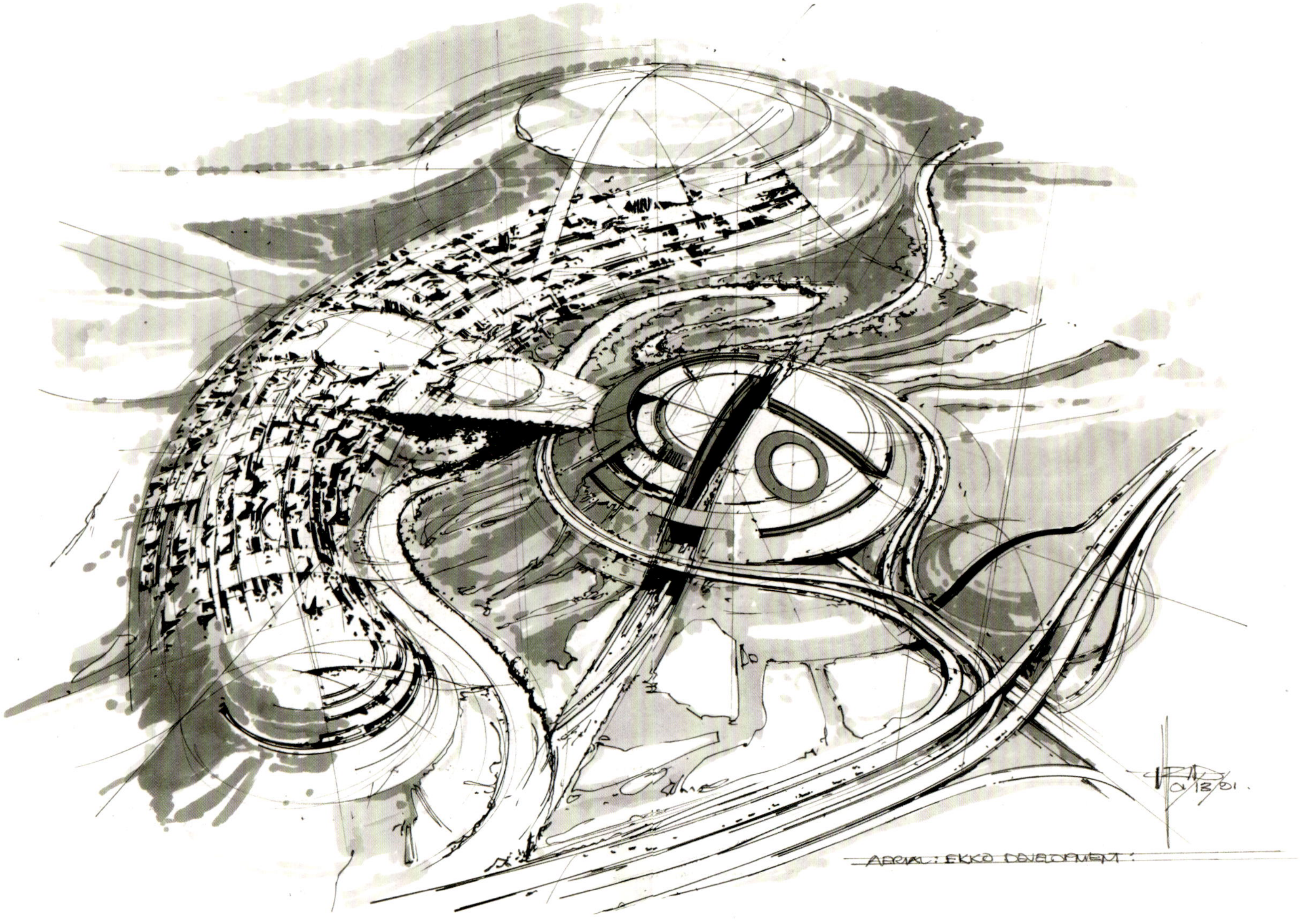

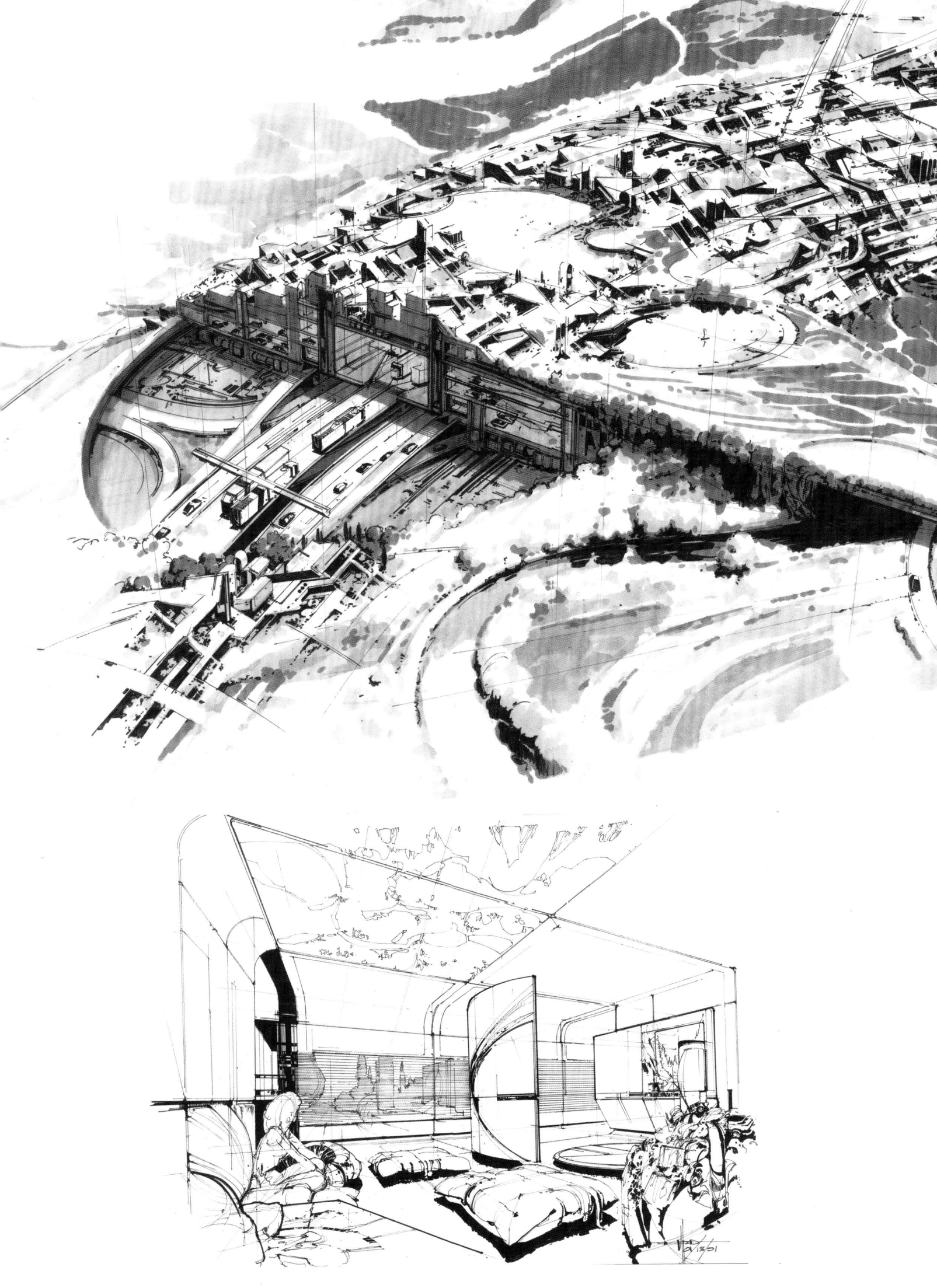

ESCORT
KINDER TRAP

Mead contributed these sketches for a science-fiction movie about a 'mother' who uses children and their genetic material to manufacture an army of robotic clones. As so often happens, unfortunately the movie failed to secure financing and was never made. As Mead explains of the concepts on these pages, "These sketches explore two automated security vehicles which were to be the safe-haven transport that allowed the younger characters to access a secret government site. They contained no offensive systems of their own, but were intended to provide protection for their occupants from any number of weapons."

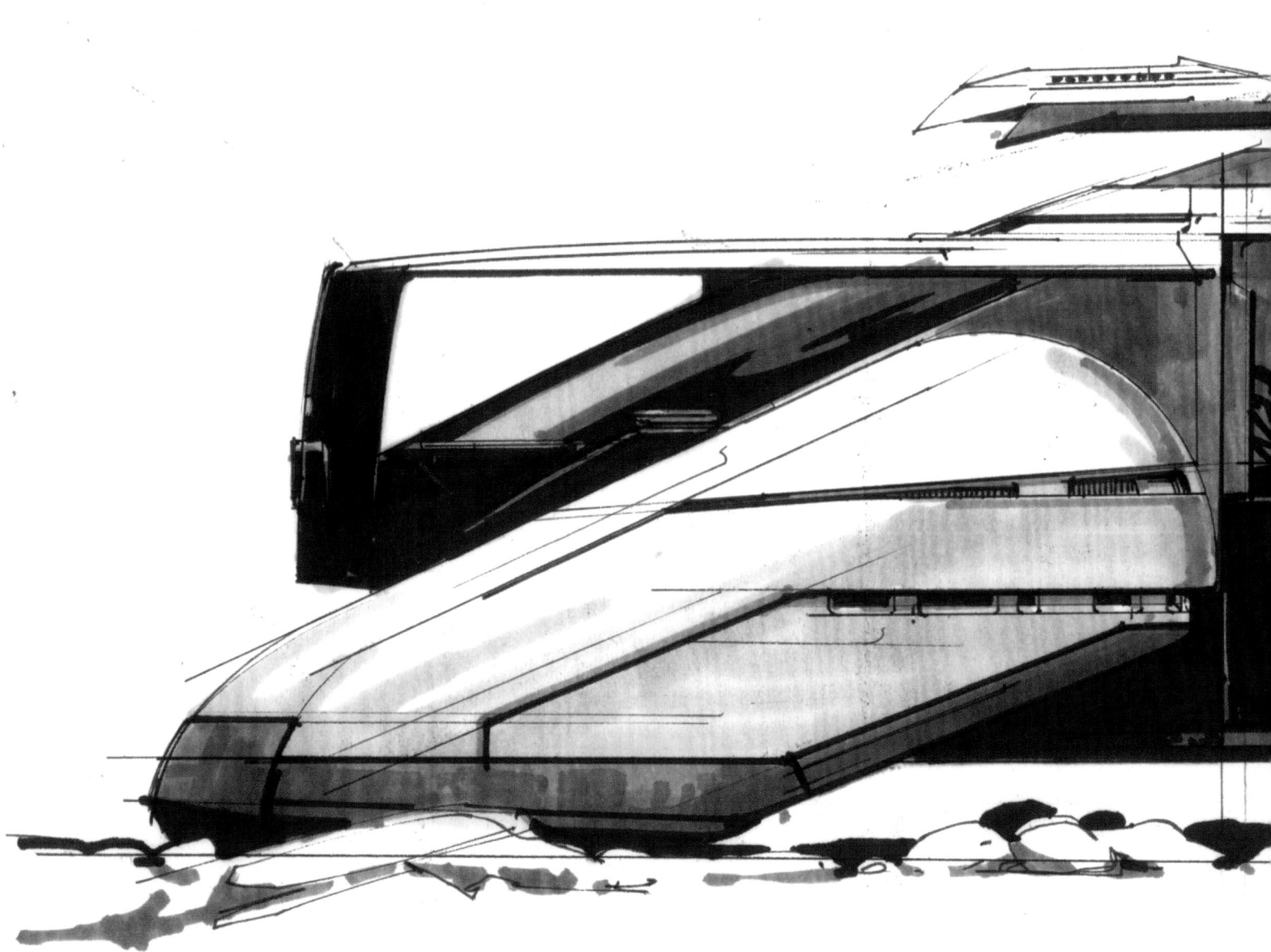

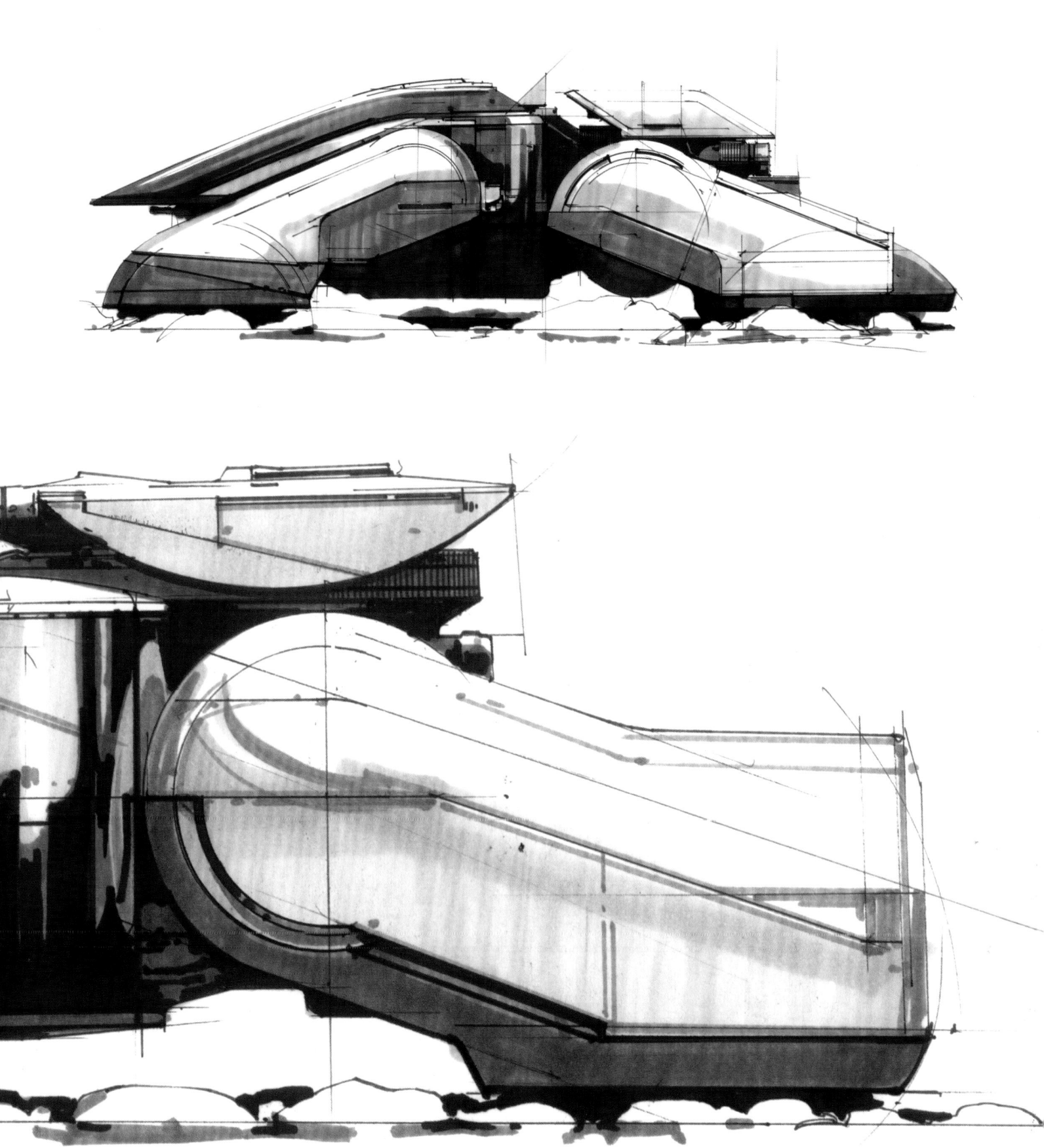

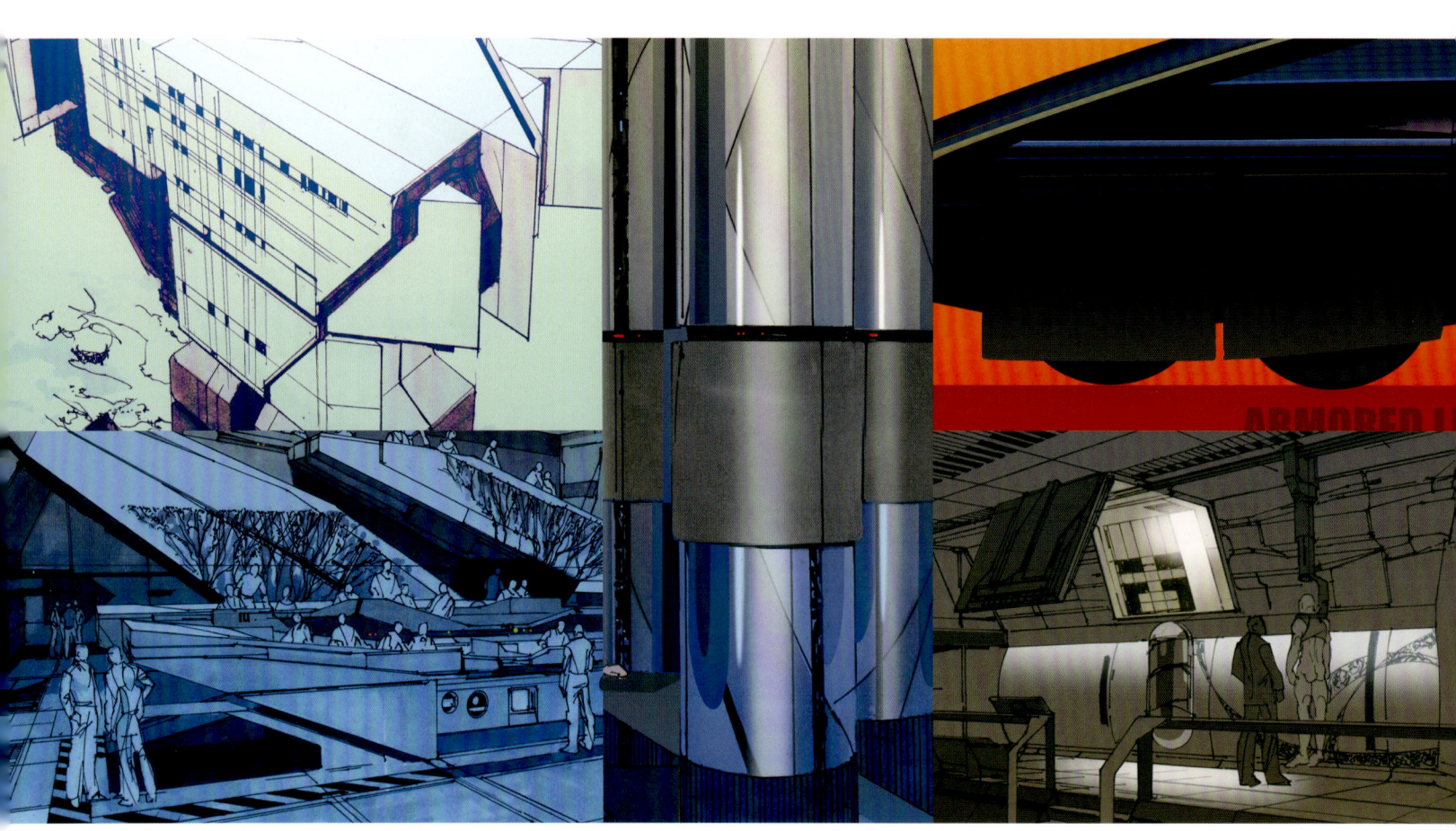

ELYSIUM

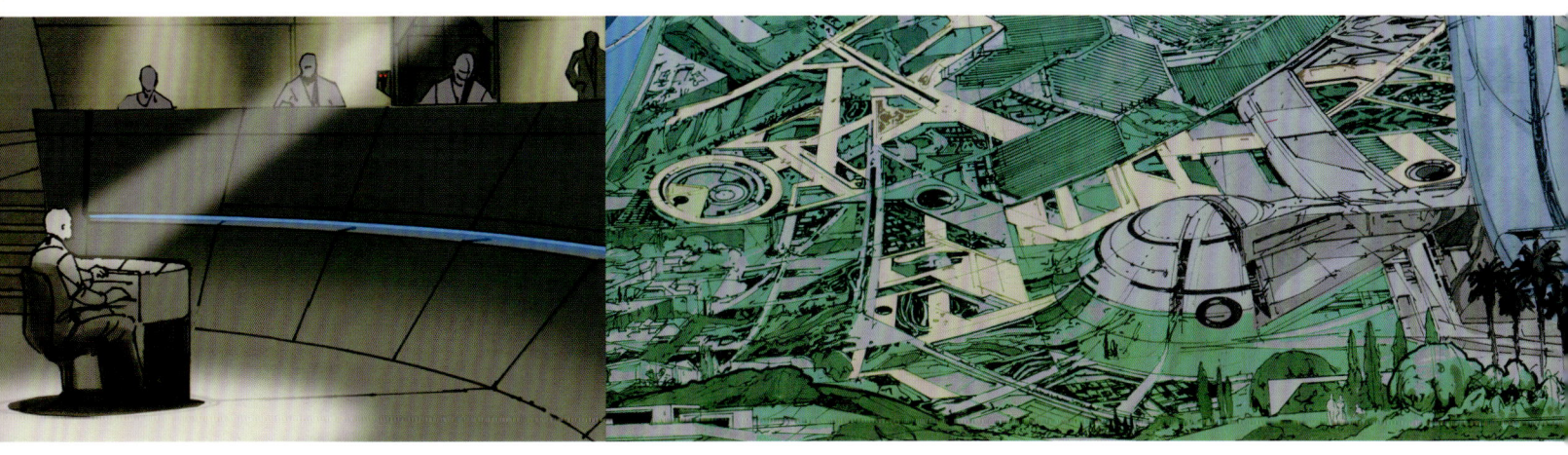

ORBITING PARADISE

The ultimate version of the future dichotomy between rich and poor presaged by films and novels alike came to perhaps its most pointed expression with this 2013 production, starring Matt Damon.

After the much-acclaimed *District Nine*, director Neil Blomkamp came upon one of Mead's drawings of an inverse world in outer space which he'd created for National Geographic Magazine decades before, and sent him the script for *Elysium*. As Blomkamp had broken into film by way of computer animation, he was no stranger to design, which contributed to an affable creative relationship between the two men. Using terms like organic, more organic, and mechanical, Mead's early sketches reflect the search for the film's visual metaphors, which sometimes reflected the socio-political sub themes of the plot, which, to Mead, flirted with depictions of a fascist government that, he says, "lets you do what you want, but not really".

It is no surprise, then, that the design of the colony became the focus of those discussions. Mead's native design objectives—the sheen of surfaces, the industrial patina, the geometry of volumes—may have seemed an obvious answer for a colony whirling like a giant Ferris wheel in space, but Blomkamp had different ideas, vetoing Mead's interlocking hexagonal grid for a more "suburban" look, which would bring to mind a verdant, Beverly Hills-like aura.

Mead's sketches, which never made it to the screen, depict a kind of heavy metal future, imbued with a darker, brooding quality seemingly at odds with the film's title, perhaps anchored in the dystopian future images which he himself had helped to nurture in films like *Blade Runner* and *Aliens*.

Nevertheless, the images on these pages, depicting a mushroom-cloud-like residence towering over a dystopian landscape are a dark reminder of the perils of a future in which haves and have-nots are doomed to a perpetual *pas de deux,* often resulting in a disrupted, tortured dichotomy. Mead's head-on depiction of a garrisoned retreat high over a wasted landscape, its references to military architecture, and its aggressive, armored profile underscores the social tension implicit in the screenplay, which the film's final version seems to avoid in favor of a high-tech retreat.

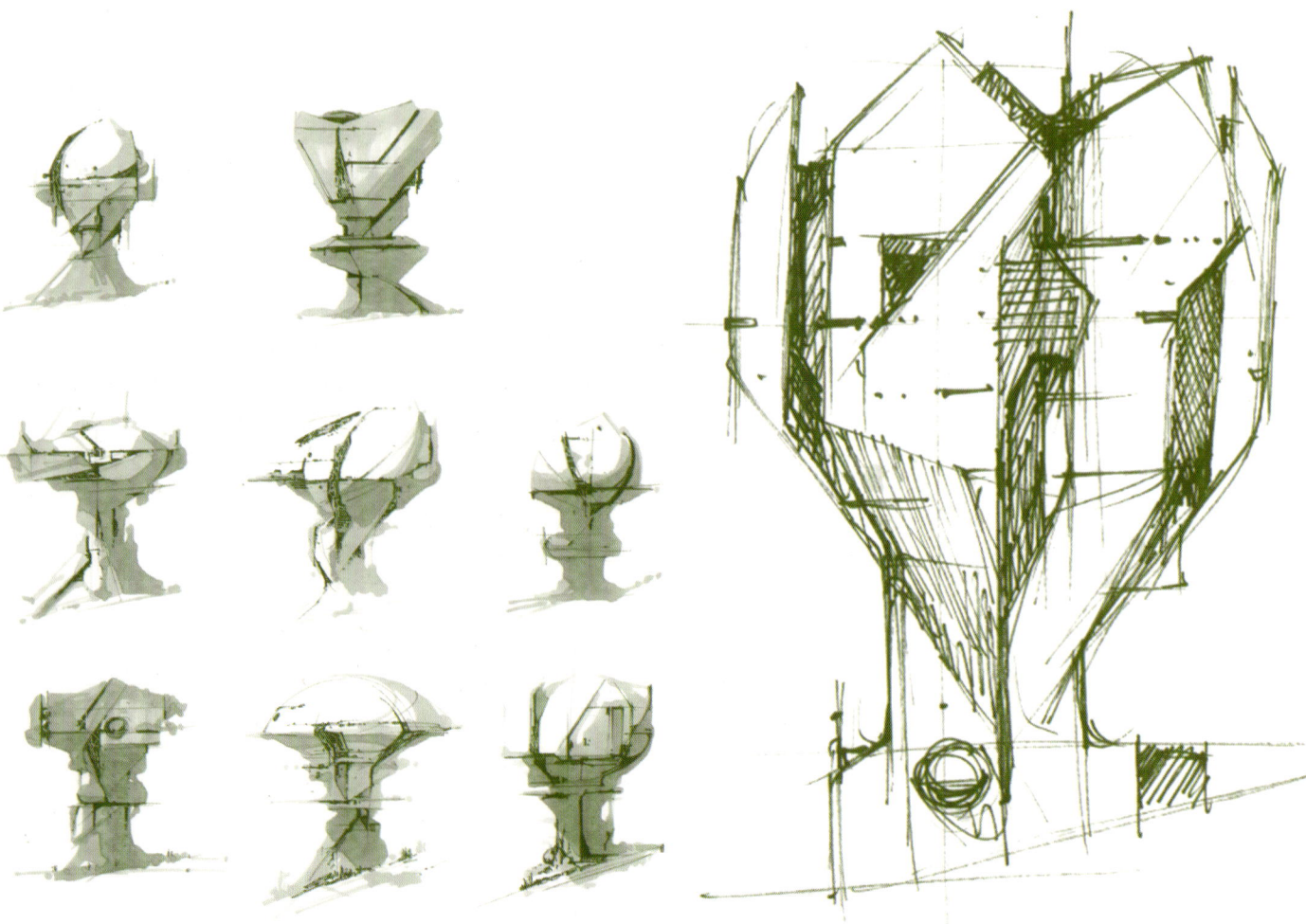

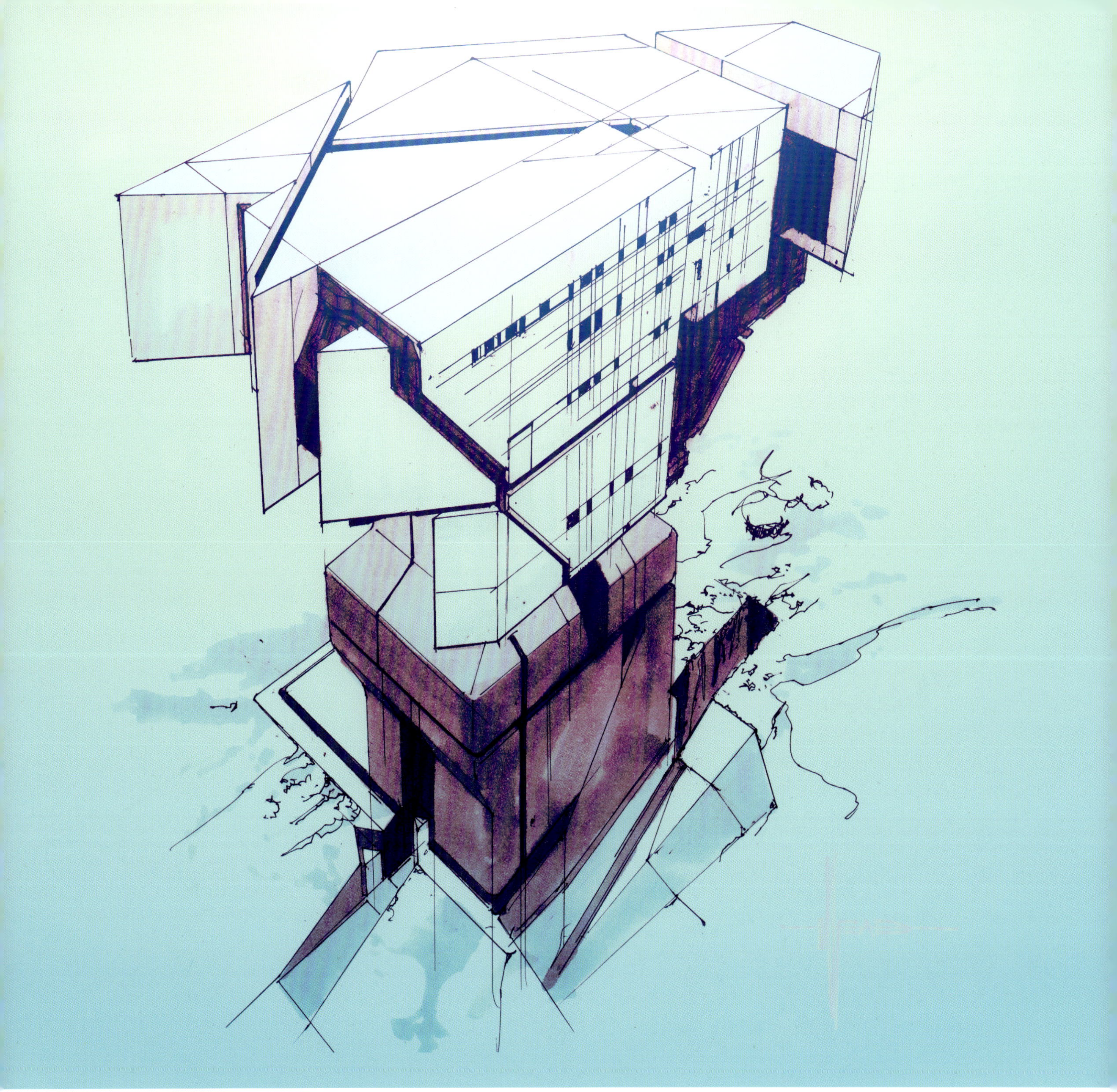

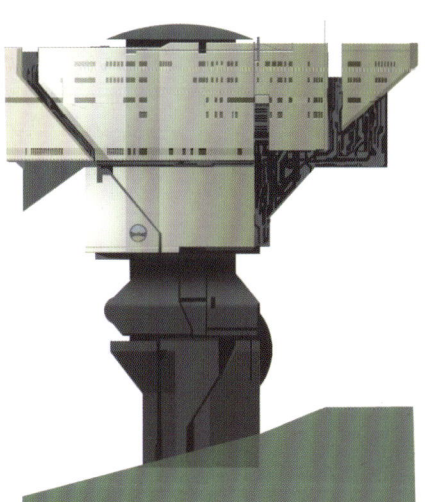

FOR THE HAVE-NOTS IN THE METAPHORIC SOCIAL STRUCTURE OF THE FILM, BLOMKAMP ELECTED A LOCATION ADJACENT TO A GARBAGE DUMP IN TIJUANA WHERE, MEAD SAYS, THE SMELL WAS SO OVERPOWERING THE PRODUCTION HAD TO COVER IT WITH IMPORTED CLEAN SOIL.

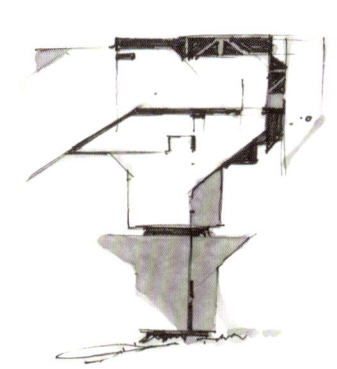
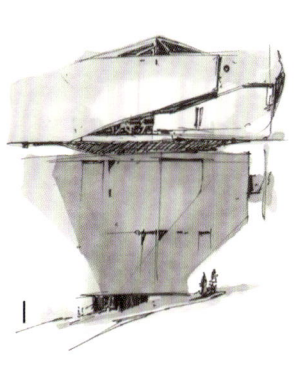
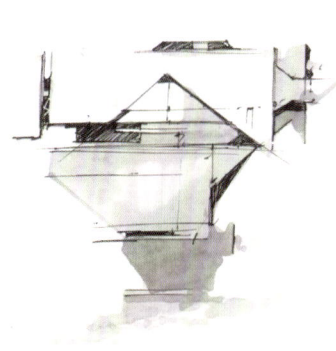

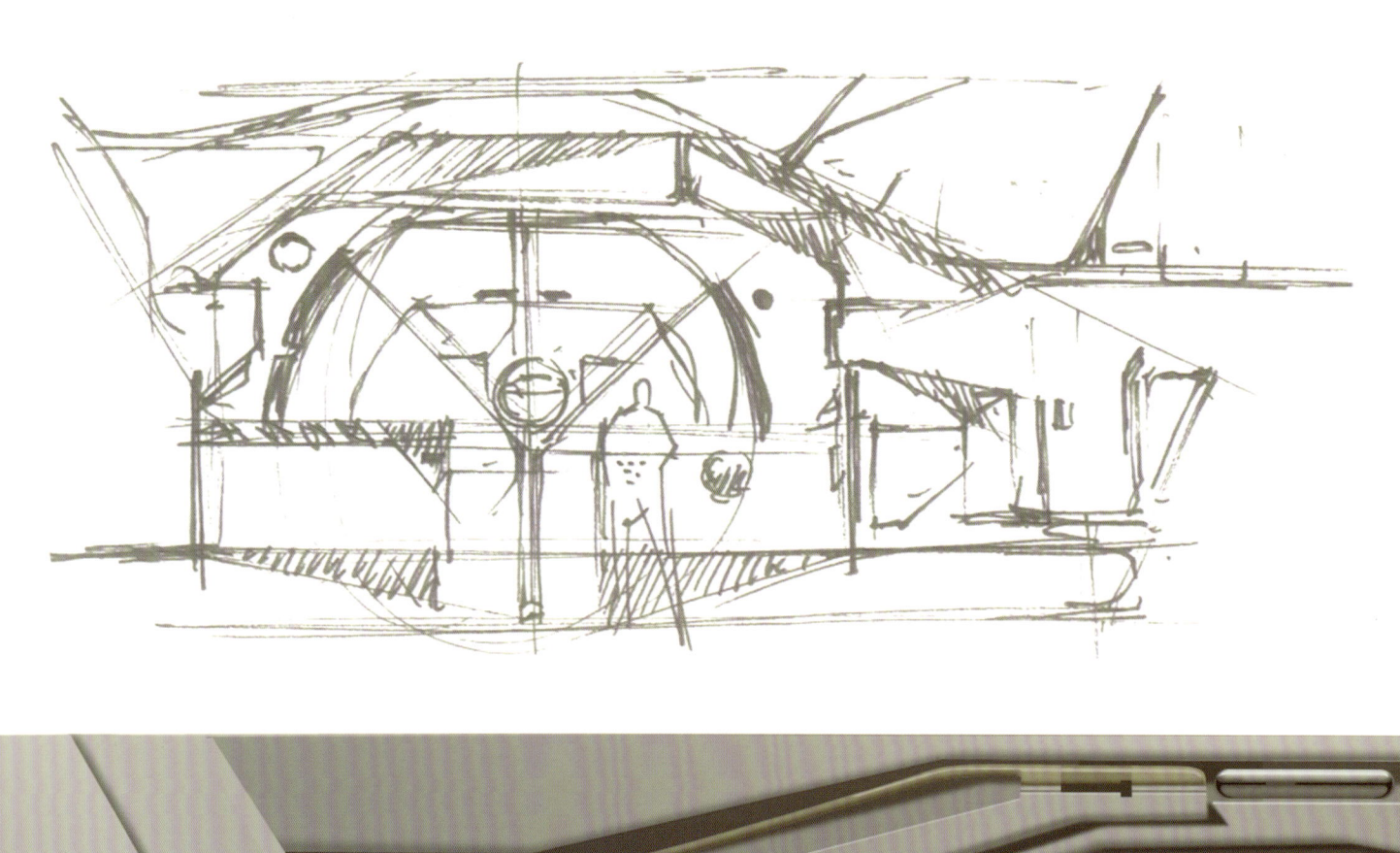

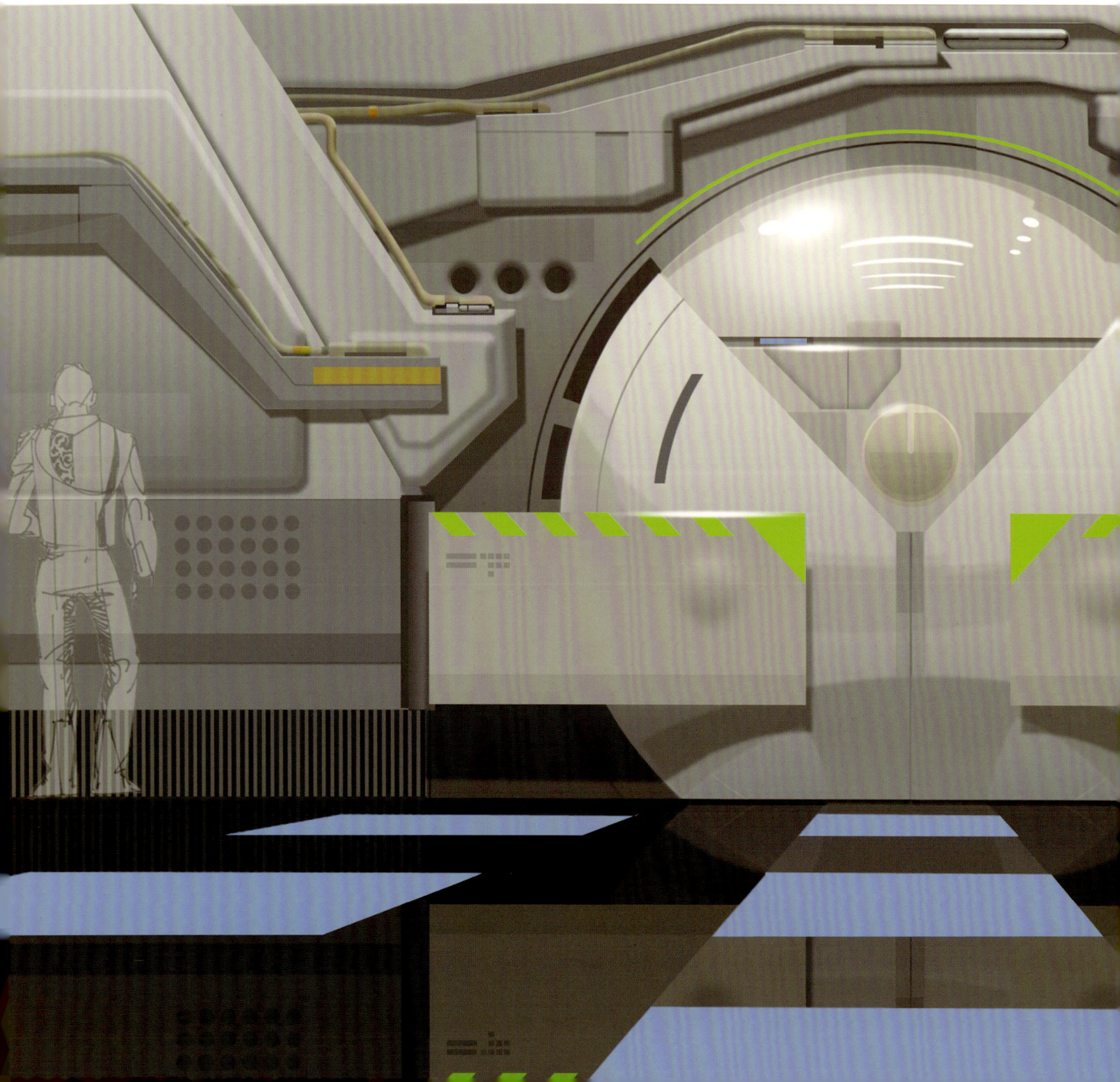

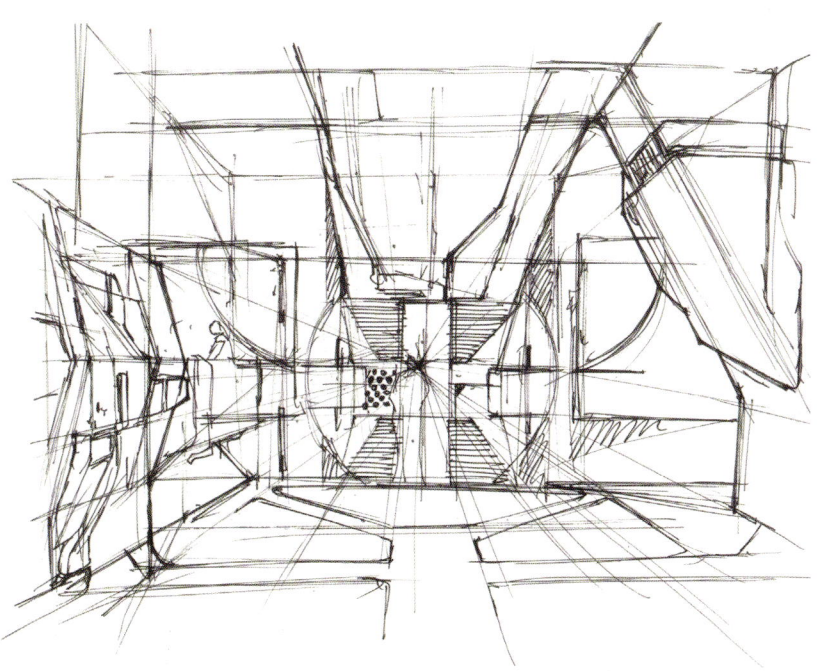

Mead saw this air lock as a symbol of the dramatic disconnect between the elite inhabitants of Elysium and the unfortunate outcasts on earth. As such, he reasoned that it needed to look the part, creating a massive structure of interlocking geometries that, by its very presence, signaled a social, economic, and cultural divide.

The design also introduces an entirely new operating regimen for such a devise, proposing to pivot two fan-shaped doors upwards to kiss at the apogee rather than sliding horizontally or traveling upwards like a medieval castle gate.

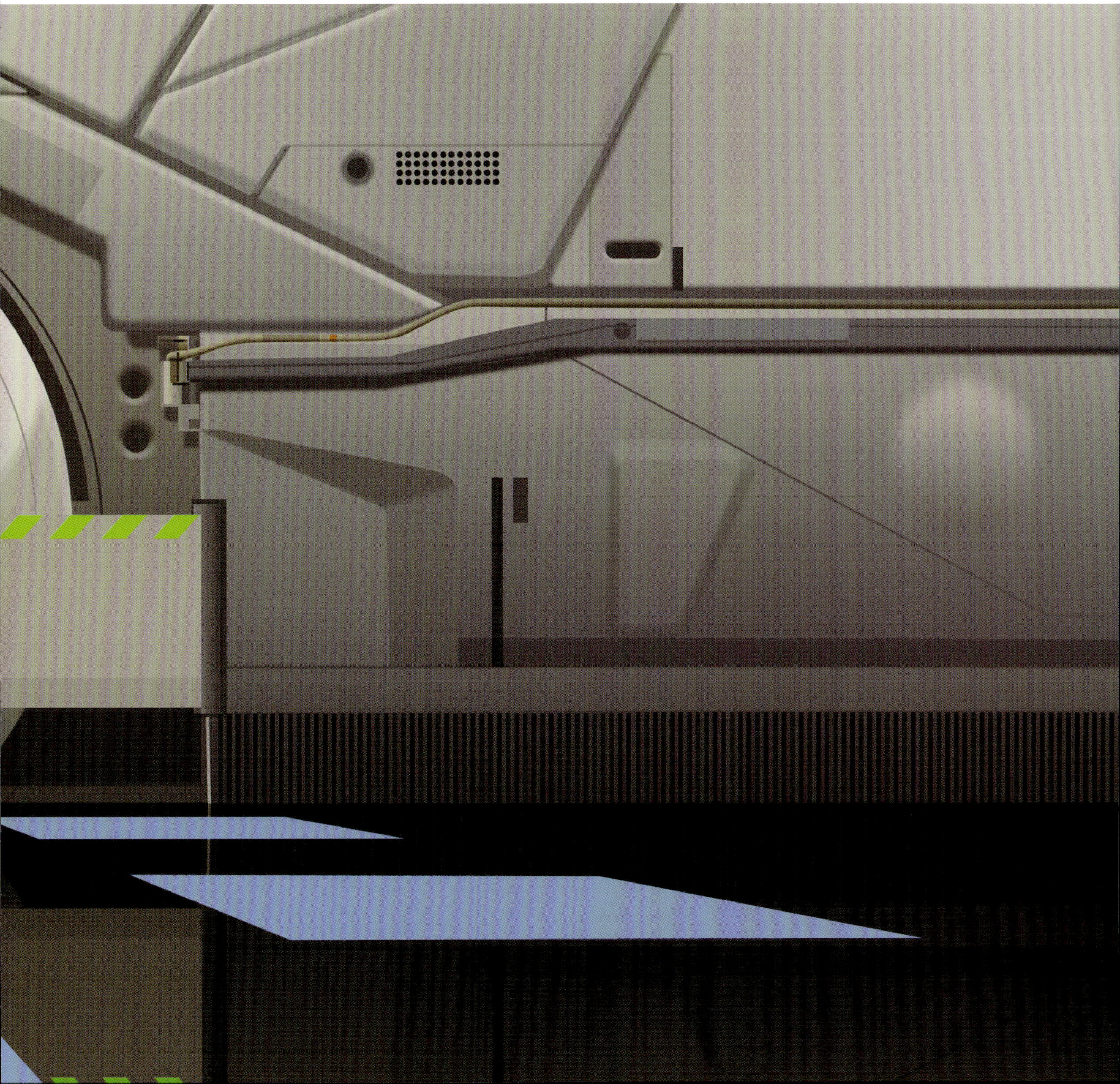

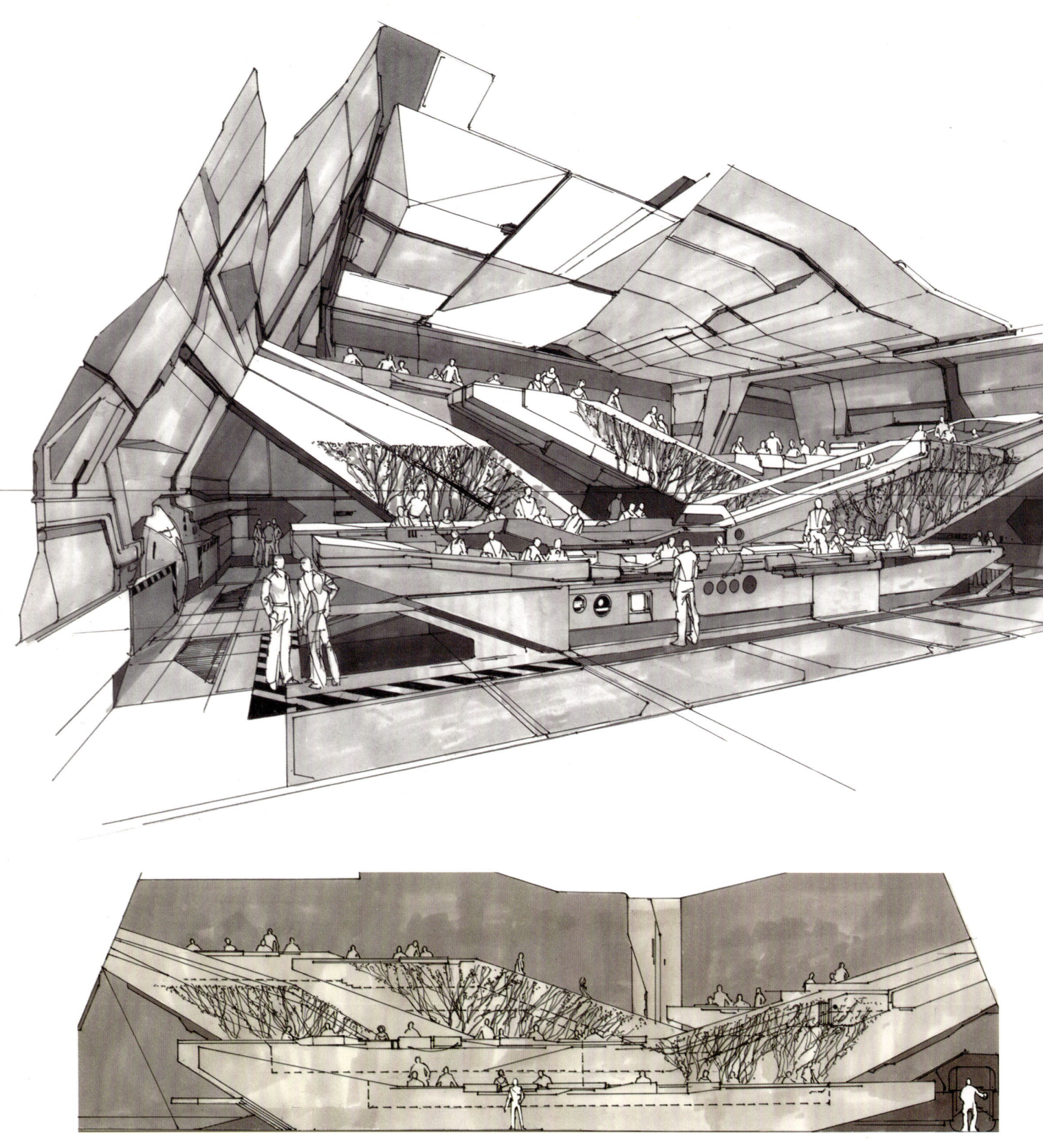

The images on these pages and overleaf are various concepts and sketches of a vast operations chamber. The overlapping staff pods came to exemplify a society in which the symbols of hierarchy and status conferred power on the ruling class. In these sketches it appears that the pods would, ideally, pivot to direct the seated judiciary to scrutinize the subject.

Concepts such as these are in fact practical within the bounds of current technologies and also commonly appear in science-fiction movies in one iteration or another. They could lead, if implemented, to entirely new forms of performance, sports events, or video gaming.

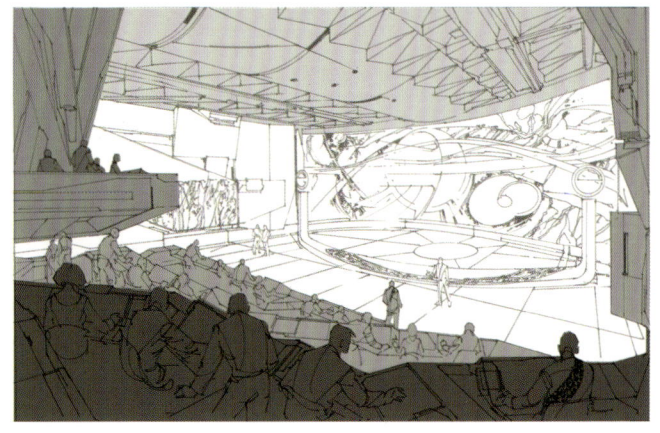

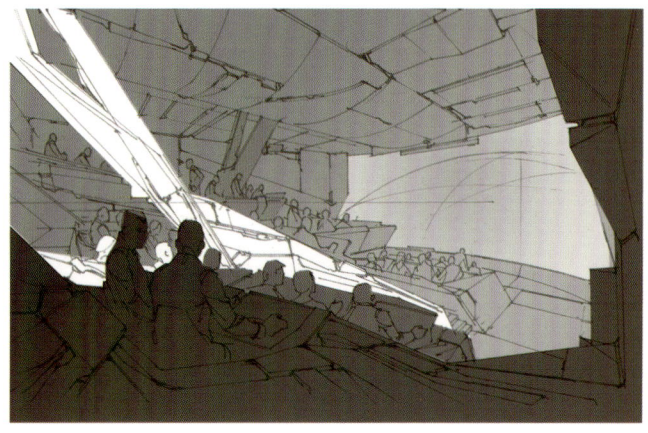

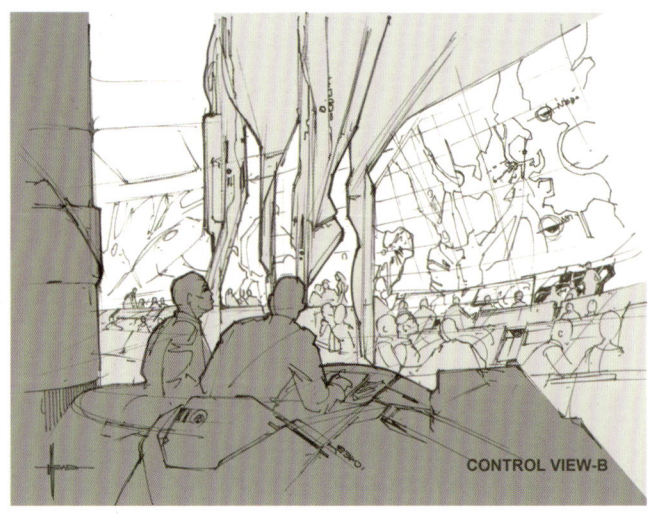

CONTROL VIEW-B

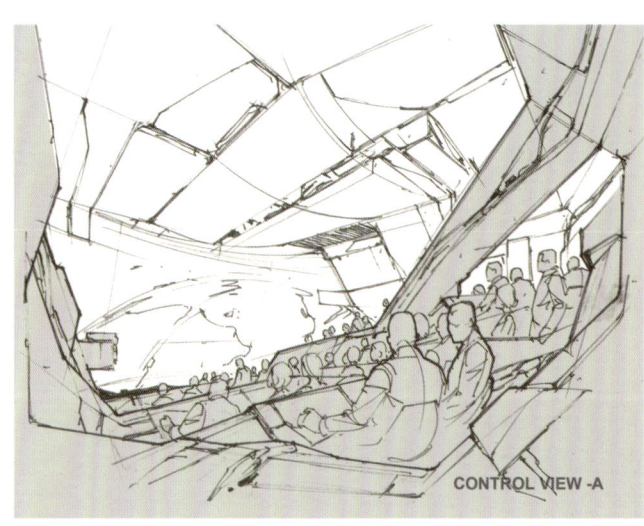

CONTROL VIEW -A

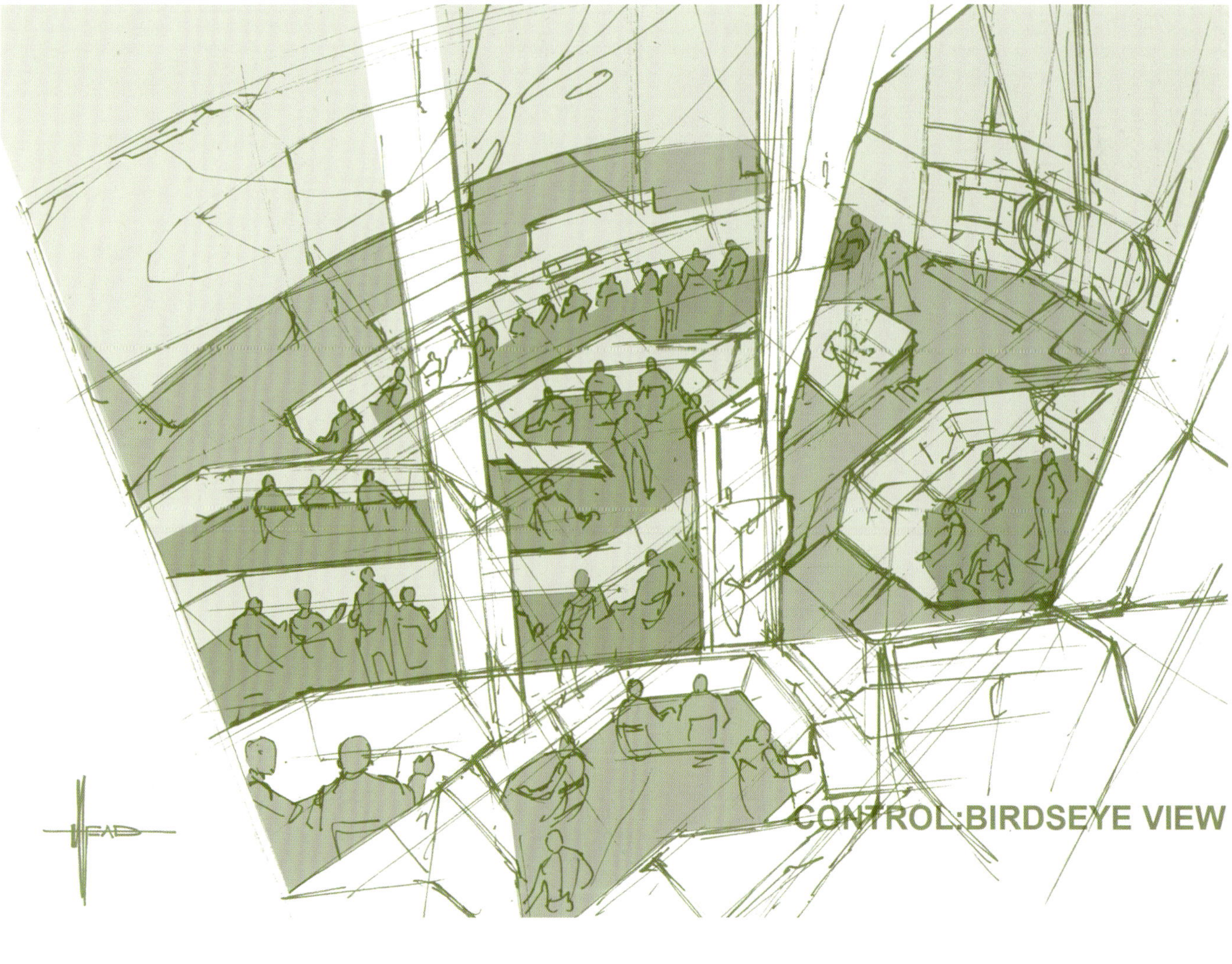

CONTROL:BIRDSEYE VIEW

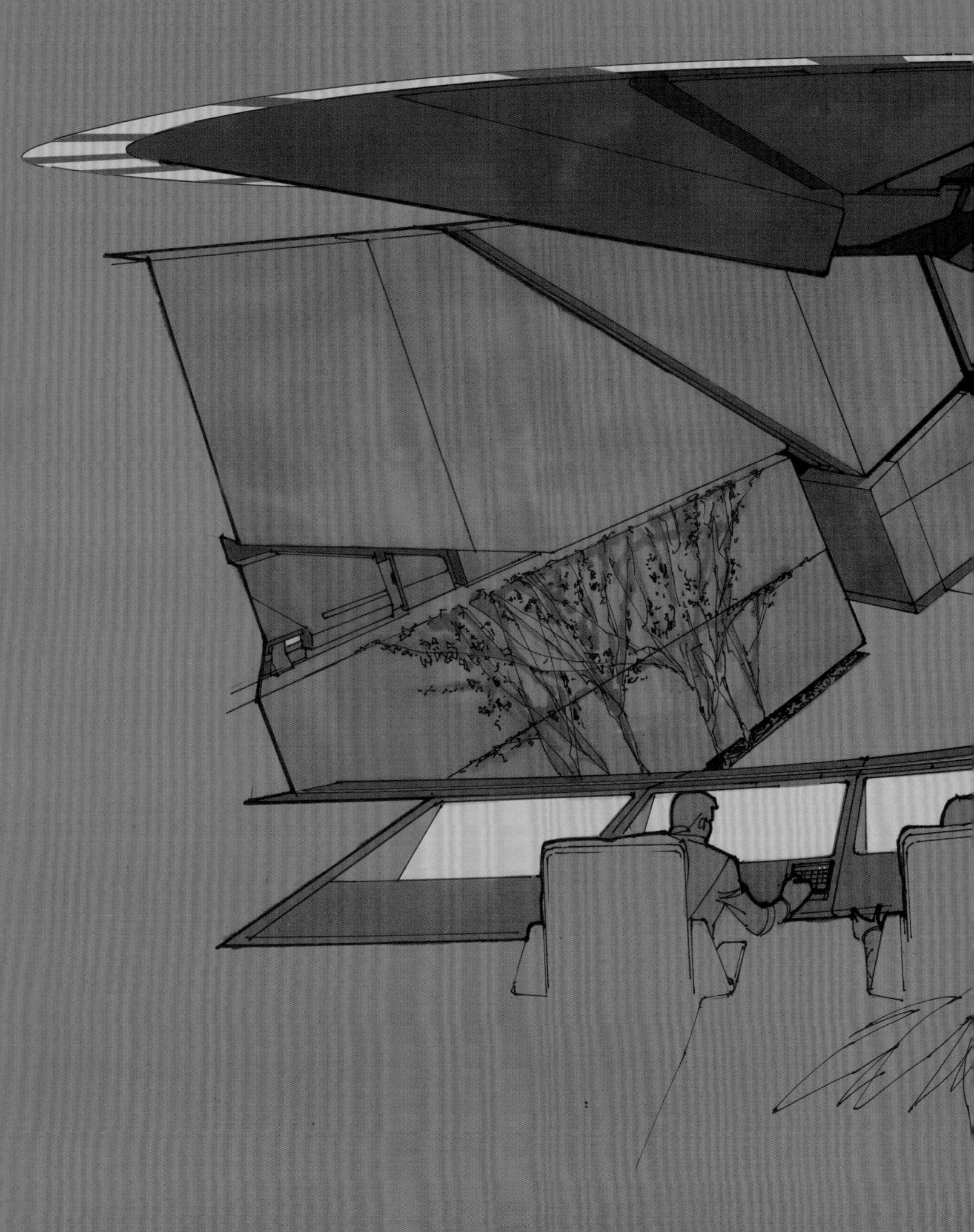

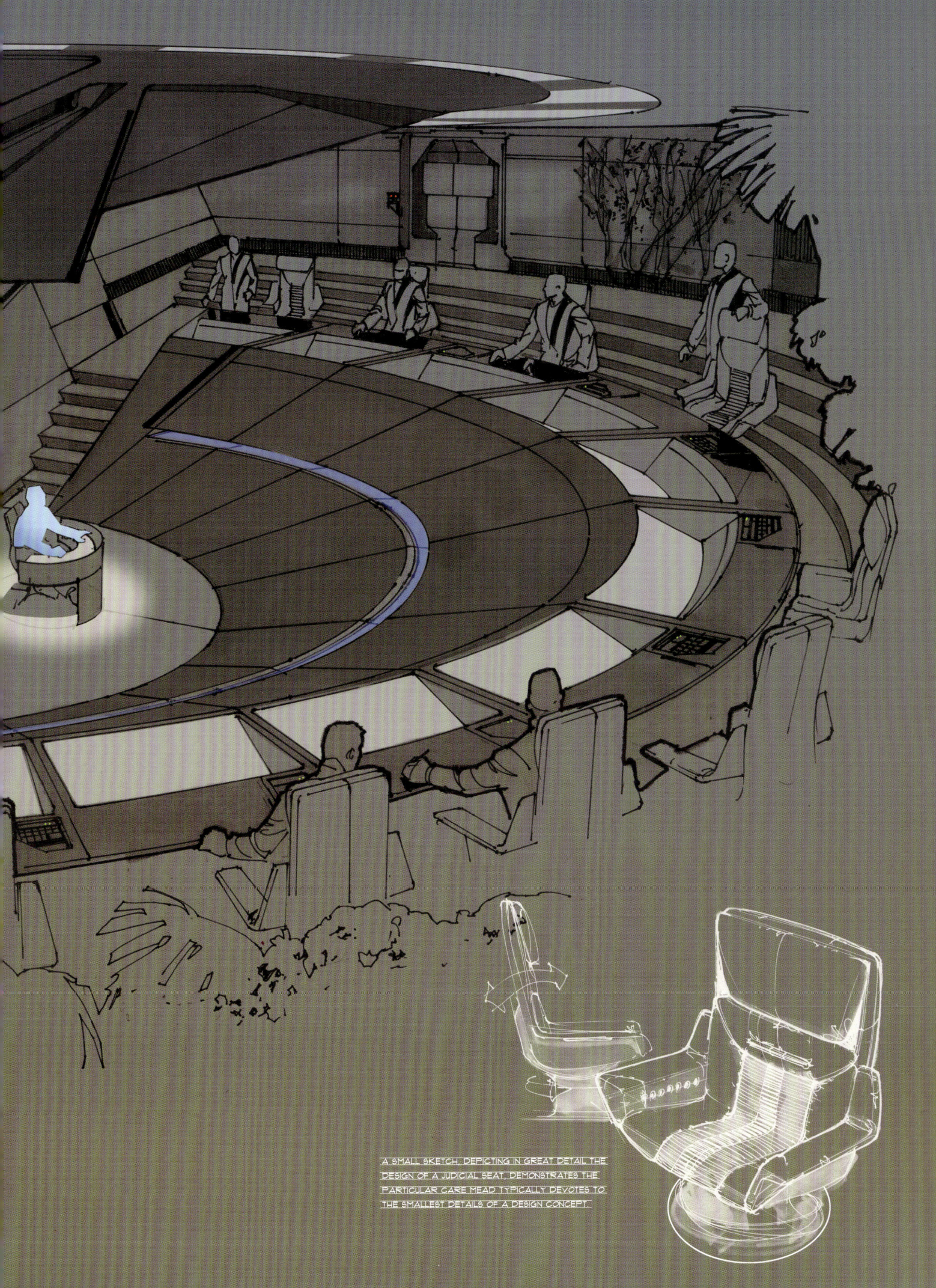

A SMALL SKETCH, DEPICTING IN GREAT DETAIL THE
DESIGN OF A JUDICIAL SEAT, DEMONSTRATES THE
PARTICULAR CARE MEAD TYPICALLY DEVOTES TO
THE SMALLEST DETAILS OF A DESIGN CONCEPT.

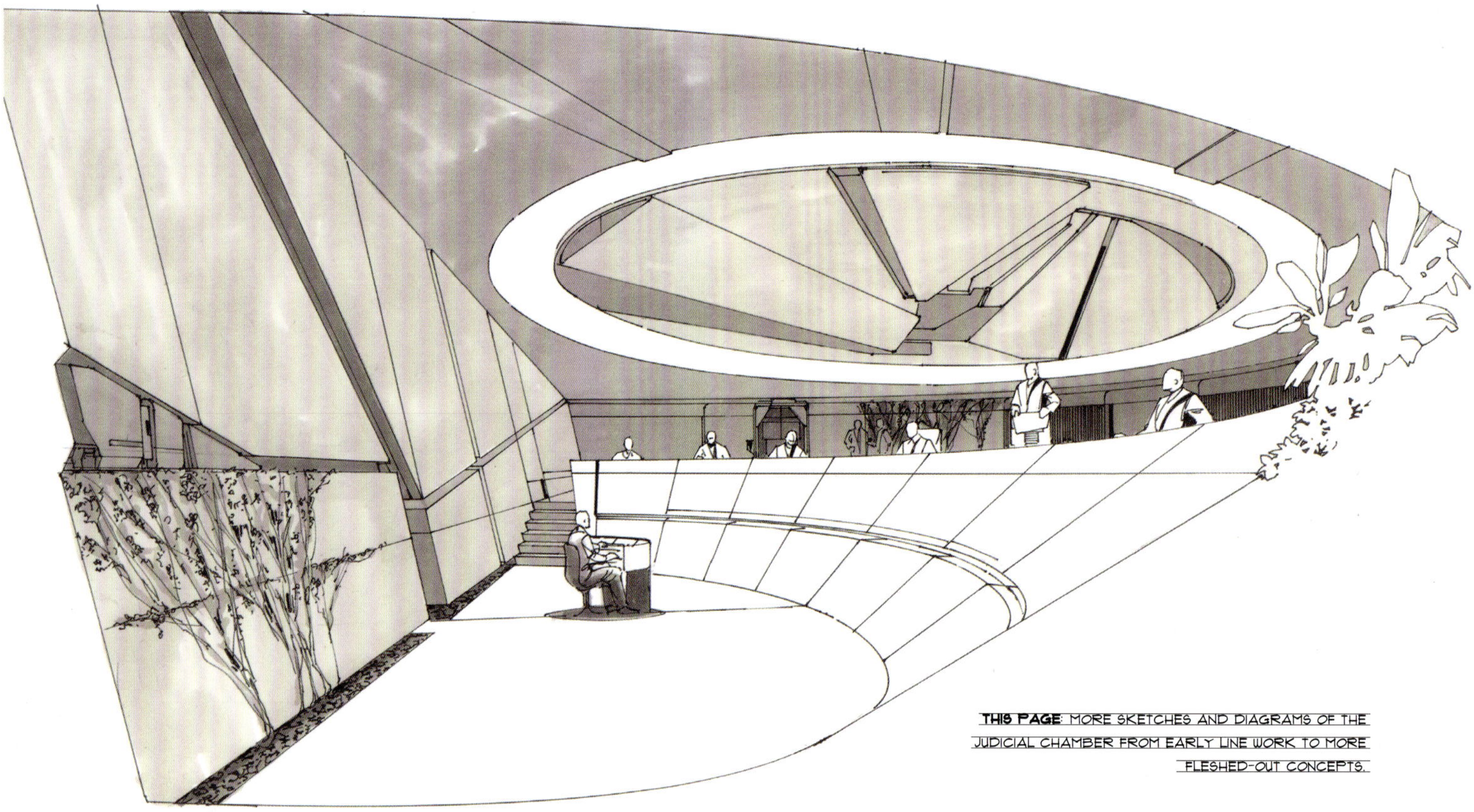

THIS PAGE: MORE SKETCHES AND DIAGRAMS OF THE JUDICIAL CHAMBER FROM EARLY LINE WORK TO MORE FLESHED-OUT CONCEPTS.

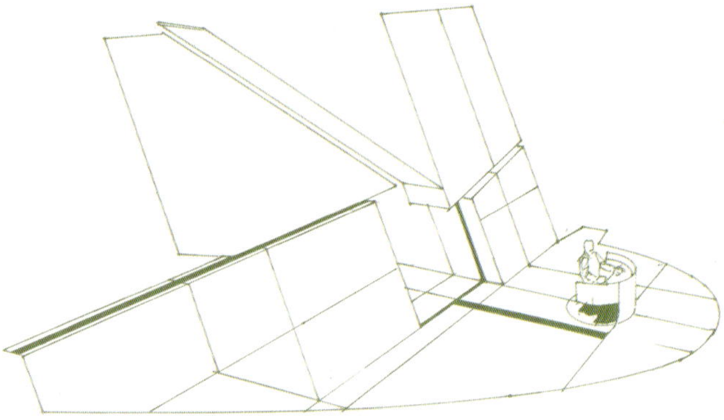

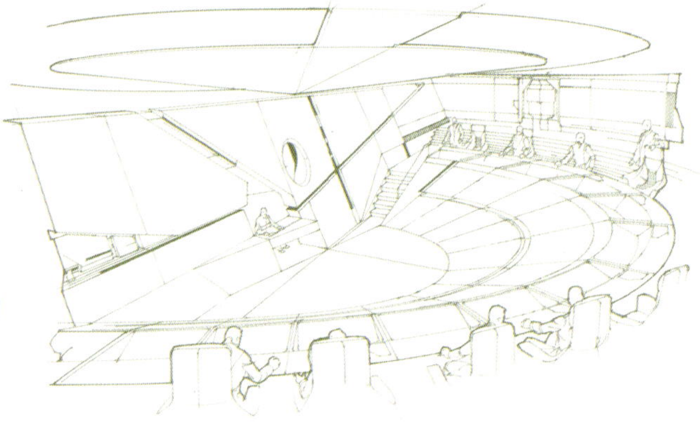

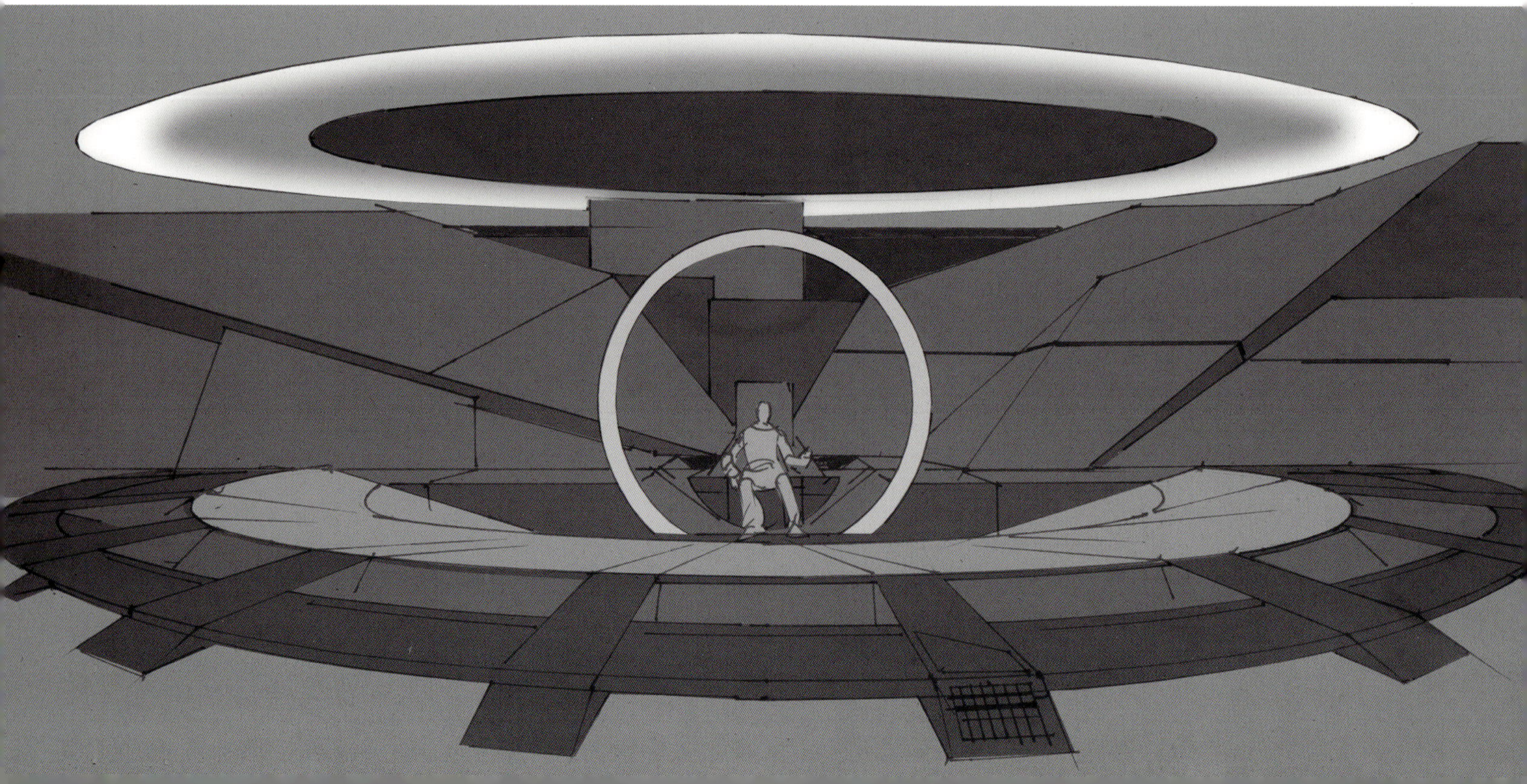

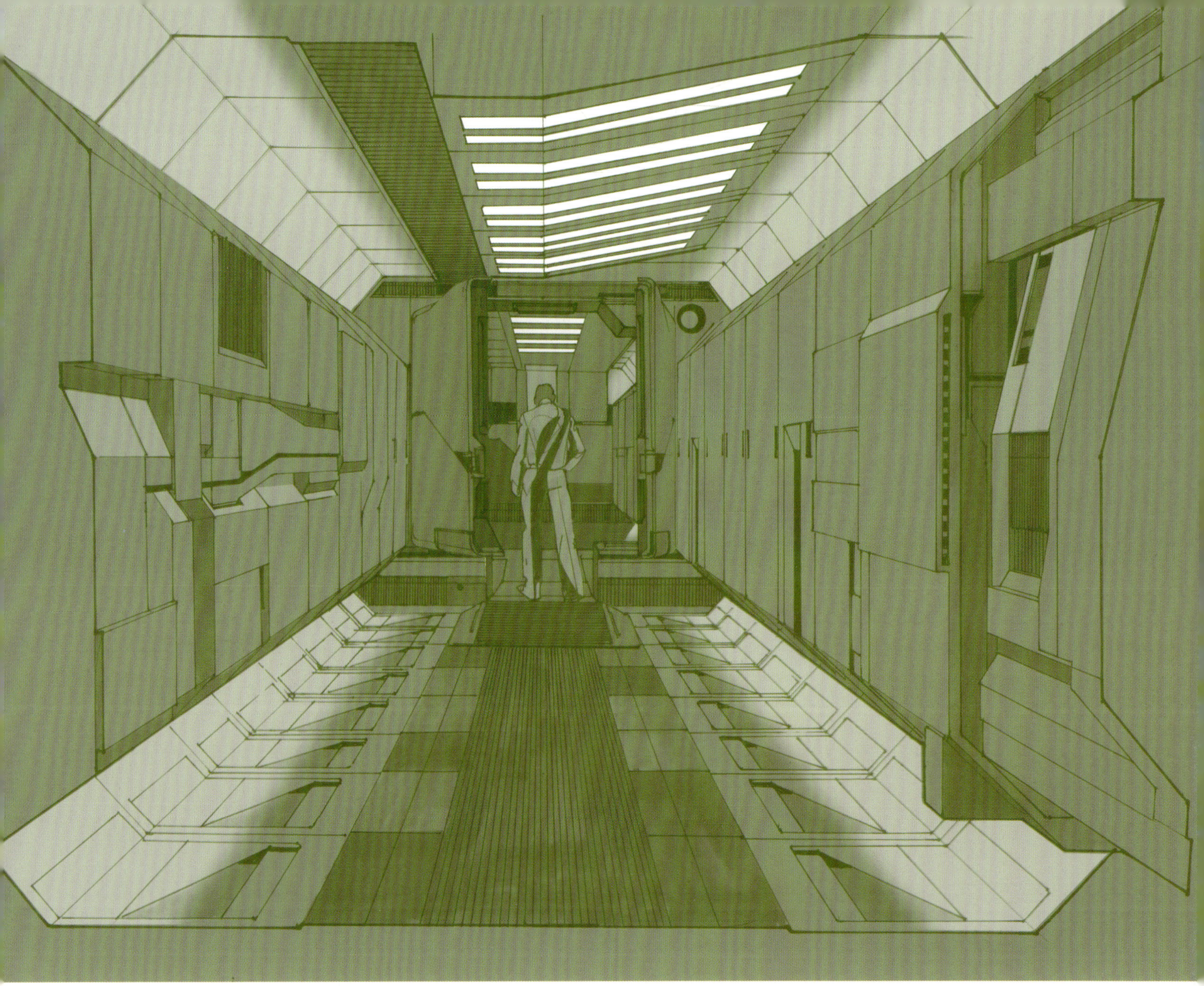

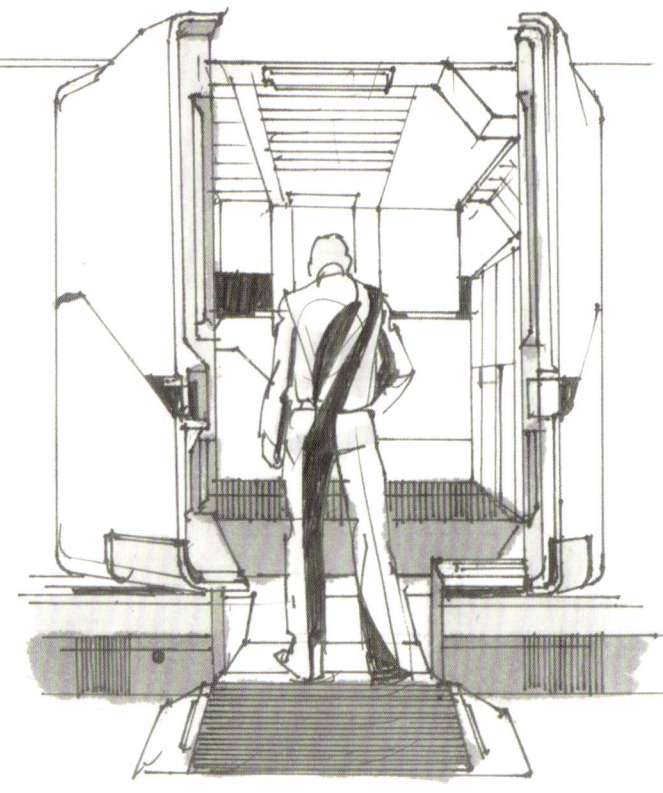

These sketches reveal a disciplined three-dimensional approach which takes a step beyond illustration to create a rigorous, dimensionally consistent design which is ready to commit to the set construction crew. Of particular interest is the sectional view of the corridor (below) in context with the perspective view above, and the detailed line drawings which form the basis for construction drawings by the movie's scene shop.

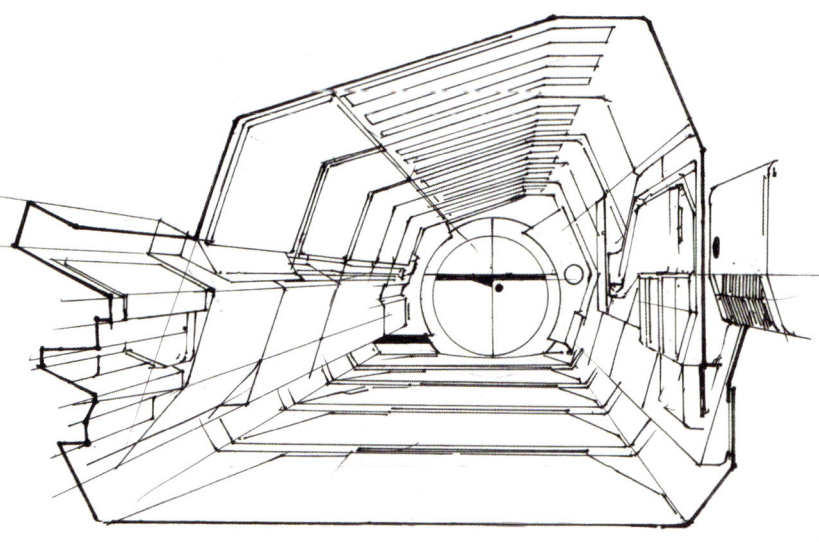

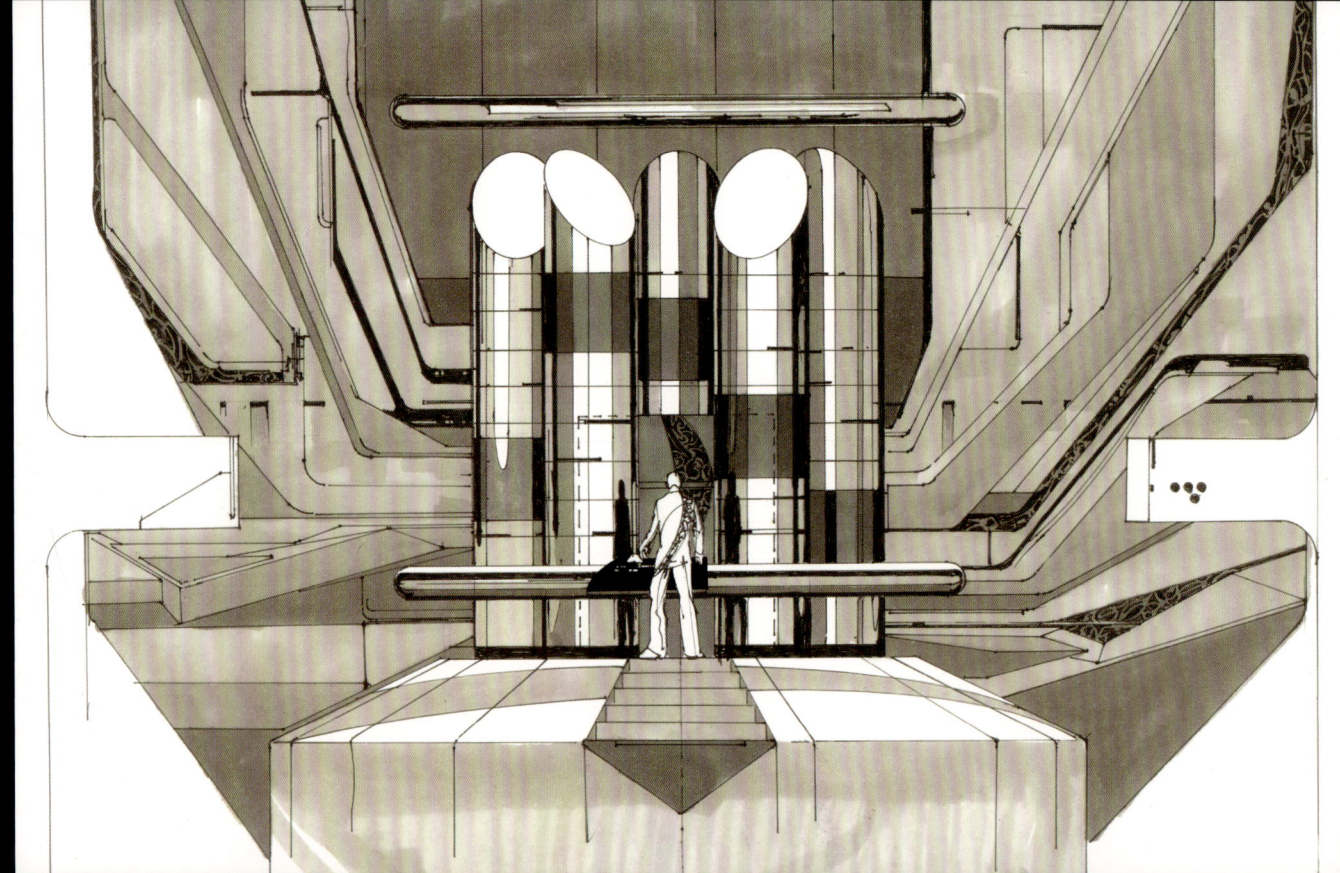

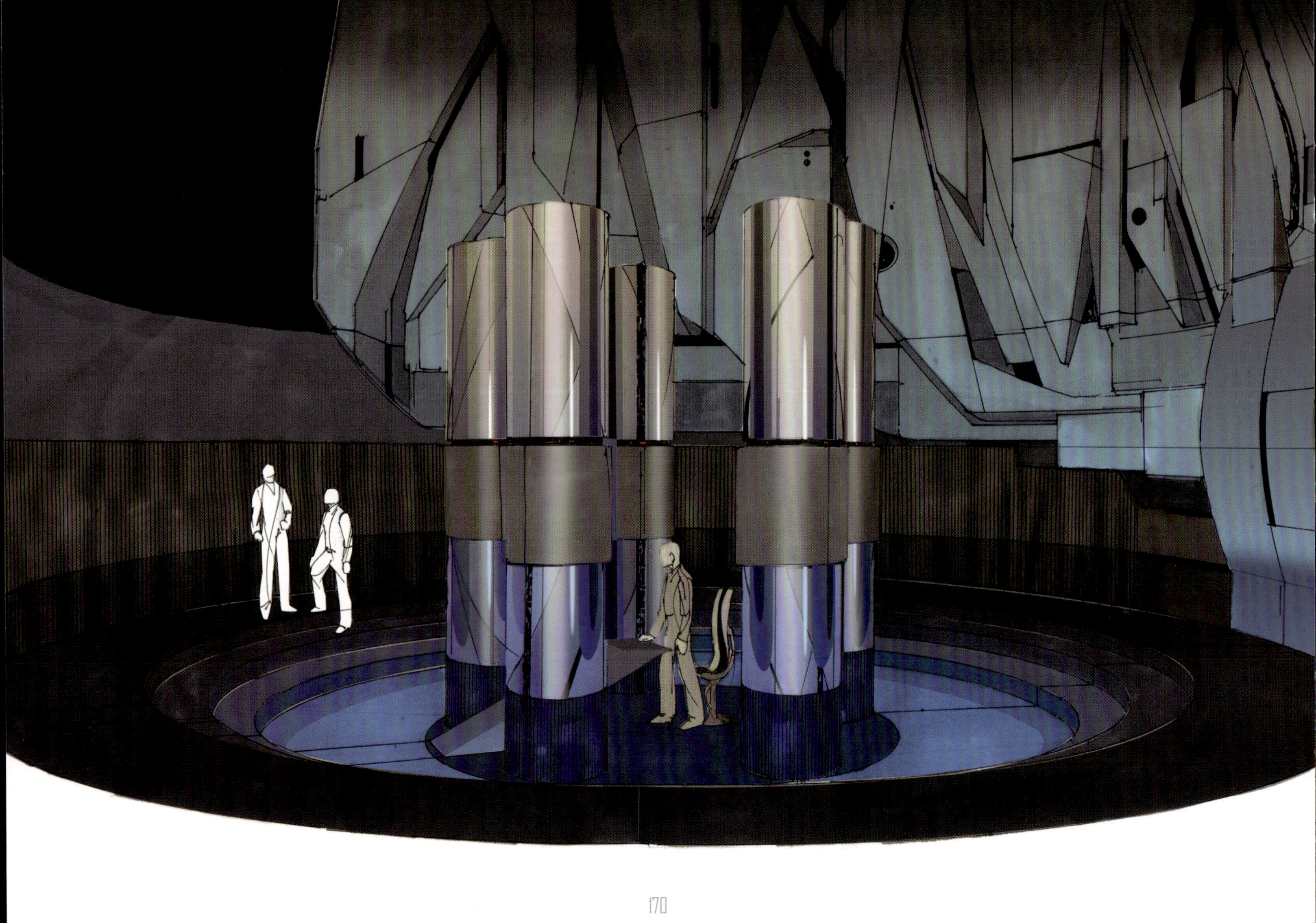

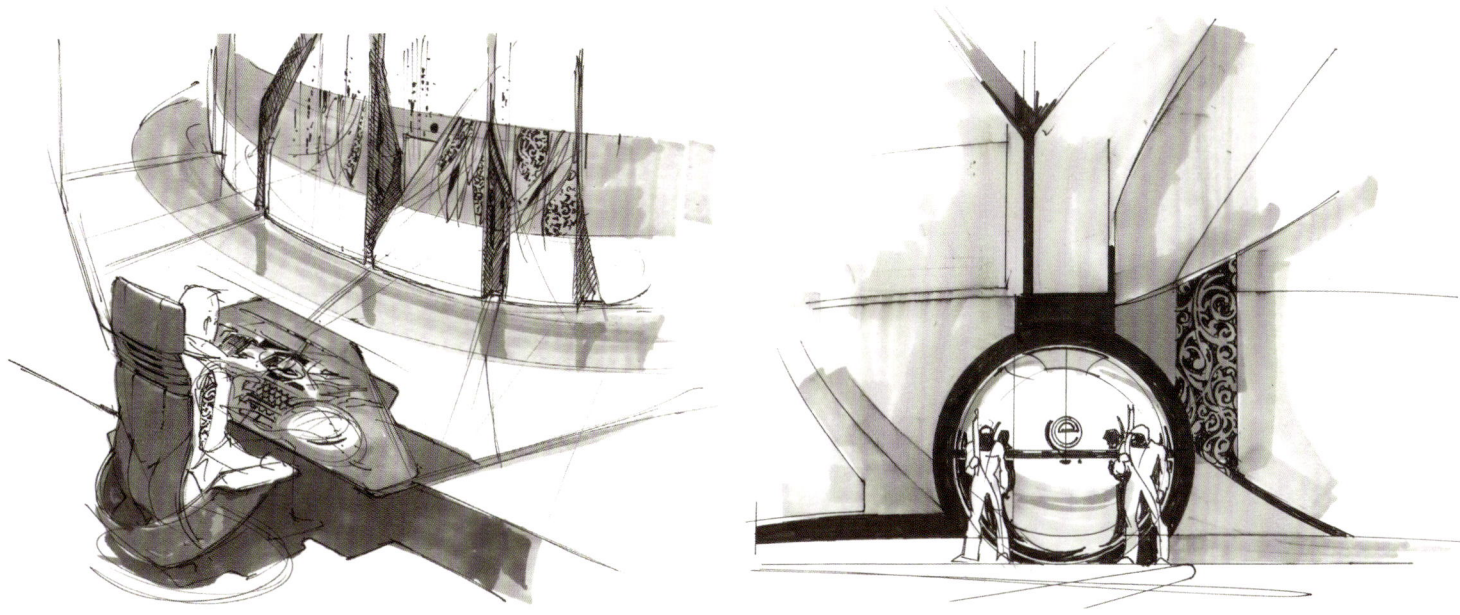

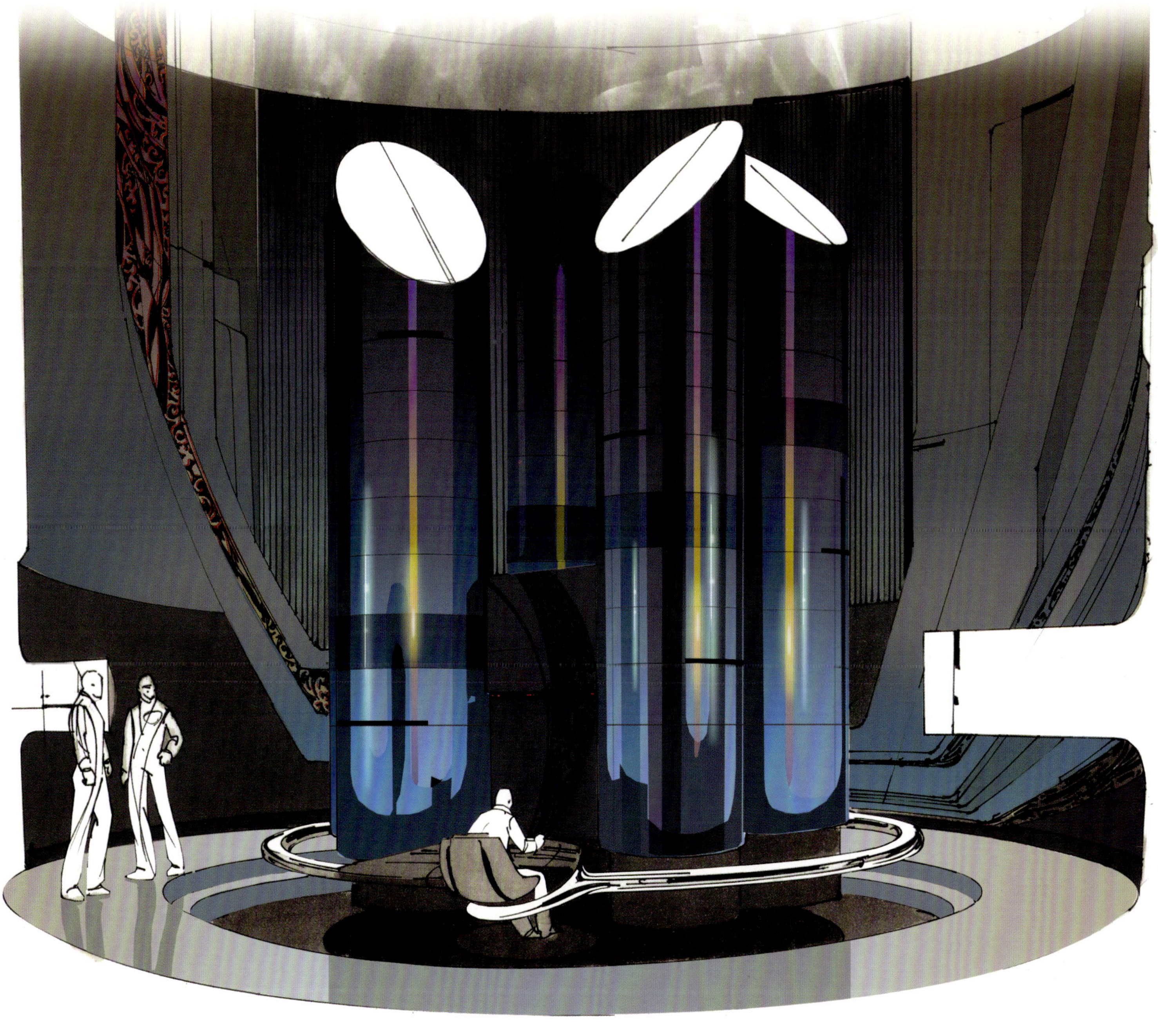

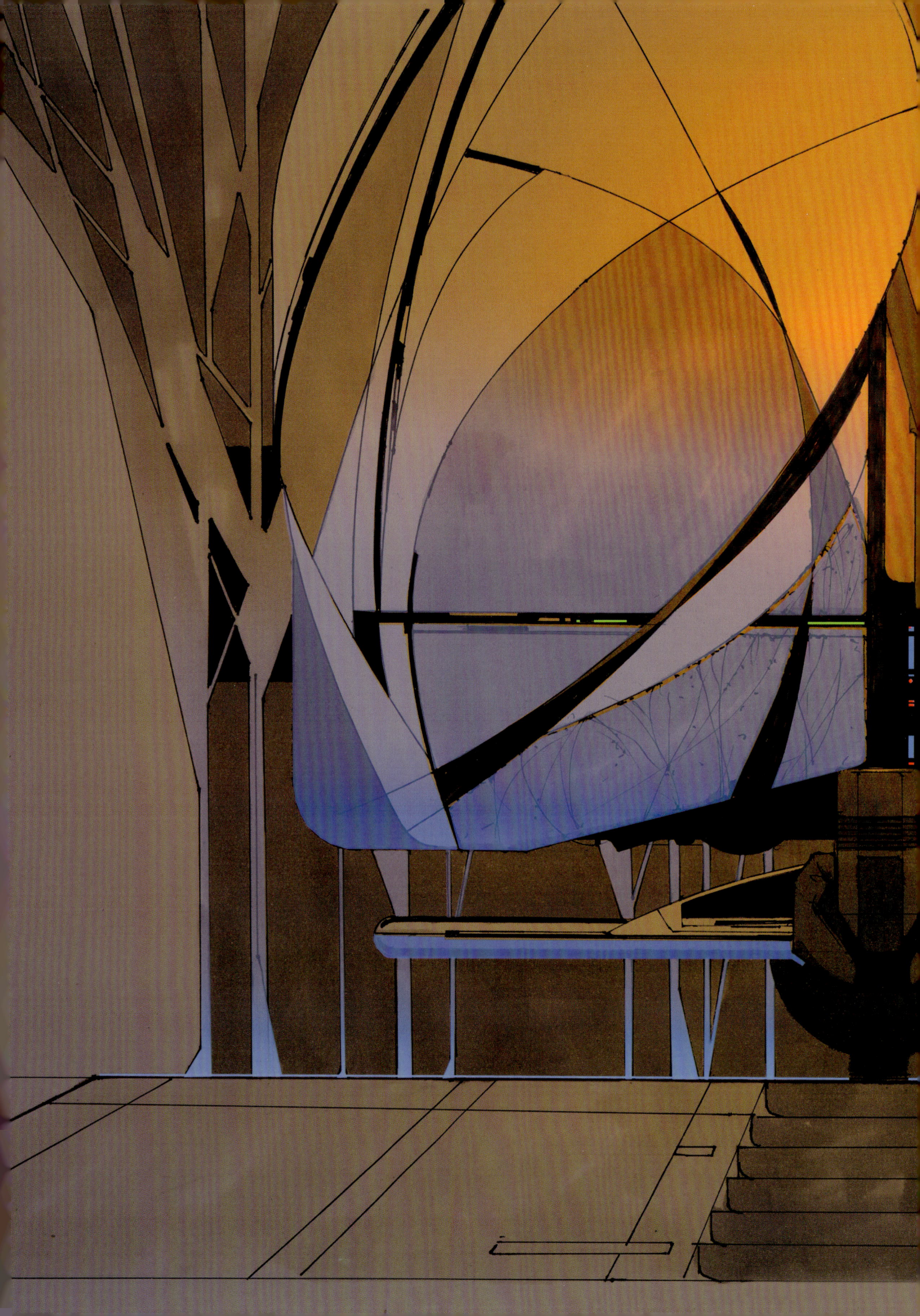

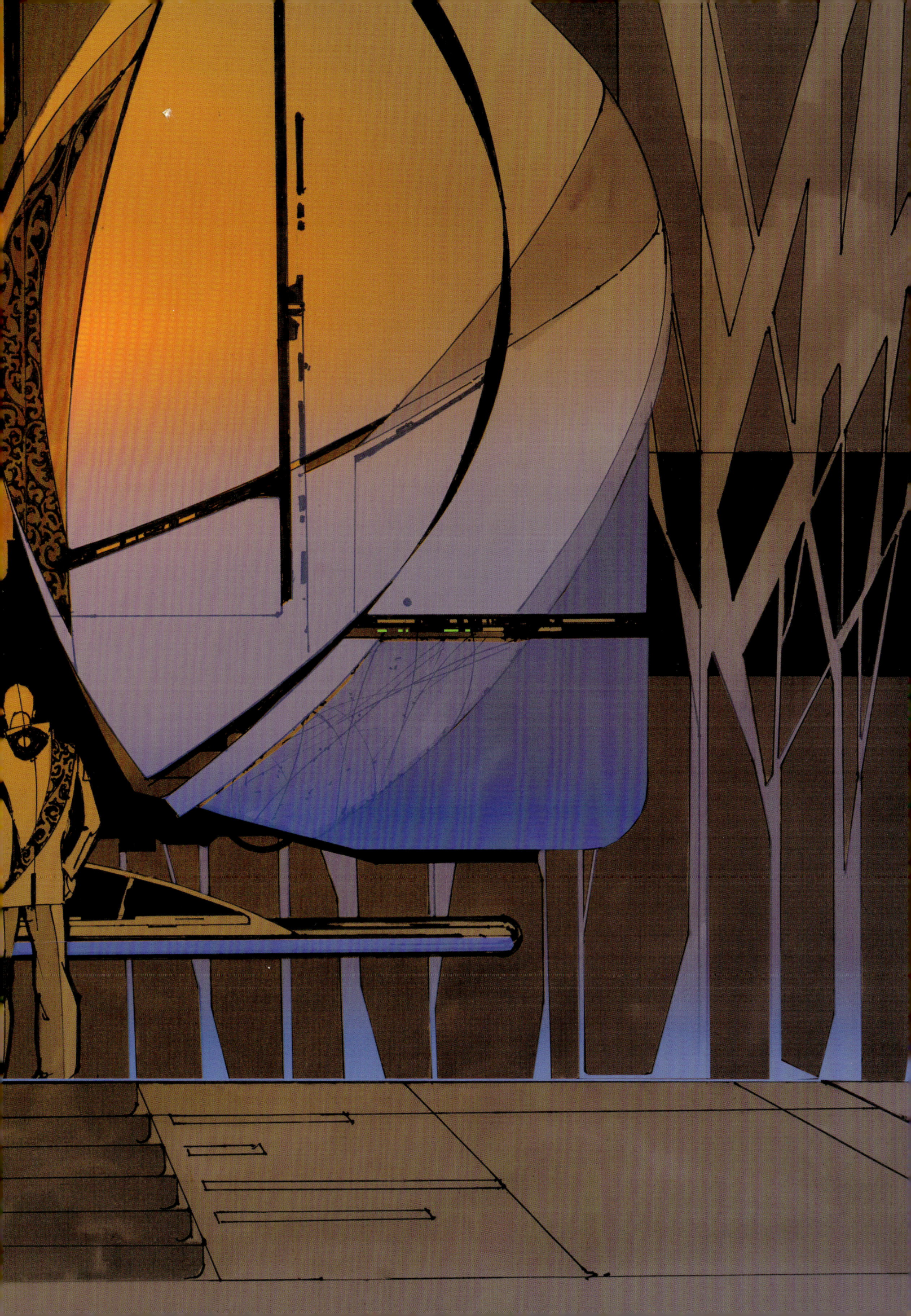

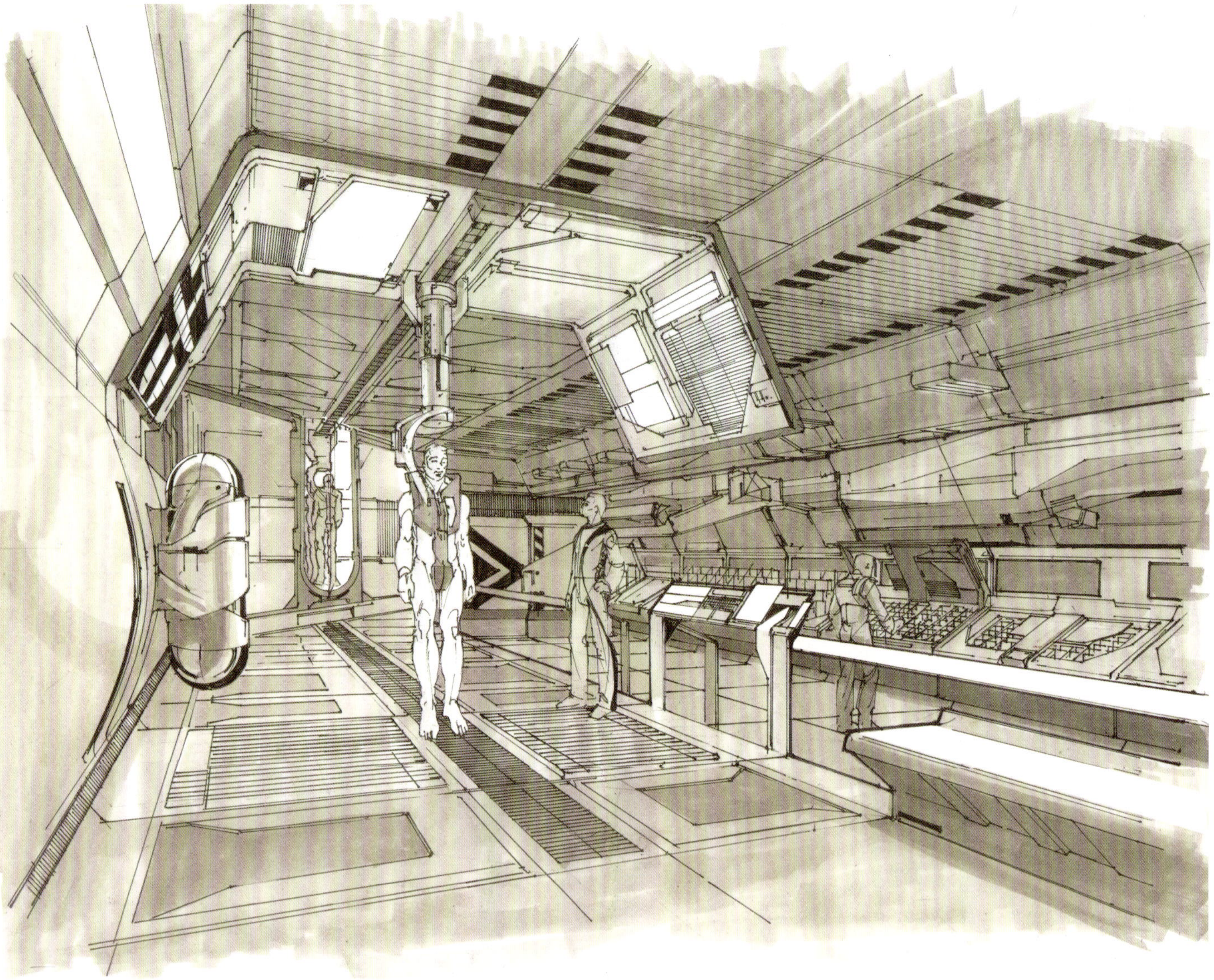

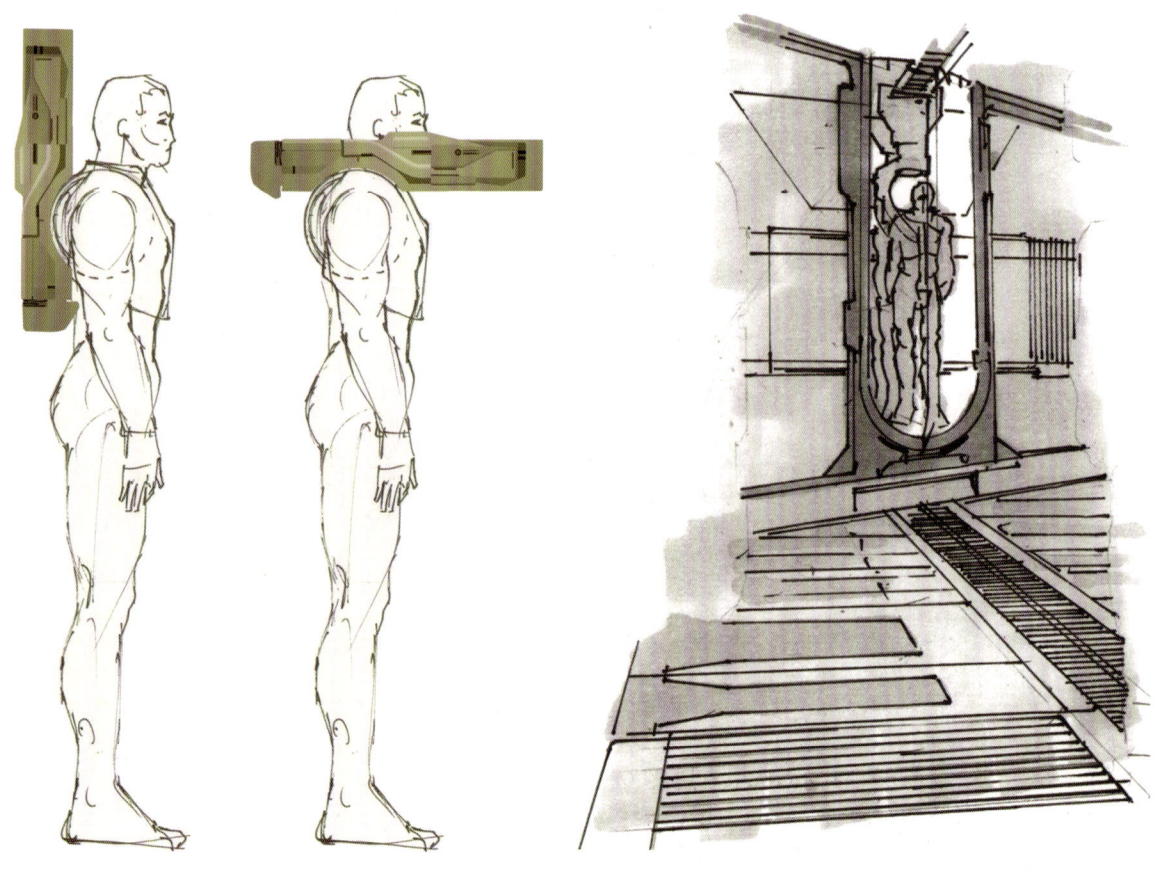

A human gantry (left) initiates a process for those who wish to become residents of Elysium. Equipped with multiple sensors and a moving, treadmill-like track, entry to the processing portal, where their bodies are exchanged for those suitable for their new life, is accomplished with a thorough, machine-like regularity. Thus transformed, the reconfigured *émigrés* are deposited in their new, 'idealized' environment.

Ergonomics, visible drama, and practical application coincide in the concept for guards and security personnel, who were to carry visible arms. Mead embellished the traditional gun sling (bottom left) with a clever vertical 'holster' from which a weapon could instantly come to the ready by pivoting over the carrier's shoulder.

Below, an unusual suspension system on the typical Elysium automobile envisions a pair of steering wheels much like the famous Tyrell P34 racing car which finished first and second in the Swedish Grand Prix of 1976. Other features of the design, such as the twin aerodynamic doors over the forward wheels, and the steeply raked windscreen are surprisingly contemporary, with recent prototypes from Mercedes and Rolls Royce sharing the concept in 2017.

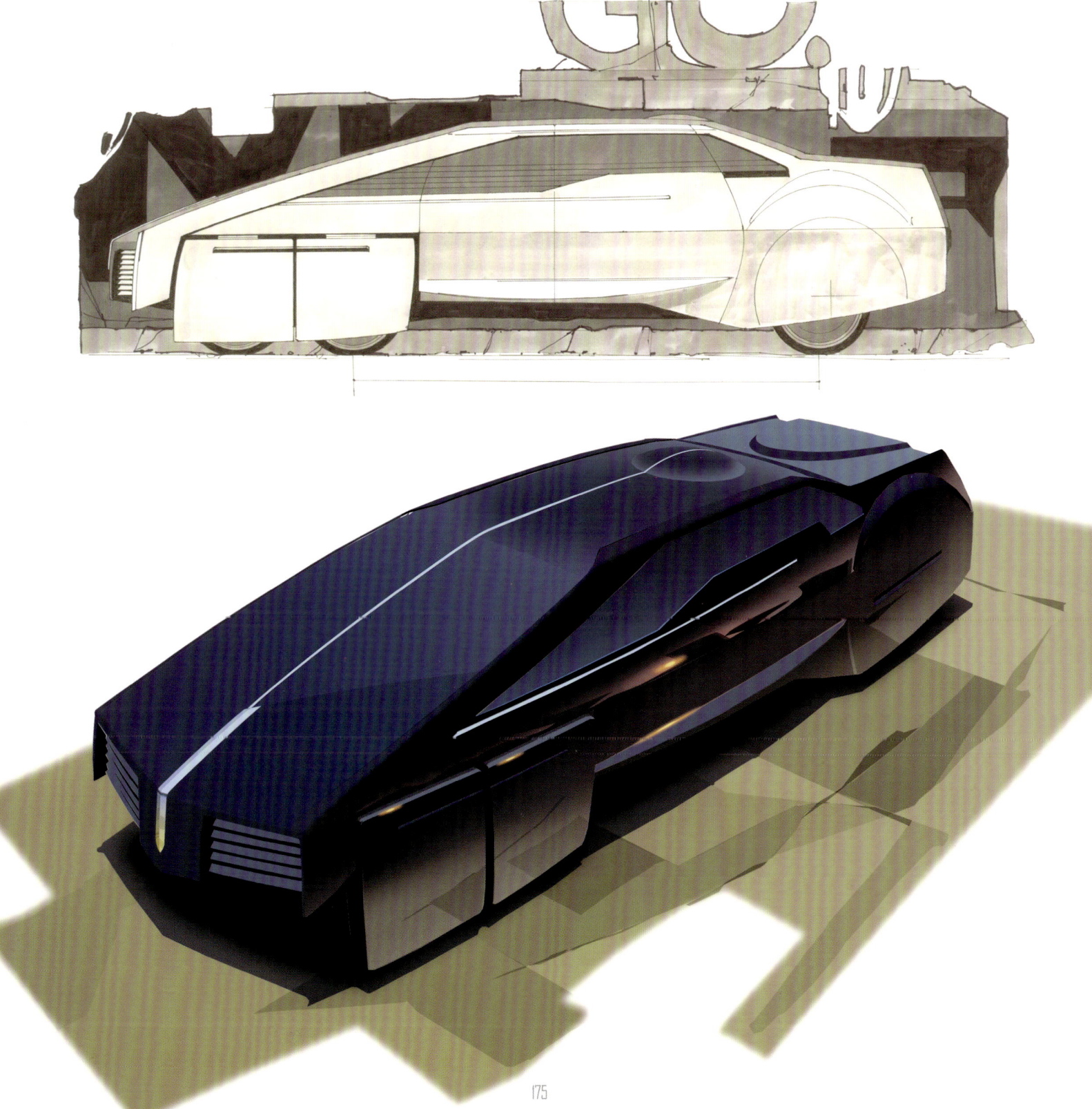

Elysium is conceived as a vast landscape arrayed along the inner periphery of a rotating, orbiting space station. With centrifugal force providing artificial gravity, the immense ring-like landscape becomes *terra firma* for practical purposes, to enable 'normal' activities, where 'up' is 'up' and 'down' is towards the circumference. Thus, Mead's concept of a 'normal' collection of roads, urban infrastructure, and landscape features is a plausible, even scientifically accurate approach to design in the gravity free reaches of outer space.

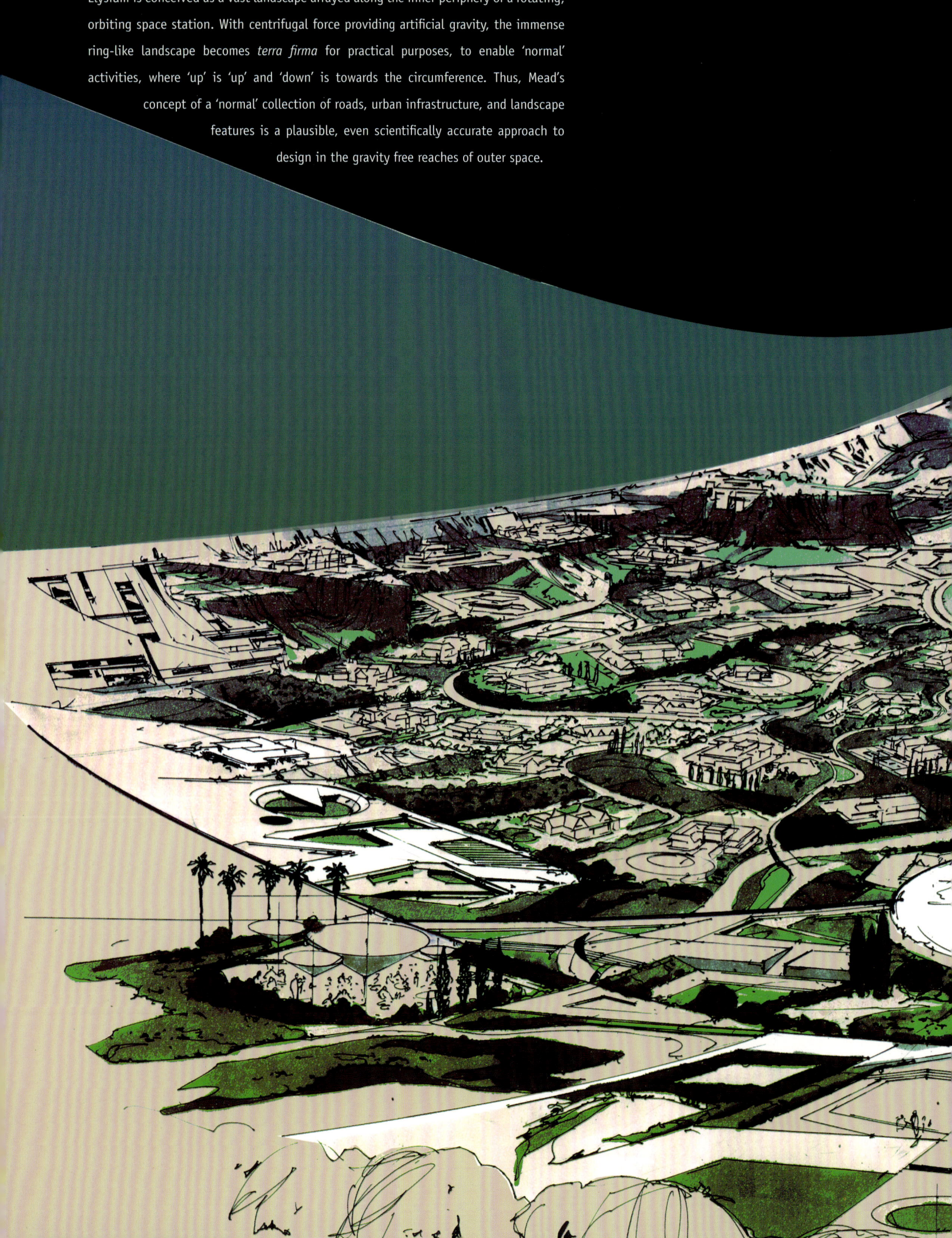

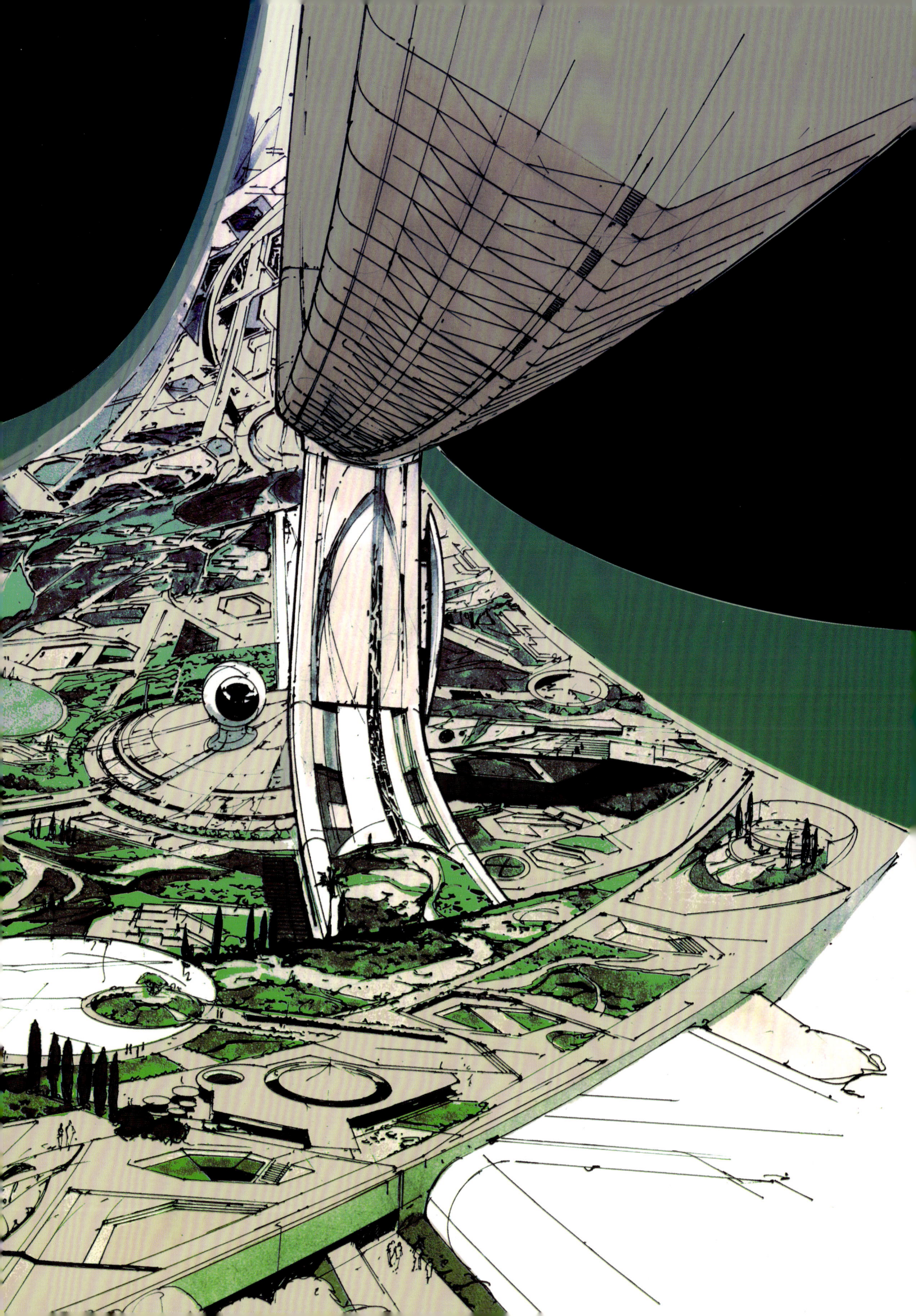

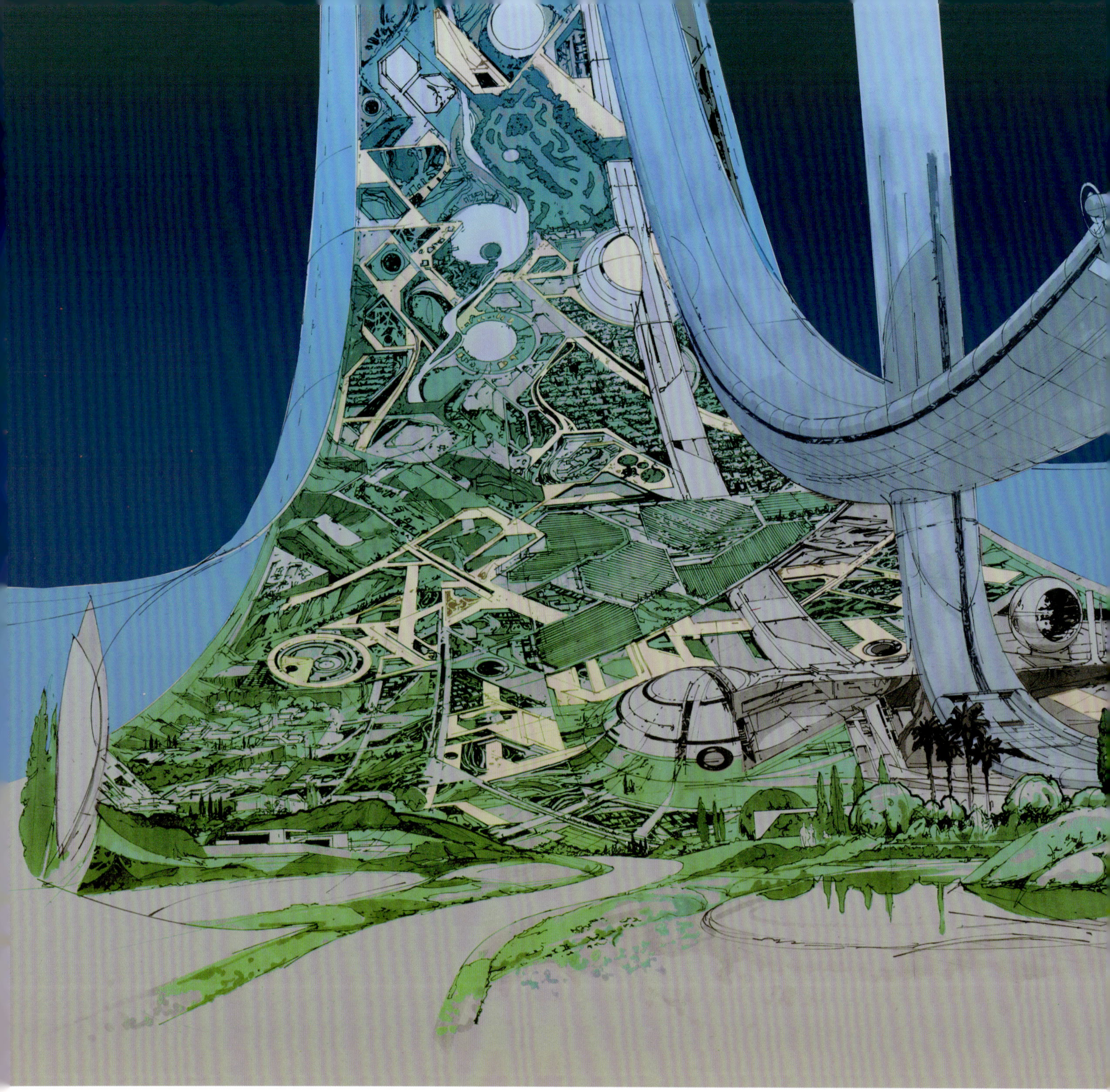

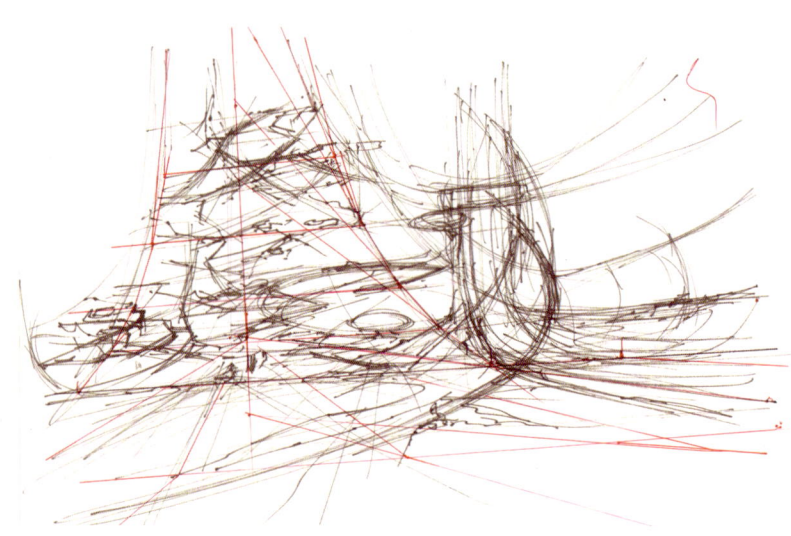
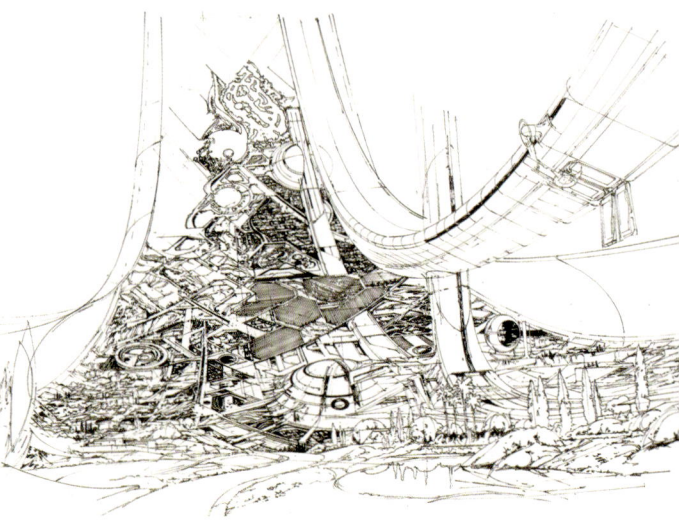

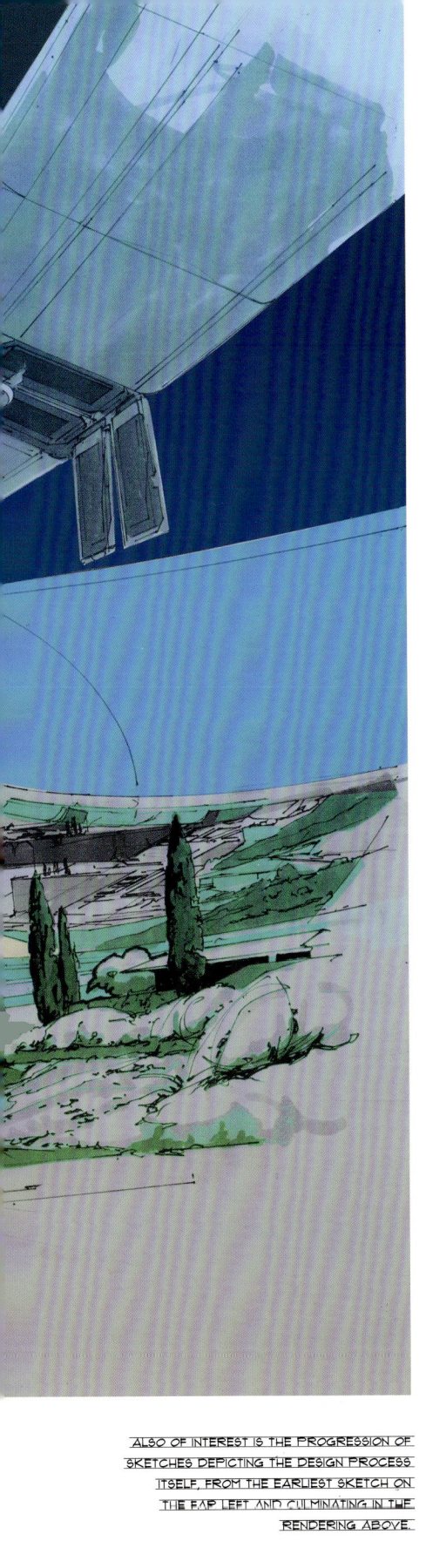

Further elaboration of the design concepts for the orbiting Elysium habitat suggests a sophisticated engineering approach to the design of the station, which owes a debt to Mead's early career as an automobile designer. Here, he pays respect to the particulars of the concept providing a cradle-like, articulated structural 'backbone' for the orbiting city-state. From an engineering point of view, this is both realistic and practical and does not sacrifice its visionary essence. By basing the design on a 'wheel within a wheel' motif, Mead succeeds in developing an approach to the structural engineering of the community which, with the 'backbone', is supported on pilot-like spokes. This creates a plausible, space-worthy construction. Details of the transparent envelop enclosing the station, while not directly expressed, suggest an inflated, balloon-like skin of transparent material.

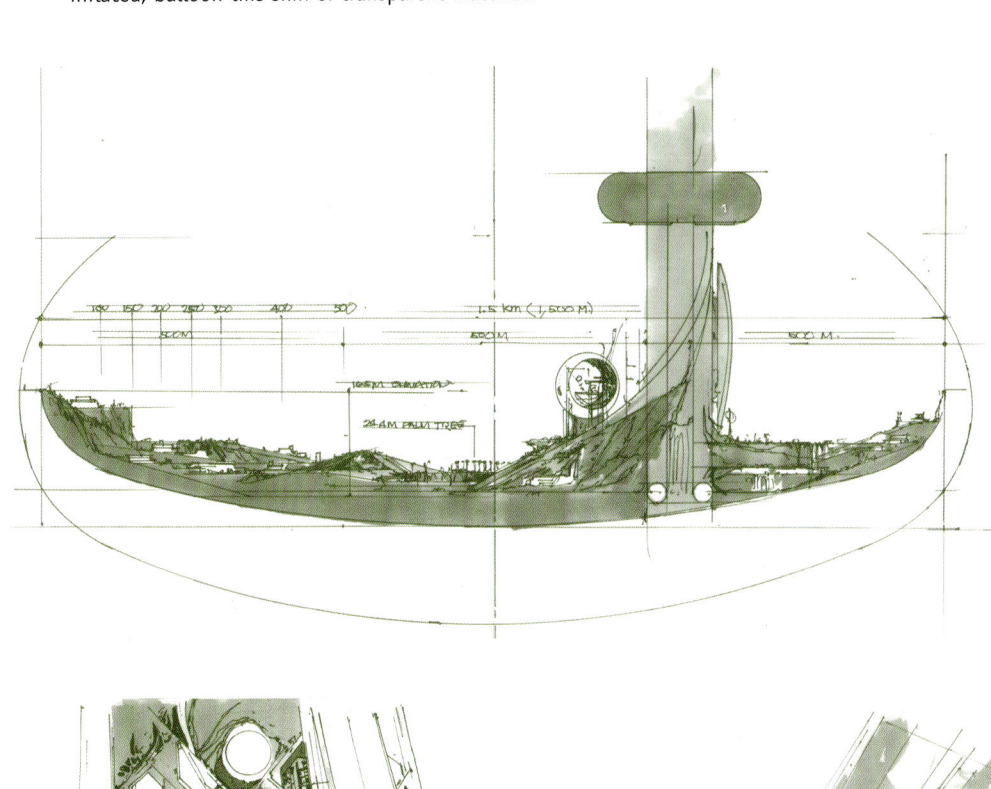

ALSO OF INTEREST IS THE PROGRESSION OF SKETCHES DEPICTING THE DESIGN PROCESS ITSELF, FROM THE EARLIEST SKETCH ON THE FAR LEFT AND CULMINATING IN THE RENDERING ABOVE.

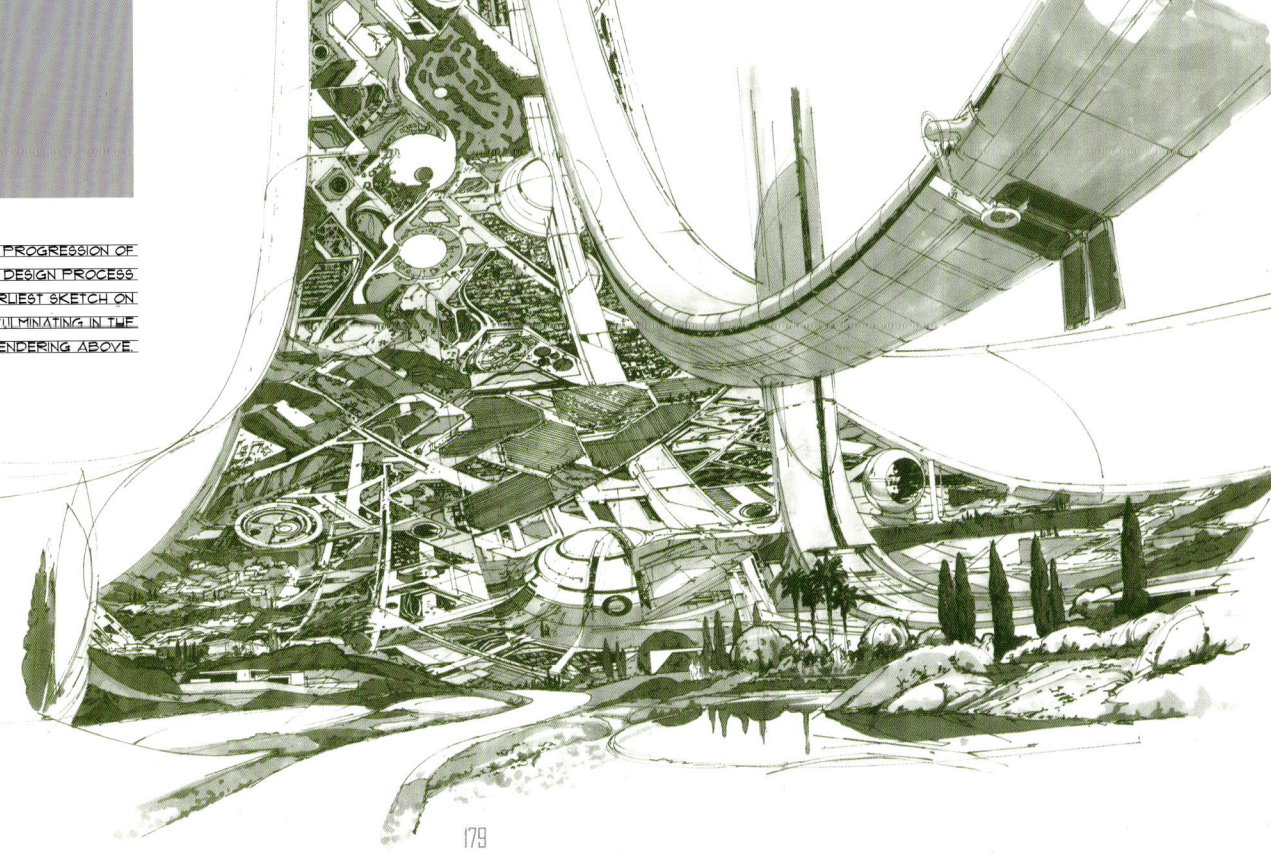

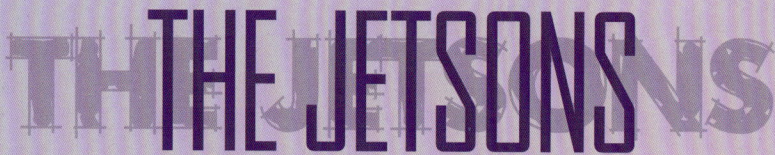

THE JETSONS

CARTOON OPERA

This reboot of the well-loved TV series was to be a mixed animation and live action production directed by Rob Minkoff, who had recently wrapped *Stuart Little* (1999), the animated movie for Warner Brothers. His vision for *The Jetsons* was to combine digital environments with live action shot on green screen backgrounds to achieve an 'operatic' scale.

Technically, this was a familiar process, but the 'cartoon-style' design direction suggested that Mead reverse course from his usual 'design with light' approach to a style he describes as "global lighting" in which highlights, shadows, and directional light are suppressed in favor of a soft overall light.

Ultimately the movie was not made so the mix of live action and two-dimensional cartoon-like images was an exciting design challenge that was never tackled.

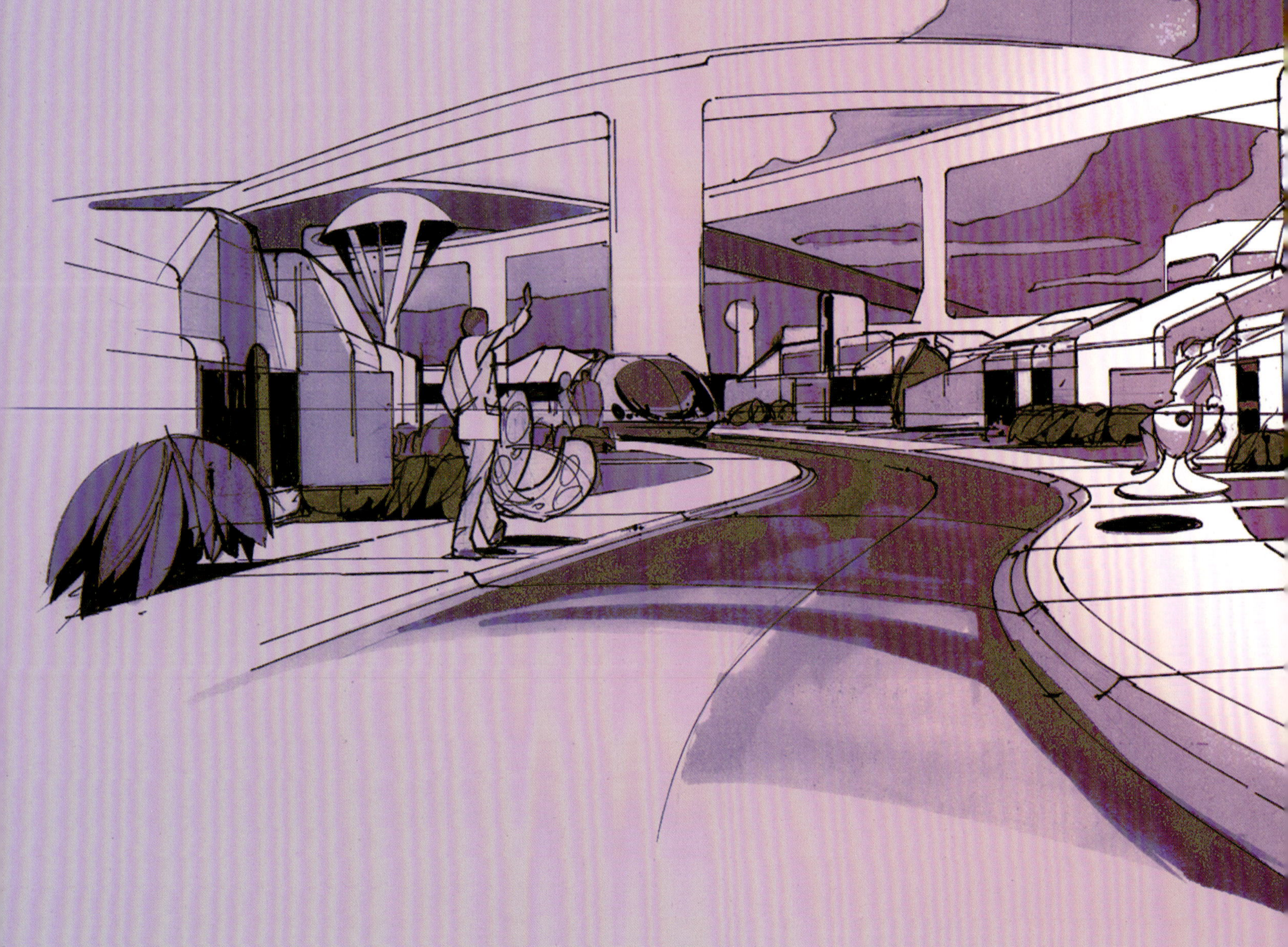

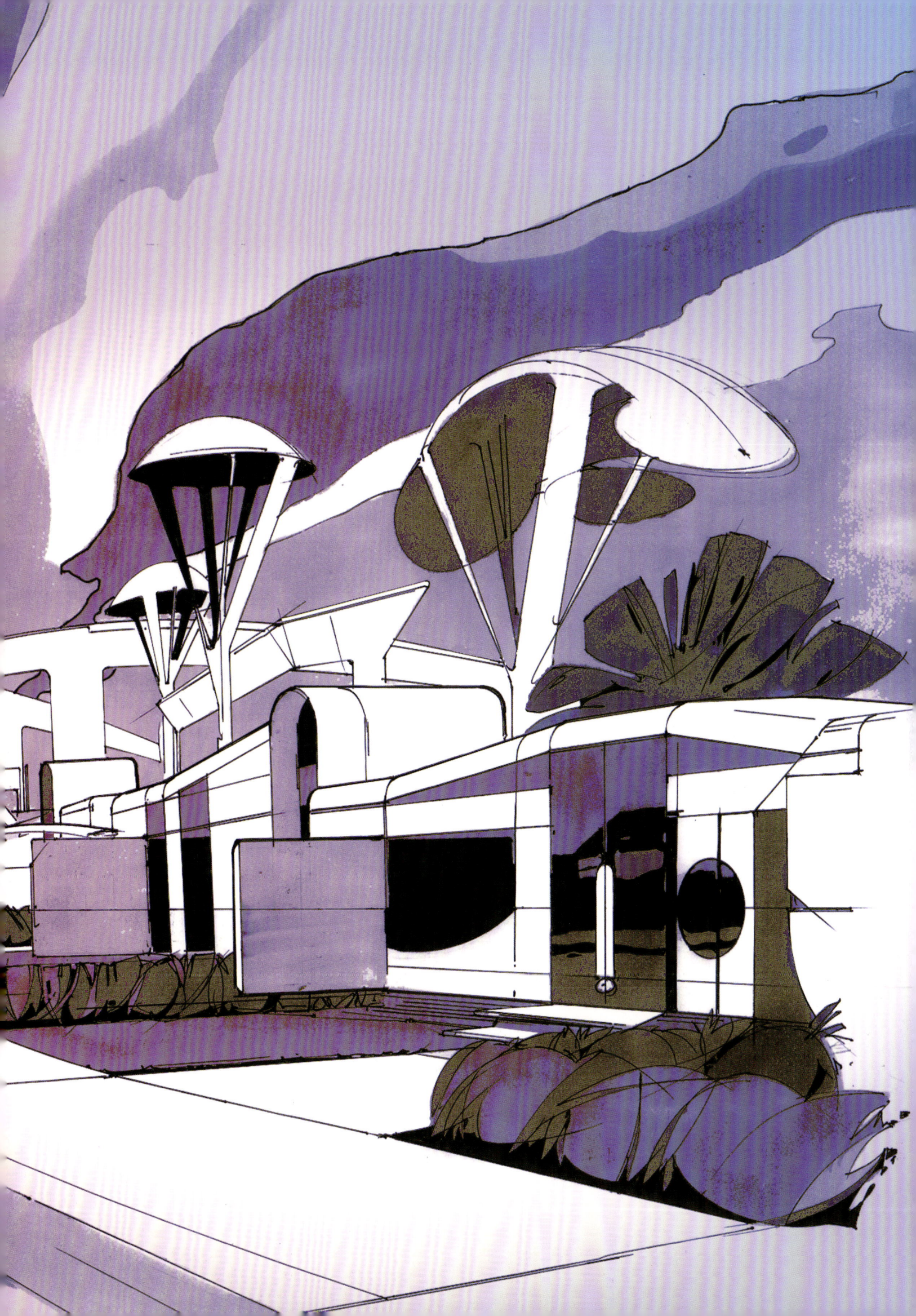

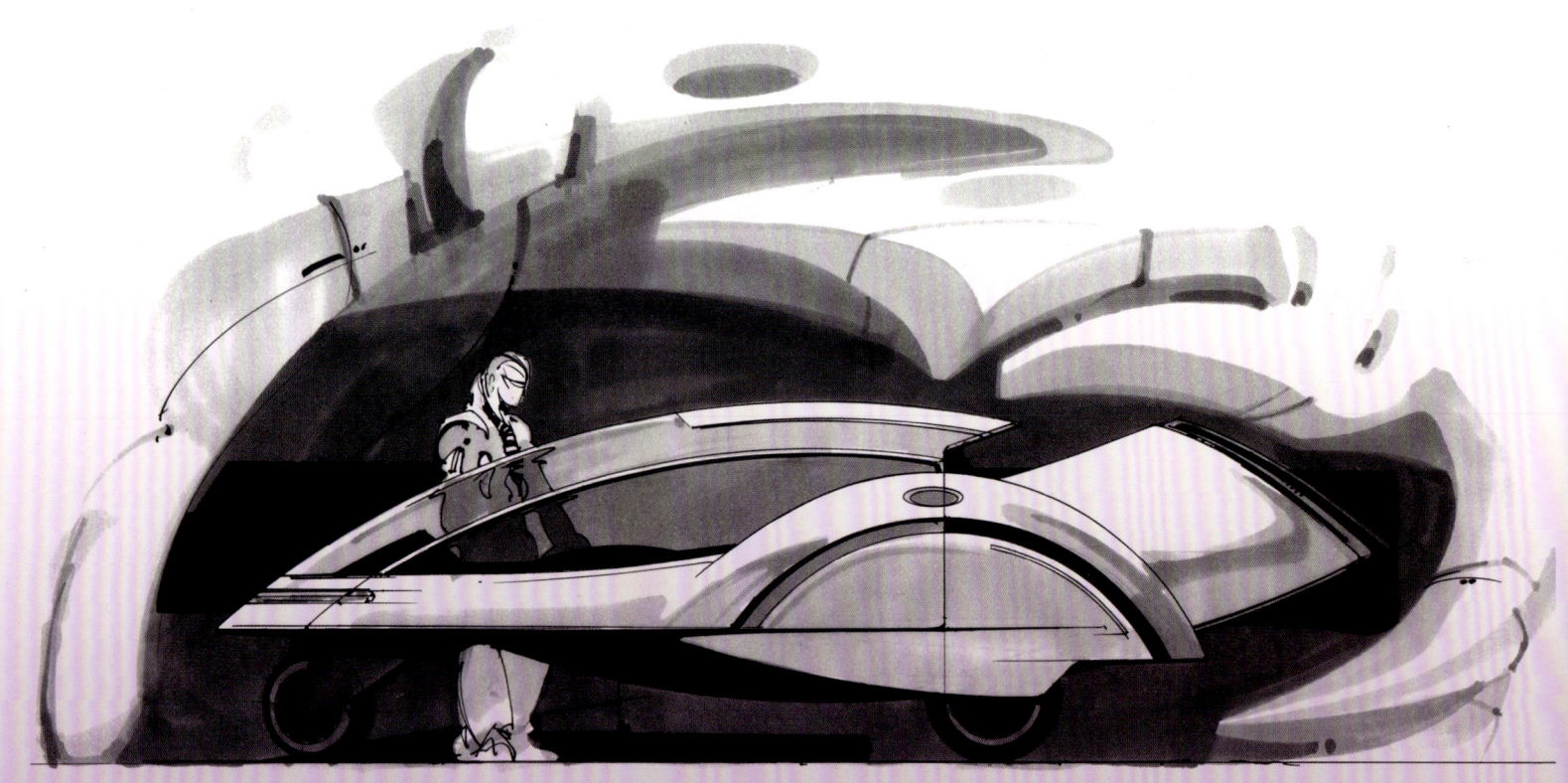

This challenge was especially apparent in the design of the Jetsons' car—a jellybean shape in the TV series but a functional prop in the proposed film. Mead re-conceptualized the car as a sphere, with logic that it could be positioned in any orientation without requiring tailor-made masking, thus making it much easier to superimpose the live action of the Jetsons and their pet dog on the background scene.

In this version (this spread and overleaf), stubby wings, a sliding canopy, and minuscule thrusters combine to create a hybrid vehicle which would be as capable on the road as in the air.

The DNA of the Jetson's family car can be traced all the way back to the spinner in *Blade Runner*, but with a more playful sensibility. Yet the hawkish countenance, the predatory stance, and the exaggerated functionality are much in evidence. A beautifully balanced, semi-circular cabin references the earlier TV version, while the vertical fin, with its slightly inflated cross section hints at a kinder softer future.

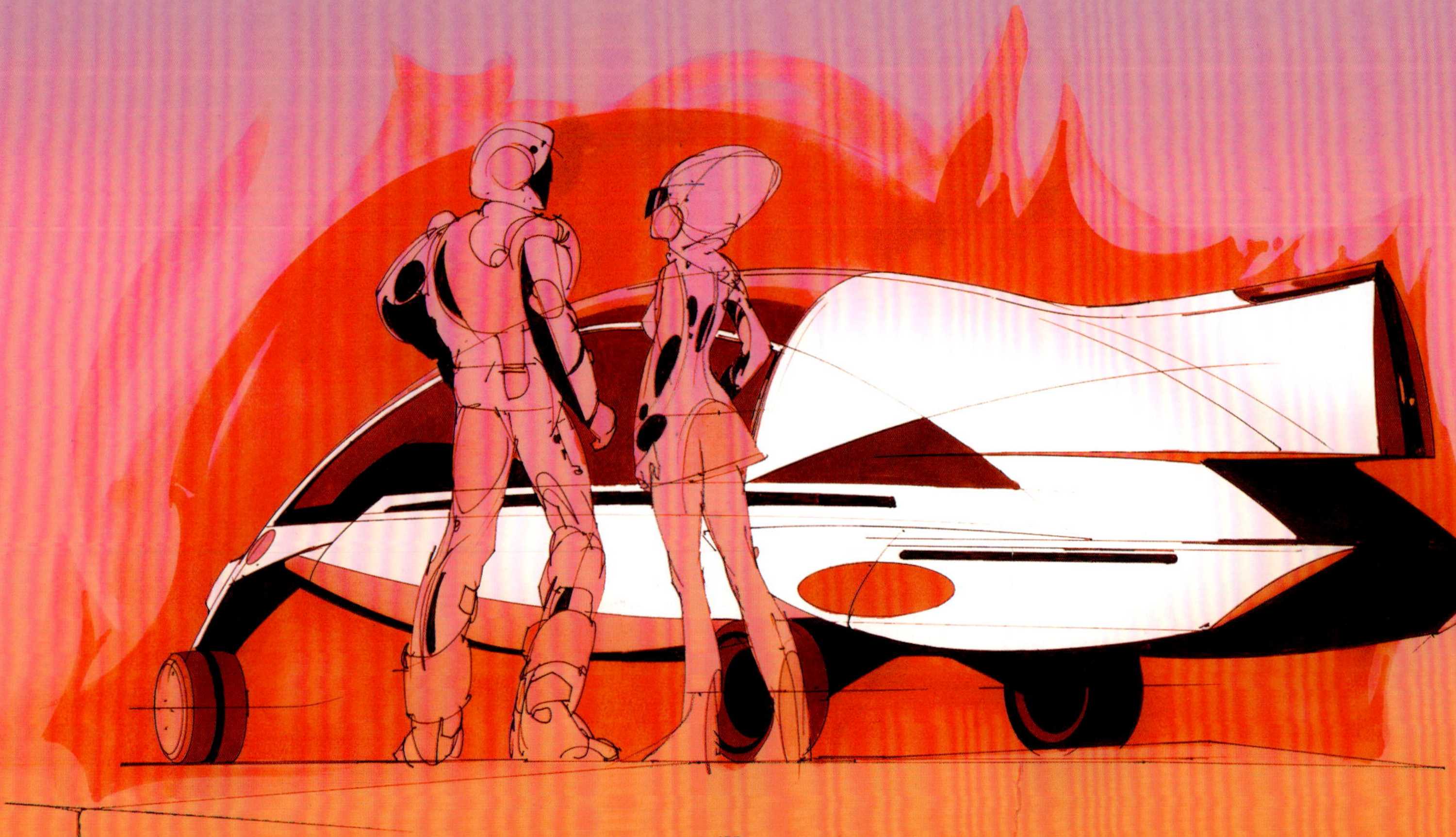

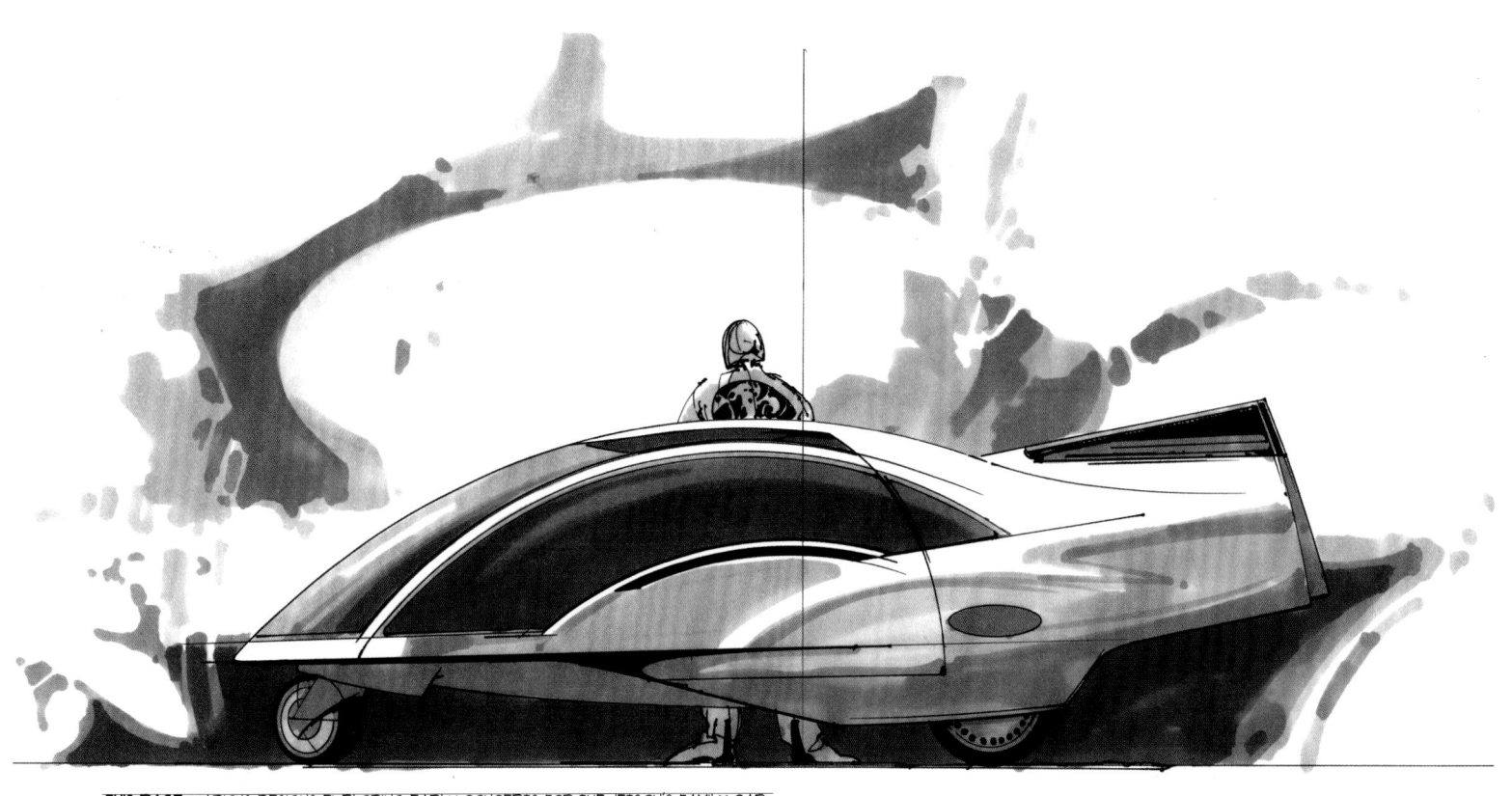

THIS PAGE: VARIOUS DESIGNS EXPLORING EARLY CONCEPTS FOR THE JETSON'S FAMILY CAR.

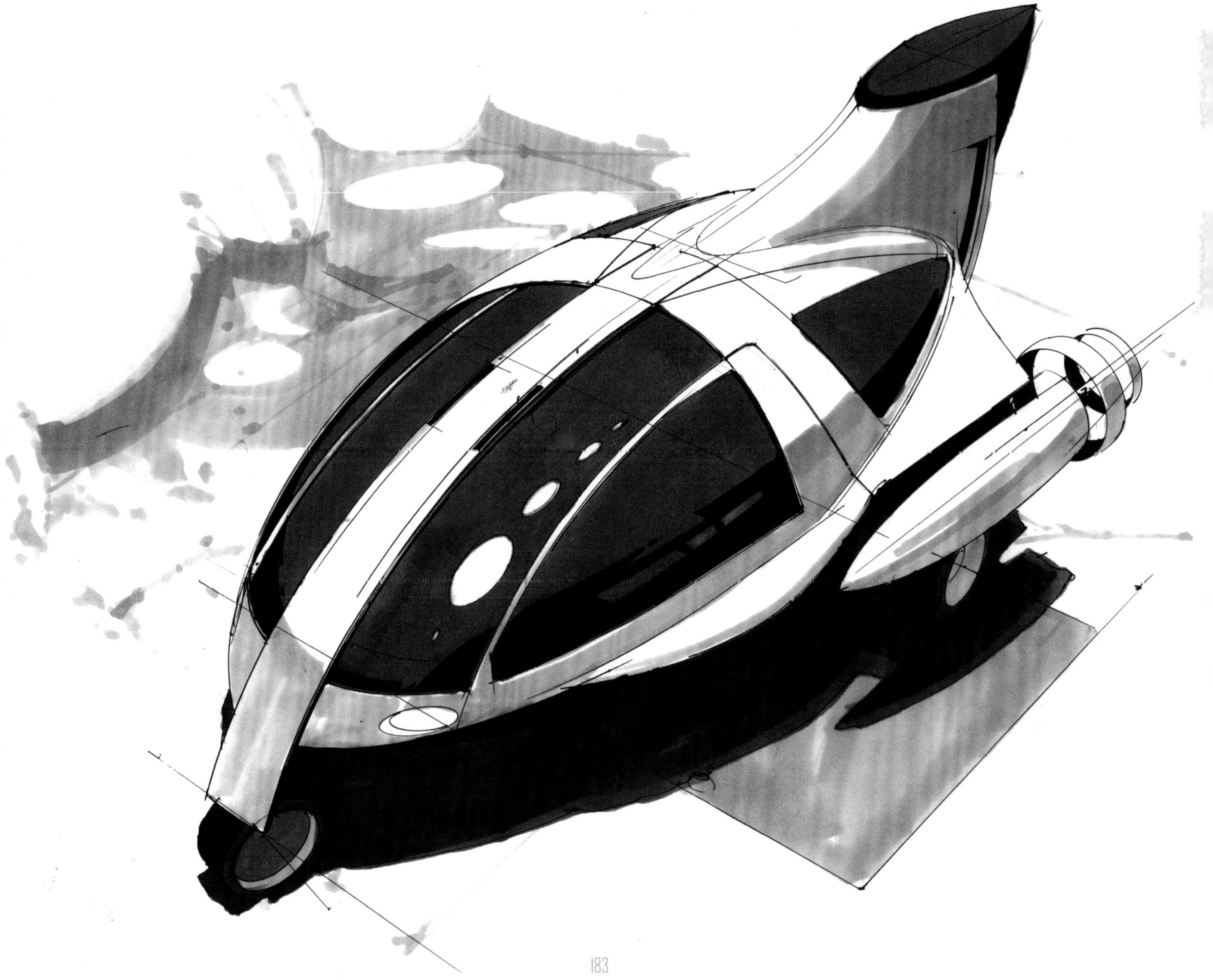

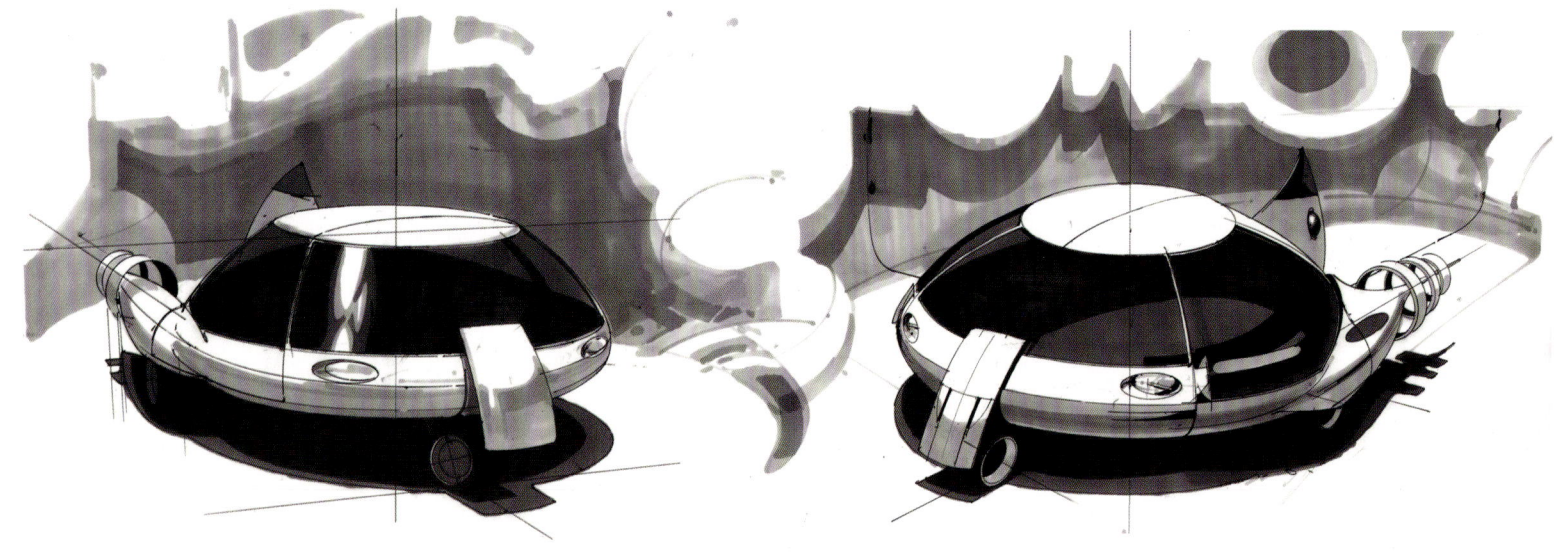

ABOVE AND BELOW: FURTHER CONCEPTS EXPLORING ALTERNATE DESIGN DIRECTIONS FOR THE CAR.

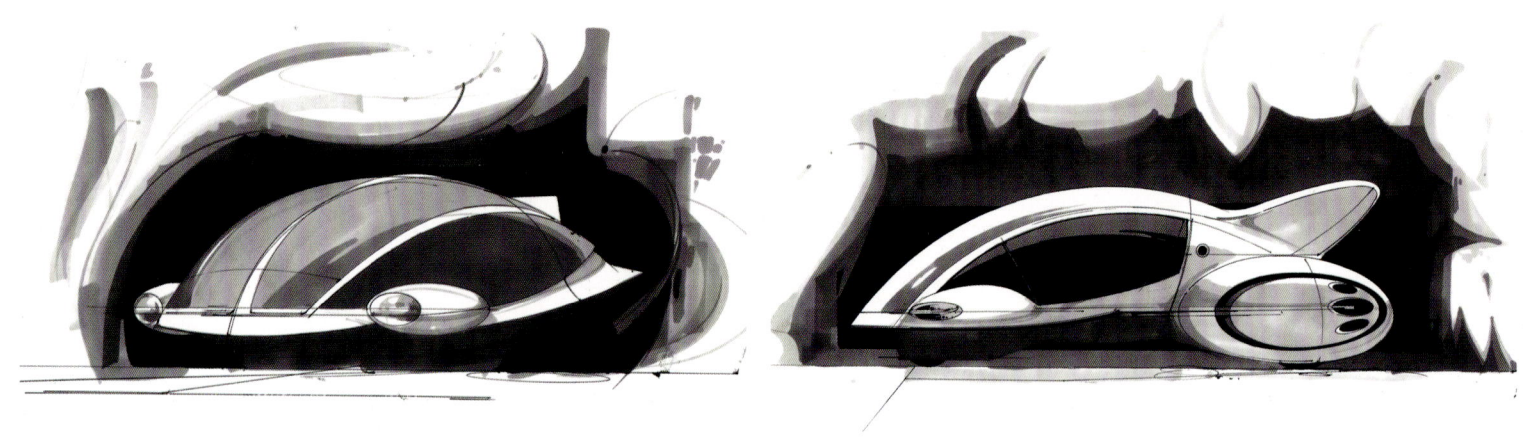

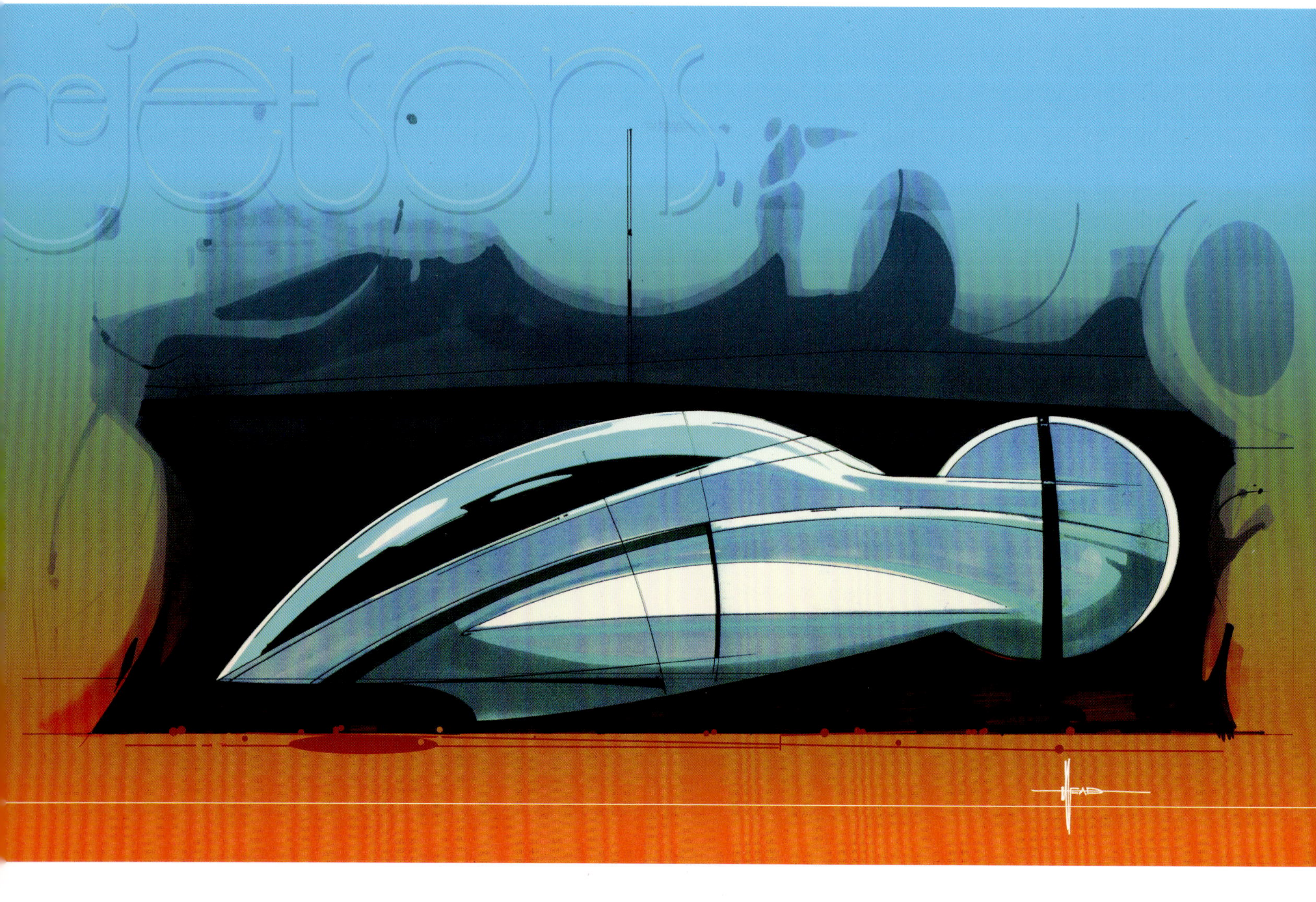

184

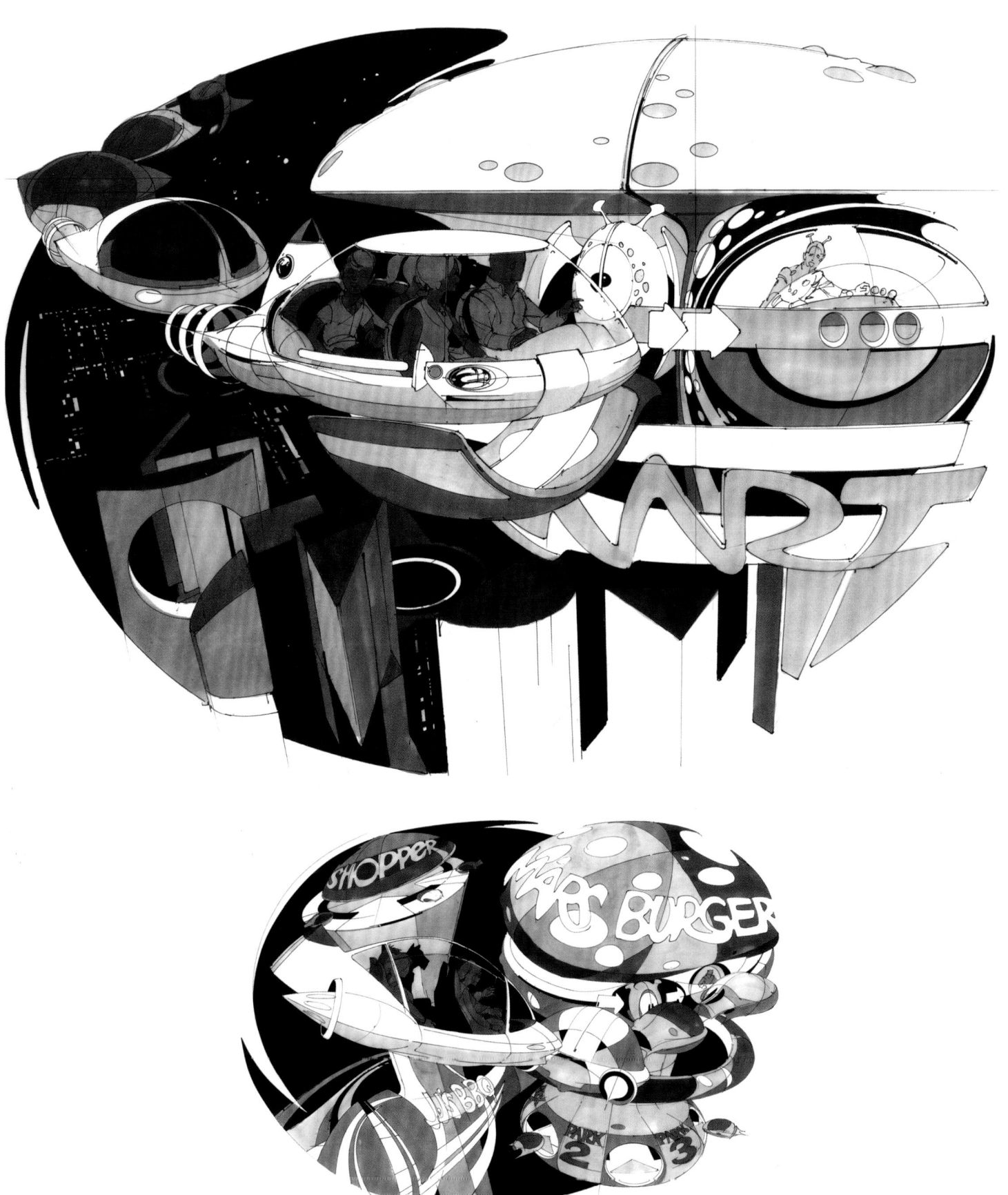

A case in point is the line-up of cars as Fred waits for a 'Marsburger' at the drive-in. Mead's vision is of a kind of kaleidoscopic line-up of candy-colored vehicles curving—floating, really—like a string of balloons. It's a kind of charm and innocence totally lacking in his other, darker projects, and casts a light on a little known facet of Mead's persona—he's funny! And many of his comments on projects end with the observation, "It was fun to do."

Hints of the aerodynamics that confer a plausible reality on the Jetsons' family car are here in abundance; the vestigial wings terminating in turbines or ducted fans, the bird-like landing gear, and the structural backbone dividing the cockpit all point to Mead's thoughtful—even practical—approach to the design of what would be an ever-present, highly visible part of the *mise en scène*, yet the rendition of the figures, in Mead's trademark style, seem at odds with the original's loopy futurism, and point to a more turbulent, tense future.

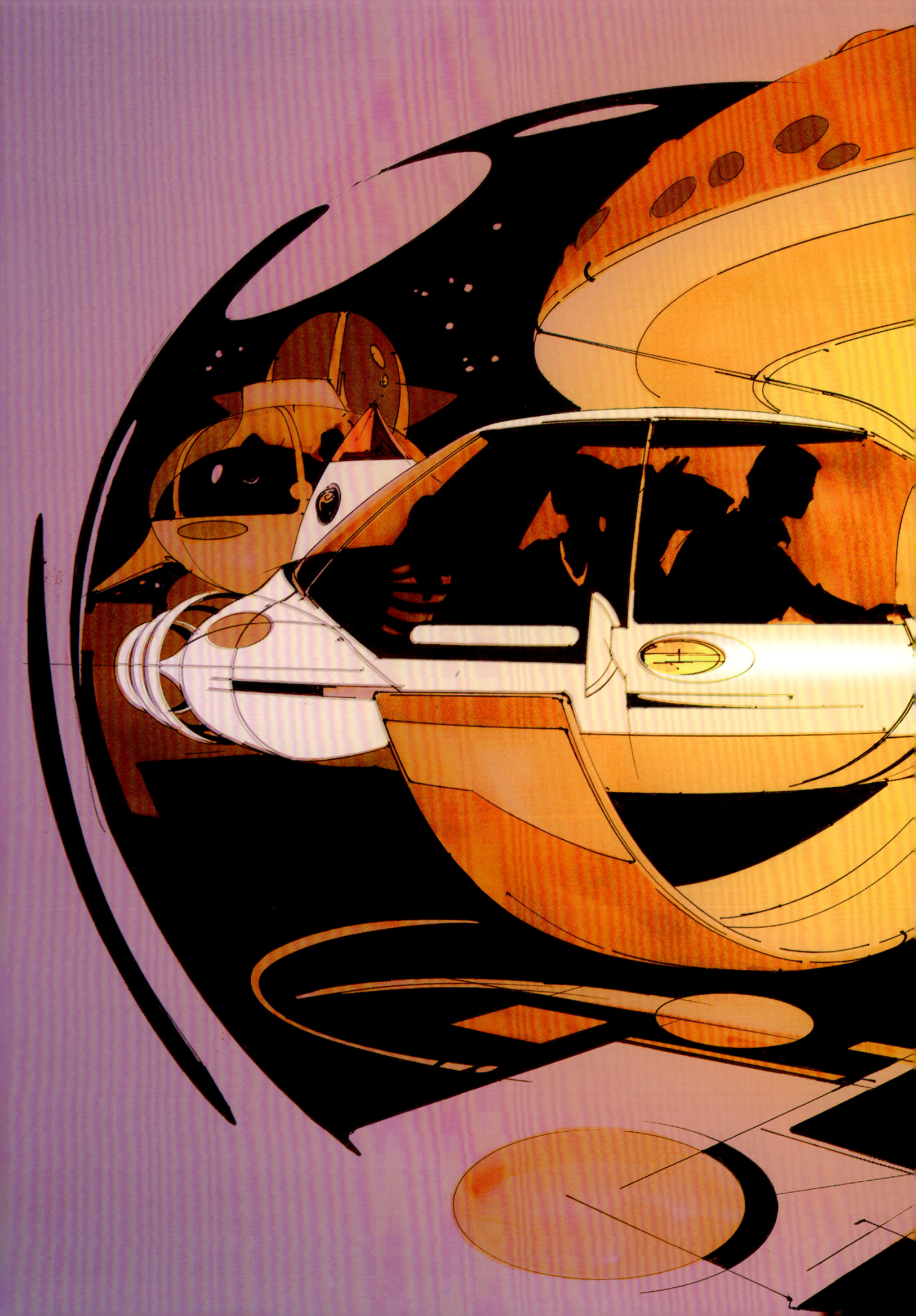

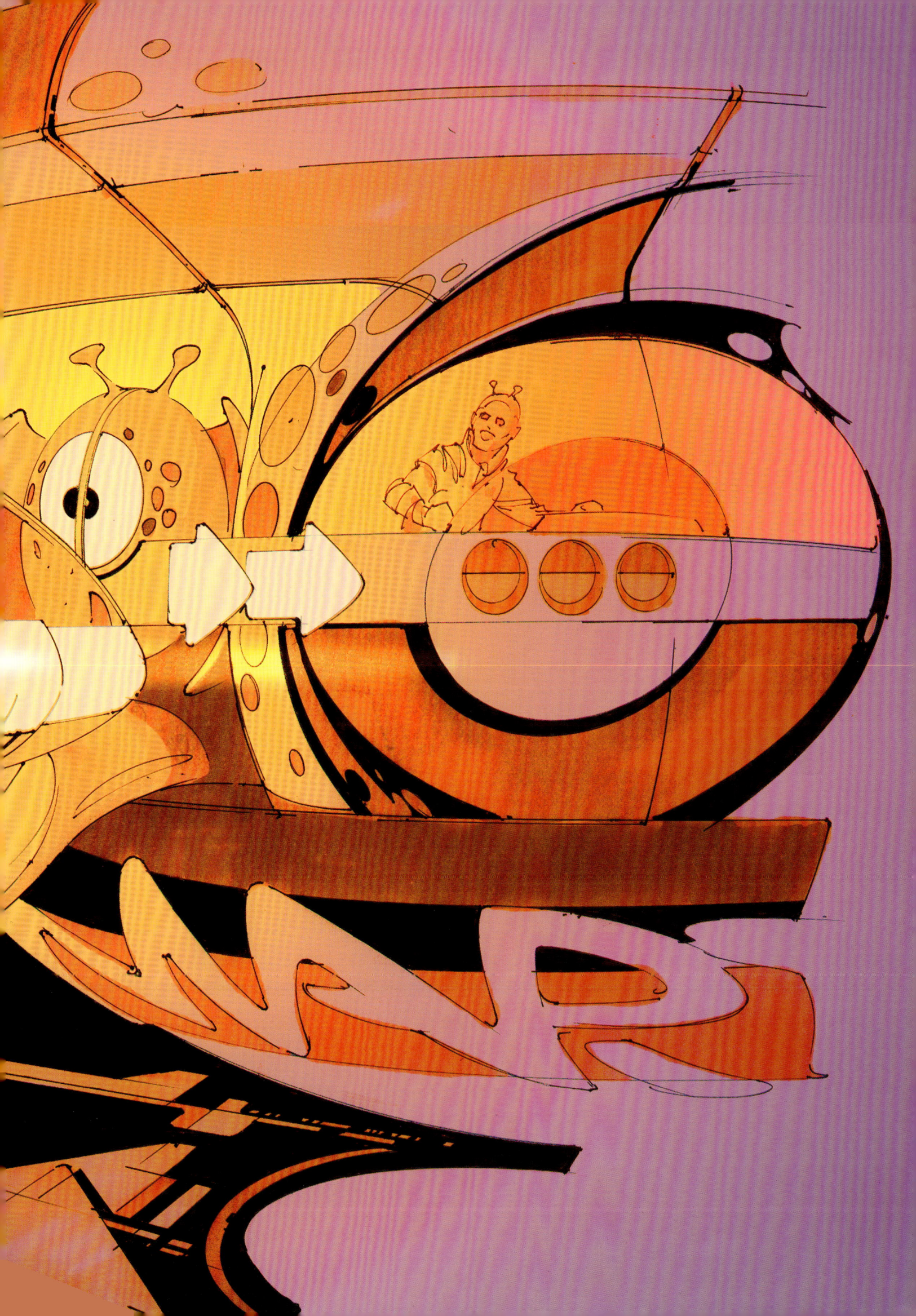

Here we are, in a future suburb crisscrossed by streamlined freeways, in a composition that, despite its mission to be 'ordinary', is undeniably filtered through the eyes of Syd Mead. For starters, there are the twisting, intertwined trajectories of the sidewalks, cloud formations and freeway overpasses which visually structure the frame. Playing against them, and carrying the eye into the distance, are the diminishing, repeated rectangular forms, and finally, the

coloration which ostensibly depicts shade and shadow but in fact focuses our attention on the foreground.

Mead on light: *"Here the shadows are maybe directly underneath, the light source could be completely unexplained: and these are procedurally lighted black and white sketches. This is not tempera; these are just line drawings shaded in markers, scanned in the color format, and then deliberately tied off with a mask, and then lighted.*

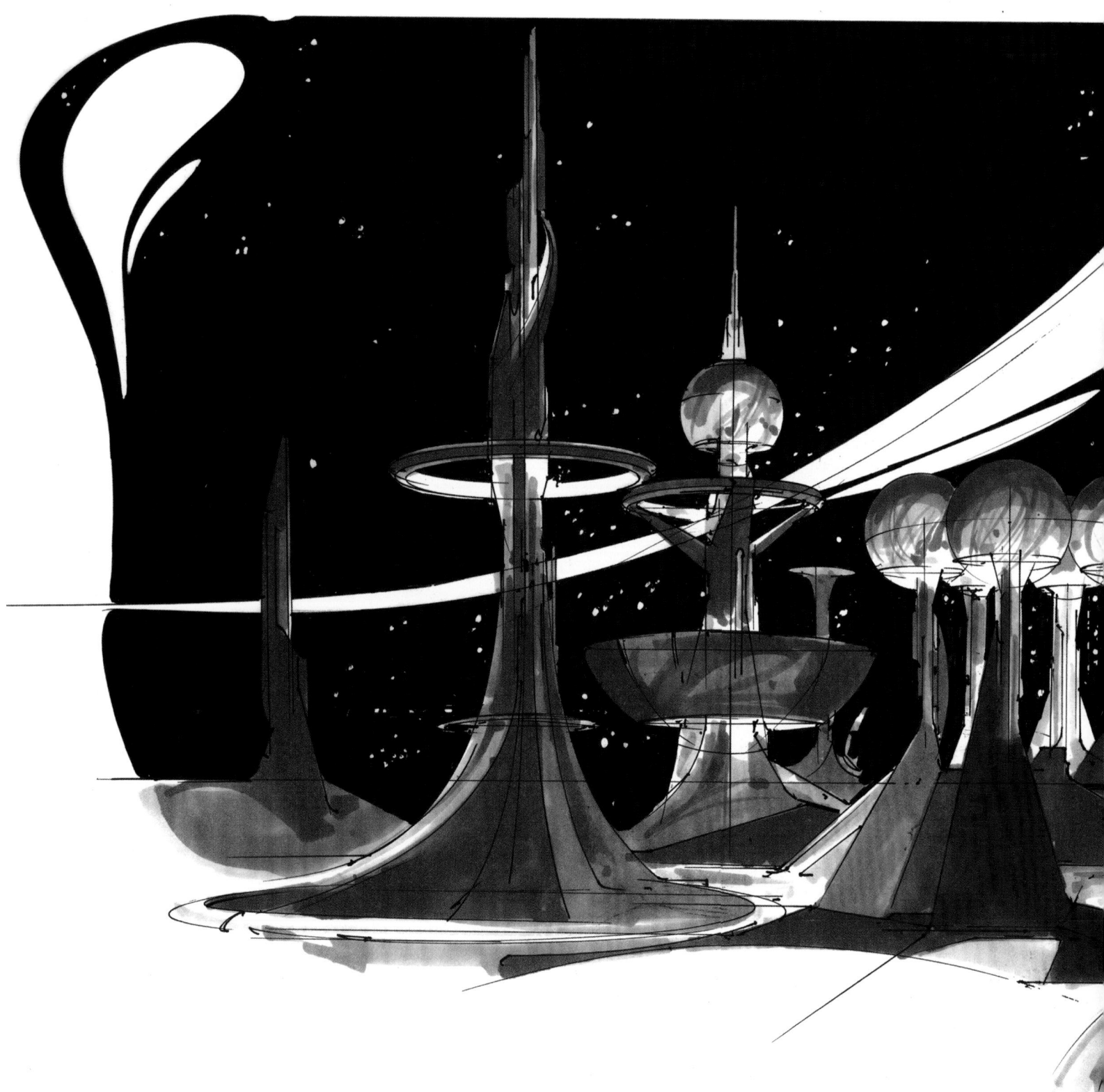

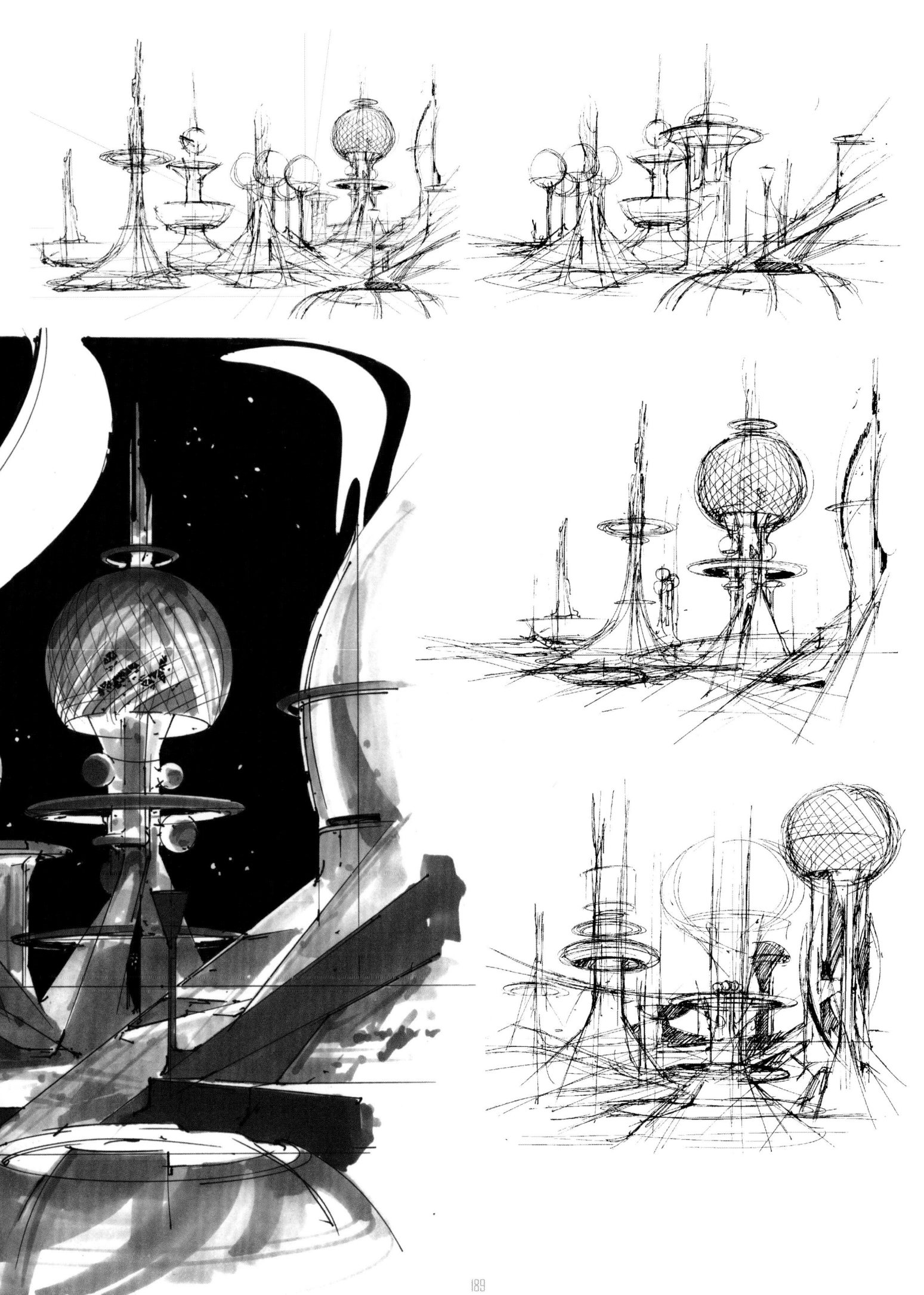

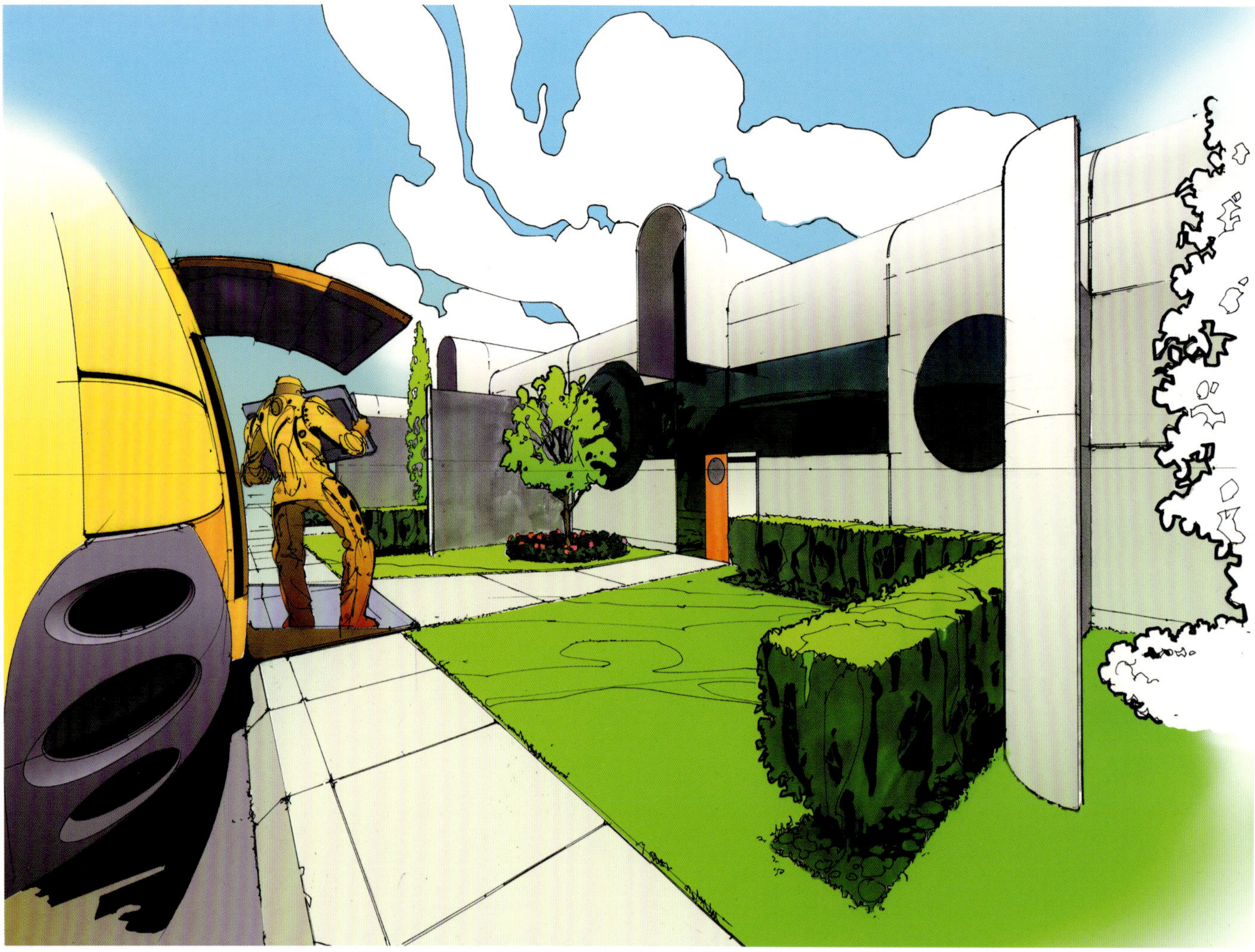

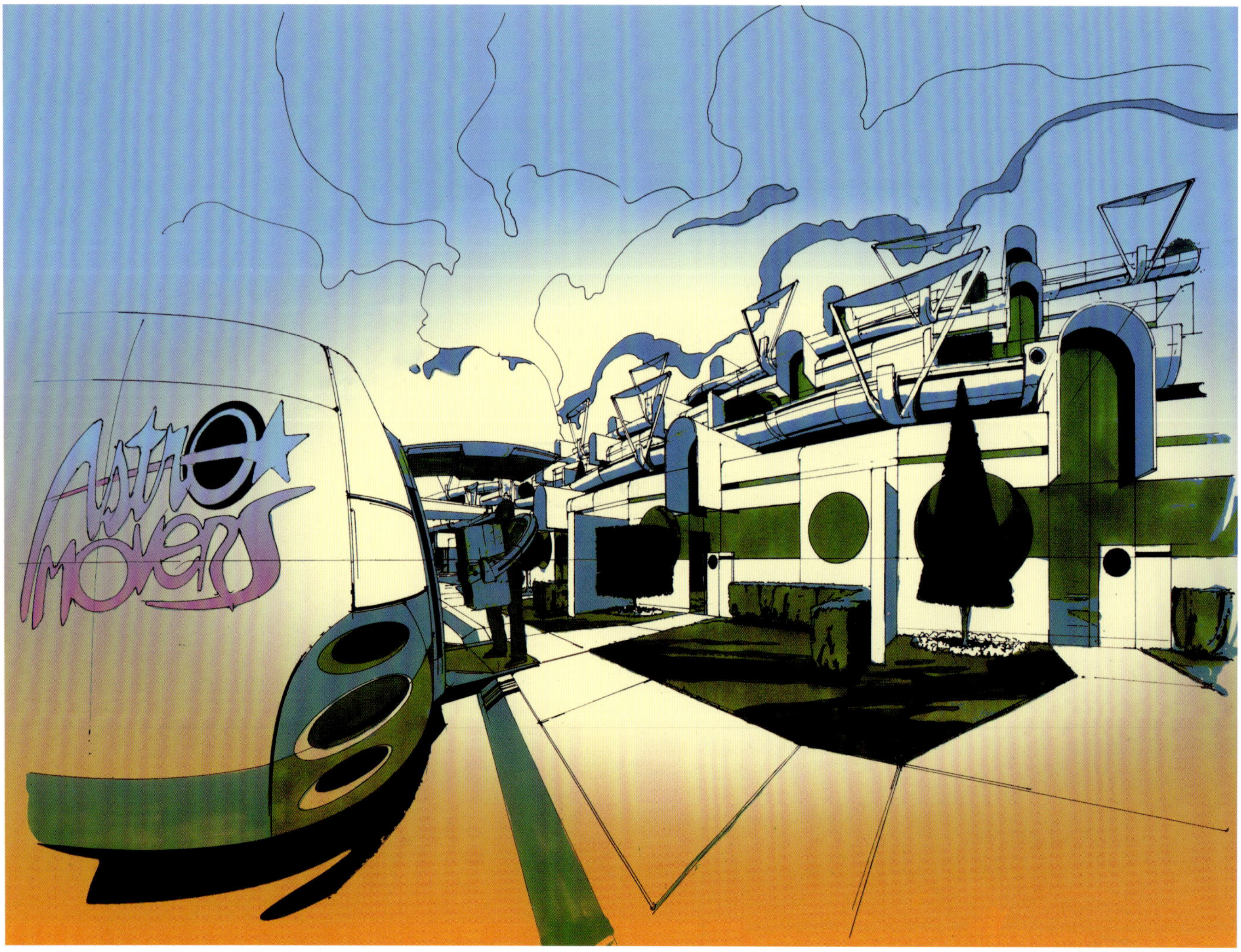
Astro movers

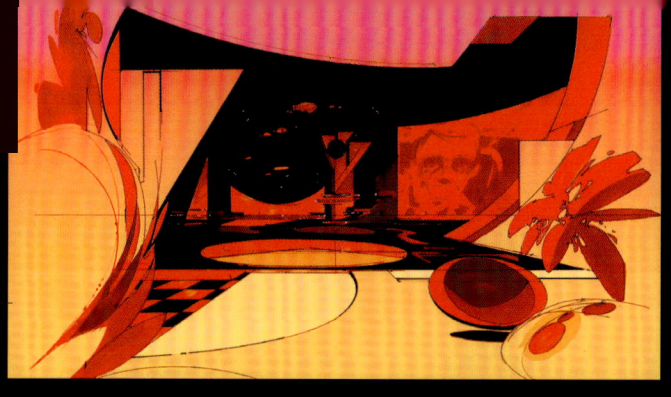
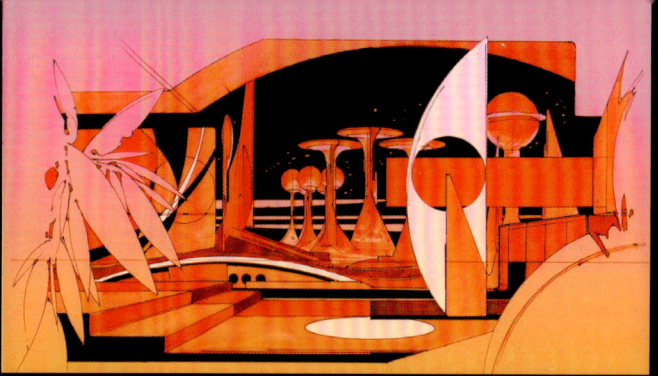

The center of the lighting sphere is right here and sort of expands out to what I've allowed to show through the mask. And it works, it looks really nice".

To compare the design elements of Mead's fresh take is to contrast the naïve future imagery of post-war America with a future bruised by political and social rifts that render that trusting vision improbable if not impossible. So that Mead's images – darker, with sharper edges and a palette far removed from the sunny primaries of the cartoon series fits uncomfortably within the Americana of the original. Yet those spires, perched like golf balls on spindly tees have, in their collective effervescence, a fantasy element entirely lacking in Hanna-Barbera's version.

It would have been delightful to cruise through George Jetson's city of levitating spheres "dancing like water drops", says Mead.

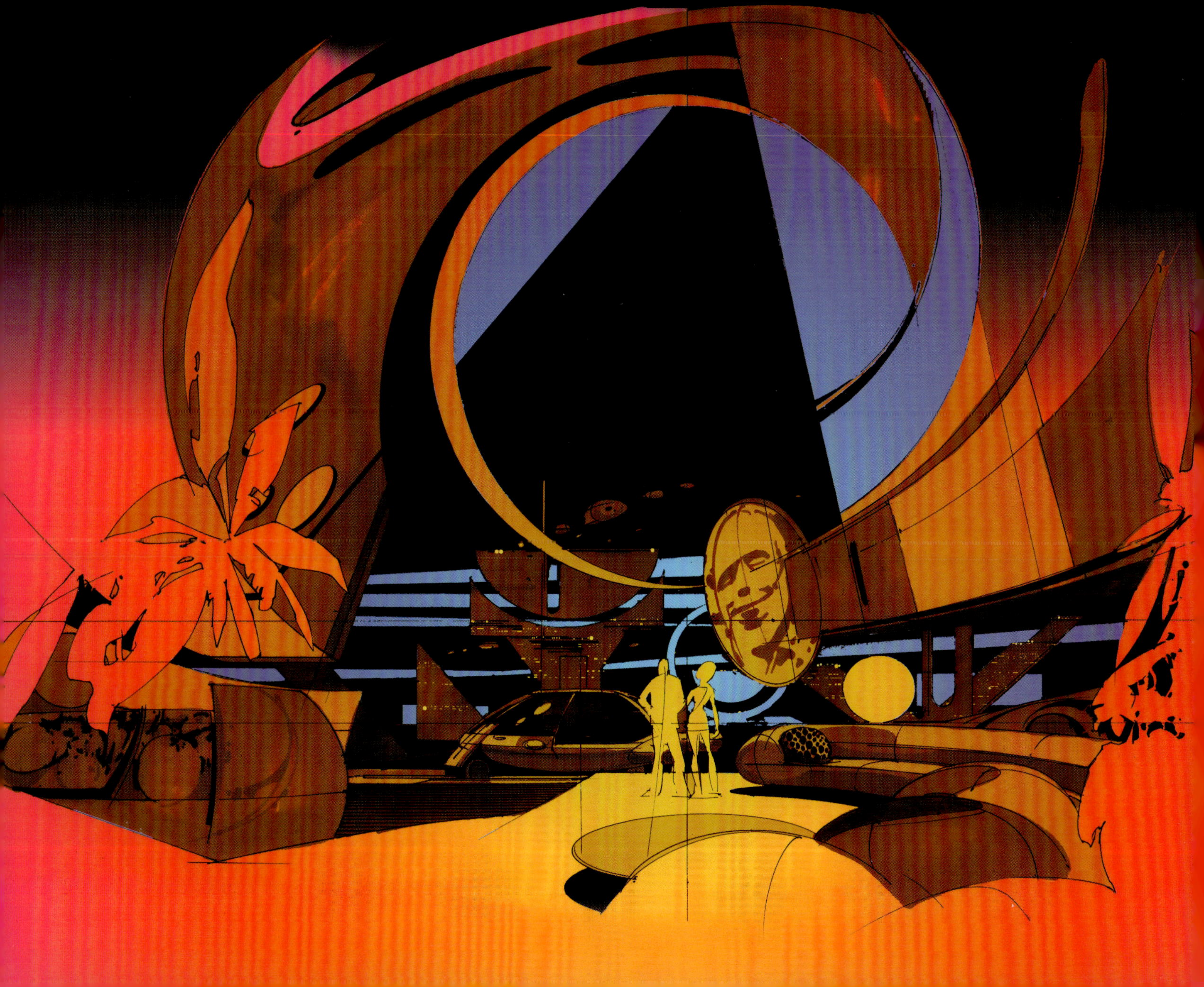

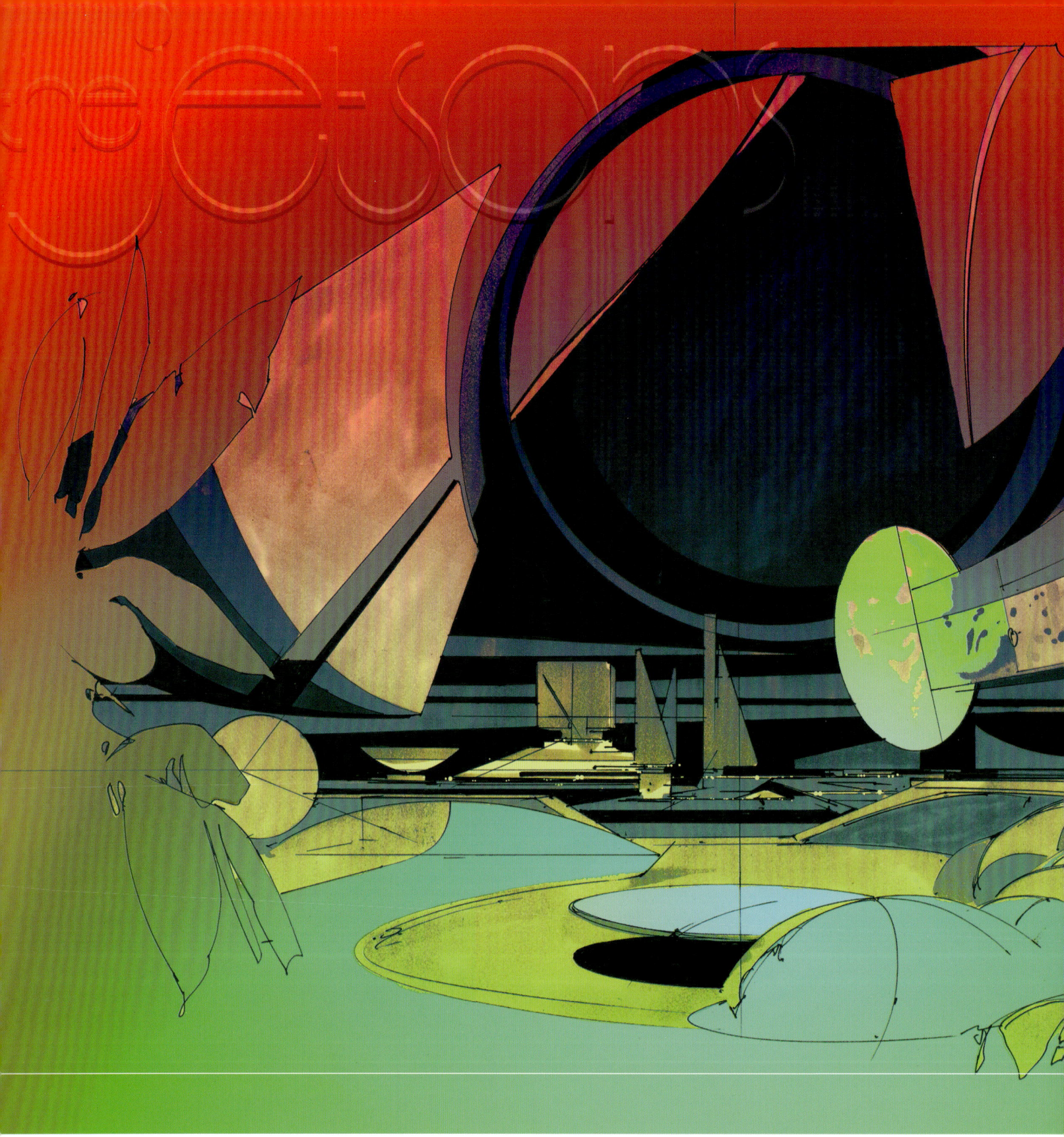

Here the Jetson's Orbit City home is sharply delineated with multiple layers, swirling geometry and imagery very much at odds with cartoon depictions of the future, and Mead, no cartoonist, doesn't shy away from a deeper, more complex and challenging domestic environment.

Syd's imagery, while likely to be gobbled up by a contemporary audience who may have not heard of the TV series, could not have been farther away from the original.

Mead's moody images for a studio production based on the fifties TV series *The Jetsons* recast the streamline, cartoon-like style of the original in a more contemporary idiom which, in some ways presaged the *avant-garde* design of masters like John Lautner and Raphael Soriano. With bubble-like furnishings and what appears to be an homage to Brancusi's *Bird in Space* sculpture in the garden, the images carry a level of meaning and weight that only Mead's artwork can so easily convey.

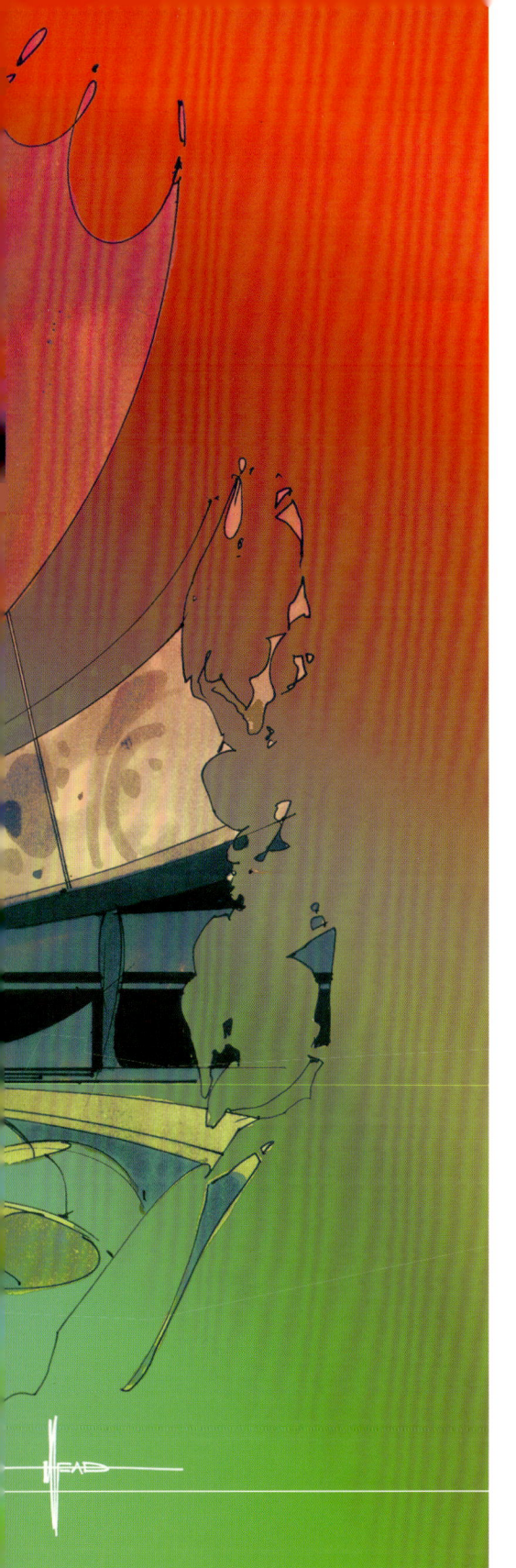

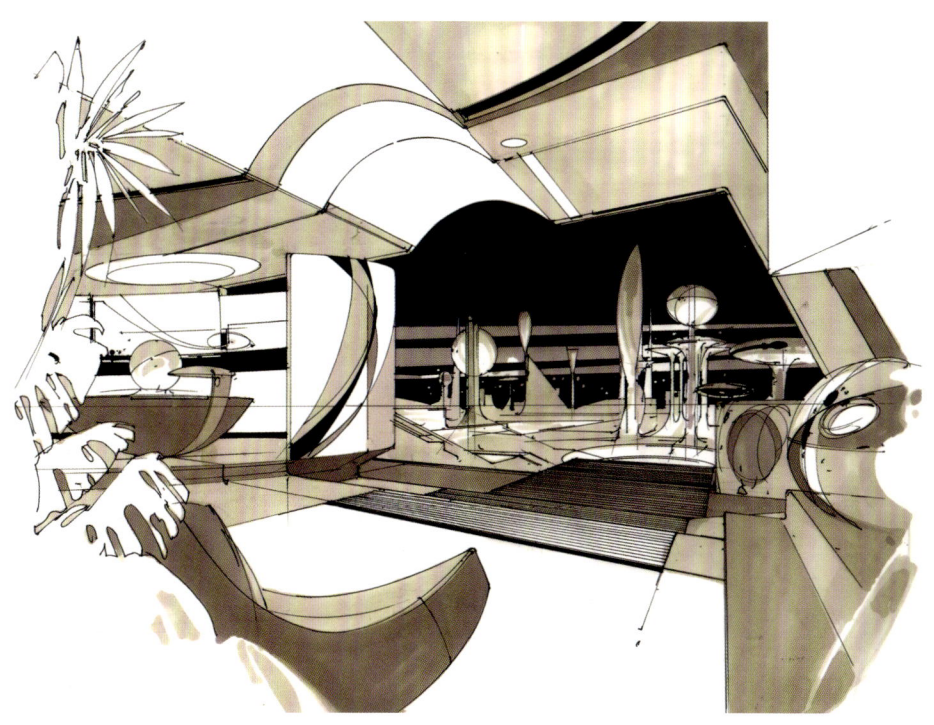

COMING HOME AND HOOKING UP TO THEIR LIVING POD WITH THEIR FAMILY DOG IN THEIR FAMILY CAR, THE JETSONS ARE WELCOMED BY THEIR HOUSEMAID, WHO IS PREPARING THE EVENING MEAL

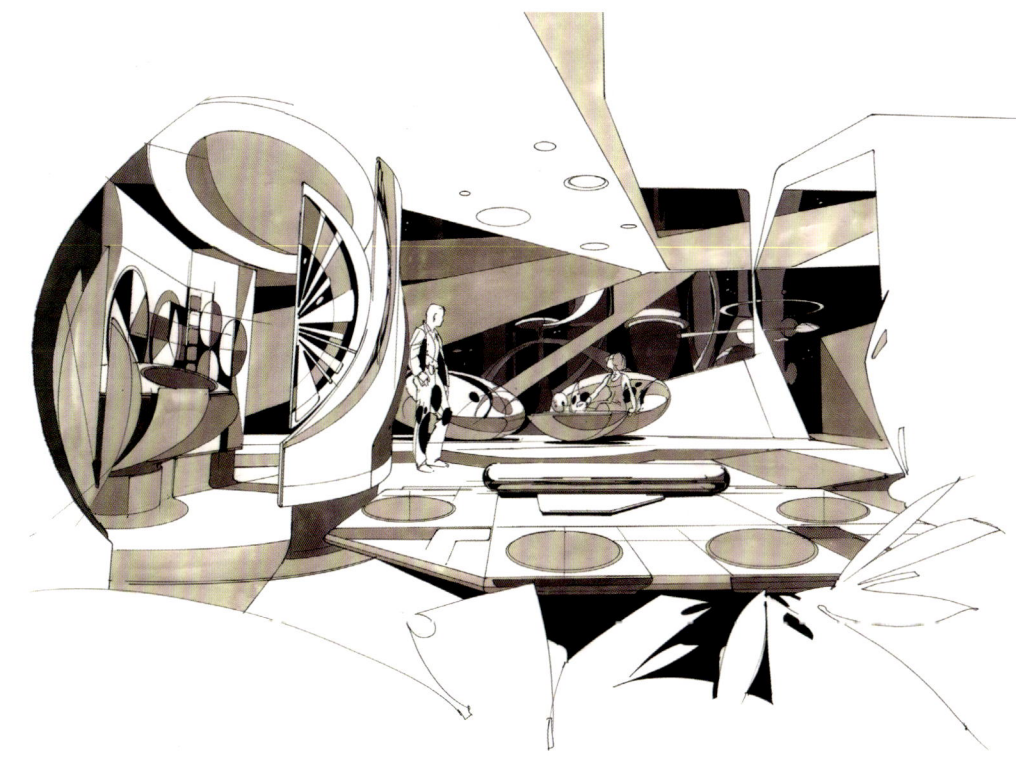

the jetsons

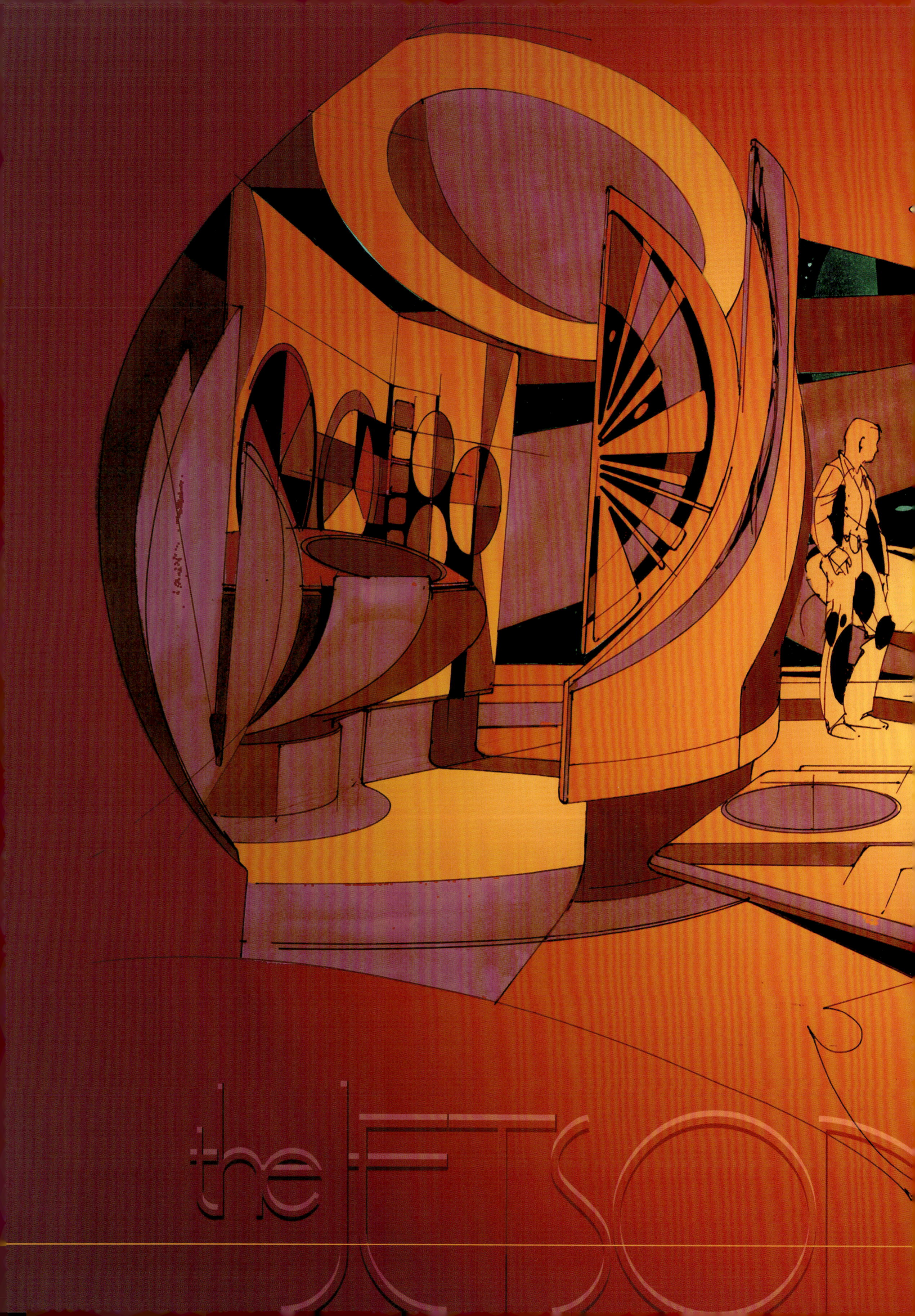

the JETSON

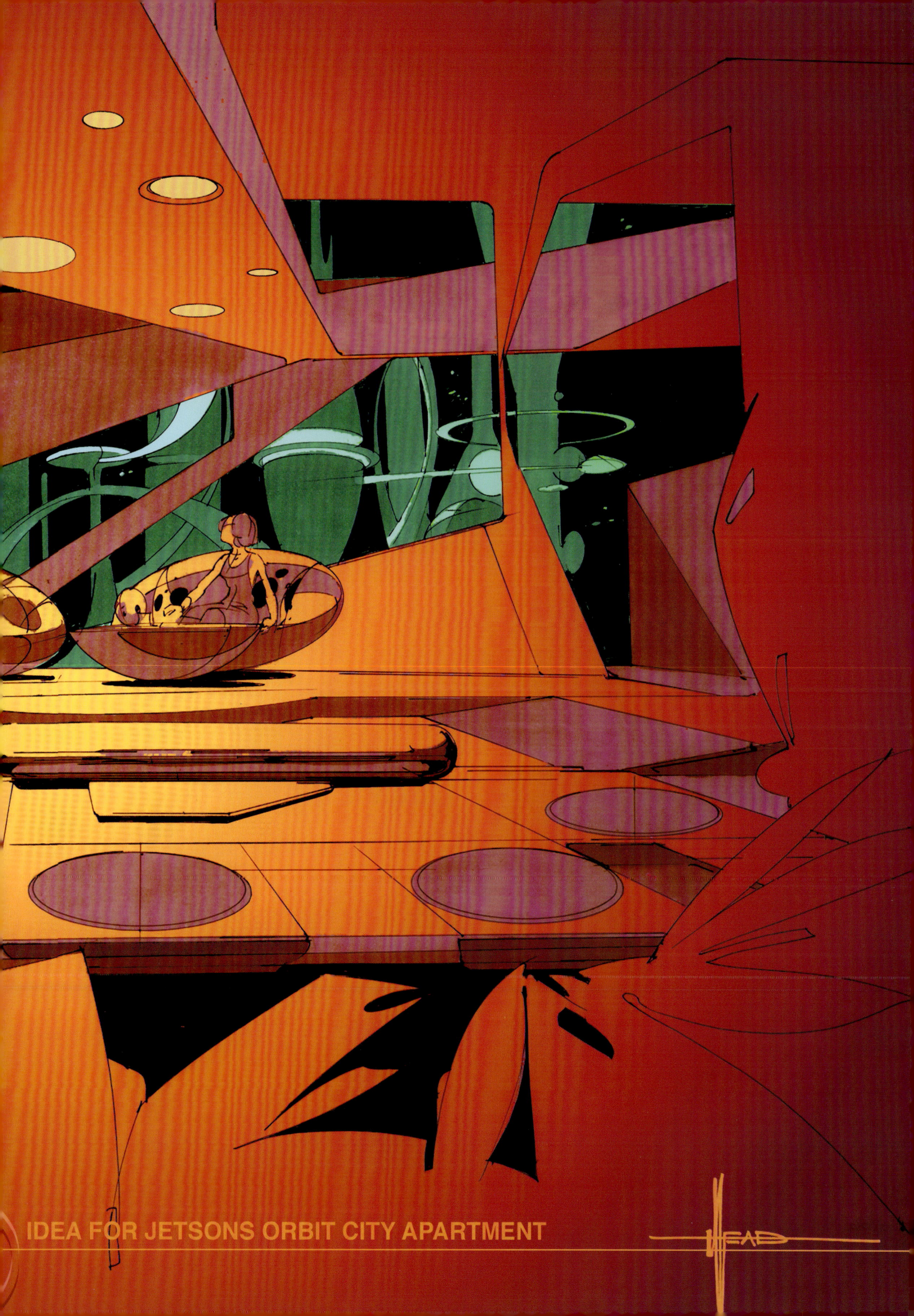

IDEA FOR JETSONS ORBIT CITY APARTMENT

JOHNNY MNEMONIC

BIOMECHANICAL FISH

In this 1995 adaptation and expansion of a William Gibson short story originally written for an exhibition at the San Francisco Museum of Art, it is 2021, the whole world is connected by the internet, and almost half of the population is suffering from "nerve attenuation syndrome" (NAS). Keanu Reeves plays the eponymous Johnny, a cybernetic "mule" whose brain has been programmed via an embedded wet-wired cranial chip to transport a downloaded "fix" to Newark, NJ, where Pharmakon Industries awaits him.

Originally conceived as a low-budget "art film", the director was Robert Longo, a NYC artist known for large-scale vertigo-inducing images of falling figures, who was making his directorial debut.

MEAD'S DESIGN OF THE DOLPHIN'S *BIOMEK* PACK AND NOSE GUARD, REPRESENTED BELOW AND RIGHT IN SKETCH FORM AS WELL AS THE FINAL RENDERING MARKS A FILM DEBUT FOR WHAT BECAME A SUB-GENRE IN BIO-MECHANICAL TRANSFORMATIONS, AND WAS THE IMAGE EMPLOYED BY GIBSON AND LONGO AS THEY SOUGHT FUNDING FOR THE FILM.

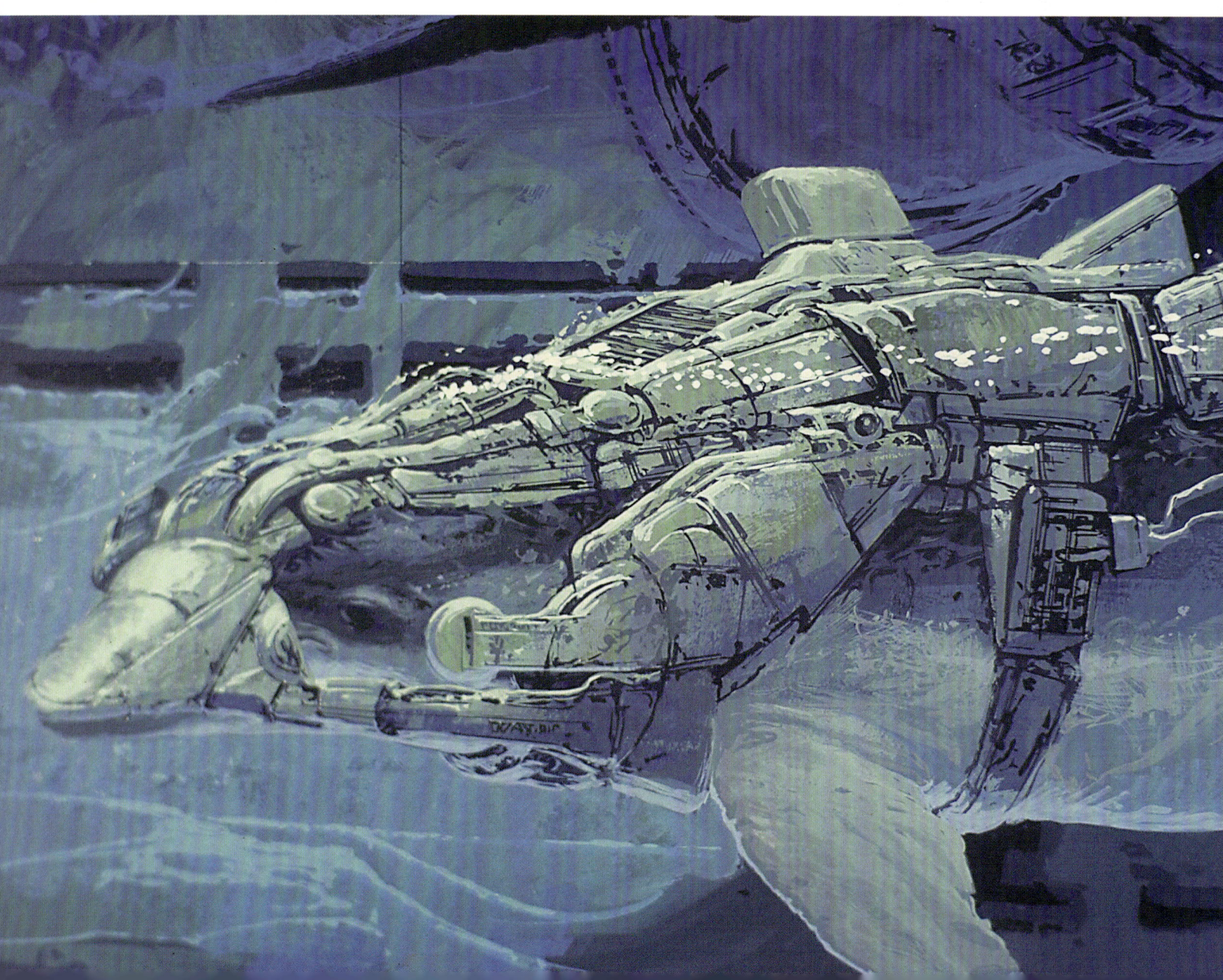

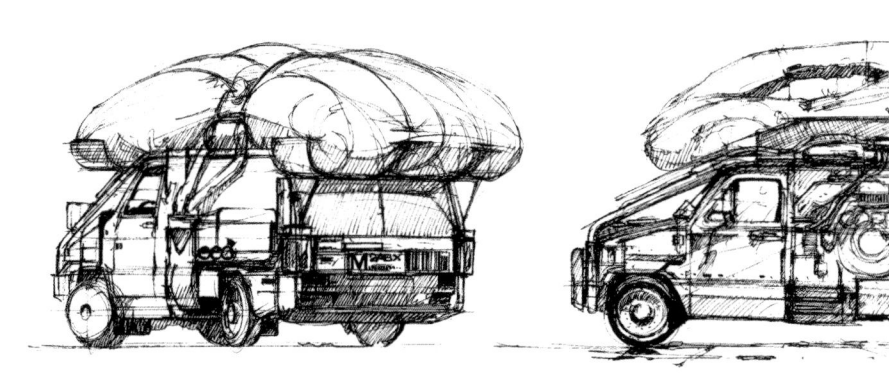
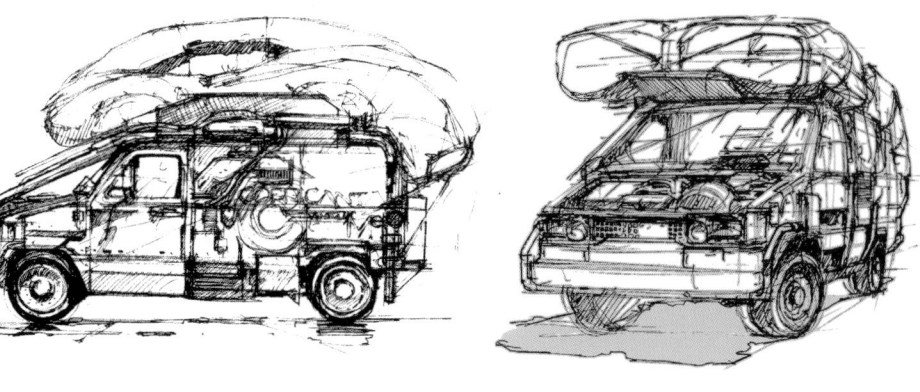

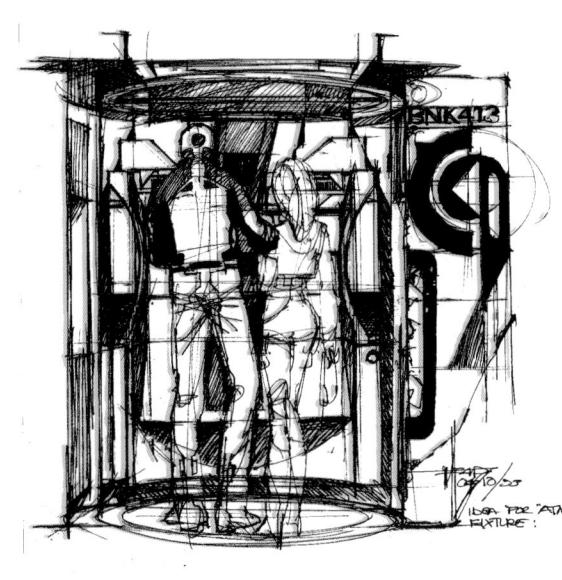
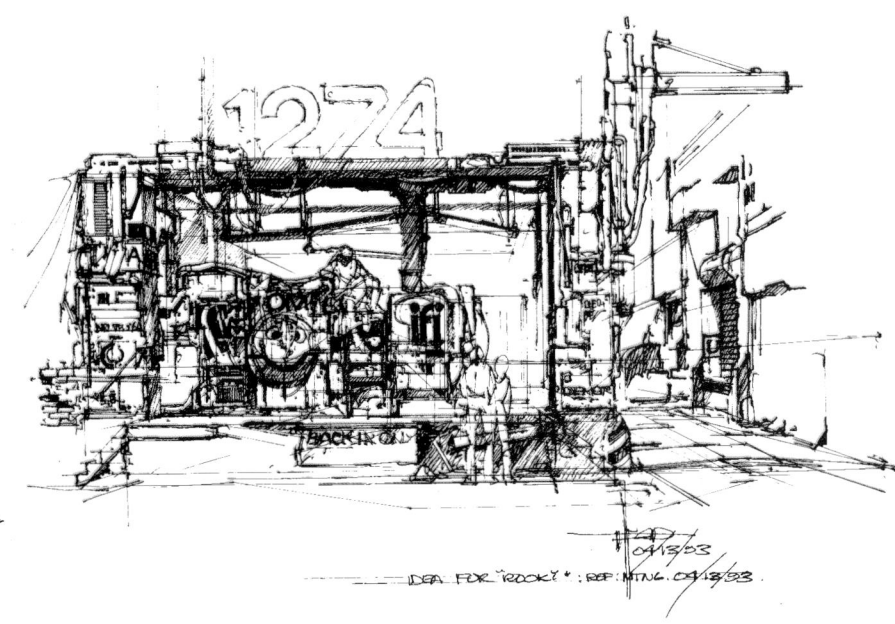

ABOVE: EARLY SKETCHES OF A VEHICLE AND
DIFFERENT LOCATIONS IN THE FILM.

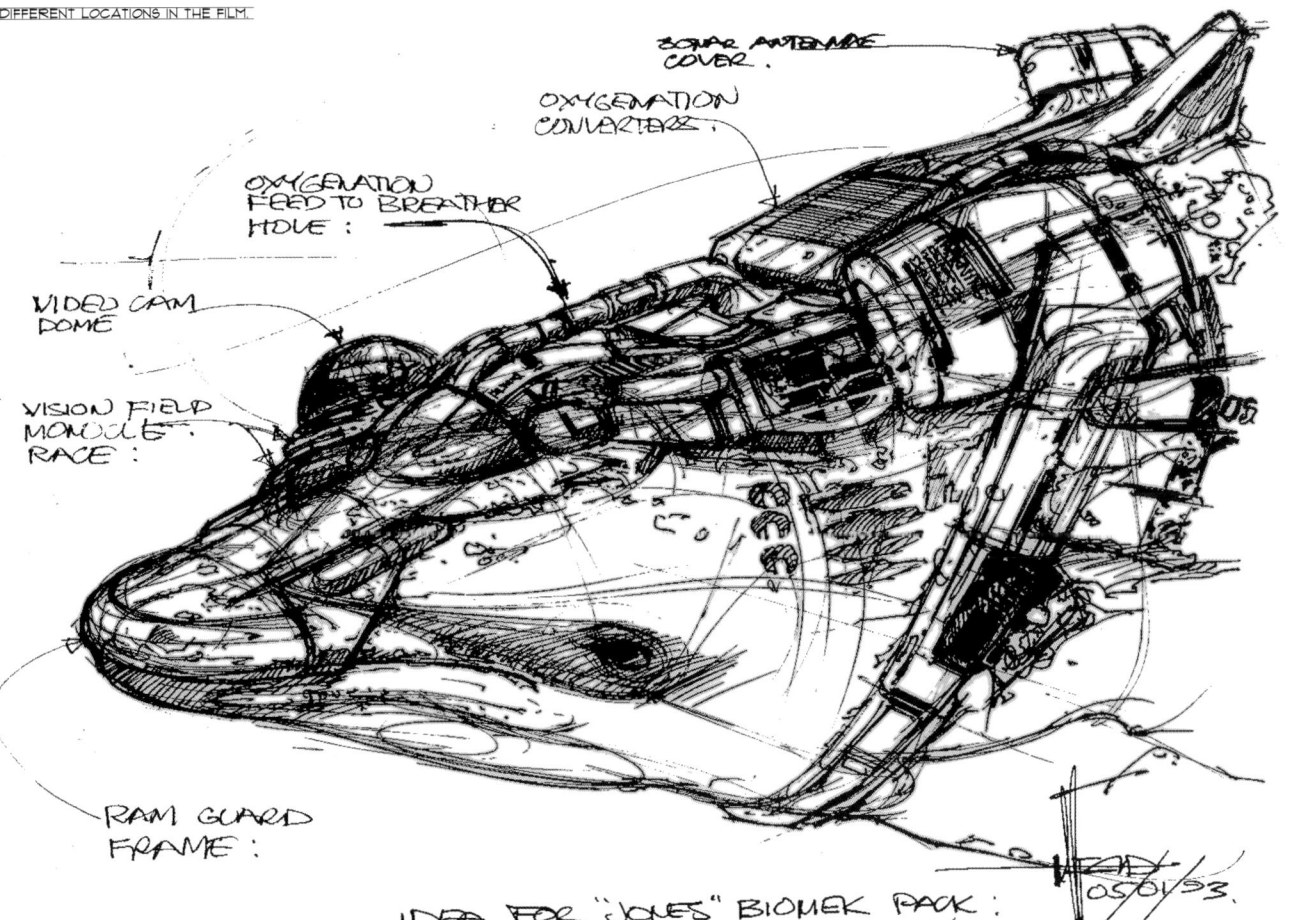

197

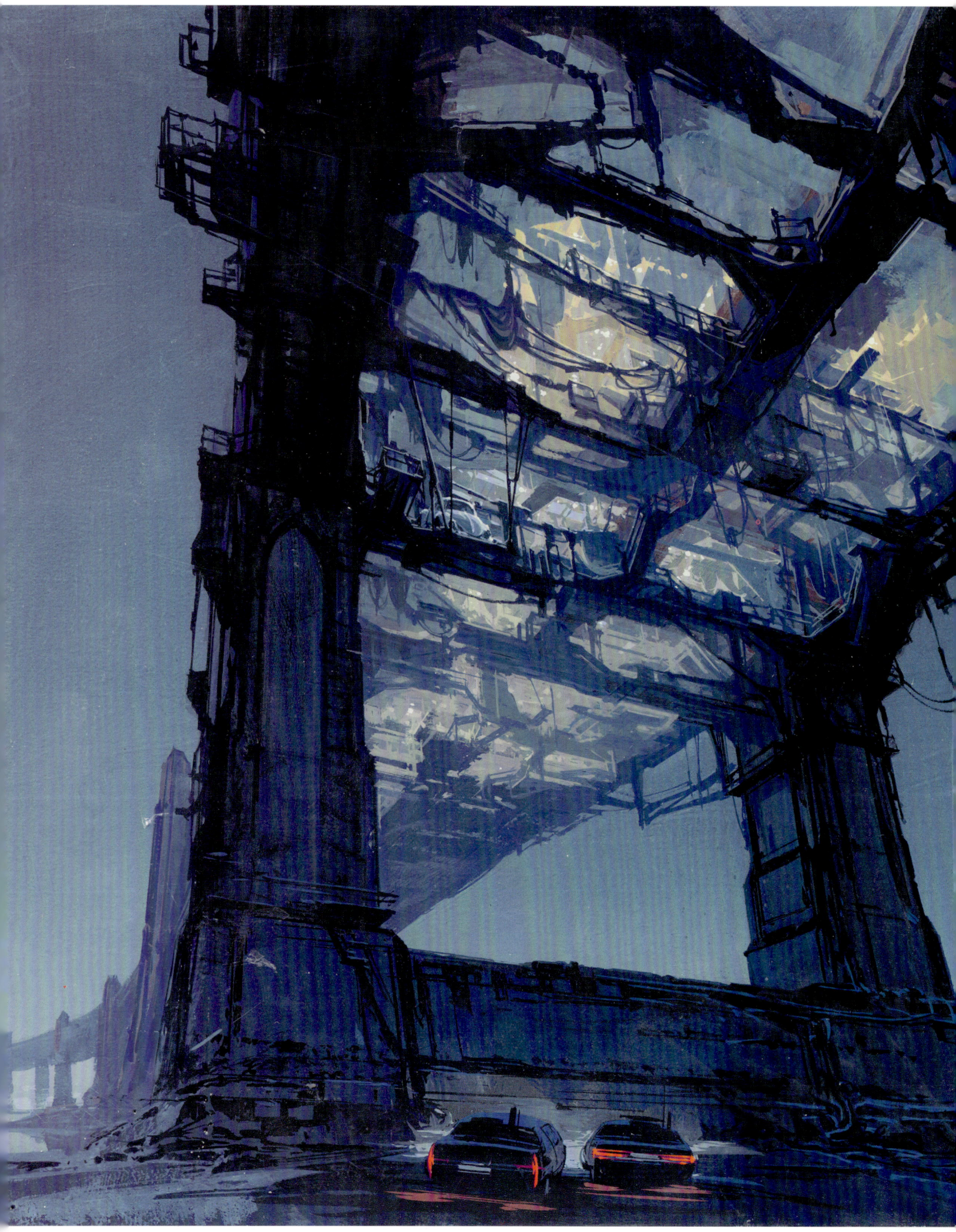

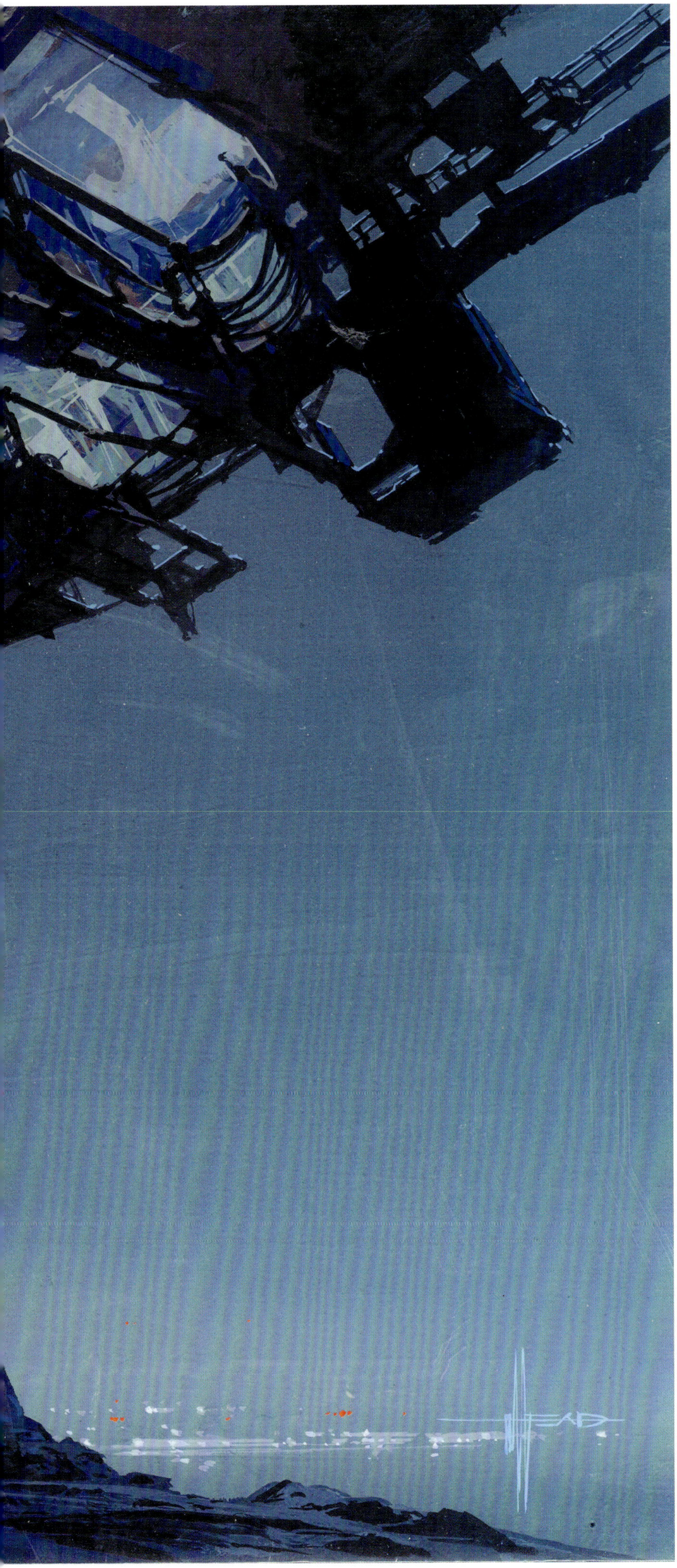

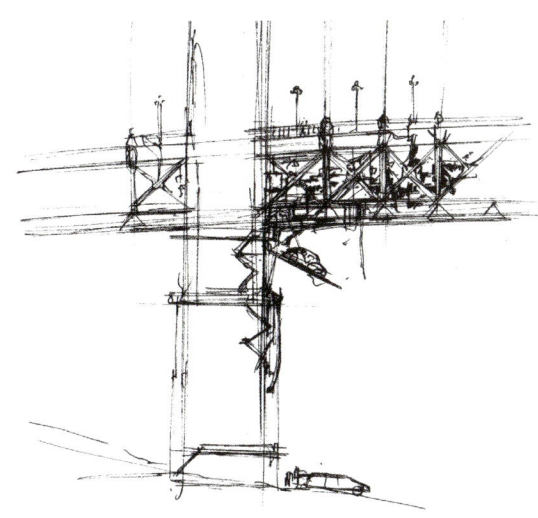

Mead's vision of a crumbling, rusted, hulking bridge occupied by a rebellious cyberpunk colony is the destination for the title's ill-fated messenger, whose brain has been injected with a computer chip containing highly classified material. In the climatic final scenes, as various forces vie to capture Johnny, and with him, the information on the chip, it is revealed that the recipient of the transfer is a specially equipped dolphin uniquely able to interpret the material.

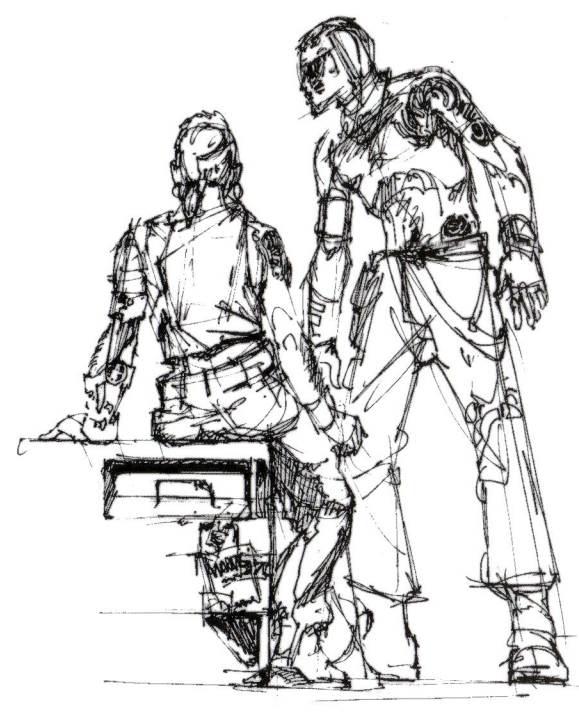

LUNAR SCOUT COMMANDOS

LIFE UNDER GLASS

In this youth-oriented science-fiction project, the lunar scouts of the title take on the bad guys who are bent on disrupting life at a human outpost on the moon. Fortunately for them, and for the colony itself, the father of one of the scouts is the head man, giving them access to the control center from which they mount their attack.

Mead's pre-production images were developed before there was a shooting script, or even a finalized story line, yet it contains some of the most compelling images to be found in the annals of his work.

By envisioning the lunar colony called for in the outline as a cluster of shallow dome-like structures with varying shading devices, Mead's design proposes a replica of San Francisco "under glass", with outlying domes roughly filling the role of suburbs, and iconic references, like the Golden Gate Bridge, to provide opportunities for story development. This approach, like a ship in a bottle, would enable the producers to use "real" locations as dressing for the "unreal" story line with a minimum of the expense that might be required if full-scale sets were to be employed.

The progress of the design, from a rough sketch (right) depicting a lunar colony, to a final, detailed image (below) illustrates the simultaneous development of visual imagery and disciplined, reality based engineering which differentiates Mead's work from that of other visionary illustrators.

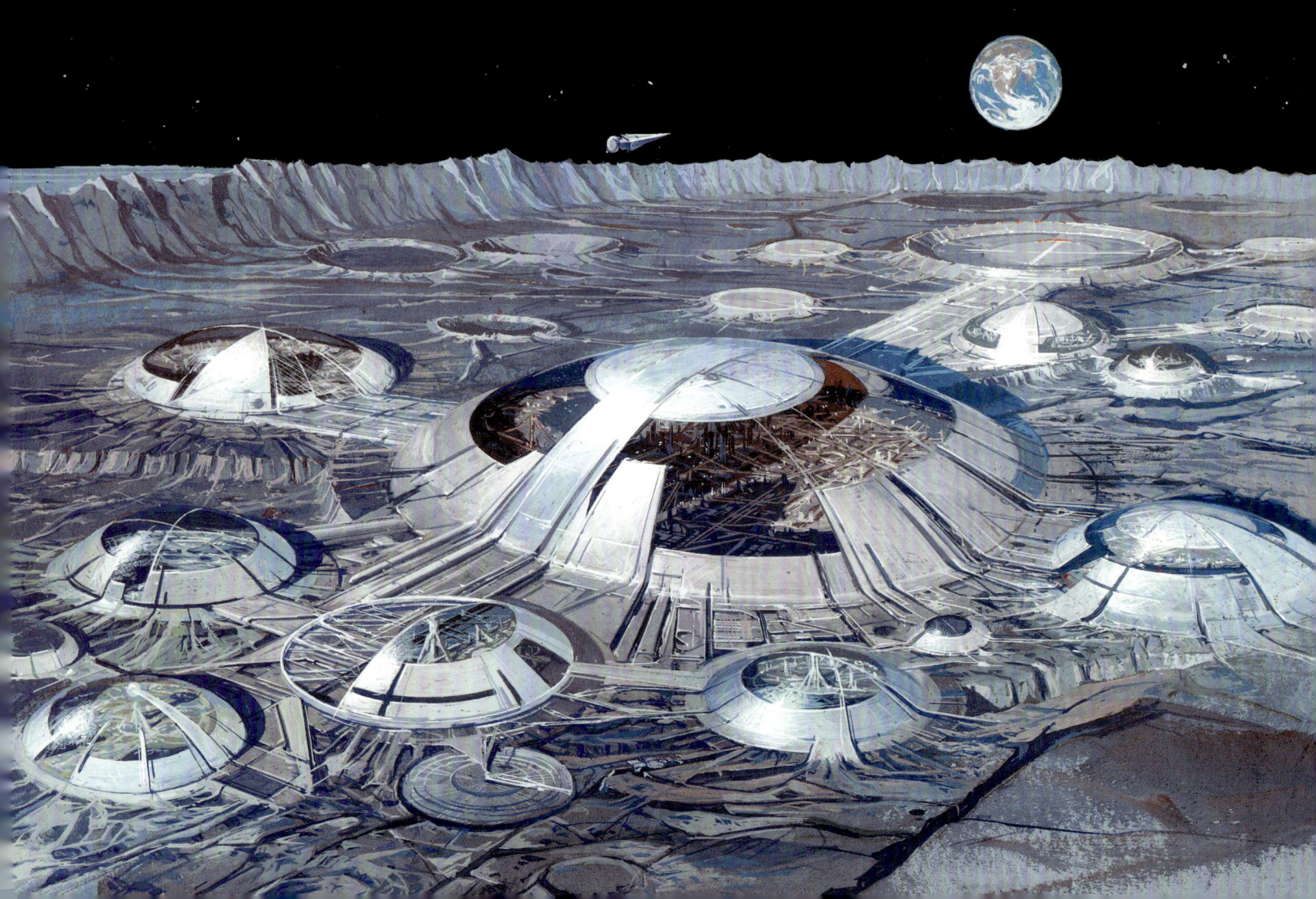

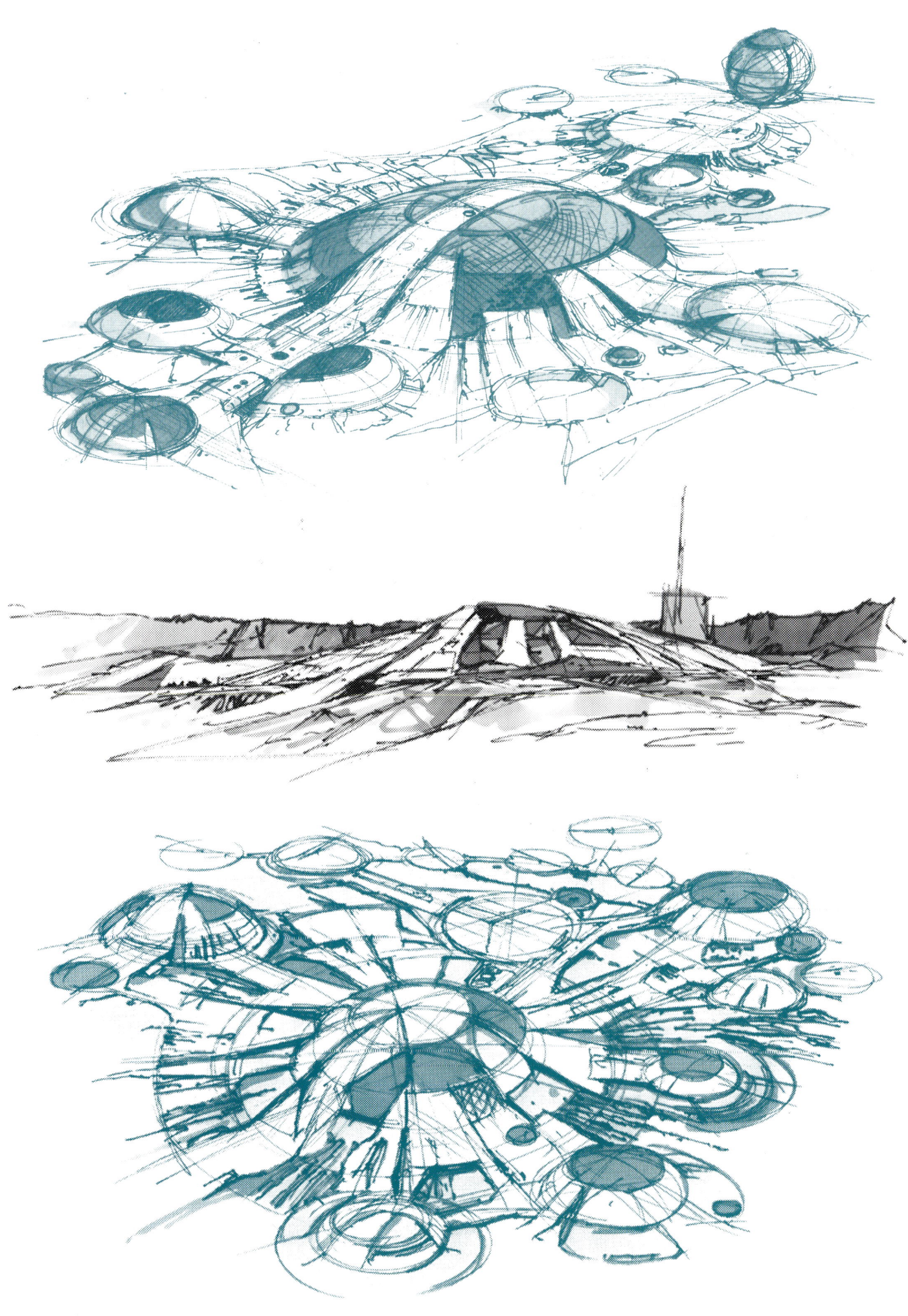

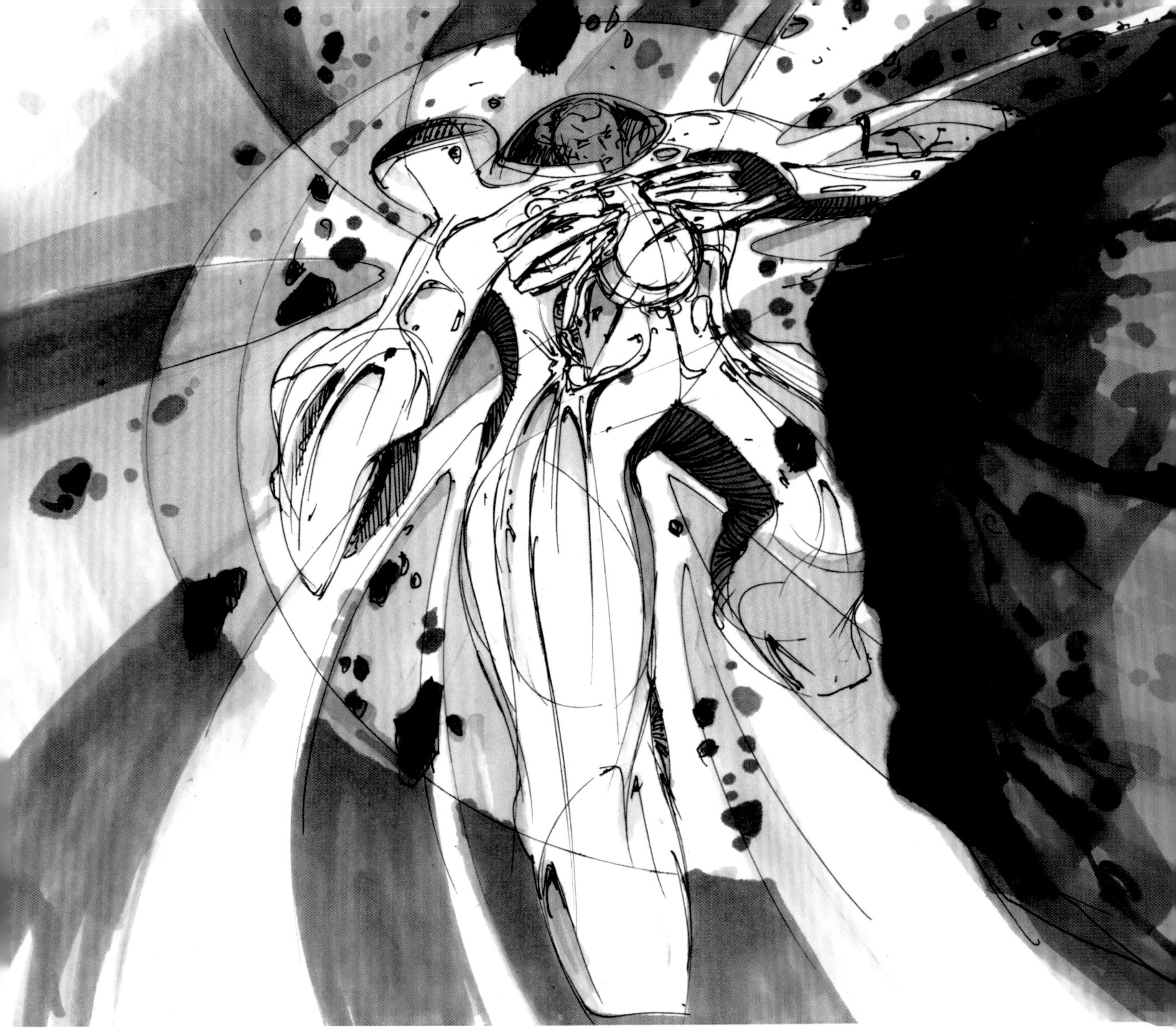

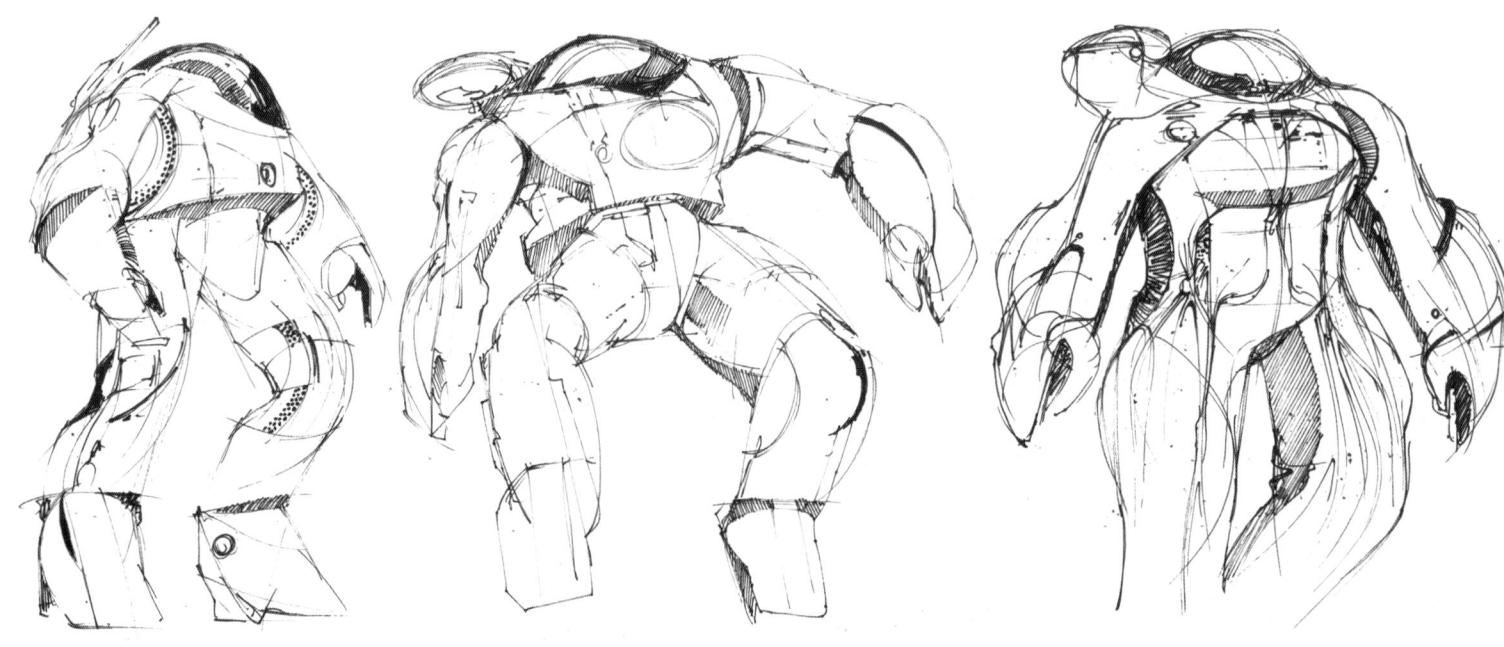

BREAKING WITH TRADITIONAL SPACESUIT TYPOLOGY, MEAD PROPOSES AN ALL-ENCOMPASSING EVERYDAY PRESSURE SUIT IN WHICH A MASSIVE SHOULDER UNIT ENCLOSES MUCH OF THE USER'S HEAD, AS WELL AS A MECHANISM TO SYNTHESIZE OXYGEN IN THE EVENT OF A CATASTROPHIC FAILURE OF THE ARTIFICIAL ATMOSPHERE.

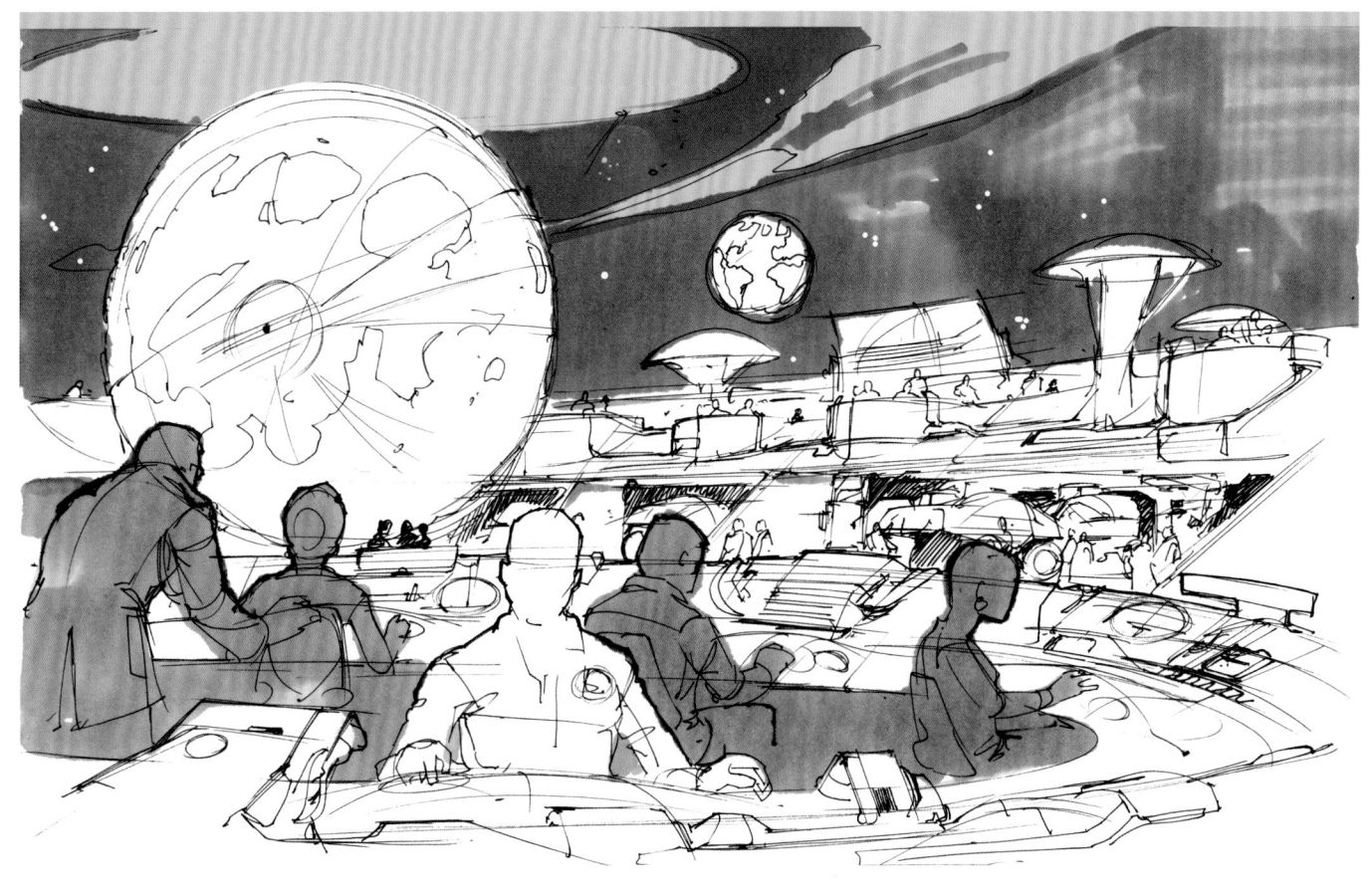

IN THESE SKETCHS FOR THE HERO RENDERING (OVERLEAF) OF THE CONTROL CENTER, MEAD DEPICTS THE FIGHTING SHIPS, RANK UPON RANK OF SPACE SUITS, AND A HOLOGRAPHIC MOON SO THAT THE LUNAR SCOUTS COULD FORM THEIR BATTLE PLANS.

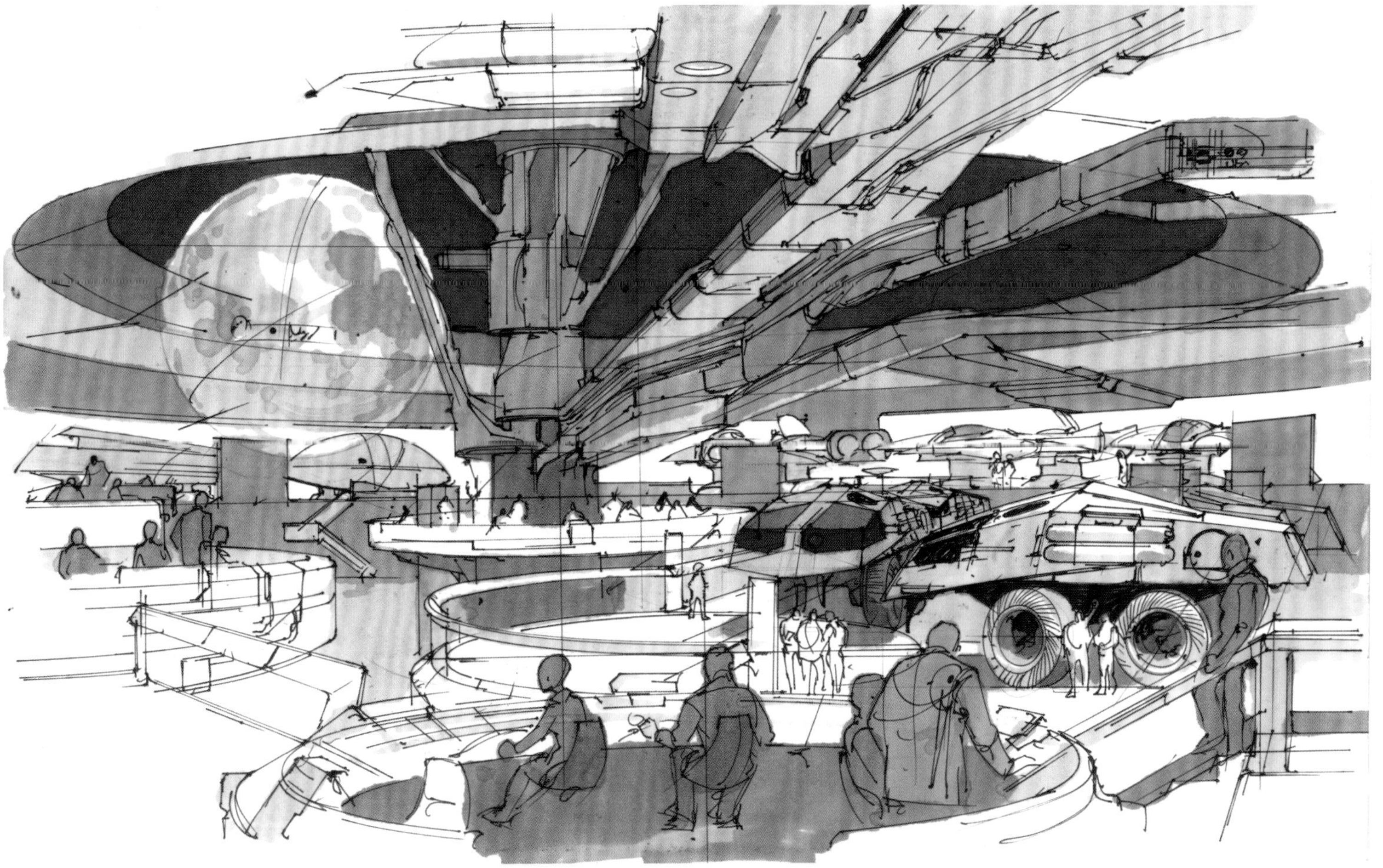

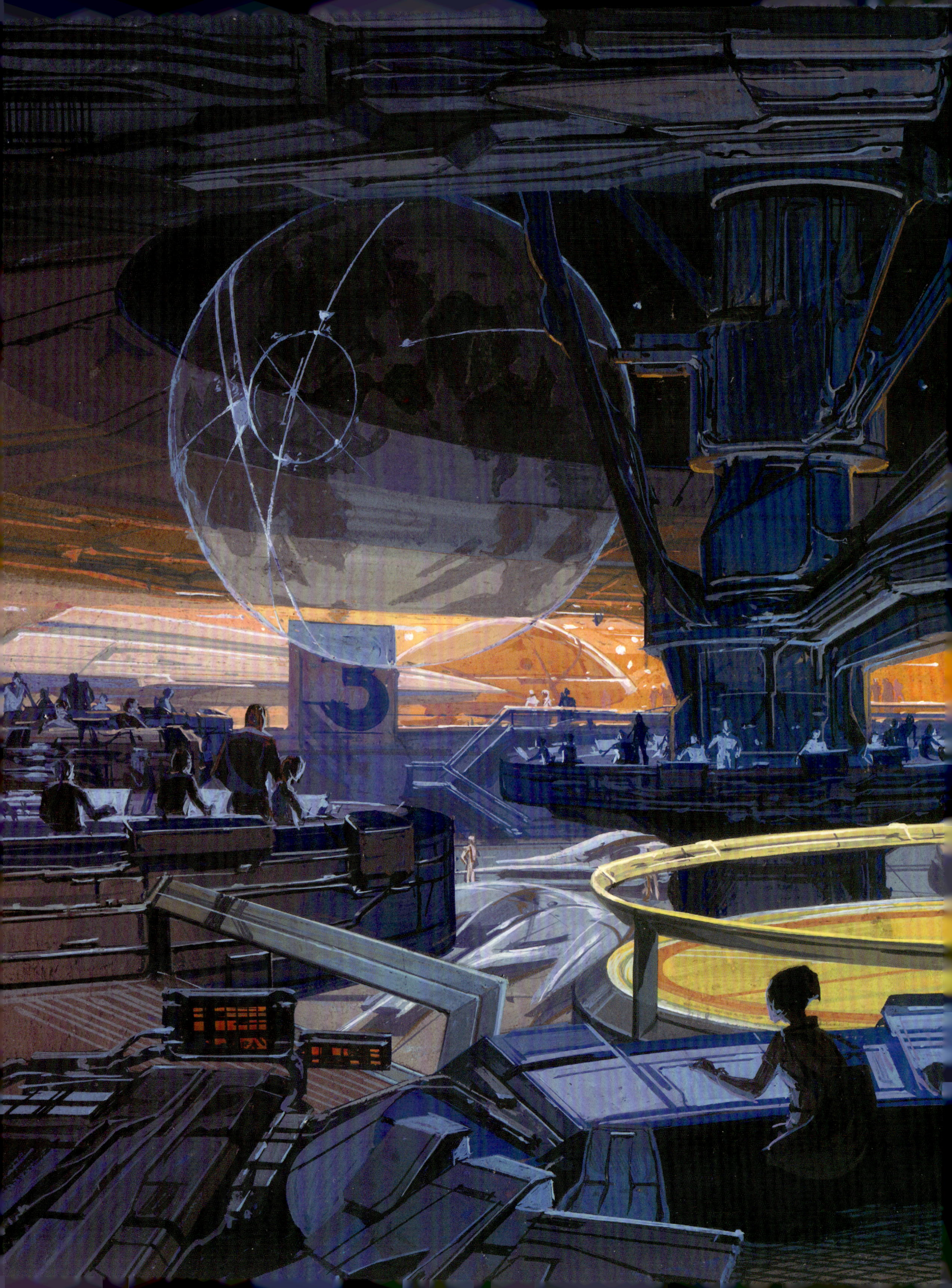

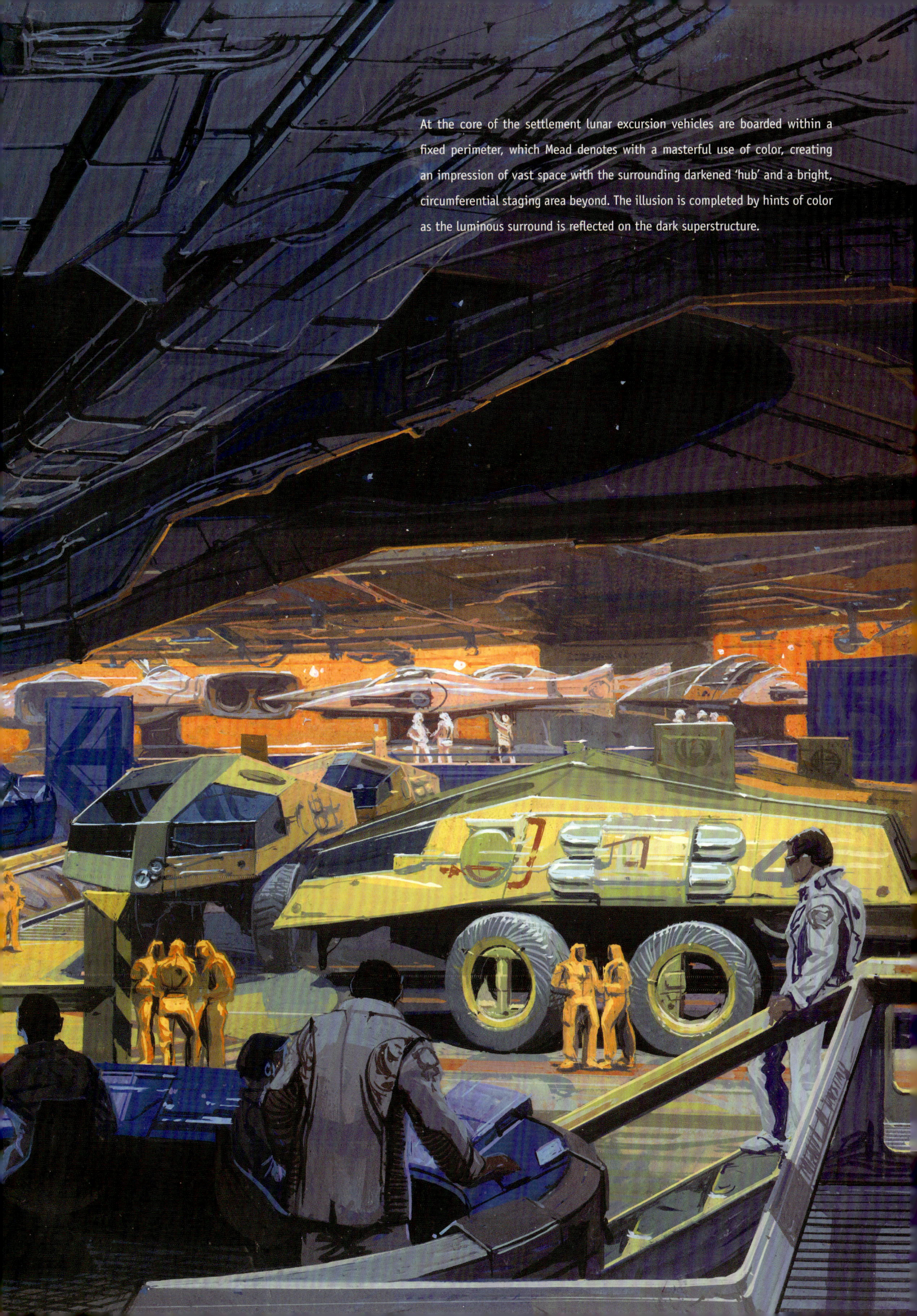

At the core of the settlement lunar excursion vehicles are boarded within a fixed perimeter, which Mead denotes with a masterful use of color, creating an impression of vast space with the surrounding darkened 'hub' and a bright, circumferential staging area beyond. The illusion is completed by hints of color as the luminous surround is reflected on the dark superstructure.

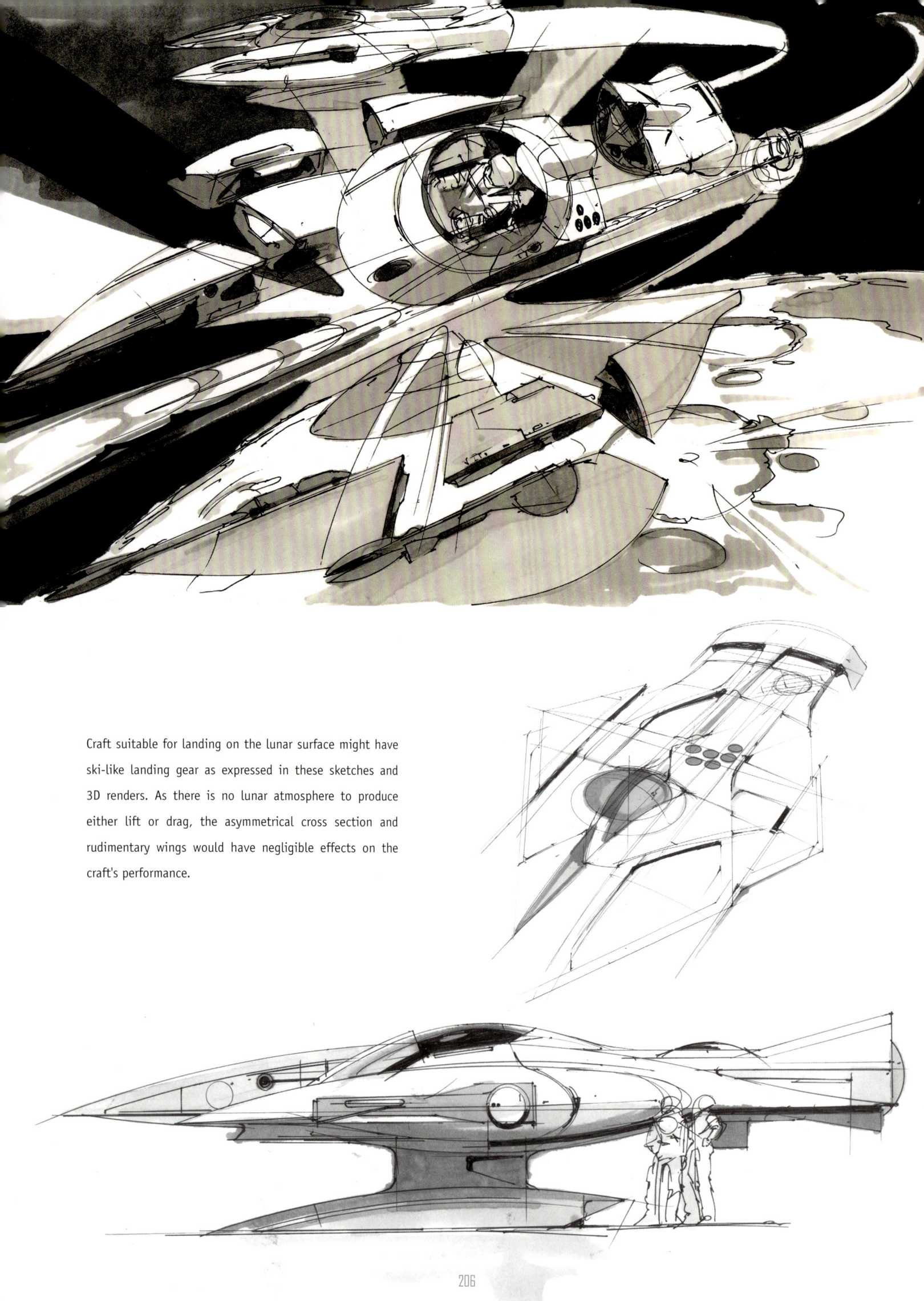

Craft suitable for landing on the lunar surface might have ski-like landing gear as expressed in these sketches and 3D renders. As there is no lunar atmosphere to produce either lift or drag, the asymmetrical cross section and rudimentary wings would have negligible effects on the craft's performance.

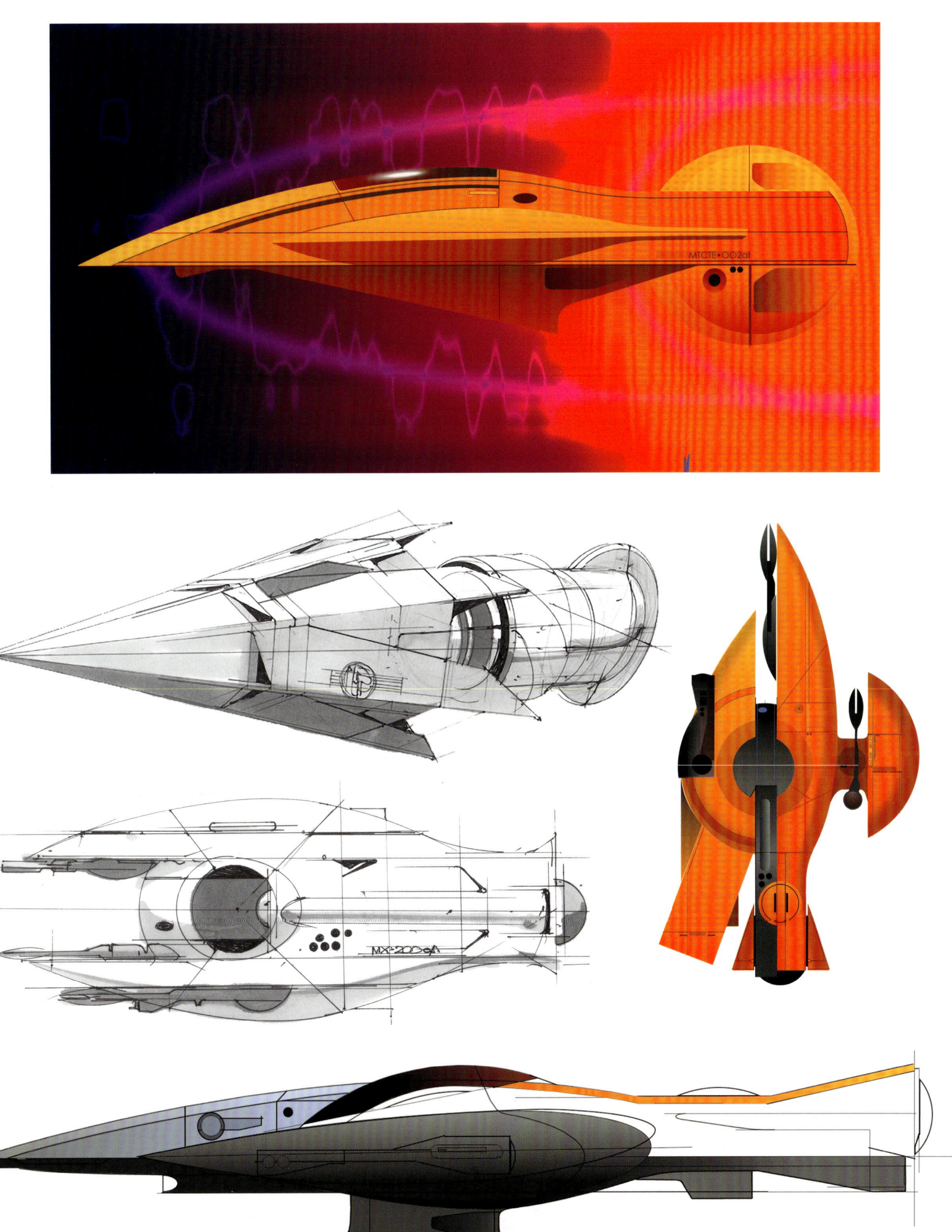

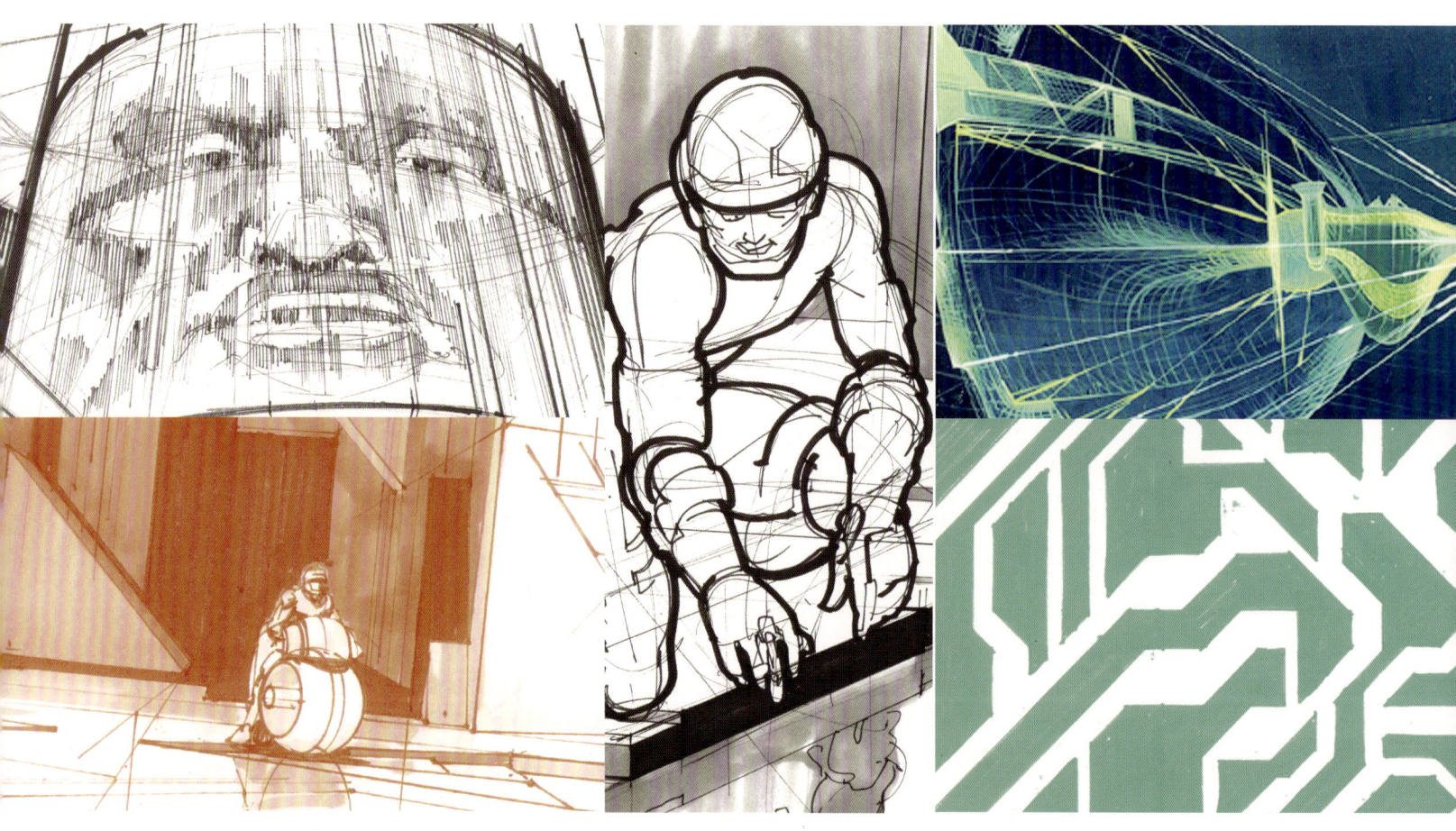

TRON

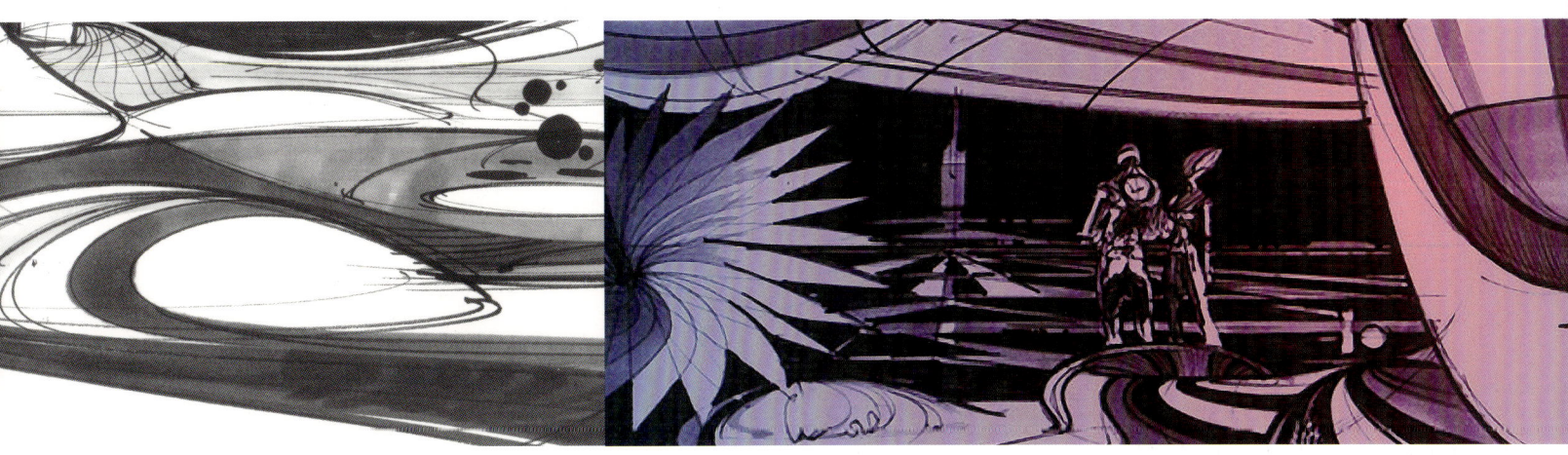

The 1980s saw two of Mead's most demanding assignments come about when two directors simultaneously tapped him to conceive the looks of two of the most visually and tonally distinct films ever made. The world of *TRON* (released in 1982) and that of *Aliens* (1986) demand vastly different special effects, as well as, in the case of *TRON,* pioneering 3D computer modelling.

As the action in *TRON* takes place *within* a computer chip, Mead was challenged to create a convincing digital realm, and to address the incongruity of a world within a solid state device, while at the same time creating costumes and props to support that admittedly improbable concept.

While working for the first time with computer 3D modelling, Mead discovered unique creative opportunities and began thinking of the possibilities offered by a new set of digital tools and what they would allow you to do. Inspired by the graphic patterns of a computer motherboard, and exploiting the creative potential of 3D modelling, Mead generated a surface model of the *TRON* landscape composed of sixteen squares which could be rearranged to produce a convincing digital "world".

BELOW: EMBEDDED CIRCUITRY BLENDS THE ACTOR'S PRESENCE WITH THE IMAGERY OF THE ENVIRONMENT TO IMPLY THAT THEY ARE SIMPLY AN ACTIVE ENERGY SOURCE. MEAD'S ATTENTION TO DETAIL EXTENDS TO THE DESIGN OF THE ACTOR'S BODY, DEFINING TRON'S IMAGE (RIGHT) AS LITHE AS A DANCER'S AND DELINEATING MUSCLE MASS WITH A SCULPTOR'S EYE.

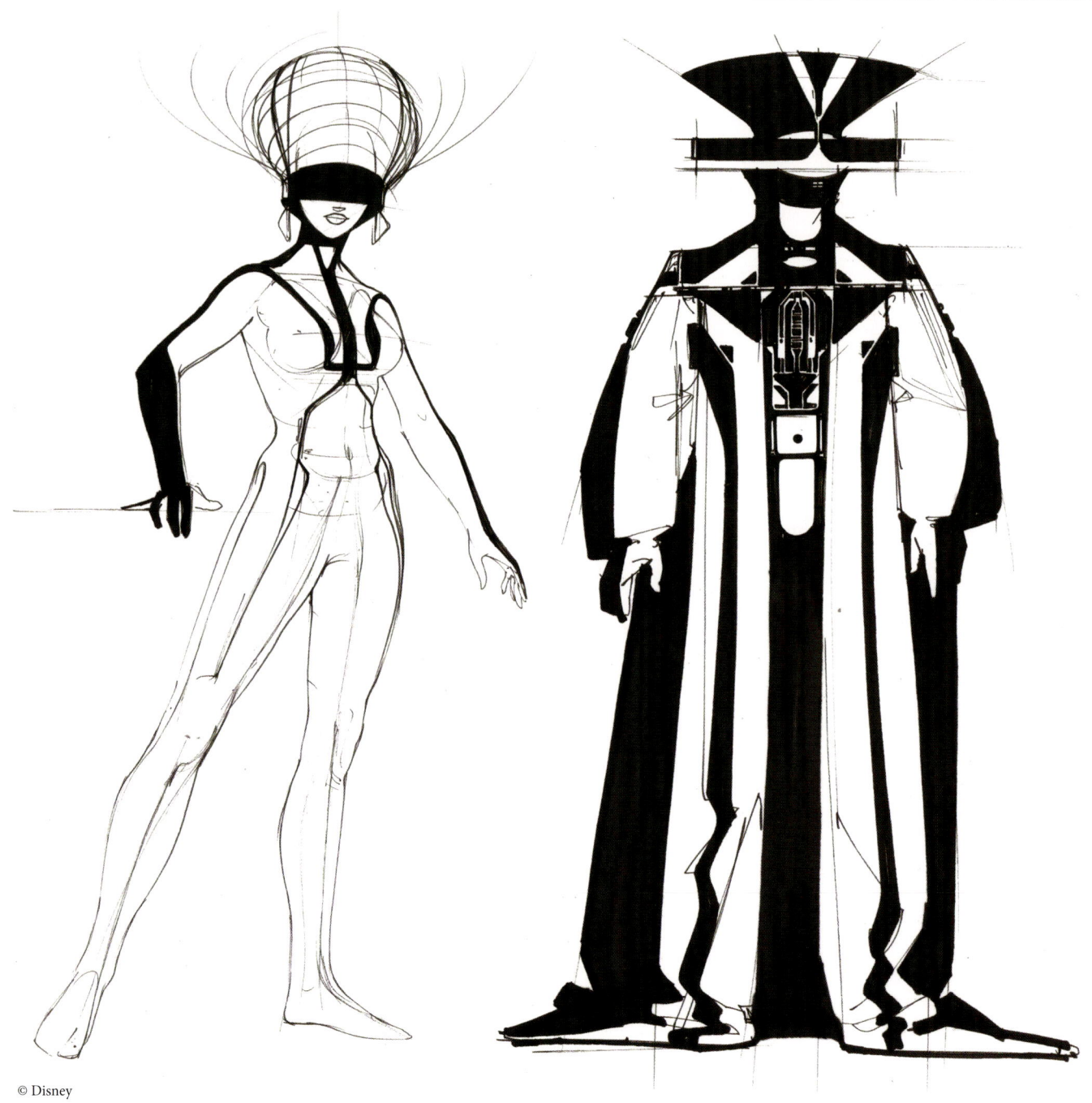

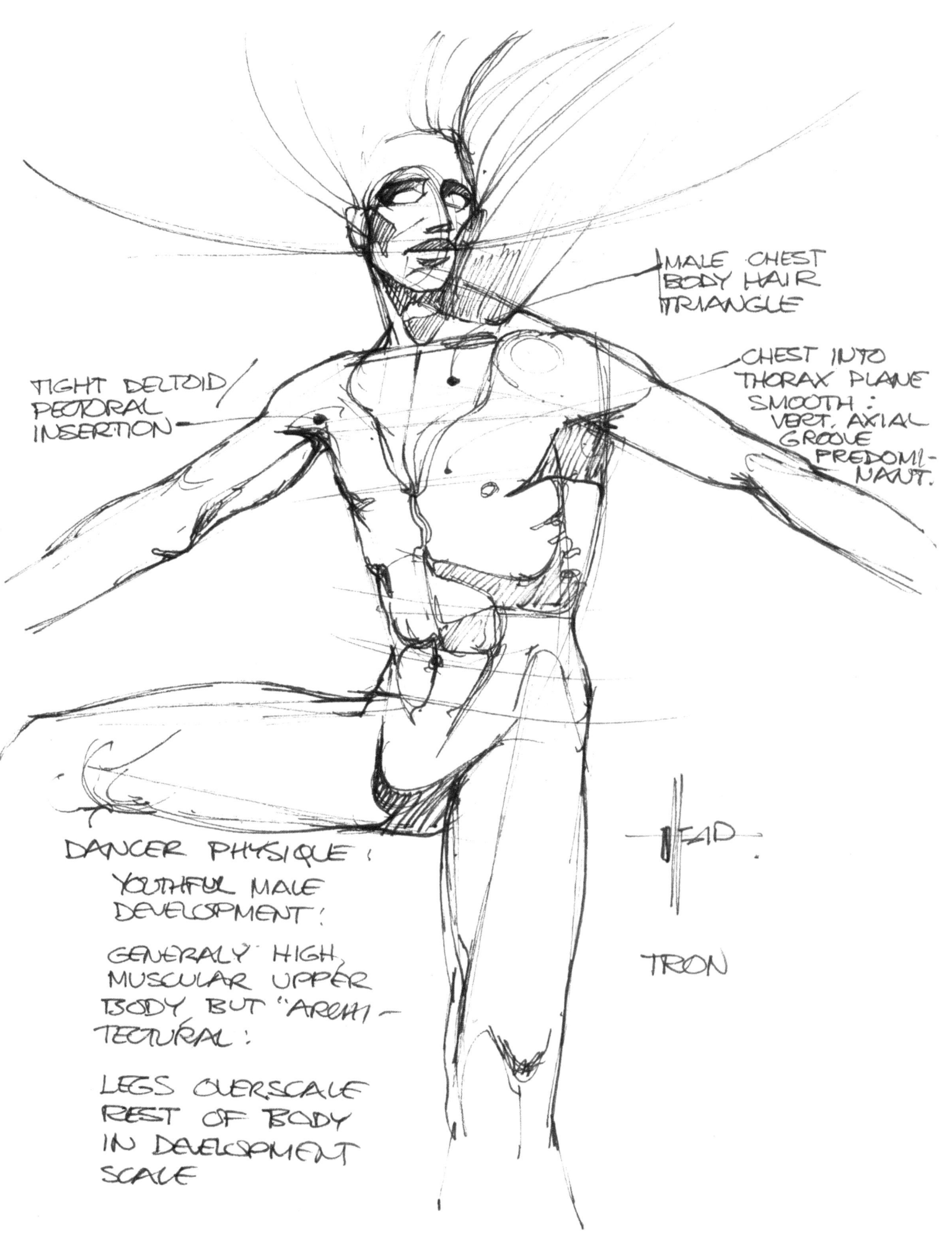

MALE CHEST
BODY HAIR
TRIANGLE

CHEST INTO
THORAX PLANE
SMOOTH :
VERT. AXIAL
GROOVE
PREDOMI-
NANT.

TIGHT DELTOID/
PECTORAL
INSERTION

DANCER PHYSIQUE :

YOUTHFUL MALE
DEVELOPMENT :

GENERALY HIGH
MUSCULAR UPPER
BODY BUT "ARCHI-
TECTURAL :

LEGS OVERSCALE
REST OF BODY
IN DEVELOPMENT
SCALE

HEAD.

TRON

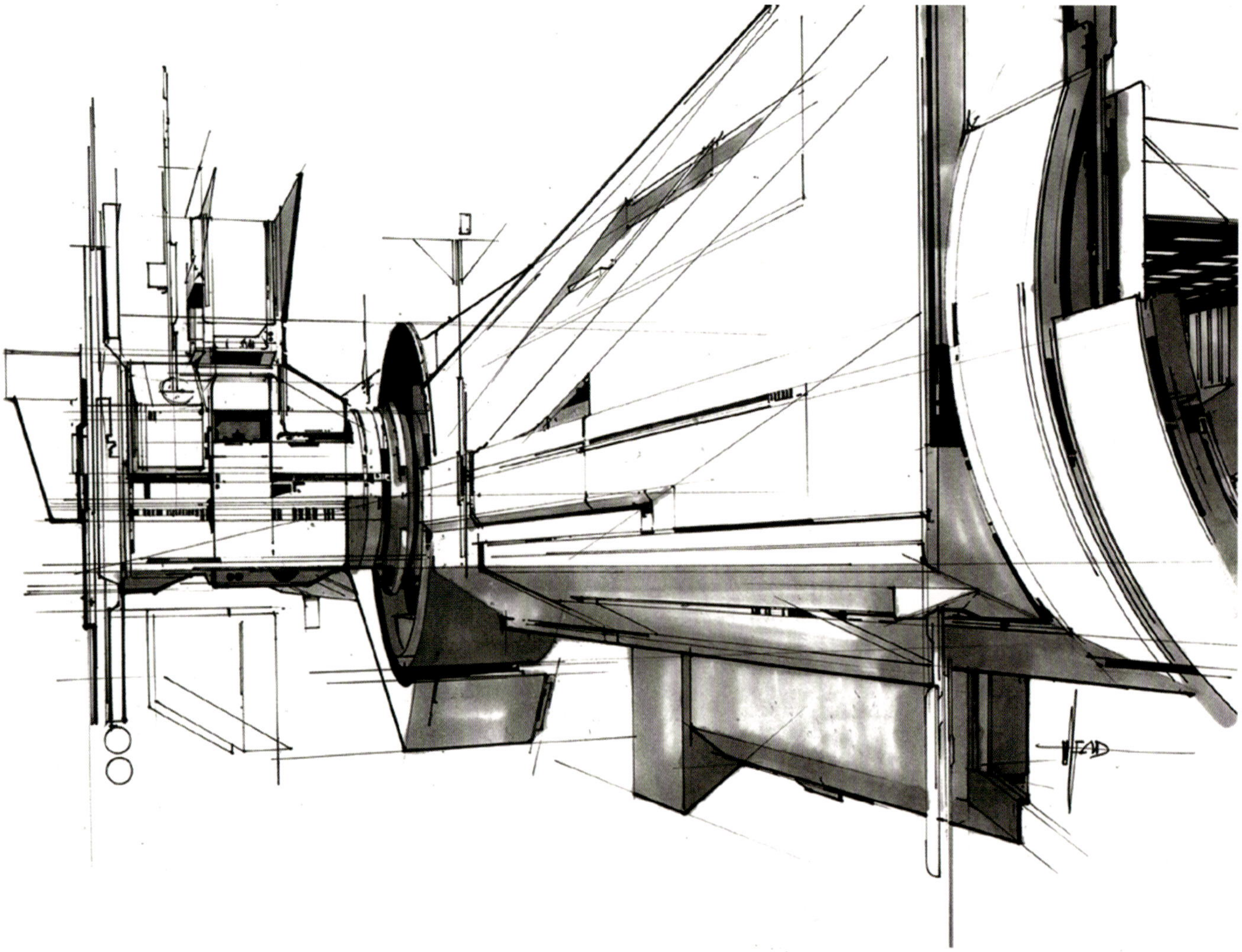

This was the challenge: create a vivid, three-dimensional representation of an environment made up of electrons, solid state switching devices, Nano-thin surfaces of silicon and the steady pulse of binary code. Now add people, government agency, and a civilization dominated by binary, either/or decisions.

The first time around, the story and graphics almost wrote themselves: boy meets computer game, is sucked into an electronic world, has near-death confrontations with denizens of that world, and escapes via a clever application.

The struggle, of course, was to unite the graphic treatment of the 3D digital models with live action costuming and props.

The look, extrapolated from the linear arrangement of circuitry on a generic motherboard, was nearly inevitable: glowing paths stretching to infinity, and costumes featuring glowing tracery reminiscent of printed circuits. On a technical level, considering it was 1982, it required ingenuity and the creation of unprecedented luminous costumes to achieve the desired effect.

By the time of the reboot, the game had changed: the world of electronics was native to computer simulation and the zeroes and ones of digital design presented an almost too easy analogue to the interior world of a computer game.

TWO STUDIES OF TYPICAL PATTERNS FOUND ON COMPUTER CIRCUIT BOARDS. NOTE THE CONSISTENT ANGULAR PATHS, THE THICKENING OF VECTORS, AND THE INTRICATE LAYERING WHICH TARGETS SPECIFIC COMPONENTS.

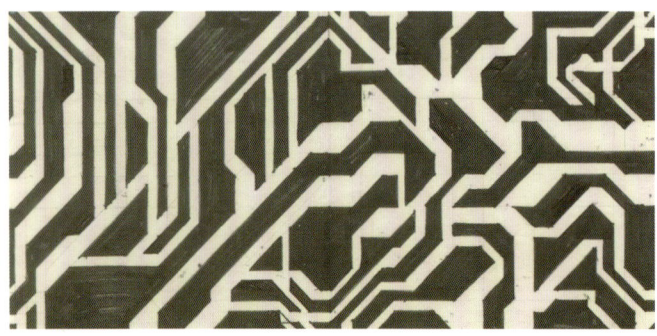
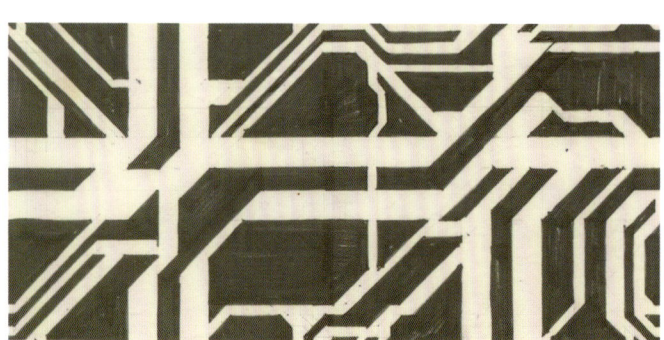

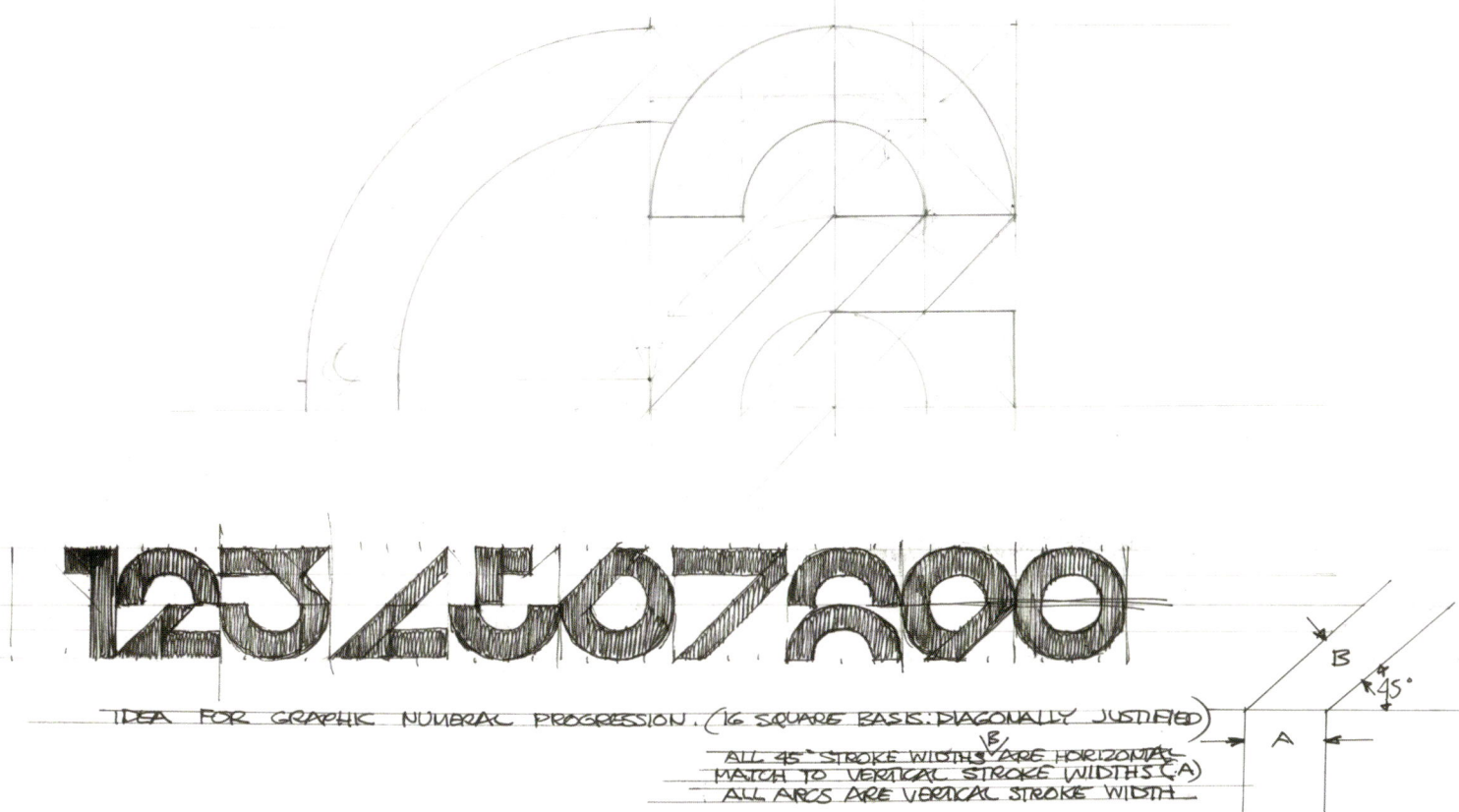

1 2 3 4 5 6 7 8 9 0

IDEA FOR GRAPHIC NUMERAL PROGRESSION. (16 SQUARE BASIS: DIAGONALLY JUSTIFIED)

ALL 45° STROKE WIDTHS ARE HORIZONTAL
MATCH TO VERTICAL STROKE WIDTHS (A)
ALL ARCS ARE VERTICAL STROKE WIDTH

B

45°

A

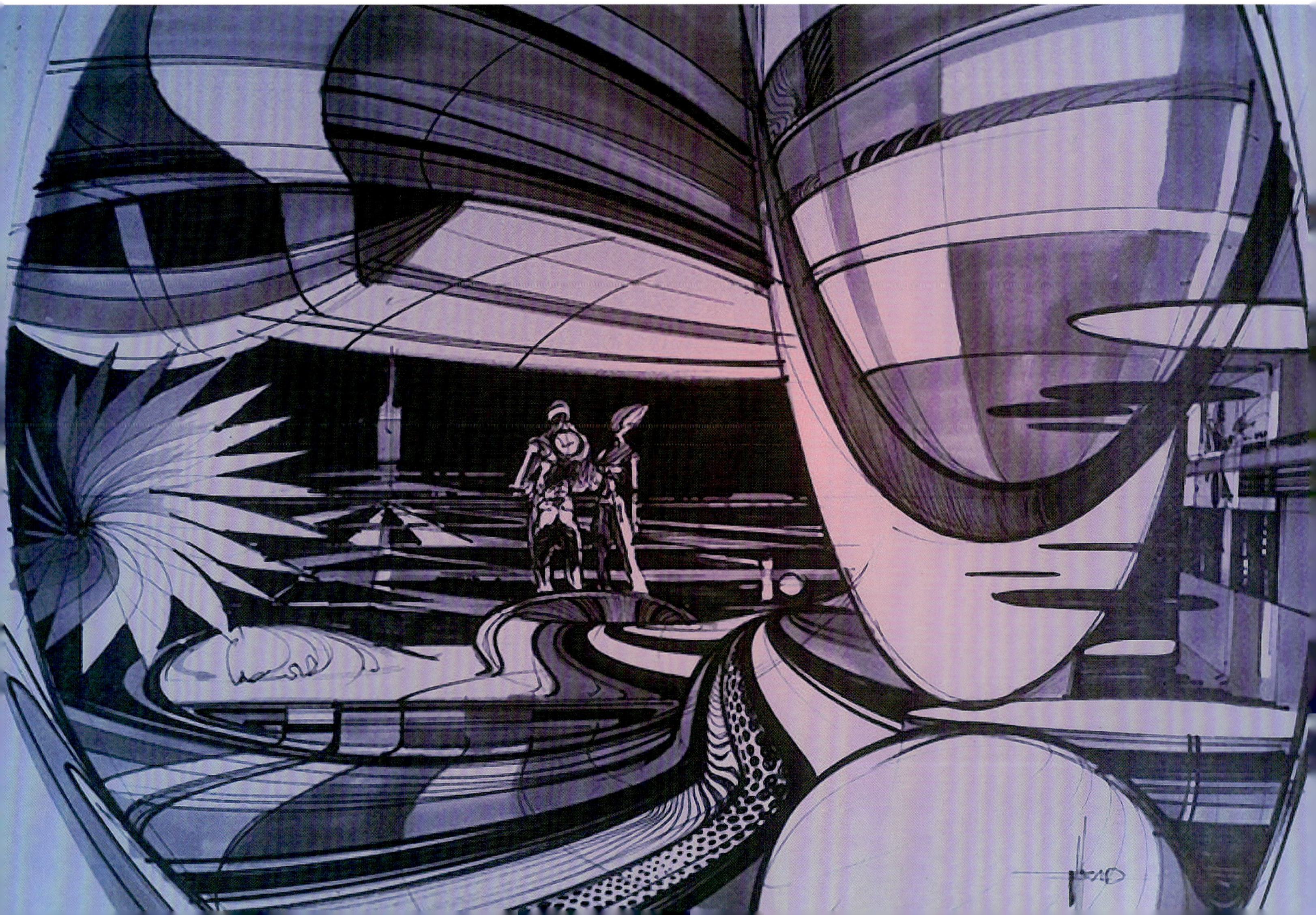

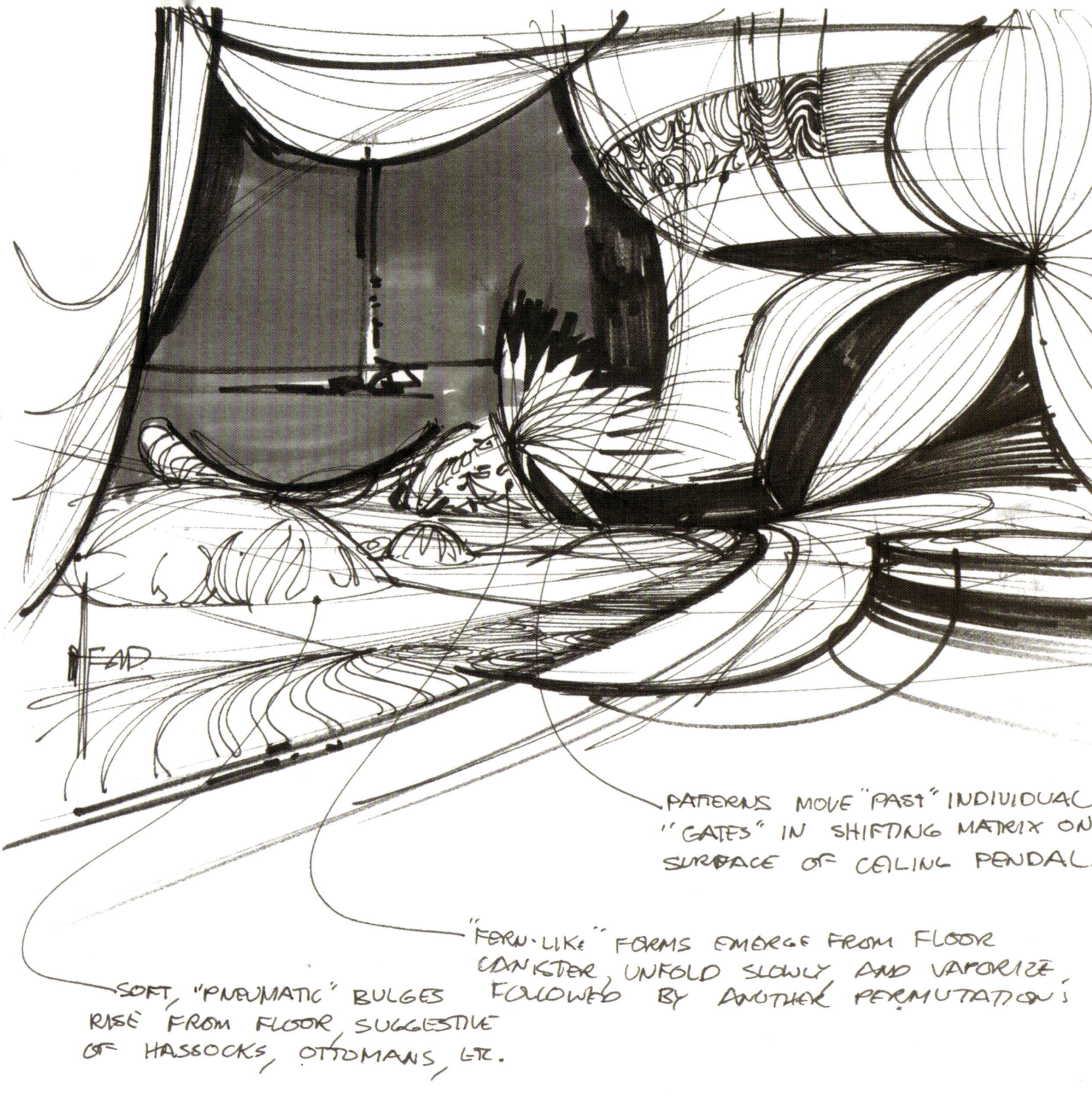

HEAD.

PATTERNS MOVE "PAST" INDIVIDUAL "GATES" IN SHIFTING MATRIX ON SURFACE OF CEILING PENDAL.

"FERN-LIKE" FORMS EMERGE FROM FLOOR CANISTER, UNFOLD SLOWLY AND VAPORIZE, FOLLOWED BY ANOTHER PERMUTATION.

SOFT, "PNEUMATIC" BULGES RISE FROM FLOOR, SUGGESTIVE OF HASSOCKS, OTTOMANS, ETC.

AMBIENCE:- COZY : COMFY : INTIMATE : DEN-LIKE :

ELEMENTS : DRAPERY: MULTIPLE PATTERN OVERLAYS (TEXTURE & INTRICACY)
PLANTS: NON-FORMAL SIT/LOUNGE FIXTURES-
LEVEL CHANGES, BOTH IN FLOOR & CEILING PLANES
INTERESTING PLAN-VIEW ARRANGEMENT:
(TO FAVOR CERTAIN PERSPECTIVES, A LA JAPANESE)

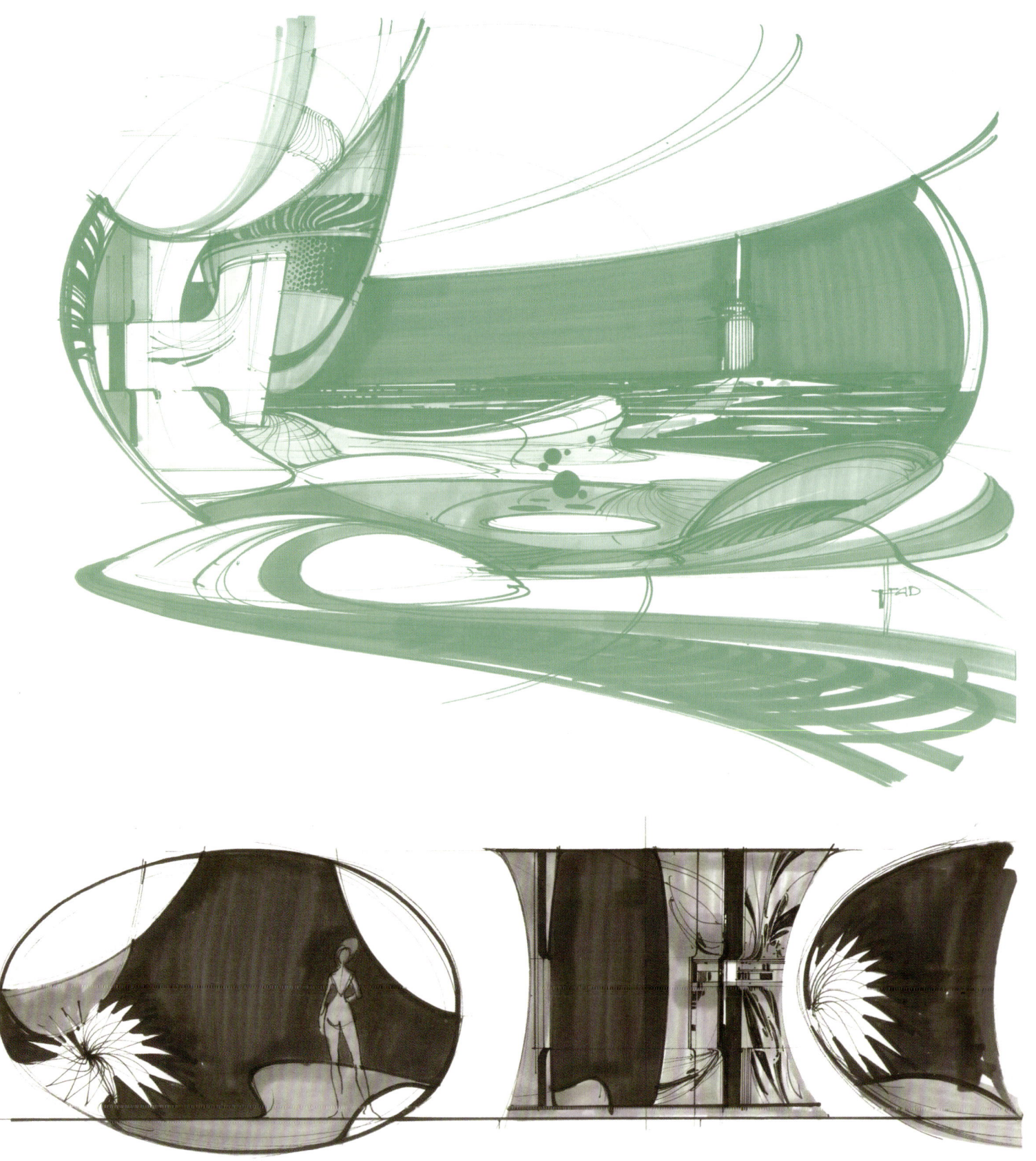

VIGNETTE SKETCHES EMPHASIZE THE DETAILED NATURE OF MEAD'S VISION TO
MANIPULATE THE PERVASIVE SILICON CRYSTAL STRUCTURE TO FORM A DIGITAL CAVE.
MEAD SAYS IT INCLUDES "ALL SORTS OF WEIRD STUFF. IT TOOK A WHOLE DAY AND
WAS REALLY FUN TO DRAW".

The powerful, primary geometry of the *TRON* environment conveyed a uniform aesthetic at multiple scales, implying that, like crystalline formations, even smaller elements, such as a speaker's podium, shared the same basic form as the immense volumes framing the action. Like the Renaissance engravings of Paranesi, whose 'imaginary prisons' or *carceri* represented a "negation of time, incoherence of space," the spatial constructs in these sketches, with their labyrinthine pathways, are designed to imprison, and ultimately defeat Tron's progress.

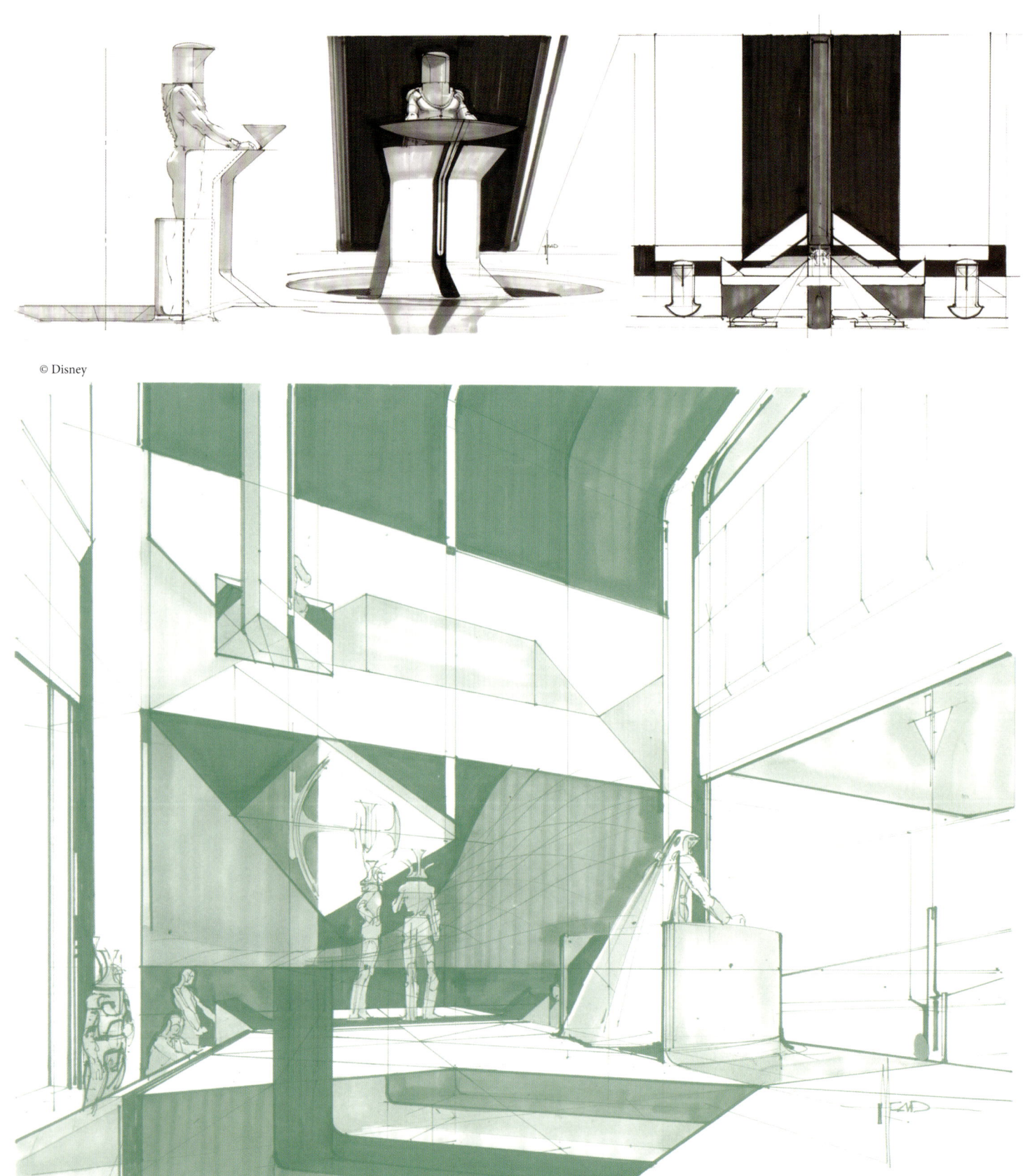

© Disney

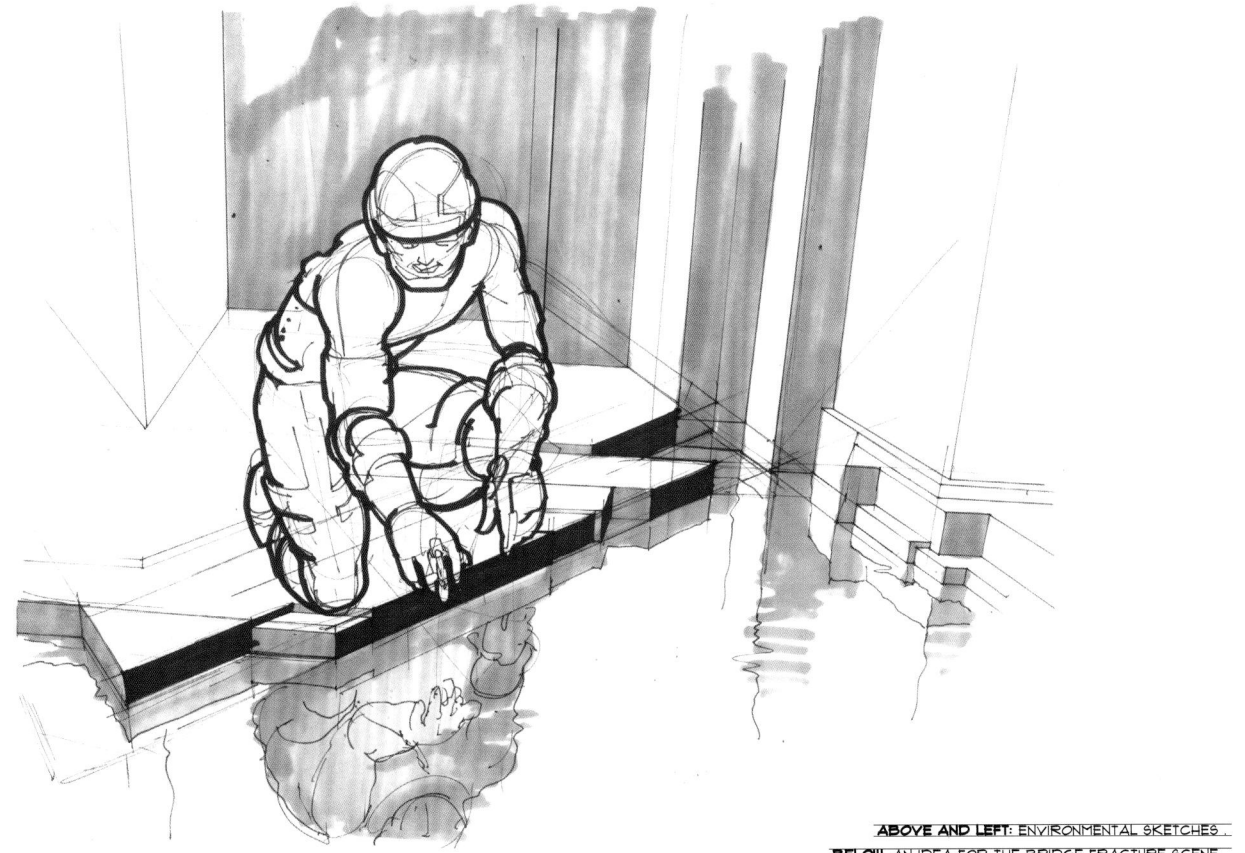

ABOVE AND LEFT: ENVIRONMENTAL SKETCHES.
BELOW, AN IDEA FOR THE BRIDGE FRACTURE SCENE.

IDEA FOR BRIDGE
FRACTURE:

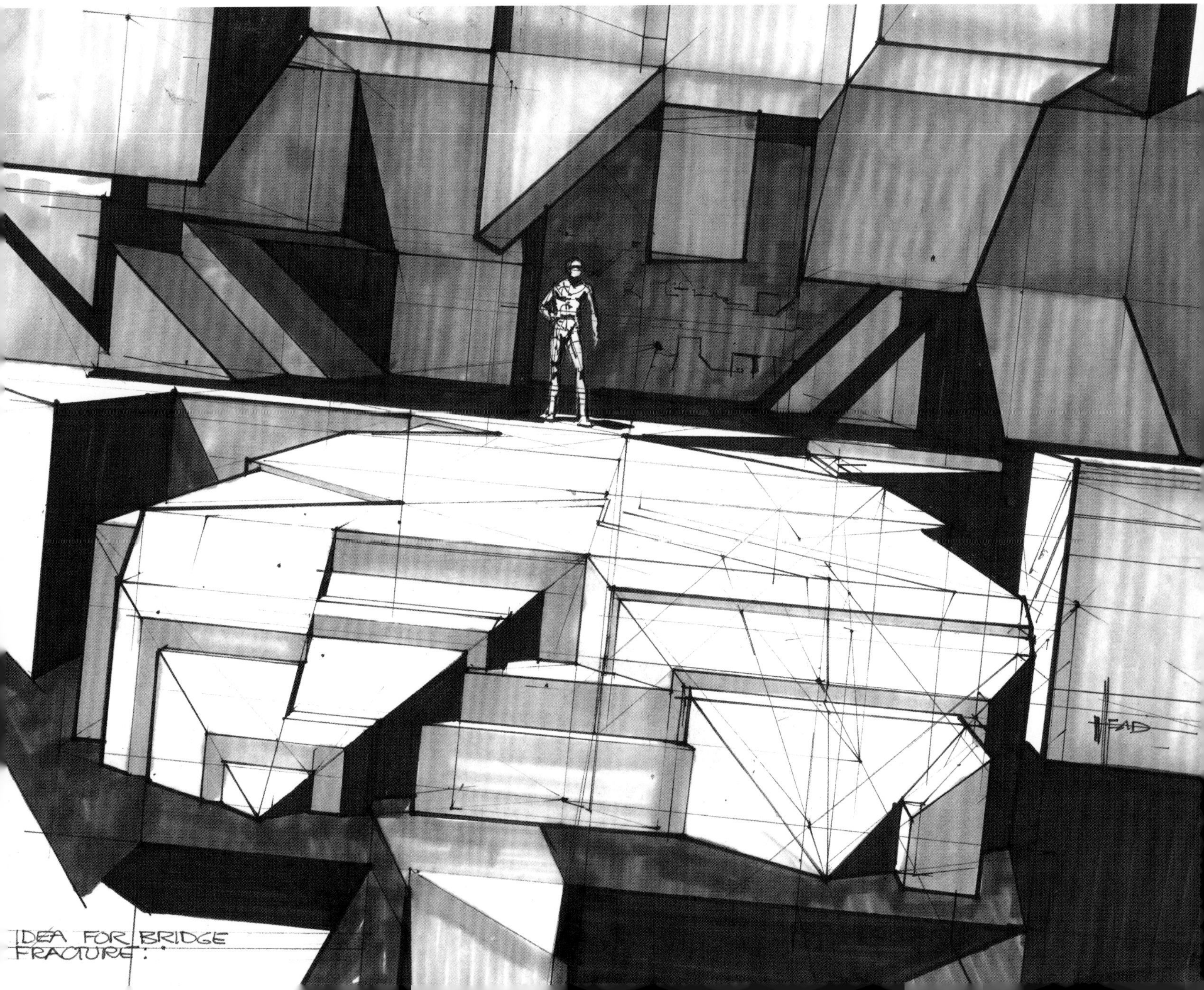

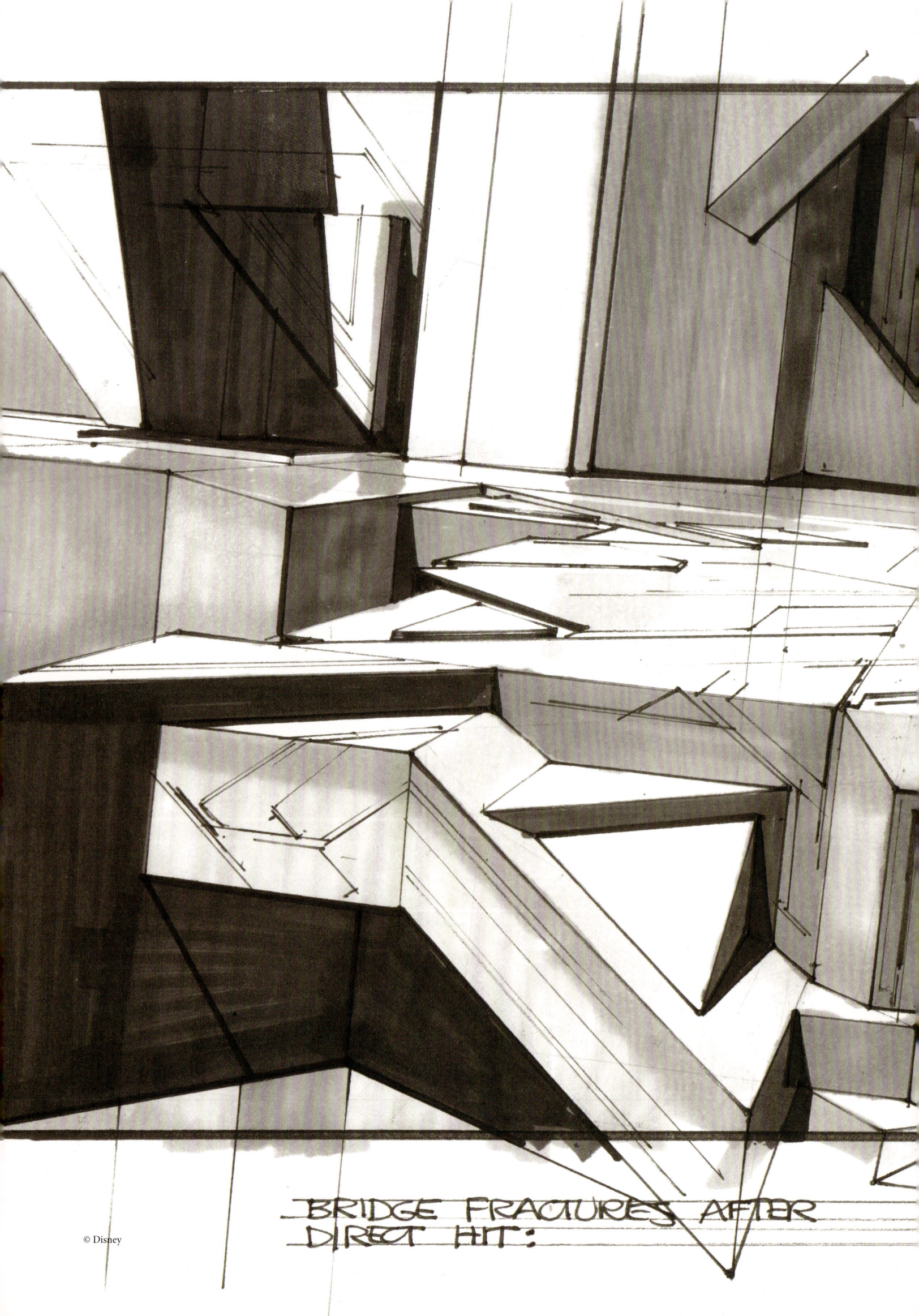

BRIDGE FRACTURES AFTER
DIRECT HIT:

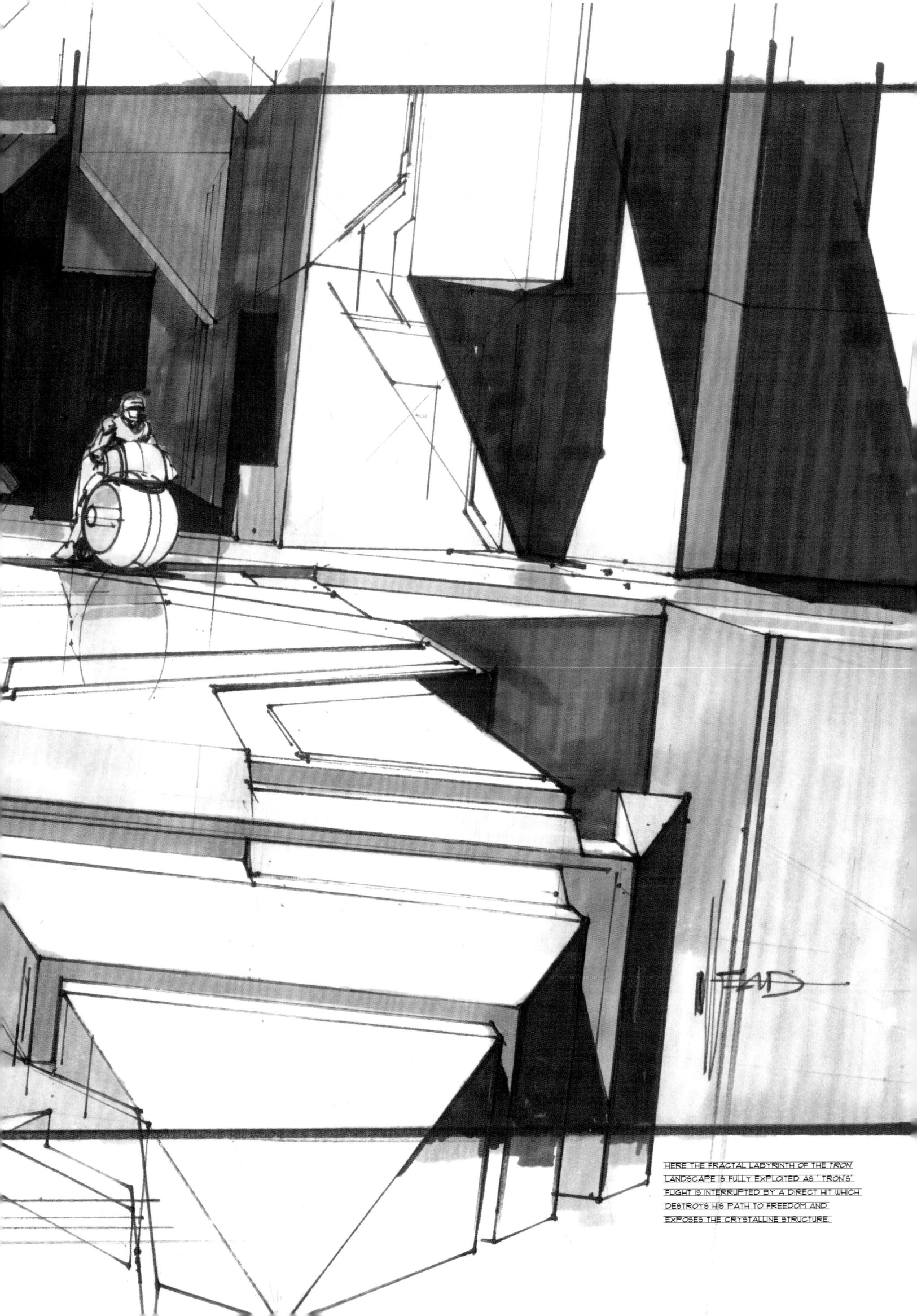

HERE THE FRACTAL LABYRINTH OF THE *TRON*
LANDSCAPE IS FULLY EXPLOITED AS "TRON'S"
FLIGHT IS INTERRUPTED BY A DIRECT HIT WHICH
DESTROYS HIS PATH TO FREEDOM AND
EXPOSES THE CRYSTALLINE STRUCTURE

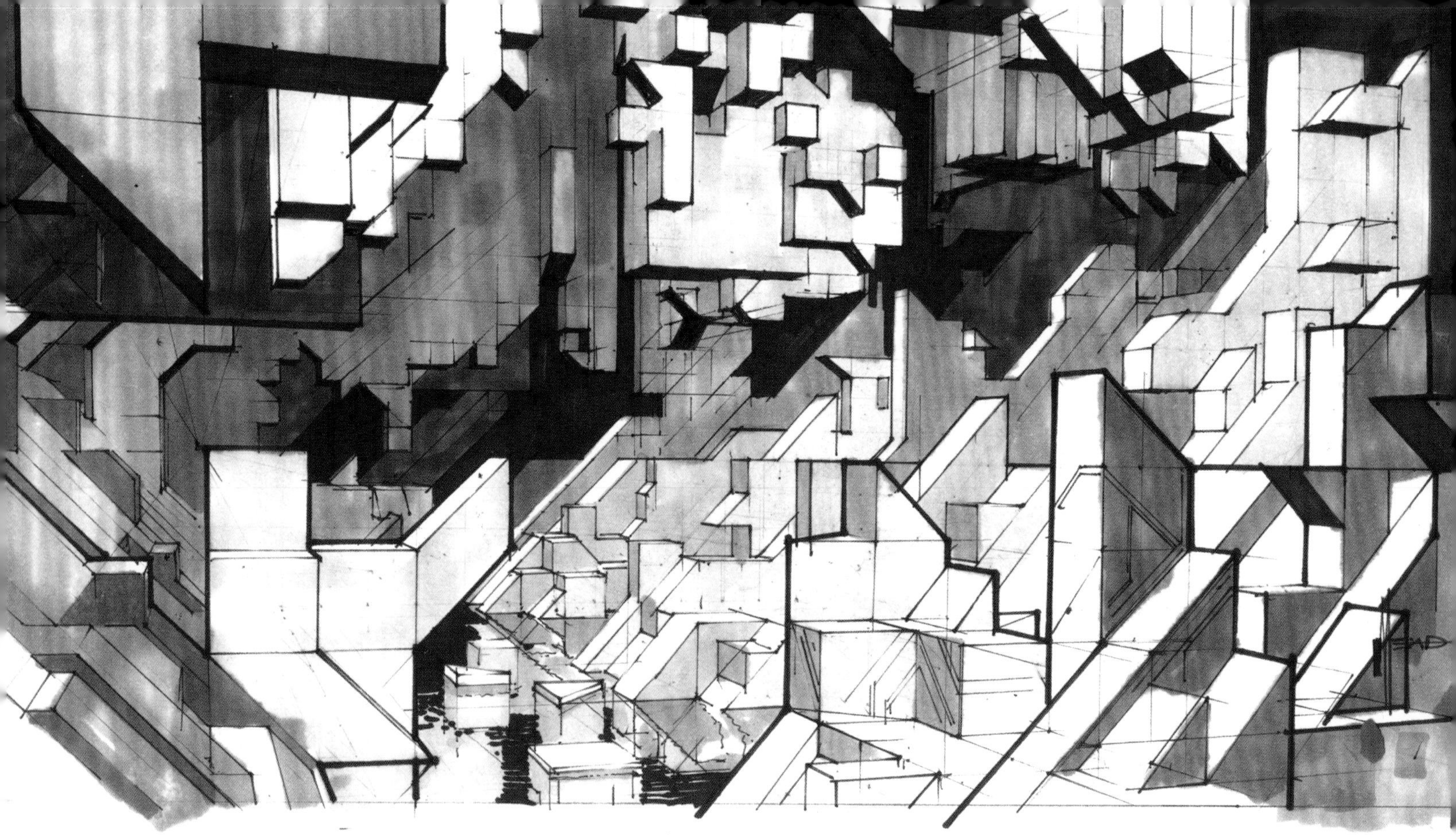

THE SEARCH FOR APPROPRIATE IMAGERY FOR TRON FOUND MEAD STRETCHING HIS VISION TO INCLUDE SOLID-STATE DEVICES, WIRING DIAGRAMS, AND ELECTROLUMINESCENCE, AS WELL AS THE MICRO-STRUCTURE OF THE SILICON CRYSTAL.

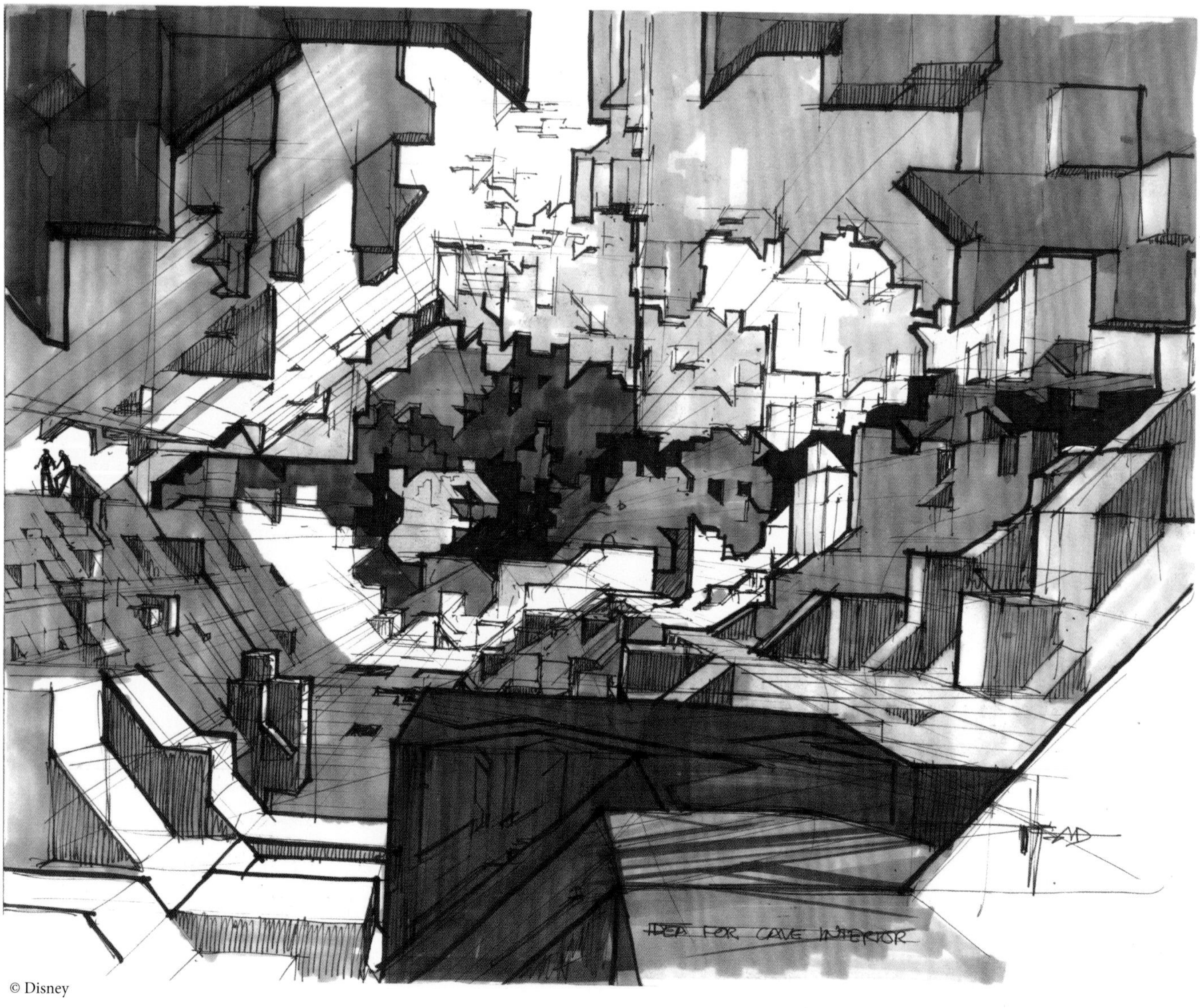

IDEA FOR CAVE INTERIOR

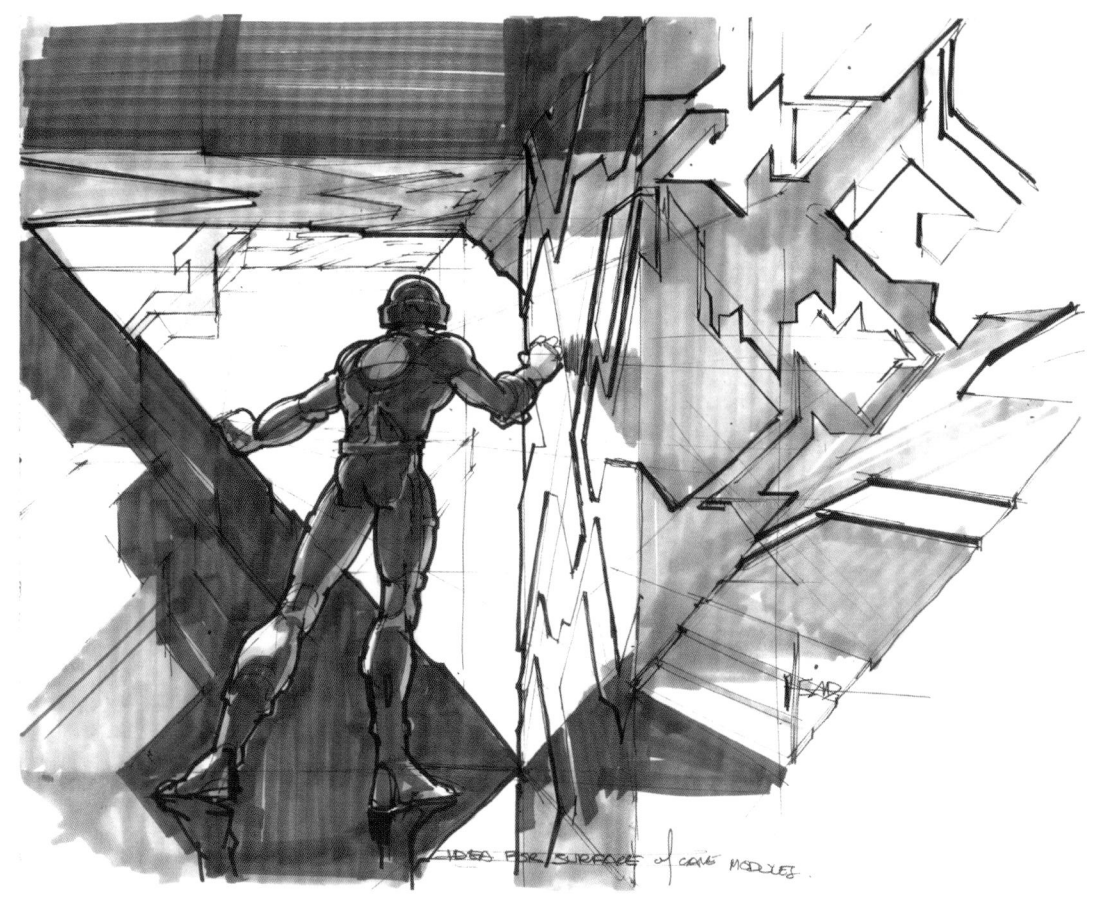

IDEA FOR SURFACE of CAVE MODULES

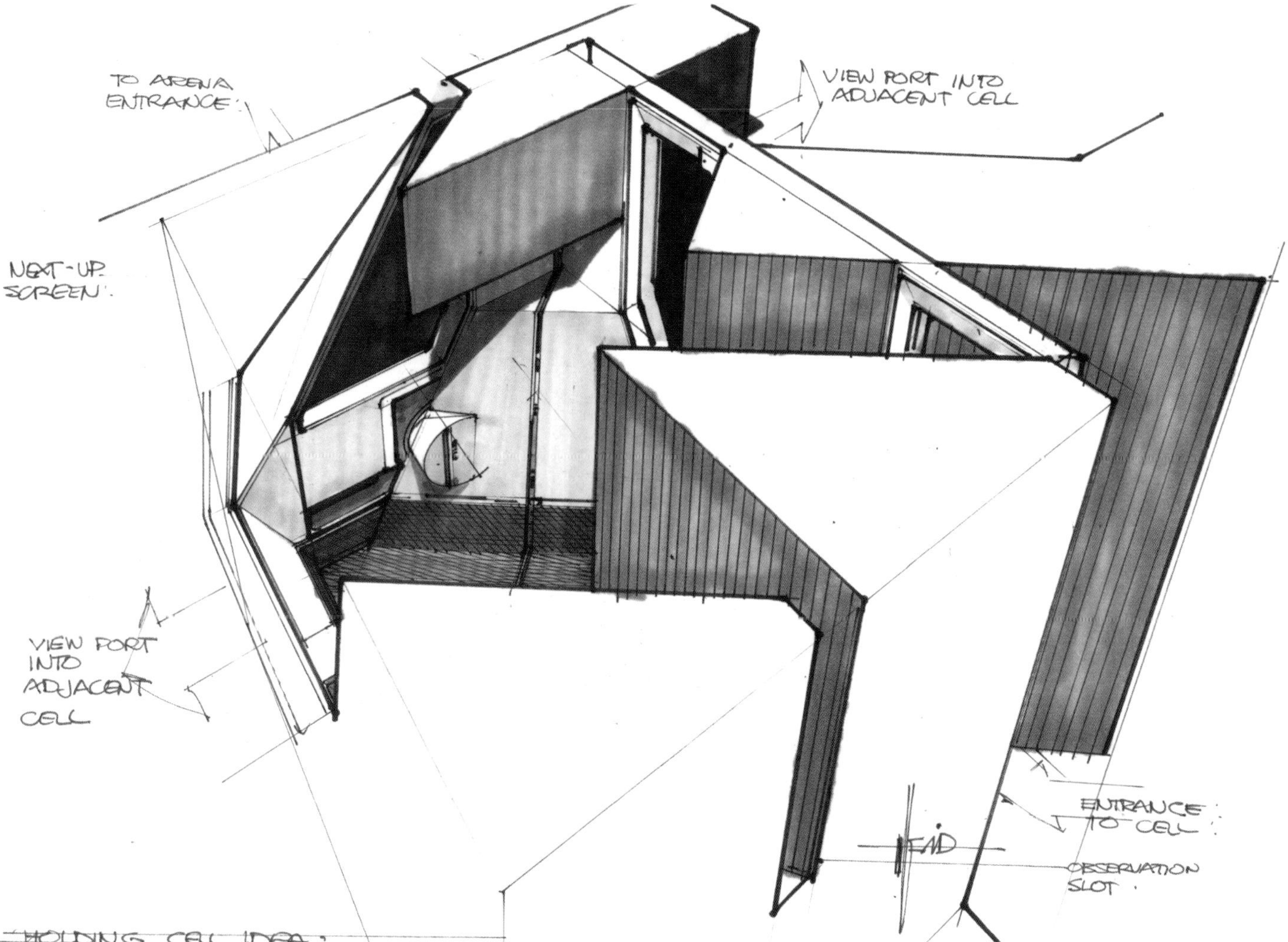

VIEW PORT INTO
ADJACENT CELL

TO ARENA
ENTRANCE

NEXT-UP
SCREEN

VIEW PORT
INTO
ADJACENT
CELL

ENTRANCE
TO CELL

OBSERVATION
SLOT

HEAD

HOLDING CELL IDEA:
NO PLACE TO "SIT": NO RELAXATION:
INTRUSIVE EDGES CORNERS: VOLUMES:
CONSTANT AWARENESS OF "DON'T FIT":

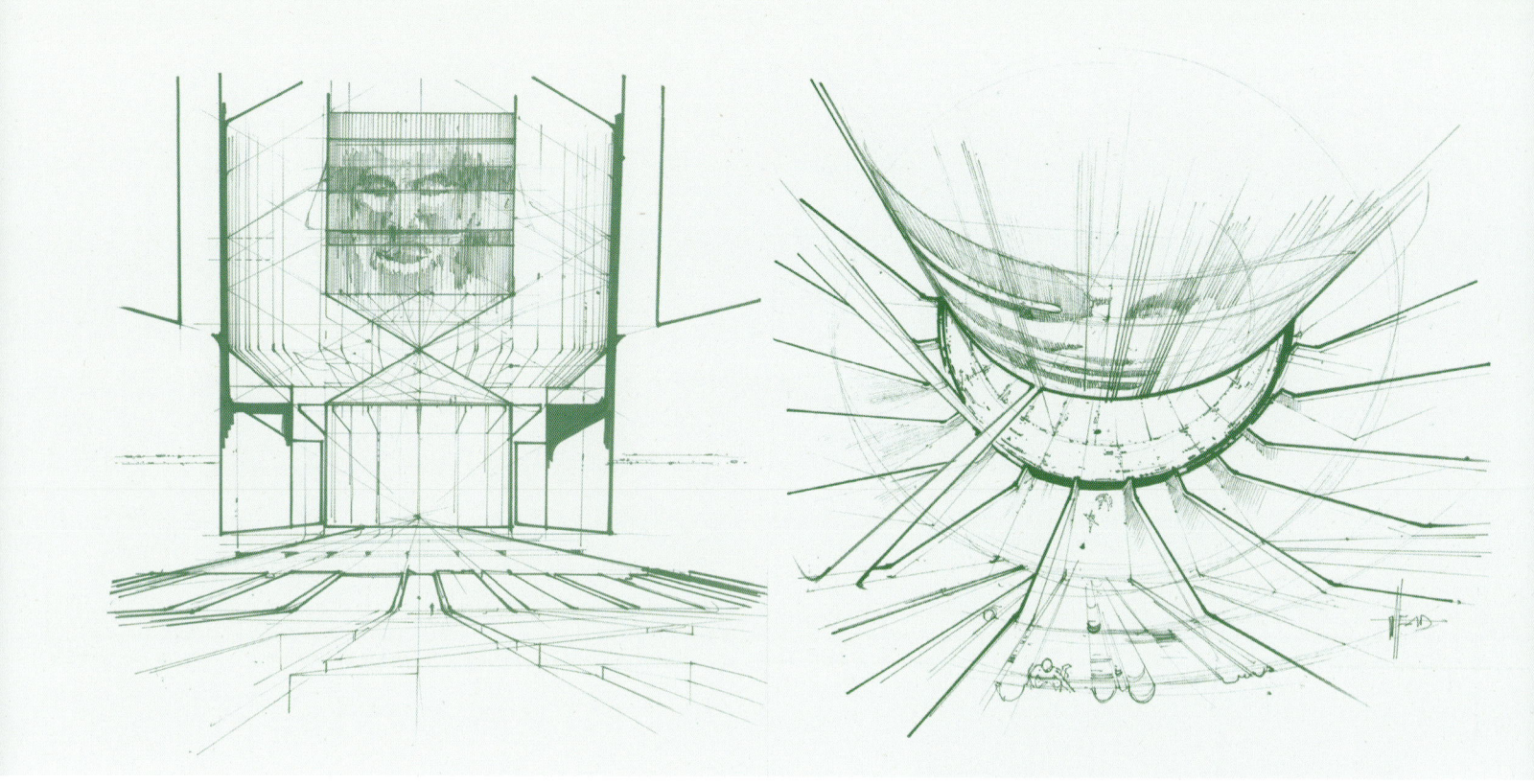

THESE PAGES: SKETCHES OF THE ICONIC MASTER CONTROL PROGRAM (MCP) THE TINY FIGURE IN THE FOREGROUND SERVES TO REMIND US OF THE SCALE OF MCP AND THE WORLD, AND THE SIZE OF THE CHALLENGE FACED BY FLYNN, TRON AND YORI.

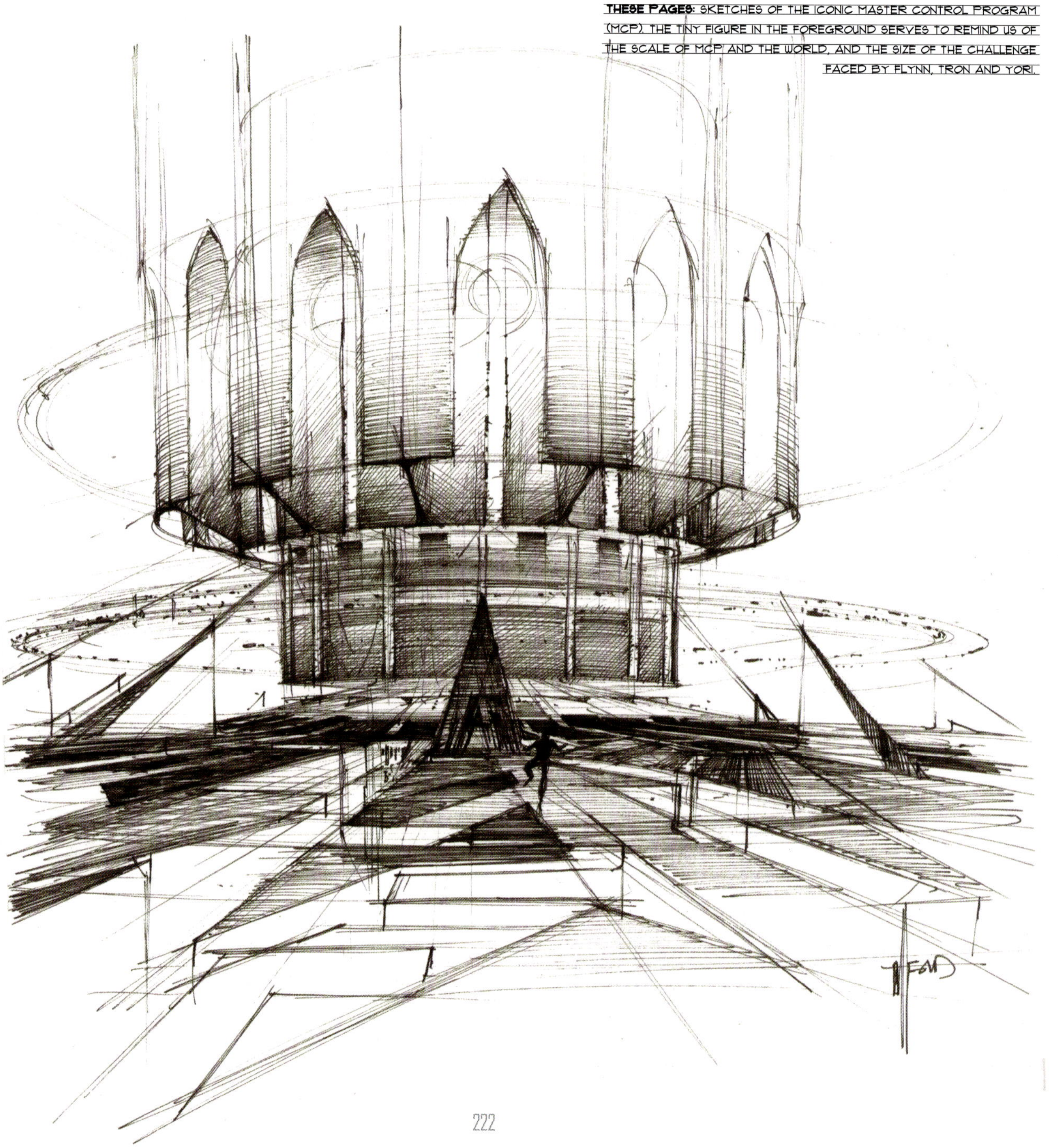

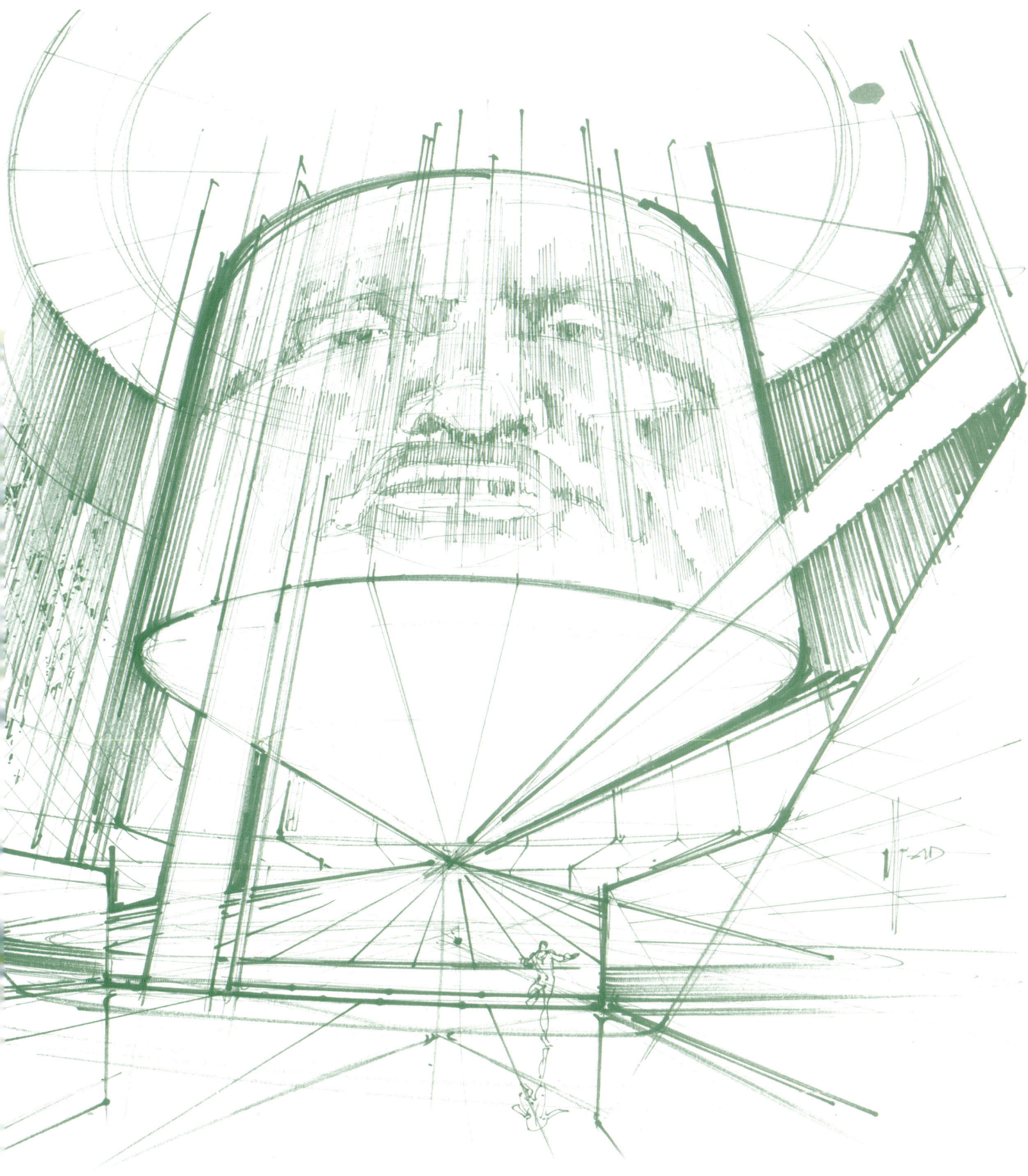

Mead created a maze-like environment of crystalline shapes that metastasize to form surfaces in which vestiges of heat sink. Transistors and condensers commonly found within the sleek faces of today's computers materialize as monumental artifacts of an oppressive regime, realised fully on this spread depicting the Master Control Program (MCP). In anticipation of the build-out of full-scale settings, a system of secondary supports congruent with, and geometrically consistent, can be employed where necessary to achieve structural integrity.

GRAND ODYSSEY
GRAND ODYSSEY

BACK TO EARTH, OVER

For Mead, his involvement with *Grand Odyssey* started at the Aichi Tech Expo in 2003, with the design of a themed attraction featuring a quartet of spaceships meant to be sent out to colonize a 'New Earth'. The installation featured an innovative face-scanning technology which enabled visitors to the exhibit to see their own face, randomly, behind the faceplate of a spacesuit as a member of the crew. This was a ground-breaking experience at the time, for which visitors stood in line for hours, sometimes returning for seconds.

The design of the ship is based on the storyline of an outer space *rendezvous* in which the ships join up to return to a now habitable Earth. Although not a movie in the traditional sense, *Grand Odyssey* is an immersive experience which allows the audience to participate in the story. Based on the success of the Expo installation, the *Grand Odyssey* attraction was re-installed at the Huis Ten Bosch theme park in Nagasaki where it continues to offer, in the words of the park, "the only casting entertainment system that makes the audience (play a) role in the movie."

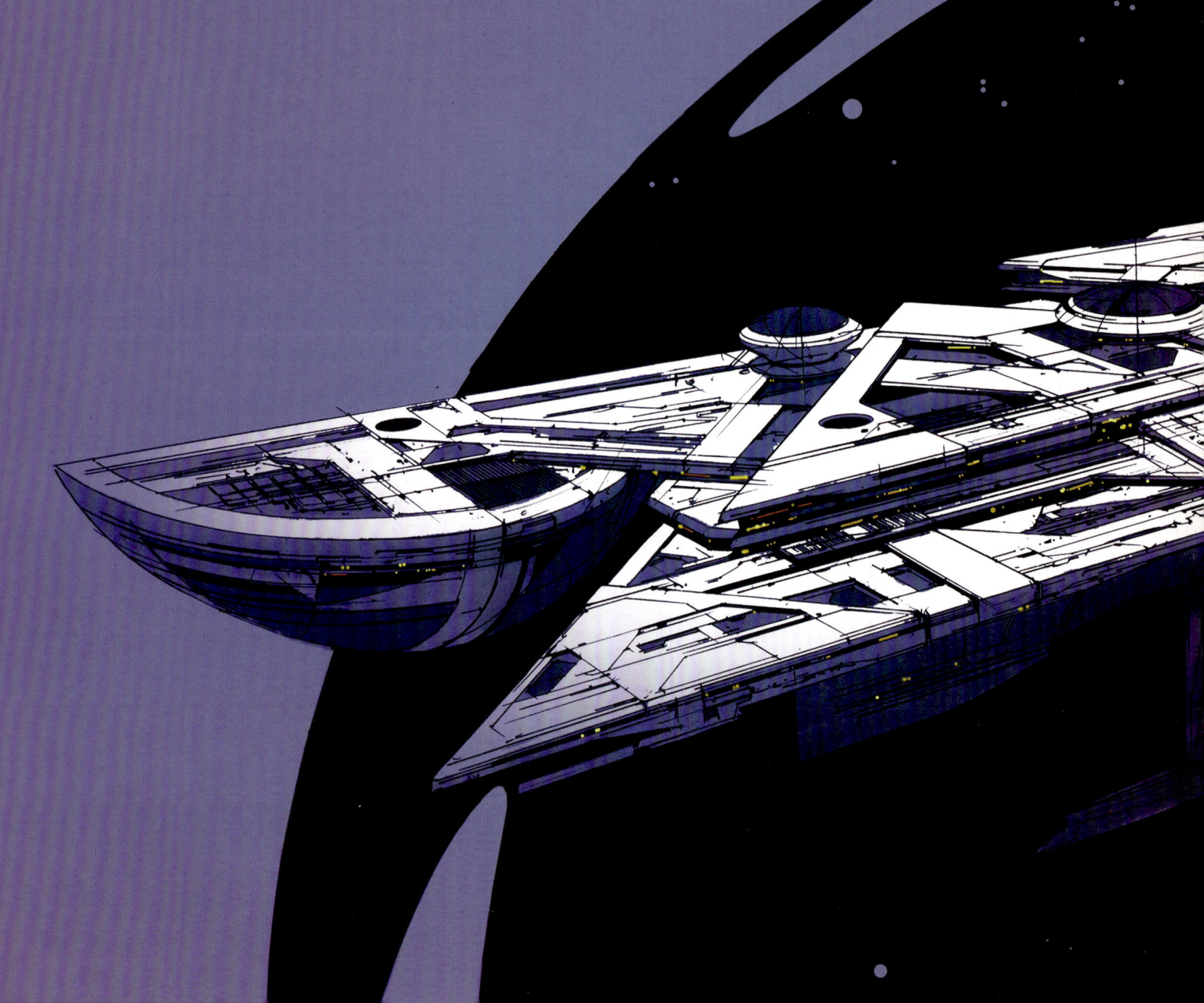

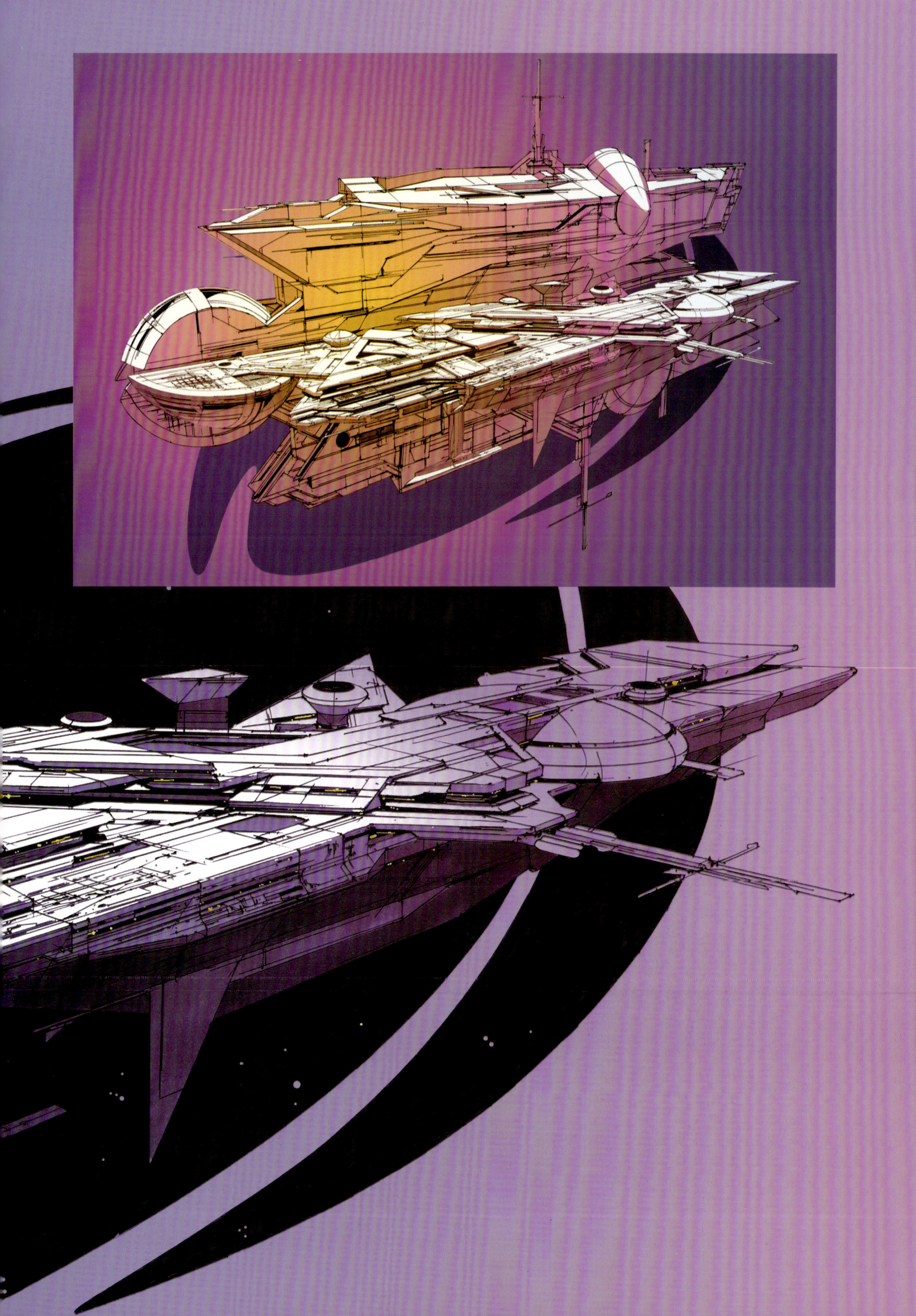

MISSION: IMPOSSIBLE III

HEAD CASE

A key story point in *Mission: Impossible III* occurs as Ethan Hunt (Tom Cruise) activates a high-tech machine capable of creating a prosthetic "face" with which to transform his identity. Initial design ideas were deemed too prosaic by the director, who asked Mead to create something technically plausible yet visually astounding. "Visceral", says Mead whose solution was a laser-scanning device in a suitcase which opened to reveal a 3D model of Hunt's head. In operation the device was designed to scan up and down to capture minute imperfections, pores, and so on prior to a second "coloring" scan in which details of complexion were to be mapped and printed onto a plastic "skin". Hunt would then remove and pull the skin over his head to complete the transformation.

Again, an industrial engineering approach is apparent. So much so, that its gimmick-free design could very well wind up as a consumer product, utilizing 3D printing technology and bespoke polythene.

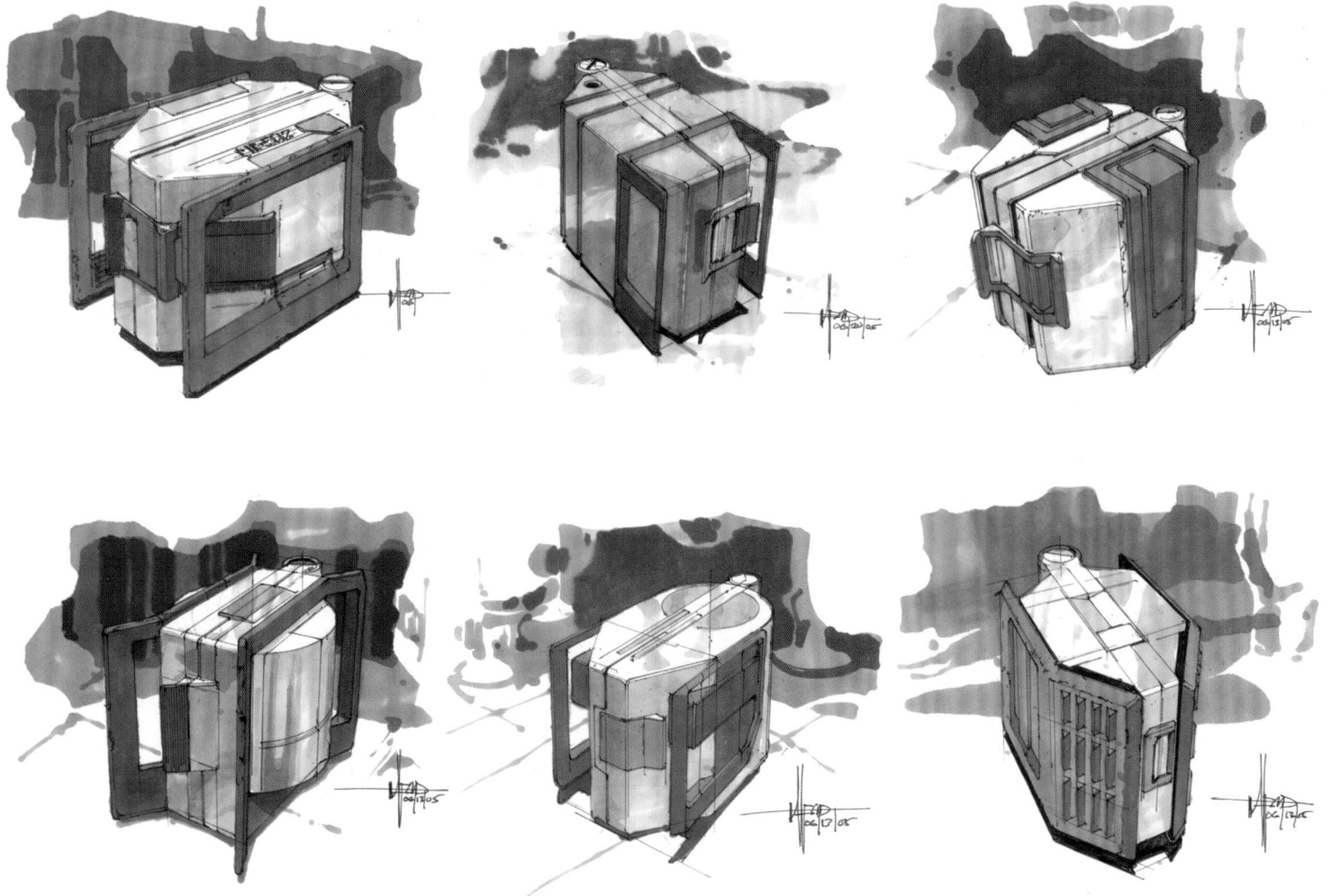

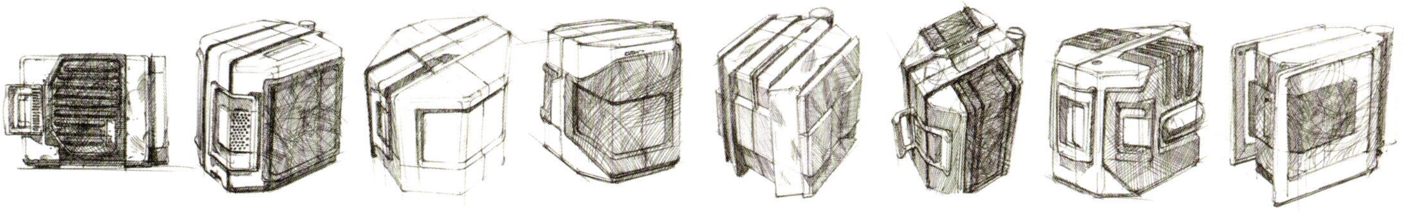

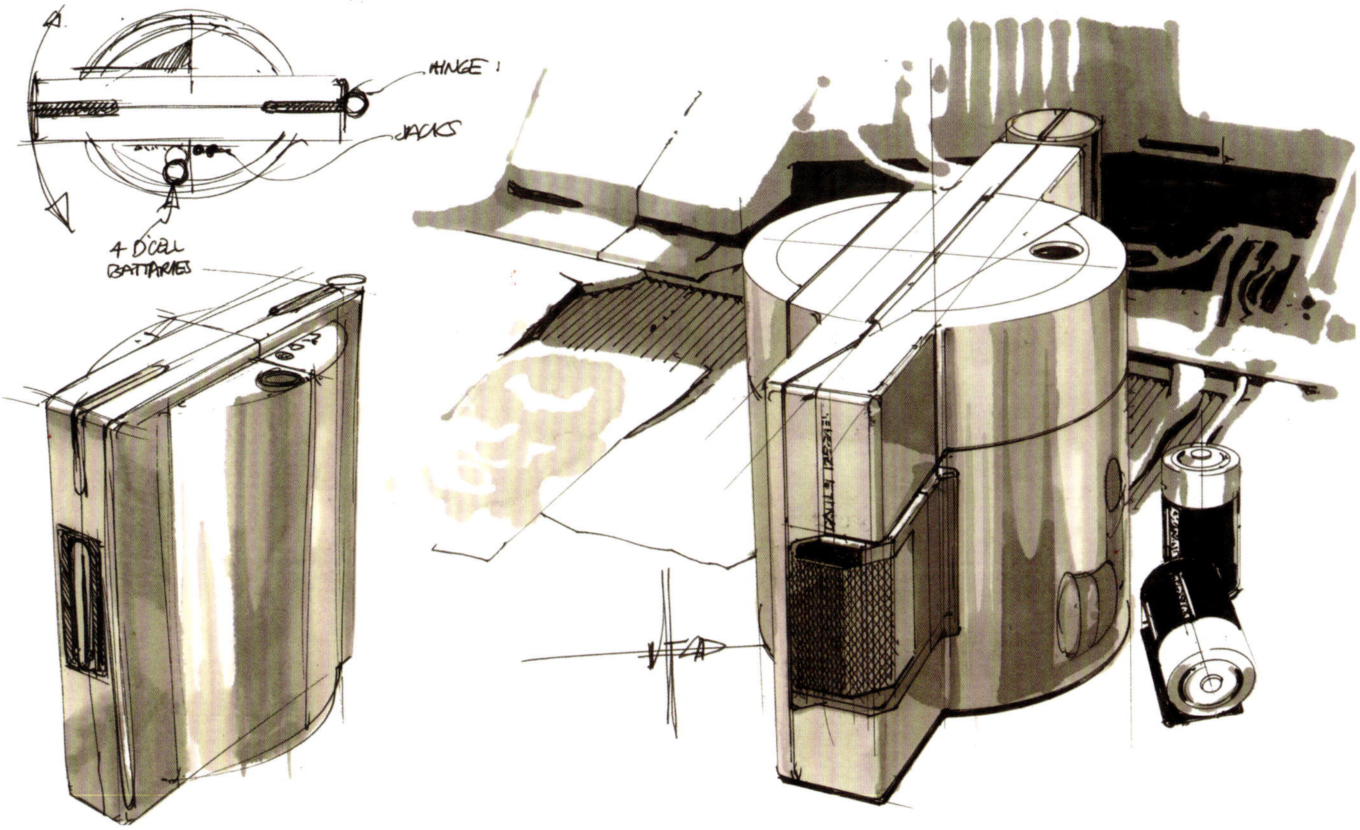

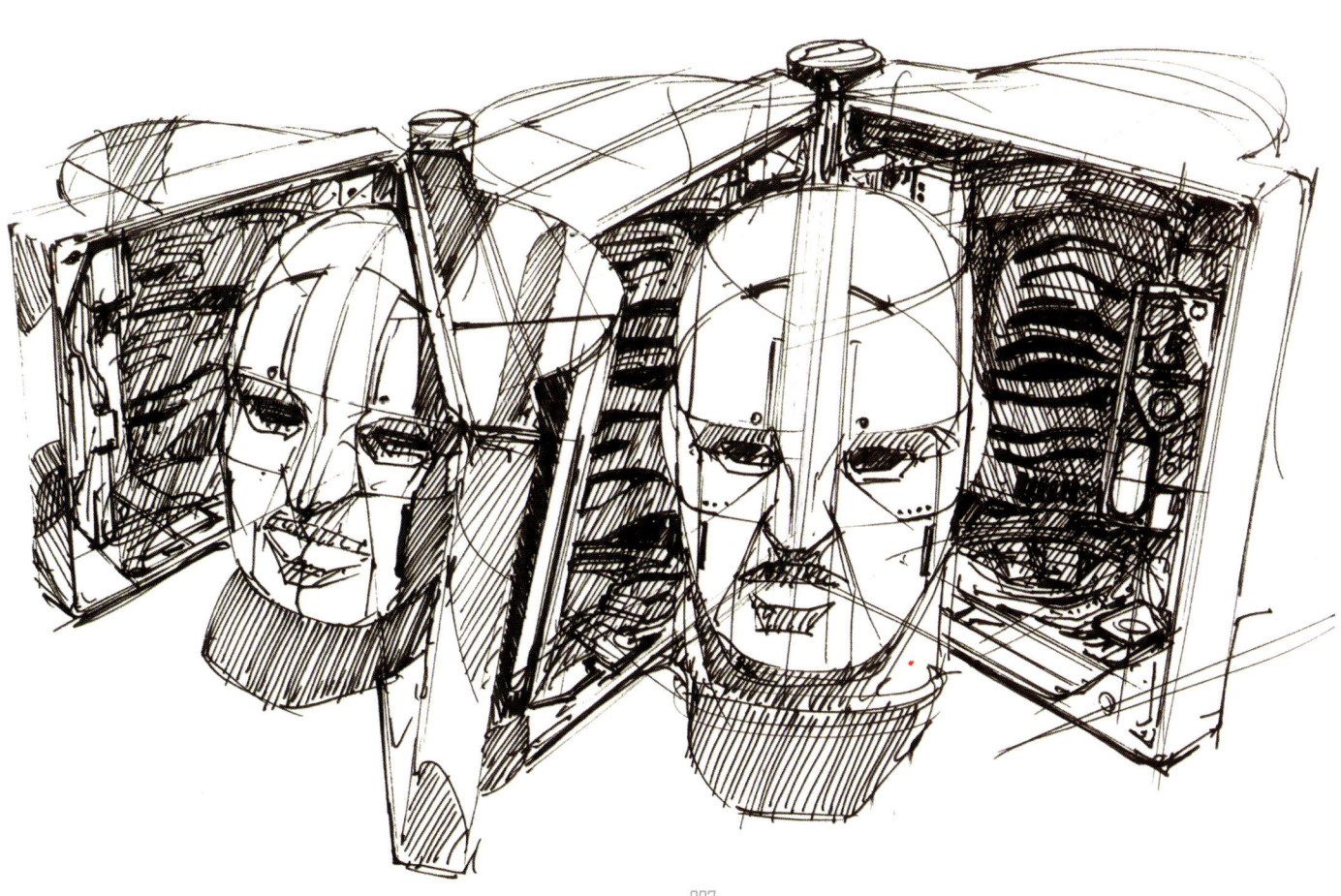

ABOVE: EARLY VARIANTS OF THE CASE SHOWING ALL SIDES AND ANGLES FOR FILMING

BELOW: A SKETCH OF THE FINISHED "MASK" IN PROCESS

HINGE

JACKS

4 D CELL BATTERIES

As these iterations make clear, even the casework underwent considerable revisions, from a vaguely faceted bulge reflecting the volume of the molded head to a semi-cylindrical bump, while the interior mechanics of the device evolved from a slack umbilical to one structured to preserve the geometric constraints of the film's techno-aesthetic.

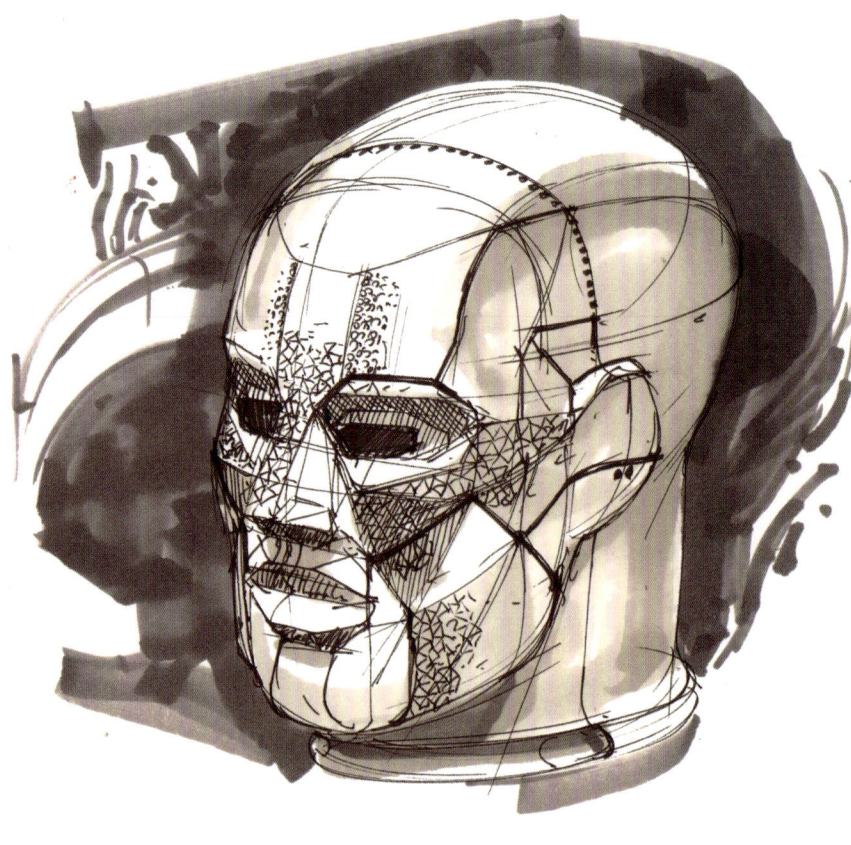

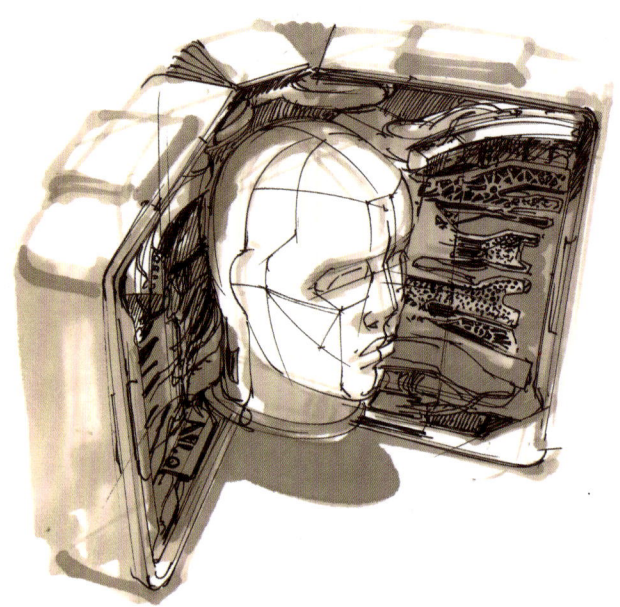

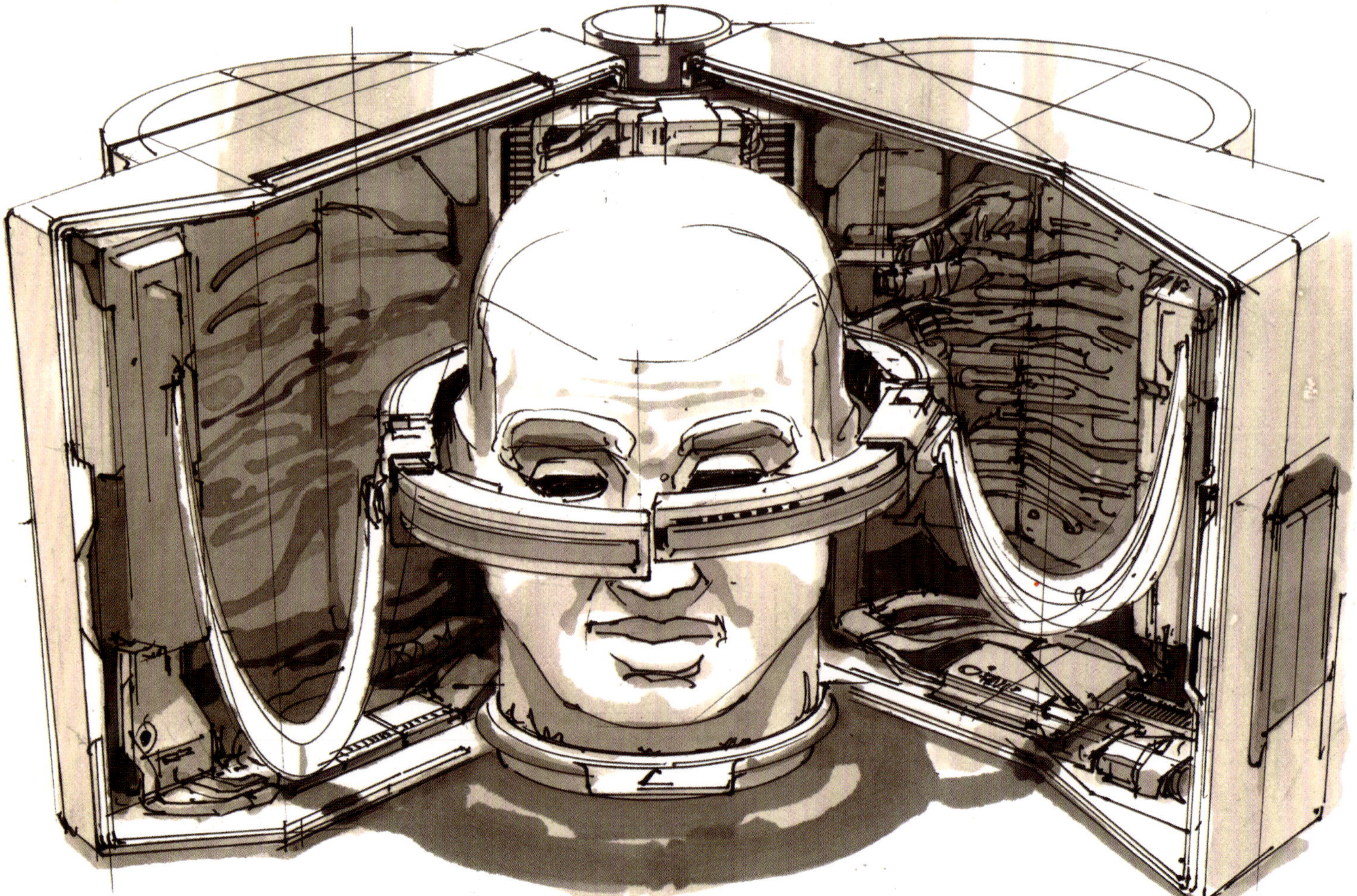

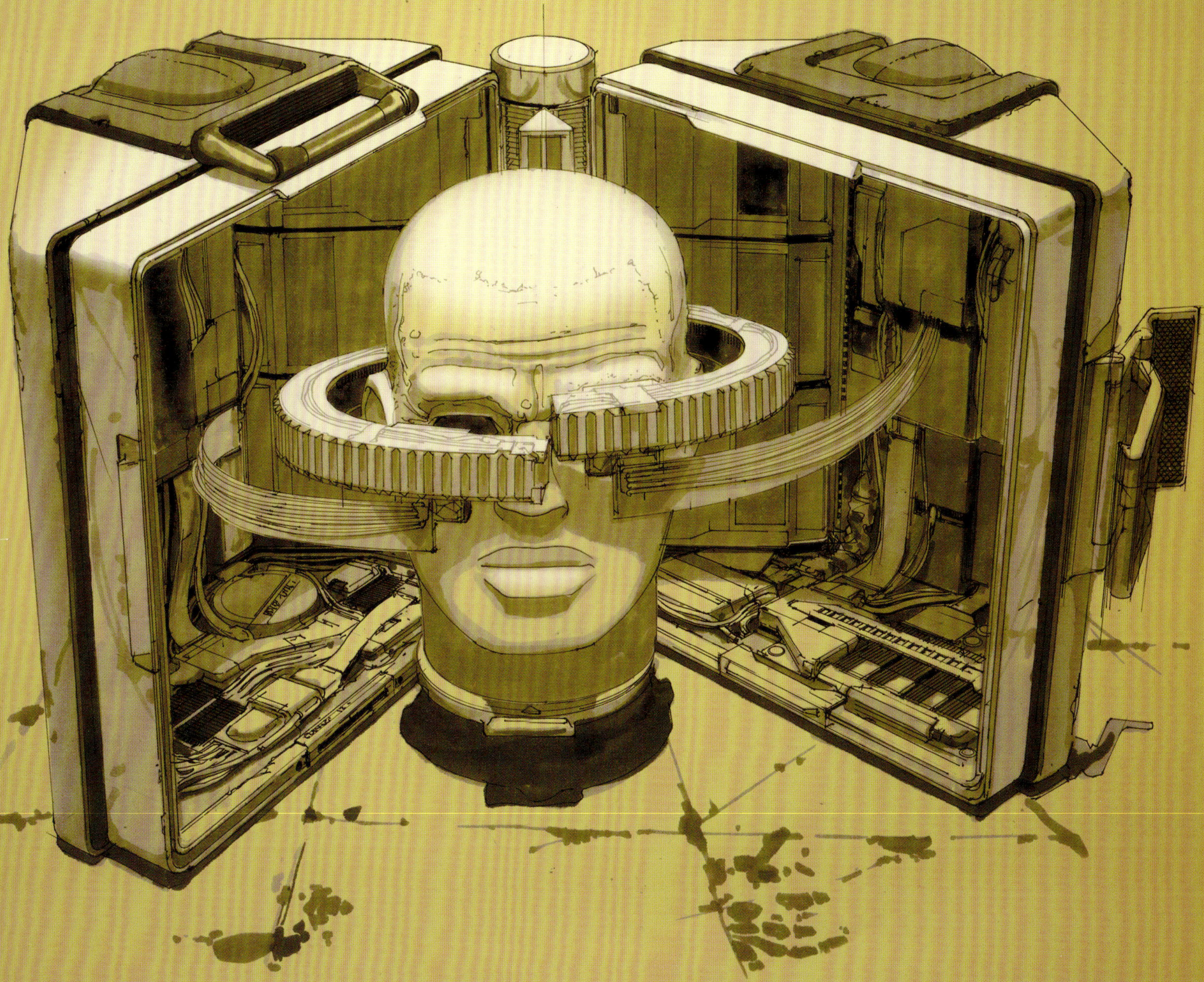

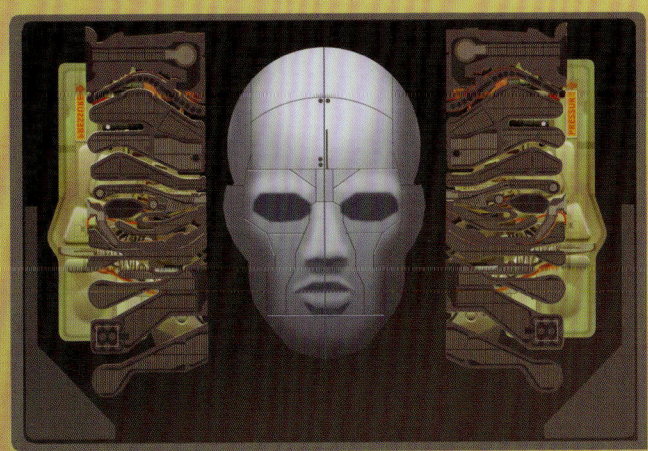
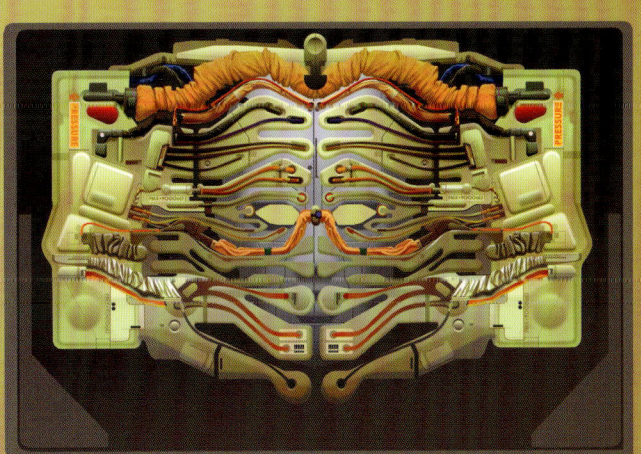

LEFT: SKETCHES OF THE MASK CREATION IN PROGRESS AND; ABOVE: 3D RENDERS OF THE PROCESS.

MISSION TO MARS

GLARE

In this 2000 telling by director Brian de Palma, a rescue expedition to Mars turns into a quasi-mystical spiritual quest. Once there, after a series of mishaps which render the rescuers themselves imperiled, they are able to rendezvous with the sole remaining member of the lost mission and together seek out the source of an electrochromatic DNA strain that turns out to have the key to the origin of the human race.

Mead's pre-production imagery was derived from research on the nature of the red planet: its powdery soil, the glare of the sun, and the pervasive winds dictated an inverse, upside-down slant to the windows of the vehicle. The wheels were modelled on an experimental suspension developed by NASA, which replaced the usual assembly of springs, struts, and inflated tires with a ring made up of flexible fins that could provide both resilience and traction. Note also the cameras which are able to travel around a circular track mounted on the roof of the vehicle.

As is often the case, a change in director led to a different visual and technological approach so Mead's designs weren't used.

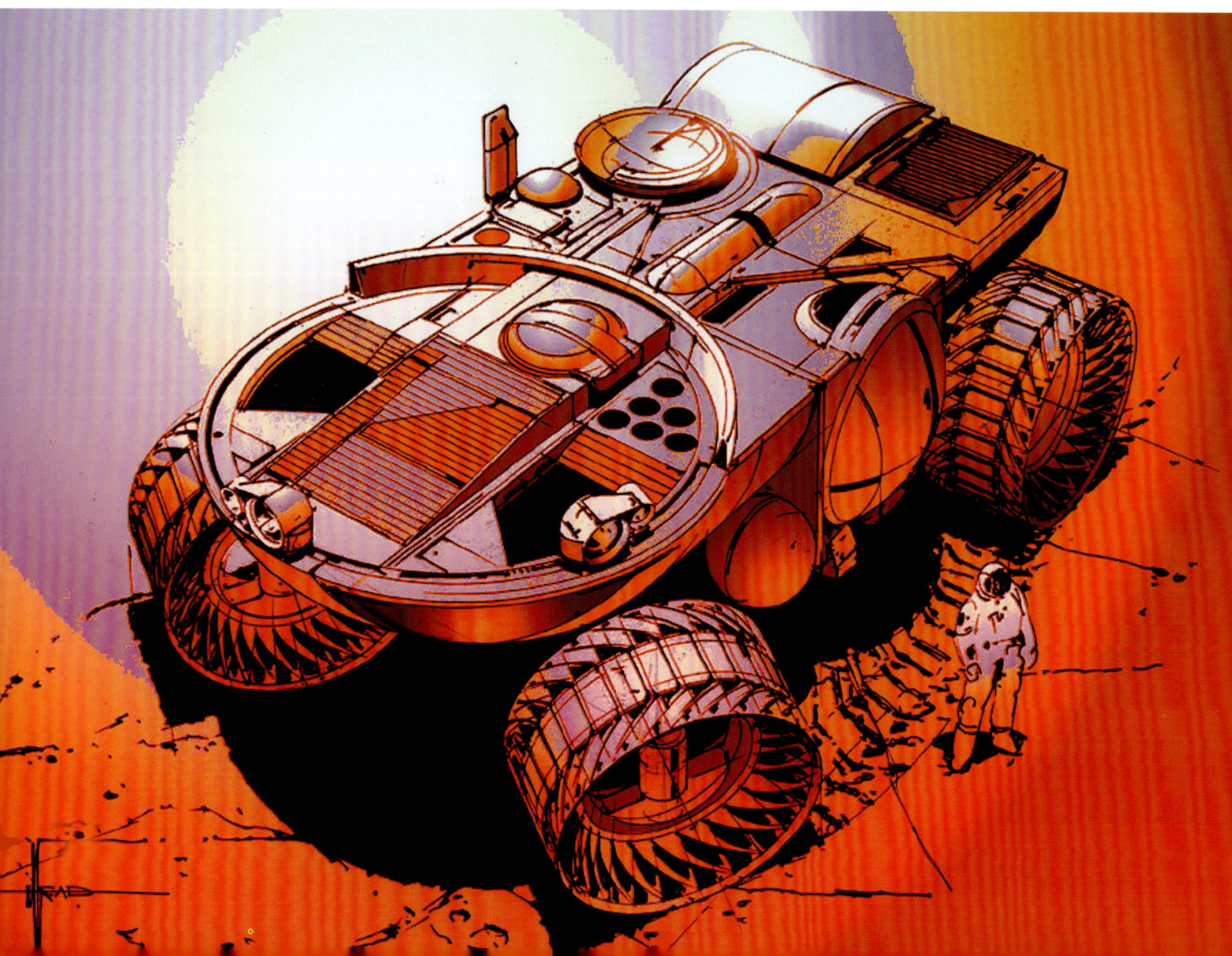

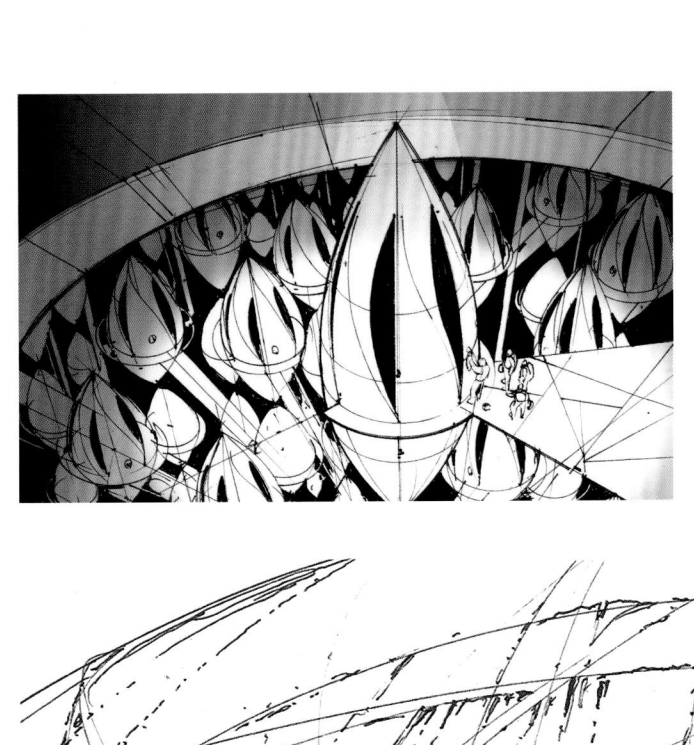

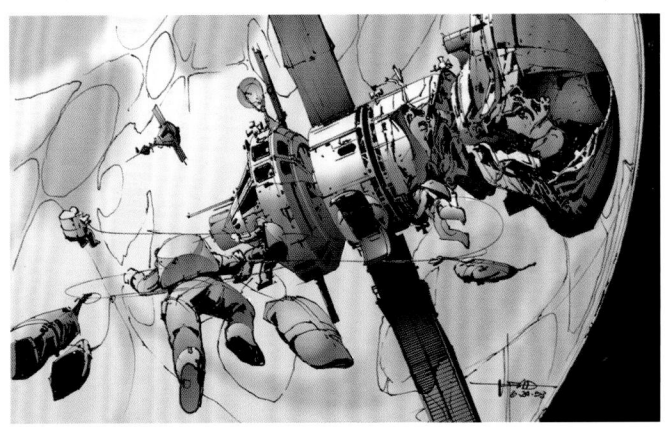

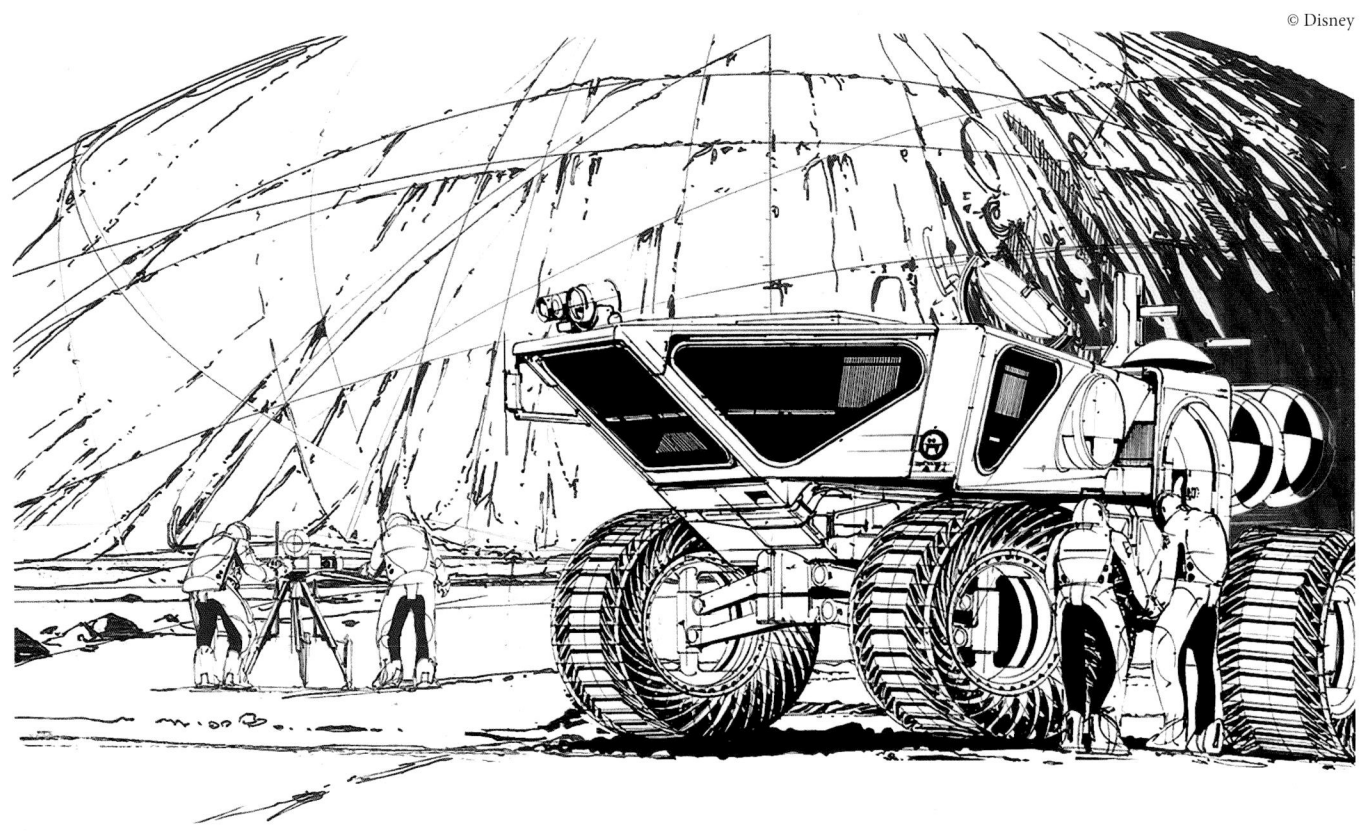

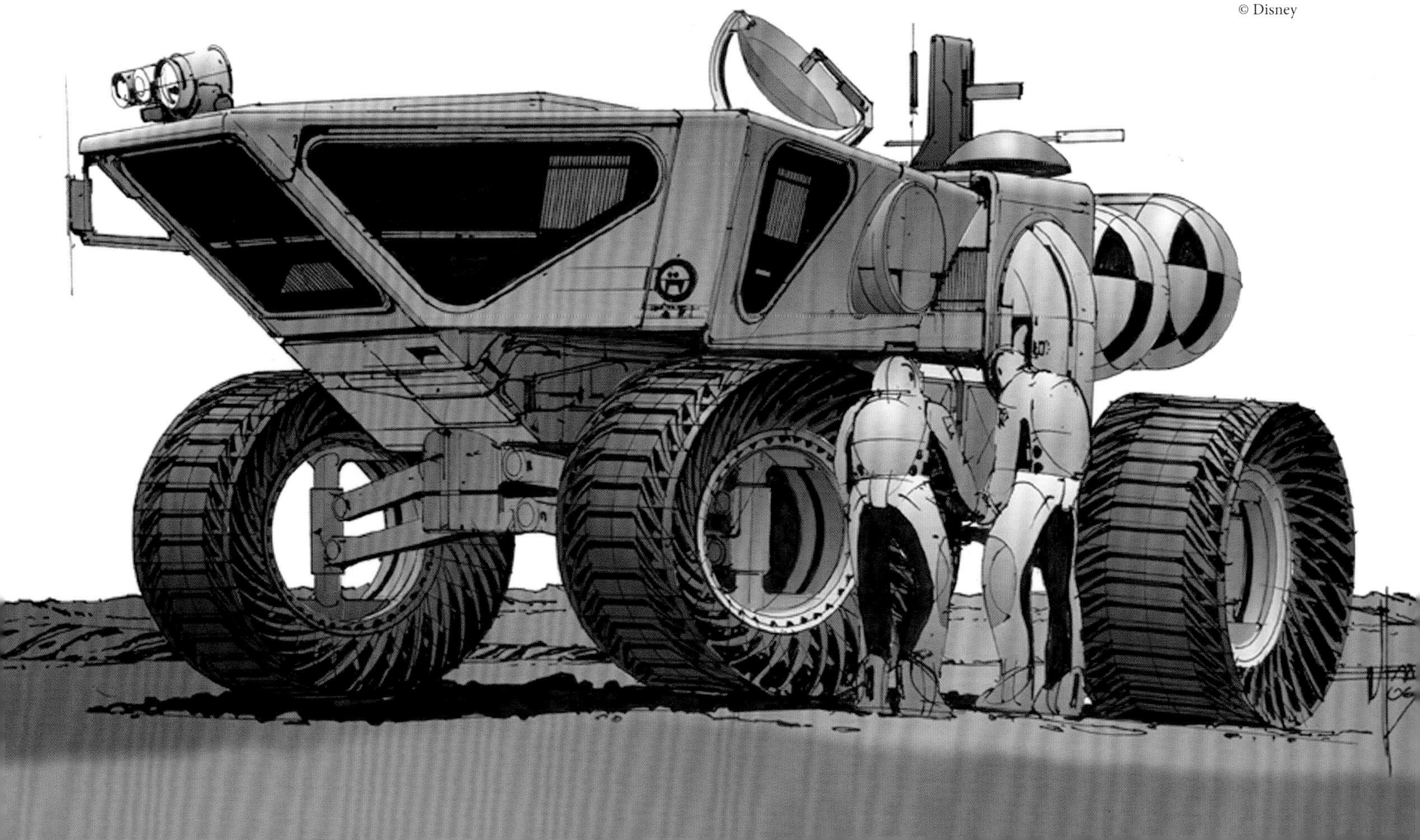

SHORT CIRCUIT

MACHINE EMPATHY

n the story of *Short Circuit* (1986), a prototype military robot is transformed and given human insight by an electrical storm. The project demanded an empathetic approach to the design, which Mead suggested by mixing metaphors and engineering principles to create a hapless, yet emotionally appealing survivor. By departing from the formulaic 'robotic' vocabulary, Mead's design featured an asymmetrical approach, enormous, clumsy tracks, and a wobbly, uncertain head which was repurposed from Douglas Trumbell's special effects shop.

The film's director, John Badham, envisioned the amiable robot, known as Number 5, folded into a garbage can. This further complicated the design process but resulted, ultimately, in the gangly torso which, according to the director's mandate did not look as though an actor was hiding within. Festooned with sensors and requiring several duplicates capable of different tasks, the completed Number 5 was to be the film's star, and the most expensive single element in the production.

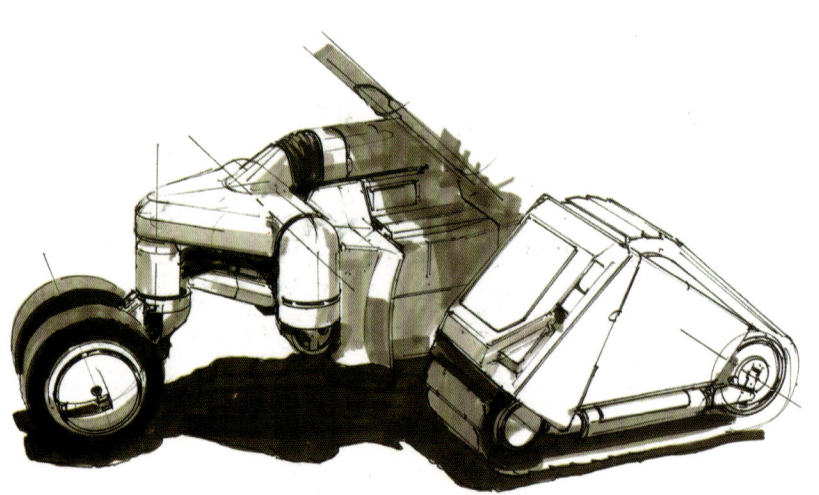

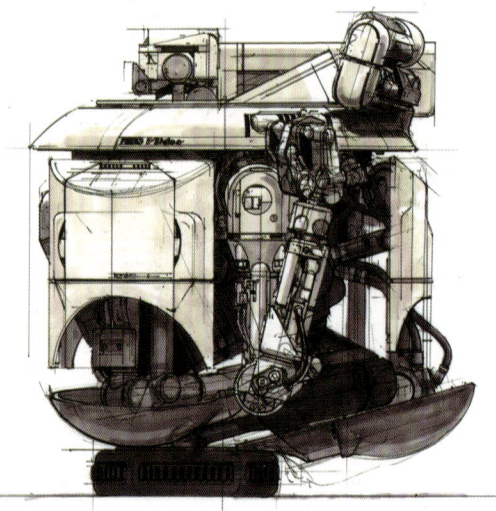

THIS PAGE: EXPLORATION OF HOW NUMBER 5 COULD FOLD UP AND COMPACT ITSELF TO FIT INSIDE A TRASH CAN

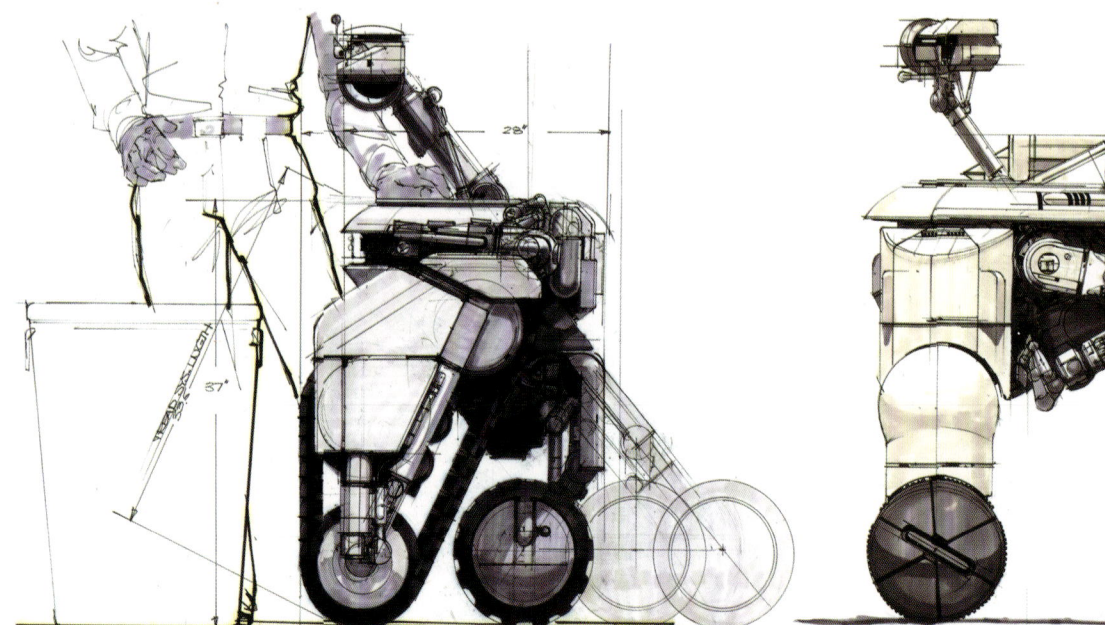

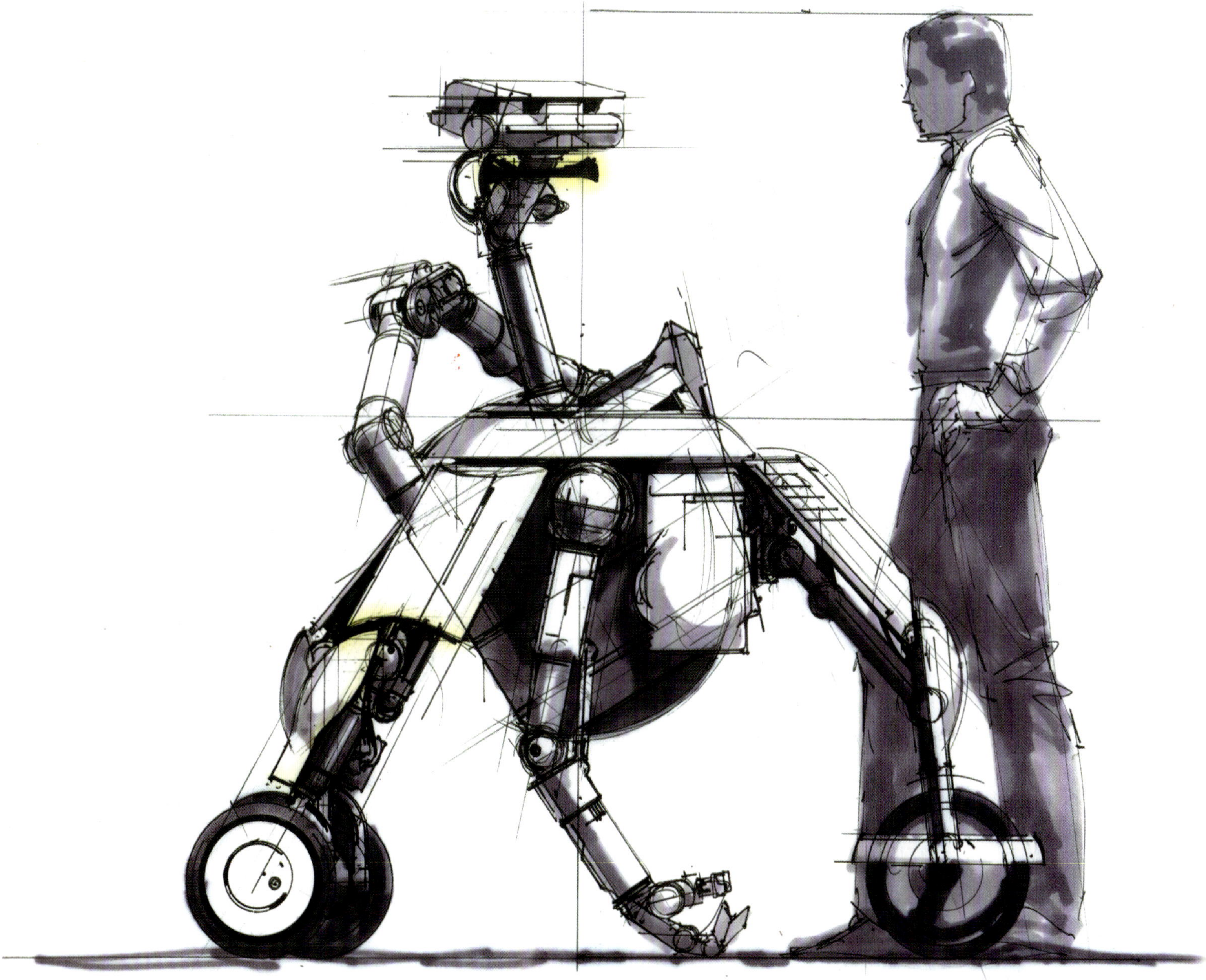

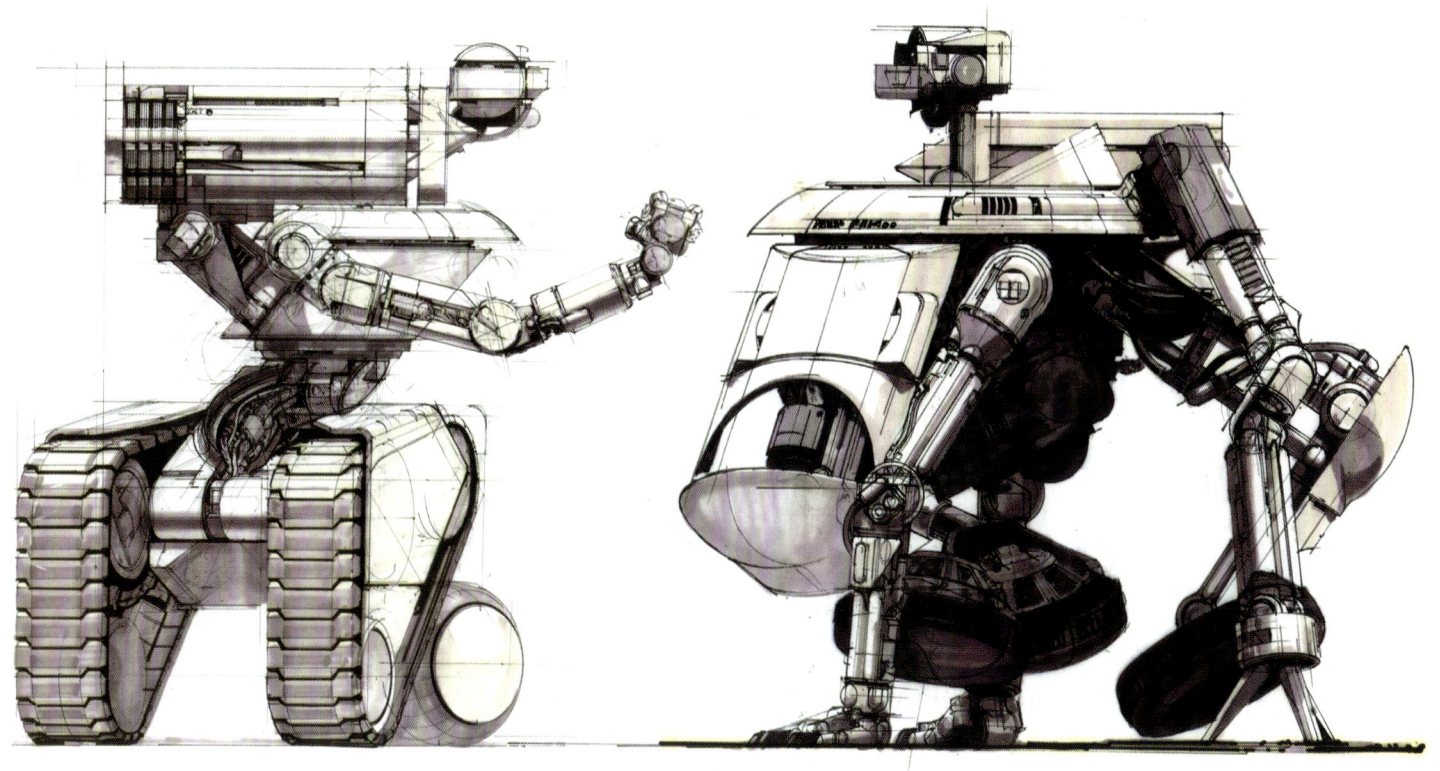

THIS PAGE: EARLY SKETCHES EXPLORING DIFFERENT LOOKS FOR NUMBER 5'S LOOK, CONSTRUCTION, SIZE AND FUNCTION.

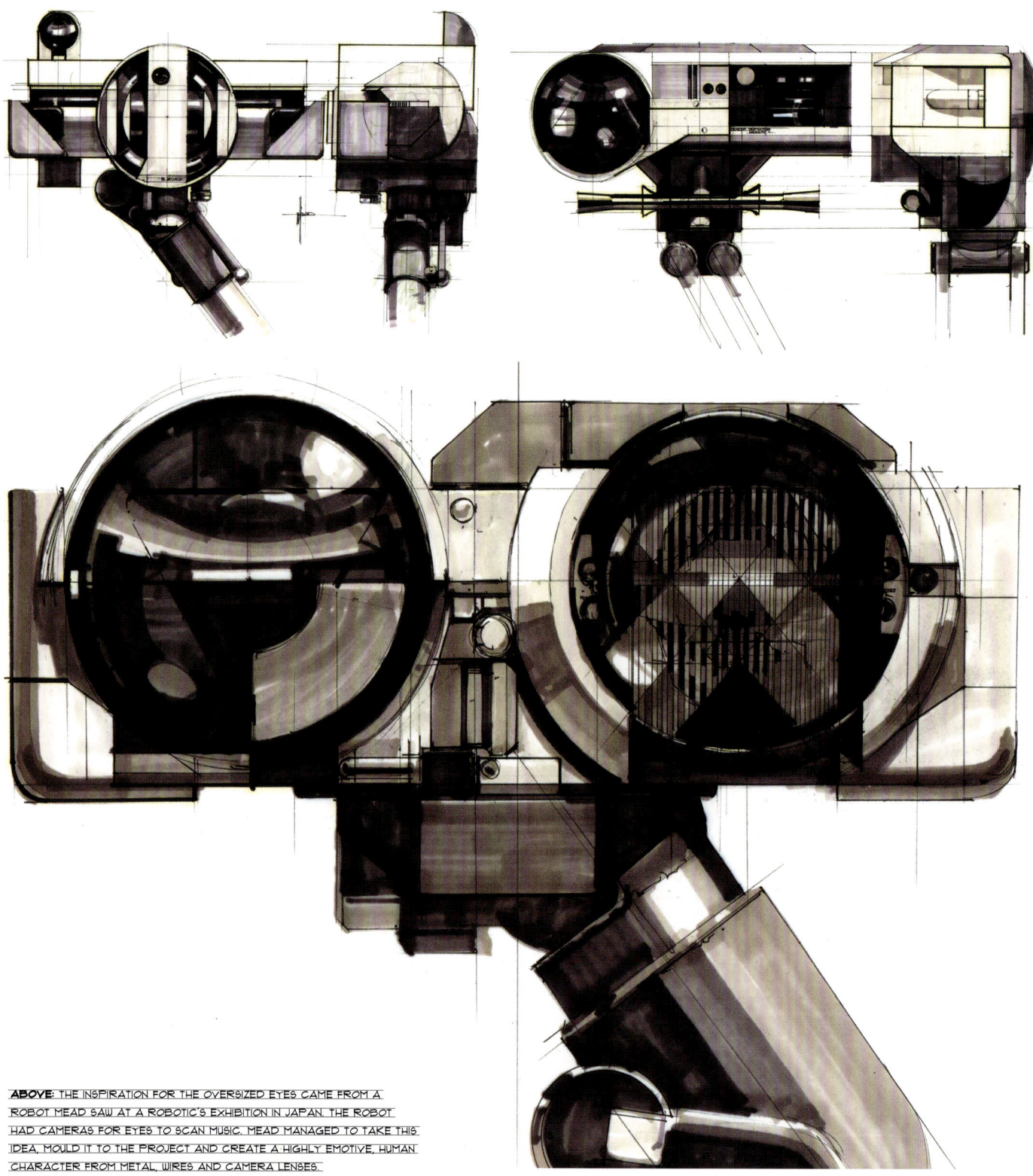

But, as anyone who has followed Syd's work knows those requirements simply fueled his creative impulses, resulting in the ability of the tank-like treads to pivot to a vertical disposition whereby Number 5's attitude rather resembled that of a dog begging for a treat.

If, as the saying goes, "the eyes are the windows of the soul", then Number 5 must have a deep and profoundly interesting one. The koala bear elicits our sympathy for similar reasons, as do Disney's Bambi and other doe-eyed animated creatures. The design for

Number 5, however, can lay claim to being one of the only robots in cinema history to employ the same, emotionally appealing device in a mechanical, metallic form.

The juxtaposition of such an emotionally appealing, fragile even, icon with an ungainly torso, combat-grade caterpillar treads and ready weaponry, yields a kind of dissonance often employed by surrealist artists, such as Cocteau's infamous image of an eye being sliced by razor, but rarely, if ever encountered in the seamless world of mainstream cinematic imagery.

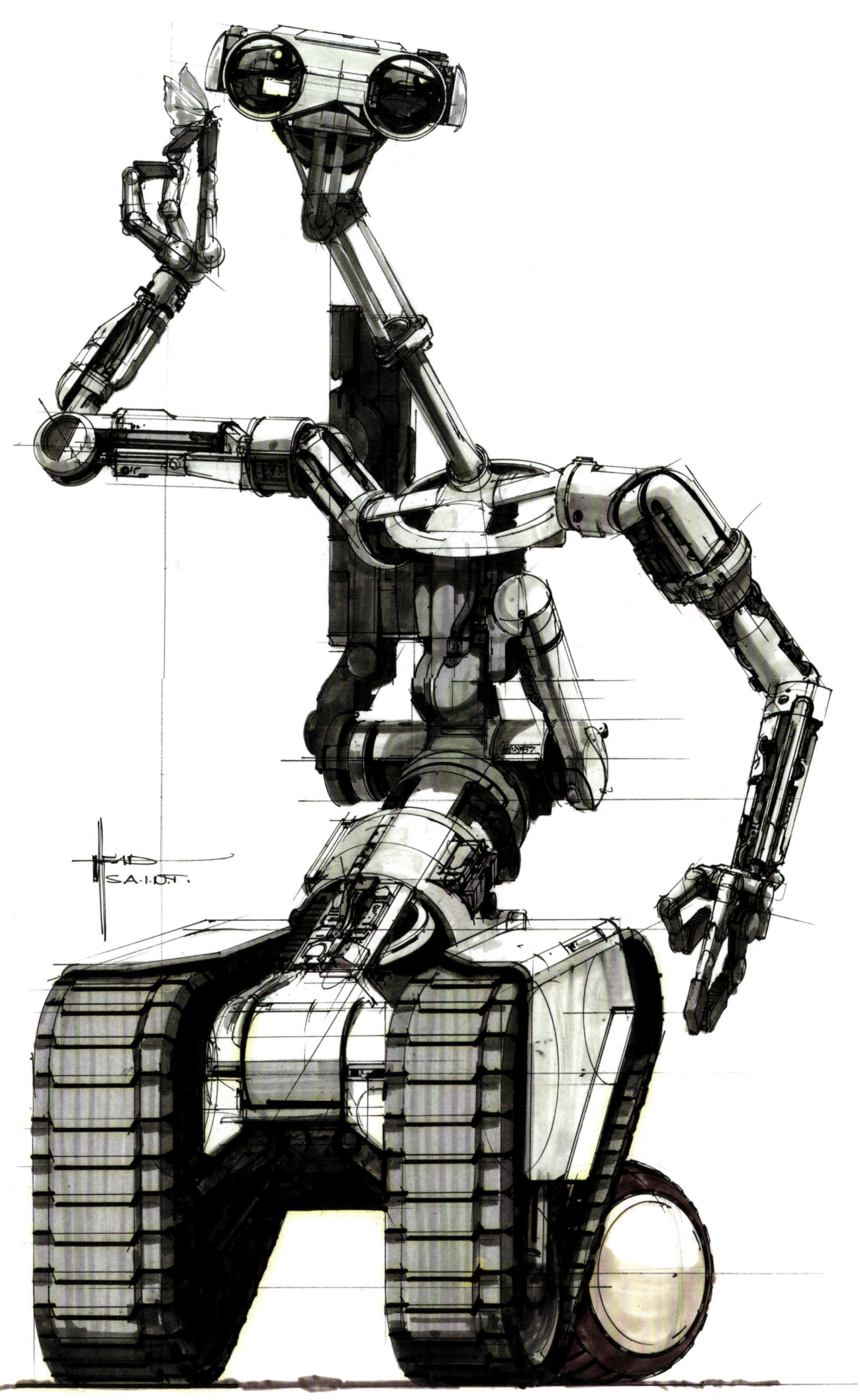

A SOUND OF THUNDER

A SOUND OF THUNDER

TITANS OF SCI-FI

Drawn from the imagination of two legendary figures from the universe of science fiction, *A Sound of Thunder* (2005) is based on a story by Ray Bradbury, with designs by Syd Mead. Directed by Peter Hyams, it is a cautionary tale of the precarious relationship between cause and effect, time travel and the devastating repercussions of a break in the primordial chain of events.

The challenge for Mead was to create visually arresting vehicles and props while basing their shape on existing platforms, which could then be retrofitted with fiberglass shells or additional elements.

While working on a vehicle, Mead superimposed a parallelogram over the profile of the van the production company planned to use, and detailed it with integrated alarm systems, antennae, impact accessories, and lighting packages. Below, the design of the holorecorder (left) and cartridge (right) are recognisable as real life objects but are here given a battered look with odd angles and extra accessories and wires to match the futurism of the project.

The expedition's protective clothing (right) strikes a balance between the foreseeable future and high tech science fiction—a vernacular extrapolated from a mash-up of contemporary gear and the imagined demands of time travel.

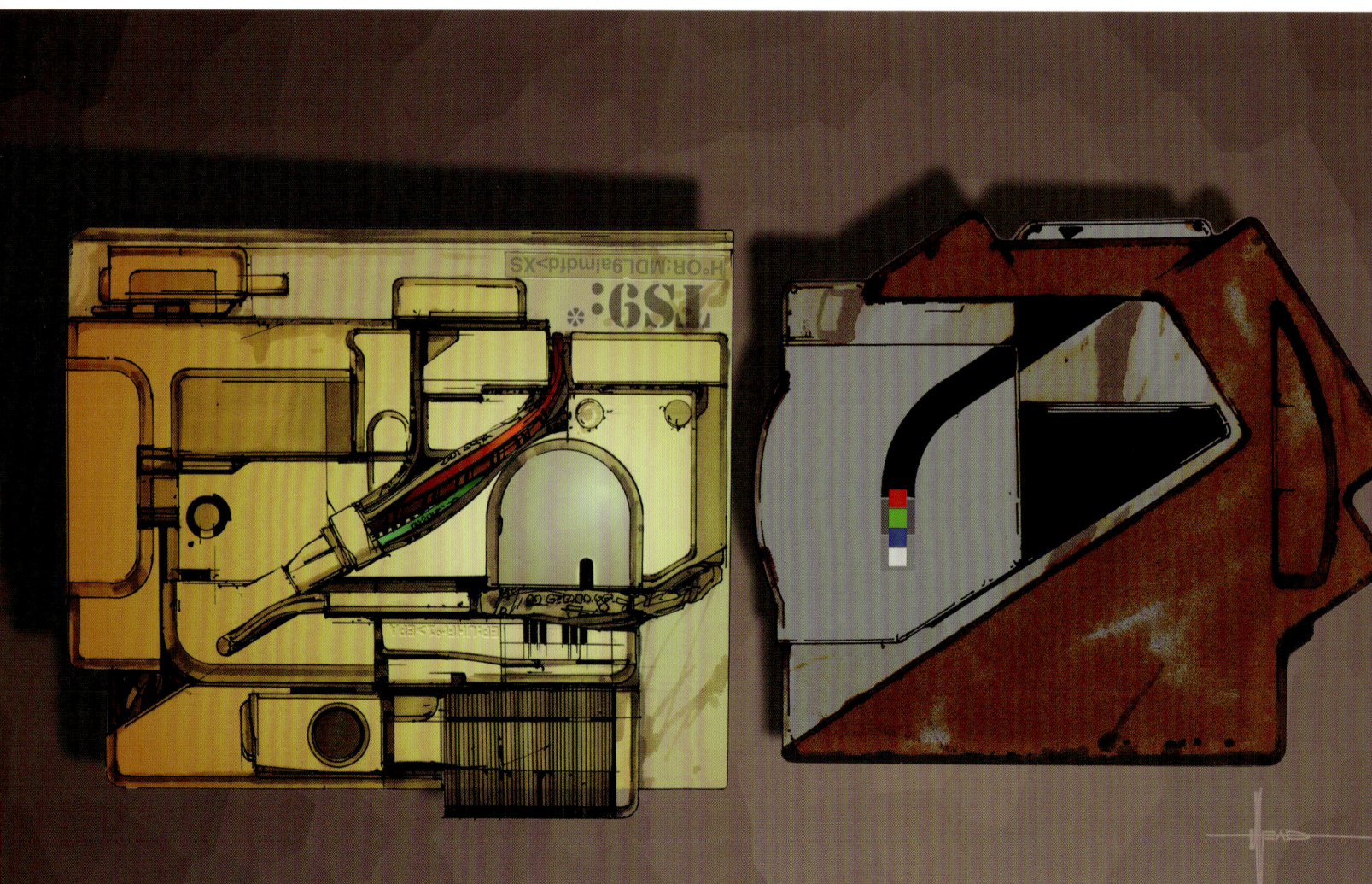

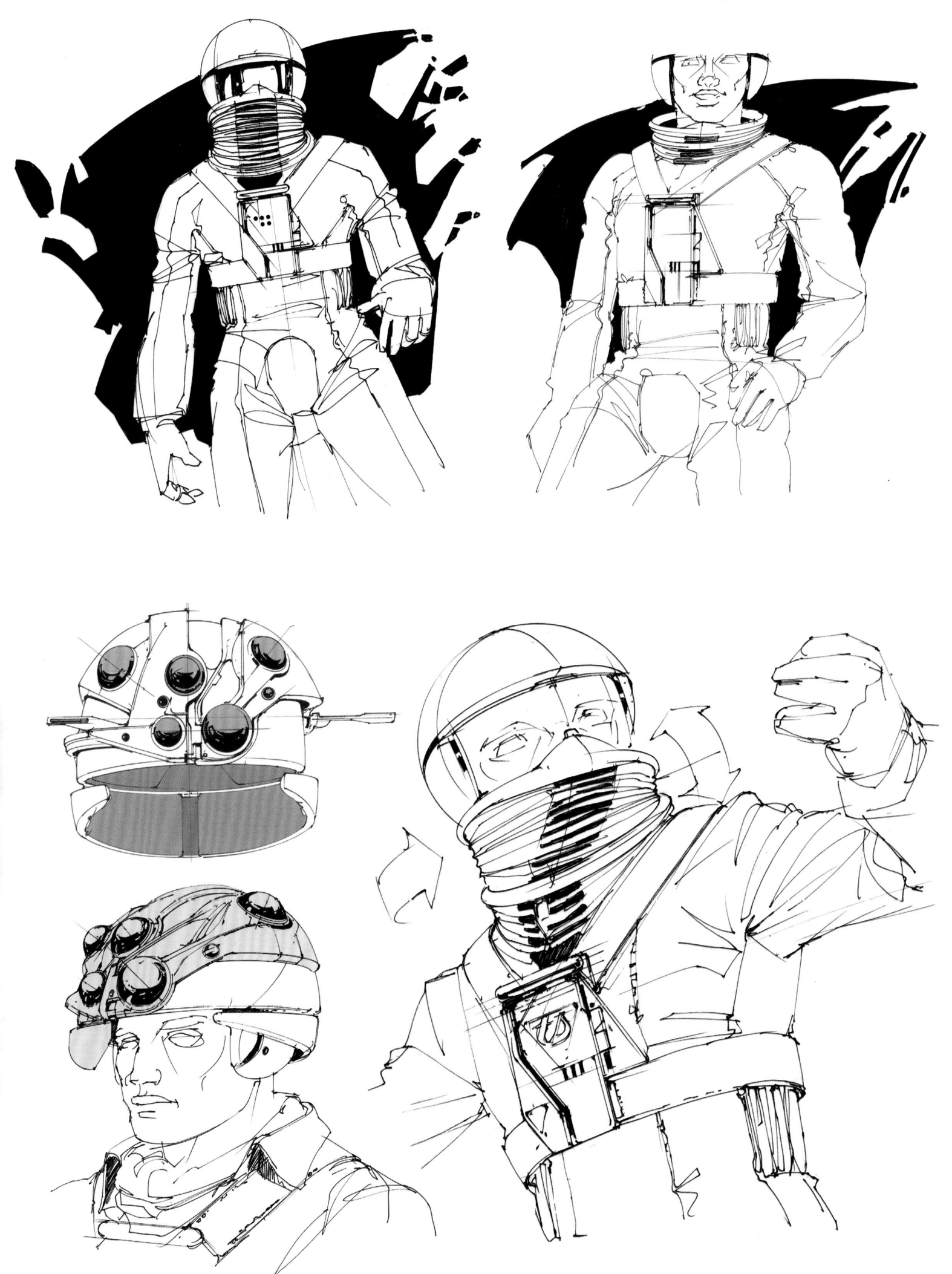

SCHIZOID

ZERO GRAVITY

This outer space film was to feature a S.W.A.T-like team of orbiting astronauts who can descend to earth to intervene when there is trouble. Mead reports on a meeting with the writer-director in which he explained the logic of a centrifuge when the writer asked about a cylindrical object in the concept sketches, to which Mead responded, "It's the centrifuge, to produce gravity, because these guys are up in space for weeks, months, I don't know how long. If you don't have gravity, your muscle structure just goes to hell. Your organs change position," and he concluded, "If they don't have gravity, they'd descend to earth and crumble to the ground like a wet noodle". When the writer asked, "Really?", it became clear to Mead that there had not been sufficient research into the demands of the concept, and the project was abandoned shortly thereafter.

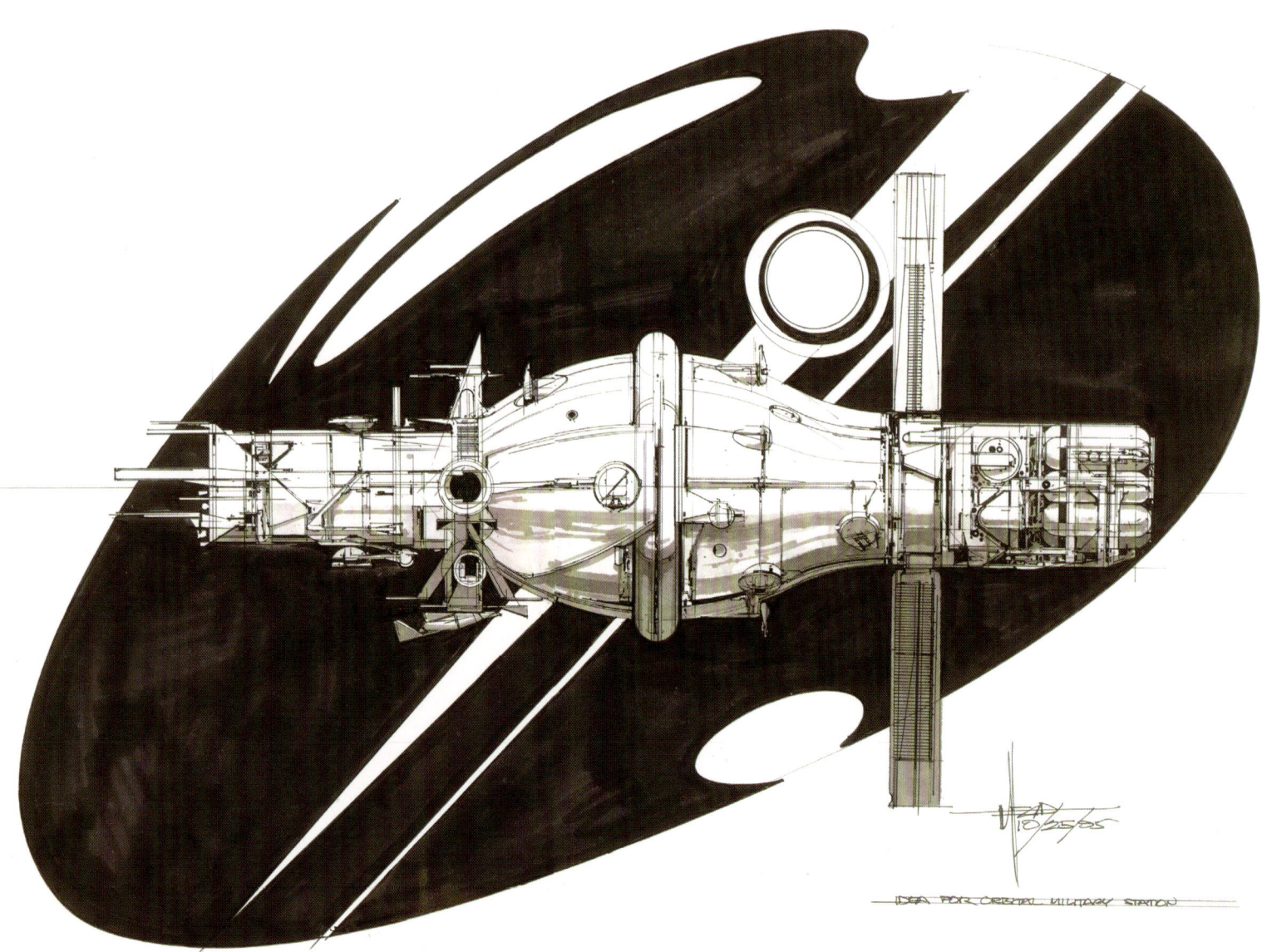

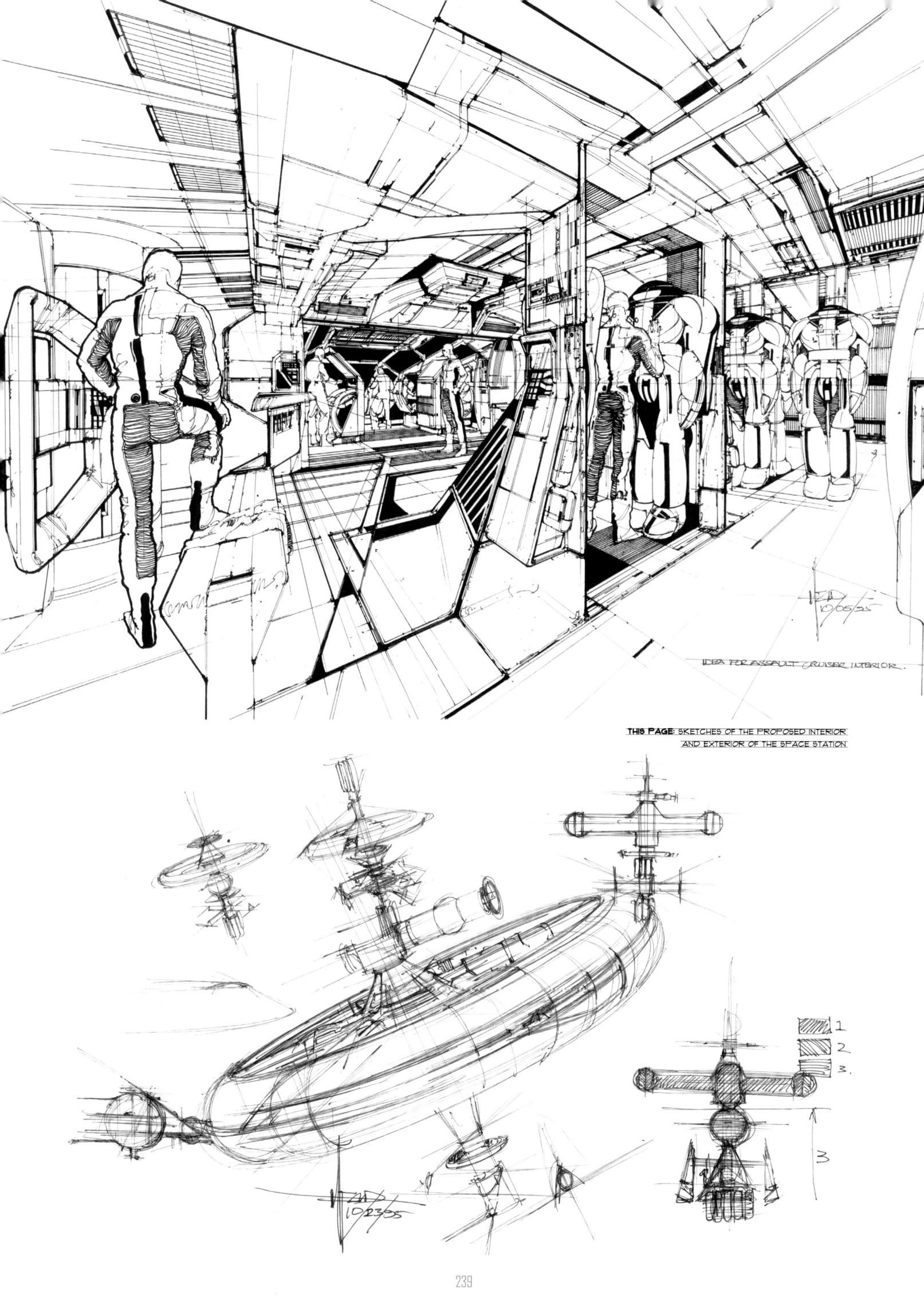

IDEA FOR ASSAULT CRUISER INTERIOR.

THIS PAGE: SKETCHES OF THE PROPOSED INTERIOR
AND EXTERIOR OF THE SPACE STATION

SANDBLAST

CHANGES

In what is a paean to patience, forbearance, and flexibility, the design of the hero prop for this never-to-be-made film went through innumerable revisions as the script was being written and re-written. Originally envisioned as a long articulated Weapon of Mass Destruction characterized by an enigmatic mechanical geometry, it morphed during pre-production into, in Syd's words, "a bulky combination of transit cradle, cryogenic cooling mantles, readout mantissas, parachute canister and jettisonable casing", losing, in the process, the genesis of the prop itself.

While the premise of the film evolved, Mead produced a series of thoughtful variations of what was meant to be a WMD that could be carried by one man as he ran to leap into a waiting helicopter.

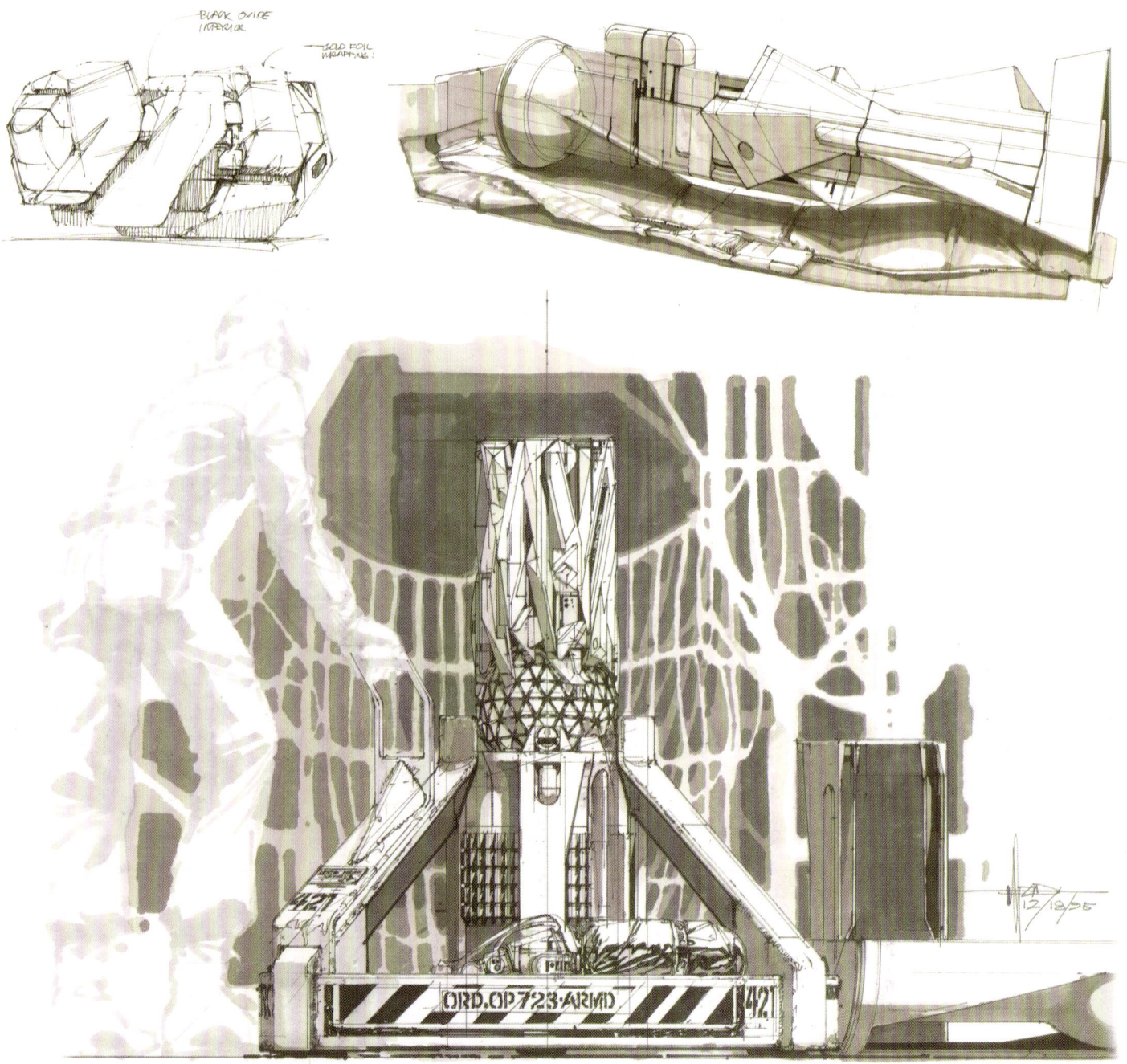

FORBIDDEN PLANET

FORSAKEN REBOOT

Having never seen the original film, when Mead was invited to design elements of the reboot of *Forbidden Planet* by three-time Oscar-winning production designer Richard Sylbert, the first thing he did was to view the original version. Upon grasping the significance of the back story, namely that the entrance to the ancient habitat of the now extinct Krell was via a fragment of the ship originally piloted by the human colonists, Mead reasoned that the design of the cabin module of the rescue ship ought to contain similar design cues.

By then no stranger to the whims of filmmaking, Mead redesigned the original flying saucer-shaped ship as a sleek, flat, ovoid vessel (below) which would offer more opportunities to the filmmakers. Within, rather than the switches and gauges then in vogue, the control console featured a touch-sensitive surface, framed by a vocabulary of sweeping, intersecting curves that divided the cabin into discreet sectors.

If produced, Mead's vision of hyper-light travel called for the starship's computers to sequentially scan the ship and its occupants and stream the data towards its destination where the ship itself would be reassembled in physical form.

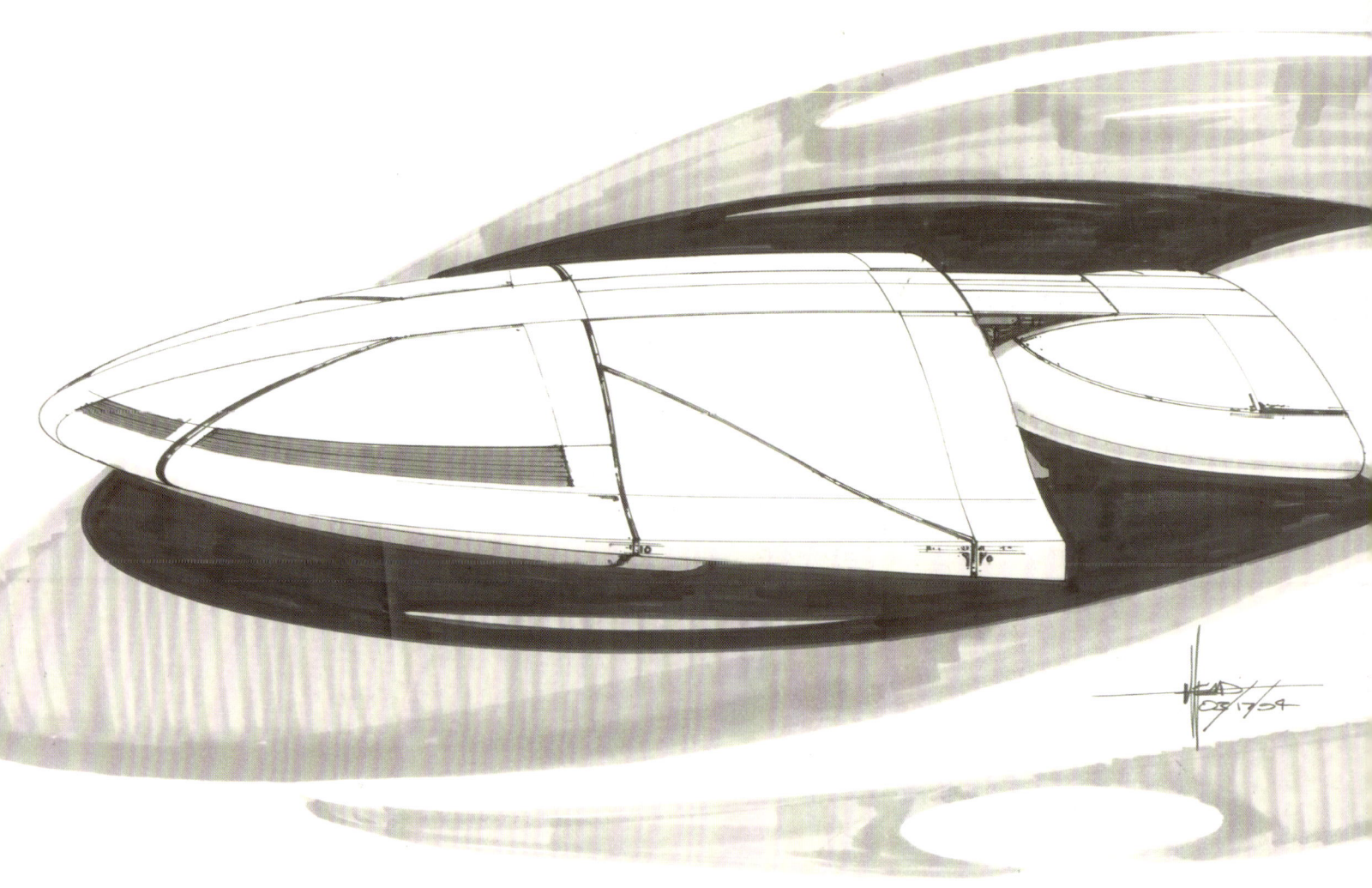

YAMATO 2520

MASTERS OF ANIME

The passionate, mythic, images created by Mead for the revival of the legendary Japanese anime series reflect his fascination with the culture of anime, and the all-encompassing world of the fabled battleship. Here was an opportunity to work closely with the masters of the medium, who Mead came to admire, and to forge a true creative partnership with the storytellers, animators, and voices, that were to bring the story to life.

Mead, already a near deity in Japan, was invited to give form to a successor ship to the venerable *Yamato* which, much like the starship *Enterprise,* had become an icon of the series, with fetish-finished models, interpretive text, and posters depicting it in constant demand.

As Mead explains, he was both honored and somewhat awed by the challenge. He explains, "The design had to embody the mystique of the original story ship designed by venerable animation guru Matsumoto. Design for the new Yamato 2520 went way beyond any movie project I have worked on... [It] was an elaborately funded and elaborately staged design tour de force stretching over many years".

The medium of anime, unlike live film, is a graphic artist's medium, revealing, in lingering image after lingering image the precision of Mead's designs, unadulterated for the most part, by the vagaries of motion and lighting that so often consign intricately designed props to fleeting impressions.

THIS POINT-OF-VIEW IMAGE OF THE CONTROL DECK IS DEVISED TO PERFECTLY FRAME THE ARCHING LINES OF A VAST TRANSPARENT CANOPY BEYOND A BEVELED OPERATIONS CONSOLE.

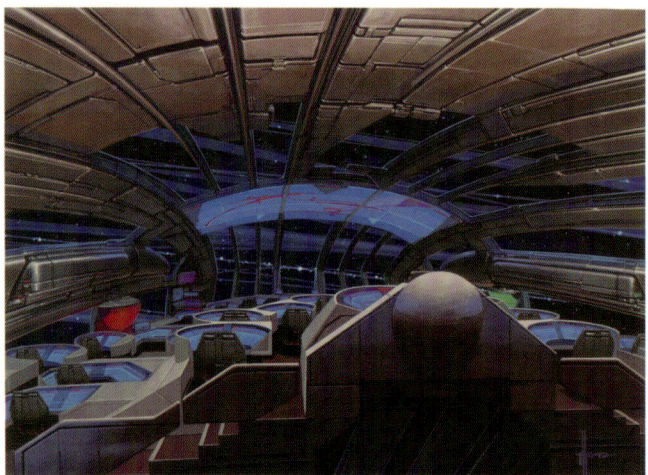
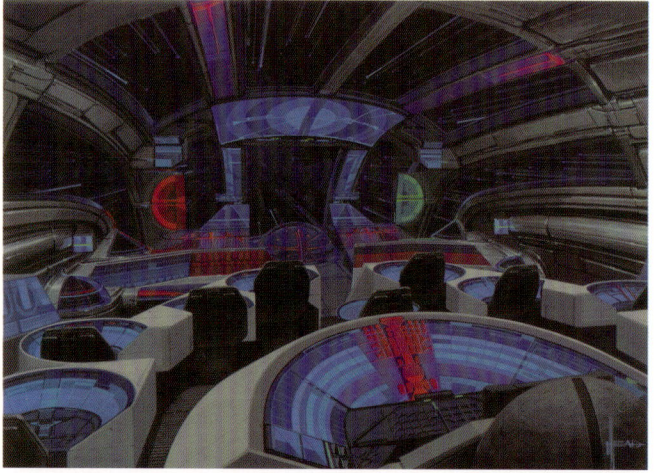
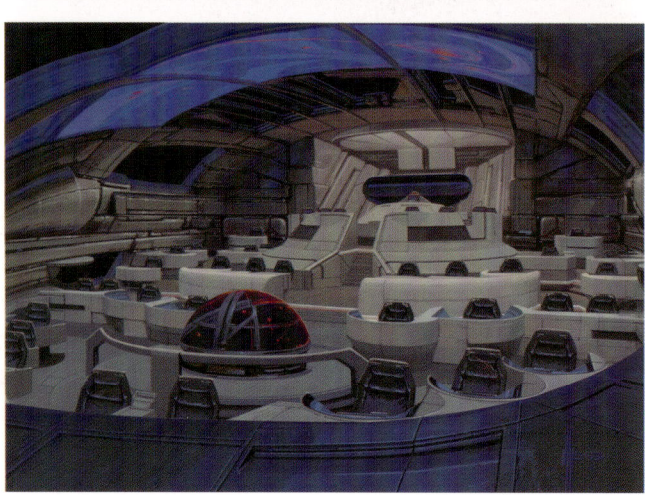
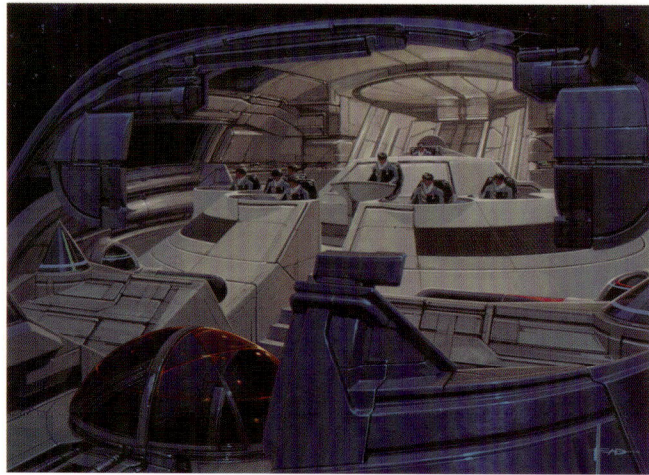

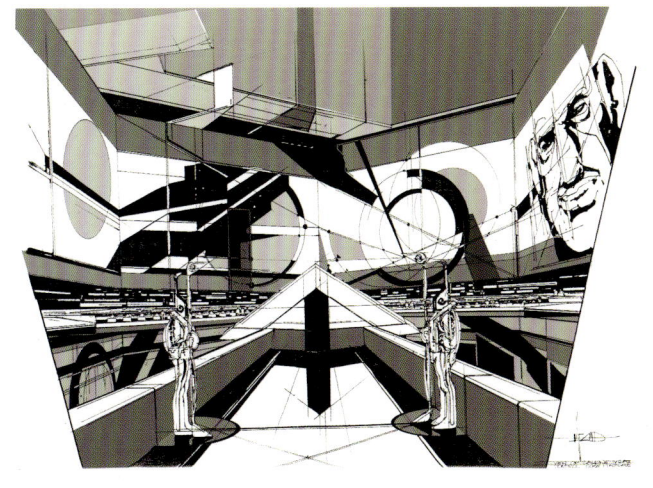

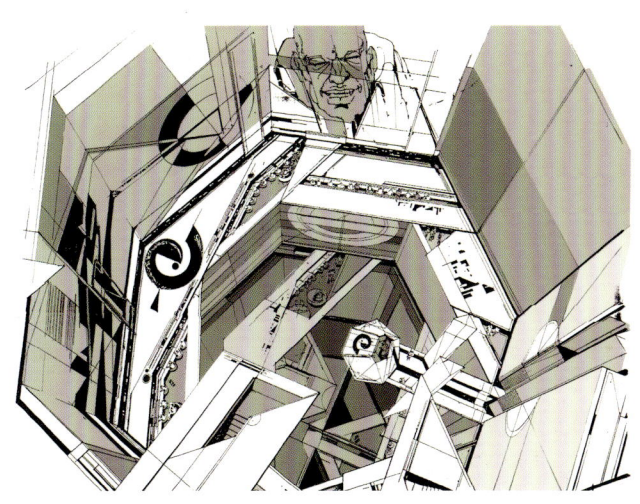

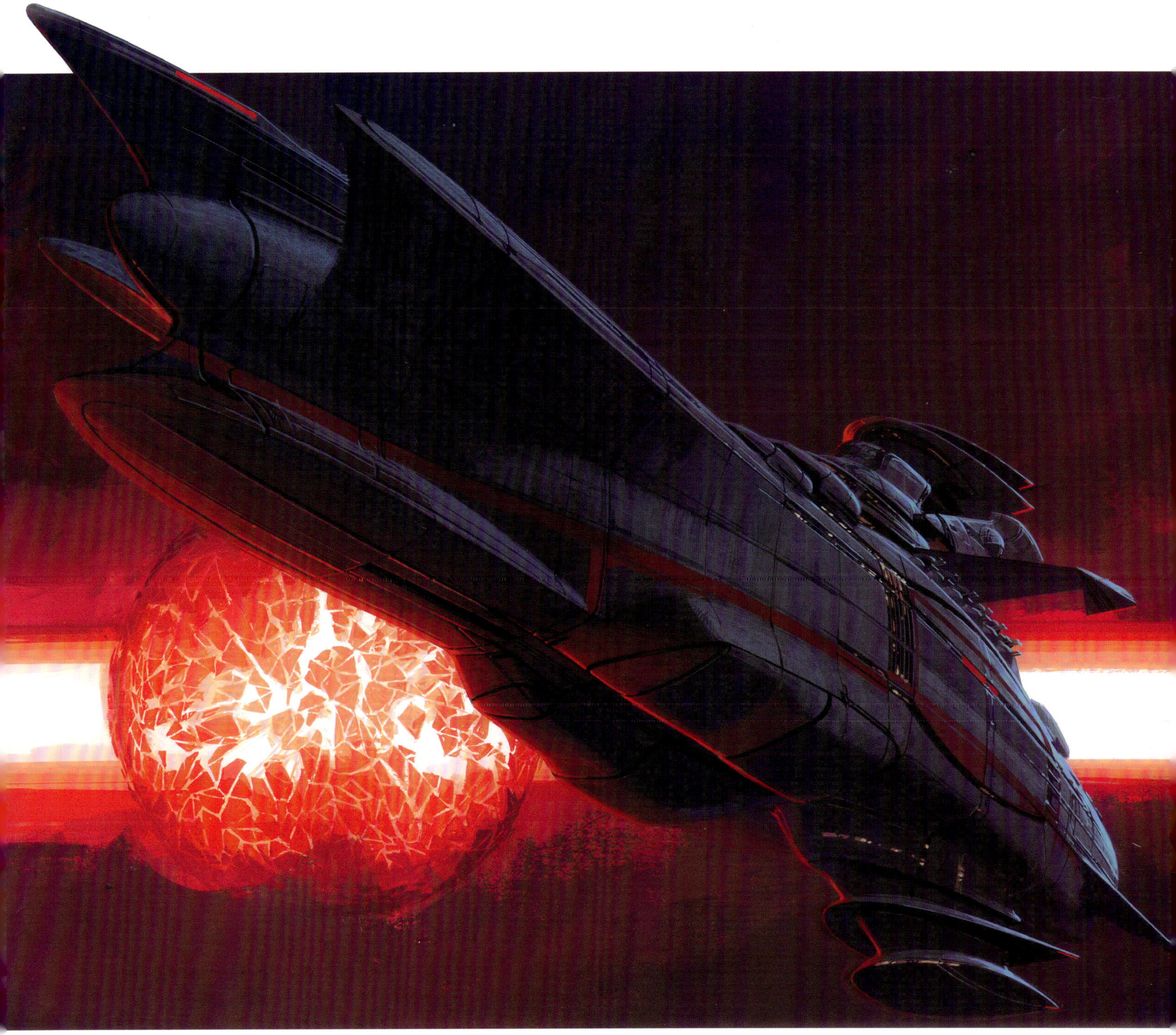

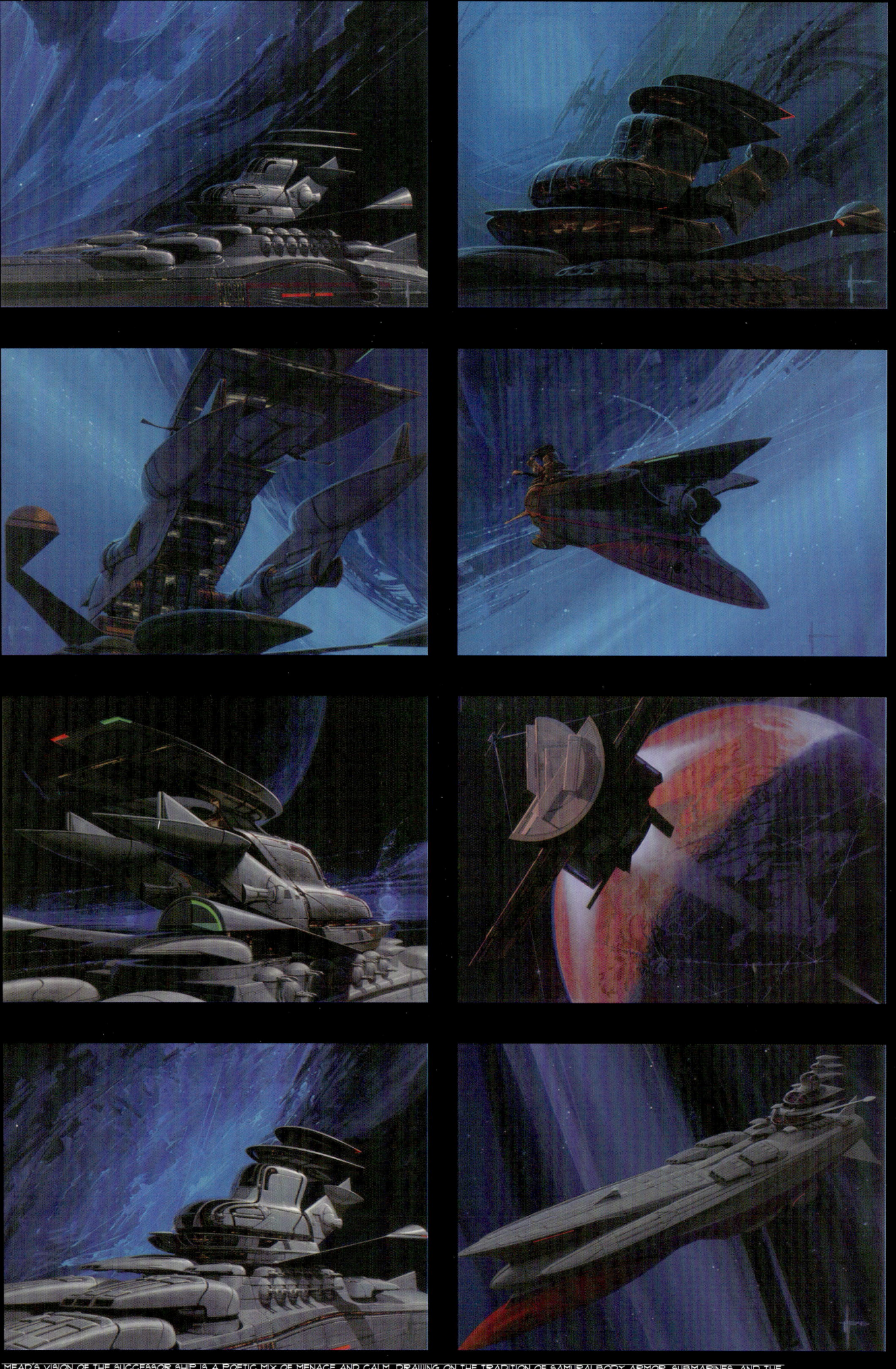

MEAD'S VISION OF THE SUCCESSOR SHIP IS A POETIC MIX OF MENACE AND CALM. DRAWING ON THE TRADITION OF SAMURAI BODY ARMOR, SUBMARINES, AND THE PUFFY GUN TURRETS OF WORLD WAR TWO JAPANESE BATTLESHIPS, AND BRISTLING WITH PROBES, THE YAMATO ESTABLISHED A NEW GENRE FOR SCI-FI BATTLE CRUISERS.

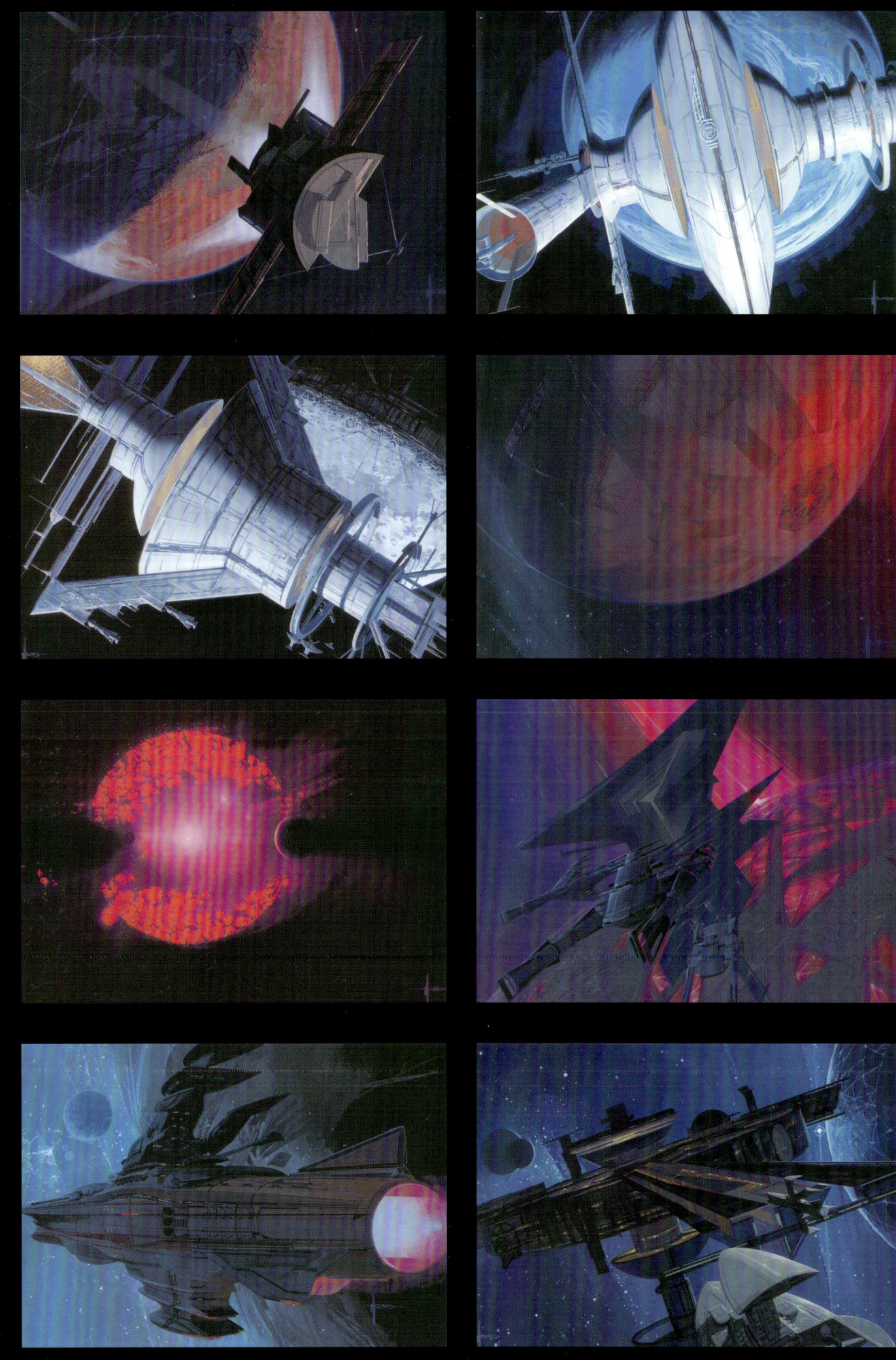

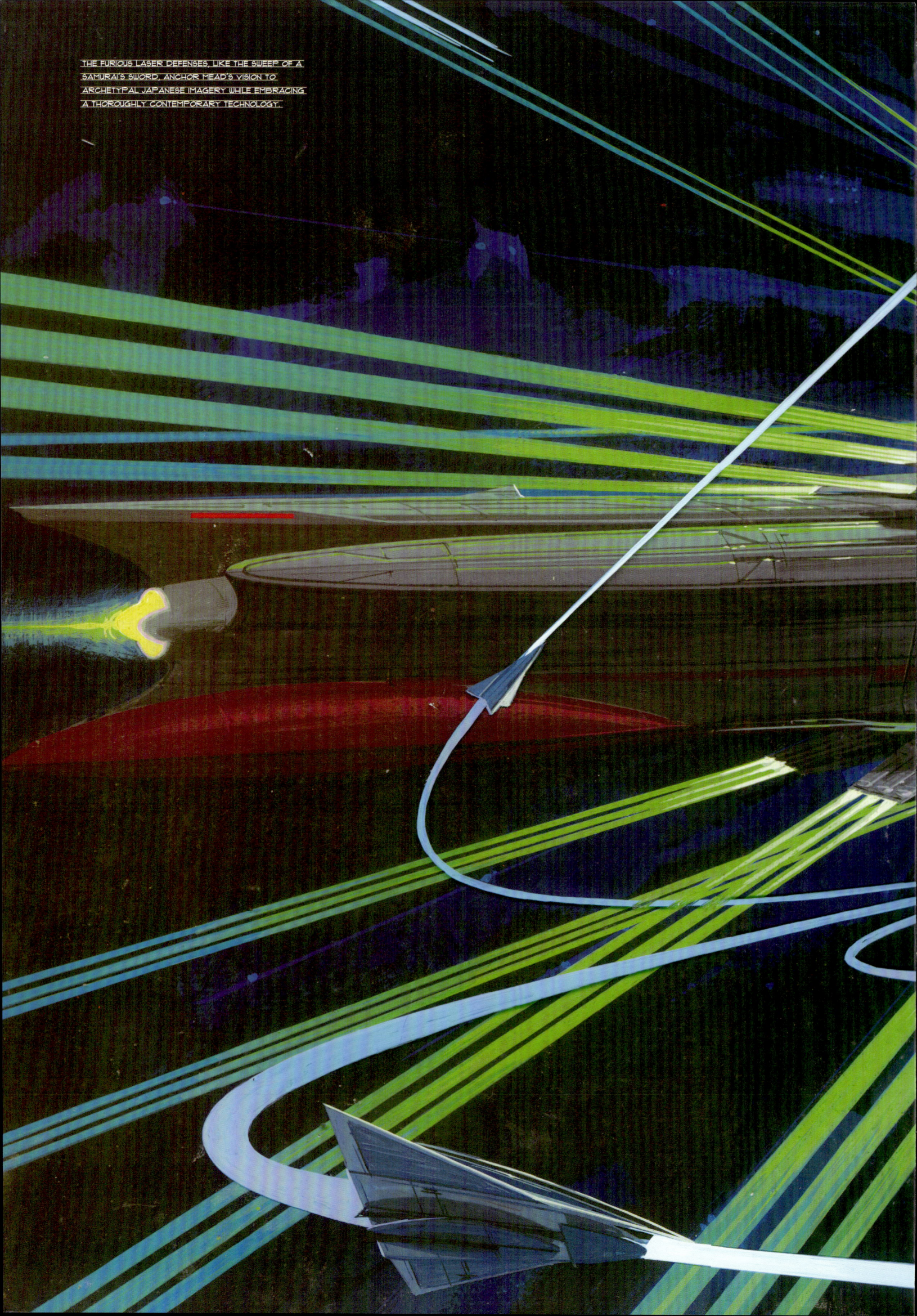

THE FURIOUS LASER DEFENSES, LIKE THE SWEEP OF A
SAMURAI'S SWORD, ANCHOR MEAD'S VISION TO
ARCHETYPAL JAPANESE IMAGERY WHILE EMBRACING
A THOROUGHLY CONTEMPORARY TECHNOLOGY.

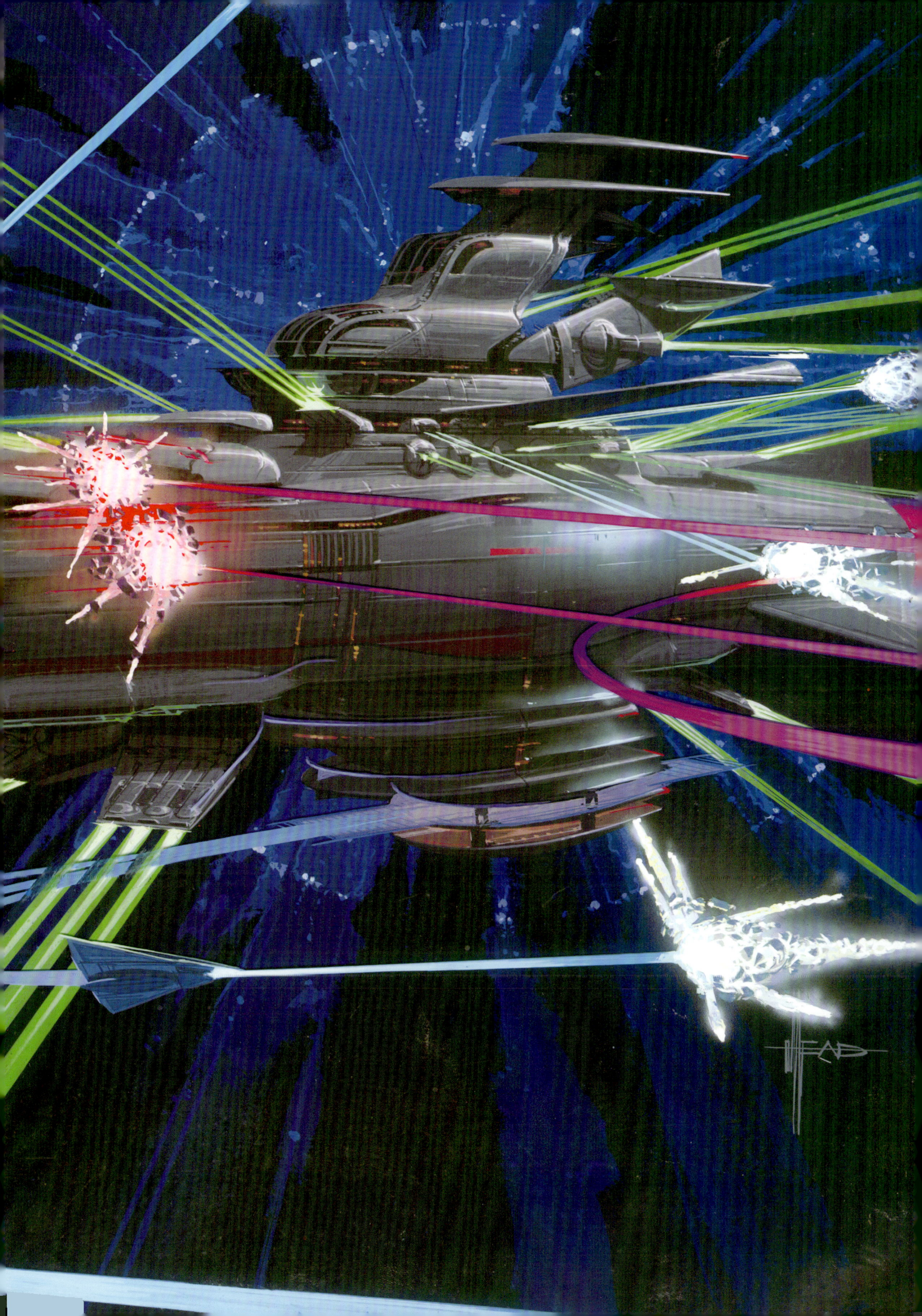

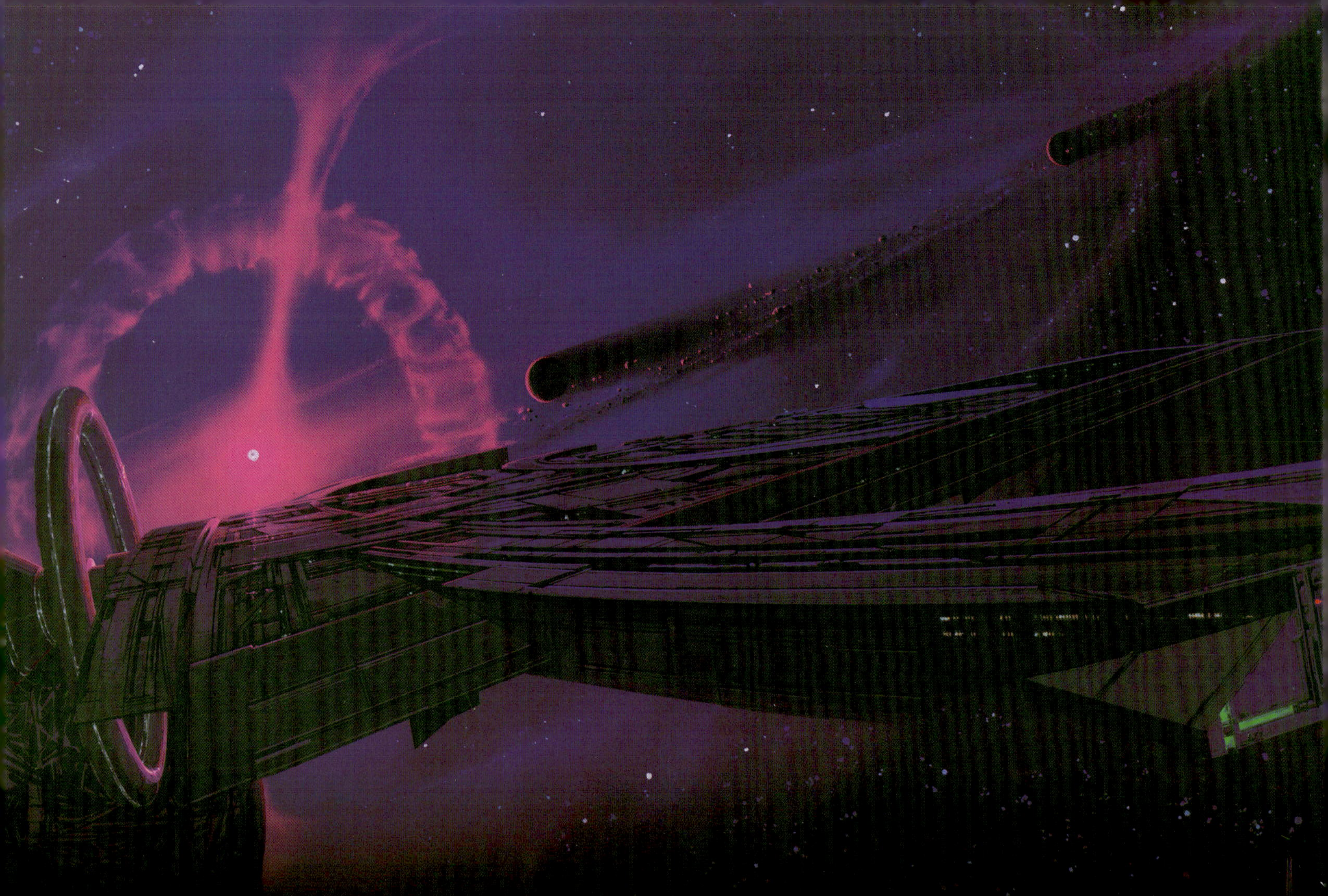

The cosmic sweep of the compositions for *Yamato 2520* permeates space, time and even tranquil, earth-bound environments, endowing each image with an epic stature fitting the legacy of the original series.

They are among the most compelling of Mead's long career, imbued with the gravitas of pure geometry as pure energy arches into the infinite reaches of outer space, as well as in the green-edged pools of the earth's surface.

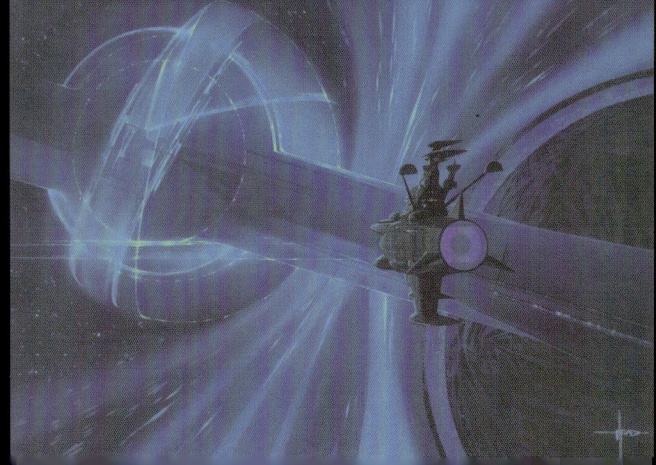

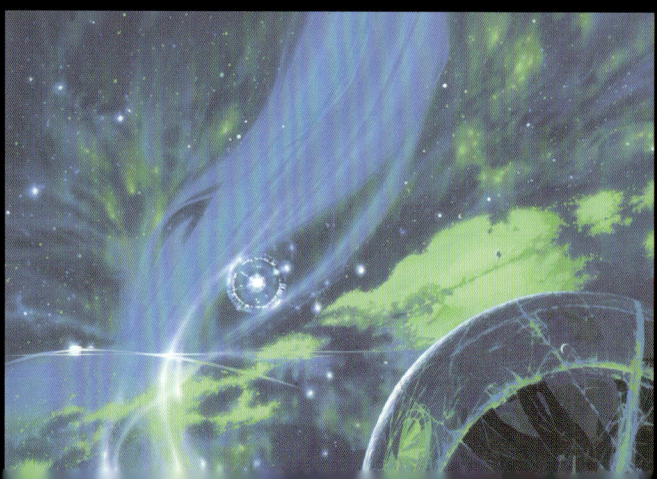

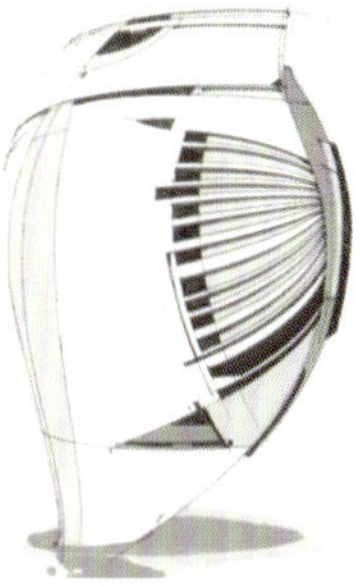

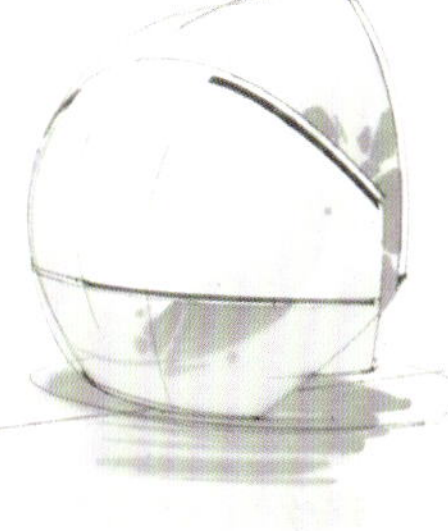

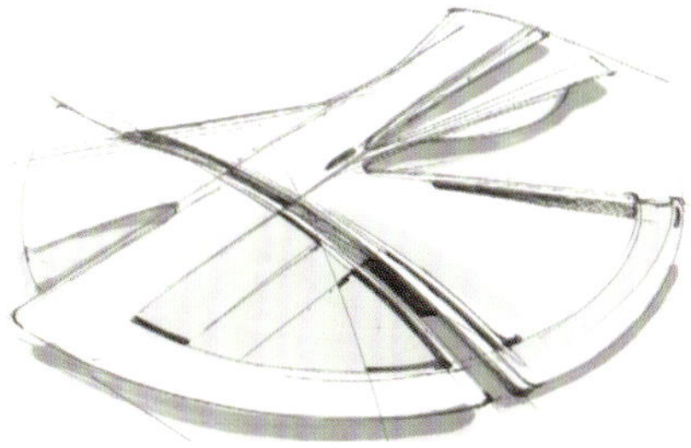

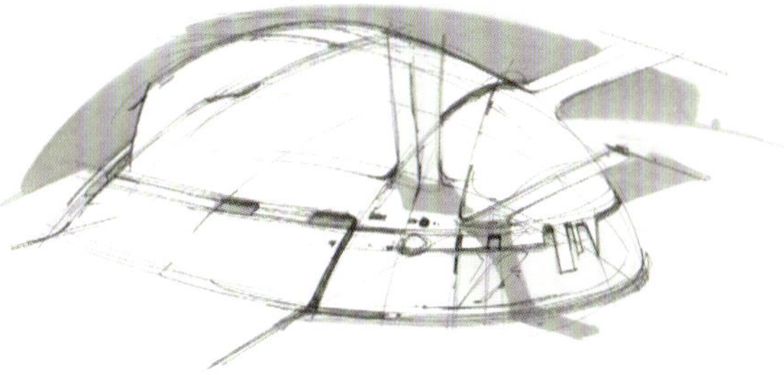

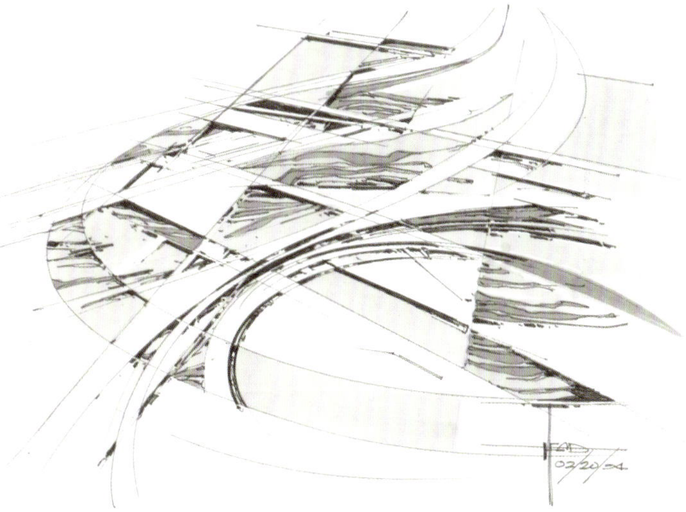
02/20/04

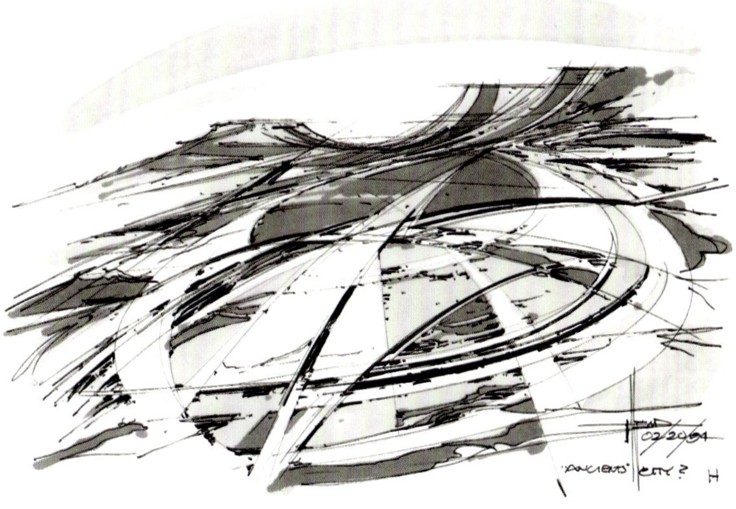
02/20/04
'ANCIENTS' CITY?

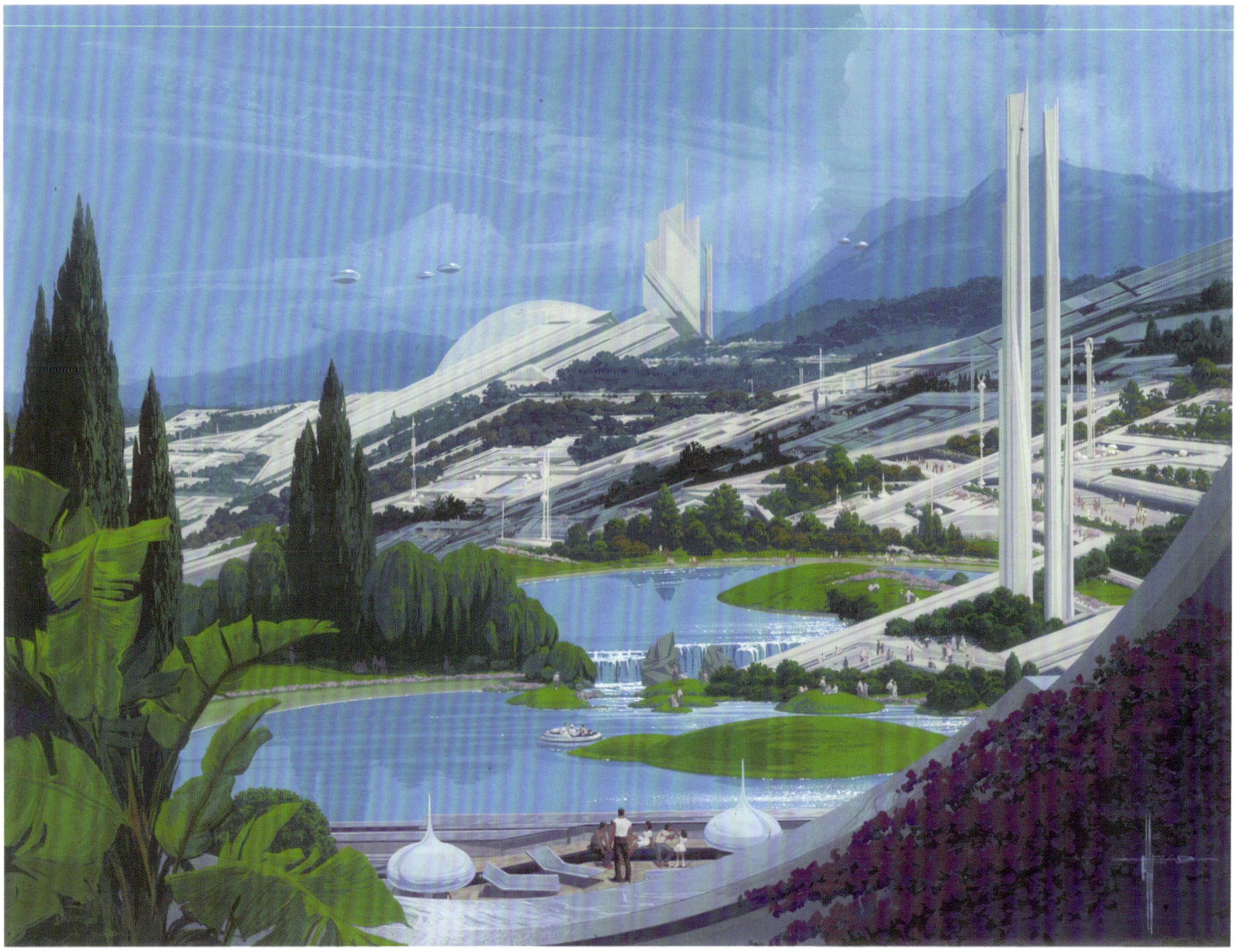

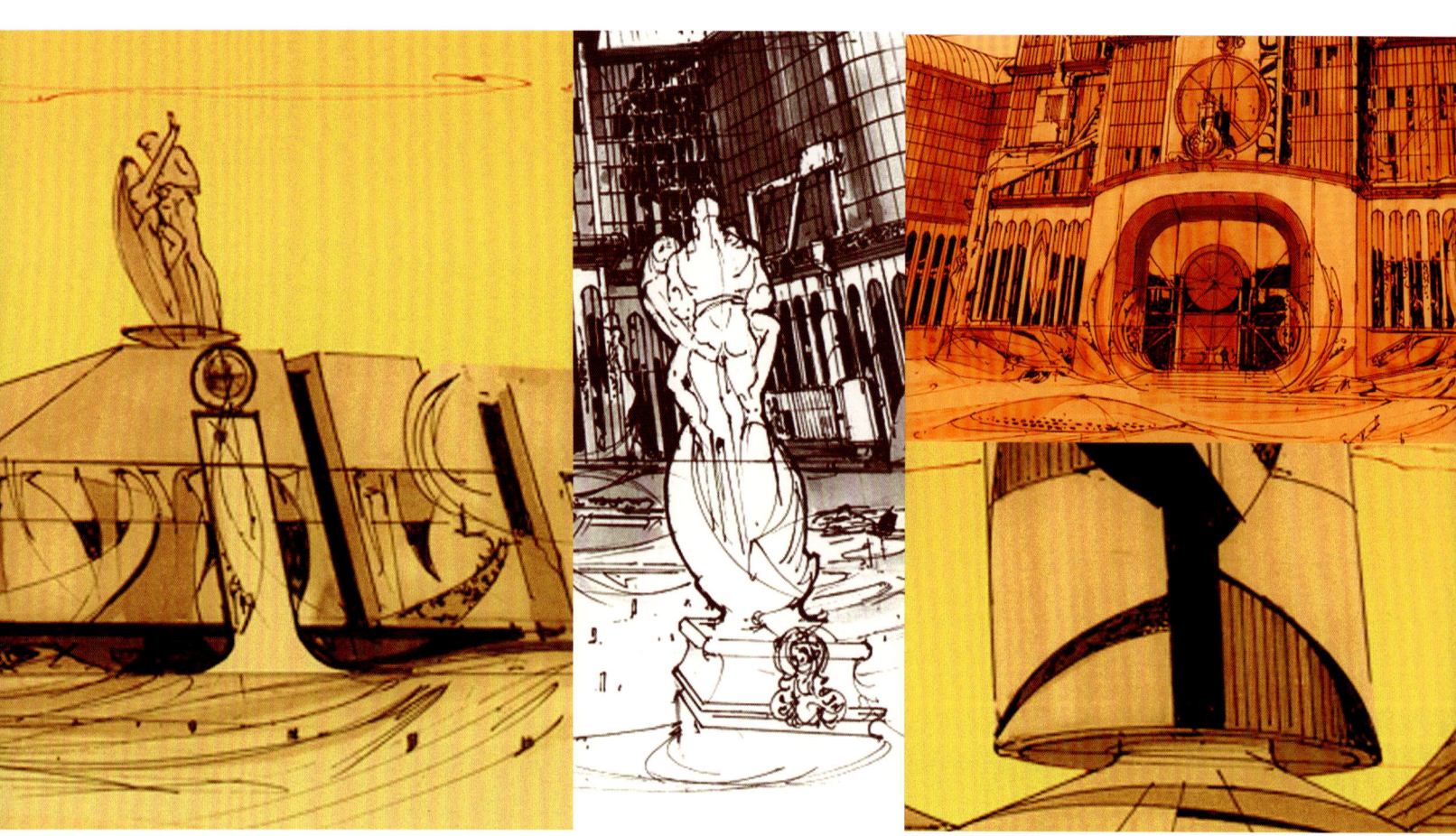

BLADE RUNNER
2049

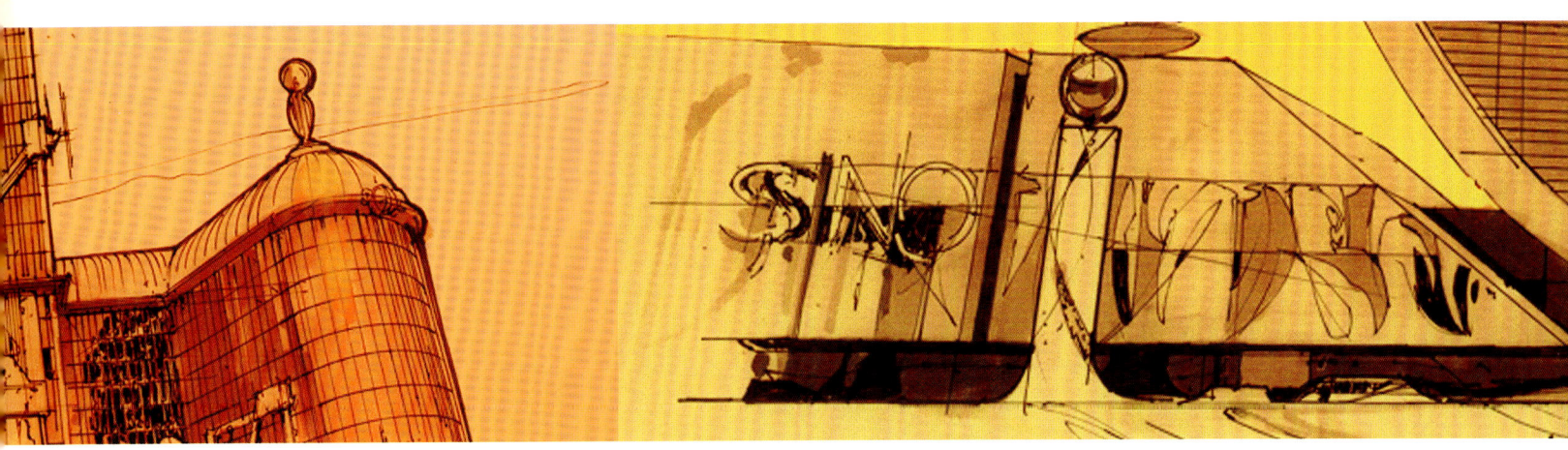

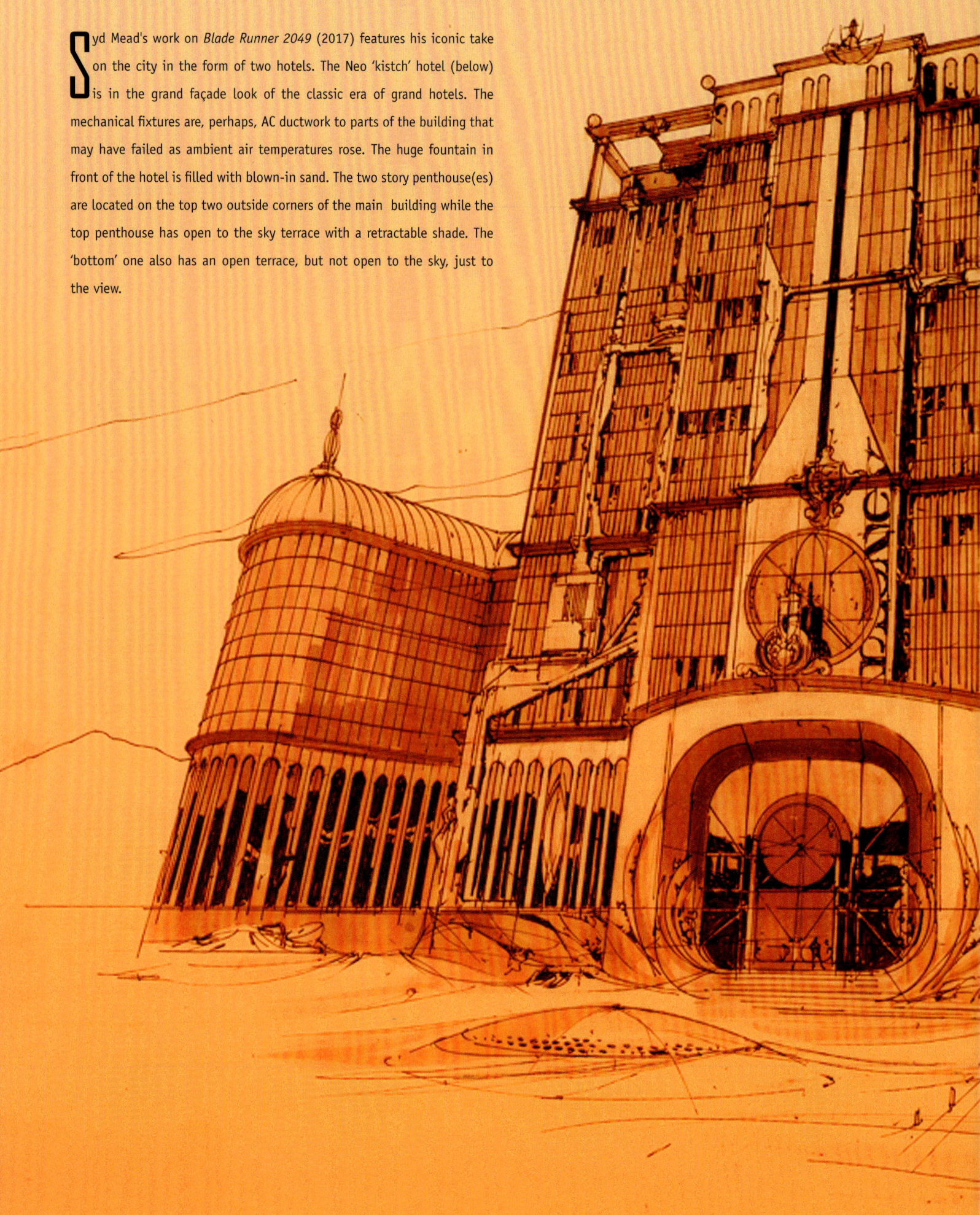

yd Mead's work on *Blade Runner 2049* (2017) features his iconic take on the city in the form of two hotels. The Neo 'kistch' hotel (below) is in the grand façade look of the classic era of grand hotels. The mechanical fixtures are, perhaps, AC ductwork to parts of the building that may have failed as ambient air temperatures rose. The huge fountain in front of the hotel is filled with blown-in sand. The two story penthouse(es) are located on the top two outside corners of the main building while the top penthouse has open to the sky terrace with a retractable shade. The 'bottom' one also has an open terrace, but not open to the sky, just to the view.

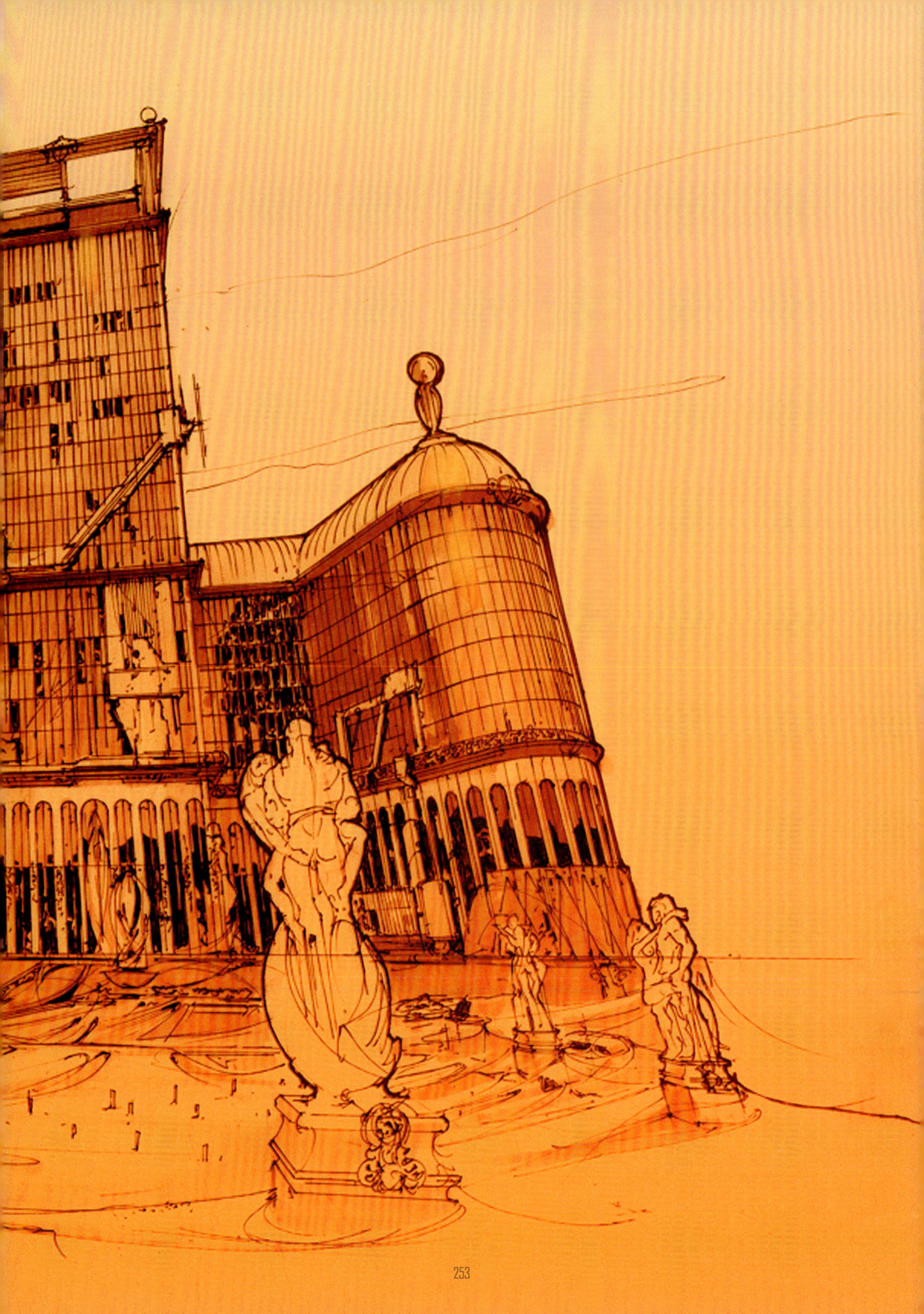

The Neo-modern hotel (below) drawing shows a sleek vertical tower with penthouse terraces on the top two floors. The marquee is actually under the conical lower part of the hotel. The extensions at either side are conference space, and perhaps a casino at the extreme left? Mead says, "These two sets are simply for me to get an idea of a visual stylistic direction... all 'modern, sleek' combined with 'traditional' style, etc". The director indicated he would like to see a 'classic casino' next to a modern 'Syd Mead' hotel, suggesting the hotel was a property upgrade. Mead says, "What is a 'classic' casino? Would it be like the Casino de Monaco for instance? These first sketches were simply to establish a start-off visual dialogue with the director for further development."

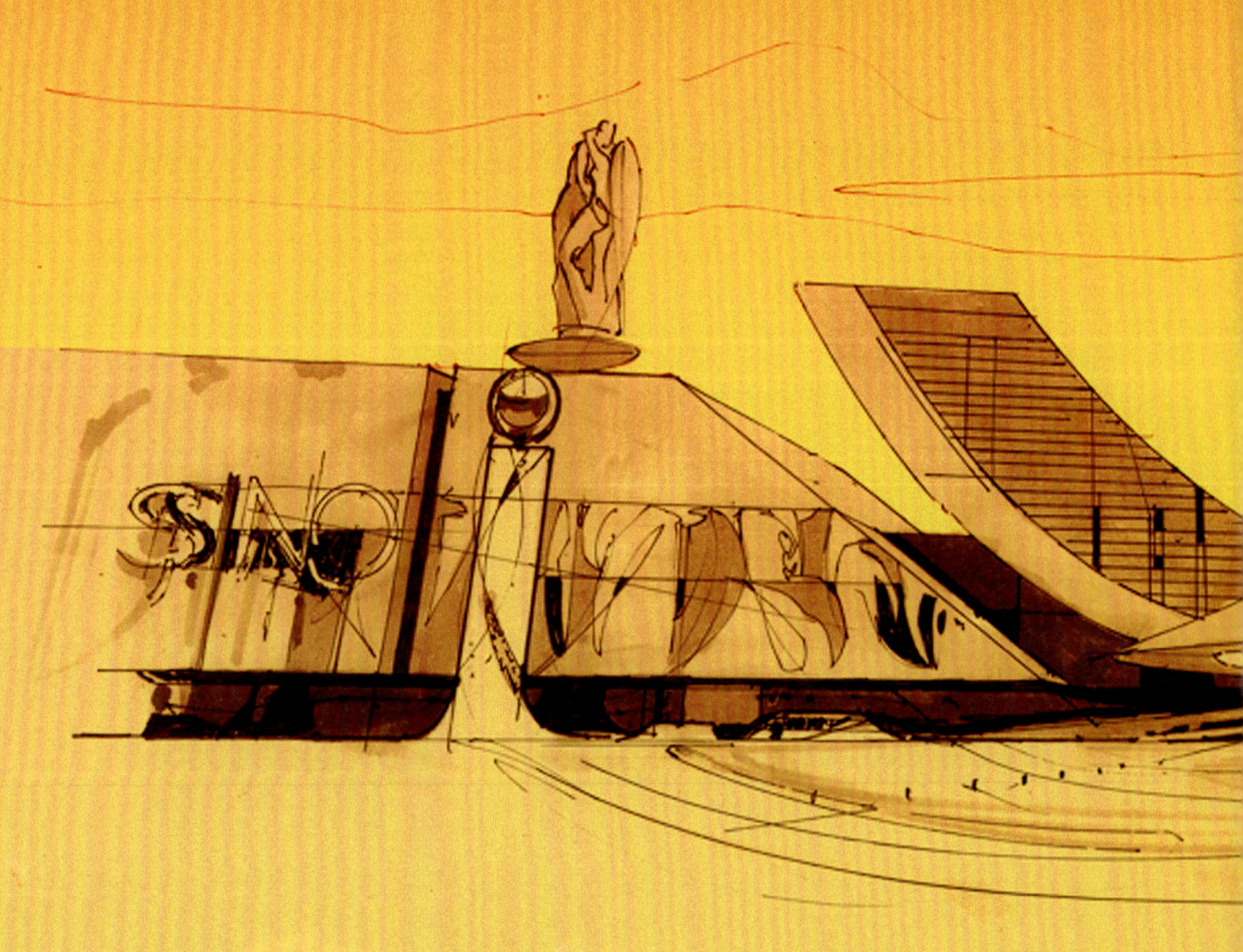

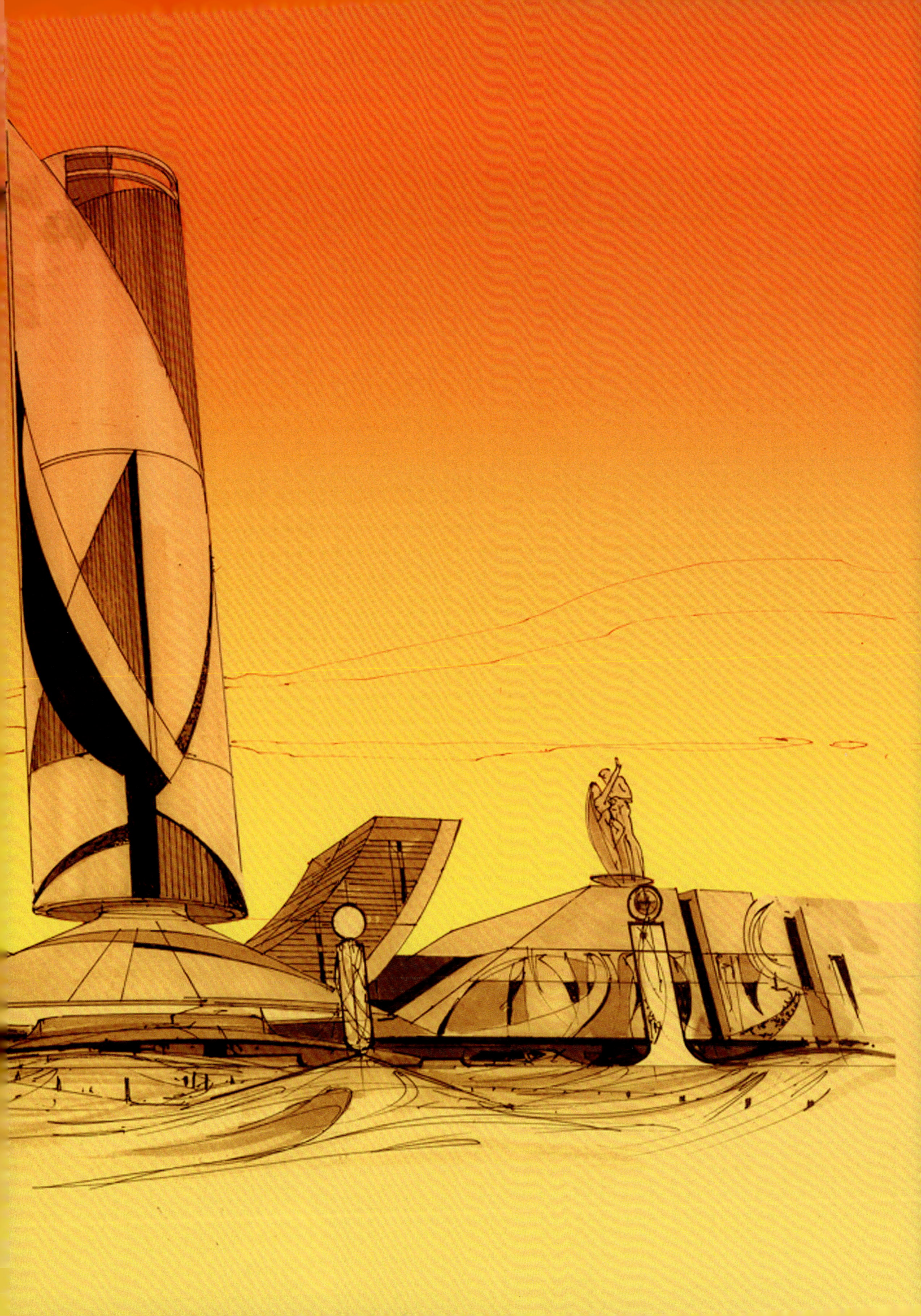

ACKNOWLEDGMENTS

ACKNOWLEDGMENTS

FROM THE AUTHOR

This book would not have been possible without the good cucumber sandwiches and matching soda which fueled my conversations with Syd and Roger, nor without the humor and candor which they offered in large helpings.

I'd like to thank Hsinming Fung, my "partner-in-all-things" for her encouragement and forebearance as the "Syd Thing" dominated our evenings for weeks and weeks, and also Allie Bogle who literally brought the manuscript back from the grave when the text was inextricably scrambled due to a computer mishap.

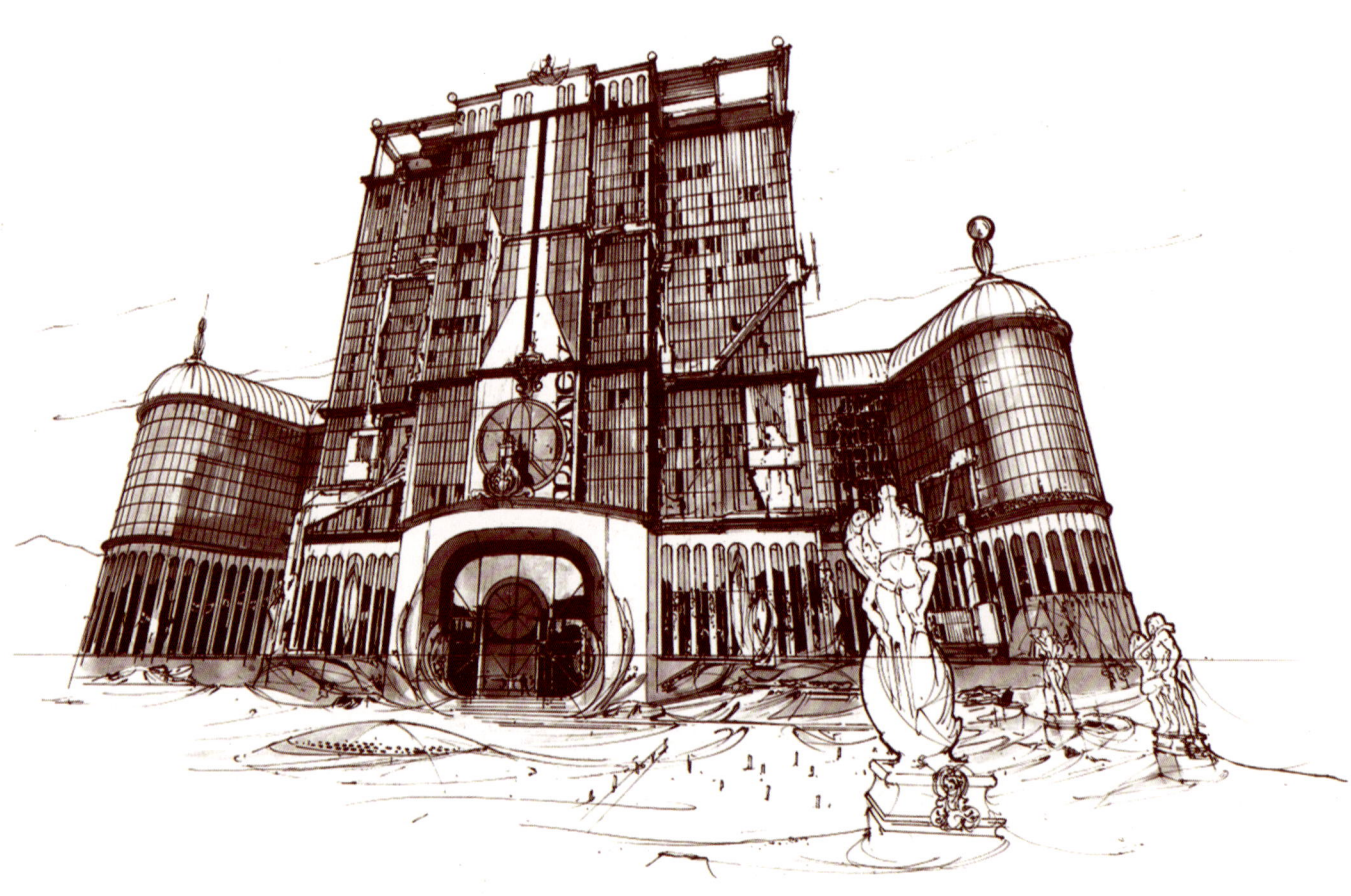

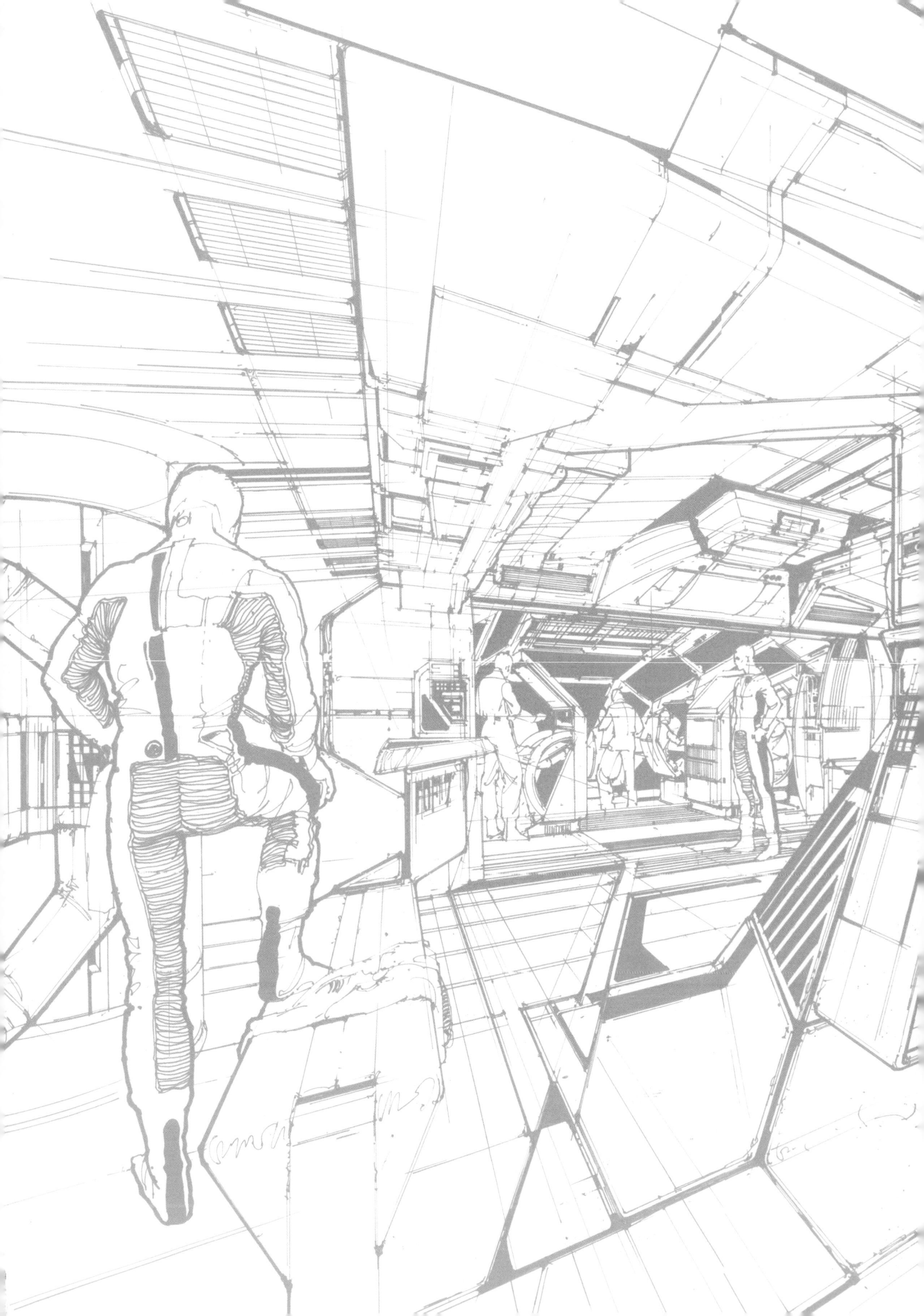

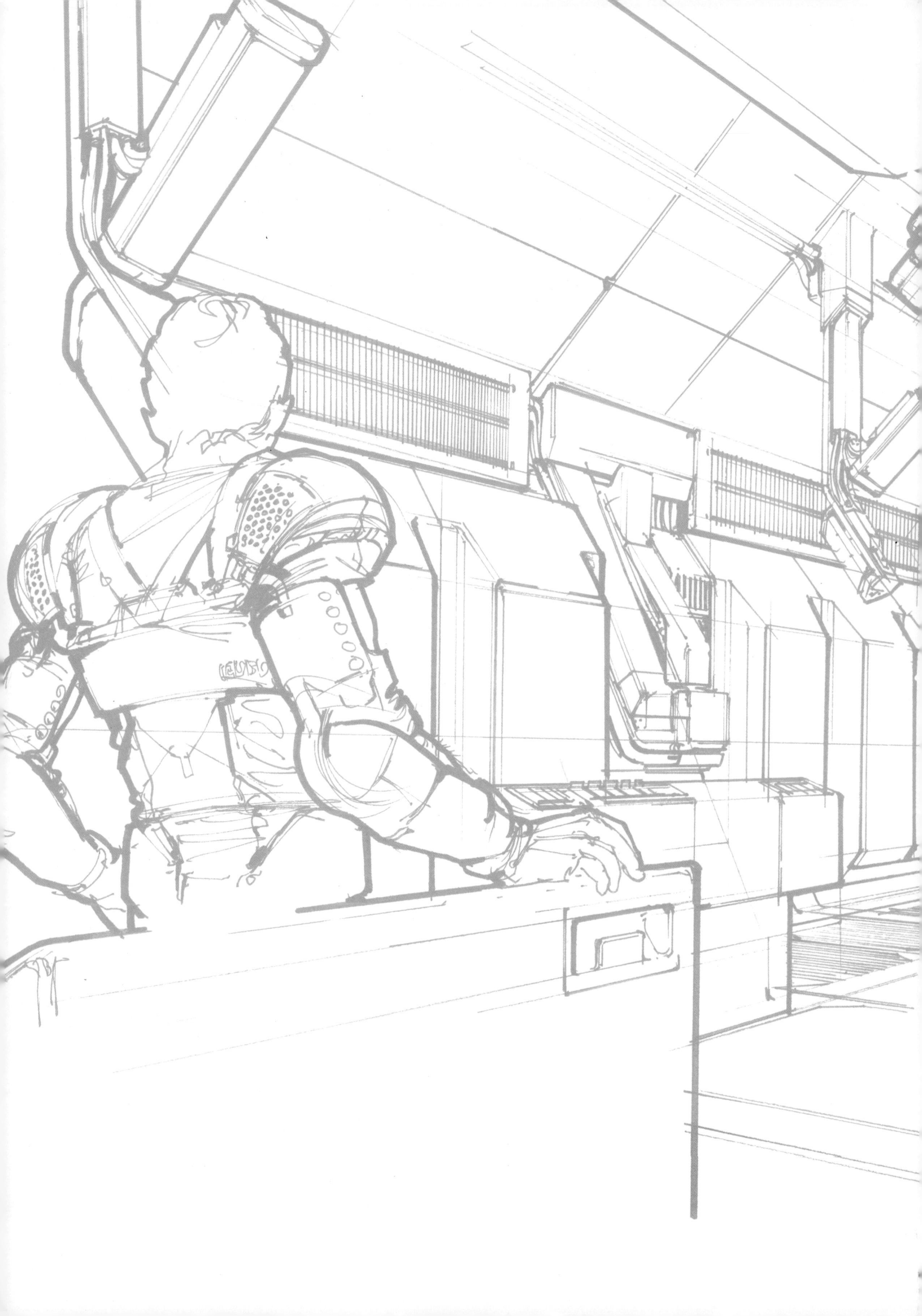